Early Negro Writing
1760-1837

EARLY NEGRO WRITING
1760 - 1837

Selected and introduced by
Dorothy Porter

Black Classic Press
Baltimore

EARLY NEGRO WRITING

Published 1995 by
Black Classic Press
Copyright 1971 by Dorothy Porter
Cover art by W. Paul Coates and Carles Juzang

Library of Congress Catalog Card Number: 94-78761
ISBN: 0-933121-59-8 Paperbound
ISBN: 0-933121-60-1 Hardbound

Printed on acid free paper to assure long life

Founded in 1978, Black Classic Press specializes in bringing to light obscure and significant works by and about people of African descent. If our books are not available in your area, ask your local bookseller to order them. Our current list of titles can be obtained by writing:

Black Classic Press
c/o List
P.O. Box 13414
Baltimore, MD 21203

A Young Press With Some Very Old Ideas

To Coni

CONTENTS

Introduction   *1*

PART I
MUTUAL AID AND FRATERNAL ORGANIZATIONS, 1792–1833
5

Laws of the African Society, Instituted at Boston, 1796.   *9*

The Sons of Africans: An Essay on Freedom. With Observations on the Origin of Slavery. 1808. BY A MEMBER OF THE AFRICAN SOCIETY IN BOSTON   *13*

Constitution and Rules to be Observed and Kept by the Friendly Society of St. Thomas's African Church, of Philadelphia, 1797.   *28*

An Address to the New York African Society, for Mutual Relief, Delivered in the Universalist Church, January 2, 1809. BY WILLIAM HAMILTON   *33*

Constitution of the African Marine Fund, For the Relief of the Distressed Orphans, and Poor Members of this Fund, 1810.   *42*

Constitution of the New-York African Clarkson Association, 1825.   *45*

Constitution and By-Laws of the Brotherly Union Society, Instituted, April 1833.   *51*

A Charge Delivered to the Brethren of the African Lodge on the 25th of June, 1792. BY PRINCE HALL   *63*

vii

A Charge, Delivered to the African Lodge, June 24, 1797, at Menotomy. BY PRINCE HALL   70

PART II

SOCIETIES FOR EDUCATIONAL IMPROVEMENT, 1808–1836

79

Constitution of the African Benevolent Society, 1808.   84

An Address, Delivered at Bethel Church, Philadelphia; on the 30th of September, 1818. Before the Pennsylvania Augustine Society, for the Education of People of Colour. To Which is Annexed the Constitution of the Society, 1818. BY PRINCE SAUNDERS   87

An Oration Delivered in the African Zion Church, on the Fourth of July, 1827, in Commemoration of the Abolition of Domestic Slavery in this State, 1827. BY WILLIAM HAMILTON   96

An Address Delivered in Wesley Church on the Evening of June 12, before the Colored Reading Society of Philadelphia, for Mental Improvement, 1828. BY WILLIAM WHIPPER   105

Preamble and Constitution of the Pittsburgh African Education Society, January 1832.   120

Duty of Females, 1832. SIGNED L. H.   123

Address to the Female Literary Association of Philadelphia, May 1832.   127

An Address Delivered at the African Masonic Hall, Boston, February 27, 1833. BY MARIA W. STEWART   129

A Lecture at the Franklin Hall, Boston, September 21, 1832. BY MARIA W. STEWART   136

Address and Constitution of the Phoenix Society of New York and of the Auxiliary Ward Associations. 1833.   141

Address Delivered Before the Humane Mechanics' Society, on the 4th of July, 1834. BY JOSEPH M. CORR   146

Address Delivered Before the Moral Reform Society in Philadelphia, August 8, 1836. BY WILLIAM WATKINS   *155*

PART III
SIGNIFICANT ANNUAL CONFERENCES, 1831–1837
167

Constitution of the American Society of Free Persons of Colour, for improving Their Condition in the United States; For Purchasing Lands; and for the Establishment of a Settlement in Upper Canada. Also The Proceedings of the Convention, With Their Address to the Free Persons of Colour in the United States. 1831.   *172*

Minutes of the Four Last Annual Conferences of the African Methodist Episcopal Church; held at Pittsburg, (Pa.,) Washington, (D.C.,) Philadelphia, and New York, 1833–4.   *182*

The Minutes and Proceedings of the First Annual Meeting of the American Moral Reform Society, Held at Philadelphia, In the Presbyterian Church in Seventh Street, below Shippen, from the 14th to the 19th of August, 1837. CONTAINS SPEECHES BY WILLIAM J. WHIPPER, JAMES FORTEN, JR., AND JOHN F. COOK   *200*

PART IV
TO EMIGRATE OR REMAIN AT HOME? 1773–1833
249

Petition Addressed to the Representative of the Town of Thompson, April 20, 1773. SIGNED BY PETER BESTES, SAMBO FREEMAN, FELIX HOLBROOK, AND CHESTER JOIE   *254*

A Brief Account of the Settlement and Present Situation of the Colony of Sierra Leone, in Africa, 1812, *by* PAUL CUFFE   *256*

To the Humane and Benevolent Inhabitants of the City and County of Philadelphia, Address delivered August 10, 1817. BY JAMES FORTEN AND RUSSELL PARROTT   *265*

A Memoir Presented to the American Convention for Promoting the

x   Contents

Abolition of Slavery, and Improving the Condition of the African Race, December 11, 1818. BY PRINCE SAUNDERS   *269*

Letter Relative to Conditions in Hayti, July 1, 1824, Written to the Editor of the Columbian Sentinel. BY THOMAS PAUL   *279*

Resolutions of the People of Color, at a Meeting held on the 25th of January, 1831. With an Address to the Citizens of New York, 1831. In answer to Those of the New York Colonization Society. SIGNED BY SAMUEL ENNALS AND PHILIP BELL   *281*

Speech of Nathaniel Paul delivered at the Anti-Colonization Meeting, London, 1833.   *286*

Emigration to Mexico, 1832, by a Colored Female of Philadelphia.   *292*

A Discourse Delivered in St. Philip's Church, for the Benefit of the Coloured Community of Wilberforce in Upper Canada, on the Fourth of July, 1830. BY PETER WILLIAMS   *294*

Opinions of a Freeman of Colour in Charleston, 1832. SIGNED, A SOUTH CAROLINIAN   *303*

PART V

SPOKESMEN IN BEHALF OF THEIR "COLORED FELLOW CITIZENS," 1787–1815

309

An Address to the Negroes in the State of New York, 1787. BY JUPITER HAMMON   *313*

Copy of a Letter from Benjamin Banneker, To the Secretary of State, With his answer, 1792. BY BENJAMIN BANNEKER   *324*

The Petition of the People of Colour, Free Men, Within the City and Suburbs of Philadelphia. To the President, Senate, and House of Representatives, December 30, 1799. SIGNED BY ABSALOM JONES AND OTHERS   *330*

Contents xi

Letter Addressed To the Honourable George Thatcher, Member of Congress, 1799. BY JAMES FORTEN   333

A Thanksgiving Sermon, Preached January 1, 1808, In St. Thomas's, or, The African Episcopal Church, Philadelphia: On Account of the Abolition of the African Slave Trade, on That Day, By the Congress of the United States, 1808. BY ABSALOM JONES   335

An Oration on the Abolition of the Slave Trade: Delivered in the African Church, in The City of New York, January 1, 1808. With an Introductory Essay by Henry Sipkins. BY PETER WILLIAMS   343

An Oration Commemorative of the Abolition of the Slave Trade; Delivered Before the Wilberforce Philanthropic Association, in the City of New York, on the Second of January, 1809. BY JOSEPH SIDNEY   355

An Oration on the Abolition of the Slave Trade; Delivered in The African Church, in The City of New York, January 2, 1809. With an Introductory Address by Henry Johnson. BY HENRY SIPKINS   365

Oration on the Abolition of the Slave Trade, Delivered on the First Day of January, 1813, in The African Methodist Episcopal Church, 1813. With an Address by Peter Malachi Eagans. BY GEORGE LAWRENCE   374

An Oration on the Abolition of the Slave Trade Delivered on the First of January, 1814, at the African Church of St. Thomas. BY RUSSELL PARROTT   383

An Oration, on the Abolition of the Slave Trade, Delivered in the Episcopal Asbury African Church, in Elizabeth St., New York, January 2, 1815. BY WILLIAM HAMILTON   391

PART VI
SAINTS AND SINNERS, 1786–1836
401

The Life and Confession of Johnson Green, who is To be Executed This Day, August 17th, 1786, for the Atrocious Crime of Burglary; Together With His Last and Dying Words. A Broadside.   405

Confessions of John Joyce, alias Davis, Who was Executed on Monday, the 14th of March, 1808. For the Murder of Mrs. Sarah Cross; With an Address to the Public and People of Colour By Richard Allen, Together With the Substance of the Trial and the Address of Chief Justice Tilghman, on his Condemnation.   *414*

A Narrative of the Lord's Wonderful Dealings With John Marrant, a Black, 1802. BY JOHN MARRANT   *427*

Universal Salvation: A Very Ancient Doctrine: With Some Account of the Life and Character of its Author. A Sermon Delivered at Rutland, West Parish in the Year 1805. BY LEMUEL HAYNES   *448*

An Address to the Wyandott Nation and Accompanying Letter to William Walker, dated May 25, 1817. BY JOHN STEWART   *455*

Religion and the Pure Principles of Morality. The Sure Foundation on Which We Must Build, October 1831. BY MARIA STEWART   *460*

A Pastoral Letter, Addressed to the Colored Presbyterian Church in the City of New York, June 20th, 1832. BY THEODORE WRIGHT   *472*

The Abrogation of the Seventh Commandment, by the American Churches, 1835. Signed—A Puritan. BY DAVID RUGGLES   *478*

Life of Jarena Lee. 1836. BY JARENA LEE   *494*

PART VII
NARRATIVES, POEMS AND ESSAYS, 1760–1835
515

A Narrative of the Uncommon Sufferings, and Surprizing Deliverance of Briton Hammon, Negro Man, Servant to General Winslow, of Marshfield, in New England. 1760.   *522*

An Evening Thought, Salvation By Christ, With Penetential Cries, 1760. A Broadside. BY JUPITER HAMMON   *529*

An Elegiac Poem on the Death of That Celebrated Divine, and Eminent Servant of Jesus Christ, the late Reverend, and Pious George Whitefield, 1770. A Broadside. BY PHILLIS WHEATLEY   *532*

Contents   xiii

An Address To Miss Phillis Wheatley, Ethiopian Poetess in Boston
. . . 1778. A Broadside. BY JUPITER HAMMON   535

A Narrative of the Life and Adventures of Venture, A Native of
Africa: But Resident Above Sixty Years in The United States of
America. 1798. BY VENTURE SMITH   538

Spiritual Song. n.d. BY RICHARD ALLEN   559

Anthems and Hymns, 1808–1814. BY MICHAEL FORTUNE, ROBERT Y.
SIDNEY, PETER WILLIAMS, AND WILLIAM HAMILTON   562

Essay—To the American Convention for Promoting the Abolition of
Slavery, 1828.   572

Poem—On Slavery, 1828. BY GEORGE R. ALLEN   574

Poem—On Freedom, 1828. BY THOMAS S. SIDNEY   574

Essay, 1828. BY ISAIAH G. DE GRASS   576

Selections from The Hope of Liberty, 1829. BY GEORGE MOSES
HORTON   578

A Narrative of Some Remarkable Incidents, In the Life of Solomon
Bayley, 1825.   587

The Origin, Horrors, and Results of Slavery, 1834. BY WILLIAM PAUL
QUINN   614

Appeal To the Colored Citizens of New York and Elsewhere in
Behalf of the Press, 1835. BY DAVID RUGGLES   637

Index of Authors   657

Author's note to the
Black Classic Press edition

Early Negro Writing, 1760-1837 was well received when
it was first published in 1971. It has been out of print and
generally unavailable for a number of years. Since it is
still being used by researchers, teachers and students, when
a copy can be located, it seemed to the compiler that a
reprint of the original edition would be pertinent at this
time. I am grateful to Black Classic Press for reprinting this
edition from the original. No attempt has been made by the
author to include additional entries or to prepare a subject
index at this time. However, eight pages of illustrations
have been included which enhance this edition.

Dorothy Porter
June, 1995

INTRODUCTION

Source materials documenting the role of the Afro-American in our history are being made increasingly available as numerous publishing houses reprint volumes long out of print. However, many of the rarities of early Afro-Americana are yet to be collected. Documents permitting the extension of Negro history deeper into the American past do exist, and in time will be used by those whose task is the rewriting of early Negro history.

The primary purpose of this book is to make available a selected number of writings by Afro-Americans which have appeared in print as books, pamphlets, broadsides, or as parts of books between the years 1760 and 1837. The year 1760 marks the publication of works by the two earliest Negro authors, Briton Hammon and Jupiter Hammon, who have the same surname but were unrelated. By 1837, blacks were engaged locally and nationally in efforts toward emancipation of the slaves, the improvement of living conditions for free blacks, and in debates over colonization. The following decade saw the emergence of more able black writers as well as articulate and forceful leaders—the men who helped to shape the struggle for freedom and advancement of black people.

The writings included in this volume comprise constitutions and laws of beneficial societies; speeches before mutual aid and educational societies; the report of the earliest annual convention for the improvement of the free people of color; arguments for and against colonization; printed letters, sermons, petitions, orations, lectures, essays, religious and moral treatises, and such creative manifestations as poems, prose narratives, and short essays.

Mutual benefit organizations were among the first organized expressions of social consciousness by blacks residing in cities of the North. Such organizations flourished between 1792 and 1835. Adherents rallied to accomplish a variety of purposes, to provide not just for a particular class of blacks but for all those in need of financial help, protection, or enlightened leadership. This early disposition to associate together for mutual improvement provided a training ground for the half-educated as well as for the educated and ambitious among the sons of Africa in the United States. The very titles of some of these organizations suggest that they were directed in the main to the improvement of the social and political status of the blacks.

Educational societies were created largely because of the lack of schools for the young; in fact, opportunities for education were generally denied blacks in Northern cities throughout the Colonial and Federalist periods.

Early organizations were also remarkable for the opportunity they afforded numerous black leaders to use their assemblies as a sounding board for opinion and the advocacy of programs of social action, thus providing a platform for some of the earliest instigators of the abolition movement. While educational societies had more humanistic aims, as shown by attempts to improve the reading ability of the members and to disseminate a taste for good literature, yet these too were sometimes caught up in the prevailing atmosphere of protest and reform.

The pioneer colonization projects of Paul Cuffe and Daniel Coker in Sierra Leone reflect the Afro-American's world view of race and of race destiny for the blacks as they established communities overseas. Many Afro-Americans had significant connections with African, Haitian, and other black communities abroad. The stimulus of the British antislavery movement served to enhance Afro-American prospects for emigration to lands where their people might be free.

On the other hand, the anticolonization stand taken by James Forten, Russell Parrott, Philip A. Bell, and others, together with the resolutions of the people of color expressed the feelings of those who believed the American Colonization Society to be "the enemy of immediate emancipation, aiming to expel from the land of their birth the colored population, not for 'any color of crime, but for the crime of color,' and preventing, as far as possible, their elevation in the United States."

The gathering thunder of abolition is reflected in the group of letters, orations, lectures, and essays which have made the moral convictions and courageous actions of such people as Absalom Jones, Peter Williams, Prince Saunders, William Hamilton, David Ruggles, and William Paul Quinn memorable. Their often vehemently expressed convictions not only influenced many public men, but helped to awaken the conscience of the entire country to the evils of slavery. In a very real sense such writings as are reproduced here were an inspiration to the later antislavery giants—Douglass, Remond, Ward, and others who helped place the capstone on the antislavery edifice.

Many early Negro leaders were noted for their oratorical powers rather than for their effectiveness as writers. Nonetheless, the pamphlets and selections collected here testify to much native talent on the part of early Negro writers, particularly in view of the limited opportunities which they had for formal schooling or even leisure for self-education. In short, it was the urgency of the times that helped create such substantial figures as Richard Allen and David Ruggles.

Among the earliest outpourings of song and story, one finds the writings of Phillis Wheatley and Jupiter Hammon, the first of the black poets. Their productions were striking enough for their day and were seldom matched by such occasional expressions as hymns, spiritual songs, or didactic verse, however impassioned, on the subjects of freedom, slavery, or other-worldly bliss. The remarkable thing is that these early black expressions were genuine, sometimes moving, and often pleasing specimens of narrative writing or poetry describing the condition, the aspirations, or the sufferings of black genius. And, of course, they voiced the hopes of the race.

Students of these early writings have little to say about the vocations and origins of these authors because so little is known about them. It would be interesting to know more about such persons as Michael Fortune, the Sidneys, George R. Allen, and William Hamilton, each of whom have left us a single, or at most a few, works. But it may be enough to realize that here we have the beginnings of the Afro-American's artistic consciousness—indeed, the first articulations of the appeal of beauty and the moral sense—a phenomenon of unexpected early appearance in the course of black experience in America.

From his very beginning in this country the articulate Negro writer expressed not only his sentiments or his inner feelings, but also his attitudes toward social conditions. Specifically, he pronounced on slavery and its abolition, colonization, politics, morals, temperance, religion, education, military service, and racial injustice. In addition, blacks gave their energy, money, and time to guiding and directing their fellow countrymen, whether slave or freeman. Their thoughts and ideas were made available through pamphlets which cost little and which, moreover, were easy to distribute or to carry about. Many were printed in more than one edition: some ran to as many as nine editions.

Today, scholars of all colors and creeds eagerly seek out historical documentation that will help to restore the Negro to his rightful place in history. An analysis of the Afro-American mind as reflected in the writings included in this volume may go far to repair what slavery and the effects of neglectful time have destroyed or mutilated.

Part I

Mutual Aid and Fraternal Organizations, 1792–1833

The lack of economic security, the desire for social contact, the necessity for moral and educational improvement, and the need for spiritual expression constituted the primary reasons for the establishment of mutual aid societies—fraternal, educational, temperance, and religious organizations—by the free Negro in the North and South during the latter part of the eighteenth century. Probably the earliest effort to organize for mutual benefit occurred in Newport, Rhode Island, on November 10, 1780, when Newport Gardner and his friends met together to establish the African Union Society for the expressed purpose of promoting "the welfare of the colored community by providing a record of births, deaths and marriages; by helping to apprentice Negroes; and by assisting members in time of distress." This society was also instrumental in exercising moral influence over its members.[1]

In Philadelphia, on April 12, 1787, black Methodists organized the Free African Society for benevolent and religious purposes, largely as a result of discriminatory practices encountered as they attended services along with whites at St. George's Methodist Episcopal Church. As the popular Reverend Richard Allen through his preaching spread the Gospel of Methodism, their attendance increased and the whites soon demanded the seats occupied by the Negroes. Rather than move to the gallery and rear of the Church, the Negro worshippers along with their religious leaders, Richard Allen and Absalom Jones, left St. George's and formed the Free African Society which later developed into St. Thomas Protestant

---

[1] Irving H. Bartlett, *From Slave to Citizen: The Story of the Negro in Rhode Island* (Providence, R.I., 1954), p. 35; *Rhode Island History*, January, 1948, pp. 20–23.

Episcopal Church, dedicated on July 17, 1794, and Bethel African Methodist Episcopal Church, dedicated July 29, 1794.

In other cities in the North and South beneficial societies were soon formed.[2] The African Society in Boston published its rules and regulations in 1796, the year it was established. Its foremost concern was care for its sick and impoverished members, particularly widows and children. Travelling members left wills with the Society; in the event of death, or if they did not return and no wife survived, their assets went to the Society.[3]

The *Essay on Freedom with Observations on the Origins of Slavery*, written by a member of The Sons of the African Society formed in 1798, expressed the desirability of freedom and the difficulty encountered seeking it. The writer mentions the city of Salem, Massachusetts, as particularly benevolent to Africans noting that it had showed signs of its "approbation of the Africans' freedom."

The Friendly Society of St. Thomas in Philadelphia, whose 1797 Constitution is included in this work, made loans to its members when funds were available. One of its aims was to purchase land for the use of the Society and its successors. The original and only extant copy of the Constitution and Rules of this Society is in the Library Company, Ridgway Branch, in Philadelphia.

The slave trade was abolished in New York State in 1808. Immediately thereafter, Peter Williams, Jr., Rector of St. Philip's Church in New York City, and others organized to improve the conditions of the Negro. They petitioned the legislature for a Charter of Incorporation on March 23, 1810, which was granted.

---

[2] In 1790, a group of free colored men of Charleston, South Carolina, organized The Brown Fellowship Society. See *Rules and Regulations of the Brown Fellowship Society, established at Charleston, South Carolina, 1st November, 1790* (Charleston, 1844). Ninety-four free blacks and other persons of color formed a Temperance Society in Frankfurt, Kentucky, as early as 1832. See *Genius of Universal Emancipation*, Vol. III, No. 3, Third Series, January 1833, p. 43. For an account of burial Societies organized in 1815 in Virginia see Luther P. Jackson, "The Early Strivings of the Negro in Virginia," *Journal of Negro History*, 25:25–34, January, 1940.

[3] The August 4, 1832, issue of the *Liberator* republished the Constitution of this society as "an evidence of the early disposition of the colored inhabitants of Boston to associate themselves together for mutual improvement, protection and support." The brief notice added that this society no longer existed or it had merged with another of similar character and that of the original membership of 40, only 5 were known to have survived. Their names were Thomas Burdine, James Ball, Hamlet Earl, Lewis Jones, and Derby Vassall. (*Liberator*, Vol. 2, No. 31, August 4, 1832.)

The New York African Society for Mutual Relief primarily gave monetary relief to the widows and orphans of deceased members. By August 1820 the Society had constructed a building on Orange Street, now Baxter Street. It served as a model for the formation of the New York Societies such as The Union Society, The Clarkson Association, The Wilberforce Benevolent Society, and the Woolman Society of Brooklyn. The Society is still in existence.[4]

The Brotherly Union Society, organized in Philadelphia in 1832 "for relieving the wants and distress of each other" provided that funds remaining after relief was given to its members were to be invested in real estate, bonds, and mortgages not "to exceed a yearly value of 500 pounds." The Secretary and Assistant Secretary were paid $6.00 and $4.00 per year, respectively, for their services. The Society maintained high moral standards for its members, expelling them if guilty of "fraudulent, base or immoral conduct," or "for gambling, 'tippling' in shops, or spending time in brothels." Members caught "sleeping, lying down or disturbing the harmony of meetings of the Society" were fined 12½ cents.

Masonic and other lodges have always occupied an important position in the Negro community. African Lodge No. 459 was established in 1787 through the efforts of Prince Hall, an active member of the Boston Free African Society and a leader of his people in Boston. Having been made a Master Mason in a meeting of an English military lodge during the occupation of the British Army near Boston in 1775, Hall, along with other Negroes, on March 2, 1784, petitioned the Grand Lodge of England to be permitted to establish a Masonic Lodge. Permission was granted and in 1787, the lodge was established, and officers duly installed. Prince Hall, the first Negro Masonic Grand Master in America and the founder of Masonry among Negroes, sought every means to improve the economic, social, and spiritual condition of the free Negro and to secure the emancipation of slaves. This is evidenced in his Masonic charge delivered to the members of the African Lodge on June 25, 1792, at the celebration of the festival of St. John the Baptist. Prince Hall urged that members of the Masonic Lodge be "good subjects to the laws of the land" and "have no hand in any plots or conspiracies or rebellion, or side or assist in them." He believed in one supreme being and in the importance of love and charity to all the family of mankind. In his Charge, delivered to the African Lodge on June 24, 1797, Prince Hall indicated it was the duty of a Mason to "sympathize with our fellow men under their

[4] Roi Ottley and William J. Weatherby, *The Negro in New York* (New York, 1967), p. 60.

troubles, with the families of our brethren who are gone." He told his listeners that they should have feelings for the slaves, their "distressed brethren" for "many cannot read" but "by our searches and researchers into men and things, we have supplied that defect."[5]

The documents included in this section clearly illustrate the ability of the free Negro to direct his energies and finances to the aid of any of his people in need of welfare assistance, encouragement in their various pursuits, and support in moral and spiritual endeavors.

[5] See George W. Crawford *Prince Hall and His Followers Being a Monograph on the Legitimacy of Negro Masonry* (New York, 1914); Harved Van Voorhis *Negro Masonry in the United States* (New York, 1940).

LAWS

OF THE

AFRICAN SOCIETY,

Instituted at

Boston, Anno Domini 1796.

BOSTON:
PRINTED FOR THE SOCIETY. 1802.

1st. We, the African Members, form ourselves into a Society, under the above name, for the mutual benefit of each other, which may from time to time offer; behaving ourselves at the same time as true and faithful citizens of the Commonwealth in which we live; and that we take no one into the Society, who shall commit any injustice or outrage against the laws of their country.

2d. That before any person can become a Member of the Society, he must be presented by three of the Members of the same; and the person, or persons, wishing to become Members, must make application one month at least beforehand, and that at one of the monthly, or three monthly meetings. Person or persons, if approved of, shall be received into the Society. And, that before the admittance of any person into the Society, he shall be obliged to read the rules, or cause the same to be read to him; and not be admitted as a member unless he approves them.

3d. That each Member on admittance shall pay one quarter of a dollar to the Treasurer and be credited for the same, in the books of the Society, and his name added to the list of the Members.

4th. That each Member shall pay one quarter of a dollar per month to the Treasurer, and be credited for the same on the book;

but no benefit can be tendered to any Member until he has belonged to the Society one year.

5th. That any Member, or Members, not able to attend the regular meetings of the Society, may pay their part by appointing one of their brothers to pay the same for him: so any traveling at a distance by sea or land may, by appointing any person to pay their subscription will be, though absent for any length of time, or on their return, will pay up the same, shall be considered as brothers, and belonging to the Society.

6th. That no money shall be returned to anyone that shall leave the Society; but if the Society should see fit to dismiss anyone from their community, it shall then be put to a vote whether the one thus dismissed shall have his money again, if he should have any left, when the expenses he may have been to the Society are deducted.

7th. That any Member absenting himself from the Society for the space of one year shall be considered as separating himself from the same; but, if he should return at the end of that time, and pay up his subscription, he shall in six months be re-established in all the benefits of a Societain: but after that time he shall be considered as a new Member.

8th. That a committee, consisting of three or five persons, shall be chosen by the Members every three months; and that their chief care shall be to attend to the sick, and see that they want nothing that the Society can give, and inform the Society, at their next meeting, of those who stand in need of the assistance of the Society, and of what was done during the time of their committeement. The committee shall likewise be empowered to call the Society together as often as may be necessary.

9th. That all monies paid into the Society shall be credited to the payers; and all going out, shall be debted to whom, or what for; and a regular account kept by one chosen by the Society for that purpose.

10th. When any Member, or Members, of the Society is sick, and not able to supply themselves with necessaries suitable to their situations, the committee shall then tender to them and their family whatever the Society have, or may think fit for them. And should any Member die, and not leave wherewith to pay the expenses of his funeral, the Society shall then see that any so situated be decently buried. But it must be remembered, that any Member bringing on himself any sickness or disorder by intemperance, shall not be considered as entitled to any benefits or assistance from the Society.

11th. Should any Member die, and leave a lawful widow and children, the Society shall consider themselves bound to relieve her necessities, so long as she behaves herself decently, and remains a widow; and that the Society do the best in their power to place the children so that they may in time be capable of getting an honest living.

12th. Should the Society, with the blessing of Heaven, acquire a sum suitable to bear interest, they will then take into consideration the best method they can of making it useful.

13th. The Members will watch over each other in their spiritual concerns; and by advice, exhortation, and prayer excite each other to grow in Grace, and in the knowledge of our Lord and Saviour Jesus Christ, and to live soberly, righteously, and Godly in this present world, that we may all be accepted of the Redeemer, and live together with him in Glory hereafter.

14th. That each member traveling for any length of time, by sea or land, shall leave a will with the Society, or being married, with his wife; all other Members to leave a will with the Society, for to enable them to recover their effects, if they should not return. But on their return, this will is to be returned to the one that gave it; but if he should not return, and leave a lawful heir, the property is to be delivered to him; otherwise deemed to the Society.

The African Society have a Charity Lecture quarterly, on the second Tuesday in every third Month.

A LIST OF THE MEMBERS NAMES

*Plato Alderson.
*Hannible Allen.
Thomas Burdine.
Peter Bailey. Joseph Ball.
*Peter Branch.
Prince Brown.
Boston Ballard.
Anthoney Battis.
Serico Collens.
Rufus Callehorn.

John Clark.
Scipio Dalton.
Aurther Davis.
John Decruse.
Hamlet Earl.
Ceazer Fayerweather.
Mingo Freeman.
Cato Gardner.
Jeramiah Green.
*James Hawkins.

John Harrison.
  *Glosaster Haskins.
  *Prince M. Harris.
Juber Howland.
Richard Holsted.
Thomas Jackson.
George Jackson.
Lewis Jones.
Isaac Johnson.
John Johnson.
Sear Kimball.
  *Thomas Lewis.

Joseph Low.
George Middleton.
Derby Miller.
Cato Morey.
Richard Marshal.
Joseph Ocraman.
  *John Phillips.
Cato Rawson.
  *Richard Standley.
Cyrus Vassall.
Derby Vassall.

* Those with a Star are dead.

THE SONS OF AFRICANS:

AN

ESSAY ON FREEDOM.

WITH

OBSERVATIONS ON THE ORIGIN OF SLAVERY.

BY

A MEMBER OF THE AFRICAN SOCIETY IN BOSTON.

BOSTON:

PRINTED FOR THE MEMBERS OF THE SOCIETY.

1808.

FREEDOM, a thing so desirable to most men, and so hard to be obtained by many at the present time, will be the theme of our contemplation. Although none can rightly estimate its worth, but those who have been deprived of that invaluable blessing, and through the interposition of Divine Providence have been brought to the enjoyment of the same, yet we may all have a faint idea concerning its worth, if we would contrast our present circumstances with many which we might mention. Although the Sovereign Parent of the universe formed one man, and from whom have proceeded all the nations of the earth, Adam by name; his Maker placed him as head over this lower world, and gave him power and dominion both over the fishes of the sea, the fowls of the air, and the beasts of the field, and all that the earth produced, so that both animal and vegetable creation was for his use and service, one tree only prohibited, which his Maker had designed for a different purpose: after which the all-wise Being thought it fit to form a companion for him, that he might not indulge the melancholy thought of being alone in this vast region: thus they were created moral, intelligent and free agents, left to the freedom of their own will, either to

13

choose or refuse whatsoever was presented to their view. But it
seems as if that happy pair soon marred their happiness, by par-
taking of that forbidden fruit, which was the consequence of bringing them and all their posterity into spiritual darkness, bondage, and
misery, and so completely diffused sin into their immortal part, as
to lay the grand basis for the enemy of souls to triumph, and
spread his baleful influence over the hearts and minds of the children of men, and to be the means of increasing, cherishing, and
cultivating all those evil emotions, inventions, and appetites which
we find mankind infested with; and to incline men to strive to divest
God of his honour, and to deprive their fellow-men of their right—
Yea, an inlet to every vice that can be mentioned. Even when there
was but one family upon the earth, there we find sin increasing in
all its odious colours, in which was exhibited the spirit of an oppressor, the spirit of tyranny, and the spirit of a murderer. Cain was
somewhat affected with the evil root that sprung from the rebellion
of our first parents. If not, would he have envied his brother? Would
he have exerted the utmost of his power to oppress or distress him?
Yea, would he have attempted to deprive him of his freedom, and,
in fine, to take away his life? No, surely not, if this had not been the
case. In the disobedience of our first parents the seed of discord
was completely sown, and each of their sons are affected with the
same. With the death of Cain we do not find sin to be entirely
eradicated from the world, for when it loseth one companion, it
appears to be ready to embrace another, as it chooseth to be a companion for all the sons and daughters of Adam.

O sin, thou monster! Wast thou not ashamed of thy conduct
toward righteous Abel? Didst thou not exhibit thy mischievous
nature enough there, to the view of the world? Hast thou not created
confusion enough in Adam's family? Hast thou not set brothers at
variance, even to shed innocent blood, and what more? Why will
not this suffice? Hath not thy progress been great enough? Why wilt
thou vex the children of men any more? But sin will not stop here;
but it will still proceed, and it spreads far and wide, as the inhabitants of the earth increase—and it branches out in various forms and
means, different complexions, too numerous to mention. Yea, it becomes one of the most extensive plants which this world hath ever
produced—but its production is death, temporal, spiritual, and
eternal, and very void of good fruit. We might trace its various
windings still further, and see what a rapid progress it hath made in
the world.

But we will for a moment collect our ideas to contemplate bondage, oppression, or slavery, as they are the reverse from freedom,

as we are at the present time to suggest the idea of freedom's being valuable. This we cannot have so consistent ideas of, unless we refer back to some of the earliest periods of time, or rove from our present situation into foreign climes, by way of contemplation, and see how sin hath introduced those various abominations in the world; amongst which slavery is the capital that we shall mention at the present time.

We find, soon after the earth began to be inhabited by men, sin continued its progress in the hearts of the children of men. Their wicked ambition began to rise, in which their evil disposition was soon discoverable by their being unwilling to have their fellow men enjoy those rights and privileges which God, in the course of his divine providence, had conferred upon them. We find instances of it in so early an age of the world as in Jacob, the patriarch's family, where the brethren of Joseph gave vent to their malicious designs, by selling their brother Joseph to the Ishmaelites, through the means of which he became a servant unto Pharaoh, and in consequence of that ungodly woman, Pharaoh's wife's false report, was cast into prison, and treated both unhospitably and unkindly, as the Hebrew servants in that day used to be treated. About this time appeared to be the commencement of slavery. Soon after that we find all the family of Jacob was become slaves to the Egyptians; and that Pharaoh, that impenitent monster, would not let them go, even when the Lord commanded them to go, that they might enjoy freedom in their own land. Freedom undoubtedly was their right, if they were authorised by the sovereign majesty of heaven and earth to pursue it. But Pharaoh, in opposition to the commands of God, made their servitude more severe, and demanded of them the most unreasonable service. There was a spirit of a tyrant exhibited in a most dreadful manner. His oppression in slaying all the Hebrew infants, was another display of his folly and wickedness; in which, when Moses was born, he must be consigned to the water, in order to preserve his life, while his sister implored the benediction of heaven for the same. The governor of heaven hears and answers her request; protects him from the boisterous waves, and from the devouring monsters of the same, and even brought him to be nursed in the house of Pharaoh, his inveterate foe, and there to be raised up to set his kinsmen free. Moses's mother knew too well what must have been the consequence if he was found in her own house; he, like the other infants, undoubtedly must have shared the same fate —but when God designs to raise up men for valuable purposes, he oft times takes the most unlikely ways, in the view of mortals, to perform it. No one could think that the river Nile would be a place of safety, or a place in which an infant's life might be preserved; but God had designed that he should lead the children of Israel from the bondage of Pharaoh, therefore he was raised for that purpose.

The miraculous ways in which it was brought about, concerning Moses's being made an instrument, in the hands of God, to liberate the children of Israel from the bondage of Pharaoh, seems to demonstrate a truth like this: that it was displeasing to God to have any of the children of men exercise such a spirit of tyranny as Pharaoh there exhibited. Notwithstanding all the dealings of God towards him, both in way of mercy and judgment, yet that obstinate wretch dares go abreast to them all, and after he had even given them liberty to go, he felt so unwilling that they should be free from being under his dominion, that he calls his army to go with him and pursue them, even to the Red Sea, where God displayed his wrath and indignation upon that oppressor by drowning him there. It was a striking display of God's disapprobation of tyrants' conduct, and surely ought be a warning to any or all who exercise a similar spirit as Pharaoh hath. Thus we see the folly of that cruel tyrant's conduct. When power is put in the hands of a fool, then he is furnished with an opportunity to display his folly: this was the case of Pharaoh, and is the case of many others in the present world. But as that oppressor was destroyed, so will all others be, and meet with their reward either in this or in the world to come.

But it is unnecessary to take up too much of our time in contemplating what was done in the first, second, or third age of the world, since the oppressors and the oppressed that were then on the stage of action, have gone to that impartial Judge that treats every man according as his conduct is, whether it be good or bad.

Those three characters that we have mentioned, plainly testify that men are selfish, and that some will even murder their own brethren, rather than they should have the ascendancy over them, or enjoy an equal privilege with them.

The second instance carrieth an evidence to our minds, that if some dare not go to such an extreme length as to murder their brethren, on account of the boundary which the law of God or men have set, yet they dare to sell and enslave them, and inflict upon them the most severe bondage that human beings can be made the subjects of.

The third instance, which was Pharaoh's conduct, evinces a truth like this: that for the sake of honour, power, dominion, or some worldly object, some men would risk their own lives, yea, lose them, rather than not gain the pre-eminence over their fellow men. To confirm this, we might mention some of those bloody scenes that have taken place from one age to another, even from the death of the Egyptians until the coming of Christ; but time will not permit. However, we would just add this, as a confirmation of the truths which we have mentioned, that in all nations more or less of that spirit prevails amongst men: even in a short debate between the Jews and Romans, we find such an hostile spirit there exhibited, that the issue of it was the blood of twelve thousand men spilt; and many more such instances we might mention, but we hasten our contemplations on more modern times.

There have been divisions in all ages of the world, even from the days of Abel until the present time. The sin of men's enslaving each other, hath made so rapid a progress in the world, that in many parts of it a free man is rarely to be found, unless some who assume the title of lord, or some kingly office, wherein they may domineer over their fellow men, and exercise their authority to the greatest degree. Yea, many have had so great a desire for power, that it seems to have been their delight to oppress and distress their fellow men, which the Africans, I say, the poor Africans, have too often felt the dire effect of, by being made subservient to the will of other nations. Is this not far from acting the part of a man? How far from exhibiting a love for that golden rule which God enjoined upon all his creatures, which is, *Love thy neighbour as thyself,* which would be the best way to confer happiness on ourselves, and a means of advancing great good in the world. But instead of that, a spirit is exhibited quite the reverse, which is the cause of so much discord and confusion. We have no need to query to know who our neighbours are, sinice all men claim the patrimonial connection with Adam. Men, of whatever name or nation, complexion or size; however far remote or near by; however wise or ignorant; all appear to be affected with one blood, for *of one blood was all the nations of the earth formed:* If so, then why this division? Why these discords between nations? Why is the thought so disgustful to many that they cannot bear it? And why should it raise the indignation of many to such a degree that they would enslave all those nations which they viewed inferior to themselves?

All the Africans, at the present day, seem to be the butt of the nations over which men choose to tyrannise, enslave, and oppress. The same spirit still prevails amongst the inhabitants of the earth at the present day as did in the days of Pharaoh. Men pursue the same line of conduct now that Joseph's brethren exhibited towards him, only in a more forcible and severe manner.

When Joseph speaks of himself as coming down to Egypt, he saith, *I was stolen and brought down here and sold.* So, many

Africans may use the same language, or similar expressions—I was brought to America and sold. Men have exercised authority over our nation as if we were their property, by depriving us of our freedom, as though they had a command from heaven thus to do. But, we ask, if freedom is the right of one nation, why not the right of all the nations of the earth? Doth not the sun shine to enlighten each nation? Doth not the rain descend to refresh every land? Why is it then that any of the children of men should make sad the hearts of those whom God hath not made sad, by taking from them the rights and privileges which Providence hath allotted them? Why is such an austere spirit exhibited towards mankind by each other, when the God of nature knows no such distinction?

Some men that we are conversant with, however, are ready to say that a black man, or an African, ought never to be free. But this assertion is groundless, since it is founded on so shallow a foundation as to scarcely bear bringing up to remembrance as an argument, that because many are slaves they all ought to be. But surely this can be no reason, neither would a benevolent man offer such an argument as a reason; one that regarded the welfare of his fellow men would not wish to be guilty of such language. Suppose, yea, there is, in North Carolina, one million thirty-three thousand two hundred and ninety-six, and in Georgia, fifty-nine thousand six hundred and ninety-nine, and in New Jersey, twelve thousand four hundred and twenty-two slaves; and in many other parts of the world a vast multitude of slaves; this doth not argue that they all ought to be; but the reverse. If there are so many that are now slaves, then, surely, those that remain ought to be free, as it is the right and privilege of every man.

Did not America think it was a privilege truly desirable to be enjoyed, when her mother nation was about to invade her land, and bring her under their dominion; did she not greatly regret the thought of a deprivation of her freedom when she asked the assistance of her sister nation, France, to vindicate her cause against Britain with her? If desirable, I say, to America under such circumstances, why not to any or all the nations of the earth? I answer, equally desirable to all. Well, if so desirable to America as that they exerted all their powers to obtain it, why then are they not willing to have it universal? Would not the inhabitants of America think it an act of unkindness in the Turks, the Spanish, or Portuguese, or the more inhospitable nations, if they should take their men, women, and children captive to their own country, and there enslave them with the oppressive yoke of bondage in its awful severity? Most assuredly they would think they divested of all humanity, nor would it be uncharitable judging, as America hath an equal right to their privileges with any nation of the earth. Well, if so, what must be said of America, or especially that part which treats the African in ways similar to those which we have mentioned? This we leave for their own consciences to answer. If they, being apprehensive of such an evil taking place as the loss of freedom, were filled with fear, then surely its enjoyment is desirable. I say, then surely the enjoyment of freedom is desirable. It is desirable on various accounts. We may prove, first, freedom is desirable, as a bound man, or slave, is prohibited from being beneficial to society, or to the church of Christ, as a free man could be. Even on these accounts freedom is to be desired. A man that is bound, or in other words a slave, cannot carry into effect those lawful designs, which otherways he might, if he was free. Although it may be in his heart to relieve the necessities of his fellow men, or to offer some charitable contribution for the cause of his Redeemer, and the interest of religion in the world, but bondage prevents it. Freedom is desirable on another account, that is, on the account of getting knowledge both of our duty to God and our fellow men; as the slave or bound man labours under a great disadvantage of obtaining this knowledge; for their oppressors are apt to keep them in ignorance, lest they should discover their wickedness in the oppression, and find out a way to rid themselves from their hands. Freedom is still desirable on another account; as the free man is indulged with the privilege of commanding his own household, and training up his children in the fear of the Lord, and making them useful both in church and state. Again, it is desirable as we are social beings, and much of our happiness consisteth in those friendly interviews with each other, by way of conversation about various objects which may occur to our minds from time to time; such as the revolution of nations, states, and kingdoms, and things of ancient and more modern times, and likewise friendly intercourse with christian brethren, which afford a great source of happiness; while the slave is in a greater or less degree deprived of that enjoyment.

Once more: Freedom is to be desired, as all men are liable to the decays of nature, either by sickness or age, which in such a season it is highly necessary to be a possessor of some of the comforts and conveniences of this life, which such a season would loudly call for, to make our bodies comfortable, and which the bondman or slave may not have it in his power to obtain.

Slavery hath ever had a tendency to spread ignorance and darkness, poverty and distress in the world. Although it hath advanced a few, yet many have been the sufferers; it was first invented by men of the most malicious dispositions, and has been carried on by men of similar character.

The first man that we have any account of, as being sold, we are informed was done by his envious brethren. Well, if so, O that American christians would no longer follow so pernicious an example, or imitate that, whose origin is of sin. However many attempt to excuse the matter, concerning their trade with the Africans, and pretend to say, if they did not trade with them thus they would destroy themselves by fighting with each other:—but we are apt to persuade ourselves to the contrary, and believe such scenes of havoc and destruction would never have taken place, if the nations round about them had not influenced them thus to do, by promising them something lucrative, to exhilarate their spirits, and to induce them to engage in combat with each other; which by no means render them so blameable as those who trade with them—for men to say, that they would destroy each other, is no excuse for them to perpetrate a similar crime; neither was that the motive that first induced them to proceed in that business. If they had spilled their own blood, it would have been at their own expense, and would have injured none, perhaps, but their own selves. But why should men reason thus about them, as to say, if they were left alone they would destroy themselves? Are they a more morose, blood-thirsty nation than any other on the globe? If not, I see no propriety in such reasoning, and believe it to be evidently demonstrable that this excuse was only a cloak to cover their wickedness, which all good judges must allow to be a wicked act. Neither will it answer to say that they purchased them of their own nation; neither is that an excuse, unless it can be proved that they have a right to them, which perhaps they would meet with more difficulty to prove this, than we should to prove the reverse. I say, perhaps it might be attended with more difficulty to produce arguments to support their right, which they claim to them, than a man of reason would to prove that they had no right to them. Doth it prove that a man hath a right to another, because he is stronger and gains the mastery over him? Is it a sufficient evidence that one neighbour hath a right to another, because he is so sagacious as to rob his neighbour of his wife and children, and sell them to another neighbour for half the value? Neither could it be said of the purchaser, that he had any right to purchase that of another which he knew was gotten by dishonesty; which we know, in every instance in which the Africans have been made to experience similar treatment, is equally as dishonest as that. Let us, for a moment, condole the situations of the bereaved Africans, by way of comparison, and then draw up a conclusion in our own minds, and see whether men have exhibited that benevolent feeling toward them that becomes human beings.

Then let us for once ask, where are the affectionate parents that can bear to see their tender offspring snatched from their bosoms, or dragged from their nurseries, or taken from cradles, without feeling somewhat affected at so horrid a scene? Where is the affectionate husband, the tender wife, the loving brother, the intimate friend, in America, or in any other part of the world, that can bear to be thus severed, without feeling themselves burdened with a load almost insupportable?

Ah! if so, what must be the trials, the anxiety and the distress of the Africans? They who are thus separated, the husband from the wife, and the wife from the husband; the parents from the children, and the parents and neighbours from neighbours, when they have raised expectations of future blessings, and then to be thus deprived of the same; surely it must fill their minds with the greatest anxiety and distress, unless they were drowned in the deepest ocean of insensibility. Surely he must be an unfeeling wretch, indeed, who would prevent his eye from tears, or his heart from sympathy, at the thoughts of having his fellow mortals carried into captivity by their fellow men, who have no right to them or their services? When we are called to part with our fellow mortals by death, we are ready to complain. How frequently do we visit the solitary mansions of the tombs, and there pour out our flood of tears over their silent clay; how do we exclaim against death and the grave. We are ready to say to death: thou cruel monster, why hast thou destroyed the life of this my friend? Why hast thou seized his breath and deprived him of all his earthly comforts? And to the grave: why hast thou bound him in this dark prison, and confined him with these gloomy fetters, that he never shall go free again? And then we complain against God, and with his dealings towards us, whose right and prerogative it is to deal with us as he pleaseth, as we are his property. Every being, both great and small, hath a right to their own, but not to another's; as all men are the Lord's, he hath a right to them and all their services—then surely it would be unjust in us to complain at his government, or repine at his dealings; but men ought not to assume that authority that belongs to God alone. Surely if men complain at the just dealings of God, whose right and prerogative it is to take who, what, or where he pleaseth, no wonder if they exclaim against their fellow men, who attempt thus to do as they have no right to them. If they have no right to them, as it is evident they have not, why then should men assume that authority they do, by taking them from their native country and enslaving them, as they presume to do, by leading them into captivity, when they have as equal right to liberty as those who oppress them? Ah! most assuredly all men have an equal and undoubted right to freedom, either in their own land or in whatsoever part of the world God, in the course of his divine providence, may cast our lot; unless we have done something worthy of confinement, and something for which legal government should think it best that their subjects should be confined, or punished in some other equivalent to their crimes. Men must and ought submit to the government of God, as it is good, and as he has a sovereign right to command us, and as we are under particular obligations to obey him; but not to the government of man, if it is unreasonable and unjust. No one could call that government a good one that would tolerate the keeping of slaves or trafficking in them, if he was possessed of much disinterested benevolence.

The present government, or in other words, that of this state, namely, Massachusetts, is greatly to be valued for the peculiar advantage which we enjoy, as it respects our freedom. Each man hath liberty to enjoy his own opinion, as it respects religious and civil matters; to contrast our circumstances with almost any people, ours would shine with a most superior lustre. The town of Salem, in the state of Massachusetts, may, with great propriety, be distinguished from many other towns in America, on account of their peculiar partiality to freedom, and likewise for their particular benevolence to the Africans, in which they have exhibited visible tokens of their approbation of the African's freedom. Twice we might mention, in March 20th, 1806, and in July 16th, 1807, wherein they rather seem to justify freedom than condemn it: they knowing the worth of that invaluable blessing, freedom, appear to be willing to have the Africans enjoy the same blessing with them; in which they exhibit the character of gentlemen, valuable citizens, yea, of christians. If many, who discover the reverse temper, should be found to exhibit a similar temper, or that candor and benevolence which the town before mentioned doth, we then might with great propriety say, they were a reformed people; yea, might we not say they were christians?

But to return, to support the idea of freedom. Freedom is desirable; if not, would men sacrifice their time, their property, and finally lose their lives in the pursuit of it? If it was not a thing that was truly valuable, should we see whole nations engaged in hostility, to procure it for their country, wives, and children? Yea, I say there is something so dreadful in slavery that some had rather die than experience it. Although there are various kinds of bondage, yet an alleviation from them all is truly desirable. It matters not what the bondage is, while its severity is felt to be a burden; whether it is a contract of our own engagements, or imposed upon us by supreme authority; whether verbal or written. It is evident that there are various kinds of bondage, some of which we shall mention at the present time. It may be called a bondage to persons, when they engage in matrimonial covenant, and are afflicted with a cruel, morose companion; one who tries to irritate the mind of the other, either by insulting language, or absurd conduct. A man may be said to be in bondage, when his station in life is with dishonest neighbours, who would either destroy his property or take away his character. It may, with propriety, be called a bondage of a man, who labours hard to obtain a little of the comforts of this world, and then through his inattention he is not sagacious enough to retain it. From these things, and many others which we might mention, freedom is desirable; such as a violent temper, a profane tongue, and reigning lusts, that oft times bring men in subjection, by the means of which they act a most unbecoming part. So bondage doth not altogether consist in being under the control of overseers, and the severity of their conduct, which we may experience from them; but a freedom, from those other bondages is equally desirable. But we shall not dwell so particularly on those various bondages which mankind are oft times involved in, since that capital bondage of man's enslaving each other, or a freedom from the same, so strongly engrosses our attention and contemplation at the present time.

To assist our contemplation at this time, let us for a moment take a survey of the many thousands of our fellow men, who feel the oppressive yoke. Tyrants—some in one way and some in another, men have racked their minds to invent ways to oppress their fellow men; while they have enclosed some in dungeons, others have been confined in mines, others rowing at the galley, and drawing heavy burdens, grievous to be borne, and labouring in the heat of the day; and if weary and faint, and not fit to perform their daily task, then a whip is prepared for them; which their overseers are not backward in performing their office of putting it on their backs, and that in the most cruel manner; and if hungry and fatigued, but a small quantity of food to supply their gnawing appetites, and that neither wholesome or palatable. And when burdened with age, so that they are not so profitable, they must either be instantly destroyed, or placed in such situations as that they cannot extricate themselves from destruction. Ah! if so, no wonder that the free man exclaims against slavery, and pleads for freedom. If the slave enjoyed food even to the full, [as well as] many other blessings which they now are deprived of, yet their servitude is so severe that they would desire freedom. Even those who have never enjoyed freedom, or experienced it, have such an idea of its value, that they would willingly sacrifice many earthly comforts for its enjoyment.

If there should be a general proclamation of freedom made to those who are thus enslaved, as many of mankind are in some of the ways which we have mentioned, undoubtedly their united voice would be for freedom—how would they hail that auspicious era? how gladly would they receive that melodious sound? A thing so long desired, so ardently wished for, but so unexpected, even the anticipation of which would invigorate their spirits and incline them to bear their present burden with great exhilaration. However, there might be a few of that servile temper, who, like the Hebrew servant of old, that would reply against it, and say, I love my master, my wife, and my children, and will not go free. But then, when compared to the whole, I persuade myself the number of these characters would be few. Undoubtedly the most of them would feel a new joy created in their hearts at so glorious a proclamation as that, and they would with joyful hearts pursue it, and that with the greatest earnestness. Well, if freedom is so desirable to those who are bound, how we who possess it ought to praise it. I say: we Africans in this state, how we ought to praise such an invaluable blessing as it is. It might have been our unhappy lot to have been thus enslaved—we might have felt that awful severity which they now experience, or the bondage which our fathers were under might have been continued unto us. When we refer back but a few years since, and we call to our recollection slavery general throughout all these United States of America, and them men of our complexion, we Africans, who inhabit 'Massachusetts, have great reason to praise the name of the Lord for the same, that peace and freedom in our case have met and embraced each other, and the hope of its continuance is as an anchor for our support. Yea, we would render our unfeigned gratitude to the Almighty for his kind interposition in our deliverance; and would likewise render our most respectful regard to the inhabitants of this state, for the particular benefits and blessings which they have conferred upon us. Although freedom was our right, as it is the right of every other man, yet it was in their power to have held us in slavery and oppression. But a more pleasing prospect presents itself to our view; a thing that affords so much happiness we are now in the possession of; a thing from which so many blessings and benefits proceed, which we humbly pray God would continue to us and to our posterity after us.

If such blessings and benefits are the result of freedom, as we have mentioned, and if slavery is the producer of so many evils, and is attended with such a train of difficulties, then we may learn how amazingly criminal those must be who love freedom themselves, to prevent any from its enjoyment; and likewise learn how much real injury it doth both to church and state to have men enslaved. When, if the same men were but free, they might be useful members of society, valuable citizens, and perhaps eminent in the church of God; and in one way and in another, one man that was free might do vastly more good in the world than a multitude of slaves could possibly do. The objector is now ready to say, that if all other men are free the Africans ought not to be free. Mr. Objector, why ought not the Africans be free? To your question, I answer, because some of them do not conduct with that propriety which becomes human beings. But as we are not to judge men, then surely we ought not to condemn all for one's transaction. How unwise should we esteem the merchant that would destroy a large sum of gold, because a piece of dross was found amongst it. This, I say, would be acting foolishly, judging partially, and condemning wrongfully. It is true, many of our complexion conduct with great impropriety; notwithstanding, as they must answer for their conduct, it doth not militate against those having freedom who do conduct with propriety. Again, we would insist on the universality of freedom, because we believe it to be the right of every rational creature. Yea, we might prove it from various observations—but each man, of an enlightened understanding, is so well acquainted with his rights, that it needs no arguments to prove this assertion.

We would equally condemn a tyrannical spirit in all nations. Although there are particular characters, who we acknowledge, in the world, are not fit subjects to enjoy freedom; some of which our curiosity prompts us to mention. First, the man that is deranged is not a fit subject to enjoy freedom; whether deranged by intemperance or some providential dealing of God, so that his reason hath left him. Such a man, we all would conceive, ought be confined, lest be would do great injury if at large. The idiot, or one that is born into the world void of sense, and groweth even to manhood, but never retains it, but as readily runs into the way of danger as of safety. Such ones need some one to have a cautious eye over them, lest they soon destroy themselves, or injury others. Once more—the third character which we shall mention is the infant, whose mind is weak and feeble, dull of apprehension, and comprehension short, and bodies equally as feeble as their minds; yea, and are not capable of preserving themselves, either from the fire or from the water. Surely such ones need one for their guardian. Again—the high minded man may do much hurt in the world; one who feels his own superiority to his fellow men, and wishes to exercise his authority over mankind. Yes, I say, the tyrant too often exhibits a spirit more fit to be a slave than many of his domestics.

The three first characters which we have mentioned, however unfit they are to enjoy freedom, yet they ought not be treated with harshness or severity, but in the most kind and sympathetic manner. But this last character, as it is so turbulent and hostile, it needs more and stronger force to subdue it, than bare leniency.

Surely, for men who boast of having reason, to conduct more rationally than those who have it not, by taking advantage of them who labour under the disadvantage of the loss of their reason, surely if any men deserve to be deprived of their freedom, those who thus conduct are the men. Again—according to our contemplations, we observed, the slave is surrounded with a multitude of discouragements; but notwithstanding, there are a few encouraging words found in the word of God for him, which, if his heart is right with God, they may afford him a great source of comfort. While he realizes his master enjoying freedom, and is deprived of it, he forgets, or never knew, that it is written in God's word, *that he that hath, it shall be taken from him that which he hath, and to him that hath not, it shall be given.*

It is no real sign that a man is rejected of God because he is enslaved by man. The Israelites, after a long series of hardships by the oppressive hand of Pharaoh, were carried into captivity ten times. Although, perhaps, they did not experience slavery in that awful severity that their fathers did: yet they experienced it in such a manner, as in which, when they were delivered, it was so delightful a thing that *their mouths were filled with laughter and their tongues broke forth in singing.* Yea, freedom hath been so desirable in all ages of the world, that when any had been deprived for a time of it, their joy was so great to them, that it only appeared as a dream. Although the Israelites were carried into captivity ten times, yet they often had a different master; four times by the hand of Sertacherib, and four times by Nebuchadnezzar, and once by Vespasian, and once by the superstitious Adrian. Although their masters' different bondage varied, yet they were God's particular people still. From this thought may the slave take encouragement, to put his trust in the Lord. This was Moses's support when passing through the Red Sea—this was Daniel's comfort when in the lion's den—this was David's hope when carried into captivity—this hath been the consolation of many poor, disconsolate ones in these latter days. To know that the Lord reigneth, ought and will afford the slave the greatest consolation of anything in this world, if his heart is right with God. Yea, he need not be discouraged, knowing that all his oppressors shall be subdued by his Almighty hand, as he may well suppose it is displeasing to him; so, therefore, the oppressors shall not be unpunished. Once more—we would disapprove of a tyrannical spirit as much in an African as in any other man; not because they are connected with us as it respects our complexion, would we justify wicked conduct in them, for we believe that an haughty spirit did not come from the Lord, but from the son of darkness.

Once more we would take the liberty to ask the objector against freedom, before we conclude our contemplations, whether the complexion of one nation entitles them to the service and property of another? Or, in other words, whether the Africans ought be subject to the British or Americans, because they are of a dark complexion? Now the objector may have an opportunity to raise his objections; but we believe them to be so trivial, so fallacious and groundless, that we think he must have so hard a study to support it, that we think we had better postpone hearing his objection until some future period, therefore we haste to the conclusion of our present contemplation. Again, if they who feel the severity of bondage, could but realize that truth recorded in God's word, concerning a period when universal freedom should take place, in such a manner as that every man should sit beneath the shadow of his own vine and fig tree, and none to molest or make them afraid, when they shall be all their own men, the anticipation of it would create in them an universal joy: even if it was in future ages, and they did not expect to enjoy it in fruition themselves. Then it amounts to a demonstration, that even the thoughts of freedom to a slave, is truly desirable, to alleviate them under their present bondage. Well, if freedom, that inestimable blessing, which many of complexion are deprived of, is our lot, then let us be careful, lest we incur the displeasure of God by our ingratitude, as many have done, and by the means of which they have had the blessings removed from them. I say, Africans, who inhabit Massachusetts, we have great reason to rejoice in our particular favours of the Almighty, in this our distinguished privilege, as well as under renewed obligations—pray for its continuance to us and our children. But, ah! what is that temporal bondage which we have been contemplating, when compared to that spiritual bondage which all the sons of Adam are involved in? But for our encouragement it is that we read, that if the son of God, whose power alone it is to make us free, doth it, we shall be free indeed. O that we may all experience that spiritual freedom in this life, and at last be admitted to those blissful realms where peace and freedom reign uninterrupted.

CONSTITUTION

AND

RULES

TO BE

OBSERVED AND *KEPT*

BY THE

FRIENDLY SOCIETY

OF

St. Thomas's African Church,

1831.

PHILADELPHIA.

PHILADELPHIA:
PRINTED BY W. W. WOODWARD, NO. 17, CHESNUT-
STREET. 1797.

WHEREAS we the Subscribers, members of the African Episcopal Church, called ST. THOMAS's, in the City of Philadelphia, frequently conversing on that most amiable of all the social virtues, Charity, and feeling a desire to promote it in the most consistent manner, as far as our circumstances in life will admit, at the same time to make our undertaking as permanently useful as possible, have, and hereby do, conclude to associate and unite ourselves together, by the name,

title and description of "THE FRIENDLY SOCIETY OF ST. THOMAS'S
AFRICAN CHURCH, OF PHILADELPHIA," under the following

REGULATIONS

I. THE Officers of the Society shall consist of a President, Vice-
President, Treasurer, Secretary, and a Committee of Seven Members; who shall annually be chosen by the Society at large, at the
monthly meeting in November: It being expressly agreed that no
election for President shall be made in the Society, but he shall be
chosen by the seven members of the Committee from among their
number.

II. WE bind ourselves, and do hereby agree, to meet monthly in
a convenient place, to be procured by the committee. At all and
every such meeting each and every member, and such as may hereafter become members of this Society, shall deposit one quarter of a
dollar into the hands of the President, who shall cause the Secretary
to credit each member for every such payment, in a book to be kept
fair and correct for that purpose, bearing the date of the payment;
and as soon as the whole amount of the said sums shall be received,
the President shall pay the same into the hands of the Treasurer,
and shall cause the amount thereof to be entered in a book to be
kept by him, with the day on which it was paid; and the Treasurer
shall keep a book in which he shall preserve a fair and regular account of the debts and credits of all and every matter relating to
the Society, in all cases which respect his office.

III. THE duty of the President shall be as is expressed in the II.
Article, together with that of keeping order and decorum in the
Society during the meeting thereof. The duty of the Committee shall
be to call delinquent members to account, and make report thereof
to the Society: During the recess thereof the Committee shall visit
such members of the Society as reside within their district, and if a
majority of them be of the judgment that the member so visited
stands in need of assistance, they shall (with the consent of the President) have power to draw on the Treasurer for such sums of money
as they conjointly may think requisite, not exceeding one and a half
dollar per week to each member, during his inability. It shall also be
their duty to inspect all entries made in the President's book, so that
they may prove the authenticity and accuracy thereof. At every
meeting of the Society the minutes of the preceding meeting shall
be read before any other business is entered upon.

THE Treasurer shall be of good character and reputation, possessed of freehold property, and on entering on the duties of his office, he shall give such security for the faithful discharge of his trust as a majority of the Committee shall require.

IV. THE payments made by the members to the Society, shall be disposed of only for the relief and support of the orphans and widows of deceased members (so long as the widows shall remain unmarried) and for the relief of necessitous members; after which, if the funds of the Society will afford it, to any other charitable purpose that the President and a majority of the Committee may deem necessary.

V. No money whatsoever shall be drawn from the funds of the Society on any pretence, until the expiration of twelve months after the forming of the same. But if the necessities of the sick or distressed members should call for assistance before the expiration of the said twelve months, it must be a gratuitous gift from the members as they may think proper.

VI. IF the funds shall in a future time amount to one hundred pounds, clear of every charge, then the President and Treasurer shall let out one half thereof on good and sufficient security, for no longer term than twelve months, or shall purchase therewith landed property, to and for the use of the said Society and their successors; taking bond and mortgage for the same, in their own names, to and for the use of the said Society; and shall make like loans in the same proportions, as the funds of the Society may increase, always reserving one half of the stock to answer the expenses of the Society. All loans to be made with the approbation of a majority of the Committee, who shall take counter security from the President and Treasurer, for all monies loaned as aforesaid.

VII. As the business of the Committee may become arduous, such as visiting the sick, inspecting their circumstances, and supplying their necessities, with other duties already pointed out, it is agreed that they shall continue in office only twelve months, unless again elected. But in case of death, resignation or forfeiture of office by misbehaviour, another member shall be chosen to supply the vacancy.

VIII. IN case any member of the Society shall neglect paying his monthly subscription for three months, and, after being informed of the same, by the Committee, offer no good and sufficient reason for his neglect, and does not pay his arrears at the next meeting, he shall be expelled from the Society, and his subscription money forfeited for its use.

IX. If any member neglect meeting at the stated monthly meeting, he shall for every such neglect forfeit and pay one eighth of a dollar.

X. In case of the death of any member of the Society, without leaving sufficient property for his interment, the Committee shall cause him to be buried in a plain and decent manner from the Society's fund.

XI. All bye-laws shall be introduced at one meeting, and if not generally approved, they shall lay over for consideration until the next, when general notice shall be given to the members, at which time they shall be decided by a majority.

XII. Whereas, in order to make a beginning, the founders of this Society did pay a dollar at their entrance therein, it is agreed to receive all approved persons on their paying the like sum of one dollar, until twelve months after the forming of this Society, after which time they may be received as a majority may judge right.

RULES

The Society shall meet on the first Wednesday of every month. At the hour appointed the President shall take the chair, and the Society shall proceed to business, during which time the members who are met shall behave themselves in a decent and orderly manner.

Each member when speaking to the business, shall address the President, and shall not speak oftener than three times on the same subject, unless called upon by the President or requested so to do by a majority of the members present.

The President shall determine all points of order, unless his decision shall be appealed from by some of the members present, and then the point shall be decided by a majority of the meeting.

If any member shall violate any of these rules, he shall be dismissed [from] the Society for that evening, and shall not be permitted to sit therein until satisfaction be made.

If any two members shall be so imprudent as to wrangle during the time of meeting, they shall both be dismissed from the Society, and shall not be suffered to meet again until satisfaction be made.

In the absence of the President, the Vice-President shall preside at the meetings. All applications for admission of new members shall be made by a member at one meeting, and lay over for consideration until the next; and if a majority of the members present are in favor of the application, the person shall be admitted.

AN

ADDRESS

TO THE

NEW YORK AFRICAN SOCIETY,

FOR

MUTUAL RELIEF,

DELIVERED

In the Universalist Church,

January 2, 1809.

By William Hamilton.

NEW YORK:
PRINTED IN THE YEAR 1809.

ORDER OF THE DAY

First . . . The Society moved in procession from the African School Room to the Church.

Second . . . The services of the house commenced with a Solemn Address to Almighty God, by Mr. James Varick, Chaplain.

Third . . . An appropriate Hymn, sung under the direction of Mr. George Collins.

Fourth . . . The Constitution read, by Mr. Adam Carman, Assistant Secretary.

Fifth . . . The Address delivered by Mr. William Hamilton, President.

Sixth . . . An appropriate Hymn.

Seventh . . . A Collection made to defray the expenses of the day.

Eighth . . . A Hymn.

Ninth . . . The services of the day concluded with a Solemn Prayer by the Chaplain.

To Mr. William Hamilton.

SIR,

The Address which was delivered by you, on the 2d inst. having afforded us the highest satisfaction, we feel it our duty to express to you the lively sense of gratitude which we feel on that account.

We beg that you will therefore accept of our most sincere thanks, and that you will honor us by suffering a publication of that valuable and useful work.

In behalf of the New York African Society, for Mutual Relief,
PETER WILLIAMS, Jun. V.P.

New York, Jan. 9, 1809.

To the New-York African Society.

GENTLEMEN,

Your expressions of satisfaction in the Address delivered to you on the 2d inst. does much pleasure to my feelings, and your request for the publication of the address is a higher compliment paid me than I expected to receive; I shall, with the utmost cheerfulness, consent to the publication thereof, because I ever wish to act in conformity to the society's will.

I remain, Gentlemen,
With much respect,
Yours, &c.
WILLIAM HAMILTON.

ADDRESS

My Brethren and Fellow Members of the New York African Society, for Mutual Relief, I congratulate you on this first anniversary of a day which has produced an event that, for its importance to

Africans and descendants, stands unrivaled; an event that long and arduous have been the exertions of many philanthropic characters to bring forth; an event that every benevolent mind rejoices to see. This day we are met with hearts big with gratitude, to celebrate an act of congress of the United States of America, which for its justice and humanity, outstrips any that have ever passed that honorable body; by an act bearing date March the second, eighteen hundred and seven, and which became an effectual law, January the first, eighteen hundred and eight, that species of commerce designated the *slave trade* was abolished.

This abominable traffic, the most execrable and inhuman that ever was practised, had been carried on for olympiads and centuries, and the tide of misery flowing through this channel had arisen to an incalculable height. The wretched victims of the trade were not only deprived of life's first and most valuable jewel and best blessing, their liberty, not only were they torn from their native land, and all they held delightful and dear; but they were likewise doomed to pass through a train of as severe inflicted miseries as could be devised, such as at the bare recital of, the heart of sensibility sickens.

The country of our forefathers might truly be called paradise, or the scat of ease and pleasure, until the foul fiends entered—fiends did I say? yes, the name is too sacred an appellation for the base ravagers of the African coast: Until the man-stealing crew entered, peace may be said to be within her borders, and contentment in her dwelling, but the dealers in human flesh, not contented with setting the nations on to fierce, bloody, and incessant contests—not contented with making Africa groan from its sea line to its centre; but as if to be the more immediate instruments of cruelty, they obtain the captives taken in war, they kidnap thousands, they sever them from all their enjoyments! handcuff, brand, chain, clog, and scourge them, but why do we enumerate, who can recount half their sufferings, where is the artist that can delineate a full picture of their miseries— their wretched situation baffles description; let us then withdraw from, and at once acknowledge our inability to the task; but we stand confounded at the reflection that there should be found any of the human family so lost to their nature and the fine feelings of man, as to commit, unprovokedly commit, such acts of cruelty on an unoffending part of the human family.

But my Brethren, however this may be, it is for us to rejoice that the cause or source from whence these miseries sprang are removing; it is for us to rejoice not only that the sources of slavery are drying away, but that our condition is fast ameliorating; it is for us to rejoice that science has began to bud with our race, and soon shall our tree of arts bear its full burthen of rich and nectarious fruit, soon shall that contumelious assertion of the proud be proved false, to wit, that Africans do not possess minds as ingenious as other men.

The proposition has been advanced by men who claim a pre-eminence in the learned world, that Africans are inferior to white men in the structure both of body and mind; the first member of this proposition is below our notice; the reasons assigned for the second are that we have not produced any poets, mathematicians, or any to excel in any science whatever; our being oppressed and held in slavery forms no excuse, because, say they, among the Romans, their most excellent artists and greatest scientific characters were frequently their slaves, and that these, on account of their ascendant abilities, arose to superior stations in the state; and they exultingly tell us that these slaves were white men.

My Brethren, it does not require a complete master to solve this problem, nor is it necessary in order (like good logicians) to meet this argument, that we should know which is the major and the minor proposition, and the middle and extreme terms of syllogism, he must be a willful novice and blind intentionally, who cannot unfold this enigma.

Among the Romans it was only necessary for the slave to be manumitted, in order to be eligible to all the offices of state, together with the emoluments belonging thereto; no sooner was he free than there was open before him a wide field of employment for his ambition and learning and abilities with merit, were as sure to meet with their reward in him, as in any other citizen. But what station above the common employment of craftsmen and labourers would we fill, did we possess both learning and abilities; is there aught to enkindle in us one spark of emulation: must not he who makes any considerable advances under present circumstances be almost a prodigy: although it may be true we have not produced any to excel in arts and sciences, yet if our situation be properly considered, and the allowances made which ought to be, it will soon be perceived that we do not fall far behind those who boast of a superior judgment, we have produced some who have claimed attention, and whose works have been admired, yes in despite of all our embarrassments our genius does sometimes burst forth from its incumbrance. Although the productions of Phillis Wheatley may not possess the requisitions necessary to stand the test of nice criticism, and she may be denied a stand in the rank of poets, yet does she possess some original ideas that would not disgrace the pen of the best poets.—Without naming others who have appeared in the interim of her and the present time, I hold in my hand a specimen of African genius; African I term it because in the position that the present argument is offered, it makes no kind of difference whether the man is born in Africa, Asia, Europe or America, so long as he is proginized from African parents.

This book contains an introductory address and an oration on the abolition of the slave trade, delivered in the African Church, the first of January eighteen hundred and eight, by two young men whom you are generally acquainted with: the address or frontispiece to the work is a flow of tasteful language, that would do credit to the best writers; the oration or primary work is not a run of eccentric vagaries, not now a sudden gust of passionate exclamation, and then as sudden calm and an inertness of expression, but a close adherence to the plane of the subject in hand, a warm and animating description of interesting scenes, together with an easy graceful style. If we continue to produce specimens like these, we shall soon put our enemies to the blush; abashed and confounded they shall quit the field, and no longer urge their superiority of souls.

You my Brethren have formed yourselves into an association for the purpose of protecting each other from indigency, as far as in your power lies, conscious that deep poverty and distress is the bane of improvement, conscious, too, that our advancement in every point of view depends much on our being united in social bodies.

Man in the abstract is subject to almost every inconvenience that can be named, his hand is feeble, his sight short, his movements slow; but united with his fellow man he is strong, he is vigorous, he turns the channel of mighty rivers, throws down huge mountains, removes thick forests, builds great cities, pushes on the great machine of trade, his arm is next omnipotent, not only so he is formed for social life, the gloomy hermit we pity, and the snarling cynic we despise, these are men who appear to be rubbed off the list of men, they appear to have lost the fine fibres of the mind, on which it depends for expansion and growth, they appear to be sunk into a state of insensibility of the extreme happiness growing out of social life.

But my Brethren, mere socialities is not the object of our formation, but to improve the mind, soften the couch of the sick, to administer an elixir to the afflicted, to befriend the widow, and become the orphan's guardian, and is this not a noble employment, can there be found a better, you ought to be proud to be engaged in such an exercise. It is employment of this kind that raises the man up to the emperium, or highest heaven.—But in order that an association of this kind may appear to better advantage, let us take a view of the situation of man, precarious indeed, subject to continual vicissitudes.—This day strong and active, tomorrow feeble and decripped, today healthful and vigourous, tomorrow lifeless and entombed. See the rich and lordly owner of a manor, now rolling in his gilded chariot, or now sitting beneath his stately dome, surrounded by his wife and children, his hall crowded with a retinue of servants, his fine-wrought board covered with costly viands and full-flowing bowls of delicious cordials, his walls revibrating with the loud cheer of convivial friends, his sun of bliss shines clear, not a cloud to intercept its rays, but suddenly storms and tempest arise, and thick clouds overspread his horizon, he is driven as by a torrent of misfortune, and as by a whirlwind his riches all flee away, and with them, as is common, flee his friends; he is turned from his stately dwelling to give room to some hard-hearted creditor, and from a reverse of fortune, now takes up his abode in some low hovel: But does the scene of distress close here, he must not only suffer the mortification of his loss of property, friends, and pleasures, but he must likewise be subject to affliction and death, pale sickness astrides him, he is rid until his enfeebled body can sustain the pressure no longer, then Death, but oh! with what horror, what ghastly horror does he attack the man, Oh! Death thou cruel monster, thou dost not appear half so dreadful when in the field of battle, where blood and carnage spread the ground, and where from the mouth of ordnance as from a vulcano fierce flaming fire issues forth, spreading destruction in every direction, or where the battle pushed on by furious leaders to the foul entrance of a fortress kept by tube behind tube, and thou Oh! Death, standing in dread array forwarning the presumptuous invader of his fate; or when the furious tempest howls, and the angry ocean convulsed to its low foundation, swells and lifts its head as to make war with heaven, and the fierce lightning's vivid flashes, darting from the clouds, accompanied with the loud roar of thunder, the affrighted mariner in his crazy bark, dashed about from wave to wave, expecting momently the sea to be his tomb.—No, thou fell monster, thou dost not appear half so terrible in scenes like these, as to the man about to be torn from his wife and children by thy cruel fangs; at thy approach his eyes start inward, his blood retreats back to its reservoir, an icy coldness takes possession of the vacuated parts of his body, he heaves a languishing look at his family, and with his cold quivering lips, feebly exclaims, oh! my family, most merciful God, what shall be the fate of my family, gracious heaven protect my wife—my children!

But my Brethren, are scenes of distress confined to the rich made indigent by misfortune, are they the only depressed by affliction; happy indeed were this the case, would it be for the human family, but the wretched of this class stand as a mere cypher compared with the poor of mankind, the labouring part of the community, who depend on their daily earnings for their subsistance, each winter brings to these its anxieties, but let affliction attack them when it may, it is sure to bring with it additional sorrows; here then arises the necessity of societies to lessen the miseries of mankind, to participate in their sorrows and to reciprocate joy and happiness as extensively as their mutual endeavours at relief will admit.

Happy for these United States that the spirit of Liberty, improvement, and philanthropy pervades the people; societies for the purpose of spreading useful knowledge, diffusing virtuous principles, or for ameliorating the condition of man are amply encouraged; this state, and particularly this city, has produced its full proportion of useful institutions; without naming a long list of excellent associations, I shall take the liberty to mention one to which we are extremely indebt, as Africans, and their descendants, I here mean the Manumission Society: this institution was established in or about the year one thousand seven hundred and eighty-four, by a number of gentlemen of the first respectability, who were strongly attached to the principles of liberty and the rights of man; they, possessing the true spirit of patriotism, felt for the honor of their country; they saw that while the siren song of liberty and equality was sang through the land, that the groans of the oppressed made the music very discordant, and that America's fame was very much tarnished thereby; they were not contented with barely planning the means of the emancipation of large numbers of the enslaved, but they likewise established a seminary of learning, and so spirited were they in our cause, that in the year one thousand eight hundred, when, from the inadequacy of their funds to the accumulated expenses of the society, they had incurred a debt of twelve hundred dollars and upwards, the trustees of their school pledged themselves to each other to raise the just mentioned debt, by subscription, or defray the same from their own private funds.—Thou source of Benevolence, and first and main spring of all good actions, be not jealous of us, but next to thee, we owe to these men our highest tribute of gratitude, but to them as to thee, we can render nought but unprofitable thanks.

My Brethren, many and repeated attempts have been made in this city, to establish societies of various kinds among the people of colour, but whether from the impolicy of the plans, or our unripeness for those institutions, we will not say, but they have always soon perished or dwindled away to a number so small as scarcely to deserve the name of society; whether this will be the case with this institution or not, remains for futurity to say; but if we may judge from appearances, we shall predict that its standing shall be long, and that the rays of its beneficence shall make the hearts of thousands of yet unborn members dilate by its cheering effulgence and effusions of benefits in seasons of sickness and distress.

This society has not been formed three quarters of a year, and the number of its members exceed by three times the number of any civil institution yet attempted among us.

The principles on which this institution is founded are congenial not only with the wish, but likewise with the interest of its members; its principles forbid the idea of its members becoming beggars to the society for relief in time of sickness, but it is the pledge, the agreement, and the duty of this institution to pay the sums specified by its Constitution to its sick members, and the widows and orphans of deceased members who have stood as such the limited time. So long as the principles of this society remain unchanged, so long shall its limbs remain unwithered and its trunk uncorrupted, its boughs shall never refuse to bear fruit for want of nutriment in the tree; never can you, my Brethren, be so infatuated as to shake off this institution, except by the over-persuasion of some foul daemon. Guard against the enemy, for enemies we have that would make merry at our overthrow; but above all things let our meetings be conducted with order and propriety, let order be our guide and peace our way mark; let friendship and good will be our atmosphere, be attentive to the sick members, never let it justly be said that we assumed the name of *Mutual Relief* for nought.

To you, my Brethren, the Standing Committee, let me address myself. Your's is truly an exalted station in which there is much confidence and trust reposed, with you rests the credit of this society, her fame shall spread through your vigilance, it is for you to immortalize her name by your active attention to the duties imposed on you; be then attentive to the sick members, and the widows and orphans of deceased members. If there should be found any one among you who should refuse to do his duty, let him be set aside as an unfit character to have such high trust reposed in him; but surely, my Brethren, there is not one of you who would be so forgetful of his honor and the solemn pledge he has given of the strict performance of the duties assigned him.

The other Officers are no less bounden and no less responsible, and in them is reposed equal trust, and from them is expected an equal attention to their duties.

Let us all be united, my Brethren, in rearing this edifice—steady to our several departments—and so on shall be raised a wide spreading dome that shall stand the admiration and praise of succeeding generations, and on its front shall be eternally engraven

MUTUAL INTEREST,
MUTUAL BENEFIT,
AND MUTUAL RELIEF.

CONSTITUTION

OF THE

AFRICAN MARINE FUND,

FOR THE RELIEF OF

THE DISTRESSED ORPHANS,

AND

POOR MEMBERS

OF THIS FUND.

NEW YORK:
PRINTED BY JOHN C. TOTTEN,
NO. 155 CHATHAM-STREET.
1810.

PREAMBLE

THE present subscribers have for some time considered the situation of our poor Africans and descendants of our mother country. Also, considering the calamities that mankind in general are liable to fall into, more especially the Africans and their descendants,

ARTICLE I

IT is agreed that both male and female members, on their joining this society, paying the sum of *one dollar,* shall be entitled to vote for the officers of the said fund, which shall consist of a Treasurer, a President, and Secretary, with four Trustees, who shall be chosen by ballot, and the election to be adjudged by the Elders of the fund, who shall be one or each of the elder ministers of the African Zion Church in this city.

ARTICLE II

It shall be the duty of the Trustees of this fund at all meetings to make a collection, and to give a strict account of the same to the treasurer the day or evening after such collections are made.

ARTICLE III

It shall be the duty of the Secretary to make an entry of such monies collected by the Trustees, and give an account of it to the President and members, provided always one of the elders be present, once every month.

ARTICLE IV

It shall be the duty of the President to be present at all meetings; and should any difference be among the members respecting their upright walk and behaviour during their membership, he shall with the elders have a casting vote.

ARTICLE V

All monies paid in by the members, and made by collection, is to be appropriated to the use of schooling the poor African children, whose parents are unable to educate them. And as the fund increases, to give them such clothes as the Elders, President, and Trustees may think in council necessary.

ARTICLE VI

It shall also be understood that each member shall pay *twenty-five cents* every month, towards the schooling of the poor children, and the support of the sick members of the said fund. And furthermore, if any member is sick, according to this constitution they must be supported during their sickness; provided they make application to the Elder or Elders of this fund, and satisfy them respecting their circumstances.

ARTICLE VII

There shall be also a Committee appointed to visit our African brethren, and the descendants of our mother country, to give information of their several distresses and wants; and on the report of the same to the Elders, with sufficient satisfaction, the Elders may, without the consent of the Trustees, send an order to the Treasurer for such amount as in their judgment may seem sufficient to their relief.

ARTICLE VIII

It is agreed, that if any of the members of this fund should die, the Committee must immediately give notice to the Elders, who shall call a meeting and see the situation of the fund; and should the fund be not altogether sufficient to inter him or her, the members shall make a collection sufficient to bury him or her decent, and defray all the burial expenses.

Rev. June Scott
Rev. Abraham Thompson
Simon Hackett
Joseph Harman

CONSTITUTION

OF THE

New-York

AFRICAN

Clarkson Association.

NEW YORK:
PRINTED BY E. CONRAD,
4 FRANKFORT STREET.
1825.

WE, the Subscribers, having duly considered on the manifold vicissitudes of life, to which mankind are continually exposed; and actuated by a desire to improve our condition, do form ourselves into an Association, for the benevolent purpose of raising funds, to be exclusively appropriated to aid and assist the widows and orphans of deceased members, and for improvement in literature.

And furthermore we do agree, that this Association shall be known by the name and style of the NEW-YORK AFRICAN CLARKSON ASSOCIATION, and shall consist of free persons of moral character.

And for the better execution of the benevolent purpose, for which it was instituted, we jointly agree to be governed by the following CONSTITUTION

ARTICLE 1—Candidates for Membership

SECT. 1.—No person shall be admitted a member of this Association, who shall be under the age of 21 years, or over the age of 40 years—who shall be afflicted with any disorder or sickness inconsistent with ordinary health, or who may, in any probability become a charge to the Association.

SEC. 2.—Every person making application for membership, must

45

be reported by one of the members, at any one of its meetings, and the name or names of each person shall be handed over to the Board of Directors, who shall report thereon at the next meeting, when he shall be balloted for (providing his balloting be not contrary to any of the articles of the Constitution), and if a majority of the members present shall vote in his favour, he shall be declared duly elected.

SEC. 3.—If any member comes forward, previous to such person's signing the Constitution and paying the initiation fees, and states what a majority of the members present may deem a sufficient objection, he shall not be admitted.

SEC. 4.—If any person so approved of shall neglect to come forward and pay his initiation fee, and sign the Constitution, for the space of six months, his election shall be considered void.

SEC. 5.—Each candidate for membership shall assent to the following questions.

QUESTION 1.—Will you Mr. A. B. promise to demean yourself as an upright and faithful member of this Association?

Q. 2.—Will you endeavour to increase its members and extend its influence by all just and honorable means?

Q. 3.—Will you act with honesty and impartiality in whatever office, or station, to which you may be elected in this Association?

ARTICLE 2—*Of Initiation Fees and Monthly Dues*

SEC. 1.—Each person on his admission, shall pay such a sum to the Association, as they may from time to time think proper to fix upon, and the further sum of 25 cents monthly.

SEC. 2.—A member may pay up his dues at any regular meeting, but if he shall neglect to do so for the space of six months, and shall after that time receive two special notices from the Secretary to pay up his dues, and neglects to do so, his name shall be taken from the books of the Association.

ARTICLE 3—*Of Benefits*

SEC. 1.—Each member shall, at the time of signing this Constitution, or as soon after as convenient, receive a Certificate of his membership, signed by the President and Secretary.

SEC. 2.—No member shall be entitled to relief from the Association until he has been a member one year, and paid up all his dues for that time. If then sickness should prevent him from following his profession, trade, or usual employment, after he has been sick one week, he shall thence receive the sum of two dollars per week, for the space of three months; and if his sickness still continues, he shall receive one dollar and fifty cents, for three months longer; and if his sickness still continues, he shall receive such a sum as the Association may grant him weekly, the state of the funds considered.

Sec. 3.—The widows and orphan child or children of deceased members, who have been members for the space of two years, and have paid up all their dues, shall, upon proving their claims, receive at stated periods twenty dollars per year from this association, during the woman's widowhood, or until the youngest child is twelve years of age.

Sec. 4.—If any person, having been a member of this association, for the space of one year and six months, and paid up all his dues for that time, should be removed by death, it shall be the duty of the association to inter him decently; and for this purpose, a sum of money not exceeding fifteen dollars, shall be constitutionally drawn from the funds of the association.

ARTICLE 4—*Of Officers*

Sec. 1.—The officers of this association shall consist of a President and Vice President, a Secretary, a first and second Deputy Secretary, a Treasurer, a Board of Directors consisting of nine persons, and a Marshal and four Deputies, to hold their offices for one year, or until others are appointed.

Sec. 2.—All officers shall be annually elected, on the first Tuesday in June, by ballot.

Sec. 3.—There shall be a Committee of Nomination, consisting of five persons, selected indifferently from among the association, at least six weeks previous to the election. It shall be the duty of said committee to report, at the next meeting ensuing that of their appointment, two several lists of candidates for the several offices of the association for the ensuing year.

Sec. 4.—If an equality of votes should occur for two candidates, for the same office, the President shall designate the person elected.

Sec. 5.—It shall be the duty of the President to call an extra meeting of the association, to fill all vacancies that may occur among the officers of the association, either by death, resignation, or otherwise; to be conducted in the same manner as that of the regular elections.

ARTICLE 5—*Duty of the Presidents*

Sec. 1.—The President shall preserve good order and decorum in the meetings of the association; he shall read all reports of the Board of Directors, and the reports of subcommittees; state all motions, put the question, prevent any from speaking whose speech is not directed to the chair, determine who shall speak first, when more than one rises to speak at once, call the speaker to order when deviating from the subject, lay aside all unconstitutional motions (but allowing an appeal to the constitution), and sign all drafts constitutionally audited.

SEC. 2.—He shall have power to call extra meetings whenever he thinks necessary, or at the request of five members of the association.

SEC. 3.—The Vice President shall perform all the duties and powers of the President in his absence.

ARTICLE 6—*Duty of the Secretaries*

SEC. 1.—The Secretary shall keep a fair and distinct account of the transactions of the association; he shall receive all monies paid in at every regular meeting, and deposit the same with the Treasurer, always taking his receipt. He shall keep a book containing the constitution of the association, to which each member, on being admitted, shall sign his name; likewise, a book containing an exact account with each member; also a roll book, with the names of the members, in regular columns, in which an exact account must also be given; a minute book and an account book with the Treasurer. The Secretary's books shall determine all disputes that may arise concerning the payment of dues; he shall read the minutes of former meetings, and give two special notices to each member whose arrears shall be over six months.

SEC. 2.—The first Deputy Secretary shall call over the roll at every regular meeting of the association; he shall attend at each meeting of the Board of Directors, and minute down the proceedings thereof, and perform the duties of the grand Secretary in his absence.

SEC. 3.—The second Deputy Secretary shall give notice of every meeting of the association, to each one of its members; and perform all the duties of the first deputy in his absence, and assist in conducting the business of the Secretary, in the meetings of the association.

ARTICLE 7—*Duty of the Treasurer*

SEC. 1.—The Treasurer previous to his entering on the duties of his office, shall give a good and sufficient security, in a bond to the President and Directors of the association, in such a sum as they may require, which bond shall be deposited with the President, he giving a receipt for the same to the Board of Directors. The Treasurer shall receive all monies collected for the association, for which he shall give his receipt to the Secretary. He shall pay all drafts drawn in behalf of the association, and signed by the President and

Secretary: provided, such sum shall not exceed fifteen dollars, unless expressly authorised by a majority of the association, at an extra meeting called expressly for that purpose. He shall keep an exact account with the association, of all monies received and paid by him, in a book provided for that purpose. He shall report the amount of monies in the treasury every three months. He shall collect all interests, dividends on stock, and all other proceeds arising from the disposition of the funds, and all bills, bonds, and papers that belong to the funds shall be in his possession.

ARTICLE 8—*Duty of the Board of Directors*

SEC. 1.—The Board of Directors, of whom five members present shall constitute a quorum, shall meet at least once in every month. They shall report at each meeting of the association, their minutes and decisions on the case of candidates for membership. They shall carefully attend to the case of sick members: likewise, the widows and orphans. All drafts and benefits shall emanate with the Board of Directors, to which their chairman shall sign his name. They shall carefully watch over the funds and interest of the association.

SEC. 2.—The Board of Directors shall keep a book in which they shall take receipts from the persons to whom they administer benefits. They shall also report the number of sick members, widows and orphans receiving benefit from this association.

ARTICLE 9—*Of Meetings*

SEC. 1.—The regular meetings of this Association, shall be held on the evening of the first Tuesday in each month.

SEC. 2.—Twelve members shall be a sufficient number to commence the business of a regular meeting, but twenty members shall be necessary, to take a vote on business of importance.

ARTICLE 10—*Of Expelling Members*

SEC. 1.—If any member shall apply for relief, from this Association, or shall receive benefit from this Association, when he was able to, (or did actually) follow his usual trade or employment, upon due proof thereof to the Directors, he shall be expelled.

SEC. 2.—If any member shall be convicted in a court of justice, of any criminal actions, upon due proof thereof to the Association, he shall be expelled.

SEC. 3.—If any member shall neglect to come to order in the meetings of the Association, when so ordered three times by the President, he shall be fined a sum not less than one dollar, and not over five; and if he refuses to pay such a sum within a reasonable time, he shall be expelled: provided always, that no member shall be expelled but by a vote taken at an extra meeting, called expressly to consider his case; excepting the case wherein a member has been twice specially notified by the Secretary to pay up his arrears, and neglects to do so.

ARTICLE 11—*Of Sea Faring Members*

SEC. 1.—Sea Faring members shall be allowed one month to pay up their dues after their return, and if their case is distressing, two months; subject to the inspection of the Board of Directors.

SEC. 2.—It shall be their duty to announce to the Board of Directors, the date of their departure and arrival, together with the name of the captain's vessel and place of destination; a neglect of this notice, will forfeit all further indulgence.

ARTICLE 12—*Duty of the Marshal*

SEC. 1.—The duty of the Marshal shall be to keep order during the meetings of the Association, and see that all the members are seated.

SEC. 2.—The Orderly Marshals shall be subject to the Marshal, both in the meetings of the Association and in Public Processions, and in his absence perform all the duties of his office, according to the seniority of their appointment.

ARTICLE 13—*Of By-Laws*

SEC. 1.—All motions for By-Laws, shall be presented to the Board of Directors in writing, who shall report their opinion to the Association, as soon as convenient.

SEC. 2.—No By-Laws shall be altered or passed except three fourths of the members present shall vote for the same, and that a special meeting be called expressly for that purpose, at least one month previous notice being given.

SEC. 3.—It shall be lawful for the Association to pass any motion (not contrary to these By-Laws) to keep order during the evening, while they are together.

No person shall be entitled to benefit from this Association, who shall not be under the inspection of the Board of Directors, except by a majority of the members present at a meeting called expressly for that purpose.

CONSTITUTION

AND

BY-LAWS

OF THE

BROTHERLY UNION SOCIETY

Instituted, April, 1823.

PHILADELPHIA:
PRINTED BY WILLIAM BROWN,
1833.

CONSTITUTION

PREAMBLE

WE, the subscribers, coloured men, of the county of Philadelphia, citizens of the Commonwealth of Pennsylvania and of the United States of America, having associated ourselves for relieving the wants and distresses of each other, and being desirous that our association should be permanent, do agree upon the following Constitution:

ARTICLE I

The corporate name of this Society shall be: the Brotherly Union Society of the County of Philadelphia.

ARTICLE II

Sect. 1. Ten members shall form a quorum.

Sect. 2. The officers of this Society shall be a President, a Vice President, a Treasurer, a Recording Secretary, Assistant Secretary, a

Committee of nine members, five of them shall form a quorum to transact business, and shall meet the last Thursday in every month.

ARTICLE III

Sect. 1. The stated meetings of the Society shall be on the first Thursday of each and every month.

Sect. 2. The officers of the Society shall be chosen by a majority of the members present once a year, to serve for one year, at the monthly meeting in March; but the officers now chosen shall serve in their respective offices for one year from the time they were so chosen.

ARTICLE IV

The duty of the President shall be to preside at the meetings of the Society and to preserve order, and to require of other officers a performance of their duty—sign all orders upon the Treasurer for money, and call special meetings when he shall consider it proper so to do; he shall neither move or second any resolution while presiding, nor vote on any question unless the votes of the members present be equal; and it shall be the duty of the President, in the absence of the Treasurer, to receive from the members their fines and monthly dues, and pay the same over to the Treasurer at the next stated meeting of the Society.

ARTICLE V

The duty of the Vice President shall be to preside over the meetings of the committee; and in case of the absence of temporary inability of the President, the Vice President shall perform his duties; and if he is absent or unable to perform the duties, a chairman shall be chosen for the evening; and if the President die or resign, another shall be chosen to fill his place; the same, if the Vice President die or resign, or any other officer.

ARTICLE VI

Sect. 1. The duty of the Secretary shall be to make out and preserve fair minutes of the proceedings of the Society; to call the roll; to read the minutes of the preceding meeting; to record this Constitution, and such By-Laws as may be passed; to examine the state of the accounts and funds of the Society, and report the same to the Society every three months; to notify delinquent members, and prepare notices for funerals and all other occasions.

Sect. 2. The duty of the Assistant Secretary shall be to record the proceedings of the meetings of the committee, and read them at the next stated or special meeting of the Society; to assist the Secretary in the discharge of his duty when called upon, and in his absence perform all his duties.

ARTICLE VII

It shall be the duty of the Treasurer to take care of all the moneys and effects of the Society; to keep regular accounts of the state of the funds, and furnish copies of the same to the Secretary of the Society, to be reported to the same every three months; and he shall, before entering upon the duties of his office, give to the Committee such security in a bond or mortgage for the faithful discharge of his trust, as a majority of the Committee shall require, which bond or mortgage shall be placed in the hands of the President.

ARTICLE VIII

The duty of the Committee shall be to visit all sick members within twenty-four hours after receiving notice of the same, and punctually to apply such relief to them as the Constitution directs in such cases, and visit such orphans and widows of members of this Society as may apply for relief, and report all such applications to the Society, that an order may be drawn for such sum as the Society may direct from time to time.

ARTICLE IX

Sect. 1. When a member of this Society shall die, having been a member for one year, and at the time of his death not more than seventy-five cents in arrears to the Society, the sum of twenty dollars shall be allowed for defraying his funeral expenses.

Sect. 2. When a member shall die who has not been a member for one year, and regularly paid his entrance, and not more than seventy-five cents in arrears to the Society, the sum of twenty dollars shall be allowed for defraying his funeral expenses; and at the next stated meeting the members shall pay twelve and a half cents in addition to their monthly contributions.

Sect. 3. When the wife of a member shall die, the sum of twelve dollars shall be allowed him from the funds of this Society, and at the next stated meeting of the Society each and every member shall pay, in addition to his monthly contributions, the sum of twelve and a half cents.

Sect. 4. If the child of a member die, he may receive a loan of four dollars from the Committee, which he shall engage in writing to repay the Society within one year.

ARTICLE X

Any member who may be absent and in any part of the United States, shall give notice of his residence to the Society once in every four months; and if such member when he left this county shall have paid to the Society their demands upon him, he may in case of sickness make application to the President for relief, and he produce a certificate of his good conduct from respectable persons where he resides, such aid shall be afforded as the President and Committee shall think proper.

ARTICLE XI

At each and every stated meeting of the Society each and every member shall pay to the President the sum of twenty-five cents, for the use and benefit of the Society.

ARTICLE XII

The funds of the Society may be applied, by the consent of a majority of the members, to other charitable purposes than those herein particularly mentioned.

ARTICLE XIII

Sect. 1. If the funds of the Society be more than sufficient for the relief of its members and other charitable purposes, such parts of the surplus as a majority shall direct shall be invested in real estate, bonds and mortgages, or in such other way as the Society may direct; provided, that the same do not exceed in yearly value the sum of five hundred pounds.

Sect. 2. Real estate, if purchased, is to be conveyed to the Society by its corporate name; bonds and mortgages shall be made payable to the Society in the same way.

ARTICLE XIV

Sect. 1. If any member shall neglect to pay the monthly sum of twenty-five cents for three months, it shall be the duty of the Secretary to notify such delinquent member to pay his arrears; and if he does not pay the sum due to the Society at the next stated meeting, or show some sufficient cause for not paying the same, he shall be expelled from the Society, and any money he may have paid shall be forfeited to the Society.

Sect. 2. Any member who may have been guilty of fraudulent, base, or immoral conduct, may be expelled if two-thirds of the members present vote for his expulsion, provided that the accused party have a hearing and trial before the Society, at a stated meeting.

This Society shall have power to make such By-Laws, Rules and Regulations, as are necessary for the welfare and good order and government thereof, and the admission of members thereof; provided, that such By-Laws, Rules and Regulations shall not be passed unless unanimously approved of at the stated meeting at which they are proposed, but shall lie over until the next stated meeting, when a majority of the members present may decide upon and pass them; and, provided also, that such By-Laws, Rules, and Regulations, shall not be repugnant to the Constitution and laws of the United States or the Commonwealth of Pennsylvania, or this Constitution.

This Society shall not be dissolved while there are five of its members willing to continue it.

Pennsylvania, ss.

I, Thomas Elder, Attorney-General of the Commonwealth of Pennsylvania, do hereby certify that I have perused and examined the above instrument, and am of opinion the objects, articles, and conditions therein set forth and contained are lawful. Witness my hand, March 7th, 1823.

THOMAS ELDER.

Pennsylvania, to wit:

We, the Justices of the Supreme Court, do certify that we have perused the above instrument, and concur with the Attorney-General, that the objects, articles, and conditions therein set forth and contained, are lawful. Witness our hands the 24th day of March, 1823.

WILLIAM TILGHMAN,
JOHN B. GIBSON,
THOMAS DUNCAN.

Pennsylvania, ss.

In the name and by the authority of the Commonwealth of Pennsylvania,

I, Joseph Heister, Governor of the said Commonwealth, to Andrew Gregg, Esquire, Secretary of the said Commonwealth, send greeting:

Whereas, it has been duly certified to me by Thomas Elder, Esquire, Attorney-General of the said Commonwealth, and by William

Tilghman, Esquire, Chief Justice, and John B. Gibson and Thomas Duncan, Esquires, Associate Justices of the Supreme Courts of Pennsylvania, that they have respectively perused and examined the annexed act or instrument for the incorporation of the Brotherly Union Society of the county of Philadelphia, and that they concur in opinion that the objects, articles, and conditions therein set forth and contained, are lawful.

Now know you, that in pursuance of an act of the General Assembly, passed the sixth day of April, in the year of our Lord one thousand seven hundred and ninety-one, entitled "an act to confer on certain associations of the citizens of this commonwealth the powers and immunities of corporations or bodies politic in law," I have transmitted the said act or instrument of incorporation unto you the said Andrew Gregg, Secretary as aforesaid, hereby requiring you to enroll the same at the expense of the applicants, to the intent that according to the objects, articles, and conditions therein set forth and contained, the parties may become and be a corporation and body politic in law, and in fact to have continuance by the name, style, and title, in the said instrument provided and declared.

Given under my hand and the great seal of the state at Harrisburg, the twenty-first day of April, in the year of our Lord one thousand eight hundred and twenty-three, and of the Commonwealth the forty-seventh.

By the Governor.

ANDREW GREGG, Secretary,

Subscribers

Thomas Wester,	Edward Crosby,
Henry Collins,	Isaac Warren,
Gabriel Fisher,	Robert B. Wilson,
Henry Wells,	Moses Porter,
Isaac Darin,	Jacob Anderson,
Samuel Cornish,	John Walters,
Solomon Saunders,	Julius Brown,
James Purnell,	Henry Williams,
Henry Shelley, Jr.,	Cesar Murry,
Charles Corr,	Peter Gray, Jr.
Henry Shelley,	

BY-LAWS, RULES, AND REGULATIONS.

RULE I

Each member who neglects to attend the regular meetings of the Society or to send his money, shall pay a fine of twelve and a half cents, unless a good excuse be made to the Society at their meetings; and for non-attendance at the annual meetings in March, the fine shall be twenty-five cents, which will be enforced unless a good excuse be made to the satisfaction of the Society at their next meetings. Fines for nonattendance at funerals of deceased members, shall be twenty-five cents, unless a satisfactory excuse be made to the Society at their next regular meetings.

RULE II

At all meetings of the Society on funeral occasions, each and every member is required to be present in the hall at the call of the roll before they proceed to the funeral.

RULE III

Each and every member shall conduct himself in a becoming manner while going to and fro, and if any member is found with what the Society shall call misconduct while engaged with a funeral, he or they shall pay a fine of twenty-five cents at the next stated meeting of the Society.

RULE IV

The hours of the meetings of the Society and Committee shall be as follows: From the first of October to the first of April, at seven o'clock in the evening, and from the first of April to the first of October, at eight o'clock in the evening.

RULE V

No member shall be allowed to leave the room during the sitting of the Society without leave from the President or Chairman; and every member who violates or attempts to violate this rule, shall pay a fine of fifty cents at the next stated meeting of the Society, unless such an excuse be given at said stated meeting as the Society shall accept.

RULE VI

The President, in the presence of the Society, shall put the following questions to each and every applicant for membership before he signs the Constitution—which he is required to answer solemnly and truly to the best of his knowledge—otherwise should it afterwards appear that the applicant has used deception, he shall be expelled from the Society and forfeit all claims to the same:

1st. What is your name?
2d. What is your age?

3d. Are you a citizen of the Commonwealth of Pennsylvania?

4th. Are you free from all bodily infirmities?

5th. Have you been made acquainted with our Constitution and By-Laws?

6th. Will you engage to support this Constitution and these By-Laws, and act with honesty and impartiality in any office or station to which you may be elected or appointed in the Society?

RULE VII

The Society shall at the meeting previous to the annual election, appoint a committee of three members to nominate candidates for the several offices.

RULE VIII

At all elections, it shall require a majority of the votes of the members present to make it valid.

RULE IX

No member shall be entitled to any benefit from the funds of this Society until he has been twelve months a member, and paid his dues for that time—if after that period affliction should render him unable to pursue his occupation or of gaining a livelihood for the space of eight days, he shall receive, during his affliction, two dollars per week—provided his sickness does not continue longer than three months—but if it should continue longer than three months, he shall receive one dollar and fifty cents per week during the remainder of his sickness.

RULE X

Should it be proved to the satisfaction of this Society, that any member while receiving assistance from the Society, has pursued his employment in the usual manner, or spent his time in brothels, or in gambling, or in tippling shops, he shall be expelled from the Society.

RULE XI

The committee shall, in addition to the duties assigned them in the eighth article of the Constitution, scrutinize the character of every applicant for membership, and record the result of that scrutiny in the minutes of their proceedings.

RULE XII

No member of this Society shall, under any pretence whatever, make known out of the Society the cause why any applicant did not gain his election, either in the board of committee, or in the Society; and every member who shall violate this rule, shall be expelled from this Society.

RULE XIII

Every member who shall give his consent to serve in an office or on a committee, and after being elected, refuses, shall pay a fine of fifty cents for every such refusal.

RULE XIV

The President, Treasurer, and Secretary, shall be bank depositers of all monies belonging to the Society, to be deposited in the name and for the use of the Society.

RULE XV

It shall be the duty of the Marshal to attend all the meetings of the Society. He shall, together with the other members of the Society, wear whatever badge they shall choose—attend the funerals of all deceased members, and conduct the same—he shall take charge of the door during the meetings of the Society—assist the President in preserving order—and shall see all the members seated.

RULE XVI

The Deputy Marshal shall prepare the hall with lights and other necessaries for the meetings of the Society; having the same lighted up at the time appointed—he shall do all the errands during the meetings of the Society, and in the absence of the Marshal, the Deputy Marshal shall discharge the duties assigned him—the Marshal and Deputy Marshal shall serve all notices of the Society, for which they shall receive one cent per notice.

RULE XVII

No member shall be allowed to rise and speak more than three times on any question without leave from the President or Chairman, nor shall any member spend longer than three minutes at a time.

RULE XVIII

No member shall rise to speak without addressing the President or Chairman; and every member who violates this rule, shall pay a fine of twelve and a half cents, and for refusing to come to order when requested by the President or Chairman, to a fine of twenty-five cents, unless such member, when first called to order, appeals to the Society, which appeal shall be decided by a vote of the Society, and that without debate.

RULE XIX

If more than one member rise to speak at once, the President shall decide who is entitled to the floor—upon which decision the other shall come to order and take his seat—and if he refuses to come to order and be seated, he shall pay a fine of one dollar for every such offence.

RULE XX

Every person who applies to this Society for membership, must do it in writing to one of the members, stating his name, residence, and occupation, which shall be laid before the board of committee for their inspection; and if the committee approves of the applicant, the Society shall ballot for him to become a member, and if the applicant receives a majority of the votes of the members present, he shall be admitted, provided he comes forward, signs the Constitution, and pays such initiation fee as the rules of the Society require.

RULE XXI

If any member comes forward and states previous to such persons signing the Constitution, what the Society may deem a sufficient objection, he shall not be admitted a member.

RULE XXII

The election of applicants for membership will be considered void, unless they come forward within three months after they are elected, and sign the Constitution, and pay the required initiation fee.

RULE XXIII

No person shall be admitted a member of this Society under the age of twenty-one, or over the age of fifty-two.

RULE XXIV

Members of this Society applying for aid, must apply to the President, who shall immediately give notice to the acting committee, that the applicant may be visited.

RULE XXV

Seafaring members and members absent from the state shall be exempted from fines, provided that when they return, they discharge their monthly contributions within thirty days after a written demand is made upon them by the Secretary, or otherwise they will be dealt with according to the fourteenth Article of the Constitution.

RULE XXVI

The roll-book of the Society shall be settled at the stated meeting in May, in every year, at which time all fines and monthly contributions due to the Society shall be paid by the members; and it shall be the duty of the Secretary, at the stated meeting in April, to inform the Society of the approaching time of settlement.

RULE XXVII

The Vice President shall convene the committee together within seven days after their election, and appoint out of their body the committee that shall act the first month, and so continue their appointment, and the said board of committee shall have power to nominate the Vice President.

RULE XXVIII

The Secretary shall receive the sum of six dollars per year for his services.

RULE XXIX

The Assistant Secretary shall receive the sum of four dollars per year for his services.

RULE XXX

Any person who has been a member of this Society for one year and not more than seventy-five cents in arrears to the Society, when prevented from pursuing his usual occupation by rheumatism or old age, shall receive from the funds of this Society the sum of one dollar per week during such inabilities.

RULE XXXI

Every member who shall be found lying down or sleeping, or talking so as to disturb the harmony of business during the meetings of the Society, shall pay a fine of twelve and a half cents for every such offense.

RULE XXXII

Applicants for membership not recommended by the board of committee, may be balloted for by the Society.

RULE XXXIII

The committee shall, at each of their stated meetings, enter upon their minutes the names of the three acting committee, and the names of the sick in their charge, and the amount of money expended for the sick and other purposes.

RULE XXXIV

The officers of the Society, when elected, shall not enter upon the duties of their respective offices until the next regular meeting after their election, and in the intermediate time between their election and installment, the acting officers shall close all accounts belonging to their respective offices in such manner as will enable them to resign all papers and documents, of whatever kind they may have belonging to the Society, into the hands of their successors in office—which they must do at the time above specified, without any hindrance or impediment whatever.

RULE XXXV

There shall always remain in the hands of the Treasurer, the sum of sixty dollars, for the use of the Society; and when the funds shall amount to one hundred dollars more than the abovementioned sum, the Treasurer shall report to the President, who shall report the same to the Society, that it may be determined in what manner the money shall be appropriated to promote the interest of the Society.

RULE XXXVI

All elections for offices shall be conducted by ballot, for which the President and two judges and two tellers shall be appointed.

A

CHARGE

DELIVERED TO THE BRETHREN OF THE

AFRICAN LODGE

ON THE 25TH OF JUNE, 1792,

At the Hall of Brother WILLIAM SMITH,

IN CHARLESTOWN.

By the Right Worshipful Master

PRINCE HALL.

PRINTED AT THE REQUEST OF THE LODGE.

PRINTED AND SOLD AT THE BIBLE AND HEART,
CORNHILL, BOSTON.

Dearly and well beloved Brethren of the African Lodge, as through the goodness and mercy of God, we are once more met together, in order to celebrate the Festival of St. John the Baptist; it is requisite that we should on these public days, and when we appear in form, give some reason as a foundation for our so doing, but as this has been already done, in a discourse delivered in substance by our late Reverend Brother *John Marrant,* and now in print,

I shall at this time endeavour to raise part of the superstructure, for howsoever good the foundation may be, yet without this it will only prove a Babel. I shall therefore endeavour to shew the duty of a Mason; and the first thing is, that he believes in one Supreme Being, that he is the great Architect of this visible world, and that he governs all things here below by his almighty power, and his watchful eye is over all our works. Again we must be good subjects to the laws of the land in which we dwell, giving honour to our lawful Governors and Magistrates, giving honour to whom honour is due; and that we have no hand in any plots or conspiracies or rebellion, or side or assist in them: for when we consider the blood-shed, the devastation of towns and cities that hath been done by them, what heart can be so hard as not to pity those our distrest brethren, and keep at the greatest distance from them. However just it may be on the side of the opprest, yet it doth not in the least, or rather ought not, abate that love and fellow-feeling which we ought to have for our brother fellow men.

The next thing is love and benevolence to all the whole family of mankind, as God's make and creation, therefore we ought to love them all, for love or hatred is of the whole kind, for if I love a man for the sake of the image of God which is on him, I must love all, for he made all, and upholds all, and we are dependant upon him for all we do enjoy and expect to enjoy in this world and that which is to come.—Therefore he will help and assist all his fellow-men in distress, let them be of what colour or nation they may, yea even our very enemies, much more a brother Mason. I shall therefore give you a few instances of this from Holy Writ, and first, how did Abraham prevent the storm, or rebellion that was rising between Lot's servants and his? Saith Abraham to Lot, let there be no strife I pray thee between me and thee, for the land is before us, if you will go to the left, then I will go to the right, and if you will go to the right, then I will go to the left. They divided and peace was restored. I will mention the compassion of a blackman to a Prophet of the Lord, Ebedmelech, when he heard that Jeremiah was cast into the dungeon, he made intercession for him to the King, and got liberty to take him out from the jaws of death. See Jer. xxxviii, 7–13.

Also the prophet Elisha after he had led the army of the Eramites blindfold into Samaria, when the King in a deriding manner said, my *Father* (not considering that he was as much their Father as his) shall I smite, or rather kill them out of the way, as not worthy to live on the same earth, or draw the same air with himself; so eager was he to shed his brethren's blood, that he repeats his blood-thirsty demand, but the Prophet after reproaching him therefore, answers him no, but set bread and water before them; or in other words, give them a feast and let them go home in peace. See 2 Kings vi, 22–23.

I shall just mention the good deeds of the Samaritan, though at that time they were looked upon as unworthy to eat, drink or trade with their fellow-men, at least by the Jews; see the pity and compassion he had on a poor distrest and half dead stranger, see Luke x. from 30 to 37. See that you endeavour to do so likewise.—But when we consider the amazing condescending love and pity our blessed Lord had on such poor worms as we are, as not only to call us his friends, but his brothers, we are lost and can go no further in holy writ for examples to excite us to the love of our fellow-men.—But I am aware of an objection that may arise (for some men will catch at any thing) that is that they were not all Masons; we allow it, and I say that they were not all Christians, and their benevolence to strangers ought to shame us both, that there is so little, so very little of it to be seen in these enlightened days.

Another thing which is the duty of a Mason is, that he pays a strict regard to the stated meetings of the Lodge, for masonry is of a progressive nature, and must be attended to if ever he intends to be a good Mason; for the man that thinks that because he hath been made a Mason, and is called so, and at the same time will wilfully neglect to attend his Lodge, he may be assured he will never make a good Mason, nor ought he to be looked upon as a good member of the craft. For if his example was followed, where would be the Lodge; and besides what a disgrace is it, when we are at our set meetings, to hear that one of our members is at a drinking house, or at a card table, or in some worse company, this brings disgrace on the Craft: Again there are some that attend the Lodge in such a manner that sometimes their absence would be better than their Company (I would not here be understood a brother in disguise, for such an one hath no business on a level floor) for if he hath been displeased abroad or at home, the least thing that is spoken that he thinks not right, or in the least offends him, he will raise his temper to such a height as to destroy the harmony of the whole Lodge; but we have a remedy and every officer ought to see it put in execution. Another thing a Mason ought to observe, is that he should lend his helping hand to a brother in distress, and relieve him; this we may do various ways—for we may sometimes help him to a cup of cold water, and it may be better to him than a cup of wine. Good advice may be sometimes better than feeding his body, helping him to some lawful employment, better than giving him money; so defending his case and standing by him when wrongfully accused, may be better than clothing him; better to save a brother's house when on fire, than to give him one. Thus much may suffice.

I shall now cite some of our fore-fathers, for our imitation: and

the first shall be Tertullian, who defended the Christians against
their heathen false accusations, whom they charged with treason
against the empire and the Emperor, because of their silent meetings: he proved that to be false for this reason, for in their meetings,
they were wont to pray for the prosperity of the Empire, of Rome,
and him also; and they were accused of being enemies to mankind,
how can that be, said he, when their office is to love and pray for
all mankind. When they were charged with worshipping the Sun,
because they looked towards the East when they prayed; he defended them against this slander also, and proved that they were
slandered, slighted and ill-treated, not for any desert of theirs, but
only out of hatred of them and their profession. This friend of the
distrest was born in Carthage in Africa, and died Anno Christi 202.

Take another of the same city, Cyprian, for his fidelity to his profession was such, that he would rather suffer death than betray his
trust and the truth of the gospel, or approve of the impious worship
of the Gentiles: He was not only Bishop of Carthage, but of Spain
and the east, west and northern churches, who died Anno Christi
259.

But I have not time to cite but one more (out of hundreds that
I could count of our Fathers, who were not only examples to us, but
to many of their nobles and learned); that is, Augustine, who had
engraven on his table these words

> He that doth love an absent Friend to jeer,
> May hence depart, no room is for him here.

His saying was that sincere and upright Prayer pierceth heaven,
and returns not empty. That it was a shelter to the soul. A sacrifice
to God and a scourge to the Devil. There is nothing, said he, more
abateth pride and sin than the frequent meditation on death; he cannot die ill, that lives well, and seldom doth he die well, that lives ill:
Again, if men want wealth, it is not to be unjustly gotten, if they
have it they ought by good works to lay it up in heaven: And again,
he that hath tasted the sweetness of divine love will not care for
temporal sweetness. The reasonable soul made in the likeness of
God may here find much distraction, but no full satisfaction; not to be
without afflictions, but to overcome them, is blessedness. Love is as
strong as death; as death kills the body, so love of eternal life kills
worldly desires and affections. He called Ingratitude the Devil's
sponge, wherewith he wipes out all the favours of the Almighty. His
prayer was: Lord give first what thou requirest, and then require of
me what thou wilt. This good man died Anno Christi 430.

The next is Fulgentius, his speech was, why travel I in the world which can yield me no future, nor durable reward answerable to my pains? Thought it better to weep well, than to rejoice ill, yet if joy be our desire, how much more excellent is their joy, who have a good conscience before God, who dread nothing but sin, study to do nothing but to accomplish the precepts of Christ. Now therefore let me change my course, and as before I endeavoured amongst my noble friends to prove more noble, so now let my care and employment be among the humble and poor servants of Christ, and become more humble that I may help and instruct my poor and distrest brethren.

Thus, my brethren, I have quoted a few of your reverend fathers for your imitation, which I hope you will endeavour to follow, so far as your abilities will permit in your present situation and the disadvantages you labour under on account of your being deprived of the means of education in your younger days, as you see it is at this day with our children, for we see notwithstanding we are rated for that, and other Town charges, we are deprived of that blessing. But be not discouraged, have patience, and look forward to a better day; Hear what the great Architect of the universal world saith, *Aethippia shall stretch forth her hands unto me.* Hear also the strange but bold and confident language of *J. Husk,* who just before the executioner gave the last stroke, said, *I challenge you to meet me an hundred years hence.* But in the mean time let us lay by our recreations, and all superfluities, so that we may have that to educate our rising generation, which was spent in those follies. Make you this beginning, and who knows but God may raise up some friend or body of friends, as he did in *Philadelphia,* to open a School for the blacks here, as that friendly city has done there.

I shall now shew you what progress Masonry hath made since the siege and taking of Jerusalem in the year 70, by Titus Vespasian; after a long and bloody siege, a million of souls having been slain or had perished in the city, it was taken by storm and the city set on fire. There was an order of men called the order of St. John, who besides their other engagements, subscribed to another, by which they bound themselves to keep up the war against the Turks. These men defended the temple when on fire, in order to save it, so long, that Titus was amazed and went to see the reason of it; but when he came so near as to behold the *Sanctum Sanctorum,* he was amazed, and shed tears, and said, no wonder these men should so long to save it. He honored them with many honors, and large contributions were made to that order from many kingdoms; and were also knighted. They continued 88 years in Jerusalem, till that city was again retaken by the Turks, after which they resided 104 years in the Cyrean city of Ptolemy, till the remains of the Holy Conquest were lost. Whereupon they settled on the Island of Cyprus, where they continued 18 years, till they found an opportunity to take the Island Rhodes; being masters of that, they maintained it for 213 years, and from thence they were called knights of Rhodes, till in the year 1530 they took their residence in the Island of Malta, where they have continued to this day, and are distinguished by the name of the knights of Malta. Their first Master was Villaret in the year 1099. Fulco Villaret in the year 1322, took the Island of Rhodes, and was after that distinguished by the title of Grand-Master, which hath devolved to his Successors to this day.

Query, Whether at that day, when there was an African church, and perhaps the largest Christian church on earth, whether there was no African of that order; or whether, if they were all whites, they would refuse to accept them as their fellow Christians and brother Masons; or whether there were any so weak, or rather so foolish, as to say, because they were blacks, that would make their lodge or army too common or too cheap? Sure this was not our conduct in the late war; for then they marched shoulder to shoulder, brother soldier and brother soldier, to the field of battle; let who will answer; he that despises a black man for the sake of his colour, reproacheth his Maker, and he hath resented it, in the case of Aaron and Miriam. See for this Numbers xii.

But to return: In the year 1787 (the year in which we received our charter) there were 489 lodges under charge of his late Royal Highness the Duke of Cumberland; whose memory will always be esteemed by every good Mason.

And now, my African brethren, you see what a noble order you are members of. My charge to you is, that you make it your study to live up to the precepts of it, as you know that they are all good; and let it be known this day to the spectators that you have not been to a feast of Bacchus, but to a refreshment with Masons; and see to it that you behave as such, as well at home as abroad; always to keep in your minds the obligations you are under, both to God and your fellow men. And more so, you my dear brethren of Providence, who are at a distance from, and cannot attend the Lodge here but seldom; yet I hope you will endeavour to communicate to us by letters of your welfare; and remember your obligations to each other, and live in peace and love as brethren.—We thank you for your attendance with us this day, and wish you a safe return.

If thus, we by the grace of God, live up to this our Profession; we may cheerfully go the rounds of the compass of this life, having lived according to the plumb line of uprightness, the square of justice, the level of truth and sincerity. And when we are come to the end of time, we may then bid farewell to that delightful Sun and Moon, and the other planets, that move so beautifully round her in their orbits, and all things here below, and ascend to that new Jerusalem, where we shall not want these tapers, for God is the Light thereof; where the Wicked cease from troubling, and where the weary are at rest.

> Then shall we hear and see and know,
> All we desir'd and wish'd below,
> And every power find sweet employ,
> In that eternal world of joy.
> Our flesh shall slumber in the ground,
> Till the last trumpet's joyful sound,
> Then burst the chains with sweet surprize,
> And in our Saviour's image rise.

A

CHARGE,

DELIVERED TO THE

AFRICAN LODGE,

JUNE 24, 1797,

AT MENOTOMY.

BY THE RIGHT WORSHIPFUL

PRINCE HALL.

PUBLISHED BY THE DESIRE OF THE MEMBERS OF SAID LODGE.
1797.

Beloved Brethren of the African Lodge,

'Tis now five years since I deliver'd a Charge to you on some parts and points of Masonry. As one branch or superstructure on the foundation; when I endeavoured to shew you the duty of a Mason to a Mason, and charity or love to all mankind, as the mark and image of the great God, and the Father of the human race.

I shall now attempt to shew you that it is our duty to sympathise with our fellow men under their troubles, the families of our brethren who are gone: we hope to the Grand Lodge above, here to return no more. But the cheerfulness that you have ever had to relieve them, and ease their burdens, under their forrows, will never be forgotten by them; and in this manner you will never be weary in doing good.

But my brethren, although we are to begin here, we must not end here; for only look around you and you will see and hear of numbers of our fellow men crying out with holy Job, Have pity on me, O my friends, for the hand of the Lord hath touched me. And this is not to be confined to parties or colours; not to towns or states; not to a kingdom, but to the kingdoms of the whole earth, over whom Christ the king is head and grand master.

Among these numerous sons and daughters of distress, I shall begin with our friends and brethren; and first, let us see them dragg'd from their native country by the iron hand of tyranny and oppression, from their dear friends and connections, with weeping eyes and aching hearts, to a strange land and strange people, whose tender mercies are cruel; and there to bear the iron yoke of slavery & cruelty till death as a friend shall relieve them. And must not the unhappy condition of these our fellow men draw forth our hearty prayer and wishes for their deliverance from these merchants and traders, whose characters you have in the xviii chap. of the Revelations, 11, 12, & 13 verses, and who knows but these same sort of traders may in a short time, in the like manner, bewail the loss of the African traffick, to their shame and confusion: and if I mistake not, it now begins to dawn in some of the West-India islands; which puts me in mind of a nation (that I have somewhere read of) called Ethiopeans, that cannot change their skin: But God can and will change their conditions, and their hearts too; and let Boston and the world know, that He hath no respect of persons; and that that bulwark of envy, pride, scorn and contempt, which is so visible to be seen in some and felt, shall fall, to rise no more.

When we hear of the bloody wars which are now in the world, and thousands of our fellow men slain; fathers and mothers bewailing the loss of their sons; wives for the loss of their husbands; towns and cities burnt and destroy'd; what must be the heart-felt sorrow and distress of these poor and unhappy people! Though we cannot help them, the distance being so great, yet we may sympathize with them in their troubles, and mingle a tear of sorrow with them, and do as we are exhorted to—weep with those that weep.

Thus my brethren we see what a chequered world we live in. Sometimes happy in having our wives and children like olive-branches about our tables; receiving the bounties of our great Benefactor. The next year, or month, or week we may be deprived of some of them, and we go mourning about the streets, so in societies; we are this day to celebrate this Feast of St. John's, and the next week we might be called upon to attend a funeral of some one here, as we have experienced since our last in this Lodge. So in the common affairs of life we sometimes enjoy health and prosperity; at another time sickness and adversity, crosses and disappointments.

So in states and kingdoms; sometimes in tranquility, then wars and tumults; rich today, and poor tomorrow; which shews that there is not an independent mortal on earth, but dependent one upon the other, from the king to the beggar.

The great law-giver, Moses, who instructed by his father-in-law, Jethro, an Ethiopean, how to regulate his courts of justice and what sort of men to choose for the different offices; hear now my words, said he, I will give you counsel, and God shall be with you; be thou for the people to Godward, that thou mayest bring the causes unto God, and thou shall teach them ordinances and laws, and shall shew the way wherein they must walk, and the work that they must do: moreover thou shall provide out of all the people, able men, such as fear God, men of truth, hating covetousness, and place such over them, to be rulers of thousands, of hundreds and of tens.

So Moses hearkened to the voice of his father-in-law, and did all that he said. Exodus xviii. 22–24.

This is the first and grandest lecture that Moses ever received from the mouth of man; for Jethro understood geometry as well as laws, *that* a Mason may plainly see: so a little captive servant maid by whose advice Nomen, the great general of Syria's army, was healed of his leprosy; and by a servant his proud spirit was brought down: 2 Kings v. 3–14. The feelings of this little captive for this great man, her captor, was so great, that she forgot her state of captivity, and felt for the distress of her enemy. Would to God (said she to her mistress) my lord were with the prophets in Samaria, he should be healed of his leprosy: So after he went to the prophet, his proud host was so haughty that he not only disdain'd the prophet's direction, but derided the good old prophet; and had it not been for his servant he would have gone to his grave with a double leprosy, the outward and the inward, in the heart, which is the worst of leprosies; a black heart is worse than a white leprosy.

How unlike was this great general's behaviour to that of as grand a character, and as well beloved by his prince as he was; I mean Obadiah, to a like prophet. See for this 1st Kings xviii. from 7 to the 16th.

And as Obadiah was in the way, behold Elijah met him, and he knew him, and fell on his face, and said, Art not thou, my Lord, Elijah, and he told him, Yea, go and tell thy Lord, behold Elijah is here: and so on to the 16th verse. Thus we see that great and good men have, and always will have, a respect for ministers and servants

of God. Another instance of this is in Acts viii. 27 to 31, of the
European Eunuch, a man of great authority, to Philip, the apostle:
here is mutual love and friendship between them. This minister of
Jesus Christ did not think himself too good to receive the hand, and
ride in a chariot with a black man in the face of day; neither did
this great monarch (for so he was) think it beneath him to take a
poor servant of the Lord by the hand, and invite him into his carriage, though but with a staff, one coat, and no money in his pocket.
So our Grand Master, Solomon, was not asham'd to take the Queen
of Sheba by the hand, and lead her into his court, at the hour of
high twelve, and there converse with her on points of masonry (for
if ever there was a female mason in the world she was one) and
other curious matters; and gratified her, by shewing her all his
riches and curious pieces of architecture in the temple, and in his
house: After some time staying with her, he loaded her with much
rich presents: he gave her the right hand of affection and parted
in love.

I hope that no one will dare openly (tho' in fact the behaviour
of some implies as much) to say, as our Lord said on another occasion, Behold a greater than Solomon is here. But yet let them consider that our Grand Master Solomon did not divide the living
child, whatever he might do with the dead one, neither did he
pretend to make a law to forbid the parties from having free intercourse with one another without the fear of censure, or be turned
out of the synagogue.

Now my brethren, as we see and experience that all things here
are frail and changeable and nothing here to be depended upon: Let
us seek those things which are above, which are sure, and stedfast,
and unchangeable, and at the same time let us pray to Almighty
God, while we remain in the tabernacle, that he would give us the
grace of patience and strength to bear up under all our troubles,
which at this day God knows we have our share. Patience I say,
for were we not possess'd of a great measure of it you could not
bear up under the daily insults you meet with in the streets of
Boston; much more on public days of recreation, how are you
shamefully abus'd, and that at such a degree that you may truly
be said to carry your lives in your hands, and the arrows of death
are flying about your heads; helpless old women have their clothes
torn off their backs, even to the exposing of their nakedness; and
by whom are these disgraceful and abusive actions committed, not
by the men born and bred in Boston, for they are better bred;
but by a mob or horde of shameless, low-lived, envious, spiteful
persons, some of them not long since, servants in gentlemen's

kitchens, scouring knives, tending horses, and driving chaise. 'Twas said by a gentleman who saw that filthy behaviour in the common, that in all the places he had been in, he never saw so cruel behaviour in all his life, and that a slave in the West-Indies, on Sunday or holidays enjoys himself and friends without any molestation. Not only this man, but many in town who hath seen their behaviour to you, and that without any provocation—twenty or thirty cowards fall upon one man—have wonder'd at the patience of the Blacks: 'tis not for want of courage in you, for they know that they dare not face you man for man, but in a mob, which we despise, and had rather suffer wrong than to do wrong, to the disturbance of the community and the disgrace of our reputation: for every good citizen doth honor to the laws of the State where he resides.

My brethren, let us not be cast down under these and many other abuses we at present labour under: for the darkest is before the break of day. My brethren, let us remember what a dark day it was with our African brethren six years ago, in the French West-Indies. Nothing but the snap of the whip was heard from morning to evening; hanging, broken on the wheel, burning, and all manner of tortures inflicted on those unhappy people for nothing else but to gratify their masters pride, wantonness, and cruelty: but blessed be God, the scene is changed; they now confess that God hath no respect of persons, and therefore receive them as their friends, and treat them as brothers. Thus doth Ethiopia begin to stretch forth her hand, from a sink of slavery to freedom and equality.

Although you are deprived of the means of education, yet you are not deprived of the means of meditation; by which I mean thinking, hearing and weighing matters, men, and things in your own mind, and making that judgment of them as you think reasonable to satisfy your minds and give an answer to those who may ask you a question. This nature hath furnished you with, without letter learning; and some have made great progress therein, some of those I have heard repeat psalms and hymns, and a great part of a sermon, only by hearing it read or preached and why not in other things in nature: how many of this class of our brethren that follow the seas can foretell a storm some days before it comes; whether it will be a heavy or light, a long or short one; foretell a hurricane, whether it will be destructive or moderate, without any other means than observation and consideration.

So in the observation of the heavenly bodies, this same class without a telescope or other apparatus have through a smoak'd glass observed the eclipse of the sun: One being ask'd what he saw through his smoaked glass, said, Saw, saw, de clipsey, or de clipseys. And what do you think of it?—Stop, dere be two. Right, and what do they look like?—Look like, why if I tell you, they look like two ships sailing one bigger than tother; so they sail by one another, and make no noise. As simple as the answers are they have a meaning, and shew that God can out of the mouth of babes and Africans shew forth his glory; let us then love and adore him as the God who defends us and supports us and will support us under our pressures, let them be ever so heavy and pressing. Let us by the blessing of God, in whatsoever state we are, or may be in, to be content; for clouds and darkness are about him; but justice and truth is his habitation; who hath said, Vengeance is mine and I will repay it, therefore let us kiss the rod and be still, and see the works of the Lord.

Another thing I would warn you against, is the slavish fear of man, which bringest a snare, saith Solomon. This passion of fear, like pride and envy, hath slain its thousands.—What but this makes so many perjure themselves; for fear of offending them at home they are a little depending on for some trifles: A man that is under a panic of fear, is afraid to be alone; you cannot hear of a robbery or house broke open or set on fire, but he hath an accomplice with him, who must share the spoil with him; whereas if he was truly bold, and void of fear, he would keep the whole plunder to himself: so when either of them is detected and not the other, he may be call'd to oath to keep it secret, but through fear, (and that passion is so strong) he will not confess, till the fatal cord is put on his neck; then death will deliver him from the fear of man, and he will confess the truth when it will not be of any good to himself or the community: nor is this passion of fear only to be found in this class of men, but among the great.

What was the reason that our African kings and princes have plunged themselves and their peaceable kingdoms into bloody wars, to the destroying of towns and kingdoms, but the fear of the report of a great gun or the glittering of arms and swords, which struck these kings near the seaports with such a panic of fear, as not only to destroy the peace and happiness of their inland brethren, but plung'd millions of their fellow countrymen into slavery and cruel bondage.

So in other countries; see Felix trembling on his throne. How many Emperors and kings have left their kingdoms and best friends at the sight of a handful of men in arms: how many have we seen that have left their estates and their friends and ran over to the stronger side as they thought; all through the fear of men, who is but a worm, and hath no more power to hurt his fellow worm, without the permission of God, than a real worm.

Thus we see, my brethren, what a miserable condition it is to be under the slavish fear of men; it is of such a destructive nature to mankind, that the scriptures every where from Genesis to the Revelations warns us against it; and even our blessed Saviour himself forbids us from this slavish fear of man, in his sermon on the mount; and the only way to avoid it is to be in the fear of God: let a man consider the greatness of his power, as the maker and upholder of all things here below, and that in Him we live, and move, and have our being, the giver of the mercies we enjoy here from day to day, and that our lives are in his hands, and that he made the heavens, the sun, moon and stars to move in their various orders; let us thus view the greatness of God, and then turn our eyes on mortal man, a worm, a shade, a wafer, and see whether he is an object of fear or not; on the contrary, you will think him in his best estate to be but vanity, feeble and a dependent mortal, and stands in need of your help, and cannot do without your assistance, in some way or other; and yet some of these poor mortals will try to make you believe they are Gods, but worship them not. My brethren, let us pay all due respect to all whom God hath put in places of honor over us: do justly and be faithful to them that hire you, and treat them with that respect they may deserve; but worship no man. Worship God, this much is your duty as christians and as masons.

We see then how becoming and necessary it is to have a fellow feeling for our distres'd brethren of the human race, in their troubles, both spiritual and temporal—How refreshing it is to a sick man, to see his sympathising friends around his bed, ready to administer all the relief in their power; although they can't relieve his bodily pain yet they may ease his mind by good instructions and cheer his heart by their company.

How doth it cheer up the heart of a man when his house is on fire, to see a number of friends coming to his relief; he is so transported that he almost forgets his loss and his danger, and fills him with love and gratitude; and their joys and sorrows are mutual.

So a man wreck'd at sea, how must it revive his drooping heart to see a ship bearing down for his relief.

How doth it rejoice the heart of a stranger in a strange land to see the people cheerful and pleasant and are ready to help him.

How did it, think you, cheer the heart of those our poor unhappy African brethren, to see a ship commissioned from God, and from a nation that without flattery faith, that all men are free and are brethren; I say to see them in an instant deliver such a number from their cruel bolts and galling chains, and to be fed like men and treated like brethren. Where is the man that has the least spark of humanity, that will not rejoice with them; and bless a righteous God who knows how and when to relieve the oppressed, as we see he did in the deliverance of the captives among the Algerines; how sudden were they delivered by the sympathising members of the Congress of the United States, who now enjoy the free air of peace and liberty, to their great joy and surprize, to them and their friends. Here we see the hand of God in various ways bringing about his own glory for the good of mankind, by the mutual help of their fellow men; which ought to teach us in all our straits, be they what they may, to put our trust in Him, firmly believing that he is able and will deliver us and defend us against all our enemies; and that no weapon form'd against us shall prosper; only let us be steady and uniform in our walks, speech and behaviour; always doing to all men as we wish and desire they would do to us in the like cases and circumstances.

Live and act as Masons, that you may die as Masons; let those despisers see, altho' many of us cannot read, yet by our searches and researches into men and things, we have supplied that defect; and if they will let us we shall call ourselves a charter'd lodge of just and lawful Masons; be always ready to give an answer to those that ask you a question; give the right hand of affection and fellow-ship to whom it justly belongs; let their colour and complexion be what it will, let their nation be what it may, for they are your brethren, and it is your indispensable duty so to do; let them as Masons deny this, and we & the world know what to think of them be they ever so grand: for we know this was Solomon's creed, Solomon's creed did I say, it is the decree of the Almighty, and all Masons have learnt it: tis plain market language, and plain and true facts need no apologies.

I shall now conclude with an old poem which I found among some papers:

> Let blind admirers handsome faces praise,
> And graceful features to great honor raise,
> The glories of the red and white express,
> I know no beauty but in holiness;
> If God of beauty be the uncreate
> Perfect idea, in this lower state,
> The greatest beauties of an human mould
> Who most resemble Him we justly hold;

Whom we resemble not in flesh and blood,
But being pure and holy, just and good:
May such a beauty fall but to my share,
For curious shape or face I'll never care.

Part II

Societies for Educational Improvement, 1808–1837

Prince Hall showed his deep concern for the education of Negro children when in his address to the African Lodge, June 25, 1792, in Boston, he said: "Let us lay by our recreations and all super-fluities so that we may have that money to educate our rising generations. . . . Make you this beginning and who knows but God may raise up some friends or body of friends, as he did in Philadelphia,[1] to open a school for the blacks here as that friendly city has done there." Six years later, in 1798 a school for Negro children was opened in Boston in the home of Prince Hall.[2] In New England after the Revolutionary War, efforts were made to educate the people of color through both the church and the school. The Quakers, Abolition societies, and churches were effective in Pennsylvania and New York in their efforts to instruct the descendants of Africa. In large cities in southern states such as Virginia, South Carolina, and Georgia, a small number of Negro children were permitted to attend certain schools.

Although some formal education was available to free Negroes, the majority of the children of free people of color and of emancipated slaves had no opportunity to receive the rudiments of elementary education. Negro leaders knew that the education of their children was necessary and expedient to "render them useful to society and acceptable to God." The idea that Negroes were an

[1] The Society for the Free Instruction of Orderly Blacks and People of Color was organized in Philadelphia in 1789. As early as 1760 two schools for the education of Negroes existed in Philadelphia. Carter Woodson, *The Education of the Negro Prior to 1861* (Washington, D.C.: The Association for the Study of Negro Life and History, 1919), pp. 37, 104.

[2] *Ibid.*, p. 95.

79

"indolent and shiftless" group had to be abolished. Study must replace idleness and intemperance and good taste and manners had to be cultivated. Whatever could be done to improve the mental, moral, and spiritual life of youth and adults was of immediate and prime importance. Wherever free people of color lived, various societies for welfare, temperance, Bible, moral reform, and education were organized by the most intelligent and best-known blacks of the time.[3]

The organizations presented in this section had as their primary function the education of youth, but many were concerned with mutual aid and moral reform as well.

The African Benevolent Society of Newport, Rhode Island, had as its primary object the "establishment and continuance of a free school, for any person of colour in this town." In 1780, the African Union Society was organized in Newport for the purpose of promoting "the welfare of the colored community" by Newport Gardner and others. It was absorbed in 1808 by the African Benevolent Society. Under the leadership of Newport Gardner, the Society provided a school which continued in operation until the city of Newport opened a school for Negro children in 1842.[4]

Free Negroes in Philadelphia were among the first to organize educational and literary societies. William Whipper, a leading representative of the men of color in Pennsylvania and a businessman in Philadelphia, lead the group of free men of color who assembled on March 20, 1828, to organize the Colored Reading Society of Philadelphia for Mental Improvement. Whipper urged those present not to sit "as idle spectators to the movement being carried on by nations to improve themselves," but because of their limited opportunities to "feel bound to open an institution to which they may repair and qualify themselves for future usefulness." The Reading Society was to acquire a library, and to place it in the care of a Librarian who would circulate the books once a week. No person was to keep a book longer than a week without paying a fine, unless he had a good excuse. Discussions at weekly meetings were to be based on the members' readings.

William Whipper was especially interested in the elevation of his people, devoting much of his time to addresses to literary societies, writing editorials, and serving as an agent of the Underground Railroad. He helped to establish The American Moral Reform Society

[3] For information on literary Societies see Dorothy Porter "The Organized Educational Activities of Negro Literary Societies, 1828–1846" *The Journal of Negro Education* Vol. 5, October, 1936, pp. 555–576.
[4] Irving H. Bartlett, *op. cit.,* p. 35.

and later became one of the editors of its organ, the *National Reformer*, published monthly in Philadelphia in 1839.[5]

A copy of Whipper's address to the Colored Reading Society has been preserved and is in the Howard University Library. A biography and collection of Whipper's writings is long overdue.

William Hamilton, the first President of the New York African Marine Society and one of the ablest orators of his day, includes in his 4th of July, 1827, Commemoration Address specific suggestions for the education of youth. He assured his audience that the path of virtue is one of pleasure, honor, and respectability—the very opposite of debasement, misery, and destruction; that the study of the sciences was not only pleasurable, but the expense involved would not be "as great as you incur for useless gratifications." He also stated that there was a "height of knowledge which you may easily attain to, that when arrived at, you will look down with amazement, at the depth of ignorance you have risen from." To young women he pointed out that it was for them "to form the manners of the men" and "by modest conduct, to lead them in the true line of decorum and gentle manners." But above all he cautioned, "improve your own minds."[6]

Reverend Joseph M. Corr, an efficient secretary of African Methodist Episcopal Conferences during the 1820s, in one of the most intellectual 4th of July orations in this collection called attention in 1834 to the "important subject of education, one of the noblest ornaments of human nature, that most noble means whereby the shackles of ignorance may be unrivetted, and man be qualified for usefulness in all the pursuits of life; for 'knowledge is light—knowledge is power.' "

Addressing the Humane Mechanics' Society organized in 1828 in Philadelphia, Corr especially encouraged his listeners to study mechanical science, for "it discovers the means of subjecting all things around us to the control of man. . . ." This well-written and inspiring address no doubt had a very wide circulation. It could very well have meaning for the youth and adults of today. One copy of the original is known to exist; it is in the Howard University Library.

In the early 1830s women in the East formed a number of literary societies for the purpose of "mental improvement in moral and literary pursuits." Many of the members wrote poetry, essays, and

---

[5] William Still has a brief reference to Whipper in his *Underground Railroad*. . . . (Philadelphia, 1872) pp. 735–740.
[6] See pp. 96–104.

short stories, all of which were criticized by the group; frequently, worthwhile productions of various members found their way into newspapers and periodicals of the day. Unfortunately, many of these publications were unsigned, or bore initials or first names only. In the essay *Duty of Females,* signed L.H. and published in the May 5, 1832, issue of the *Liberator,* the author, while stating that women should not appear in public debates, urges them to labor for the "education of the free colored people." For it is "the intelligence of these which will advance their cause; and it is their ignorance which will retard it."

Maria Stewart, one of the earliest black women to appear on the public platform in Boston and Philadelphia, addressed audiences several times in 1832 and 1833 before she had reached the age of thirty. In strong language she pleaded with her listeners to cultivate their minds and improve their natural talents. In her address on "African rights and liberty," delivered on February 27, 1833, she asks where among the people of color is there a man of science, a philosopher, an able statesman, a counsellor at law, lecturers on natural history and our critics in useful knowledge. Maria Stewart urged her people to follow the example of whites by appropriating money for schools and seminaries of learning for their children. "Had we as a people received one half the early advantages the whites have received, I would defy the government of these United States to deprive us any longer of our rights."[7]

William Watkins in his address to the American Moral Reform Society in 1836 showed that a good education was the greatest blessing that man could possess. "Give them this and they cease to grovel; give them this and they emerge from their degradation, though crushed beneath a mountain weight of prejudice; give them this and they will command respect and consideration from all who respect themselves and whose good opinions are worth having."[8]

The Phoenix Society of New York had a few white members. Its primary object was "to promote the improvement of the coloured people in morals, literature, and the mechanical arts." Its Board of Directors were the most prominent members of the black race. The Society embarked upon many projects, including the erection of a large public building to house a library, reading room, and museum or exhibition room. Ward societies, auxiliary to the Phoenix Society, were to take a census of all persons of color to determine, among

[7] See pp. 129–135.
[8] William Watkins *Address Delivered before the Moral Reform Society* (Philadelphia, 1837) p. 13.

other things, whether or not individuals could read or write. Adults were urged to attend school and to send their children to school regularly. Under the sponsorship of the Society, scientific lectures were scheduled, reading rooms and libraries were established and Temperance Societies were formed.

There is no doubt that the efforts of the organized educational Societies were responsible for increased awareness among the free people of color of the need for many kinds of education in order to combat prejudice, abolish slavery, and make it possible for Negroes to live as equals with their white brethren.

Constitution of the African Benevolent Society of Newport,

Rhode Island, 1808

INTRODUCTION.

WHEREAS the Sovereign Lord of the Universe, who *hath, of one blood, made all nations, to dwell on all the face of the earth,* hath been pleased, in various ways, to frown upon the African Nations, and hath placed us in circumstances of trial and depression; —we would humbly bow before him, and adore his mysterious justice. At the same time, sensible of the great defects of school instruction amongst us, and of the numerous benefits which would result from securing the education of our children and friends after us,—Therefore,

1st. Resolved, That we form ourselves into a Society, to be called, the *African Benevolent Society;* and that our object shall be, the establishment and continuance of a free school, for any person of colour in this town.

Of MEMBERS.

2d. Any person of colour, whether male or female, may become a member of this Society, by subscribing to the Constitution, and by paying fifty cents.

3d. Any member residing in this place, and neglecting payment one year after it is due, shall be considered no longer a member of this Society. Any member may be dismissed, by expressing his desire to any three of the Directors; who shall see the word *Dismissed* written against his name.

Of OFFICERS.

4th. There shall be a President, Vice-President, a Secretary, Treasurer, and eleven Directors.

5th. The President shall act as Moderator in the meetings of the Society; and, in his absence, the Vice-President shall act in his place.

6th. The Secretary shall record, in a book kept for that purpose, all the acts and doings of the Society; and shall write letters of correspondence, &c. according to the direction and order of the Society, and shall have the care of the writings of the Society.

7. The Treasurer shall keep the money which shall belong to the Society; and shall keep a regular account of what he receives; and shall not pay any out, unless by order, or by application of the Directors; and shall exhibit a full statement to them, quarterly, or yearly, as the Society shall direct.

8th. The Directors shall consist of four white and seven coloured persons, who shall have no power, but in the capacity of Directors. The Directors shall have the complete management of the monies of the Society. They shall also provide the place for, and the Instructors of, the school; and shall determine what part of the year the school shall be opened. In short, they shall have the complete direction of the school; and shall render a full statement of their proceedings to the Society, at every annual meeting; and they shall consult and unite, as far as they shall feel it a duty to promote the welfare of the Africans, with the Rhode Island Missionary Society.

VOTES of the SOCIETY and DIRECTORS.

9th. Two thirds of the male members, residing in this place, shall be necessary to transact any business. In any question before the Society, a majority shall carry a vote. The officers shall be elected orally or by ballot.

10th. Seven of the Directors shall be the least number to transact business; and of the seven, two shall be white. Also no vote shall be carried by the Directors, without the concurrence of a majority of the coloured, and at least two of the white Directors.

Of the SCHOOL.

11th. The Instructor shall be one who believes in the duty of Prayer, and conscientiously conforms to it: and he shall cause the Scriptures to be read in school daily.

He shall, also, pay special attention to the morals of the scholars; and shall have power to enquire into their conduct out of school: and the school shall be visited quarterly by the Directors, who shall examine into the conduct and progress of the scholars.

Of MEETINGS.

12th. The Society shall open and close their meetings with prayer. They shall meet annually, on the first Wednesday in January, for the purpose of paying their tax, of choosing officers, and of making arrangements for a public meeting, annually, on the second

Thursday of April. At this meeting the Society shall elect, orally, or by ballot, some minister of this place, to deliver a discourse; or may agree to meet with the *Friends,* if they appoint a meeting for them, on the said second Thursday of April; at which time the Friends of their Society shall be publicly invited, through the medium of the newspaper, to attend, and to aid their object by a collection.—Also at this meeting a general statement of their circumstances shall be publicly made.

Of amending the CONSTITUTION.

13th. Any laws may be added by the Society; but the Articles concerning the manner of elections, and concerning the number of persons and power of the Directors, shall never be varied.

AN

ADDRESS,

DELIVERED AT

BETHEL CHURCH,

PHILADELPHIA;

ON THE 30TH OF SEPTEMBER, 1818.

BEFORE THE

PENNSYLVANIA

AUGUSTINE SOCIETY,

For the Education of People of Colour.

BY PRINCE SAUNDERS.

TO WHICH IS ANNEXED

The Constitution of the Society.

PHILADELPHIA:
PRINTED BY JOSEPH RAKESTRAW.
1818.

Mr. P. Saunders:

Sir,

Permit us, in the name of the Pennsylvania Augustine Education Society, to tender you our grateful thanks, for the eloquent and appropriate discourse, delivered before them on Wednesday evening, September 30th. Allow us to solicit a copy for publication.

JOHN SUMMERSETT,

JOSEPH CASSEY, and

RUSSELL PARROTT, *Committee of Arrangement.*

Philad. Oct. 1, 1818.

Gentlemen of the Committee of Arrangement, of the Pennsylvania Augustine Education Society.

My Dear Friends,

Since it is to your Society's care, that the intellectual, social, moral and political improvements of the rising generation of the people of our complexion are committed; if in your opinion, my Address will be of any service, in the promotion of these invaluable objects, you have my hearty consent for its publication.

I have the honour to be,

my dear Sirs,

your very humble and obedient Servant,

PRINCE SAUNDERS.

To Mess'rs John Summersett,

Joseph Cassey, and

Russell Parrott.

AN ADDRESS, &c.

THE human heart is a parti-coloured piece of mosaic. But notwithstanding its variegated appearances, the whited inlayings of those genuine excellencies, and of those ennobling affections, which encompass humanity with glory and honour, are but seldom to be found its innate, or, as it were, its spontaneous ornaments.

We hence descry some of the grounds for that invaluable importance which has uniformly been given to education, in supplying the mind with intellectual acquisitions, and for adorning it with those elevated accomplishments which have generally been considered as its peculiar fruits, by the virtuous and contemplative of every age and nation; where the genial influences of the Sun of

Science have been experienced, and where the blessings of civilized society have been enjoyed. If by investigating the historic page of antiquity, we take a retrospective view of the numerous votaries of literature and the useful arts who flourished at those early periods when the improving influences of knowledge and civilization were wholly confined to the oriental regions, we shall then discover some traces of their views of the intrinsic utility of mutually associating, to aid the progress of those who were aspiring to taste the Castilian spring, while ascending the towering heights of Parnassus, that there they might behold the magnificent temple of the Ruler of the Muses, and hear his venerated oracle.

We have heard of the early distinguishing attainments of the celebrated Aristotle, who improved so much at seventeen years of age, that the immortal Plato, (his preceptor,) gave him the appellation of a Lover of the Truth. He soon afterwards became tutor to Alexander the great, and founder of the sublime researches of the ancient Peripotetici. The accomplished and eloquent youth, Antonius Gripho, a native of Gaul, came to Rome, and taught rhetoric and poetry at the house of Julius Cæsar, when a mere boy; and historians tell us that his school was frequented by Cicero and others of the most eminent literati of the age.

Many, in different periods, by cultivating the arts and sciences, have contributed to human happiness and improvement, by that invincible zeal for moral virtue and intellectual excellence, which their example has inspired in other minds and hearts, as well as by the sublimity of those traces of truth with which they have illumined the world, and dignified the intercourse of civilized society.

Perhaps there never was a period when the attention of so many enlightened men was so vigorously awakened to a sense of the importance of a universal dissemination of the blessings of instruction, as at this enlightened age, in this, in the northern and eastern sections of our country, in some portions of Europe, and in the island of Hayti.

The hope is encouraged that in the above-mentioned portions of the world, the means of acquiring knowledge sufficient to read and understand the sacred Scriptures, and to manage with propriety the ordinary concerns of domestic and social life, will soon be within the reach of every individual. Then, we trust, that we shall see a practical exemplification of the beauty and excellence of those celestial precepts and commandments which came from heaven, and which are equally applicable to all descriptions of men. They address themselves to the king upon the throne; they visit the obscurity of the humblest dwelling; they call upon the poor man to cultivate every good principle of action, as well as the man of a more elevated rank, and to aim at a life of purity, innocence, elevated virtue, and moral excellence, with the assurance that he too shall reap his reward in that better scene of human destination, to which Christianity has called all those who fear God and work righteousness.

Wherever these lofty and commanding views of piety and virtue have been encouraged, a high sense of the social, moral, and practical obligations and duties of life have been cherished and cultivated with an elevated and an invincible zeal.

Under the influence of this spirit, this benevolent spirit, practical Christians of every denomination, have elevated their views far beyond the circumscribed boundaries of selfishness, sectarianism, and party zeal; and, being bound together by the indissoluble links of that golden chain of charity and kind affection with which Christianity invariably connects its sincere votaries, and standing upon the common ground of Christian equality, they encircle the great community of those who profess the religion of our divine Master in the arms of their charity and love, and become co-workers and fellow-labourers in the illumination, the improvement, and the ultimate felicity of those who will, undoubtedly, eventually belong to the commonwealth of the Israel of our God.

In such improved sections of the world, the gardens of the Academy are thronged with youth, whose ardour to reap its fairest flowers, would even vie with that evinced by the hazardous enterprize of the intrepid Jason of antiquity, when he cast the watchful Dragon, and seized that invaluable prize, the Golden Fleece.

We have reason to be grateful, my friends, that it has pleased God to permit us to witness a period when those unjust prejudices, and those hitherto insuperable barriers to the instruction, and, consequently, to the intellectual, the moral, and the religious improvement and elevation of the people of colour, under which our fathers groaned, are beginning to subside.

And now, in the true spirit of the religion of that beneficent Parent, who has made of one blood all nations of men who dwell upon the face of the whole earth, many persons of different regions and various nations have been led to the contemplation of the interesting relations in which the human race stand to each other. They have seen that man, as a solitary individual, is a very wretched being. As long as he stands detached from his kind, he is possessed neither of happiness nor of strength. We are formed by nature to unite; we are impelled towards each other by the benevolent instincts in our frames; we are linked by a thousand connexions, founded on common wants.

Benevolent affection therefore, or, as it is very properly termed, humanity, is what man, as such, in every station, owes to man. To be inaccessible, contemptuous, avaricious, and hard-hearted, is to revolt against our very reason and nature; it is, according to the language of inspiration, to "hide ourselves from our own flesh."

The genuine kind affections, and the elevated sensibilities of Christianity, as they are exhibited to us in the conduct and character of our blessed Saviour, during his residence in this scene of our pilgrimage, are suited to call forth into vigorous exercise the best sentiments, feelings and dispositions of the human heart; while they disclose to the admiring view of his obedient followers, those indissoluble and ennobling moral ties which connect earth with heaven, and which assimilate man to the benevolent Author of his being.

Wherever Christianity is considered as a religion of the affections, every well instructed, practical Christian habitually aspires at an entire imitation of the example, and to yield a cheerful and unreserved obedience to the precepts and instructions of its heavenly founder. So peculiar is the adaptation of Christianity to become a universal religion; for wherever its spirit enters into the councils of nations, we find it unbinding the chains of corporeal and mental captivity, and diffusing over the whole world the maxims of impartial justice, and of enlightened benevolence.

Such, and so sublimely excellent, are the fruits of a spirit of Christian charity and practical beneficence; for to it alone the glory is due of having placed the weak under the protection of their stronger brethren; for she unceasingly labours to improve all the varying circumstances and conditions of mankind: so that, among those who profess her true spirit, the love of our neighbour is not an inactive principle, but it is real beneficence; and they, like the good Samaritan in the gospel, evince their sincerity by ministering to the necessities, and in labouring for the welfare, improvement and happiness of mankind.

Mess'rs Vice-Presidents, and Gentlemen of the
Pennsylvania Augustine Education Society.

ALTHOUGH the seat of your respected President is vacant on this interesting occasion, on account of the severe indisposition with which he is visited, still we trust that his heart is with you, and that you have his best wishes and his prayers for the prosperity of this excellent establishment. The hope is encouraged that you will never be weary in labouring for the promotion of the cause and interests of science and literature among the rising generation of the people of colour. For upon their intellectual, moral and religious improvements depend the future elevation of their standing in the social, civil and ecclesiastical community. Surely then, my friends, you are associated for the most laudable, interesting, and invaluable purposes.

Therefore, let it be the unceasing labour, the undeviating and the inflexibly firm purpose of the members of this Association—individually and collectively—to inspire all within the sphere of their influence with a sense of the value and importance of giving their children a good education. Hear the words of revelation, calling upon you who profess to be Christians, to "train up your children in the way they should go," and to "bring them up in the nurture and admonition of the Lord." And if you believe this high authority, how can you be excused if you neglect to give them the means of acquiring a knowledge of their duty to that divine instructor who came to call them to glory, to virtue, and to immortality.

Permit me again to entreat you, duly to appreciate the importance of religiously educating your children. For a Christian education is not only of great utility while sojourning in this scene of discipline and probation, but it is more transcendently excellent in that more elevated scene of human destination to which we are hastening. For even the ruthless hand of death itself cannot disrobe the soul of those virtuous principles which are sometimes acquired through the medium of a virtuous education, and "which, when transplanted to the skies, in heaven's immortal garden bloom."

CONSTITUTION

WE the Subscribers, persons of colour of the city of Philadelphia, in the State of Pennsylvania, sensibly impressed with the high importance of education towards the improvement of our species, in an individual as well as a social capacity; and fully persuaded, that it is to the prominently defective system of instruction, as it now exists among us, that we must in a great measure attribute the contemptible and degraded station which we occupy in society, and most of the disadvantages under which we suffer; and viewing, with serious concern, the formidable barriers that prejudices, powerful as they are unjust, have reared to impede our progress in the paths of science and of virtue, rendering it almost impossible to obtain for our offspring such instruction as we deem essentially necessary to qualify them for the useful walks of society: We therefore are convinced, that it is an unquestionable duty which we owe to ourselves, to our posterity, and to our God, who has endued us with intellectual powers, to use the best energies of our minds and of our hearts in devising and adapting the most effectual means to procure for our children a more extensive and useful education than we have heretofore had in our power to effect; and now, confidently relying upon the zealous and unanimous support of our coloured brethren, under the protection of divine providence, have resolved to unite and form ourselves into a society, to be known by the name of THE AUGUSTINE EDUCATION SOCIETY OF PENNSYLVANIA, for the establishment and maintenance of a Seminary, in which children of colour shall be taught all the useful and scientific branches of education, as far as may be found practicable, under the following regulations:

ARTICLE I

THE persons associated by subscribing to this Constitution, shall be known by the name of THE AUGUSTINE EDUCATION SOCIETY OF PENNSYLVANIA.

ARTICLE II

Every person that shall subscribe, and pay one dollar to the Society, and a further sum of twenty-five cents at each of the quarterly meetings, for the support of the said Seminary, shall be a member of the Institution, and entitled to all its privileges and immunities.

ARTICLE III

The quarterly meetings of the Society shall be held on the first Mondays of April, July, October and January.

ARTICLE IV

At the January meeting of the Society, there shall be elected by the members present, twenty managers, five of whom shall be men of science.

ARTICLE V

Within five days after their election, the managers shall be convened by the persons whose names shall be first on the list, and shall proceed to elect from their number, a President, two Vice-Presidents, a Treasurer, a Secretary, a Committee of Superintendence, to consist of five persons, and a Committee of Finance, to consist of ten.

ARTICLE VI

After the first meeting of the managers, they shall meet upon their own adjournment, and at the call of the President, or in his absence, the two Vice-Presidents.

ARTICLE VII

It shall be the object of the Society to originate and maintain a Seminary, in which children of colour shall be taught, so far as practicable, the arts and sciences.

ARTICLE VIII

The committee of superintendence shall appoint, with the concurrence of the rest of the managers, one or more teachers in the Seminary, as the state of the funds shall permit; and after the appointment of the teacher or teachers, they shall be under the directions of the committee of superintendence.

ARTICLE IX

The Treasurer shall keep clear and correct accounts of the receipts and expenditures, and shall pay all orders drawn upon him, when signed by the President, or in his absence, one of the Vice-Presidents; he shall submit his accounts to the inspection of the board of managers, when called for by them; he shall give to the board of managers such security as a majority of them may deem proper, and his security shall cause to be delivered over to the managers, in case of his death, resignation, or forfeiture of office by improper behaviour, all books, vouchers and documents appertaining to the business of the Society.

ARTICLE X

The Secretary shall record, in a book, all the transactions of the Society and of the managers.

ARTICLE XI

Any religious, auxiliary, or civil Society, who shall contribute 10 dollars annually, in aid of the funds of this Society, shall have the privilege of appointing a manager.

ARTICLE XII

All monies that may be subscribed, either as donations or subscriptions, shall, in the event of the objects of the Society not being carried into operation, be returned to the respective subscribers, the whole amount of donations in the first instance; and the balance shall be divided among the annual subscribers, or members, after the incidental expenses incurred in attempting to promote the views of the Society shall have been defrayed.

Rev. John Gloucester, *President.*
James Forten, *First Vice-President.*
Rev. Jacob Tapsico, *Second Do.*
Robert Douglass, *Treasurer.*
Samuel Cornish, *Secretary.*

Committee of Finance.
Robert C. Gordon.
Russell Parrott.
John Summersett.
John G. Paul.
Joseph Cassey.
John Morris.
James Wilson.
Francis Webb.
Jeffry Bueley.
Quamino Clarkson, *Sec'ry.*

AN

ORATION

DELIVERED

IN THE

AFRICAN ZION CHURCH,

ON THE

Fourth of July, 1827,

IN COMMEMORATION OF THE ABOLITION OF DOMESTIC

SLAVERY IN THIS STATE.

BY WILLIAM HAMILTON.

NEW YORK:
PRINTED BY GRAY & BUNCE, 224 CHERRY-STREET.
1827.

LIBERTY! kind goddess! brightest of the heavenly deities that guide the affairs of men.

Oh Liberty! where thou art resisted and irritated, thou art terrible as the raging sea, and dreadful as a tornado. But where thou art listened to, and obeyed, thou art gentle as the purling stream that meanders through the mead; as soft and as cheerful as the zephyrs that dance upon the summer's breeze, and as bounteous as autumn's harvest.

To thee, the sons of Afric, in this once dark, gloomy, hopeless, but now fairest, brightest, and most cheerful of thy domain, do owe a double oblation of gratitude. Thou hast entwined and bound fast the cruel hand of oppression—thou hast by the powerful charm of reason, deprived the monster of his strength—he dies, he sinks to rise no more.

Thou hast loosened the hard bound fetters by which we were held; and by a voice sweet as the music of heaven, yet strong and powerful, reaching to the extreme boundaries of the state of New York, hath declared that we the people of colour, the sons of Afric, are free!

My brethren and fellow citizens, I hail you all. This day we stand redeemed from a bitter thralldom. Of us it may be truly said, "the last agony is o'er," the africans are restored! No more shall the accursed name of slave be attached to us—no more shall *negro* and *slave* be synonymous.

Fellow citizens, I come to felicitate you on the victory obtained —not by a sanguinary conflict with the foe—there are left no fields teeming with blood; not a victory obtained by fierce-flaming, death-dealing ordnance, vomiting forth fire and horrible destruction—no thousands made to lick the dust—no groans of the wounded and the dying. But I come to felicitate you on the victory obtained by the principles of liberty, such as are broadly and indelibly laid down by the glorious sons of '76; and are contained in the ever memorable words prefixed to the Declaration of Independence of these United States: viz. "We hold these truths to be self-evident, that all men are created equal, and endowed by their Creator with certain unalienable rights; and that among these are life, liberty, and the pursuit of happiness." A victory obtained by these principles over prejudice, injustice, and foul oppression.

This day has the state of New York regenerated herself—this day has she been cleansed of a most foul, poisonous and damnable stain. I stand amazed at the quiet, yet rapid progress the principles of liberty have made. A semi-century ago, the people of colour, with scarcely an exception, were all slaves. It is true, that many in the city, who remained here in the time of the revolution (when their masters left at the approach of the British), and many too from the country, who became a kind of refugee, obtained their liberty by leaving the country at the close of the war, or a few years respite from slavery: for such as were found remaining after the revolution, were again claimed by their masters. Yes, we were in the most abject state of slavery that can be conceived, except that of our brethren at the South, whose miseries are a little more enhanced. Without going back to the times of Negro plot, when a kind of fanaticism seized the people of New York, something similar in its bearing and effect to the sad circumstance that took place among the people of New England, in their more puritanic times, and about a half century before the fancied plot, when they put to death the good people for being witches.

Yes, my brethren, in this state we have been advertised, and bought, and sold like any commodity. In this state we have suffered cruelly; suffered by imprisonment, by whipping, and by scourging.

I have seen men chained with iron collars to their necks. I have seen—but hold! Let me proceed no farther. Why enter into the blood-chilling detail of our miseries? It would only dampen those joys that ought to glow and sparkle on every countenance: it would only give vent to feelings that would not be reconcileable with the object of our assembling.

The cause of emancipation has ever had its votaries, but they stood single and alone. After the revolution, they drew nearer together.

That venerable body of religionists, called Friends, ought ever to be held in grateful remembrance by us. Their public speakers were the first to enter their protest against the deadly sin of slaveholding; and so zealous did its members become, that the church, or more technically, the meeting, passed laws; first forbidding its members from holding slaves for life, next forbidding the use of slaves altogether. But the most powerful lever, or propelling cause, was the Manumission Society. Although many of its members belonged to the just-named society, yet very many were members of other religious societies, and some did not belong to any, but who were philanthropists indeed. How sweet it is to speak of good men! Nature hath not made us calumniators—calumny yields us no pleasure: if it does, it is satanic pleasure: but to speak of good men yields a pleasure such as the young feel, when talking of their lovers, or the parent feels, when telling of the prattle of their infants.

In speaking of the Manumission Society, we are naturally drawn to its first founders. These must have been good men: the prejudice of the times forbade any other but men of good and virtuous minds from having any lot or part in the matter. Any other must have shrunk from the undertaking. I am, therefore, about to name men who ought to be deeply inscribed on your memories, and in your hearts: The names of Washington and Jefferson should not be pronounced in the hearing of your children, until they could clearly and distinctly pronounce the names I am about to give. First, that great and good statesman, the right honourable John Jay, the first President of the Manumission Society. Blessed God! how good it is, he has lived to see, as a reward, the finishing of a work he helped to begin.

Next, the good John Murray, peace attends his memory, he was a man that calumny never did approach, but what she bit her tongue: he was the first Treasurer: next, the not only harmless, but good Samuel Franklin, the first-Vice-President; next the zealous, the virtuous, the industrious John Keese, the first Secretary; next, general Alexander Hamilton, that excellent soldier, and most able civilian and financier, and first of his profession at the bar. Next, that man of more than sterling worth, Robert Bowne.

The other names which I shall give, are of equal worth with those already mentioned, and are as follows:

Alexander M'Dougal, Colonel Robert Troup, John Lawrence, Peter Yates, Melancton Smith, William Goforth, Ebenezer S. Burling, Laurence Embree, Zebulon Bartow, Elijah Cock, William Shotwell, Joseph Laurence, James Cogswell, Matthew Vicker, William Backhouse, William Cartman, Thomas Burling, Thomas Bowne, Leonard M. Cutting.

These are the men that formed the Manumission Society, and stamped it with those best of principles, found in the preamble to the constitution, framed by them. It is too excellent to pass over, and is as follows: "The benevolent Creator, and Father of all men; having given to them all an equal right to life, liberty and property, no sovereign power on earth can justly deprive them of either but in conformity to impartial laws, to which they have expressly or tacitly consented; it is our duty both as free citizens and Christians, not only to regard with compassion the injustice done to those among us, who are held as slaves, but to endeavour by all lawful ways and means, to enable them to share equally with us, that civil and religious liberty, with which an indulgent Providence has blessed these states; and to which these our brethren are as much entitled as ourselves."

It was on the 25th January, 1785, these gentlemen held their first meeting, and on the fourth of the following month, they adopted a constitution, headed by the just mentioned most liberal and excellent preamble.

To enter into a detail of the services rendered us by this society would be out of my power. Even those that have come within my knowledge would occupy more time (though pleasing to relate) by far than we have on hand. Suffice it to say that through the efforts of this society, our situation has been much meliorated, and very many of our brethren have been liberated from slavery. The society, between the time of its formation and 1813, obtained many salutary laws relative to our emancipation and well usage. But by a revision of the laws of the state about this time, some had been changed in their intent, while others had become nugatory.

Being alarmed, the Society made strong efforts to regain the lost ground. The years between 1813 and 1817 were spent by the Society in vigorous efforts, by which, however, they gained little more than an accession of strength. But prior to the session that brought forth the law that gave rise to this rejoicing, three gentlemen, whom I shall name with pride and much glorying, viz. Mr. Joseph Curtis, Mr. John Murray, and Mr. Thomas Addis Emmet, waited on the then governor Mr. Daniel D. Tompkins. He was a man, who, if he had faults, his virtues overwhelmed them, angels vied with each other the privilege of conveying him to a better state. From the governor, who always was our friend, these gentlemen obtained a ready promise that he would introduce the subject of emancipation in his message to the legislature, and recommend to them the fixing on a time for its accomplishment, which promise he faithfully performed.

I have named some of the men to whom our gratitude is due. Did I name them as they rise on the altar of my heart, I should name many equally worthy, and equally noted; and some, although not of so public a character, who have yet rendered equal services. The Manumission Society have laboured hard and incessantly in order to bring us from our degraded situation, and restore us to the rights of men. It has stood, a phalanx, firm and undaunted, amid the flames of prejudice, and the shafts of calumny. How pleasing it is, they have a reward. Our Heavenly Father hath fixed the highest sensations of pleasure to good and virtuous actions.

My brethren, our enemies have assumed various attitudes: sometimes they have worn a daring front, and blasphemously have said, the Negroes have no souls, they are not men, they are a species of the ourang outang. Sometimes, in more mild form, they say, they are a species inferior to white men. Then again they turn to blasphemy, and say, God hath made them to be slaves.

Let us look at them, and we shall see, with all their pomp, and pride, and hauteur, they are more the objects of pity and commiseration, than of anger and hate. Well may it be said, "the wicked are like the troubled sea." It is hard breathing in their atmosphere. Are not deeds of injustice the harrowers up of fears of revenge, in proportion to their turpitude? We have a fair portrait in the Southern states. In order to see it more clearly, contrast the Southern and Northern sections of the union. Would the people of the North exchange situations for the slaves of the South, ten times told? Reverse the question, and what must be the answer? Do the people of the

North need nightly patrols to save them from insurrections? How sweet is the sleep of the virtuous! The hoverings around their nocturnal rest are soothing angels—the wicked dream of being pursued by furies. In the South, a poor, single, solitary man of colour, cannot enter their country, but through their dread of soul, they seize him and imprison him. They are like him that has murdered his neighbour, who starts at every one that looks him in the face.

It would be foolishness in me, my brethren, to tell you that by all the rules laid down by naturalists for determining the species of a creature, that we have souls, and are men. We too irresistibly feel that we have, and are such. We can more easily doubt that we exist, than doubt that we are men. To the second proposition, and my soul for it, if there is any difference in the species, that difference is in favour of the people of colour.

Man is a moral being, and ought to be governed by his reason. The lessons of reason are the lessons of morality. If we measure souls at all, we ought to measure them by the scale of morality. What does he gain that can enter into the most abstruse reasoning about matter and its properties; that is acquainted with the anatomy of every creature; or can tell you of all the heavenly bodies, of planets, and their satellites, of their diameters, and their distances, their diurnal rotations, their revolutions around their primaries, and degrees of their inclination to their orbits, and times of their revolution around the sun, if when he is done, he sits down to the intoxicating draught, until he is deprived of his reason, and becomes like a stupid beast? How much does such an abstruse reasoner gain, by the proper rule over him, who only reasons himself into sober and virtuous habits?

I know that I ought to speak with caution; but an ambidexter philosopher, who can reason contrarywise, first tells you "that all men are created equal, and that they are endowed with the unalienable rights of life, liberty, and the pursuit of happiness," next proves that one class of men are not equal to another, which by the bye, does not agree with axioms in geometry, that deny that things can be equal, and at the same time unequal to one another—suppose that such philosopher should keep around him a number of slaves, and at the same time should tell you, that God hath no attribute to favour the cause of the master in case of an insurrection of the slaves. Would not such a reasoner only show a heterogeneous mind? although he should be called an abstruse reasoner, what kind of superiority does he discover? Does he not reason, and act, like one that battles with the elements? Does he reason like a man of true moral principles? Does he set a good example? Does he act in conformity to true philosophy? True philosophy teaches, that man should act in conformity to his reason, and reason, and the law of God and nature, declare that all men are equal, and that life, liberty, and the pursuit of happiness are their unalienable rights.

It is a maxim among civilians that the principles of government and acts of the legislator should be in unison. What ought to be considered the most vital principles of our general government, are contained in the words already mentioned, as standing in front of the Declaration of Independence; and in that article of the constitution, that declares that no person shall be deprived of life, liberty, or property, without due course of law. What a jargon does that law of the United States form with the principles here laid down, that gives to one class of men the right to arrest, wherever they may find them within its jurisdiction, another class of men, and retain them as their lawful property? This, no doubt, is superior legislation, and bespeaks superior minds.

In these United States, among white men, there is an almost universal prejudice against the amalgamation of the blood of the white and black population, which goes so far as to create in them the supercilious fear, or rather the horrible sensation, that the pretty white will be changed thereby to the dingy mulatto. Yes, true it is, and true though it is white men masters do amalgamate the blood, and the children of such amalgamation they hold as slaves: and worse, they sell as slaves. It is said by a Frenchman of high note, that the American will sell his dog for money; I do not know that the Frenchman will not do the same. But this I do know, that white men sell the children of their own begetting, for sordid gold.

Authority and gold are their gods, their household gods, their sanctuary gods, and the highest gods of their sanctum sanctorum. What titillation of soul they receive from these gods! How bold! how venturous! how stubborn! how pliant! how wise! how simple! how every thing but virtuous they are!

I am sorry to break from this unravelling so soon, for I did mean to unravel this mystery of superiority. But it is necessary that we devote a few moments to a subject of vital interest to us. And here let me particularly address the youth. With you rests the high responsibility of redeeming the character of our people. White men say you are not capable of the study of what may be called abstruse literature, and that you are deficient in moral character. I feel, I know, that these assertions are as false as hell. Yet I do know, you are sunk into the deepest frivolity and lethargy that any people can be sunk. Oh Heavens! that I could rouse you. Has this frivolity taken from you all shame? Has this lethargy taken from you all ambition?

Youth of my people, I look to you. Shall this degrading charge stand unrepelled by contrary facts? Oh! that I could enflame you with proper ambition. Your honour, your character, your happiness, your well-being, all, all are at stake, and involved in the question at issue. And it is for you to retrieve or acknowledge that your fathers have been slaves deservedly.

First, my young friends, let me invite you to the path of virtue. It is a straight, open path, strewed with the sweetest aromatics: it is the path of pleasure, the path of honour, the path of respectability. Vice, from which I would call you, is its opposite; it is a crooked, thorny way, full of stinking weeds, the path of trouble, debasement, misery, and destruction.

Next, I would invite you to the study of the sciences. Here lies an open field of pleasure, that is increased at every step you take therein. If you have labour, be assured that your compensation is infinite. It has been the policy of white men to give you a high opinion of your advancement, when you have made but smattering attainments. They know that a little education is necessary for the better accomplishing the menial services you are in the habit of performing for them. They do not wish you to be equal with them—much less superior. Therefore, in all advancements they assist in (I speak of them generally) they will take care that you do not rise above mediocrity.

My young friends, it is a laudable ambition that prompts us to the highest standing in literature. Is there any thing noble or praiseworthy obtained by sneaking conduct? Why look up to others, when we may obtain the highest standing ourselves? There is a height of knowledge which you may easily attain to, that when arrived at, you will look down with amazement, at the depth of ignorance you have risen from. I am sorry to say it; but I speak with the intention to quicken you, that, properly speaking, there is none learned among us. If there is, now is the time to show themselves; it is worse than felony to keep back. It is too true, that men of prime genius among us, that have possessed high talents for improvement, have suffered improper considerations to keep them down. Therefore, my young friends, I look to you, and pray you, by all that proper pride you feel in being men, that you show yourselves such, by performing acts of worth equal with other men. Why not form yourselves into literary companies for the study of the sciences? The expense would not be as great as you incur for useless gratifications, beside the advantage of receiving pleasure, infinitely beyond what those gratifications afford.

I would now turn to the female part of this assembly, particularly the young. It is for you to form the manners of the men. My female friends, it is for you, not by proud, but modest conduct, to lead them in the true line of decorum and gentle manners. First, I would have you discountenance that loud vocability of gabble, that too much characterizes us in the street: I would look upon him, or her, that hailed me with too loud, or vulgar accents, as one who had forgot what is due to female modesty. Next, and most of consequence, I would have you prefer his affections and company most, who endeavours most to improve his mind. If you give preference to men of understanding, depend on it, they will endeavour to make themselves suitable to your wishes. But above all, endeavour to improve your own minds. I know that in the ability to improve, you are more than a match for white females, in all proper female education. Here, let me close, with our best thanks and wishes to the State of New York.

AN ADDRESS

DELIVERED IN

WESLEY CHURCH

ON THE EVENING OF JUNE 12,

BEFORE THE

COLORED READING SOCIETY

of Philadelphia,

For Mental Improvement.

BY WILLIAM WHIPPER.

PUBLISHED BY JOHN B. ROBERTS, 25 CURRANT ALLEY.

PHILADELPHIA:
PRINTED BY JOHN YOUNG, 3 BLACK HORSE ALLEY,
SOUTH SECOND ST.
1828.

COMMUNICATIONS

SIR,

It having passed the board that an address should be delivered in favour of the Reading Society; when you were unanimously appointed to this service.

Your's &c.

JOHN R. ROBERTS, *Chairman.*

THOS. F. CRAIG, *Ass't. Sec'ry.*

105

DEAR SIR,

I received your polite invitation to devote my service to you at some future period, in expressing my sentiments in favour of our Society. I feel sorry that the task had not devolved on some one more competent to do justice to this important subject. If no necessary apology will be received for my inadequacy, I beg your indulgence, whilst with the greatest of humility, I accept the service, for no other purpose than for to discharge my duty on every occasion.

WM. WHIPPER.

Philadelphia, June 14th, 1828.

DEAR SIR,

I humbly solicit from you a copy of your address which you delivered before the colored Reading Society of Philadelphia for Mental Improvement, on the 12th instant, it being my intention to commit it to the press.

Your's obt'ly.

J. B. ROBERTS.

MR. WM. WHIPPER.

DEAR SIR,

I received your favour of the 14th, requesting a copy of my address: it was not my intention to have had it printed, therefore I hope you will excuse my errors, while I cheerfully grant you the request; hoping that it may meet with a candid investigation by every reader. To the critic, I only ask pardon for the illiterateness of my remarks, not for the reality of my sentiments.

WM. WHIPPER.

MR. J. B. ROBERTS.
June 16th.

At a meeting of this Society—*Resolved*, that the thanks of this Society be given to Wm. Whipper, for his services on the 12th instant.

ENOS WATERFORD, *Chairman.*
THOMAS F. CRAIG, *Sec'ry*

AN ADDRESS DELIVERED BEFORE THE COLORED READING SOCIETY OF PHILADELPHIA

Friends and Fellow Citizens—

IF it be useful to cherish moral and intellectual improvement, the occasion which has called us together is one of high interest. The

establishment of a literary institution, whether we consider it as connected with the progress of science in times past, or associated with
its future advancement, is an event which we cannot regard with
feelings of indifference.

But sincerely do I regret that the task of awakening these reflections in your minds had not devolved on some one more competent
to do justice to the important subject from which they spring. To
my fellow members belonging to this institution I have made sufficient apology for my inadequacy, without transgressing on your
patience at present.

I am well aware that the age in which we live is fastidious in its
taste. It demands eloquence, figure, rhetoric, and pathos; plain,
honest, common sense is no longer attracting. No: the orator must
display the pomp of words, the magnificence of the tropes and figures, or he will be considered unfit for the duties of his profession.

But I pretend to none of these. Such high-wrought artificial lectures, however, are like beautiful paint upon windows, they rather
obscure than admit the light of the sun. Truth should always be
exhibited in such a dress as may be best suited to the state of the
audience, accompanied with every principle of science and reason.

In establishing a new institution, respect for public opinion requires us to make our motives understood. This is the golden age of
Literature; men studious of change are constantly looking for something new, and no sooner has the mind become gratified than new
means of gratification is sought for. The Literature of the day is
accommodating itself to the public taste, and brings in regular succession the condensed learning of past ages; and all the erudition
of the present. We shall make no pretentions to concentrate learning,
or display erudition, ours will be a humbler task, but not the less
important, and we humbly hope not the less useful.

1st. This Society shall be known and distinguished by the name of
The coloured Reading Society for Mental Improvement. 2ndly. All
persons initiated into this Society shall become members in the same
mode as is customary in all benevolent institutions, with the same
strictness and regard to the moral qualifications as is necessary in all
institutions to secure their welfare. 3rdly. Every person on becoming
a member of this institution, shall pay into the hands of the Treasurer his initiation fee and monthly dues. 4thly. All monies received
by this Society (with the exception of wood, light, rent, &c.) is to be
expended in useful books, such as the Society may from time to
time appropriate. 5thly. All books initiated into this Society shall be
placed in the care of the Librarian belonging to said institution, and
it shall be his duty to deliver to said members alternately, such books

as they shall demand, with strict regard that no member shall keep said book out of the library longer than one week, without paying the fine prescribed in the constitution, unless an apology for sickness or absence: those shall be the only excuses received. 6thly. It shall be the duty of this Society to meet once a week to return and receive books, to read, and express whatever sentiments they may have conceived if they think proper, and transact the necessary business relative to this institution. 7thly and lastly. It shall be our whole duty to instruct and assist each other in the improvement of our minds, as we wish to see the flame of improvement spreading amongst our brethren and friends; and the means prescribed shall be our particular province. Therefore we hope that many of our friends will avail themselves of the opportunity of becoming members of this useful institution.

I feel as though your minds have already become acquainted with the subject, as the necessity of the case demands the greatest attention. If there be any who doubt the usefulness and utility of this institution to be conducive of much to the public, I refer them to the most learned gentlemen of our city, or to our coloured brethren in the state of New York, who have established a reading room long ago, much to their credit be it said. It is a new era in the affairs of our state (transacted by men of colour) and consequently must meet with those trials and difficulties which commonly attend the origin of new institutions.

I make no doubt but at this moment there may be many objections made by some of you. It may be said that it has not had its origin amongst the most noble, the most opulent, or literate. To this I will agree, for had they used their talents, and influence, this might have been accomplished long ago. In establishing this institution, for the avowed purpose of spreading useful knowledge, we do not expect to escape the shafts of calumny and opposition.

Indeed we would rather count than shun the contest, as the very sparks which may be elicited by the clashing of our weapons will in some measure tend to dissipate the surrounding darkness, and thus facilitate the progress of those who are in search of the reality of our sentiments.

Another objection—That to acquire the necessaries of life, men's occupations will deprive them of the liberty of spending a few hours in a week to the improvement of their minds. To them I will answer —What occupation is within the boundary of our city that some of those who have been engaged in have not been seen once, twice, or three times a week, spending their time and money within the walls of a public house, when they might have been better employed?

And it is bold in me to assert that some of our most classic young men spend much of their time in public houses. Yes; men capable of doing justice to the subject I am rather abusing, and displaying themselves, and developing their profound talents, over the full-flowing bowl; and it is a fact that the most important literature amongst us is discussed in these evening conventions. This may be for want of a public institution. I cannot say but I fear, that the cup of intemperance will overtake many, do they not resist those baneful attractions.

I do not expect that any thing I have said, or will say, will have any tendency to bring about a new state of affairs. If I have digressed too far, I hope my sentiments will meet with a public refutation, that the force of truth may be the result. I have said no more than is said by almost every reflecting man on the same occasion. The only difference is that their channel of communication is private, while mine is public.

It would not have been my intention here to have aimed the blow at the learned; to all classes of citizens it is equally productive of the same ill consequences. But as the world in general are taught to expect something of the highest order from minds richly furnished with education, our respect and social happiness depend much on their conduct and outward performances.

The station of a scholar highly versed in classic lore (with the exception of a Christian preacher) is indeed higher than any other occupied by man. The purity of principle and integrity of life required to fill its several stations as it should be filled, the weighty and important duties it imposes and the magnitude of objects which must ever be in view, entitles it to this superiority. It is their particular province to instruct the unenlightened, to comfort the disconsolate, and to awaken hope in the breasts of the despondents; to convince the faithless, to check those who are rushing onward to ruin, to suppress the ebullition of lawless passion, and to invigorate reason, to put the blasphemer to shame, and in fact every duty that is characteristic in the history of civilized man, should shine conspicuously in them. It is required of them that their lives be pure as the precepts they inculcate, and that humility, self-denial, and every other virtue should ever remain as brilliant stars in their characters. Their situation is one of danger, as well as of difficulty. The ignorant and depraved by whom they are surrounded, and whose eyes are intently fixed on their steps, are ever busy with their fame, seeking with malicious industry to find something in their lives injurious to their profession, and to cast a reproach upon literature.

By such the smallest error of their judgments will be magnified into a wilful perversion of truth; and the most trifling deviation from the path of moral rectitude, into a grossly criminal violation of virtue. Their zeal will be called bigotry—their liberality want of devotion—their firmness obstinacy—and their independence and ambition thirst for power.

In order that we may become acquainted with the transacting of public affairs, it requires our strictest attention to study, or the young and rising generation that are receiving the advantages of a liberal education will look back on the present state of Science amongst us, and will speak of our times as the day of small things, in stronger and juster language than any in which we can depict the poverty of science in the days of our fathers, when they were bound by the galling chains of slavery, and the lights of knowledge not permitted to enter their beclouded minds.

The post rings incessantly in our ears of the progress of education amongst all classes; Sir Franceis Burdett cries up the march of mind; Mr. Brougham tells us the Schoolmaster is abroad; Mr. Peel boasts of the improvement of the age, and while all these have been going on it is time for us to be up and a-doing.

Perhaps I have said too much about necessity of obtaining a liberal education, and not enough about its advantages when attained. It is here my design to make a few remarks. I do not mean however to detain you with trite remarks on this subject, but shall feebly offer you my views respecting a learned education.

1st. The first object of education is to exercise, and by exercising to improve the faculties of the mind. Every faculty we possess is improveable by exercise. This is a law of nature. The acquisition of knowledge is not the only design of a liberal education; its primary design is to discipline the mind itself, to strengthen and enlarge its powers, to form habits of close and accurate thinking, and to acquire a facility of classifying and arranging, analyzing and comparing our ideas on different subjects. Without this preparatory exercise, our ideas will be superficial and obscure, and all the knowledge we acquire will be but a confused mass thrown together without arrangement, and incapable of useful application.

For this purpose the course of study pursued in most of the Seminaries is well adapted. The study of the languages under the directions of a careful instructor is admirably calculated to call forth the energies of the youthful minds, to fix the attention, to strengthen the memory, and to form habits of analyzing, comparing, abstracting, and correct reasoning.

The advantage of which we are speaking, is that which distinguishes the real scholar no less than the extent of his knowledge, and so great is it that if there were no other advantage to be derived from a liberal education, this alone would compensate for all the time and labour employed in acquiring it. But this is not all the diligent student in the mean time acquires.

2d. Another important object of education, viz: Useful knowledge. In studying the dead languages, the student acquires a knowledge of the principles of grammar, the philosophy of language, and becomes more thoroughly acquainted with his own. The authors which are studied are valuable on their own account, and the students, by going to the fountains themselves, attain advantages not to be derived from translation. A fund of ideas is acquired on a variety of subjects; the taste is greatly improved by conversing with the best models; the imagination is enriched by the fine scenery with which the classics abound; and an acquaintance is formed with human nature, together with the history, customs and manners of antiquity. Without some knowledge of the ancient classics it is impossible to see the beauty and understand many of the illusions of our best English writers, who imbibed the spirit and were formed on the model of the ancients. In addition to all this we may add the advantage of being able to read the sacred oracles of God in the languages in which they were originally written.

I have dwelt longer on this course of study than is necessary or useful to us who have arrived to the years of maturity. My chief design was to exhibit to you the great importance and benefit that youth derive from this study to prepare them for future usefulness.

I deem it unnecessary to dwell on the advantages to be derived from various other branches. Everyone will acknowledge the utility of geography, ancient and modern history, political economy, natural philosophy and chemistry, with the immense improvement in these sciences of late years, and their multiplied application to the ordinary purposes of life.

Whatever relates to the mind is surely of great moment, whether we consider its operations in acquiring and communicating truth, or as a subject of happiness, or as a moral agent.

It is with the greatest of pleasure we observe that the philosophy of the mind has lately assumed a new aspect. The "sublime fog" which formerly enveloped this subject, has been dispelled by the light of Scotch philosophy; and science, strictly so called, has been established, not on mere hypothesis, but on fixed principles and matters of fact. This study we desire to see at some future period, occupying a conspicuous place in all our seminaries of learning.

On the whole, each branch of learning has its issue, either as an exercise for the mind, or as subservient to other studies, as being capable of practical application, whilst all are intimately allied, having a mutual tendency to aid and illustrate one another. But in order to succeed in the communication of knowledge, there must be a capacity to receive it. In order to cultivate talents, there must be talents to be cultivated. Education cannot create; its province is to elicit and direct the faculties of the mind. It would be superfluous to make a remark of this kind, which has been made before, and which requires no depth of philosophy to suggest or comprehend, were it not for the unreasonableness of some, who expect education to do everything. At the same time, we are not to speak with unqualified contempt of modern talents; nor to consider those alone worthy of education who possess transcendent genius. Genius is a rare article, and if everything but genius were to be set aside, most of the literary or professional seats in our country would be vacated. It is a misfortune, not a crime, to lack talents. But to look for genius in everyone who may profitably receive an education is out of the question. Where there is a moderate capacity it may be cultivated with advantage, and after all has been said about genius, intellect, talent, brains, &c. the fact is that men do not differ so much from each other by original distinctions of genius as by their success in improving what they have. Men of moderate capacity have risen to eminence and respectability by industry and perseverance, whilst others of superior powers have, through negligence, sunk into contempt.

Perhaps too much has been said about mere genius, too much applause attached to it, and too little to encourage patient and persevering industry. No praise whatever is due to talents, only as it is improved and directed; but much praise is due to that man who by his own exertions has risen to eminence and usefulness.

In addition to the objects already mentioned as the primary design of a learned education, there are others of great utility intimately connected with these, and necessary to give them a proper direction and practical effects. It is not sufficient to be a mere scholar. A man may possess a vigorous mind, well disciplined, and richly furnished with learning, and yet be in a great measure useless from want of other attainments.

And this leads us to another object of importance, viz: 3d. The cultivation of taste. This, whether we consider it as a simple faculty, or as a combination, embraces in its range a great variety of objects, is to us as a source of refined enjoyments, and like other faculties admits of improvement by cultivation. Learning must furnish the material, taste must give the polish, and in many cases the capacity of useful application. It is therefore not without good reason that in a system of education so much attention is required to the study of belles lettres, to criticism, to composition, pronunciation, style, and to everything included in the name of eloquence.

'Tis vain to reject these things as useless ornaments; taste is the gift of God, and was given to be used. In the present state of society, attention to these things is absolutely necessary to usefulness and respectability.

We will here conclude our remarks on this part of our subject, and I shall feebly attempt to exhibit to you, that notwithstanding the regular mode and system of instruction, we every day view a different mode of application; we see one man a divine, another a lawyer, another a physician, &c. These are professions which are necessary to be filled, while among the most learned and enlightened statesmen that our country can boast of, we see them advocating a cause that they and their fathers groaned under a little more than half a century ago, and burst the bands of colonial bondage, and that is slavery. The wise and patriotic legislature of South Carolina, at their last convention, assembled for the purpose of discussing such questions as would be most conducive to the welfare of the state, the benefit of their constituents; and to raise themselves into respectability, passed a law that under the penalty of fine and disgraceful stripes, any white or black teaching a man of colour how to read or write. Amongst these dreadful catalogues of wrongs, we find the name of Col. D. of South Carolina (whose name shall shine bright in the history of infamy) is such a lover of his country, and the cause of injured humanity, that he has preferred to see this country drenched in blood—yea, even to a dissolution of the union, rather than see slavery banished from its soil. The Hon. J. R. of Virginia has declared that no man east of the Potomac has any right to meddle with the cause of slavery. Such philanthropists as these we cannot find in the wide extended range of creation; no, it's impossible to find its parallel; superstition and Gothic darkness would have startled at measures like these, as too base and wretched even for their gloomy policy.

And yet these avowed advocates of slavery, would wish to be classed amongst the religious, the moral, and the honest, &c., but I deny them the privilege, for there is not a slaveholder under the canopy of heaven possesses one of these titles, or else I am mistaken in the articles of justice. Where is the slaveholder who professes to love his God that has not a lie in his mouth when he says that he does unto others as he would that they should do unto him. Or in point of morality, can he say that he treats his slaves and their posterity in the same way that he would wish them to treat him and his posterity? And until there is a law enacted that will not correct the holder of stolen goods, as well as the thief, the slaveholder cannot be an honest man. Yet the dishonest slaveholders bear the name of honest upright men—men in whom the affairs of state are at pledge. Yes, and I am sorry to say, that the seat of our national government contains a majority of these misanthropists, who every day are heard exclaiming against oppressions in their conventions, and developing the same to an enlightened community on paper. We see them rejoicing in the convention of '76, that ever-memorable epoch in the annals of the nation, when their fathers declared themselves free from British tyranny—when they threw off the yoke of colonial oppression, in words as strong as it is in the power of language to express, which was "to live free or die."

Yet these wise men, who hate the very idea, form, and name of slavery as respects themselves, are holding and dooming an innocent posterity (connected to themselves in all the sublime qualities of man, differing only in the colour of their skin, which is the natural production of a tropical climate) to slavery in their own country—on their own farms—and at their own firesides, in a bondage ten times as severe as the one already mentioned, that their fathers denounced as being too ignominious to be borne by man. Yes, a race of beings only doomed to be inhabitants of this soil, by the injustice and dishonesty of their fathers who purloined our ancestors from their own country. Oh! horrible spectacle! Oh! for an asylum to hide from the knowledge of such barbarity and injustice.

May the letter and spirit of the constitution of the United States stare them in their faces—May the unalienable rights of man stand as a mirror for them to view their words, until they are ashamed of their deeds; and if not, they may see their children rise up and set the example for their fathers to look upon, ere the cold messenger of death shall summon them before a just God, where master and slave will be equal, and each judged according to their deeds. May they move on the cause of emancipation, ere the spirits of just men, such as the venerable Franklin, and immortal Rush, rise up and warn them of their awful judgement.

After all we will have need of much patience during the permitted continuance of the present night of error, until the day dawns and the shadows flee away; the time is fast approaching when this must be. It is not clear daylight! but the morning's dawn appears. Let us indulge ourselves that this gloomy night of error is far spent and that the day is at hand, the bright day long since predicted, when the light of the sun (of righteousness) shall be seven fold even as the light of seven days—

When science shall chase the clouds away, and darkness reign
  no more,
But one unclouded day shall shine, from shore to shore.

The Sacred Scriptures, those pure oracles of truth, which the
Divine Mercy of the Lord has given to fallen man, as a "light to his
feet, and a lantern to his paths," have not yet obtained their proper
rank in the Christian world, or else they would be sufficient to detect
all slaveholding doctrines, and supersede all human oppression. I
trust ere long, through the instrumentality of the Bible Societies,
they will be brought into full operation.

I hope that you will excuse my abstruse and abridged remarks
concerning the justice and humanity of some of our leading and
most enlightened men that is in our province to boast; men who
have feasted in the storehouse of science, and there conceived a plan
which justifies them in holding two millions of their fellow beings
in slavery.

I must now attempt to exhibit to you that there is an indifference
in ourselves relative to emancipating our brethren from universal
thralldom; and if this had, and would at the present be attended to,
might be the means of ameliorating our condition much, and that is
by a strict attention to education. We find that those men who have
ever been instrumental in raising a community into respectability,
have devoted their best and happiest years to this important object;
have lived laborious days and restless nights; made a sacrifice of
ease, health, and social joys; and terminated their useful career in
poverty, with the only consoling hope that they had done justice to
their fellow men, and should in their last hours of triumphant prospect lie down on the bed of fame and live to future ages.

It was a wise remark of Mr. Cobbett, whilst lecturing the present
Duke of Wellington on the new course of administration he must
pursue in order to extinguish the national debt, says: "The higher
class consider it too much trouble to enter into the arduous task,
while the middle consider they can do nothing to better their condition; and the lower class neither know nor care anything about
what good or bad effects it might produce upon the natives. And,
my brethren and friends, it is exactly so with ourselves relative to
the cause of slavery. Those who enjoy liberty, and have accumulated
considerable property are satisfied with their situation, and will not
meddle with the cause; while the middle class are too busy in pro-
curing the necessaries of life to alter their course. And the lower
class remain regardless of themselves or their brethren, who are existing in a state of ignorance and under the debasing influence of

slavery and wicked men.—Their only object is to become votaries to the cup of intemperance, and reflect disgrace on those who enjoy a more retired life and civil society.—This leads me to an important part of my subject, viz: AMBITION.

Ambition in its true and philosophical sense, takes in everything to which our thoughts can be extended, and is the very thing that will exert us to action. It has so many terms, I am not able to explain the one-tenth part. It stoops to the lowest and looks after the highest —extends to all life—moves through every sense—and fastens itself on aspiration, without which it is vain for us to attempt to read the stars, "or justly know our own minds."

It is confined to no particular part, but it embraces all, the whole extent of matter, finite and infinite—the whole immeasurable round of the universe. Hence it will be impossible for any one to dwell upon the principle of universal love, or upon its kindred, ambition, the subject matter of our performance, without taking an extensive range, looking backwards as well as forwards, and without dipping into, at once, the whole scope of human enquiry. Nevertheless it may be impossible in attempting to touch upon one subject, to be confined either to the heavens, or to the earth, to one place or another, hence, no one can attempt to philosophise upon ambition, without taking a glance at religious, moral, and political institutions, &c. And which, although it may be condemned by critics whose optics and ideas are contracted, must notwithstanding be approved of by persons of reflection.

Here we may be told that the very subject of my discourse is, and must be, of no interest to the bulk of mankind—that it can be of little or no profit to people of the higher orders, to fret themselves about that which they never can attain to; or study into the nature of a thing which is so unimportant considered with a hundred other topics. But we hope that we are not deceived in the belief that it is of all others, the most interesting theme that can possibly command our attention, or at all events it is not to be thrown away without some consideration or examination; not without, at least, some hesitation.

Again, it may be said, that ambition sounds too much like envy; that it is the parent of iniquity, has destroyed millions of lives, and deluged the world in blood; nay, it has been the downfall of many noble objects. Ambition, dreadful sound! the cause of all our woe, some may say! away with ambition; it is humility and quiet we hope to seek, and not the hum or noise and parade of a vain world; it is rest and retirement which will be most conducive to happiness, not the giddy applause of an ignorant unthankful multitude. This is excellent, and to the very point. But where, what is this rest; or to what place would one flee to, in order to have and enjoy it? In the woods among ignorance and poverty, where there is, and can be no hope? Nothing but fell despair—starvation and want? Where there are no books nor learning, hardly newspapers themselves to wipe away the falling tear?

No; Fame, Ambition, rise! proclaim! and tear us from the chains of slavery! Be alert, be free; and then forever rest.

Yes, ambition is my theme,—that "powerful source of good and ill." What, in the language of our gloomy poet, "proud world and vain." O, Young! would to heaven, that I, like thee, could do justice to the object of my choice. O, could I, in some small degree, approach to that utility, which must ever, ever, ever belong to thy Night Thoughts!

My much honoured, esteemed friends, what is it that incites mankind to virtuous actions? Is it not ambition? certainly it is, and it inspires us with a sense of our dignity, and just importance in the scale of being—elevates us into the path of our duty. I tell you, my friends, that ambition is the cornerstone of all human greatness; without it we are sunk into the grave of sublunary hope; we become nothing—nay, we become awful nuisances to society. Despair seizes hold upon us, drags us to the precipice of destruction, and chains us in his gloomy vaults for ever. Take hope from us, and this is the very foundation of ambition, and we are at once plunged into the dark Tartarian abyss, where there is, or can be nothing but wretchedness and misery; where we shudder at the very approach of man.

Ambition, high swelling word of vanity; and yet it is the grand pillow of virtue, and the very high road of honour. To that do we owe the most precious delights we enjoy. Oh! Parent of virtue, great origin of religious ambition, which can level mountains, tear the very hills from their foundations, and make rivers flow through dry land. Providence has always so ordered things, that when men, out of good motives, try earnestly to perform noble actions, to crown them in some degree with success. Achilles no sooner lays his shoulders to the wheel, than the ponderous vehicle moves directly. The truth is, that the greater the opposition one meets with in any laudable undertaking, the greater is its final triumph; it is so ordered in the nature of things; and the greater the undertaking, the higher the honour, the more extensive the benefits, the happier the result. That ambition, that incitement, which is produced by slavish fear, is not worth a straw!! This is common sense. It is in the heart all high minded intellectual good flourishes and decays; the seat of good is in the heart; there, and there only, do its bright illuminations dazzle our eyes, and tower as upon eagle's wings to the sun. We trust that enough has been offered to make everyone in some degree satisfied there is nothing terrible in the sound of ambition. It has to be sure, a bad side, but like knowledge, like water, and like fire, when properly made use of, it is of immense benefit.

We have now feebly endeavoured to touch at the main spring of true ambition. We have shown that it ought to be possessed by every useful citizen.

If climate and natural scenery have a powerful effect in forming the intellectual character of a nation, surely we have much to hope from them, and much to encourage us to action, while the literary spirit of our country is still awake. A day or an hour may sweep away a throne, but years must elapse ere any sensible change can be produced on literature. It is a cause we all ought to be deeply engaged in; it is the pillars of this empire, and the basis on which the whole superstructure of our liberty and happiness depends.

It is the hope of benefiting our condition, that has encouraged us to commence the present undertaking. It is not a spirit of rivalry or competition that has brought this institution before the public. We occupy a field till now unappropriated, and which has hitherto been regarded too limited to justify such an attempt. It is an humble hope of contributing something to the advancement of science generally amongst our brethren, as well as of elevating its character in this City, that has called us to the enterprise. And, if it should be our fortune to lay the foundation only, of an institution which shall hereafter become commensurate with the demands of this great metropolis, and the improvement of science through the country, we shall feel that we have done an honour to the undertaking, and discharged a duty that we owe to our fellow citizens. And who knows but it may be reserved to this institution to make some discovery in philosophy which shall commence a new era in science, or furnish the world with something of magnificent worth, which now eludes the powers of the universe. Who can say that it is not reserved for some member of this institution to be the happy discoverer of the solvents of the stone? Who knows but some bold and fortunate genius, who shall have his zeal first kindled in this institution, may be destined, while climbing up the rocky mountains, or exploring the vale of the Mississippi, to discover a plant or a mineral which shall prove a cure for hydrophobia, or a remedy for consumption? or find out on the shaking prairie of Louisiana, or at the mouth of the Mobile, the true nature of miasmata and its operations on the human body?

Who knows but this institution may be destined to produce a Wilberforce, a Jay, or a Clarkson, or give to the world a Franklin, a Rush, or a Wistar? Who knows but talent (who knows no man by the colour of his skin) may not bestow her treasures on some one of our brethren (who may yet belong to this institution), that from this noble seat of wisdom, he shall adorn the brows of this great empire?

My friends, you carry with you my best wishes for your welfare; may your earthly comforts remain unsullied; and when done with time, may you be admitted to still higher posts in heaven.

PITTSBURGH AFRICAN EDUCATION SOCIETY

At a meeting of the colored people of the city and vicinity of Pittsburgh, convened at the African Church, on the evening of the 16th Jan. 1832—J. B. Vashon was appointed Chairman, and Lewis Woodson, Secretary.

The object of the meeting being stated by the chairman—after some further deliberation, the following Preamble and Constitution were adopted:

PREAMBLE

WHEREAS, ignorance in all ages has been found to debase the human mind, and to subject its votaries to the lowest vices, and most abject depravity—and it must be admitted, that ignorance is the sole cause of the present degradation and bondage of the people of color in these United States—that the intellectual capacity of the black man is equal to that of the white, and that he is equally susceptible of improvement, all ancient history makes manifest; and even modern examples put beyond a single doubt.

WE, THEREFORE, the people of color, of the city and vicinity of Pittsburgh, and State of Pennsylvania, for the purpose of dispersing the moral gloom that has so long hung around us, have, under Almighty God, associated ourselves together, which association shall be known by the name of the *Pittsburgh African Education Society,* which shall have for the direction of its government, the following

CONSTITUTION

Article 1. There shall be a President, Vice-President, Secretary, Treasurer and Board of Managers, consisting of five, each of whom shall be elected, annually, by the members of the society, at its annual meeting, and shall continue in office until their successors are appointed.

Article 2. It shall be the duty of the President, to preside at all meetings of the Society, and of the Board of Managers, to preserve order in its deliberations, and to put all motions when duly made and seconded, to the decision of the meeting. To sign all orders on the

Treasurer for money. In the absence of the President, the Vice-President shall perform his duties.

Article 3. The Secretary shall keep a fair record of all the proceedings of the Society, and of the Board of Managers, in a book to be furnished him for that purpose, and shall file and keep all papers of importance to the Society. And at the expiration of his office, shall deliver over to his successor, all books and papers in his care belonging to the Society.

Article 4. The Treasurer shall keep all monies and other property belonging to the Society, committed to his care, and shall keep a fair account thereof, in a book to be furnished him for that purpose. His books shall be open for inspection at any meeting of the Society, or of the Board of Managers. And at the expiration of his office, shall deliver over to his successor, all monies and other property in his possession, belonging to the Society.

Article 5. It shall be the duty of the Board of Managers to transact the business of the Society during its recess. To purchase such books and periodicals as the Society may deem it expedient, they shall have power to raise money by subscription or otherwise, to purchase ground, and erect thereon a suitable building or buildings for the accommodation and education of youth, and a hall for the use of the Society. They shall have power, to make, alter or abolish all bye-laws and regulations necessary for their government. And to do whatever else may be conducive to the best interests of the Society.

Article 6. The President, Vice-President, Secretary and Treasurer shall be members of the Board of Managers, any five of whom shall constitute a quorum to do business.

Article 7. Any person subscribing his name to this Constitution, and paying into the hands of the Treasurer, the sum of two dollars, shall be a member of this Society; which sum the Society may alter from time to time, as they may see fit.

Article 8. The Annual Meeting for the Society shall be on the third Monday in each year, and its Monthly Meeting, on the second Monday in each month.

Article 9. No alteration shall be made in this Constitution, without the concurrence of two-thirds of its members.

The following persons were elected Officers of the Society, for the ensuing year.

John B. Vashon, President.
Job B. Thompson, Vice-President.

Lewis Woodson, Secretary.
Abraham D. Lewis, Treasurer.

Board of Managers
Richard Bryans,   Wm. J. Greenly,
Samuel Bruce,   Moses Howard,
Samuel Clingman.

[Source: *Liberator*, Vol. 2, No. 8 (February 25, 1832), p. 32.]

DUTY OF FEMALES

From whence comes the indifference manifested to the cause of the female slave? Can a claim like hers be urged in vain? Have American women turned coldly away from her pleading voice, or are the fountains of benevolence sealed in their hearts to all those guilty of "a skin not colored like their own?" We hope not, and believe that the apathy so generally to be remarked on this subject proceeds solely from the want of information, and the belief that all attempts to aid her on their part must be hopeless. They make few exertions from the idea that they shall be able to accomplish nothing. But the experiment has never been fairly tried, and we may be permitted to doubt the validity of the objection. Were slavery a small evil, it might be removed by proportionable exertions; but this is not the case; many obstacles are to be overcome, and much energy is demanded; it is great and united effort only which can effect its removal. There is a claim on women; as sufferers in a common calamity, they must assist in its removal; as those involved in the commission of a deep crime, they must lift up their voices against it. Are they not partakers of a common nature with the slave, holding dear the good gift of intellect, and feeling a proud consciousness of the soaring spirit within? Then let them realize the depth of the misery by which that nature is degraded, and mourn bitterly for that system of oppression which bows down the loftiness of a free spirit to the very dust, till the mind, that "spark of divinity," is quenched and lost. Are they alive to the call of benevolence? Let them raise up the oppressed, and give their sympathy to the sorrowing slave. Viewed only as a sufferer, she needs aid; but as a woman and a sister, her claim is on all. And may those who sit calmly down under the shadowing wing of peace, and feel their hearts expand in the soft sunlight of happiness, think of her to whom that peace is denied, and that sun shut out—who is a stranger to the motives that animate them—and on whose ear the friendly accent seldom falls. And let those who, mourning under the stroke of adversity, yet feel cheered and strengthened by the promises of God, think of her to whom his revelation is a sealed book, and the hope of the christian

123

an unknown thing. She who is not cheered by the promise of a land where sorrow entereth not, but mourns in silence, and bears on the weary load of existence, pitied only by Him who seeth in secret—can women view her misery, and feel no desire to alleviate it? Shall their compassion be a transient emotion, wasting itself on the desert air? Shall they look upon her misery, and go again to their own pleasures till the remembrance passes away, and her affliction becomes unheeded? Or shall they be awakened by the sight to deeper feeling, and roused to higher exertion, and feel animated in the cause of the oppressed?

But the enquiry is often made, what can women do? Are not their voices weak, and their aid feeble? and would not any exertions they might make be considered obtrusive, and retard rather than accelerate the progress of freedom? We trust not entirely. True, the voice of woman should not be heard in public debates, but there are other ways in which her influence would be beneficial. Let every woman seek to inform herself, to the best of her ability, of the evil of slavery, and the extent to which it is practised in this country. Where the means of information are possessed, she is inexcusable who does not employ them. We would have no unhallowed hand laid upon the ark of freedom; the touch of ignorance can do little good. Let every woman, then, who feels interested in this cause, take pains to acquire information, and the shield of wisdom will prove the best defense against the attacks of ridicule. When this knowledge is gained, let her seek to disseminate it by every means in her power, and thereby interest others in the cause of justice. The influence of some may be greater than that of others; but let every one exert herself to the extent of her ability, and some effect must be produced. Public opinion is the source of public action, and where is this opinion formed? In the shade of private life; there were those views first gained that were afterwards carried into operation in a more extended sphere. Let slavery be spoken of as a withering blight upon our prosperity, at every fireside in the land, and many would rise in their strength to wipe off the foul reproach on our nation. Let not any woman say she has no influence; hers may be the very voice needed to call into action some more powerful and able advocate. Those who imbibe her opinions and sentiments, though now obscure, may be hereafter called to direct the destinies of the nation, and will in after life retain the habits formed in childhood. Let not any woman feel that little harm is done when slavery is lightly treated in conversation; neither let them fear to declare their opinions on the subject. Their sentiments will exert an influence on those around them, and these in their turn will guide others. It is also a great thing when any opinions are exposed to the light, for their intelligent minds will examine, and be influenced by them. This subject demands such investigation.

As to the sacrifices every one is called to make for the cause of emancipation, let her own judgment and feelings be the guides. Self denial is an easy thing to a benevolent heart; but to be continued, all sacrifices must be voluntary. On this head, we remark that the maxim of the Moravians commends itself to the good sense of every one: "Never persuade any man to be a missionary." The wrongs of the slaves demand the deepest sympathy; and she who is unmoved by them, will scarcely be impelled by persuasion. This remark does not apply to those who are ignorant of the full measure of the evil; but to the after conduct of those only who are better informed.

There is one path of duty in which women should be glad to labor, viz. the education of the free colored people. It is the intelligence of these which will advance their cause; and it is their ignorance which will retard it. When the day shall arrive in which they shall become eminent for their intelligence and good qualities, the voice of reproach will be stilled, and the face of the scornful crimsoned with shame for the injury done them. Many women are placed where their influence can be felt in this way, and they should be glad to exert it. We feel that to some, no inducements are necessary to prompt them to this labor of love, and those who exert themselves in this cause will receive the blessing of Him who came to seek and to save that which was lost. We know there is a charity felt by some which seeks no paths where the laborer is not cheered by the applause of the multitude; but this is a fearful mistake, and cannot be acceptable to God, neither can the praise of man deck a benevolent action with brighter colors to his pure unsleeping eye. No! it is when we do good to the most obscure, expecting no reward but the pleasure of benevolence, that we meet the approval of God. It is these labors that cheer the spirit and make the heart happy.

We now finish this brief and imperfect statement, by desiring every woman to ask herself what she can do in this cause, and not be checked by the fear of discouragement. There is One who can turn the shadow of night into the morning. We wish that every woman should feel her accountability on this subject, and do good whenever and wherever an opportunity may be opened to her. And we would further say, that when freedom shall be given to the one slave, and safety shall be his, the gratitude of those who view him a regenerated and disenthralled being will be enhanced, if they have done aught for his cause; and the still evening of peace be more enjoyed by the reflection, that they too have borne the "heat and the burden of the day."

L. H.

[Source: *Liberator*, Vol. 2, No. 18 (May 5, 1832), p. 70.]

ADDRESS TO THE FEMALE LITERARY
ASSOCIATION OF PHILADELPHIA.

Am I not a Woman and a Sister?

My Friends—I expect you generally understand the reason why you are called together at this time. I shall be as brief as possible. I have long and ardently desired your intellectual advancement, upon which the progress of morality must mainly depend. It is nothing better than affectation to deny the influence that females possess; it is their part to train up the young mind, to instill therein principles that may govern in maturer years; principles that influence the actions of the private citizen, the patriot, philanthropist, lawgivers, yea, presidents and kings. Then what subject can more properly claim, what one more justly and loudly demands solid consideration, deep attention—and yet what one is more carelessly dismissed from the mind, what one more neglected than the proper education of females? I say the proper education, because I do not consider that usually bestowed on them efficient; on the contrary, it tends to debase the moral powers, to enervate the understanding; and renders them incapable of filling the stations allotted them with becoming dignity, or profitably discharging the duties arising from those stations. I am aware that the education of females has become a fashionable theme, that a great deal has been said and written concerning it, that many speculations have been set afloat respecting their capacity of receiving a liberal, a classical education; and I am also aware that an opinion too generally prevails that superficial learning is all that is requisite, and to this cause, may in a great measure be attributed the pravity, the embasement of society. It is not my design to descant at length upon the subject at this time; suffice it to say, I hold that the present system of education abounds with corruption and error, and I fondly anticipate the time when a complete reformation may be wrought therein. I look through the surrounding clouds and mists of prejudice for the shining forth of a light, whose rays shall dispel these vapors; then may the female character be raised to a just stand. At some future period I may explain more particularly my reasons for thinking as I do, although

127

it should elicit the exclamation of "thou art beside thyself, thy great zeal hath made thee mad." My object at present is to call your attention to the necessity of improving the mental faculties, of exalting the moral powers, and of elevating yourselves to the station of rational, intelligent beings, accountable for the use made of the talents committed to your care. The benefits resulting from combinations similar to the one proposed I need not iterate, you are no strangers to them; but allow me, my sisters, to entreat you to banish prejudice from your hearts. If any one imagines that her talents are less brilliant than others, let her not disdain to contrast their superior attainments with her own; suffer not a feeling (shall I say of envy?) to enter that sanctuary, but rather strive to imitate their virtues; seek their society, and whenever they are disposed to aid you, extend to them the right hand of fellowship. And lastly, I would remind you that an attention to your best interests will induce you to encourage those periodicals devoted to your cause. The *Genius of Universal Emancipation* and the *Liberator,* I allude to in particular. Their editors are devoting their time and talents to your service, they have subjected themselves to many privations, and despise the reproach, the calumny, so liberally bestowed upon them by interested, calculating, designing men; they merit your patronage.

Philadelphia, May, 1832

[Source: *Liberator,* Vol. 2, No. 23 (June 9, 1832), p. 91.]

AN ADDRESS

DELIVERED AT THE AFRICAN MASONIC HALL

BOSTON, FEBRUARY 27, 1833

by Maria W. Stewart

African rights and liberty is a subject that ought to fire the breast
of every free man of color in these United States, and excite in his
bosom a lively, deep, decided, and heart-felt interest. When I cast
my eyes on the long list of illustrious names that are enrolled on the
bright annals of fame among the whites, I turn my eyes within, and
ask my thoughts, "Where are the names of *our* illustrious ones?" It
must certainly have been for the want of energy on the part of the
free people of color, that they have been long willing to bear the
yoke of oppression. It must have been the want of ambition and
force that has given the whites occasion to say that our natural
abilities are not as good, and our capacities by nature inferior to
theirs. They boldly assert that, did we possess a natural independence
of soul, and feel a love for liberty within our breasts, some one of
our sable race long before this would have testified it, notwithstanding the disadvantages under which we labor. We have made ourselves appear altogether unqualified to speak in our own defence,
and are therefore looked upon as objects of pity and commiseration.
We have been imposed upon, insulted and derided on every side;
and now, if we complain, it is considered as the height of imperti-
nence. We have suffered ourselves to be considered as dastards,
cowards, mean, faint-hearted wretches; and on this account, (not because of our complexion) many despise us, and would gladly spurn
us from their presence.

These things have fired my soul with a holy indignation, and
compelled me thus to come forward, and endeavor to turn their attention to knowledge and improvement; for knowledge is power. I
would ask, is it blindness of mind, or stupidity of soul, or the want
of education, that has caused our men who are 60 or 70 years of

age, never to let their voices be heard, nor their hands be raised in behalf of their color? Or has it been for the fear of offending the whites? If it has, O ye fearful ones, throw off your fearfulness, and come forth in the name of the Lord, and in the strength of the God of Justice, and make yourselves useful and active members in society; for they admire a noble and patriotic spirit in others; and should they not admire it in us? If you are men, convince them that you possess the spirit of men; and as your day, so shall your strength be. Have the sons of Africa no souls? Feel they no ambitious desires? Shall the chains of ignorance forever confine them? Shall the insipid appellation of "clever negroes," or "good creatures," any longer content them? Where can we find among ourselves the man of science, or a philosopher, or an able statesman, or a counsellor at law? Show me our fearless and brave, our noble and gallant ones. Where are our lecturers on natural history, and our critics in useful knowledge? There may be a few such men among us, but they are rare. It is true, our fathers bled and died in the revolutionary war, and others fought bravely under the command of Jackson, in defence of liberty. But where is the man that has distinguished himself in these modern days by acting wholly in the defence of African rights and liberty? There was one; although he sleeps, his memory lives.

I am sensible that there are many highly intelligent gentlemen of color in these United States, in the force of whose arguments, doubtless, I should discover my inferiority; but if they are blest with wit and talent, friends and fortune, why have they not made themselves men of eminence, by striving to take all the reproach that is cast upon the people of color, and in endeavoring to alleviate the woes of their brethren in bondage? Talk, without effort, is nothing; you are abundantly capable, gentlemen, of making yourselves men of distinction; and this gross neglect, on your part, causes my blood to boil within me. Here is the grand cause which hinders the rise and progress of the people of color. It is their want of laudable ambition and requisite courage.

Individuals have been distinguished according to their genius and talents, ever since the first formation of man, and will continue to be while the world stands. The different grades rise to honor and respectability as their merits may deserve. History informs us that we sprung from one of the most learned nations of the whole earth; from the seat, if not the parent of science; yes, poor, despised Africa was once the resort of sages and legislators of other nations, was esteemed the school for learning, and the most illustrious men in Greece flocked thither for instruction. But it was our gross sins and abominations that provoked the Almighty to frown thus heavily upon us, and give our glory unto others. Sin and prodigality have caused the downfall of nations, kings and emperors; and were it not that God in wrath remembers mercy, we might indeed despair; but a promise is left us; "Ethiopia shall again stretch forth her hands unto God."

But it is of no use for us to boast that we sprung from this learned and enlightened nation, for this day a thick mist of moral gloom hangs over millions of our race. Our condition as a people has been low for hundreds of years, and it will continue to be so, unless, by true piety and virtue, we strive to regain that which we have lost. White Americans, by their prudence, economy and exertions, have sprung up and become one of the most flourishing nations in the world, distinguished for their knowledge of the arts and sciences, for their polite literature. While our minds are vacant, and starving for want of knowledge, theirs are filled to overflowing. Most of our color have been taught to stand in fear of the white man, from their earliest infancy, to work as soon as they could walk, and call "master," before they scarce could lisp the name of *mother*. Continual fear and laborious servitude have in some degree lessened in us that natural force and energy which belong to man; or else, in defiance of opposition, our men, before this, would have nobly and boldly contended for their rights. But give the man of color an equal opportunity with the white from the cradle to manhood, and from manhood to the grave, and you would discover the dignified statesman, the man of science, and the philosopher. But there is no such opportunity for the sons of Africa, and I fear that our powerful ones are fully determined that there never shall be. Forbid, ye Powers on high, that it should any longer be said that our men possess no force. O ye sons of Africa, when will your voices be heard in our legislative halls, in defiance of your enemies, contending for equal rights and liberty? How can you, when you reflect from what you have fallen, refrain from crying mightily unto God, to turn away from us the fierceness of his anger, and remember our transgressions against us no more forever. But a God of infinite purity will not regard the prayers of those who hold religion in one hand, and prejudice, sin and pollution in the other; he will not regard the prayers of self-righteousness and hypocrisy. Is it possible, I exclaim, that for the want of knowledge, we have labored for hundreds of years to support others, and been content to receive what they chose to give us in return? Cast your eyes about, look as far as you can see; all, all is owned by the lordly white, except here and there a lowly dwelling which the man of color, midst deprivations, fraud and opposition, has been scarce able to procure. Like king Solomon, who put neither nail nor hammer to the temple, yet received the praise; so also have the white Americans gained themselves a name, like the names of the great men that are in the earth, while in reality we have been their principal foundation and support. We have pursued the shadow, they have obtained the substance; we have performed the labor, they have received the profits; we have planted the vines, they have eaten the fruits of them.

I would implore our men, and especially our rising youth, to flee from the gambling board and the dance-hall; for we are poor, and have no money to throw away. I do not consider dancing as criminal in itself, but it is astonishing to me that our young men are so blind to their own interest and the future welfare of their children, as to spend their hard earnings for this frivolous amusement; for it has been carried on among us to such an unbecoming extent, that it has became absolutely disgusting. "Faithful are the wounds of a friend, but the kisses of an enemy are deceitful." Had those men among us, who have had an opportunity, turned their attention as assiduously to mental and moral improvement as they have to gambling and dancing, I might have remained quietly at home, and they stood contending in my place. These polite accomplishments will never enrol your names on the bright annals of fame, who admire the belle void of intellectual knowledge, or applaud the dandy that talks largely on politics, without striving to assist his fellow in the revolution, when the nerves and muscles of every other man forced him into the field of action. You have a right to rejoice, and to let your hearts cheer you in the days of your youth; yet remember that for all these things, God will bring you into judgment. Then, O ye sons of Africa, turn your mind from these perishable objects, and contend for the cause of God and the rights of man. Form yourselves into temperance societies. There are temperate men among you; then why will you any longer neglect to strive, by your example, to suppress vice in all its abhorrent forms? You have been told repeatedly of the glorious results arising from temperance, and can you bear to see the whites arising in honor and respectability, without endeavoring to grasp after that honor and respectability also?

But I forbear. Let our money, instead of being thrown away as heretofore, be appropriated for schools and seminaries of learning for our children and youth. We ought to follow the example of the whites in this respect. Nothing would raise our respectability, add to our peace and happiness, and reflect so much honor upon us, as to be ourselves the promoters of temperance, and the supporters, as far as we are able, of useful and scientific knowledge. The rays of light and knowledge have been hid from our view; we have been taught to consider ourselves as scarce superior to the brute creation; and have performed the most laborious part of American drudgery. Had we as a people received one half the early advantages the whites have received, I would defy the government of these United States to deprive us any longer of our rights.

I am informed that the agent of the Colonization Society has recently formed an association of young men, for the purpose of influencing those of us to go to Liberia who may feel disposed. The colonizationists are blind to their own interest, for should the nations of the earth make war with America, they would find their forces much weakened by our absence; or should we remain here, can our "brave soldiers," and "fellow-citizens," as they were termed in time of calamity, condescend to defend the rights of the whites, and be again deprived of their own, or sent to Liberia in return? Or, if the colonizationists are real friends to Africa, let them expend the money which they collect, in erecting a college to educate her injured sons in this land of gospel light and liberty; for it would be most thankfully received on our part, and convince us of the truth of their professions, and save time, expense and anxiety. Let them place before us noble objects, worthy of pursuit, and see if we prove ourselves to be those unambitious negroes they term us. But ah! methinks their hearts are so frozen towards us, they had rather their money should be sunk in the ocean than to administer it to our relief; and I fear, if they dared, like Pharaoh, king of Egypt, they would order every male child among us to be drowned. But the most high God is still as able to subdue the lofty pride of these white Americans, as He was the heart of that ancient rebel. They say, though we are looked upon as *things*, yet we sprang from a scientific people. Had our men the requisite force and energy, they would soon convince them by their efforts both in public and private, that they were men, or things in the shape of men. Well may the colonizationists laugh us to scorn for our negligence; well may they cry, "Shame to the sons of Africa." As the burden of the Israelites was too great for Moses to bear, so also is our burden too great for our noble advocate to bear. You must feel interested, my brethren, in what he undertakes, and hold up his hands by your good works, or in spite of himself, his soul will become discouraged, and his heart will die within him; for he has, as it were, the strong bulls of Bashan to contend with.

It is of no use for us to wait any longer for a generation of well educated men to arise. We have slumbered and slept too long already; the day is far spent; the night of death approaches; and you have sound sense and good judgment sufficient to begin with, if you feel disposed to make a right use of it. Let every man of color throughout the United States, who possesses the spirit and principles of a man, sign a petition to Congress, to abolish slavery in the District of Columbia, and grant you the rights and privileges of common free citizens; for if you had had faith as a grain of mustard seed, long before this the mountains of prejudice might have been removed. We are all sensible that the Anti-Slavery Society has taken hold of the arm of our whole population, in order to raise them out of the mire. Now all we have to do is, by a spirit of virtuous ambition to strive to raise ourselves; and I am happy to have it in my power thus publicly to say, that the colored inhabitants of this city, in some respects, are beginning to improve. Had the free people of color in these United States nobly and boldly contended for their rights, and showed a natural genius and talent, although not so brilliant as some; had they held up, encouraged and patronized each other, nothing could have hindered us from being a thriving and flourishing people. There has been a fault among us. The reason why our distinguished men have not made themselves more influential is, because they fear that the strong current of opposition through which they must pass, would cause their downfall and prove their overthrow. And what gives rise to this opposition? Envy. And what has it amounted to? Nothing. And who are the cause of it? Our whited sepulchres, who want to be great, and don't know how; who love to be called of men 'Rabbi, Rabbi, who put on false sanctity, and humble themselves to their brethren, for the sake of acquiring the highest place in the synagogue, and the uppermost seats at the feast. You, dearly beloved, who are the genuine followers of our Lord Jesus Christ, the salt of the earth and the light of the world, are not so culpable. As I told you, in the very first of my writing, I tell you again, I am but as a drop in the bucket—as one particle of the small dust of the earth. God will surely raise up those among us who will plead the cause of virtue, and the pure principles of morality, more eloquently than I am able to do.

It appears to me that America has become like the great city of Babylon, for she has boasted in her heart, "I sit a queen, and am no widow, and shall see no sorrow?" She is indeed a seller of slaves and the souls of men; she has made the Africans drunk with the wine of her fornication; she has put them completely beneath her feet, and she means to keep them there; her right hand supports the reins of government, and her left hand the wheel of power, and she is determined not to let go her grasp. But many powerful sons and daughters of Africa will shortly arise, who will put down vice and immorality among us, and declare by Him that sitteth upon the throne, that they will have their rights; and if refused, I am afraid they will spread horror and devastation around. I believe that the oppression of injured Africa has come up before the Majesty of Heaven; and when our cries shall have reached the ears of the Most High, it will be a tremendous day for the people of this land; for strong is the arm of the Lord God Almighty.

Life has almost lost its charms for me; death has lost its sting and the grave its terrors; and at times I have a strong desire to depart and dwell with Christ, which is far better. Let me entreat my white brethren to awake and save our sons from dissipation, and our daughters from ruin. Lend the hand of assistance to feeble merit, plead the cause of virtue among our sable race; so shall our curses upon you be turned into blessings; and though you should endeavor to drive us from these shores, still we will cling to you the more firmly; nor will we attempt to rise above you: we will presume to be called your equals only.

The unfriendly whites first drove the native American from his much loved home. Then they stole our fathers from their peaceful and quiet dwellings, and brought them hither, and made bond-men and bond-women of them and their little ones; they have obliged our brethren to labor, kept them in utter ignorance, nourished them in vice, and raised them in degradation; and now that we have enriched their soil, and filled their coffers, they say that we are not capable of becoming like white men, and that we never can rise to respectability in this country. They would drive us to a strange land. But before I go, the bayonet shall pierce me through. African rights and liberty is a subject that ought to fire the breast of every free man of color in these United States, and excite in his bosom a lively, deep, decided and heart-felt interest.

[Source: *Productions of Mrs. Maria W. Stewart* (Boston: Friends of Freedom and Virtue, 1835), pp. 63–72.]

A Lecture by Maria W. Stewart, given at Franklin Hall, Boston, September 21, 1832.

Why sit we here and die? If we say we will go to a foreign land, the famine and the pestilence are there, and there we shall die. If we sit here, we shall die. Come, let us plead our cause before the whites: if they save us alive, we shall love—and if they kill us, we shall but die.

Methinks I heard a spiritual interrogation—"Who shall go forward, and take of the reproach that is cast upon the people of color? Shall it be a woman?" And my heart made this reply—"If it is thy will, be it even so, Lord Jesus?"

I have heard much respecting the horrors of slavery; but may Heaven forbid that the generality of my color throughout these United States should experience any more of its horrors than to be a servant of servants, or hewers of wood and drawers of water! Tell us no more of southern slavery; for with few exceptions, although I may be very erroneous in any opinion, yet I consider our condition but little better than that. Yet, after all, methinks there are no chains so galling as the chains of ignorance—no fetters so binding as those that bind the soul, and exclude it from the vast field of useful and scientific knowledge. O, had I received the advantages of early education, my ideas would, ere now, have expanded far and wide; but, alas! I possess nothing but moral capability—no teachings but the teachings of the Holy Spirit.

I have asked several individuals of my sex, who transact business for themselves, if, providing our girls were to give them the most satisfactory references, they would not be willing to grant them an equal opportunity with others? Their reply has been—for their own part, they had no objection; but as it was not the custom, were they to take them into their employ, they would be in danger of losing the public patronage.

And such is the powerful force of prejudice.—Let our girls possess what amiable qualities of soul they may—let their characters be fair and spotless as innocence itself—let their natural taste and ingenuity be what they may—it is impossible for scarce an individual of them to rise above the condition of servants. Ah! why is this cruel and unfeeling distinction? Is it merely because God has made our complexion to vary? If it be, O shame to soft, relenting humanity! "Tell it not in Gath! publish it not in the streets of Askelon!" Yet, after all, methinks were the American free people of color to turn their attention or more assiduously to moral worth and intellectual improvement, this would be the result:—prejudice would gradually diminish, and the whites would be compelled to day,—Unloose those fetters!

> Though black their skins as shades of night,
> Their hearts are pure—their souls are white.

Few white persons of either sex, who are calculated for anything else, are willing to spend their lives and bury their talents in performing mean, servile labor. And such is the horrible idea that I entertain respecting a life of servitude, that if I conceived of their being no possibility of my rising above the condition of a servant, I would gladly hail death as a welcome messenger. O, horrible idea, indeed! to possess noble souls aspiring after high and honorable acquirements, yet confined by the chains of ignorance and poverty to lives of continual drudgery and toil. Neither do I know of any who have enriched themselves by spending their lives as house-domestics, washing windows, shaking carpets, brushing boots, or tending upon gentlemen's tables. I can but die for expressing my sentiments; and I am as willing to die by the sword as the pestilence—for I am a true born American—your blood flows in my veins, and your spirit fires my breast.

I observed a piece in the Liberator a few months since, stating that the colonizationists had published a work respecting us, asserting that we were lazy and idle. I confute them on that point. Take us generally as a people, we are neither lazy nor idle; and considering how little we have to excite or stimulate us, I am almost astonished that there are so many industrious and ambitious ones to be found—although I acknowledge, with extreme sorrow, that there are some who never were and never will be serviceable to society. And have you not a similar class among yourselves?

Again—It was asserted that we were "a ragged set, crying for liberty." I reply to it, the whites have so long and so loudly proclaimed the theme of equal rights and privileges, that our souls have caught the flame also, ragged as we are. As far as our merit deserves, we feel a common desire to rise above the condition of servants and drudges. I have learnt, by bitter experience, that continual hard labor deadens the energies of the soul, and benumbs the faculties of the mind: the ideas become confined, the mind barren, and, like the scorching sands of Arabia, produces nothing—or like the uncultivated soil, brings forth thorns and thistles.

Again, continual hard labor irritates our tempers and sours our dispositions; the whole system becomes worn out with toil and fatigue; nature herself becomes almost exhausted, and we care but little whether we live or die. It is true that the free people of color throughout these United States are neither bought nor sold, nor under the lash of the cruel driver; many obtain a comfortable support; but few, if any, have an opportunity of becoming rich and independent; and the employments we most pursue are as unprofitable to us as the spider's web or the floating bubbles that vanish into air. As servants, we are respected; but let us presume to aspire any higher, our employer regards us no longer. And were it not that the King eternal has declared that Ethiopia shall stretch forth her hands unto God, I should indeed despair.

I do not consider it derogatory, my friends, for persons to live out to service. There are many whose inclination leads them to aspire no higher—and I would highly commend the performance of almost anything for an honest livelihood; but where constitutional strength is wanting, labor of this kind, in its mildest form, is painful. And doubtless many are the prayers that have ascended to Heaven from Afric's daughters for strength to perform their work. Oh, many are the tears that have been shed for the want of that strength! Most of our color have dragged out a miserable existence of servitude from the cradle to the grave. And what literary acquirements can be made, or useful knowledge derived, from either maps, books or charts, by those who continually drudge from Monday morning until Sunday noon? O, ye fairer sisters, whose hands are never soiled, whose nerves and muscles are never strained, go learn by experience! Had we had the opportunity that you have had, to improve our moral and mental faculties, what would have hindered our intellects from being as bright, and our manners from being as dignified as yours? Had it been our lot to have been nursed in the lap of affluence and ease, and to have basked beneath the smiles and sunshine of fortune, should we not have naturally supposed that we were never made to toil? And why are not our forms as delicate, and our constitutions as slender, as yours? Is not the workmanship as curious and complete? Have pity upon us—have pity upon us, O ye who have hearts to feel for others' woes; for the hand of God has touched us. Owing to the disadvantages under which we labor, there are many flowers among us that are

born to bloom unseen,
And waste their fragrance on the desert air.

My beloved brethren, as Christ has died in vain for those who will
not accept of offered mercy, so will it be in vain for the advocates
of freedom to spend their breath in our behalf, unless with united
hearts and souls you make some mighty efforts to raise your sons
and daughters from the horrible state of servitude and degradation
in which they are placed. It is upon you that woman depends; she
can do but little besides using her influence; and it is for her sake
and yours that I have come forward and made myself a hissing and
a reproach amongst the people; for I am also one of the wretched
and miserable daughters of the descendants of fallen Africa. Do you
ask—Why are you wretched and miserable? I reply, look at many of
the most worthy and interesting of us doomed to spend our lives
in gentlemen's kitchens. Look at our young men, smart, active and
energetic, with souls filled with ambitious fire; if they look forward,
alas! what are their prospects? They can be nothing but the humblest laborers, on account of their dark complexions; hence many
of them lose their ambition, and become worthless. Look at our
middle-aged men, clad in their rusty plaids and coats—in winter,
every cent they earn goes to buy their wood and pay their rents;
their poor wives also toil beyond their strength to help support their
families. Look at our aged sires, who heads are whitened with the
frosts of seventy winters, with their old wood saws on their backs.
Alas, what keeps us so? Prejudice, ignorance and poverty. But ah!
methinks our oppression is soon to come to an end; yea, before the
majesty of heaven, our groans and cries have reached the ears of the
Lord of Sabaoth. As the prayers and tears of Christians will avail
the finally impenitent nothing; neither will the prayers and tears of
the friends of humanity avail us anything, unless we possess a spirit
of virtuous emulation within our breasts. Did the Pilgrims, when
they first landed on these shores, quietly compose themselves, and
say, "The Britons have all the money and all the power, and we
must continue their servants forever?" Did they sluggishly sigh and
say, "Our lot is hard—the Indians own the soil, and we cannot cultivate it?" No—they first made powerful efforts to raise themselves and
then God raised up those illustrious patriots, Washington and
Lafayette, to assist and defend them. And, my brethren, have you
made a powerful effort? Have you prayed the legislature for mercy's
sake to grant you all the rights and privileges of free citizens, that
your daughters may rise to that degree of respectability which true

merit deserves, and your sons above the servile situations which most of them fill?

[Source: *Liberator*, Vol. 2, No. 46 (November 17, 1832), p. 183; reprinted in *Productions of Mrs. Maria W. Stewart* (Boston: Friends of Freedom and Virtue, 1835), pp. 51–56.]

ADDRESS AND CONSTITUTION

OF THE

PHOENIX SOCIETY OF NEW YORK,

AND OF

THE AUXILIARY WARD ASSOCIATIONS.

Though it is the pride and boast of our state, that in conformity with the principles of Christianity and republicanism, no man within her precincts can now hold another as his property, yet it is obvious that the people of colour, who have always composed a very considerable part of her population, labour under much greater disadvantages than any other class of the community, and that their condition can only be meliorated by their being improved in *morals, literature,* and the *mechanic arts.*

It is no less obvious, that this important work cannot be accomplished to any great extent, but by a combination of their own powers, and the aid of benevolent white persons. The want of such combination and co-operation, has hitherto prevented the labours of philanthropists in their cause, from being more successful.

THE PHOENIX SOCIETY, whose Constitution is hereto affixed, has these objects in view. It has, therefore, a claim upon every man of colour, upon every Christian, upon every philanthropist, and every patriot. Let each of these classes duly regard its claims, and according to their ability aid its operations. Let every person of colour unite himself, or herself, to this Society, and faithfully endeavour to promote its objects—and let every one who wishes to see their condition improved, aid them in the work; and, instead of their being sunk in a state of poverty and degradation, they will rise to be a virtuous, respectable and useful portion of the community. How desirable a result! What coloured person will refuse to do his part in producing it? What good man will refuse his aid towards it? God speed it.

New York, April 20th, 1833.

141

CONSTITUTION

THIS Society shall be known by the name of the PHOENIX SOCIETY of the City of New York, the object of which shall be to promote the improvement of the coloured people in Morals, Literature, and the Mechanic Arts.

ARTICLE I.   The Society shall consist of all persons who contribute to its funds quarterly, any sum of money they may think proper.

ARTICLE II.   The Officers shall consist of a President, two Vice Presidents, a Corresponding Secretary and a Recording Secretary, and a Treasurer, who shall constitute a part of the Board of Directors.

ARTICLE III.   There shall be a Board of Directors not to exceed in number sixty, who shall meet monthly—sixteen of whom shall be a quorum to do the ordinary business.

ARTICLE IV.   The Officers and Directors, shall be chosen annually, at the annual meeting of the Society; they shall have power to fill vacancies in their Board.

ARTICLE V.   At the formation of this Society, there shall be but thirty Directors chosen, who shall have power to add to the number, not exceeding sixty in all.

ARTICLE VI.   The Board of Directors shall appoint from their own number, an Executive Committee of seven, including the President, Secretary, and Treasurer, who shall transact the business of the Society in the recesses of the Board, and shall meet weekly, and shall report to the Board at its monthly meeting, by reading their minutes.

ARTICLE VII.   The Board shall appoint an Agent to be devoted to the objects of the Society, who shall attend the meetings of the Board and of the Executive Committee, and report weekly in writing to the Executive Committee.

ARTICLE VIII.   The funds raised after the necessary expenses of the Society are paid, shall be applied to the establishment and sustaining of a Manual Labour School, and for this object an effort shall be immediately made to raise at least Ten Thousand Dollars.

ARTICLE IX.   This Constitution may be altered or amended at an annual meeting of the Society, by a majority of the members present at such meeting.

OFFICERS

REV. CHRISTOPHER RUSH, *President.*
REV. THEODORE S. WRIGHT, *First Vice-President.*

THOMAS L. JINNINGS, *Second Vice-President.*
ARTHUR TAPPAN, *Treasurer.*
BENJAMIN F. HUGHES, *Recording Secretary.*
PETER VOGELSANG, *Corresponding Secretary.*

DIRECTORS

George R. Barker,
James Barnett,
Philip A. Bell,
John Berrian,
Rev. George Bourne,
Rev. James Burton,
Platt S. Cleaveland,
George Collins,
Rev. Edmund Crosby,
Boston Crummell,
Rev. Charles C. Darliag,
Rev. Chas. W. Dennison,
Rev. Loring D. Dewey,
Thomas Downing,
Samuel Ennalls,

James Fields,
William Goodell,
Rev. Charles Hall,
William Hamilton,
Samuel Hardenburgh,
Isaac Hatch,
Rev. James Hayborn,
William L. Jeffers,
Rev. Simeon S. Jocelyn,
Richard Livingston,
Rev. Jacob Matthews,
Richard C. M'Cormick,
James Miller,
James Moore,
Ezra Morris,

John Peterson,
George L. Phillips,
Rev. William P. Quinn,
Rev. John Raymond,
Henry Scott,
Wright Seaman,
Henry Sipkins,
Charles Smith,
William Thompson,
William Turpin,
Peter Vanderhost,
Ransom F. Wake,
Rev. Peter Williams,
Aaron Wood,
James Fraser.

CONSTITUTION FOR WARD SOCIETIES

ARTICLE I. This Society shall be called the PHOENIX SOCIETY of the ———— Ward, in the City of New-York, auxiliary to the *Phoenix Society of the City of New York,* and shall consist of all persons who contribute to its funds. Its object is to promote the improvement of the people of colour of this Ward in Morals, Literature, and the Mechanic Arts.

ARTICLE II. Its Officers shall be a President, one Vice-President, a Secretary, a Treasurer, and twenty Directors, to be annually chosen, who together shall constitute a Board of Managers, and shall have power to fill vacancies in their own body.

ARTICLE III. Seven shall constitute a quorum for the transaction of business.

ARTICLE IV. All meetings of the Board shall be opened with prayer.

ARTICLE V. The Ward shall be divided into ———— Districts, and a committee of one or more members of the Board be appointed to each District, whose duty it shall be to carry into effect the objects of the Society, and to report to the Board at its regular meetings.

ARTICLE VI. The Board shall appoint Committees of Ladies to visit the Districts to promote the objects of the Society, who shall be expected to report at the meetings of the Board.

ARTICLE VII. All money collected shall be paid over to the Treasurer of the Parent Society, after the necessary expenses of the Society are provided for.

ARTICLE VIII. The Board shall meet monthly, on the ———— day of the month.

ARTICLE IX. It shall be the duty of the Secretary to make a minute report of the proceedings of this Society in writing, monthly, to the Board of the Parent Society.

ARTICLE X. The annual meeting for the choice of Officers and Directors shall be on the ————, and in case of there being no election at the appointed time, the old Board shall continue to act till such election takes place.

ARTICLE XI. This Constitution may be altered at an annual meeting.

ARTICLE XII. If any member shall absent himself from the meetings of the Board three months in succession, or shall neglect to attend to the duties assigned him, without offering a satisfactory excuse, he shall be considered as having resigned.

THIS Society will aim to accomplish the following objects. To visit every family in the Ward, and make a register of every coloured person in it—their name, sex, age, occupation, if they read, write and cipher,—to induce them, old and young and of both sexes, to become members of this Society, and make quarterly payments according to their ability;—to get the children out to infant, Sabbath and week schools, and induce the adults also to attend school and church on the Sabbath,—to encourage the females to form Dorcas Societies to help to clothe poor children of colour if they will attend school, the clothes to be loaned, and to be taken away from them if they neglect their schools; and to impress on their parents the importance of having the children punctual and regular in their attendance at school,—to establish circulating libraries formed in each ward for the use of people of colour on very moderate pay,—to establish mental feasts, and also lyceums for speaking and for lectures on the sciences, and to form moral societies,—to seek out young men of talents, and good moral character, that they may be assisted to obtain a liberal education,—to report to the Board all mechanics who are skilful and capable of conducting their trades,— to procure places at trades and with respectable farmers for lads of good moral character—giving a preference to those who have learned to read, write, and cipher,—and in every other way to endeavour to promote the happiness of the people of colour, by encouraging them to improve their minds, and to abstain from every vicious and demoralizing practice.

[Source: *Minutes and Proceedings of the Third Annual Convention for the Improvement of the Free People of Colour* (New York, 1833), pp. 37–40.]

ADDRESS

DELIVERED

BEFORE THE

HUMANE MECHANICS' SOCIETY,

ON THE

4TH OF JULY, 1834

BY THE

Rev. Joseph M. Corr,
OF THE FIRST AFRICAN EPISCOPAL METHODIST
CHURCH, AND MEMBER OF THE H. M. S.

PHILADELPHIA, 1834.

Fellow Citizens and Members of the Humane Mechanics' Society—

IN obedience to your will, I rise your humble organ, with a desire of executing an arduous duty in a manner creditable to you and no less satisfactory to myself. Today we are called upon to celebrate another anniversary of our Society; on the return of that auspicious morn that gave birth to the independence of our native and beloved country, and to an humble institution devoted to liberal and beneficent objects. Today, while the roaring cannons, the rattling drums, and sounding bells are echoing the acclamations of joy from the hearts of millions of freemen, and the halls of literature and temples of religion are abounding with the patriotic eloquence of those who are exulting in the glories of that power, with which their freedom enables them to triumph over the claims of justice, humanity and sympathy in the behalf of nearly three millions of fellow beings, whose only crime is colour—a contemptuous libel on the character and constitution of a republican government, an audacious insult offered to the Omnipotent Creator of the universe, whose wisdom is fully competent without the puny aid of mortal worms, to direct him in accomplishing his own august designs.

Today (while the clank of the chain of the poor slave is responding back the hypocritical sound of liberty and equality upon the base tramplers on human rights, with imperative appeals to the conscience and feelings of all mankind), have we assembled, apart from the noise and bustle of the tumultuous world, to celebrate the birthday of our society. Permit me, first of all things, to suggest to your ideas, the practice of virtue; that unchanging principle of heavenly origin, the peculiar effect of which is to promote happiness and true enjoyment, the rational desire of all intelligent beings, and which must arise from man's own conduct, being in accordance with the mandates of the Great Sovereign of the universe—an obedience to the requisitions of Divine command, a uniform deportment and due deference to all the moral obligations which, as rational and intelligent beings, we are continually under, to a merciful and benevolent Creator, whose bountiful providence is every pouring forth into the lap of man new and inexhaustible treasures of the choicest blessings.

Though virtue, at first sight, may appear to contract the bounds of enjoyment, it will be found upon a persevering practice, that in truth it enhances it. If it restrains the excess of some pleasures, it enlarges and increases others; it precludes from none but such as are either fantastic and imaginary, or pernicious and destructive: whatever is truly valuable in human enjoyment it allows to a good man, no less than others. It not only allows him such pleasures, but heightens them, by that grateful relish which a good conscience gives to every pleasure—it not only heightens, but adds to them also the peculiar satisfaction which flows from virtuous sentiments, from devout affections, and religious hopes. On how much worse terms is vice placed, in the midst of its boasted imaginary gratifications; the bubbles and transitory phantoms of this fading world. Enlarge as much as you please the circle of worldly pleasures, extend the bounds of carnal mirth as far as human ideas will admit, stretch your arms like seas, and grasp in all the shore, yet you are constrained to exclaim with a royal devotee of this world's pleasure, "vanity of vanities, all is vanity and vexation of spirit."

Vice and virtue, in their progress and results, as in every other respect, maintain an opposite course, and lead to a contrary end.

The beginnings of vice are enticing, beguiling and deceptive. The first tastes are flattering and attracting, but even the continuation of success blunts enjoyment, and flattens desire, while it leads on to degradation, misery and distress; and to this we may ascribe all the wretchedness which has been the inevitable fate of the wicked. Virtue at first appears laborious, but by perseverance its labours diminish and its pleasures increase. As it ripens into confirmed habits, it becomes both smoother in practice and more complete in its reward. In a vicious life, the termination of our hopes always meets our view. We see a boundary before us, beyond which we cannot reach. But the prospects of virtue are growing and endless— "For the righteous shall hold on his way, and he that hath clean hands shall wax stronger and stronger." Virtue, howsoever discouraged or oppressed for awhile, shall not be deprived of that eternal reward which an impartial and unchangeable God has promised to all who are obedient to the mandates of heaven, without distinctions or exceptions of nations or colours. The unfinished parts of the fabric of happiness, show that a future building is intended, an everlasting portion reserved for the truly virtuous; this will reasonably appear, if we consult all the other works of Jehovah, which are indeed constructed according to the most exact proportion. In the natural world nothing is redundant, nothing deficient; it is in the moral world only that we discover irregularity and defect. It falls short of that order and perfection which appears in the rest of creation. It exhibits not in its present state the same features of complete wisdom, justice and goodness. But can we believe that under the government of a Supreme Being, so full of truth and love as the great Governor of the universe, that these apparent disorders shall not be rectified, and a just and equitable state of things shall be the success and crowning triumph of virtue, and the laurel wreath of victory shall distinguish all its persevering votaries.

To ensure virtue and its blessings, let me next call your attention to the all-important subject of education, one of the noblest ornaments of human nature, that most noble means whereby the shackles of ignorance may be unrivetted, and man be qualified for usefulness in all the pursuits of life; for "knowledge is light—knowledge is power."

> 'Tis education forms the youthful mind,
> Soon as the twig is bent, the tree's inclin'd.

What is man without cultivation, of whatever colour or nation? A mental desert—a waste of ignorance and error—a wilderness of wretchedness. It is the mind that rules and governs the man, and gives one man the only real superiority and right of pre-eminence over another. In the formation of man, our great Creator has displayed the greatest manifestation of infinite wisdom and power—the human mind is the direct image of God; he has endowed it with the noble faculty of reason, a restless desire for the acquirement of knowledge, and placed it in a world surrounded with facilities to improve it, by cultivation and industry—the neglect of which results in barrenness and unfruitfulness.

If we neglect our duty, if we give place to slothfulness and inactivity; we shall never rise to that dignity of rational intelligence, nor be found capable of filling up that station in society for which a designing Providence intended us. The fruits of application and diligence in the culture of the mental soil, are as certain as the results of the labour and tillage of industrious husbandry. In proportion to our application and activity, we shall make advances in the acquisition of useful information—our intellectual faculties will be strengthened and improved, our capacities extended, and our ideas enlarged.

The Creator designed us to be the lords of his creation, to be sole governors of this lower world, and to subject to our service the laws of nature, and so be capable of improving the convenience and gratifications of human life—it is only by useful intelligence and information that these purposes can be accomplished. In a state of nature, man is, of all animals, the most helpless—until assisted by reason, he finds the means of providing for his wants, and of protecting himself from injury: his condition is little better than the brutes that roam in the desert. But when his latent powers are improved and strengthened by exercise, and grown to their full dimensions by culture—when learning sheds her light upon his understanding, and science, which so essentially promotes civilization and refinement, are assiduously attained, he becomes indeed the master-piece of creation. It is no longer a doubt that this is the exclusive privilege of all men, everywhere, wherever opportunities afford facilities to accomplish this desirable purpose.

It remains then, for us, brethren, to be up and doing; to put our shoulders to the work; to say to the great "mountain" of prejudice, by faithful perseverance and active energy, "Be thou removed," and instantaneously it disappears, before the spirited efforts of practical exertion. As parents and guardians, let us remember that we are responsible for the future destinies of our children, so far as our influence and duty have a bearing upon their future conduct—they are shortly to succeed to that unfolding glory, which, in the order of Providence, is soon to be revealed. Let us then, be careful to inculcate upon their youthful minds, let them early begin to prize the important truth, that education and elevation succeed with hasty steps, and though many may fall short of the desired end, many candidates be unsuccessful in arriving at the desired goal, yet let them "so run that they may obtain." No man can attain every object that he pursues; this cannot be reasonably expected, neither can every man obtain the same object; yet every man is under a necessary obligation to improve his own understanding, otherwise it will be a barren desert, or an overgrown forest, with the weeds and brambles of universal ignorance or infinite errors.

I shall next introduce the mechanic arts, which have always been held in the highest repute, from the ages of antiquity, but which have received a new impulse from modern improvement.

The erection of Noah's ark, the building of the ancient and noble cities of Nineveh, Babylon and Hieropolis in Egypt; the renowned pyramids, at which the Israelites laboured, in that famed land of hieroglyphics, the cradle of arts and science, has distinguished the mechanic as one of the most useful members of society, even in that remote era.

The reminiscences of Grecian artisans, the tastefulness of Gothic architecture in more modern times, are still attracting and admirable. It is mechanical science which discovers the means of subjecting all things around us to the control of man: without it the improvements of the age could never have been anticipated, much less arrived to in that order and perfection which we meet with everywhere. In a word, without science, mankind would be helpless and destitute, their comforts few, and the necessaries of life precarious: through it all things surrender to the will of man—in the most impenetrable forests are made to appear paths, to facilitate the traveller's speed— the sturdy oak and the tall cedars of Lebanon yield to his wishes, and supplies strength for his building, and beauty for his parlour: the immense hitherto unknown quarries of the richest granite become tributary to his wants, and surrender themselves to the powers of geology, and afford a foundation for his edifice and a top-stone for his temple. In subjection to his knowledge, the air wafts the freighted barge, constructed by his skill, to foreign climes to satisfy the adventurer's toil, and facilitate the friendly communications of distant nations. The winged canvas spreads before the gentle gale, and bears to distant shores the monarch's ambassage and the friendly visitor. The water is induced to give motion to the ingenious machinery, which regularly and willingly performs the desired task. Chemistry, with her innumerable analyzing processes, is always ready to furnish originals for the display of renewed species of continual inventions: and even steam, that powerful agent, whose velocity is almost irresistible, is made to obey and yield itself submissive to the direction in which he bids it act—while nature with her ten thousand spontaneous and charming productions, rendered more luxuriant by scientific culture, is continually producing the blessings of a plentiful and abundant harvest. These advantages are the undeniable results of perseverance and industrious mechanical pursuits, which are open to the grasp of all men, everywhere, of every kindred, tongue and people, wherever a successful application is the study and pursuit of those who will make themselves interested in these important concerns; for that God, who has created the bodies of all men, and that of one blood, has also endowed all with the same capacious mind.

Then let me ask the important question, Why! O why! should not the coloured American citizen be equal, in all the qualities of the heart, and the powers of the mind, with his white brother? Has nature made him inferior? Has his great Creator designed him to be less, in any respect? Has he at any time, or on any occasion, declared it? Can there be a prophet produced, a revelation quoted, an oracle consulted, to unfold such an idea, to resolve such a problem, or expound such a theory? Ask the standard of truth; let Heaven's own inspiration be heard, and God himself speak! "All souls are mine," is his express declaration, "For my ways are equal, saith the Lord God, and consequently all my works are founded on the same basis."

The pages of history furnish us with abundant proofs, from the achievements of our ancestors, that heaven has designed us to be an equal race. Both the church and the state have honoured them with an equal competition, in estimation of their services. From whence did those springs of learning and civilization originate, which has poured forth streams of light and information, when learned Greece and famed Rome were overwhelmed in heathen darkness and rude barbarianism? Ask the venerable pages of ancient literature—consult the oracles of truth and they will inform you, that when Rome was a desert, and Greece a wilderness, Moses was learned in all the wisdom of Egypt—the seat of literature and science—and in more recent times, yea, even in our own age, may we not cast our eyes around us and see the momentous struggle that is now abroad and is observable in the spirit of the times? The coloured American citizen may be everywhere discovered contending by temperance, economy, and mental ability for an admission into estimation as competitors for equal rights—the most unreasonable prejudice, and the most disgraceful encumbrances to the contrary notwithstanding—the development of the capacities of whose mind are daily convincing the enemies of human rights, that they are progressing onward, and that in spite of every effort made use of to prevent it. "We hope at last to rise," to an eminence, at least, on a level with the nations of the earth—we live in an age of wonder—let us make use of every effort as a band of mechanical brethren, to forward on this glorious cause—this is an era pregnant with the most important events which are on the eve of disclosure—the world is in commotion—the nations are shaken—the enemy has arisen from his slumber—the coloured race must be delivered—Jehovah, their God has seen their affliction, their groans are heard, and the Deliverer has come down. The Spirit of Wrongs—the Demon of Slavery has been startled from his lair by the Victorious Lion of Britain, and shall be successfully driven from all his coasts, on the 1st day of August, 1834,—and shall he find shelter alone in the fertile plains of America? Nay, we hope ere long to see him fall an easy prey to the American Eagle, there to be entombed in the pit already dug by his very votaries who now administer to his support, and who will be compelled, like the friends of mystic Babylon, to sing his funeral dirge.

That fated cause—the colonization project—that soul and body destroying experiment, that handmaid of slavery, must perish with him, and meet a similar fate. I see it in the signs of the times—in the spouting of colonizationists—in the feeble and expiring efforts of political pedagogues—in the able and spirited exertions of that philanthropic band, that a few months ago united in the greatest effort ever made use of to redeem their country's character from degradation and contempt—that heavenly band, peace to their memory, immortal be their names; but above all, I see it in the last struggles of prejudice, creeping from beneath the pen of mercenary newspaper editors, disgorging all their low calumnious slangs, and retorting them, in vain, on us and our friends, in these and in numerous other instances. "The enemy rageth, because he has but little time."

But the predictions of revelations—the prophecies of the Scriptures must be accomplished. I speak it boldly—the chain must be broken; the magic power of slavery must be destroyed; the fetters must be unrivetted; colonization must go down; it is weighed in the balance of public opinion, and ten thousand voices respond, "Thou art found wanting." Prejudice must die, as hard as the death struggle seems. God and man are united in its destruction; the daystar has already appeared; the jubilee trumpet already sounds, its echo reverberates from the British isles. "The redeemed of the Lord shall return and come home to Zion." "Thy sons shall come from afar, and thy daughters from the ends of the earth."

To the youth, let me subjoin a few admonitions. Let not this important season be barren of that improvement so essential to your future felicity and honour. Now is the seed time of life, and according to what you sow, you shall reap. Your character is now, under divine assistance, of your own forming; your fate is in some measure, put in your own hand; your natures are, as yet, pliant and soft. Habits have not established their dominion. Prejudice has not preoccupied your understanding. The world has not had time to contract and debase your affections. All your powers are more vigorous, disembarrassed, and free, than they will be at any future period. Whatever impulse you now give to your desires and passions, the direction is likely to be continued. Aim at elevation; let your study be improvement; acquire and persevere in education and the mechanic arts. Consider the employment of this important period as the highest trust which shall ever be committed to you, as in a great measure decisive of your future usefulness, and distinction in society. As in the succession of the seasons, each by the invariable laws of nature affect the productions of what is next in course, so human life—every period of our age, according as it is well or ill spent, influences the happiness of that which is to follow. Industry, diligence, and proper improvement of time, are the material duties of the young. To no purpose are you endowed with the best abilities, if the want of activity for exerting them prevails. In youth, the habits of industry are most easily acquired; the incentives to it are strongest from motives of duty, of ambition, of emulation, and from all the prospects which the beginning of life affords. Fly from idleness as the certain parent of guilt and ruin. And under idleness may be included, not mere inaction only, but all that circle of trifling occupations, in which too many saunter away their youth, perpetually engaged in frivolous society, or public amusements. Is this the foundation which you lay for future usefulness and esteem? By such accomplishments do you hope to recommend yourselves to the thinking part of mankind, and to answer the expectation of your friends, and become useful members of society? Redeem your time from such dangerous waste,—seek to fill it with employments which you may review with satisfaction. The acquisition of knowledge is one of the most honourable occupations of youth. Whatever you pursue, be emulous to excel. Let me again recall your attention to that dependence on the blessings of heaven, which, amidst all your endeavours after improvement, you ought continually to preserve.

Let me now conclude by addressing myself most especially to the brethren of the Humane Mechanics' Society: six years have elapsed since that auspicious day that gave birth to your union in this good cause—formed for the purpose of extending fellowship and good feeling, as well as motives of humanity and benevolence. You have found your most sanguine expectations to be realized; the distresses of many of your brethren have been alleviated; their necessities supplied in the hour of affliction. You have been instrumental in wiping away the falling tear from the orphan's eye, and have caused the widow's heart to dance for joy. Let us continue to progress in the discharge of these essential duties, until having finished a glorious, useful and praiseworthy career on this earthly ball, we may leave behind us an immortal standard around which successive generations may rally with delight. Let our motto then be "improvement," and our watchword "onward."

ADDRESS

DELIVERED BEFORE THE

MORAL REFORM SOCIETY,

IN

PHILADELPHIA,

AUGUST 8, 1836.

BY WILLIAM WATKINS,

OF BALTIMORE.

PHILADELPHIA:
MERRIHEW AND GUNN, PRINTERS,
NO. 7 CARTERS' ALLEY.
1836.

TO THE READER

The following Address is published in pursuance of a resolution adopted by the Moral Reform Society, before whom it was delivered. In consenting to its publication, the writer is aware that he may have betrayed more vanity than good sense—that in disregarding the dictates of his own judgment and complying with the wishes of his too partial friends, he may have unwittingly contributed to erect, though of ephemeral duration, a monument of his own folly. While some will find it no herculean task to discover inaccuracies of thought and language, others will dissent from some of the sentiments advanced, and a third party with the writer will see, that as it respects felicity of arrangement, there is yet much room for improvement. Much might be said to extenuate faults and render powerless the weapons of criticism, but it is believed that this is unnecessary in regard to those for whom the Address is intended, and should it fall into other hands the hope is indulged that it will be viewed with a charitable eye, especially when it is considered, we should not despise the day of small things.

W. W.

ADDRESS

I RISE, Mr. President, to offer, and make a few remarks to sustain, a resolution which is in the following words:

Resolved, That a good education is the most valuable blessing that we, as a people, can bestow upon the rising generation.

The thinking and observing of all civilized nations have always regarded, as of paramount importance, the education of the rising generation. They have seen, sir, in the light of a sunbeam, that when the human intellect begins to expand, and put forth its feeble energies, it must be enlightened, strengthened, and disciplined—that when the passions are beginning to be excited by external objects, they must be directed into proper channels; they must be duly regulated; they must be subjected to a judicious moral training; or otherwise the mind, in its developement, will be little else than a mental chaos, incapable of perceiving, and consequently of remedying, the moral evil that must inevitably result to society from the unchecked, the violent ebullitions, the ungovernable passions of the human heart.

It has required no extraordinary acuteness of discernment to discover that the neglect of the mind and morals is the most prolific source of ignorance and barbarism, of degradation and misery.

It has also been seen, sir, that a suitable education ameliorates the condition of man, renders him a useful member of society, promotes his own happiness, and elevates him to the true dignity of human nature. Hence that unconquerable thirst after knowledge which characterized some of the ancient nations; hence the laudable and strenuous efforts now being made by the reflecting, the enlightened, the patriotic, both of Europe and America, to diffuse useful knowledge among all classes of society.

And I rejoice, sir, to find that an ardent desire for mental and moral improvement is beginning to animate the intelligent of our people; and that they are devising means to promote these desirable objects; that among these stands pre-eminent the parent Moral Reform Society over which you preside, and which is to be the grand centre of all our future operations—a Society, sir, which I regard as a golden chain, uniting the divided energies of our people of every sect and party—a Society, sir, which will exhibit to the world in one solid and permanent nucleus, a union and concentration of much that is respectable in intelligence, excellent in morals, splendid in genius, and fervent in piety.

And here, Mr. President, you will permit me to say, that whenever I have reflected upon the elements of which this Society is composed —the magnitude of the task assigned me—my inability to perform it adequately, I have felt a strong temptation to decline the honour of an appointment which I accepted with unaffected reluctance, and which, not being able honourably to avoid, I now proceed to accomplish, though with extreme diffidence.

The resolution says, that a *good* education is the most valuable blessing that we, as a people, can bestow upon the rising generation. It tacitly admits that there is such a thing as a *bad* education. We know, sir, that man, in the incipient stages of his being, receives an education, whether he will or not—that while his infant mind is opening, it is continually receiving impressions from objects with which it is daily coming in contact—that it is perpetually forming habits which, for the most part, grow with its growth, and strengthen with its strength: and we also know with what facility it imbibes false impressions, and with what difficulty they are corrected—that to break the force of early associations, and to eradicate inveterate habits, is, too frequently, to stem a resistless torrent. And when I reflect upon the universal depravity of the human heart—the preponderance of bad example—the contagious nature of vice, I am not at all surprised that so many receive a bad education.

But it is our object to save the rising generation from a *pernicious,* and bless them with a *good* education. To accomplish this, we would have every child placed under such a course of judicious instruction and discipline as will elicit all the capabilities of his nature—as will embrace the developement and cultivation of all his faculties, whether they relate to his spiritual or physical organization—such a course of instruction and discipline, as will enable him at all times, in all places, and under all circumstances, to act up to the dignity of a being who, though, in one sense, sustaining a cognation to the brute creation, yet, in another, but little a lower than the angels.

By a good education, sir, we mean such a one as will soundly instruct this compound being, man, in the obvious principles of his nature; an education that will teach him his origin, his end—that will teach him the various relations he sustains, and instruct him in the duties which they involve to his God, to his fellow creatures, and himself.

It will not be enough to attend to the mere developement and discipline of the intellectual powers—to initiate the juvenile mind into all the mysteries of the arts and sciences—no, sir; but on the contrary, the moral and religious feelings of the heart must be cultivated, as of paramount interest. In the education of our children, we must regard them as immortal beings who are rapidly hastening through this probationary state to the eternal world, and whose unchangeable destiny there, sir, will be according to the type of their characters here. O, then, how important is it, that while the tender age of our children is such as to render them most susceptible of moral and religious impressions—that while their characters and habits are being formed, and that, for the most part, for life, how important is it that they should be thoroughly indoctrinated in the principles and practices of our holy religion. I mean, not that they are to be harnessed and disciplined in the traces of bigotry, or that they are to be baptized in, or proselyted to, the peculiar tenets of the different sects in the land—no, sir; I mean simply that our children should be taught, in all our schools, the fundamental doctrines of Christianity, the sublime morality of the Bible, and trained up in the way in which they should go, that when they are old they may not depart from it.

I can never consent to admit that mere scientific and literary attainments, though productive of vast advantages to mankind, constitute a good education. I believe, with Dr. Young, that "with the talents of an angel, a man may be a fool."

Man, sir, is but a sojourner here: "He cometh up and is cut down like a flower." He is also in a state of probation: his thoughts, words, works, have all a momentous bearing upon his interests in the world to come—upon his happiness or misery through the annals of eternity. And when I consider the shortness of life, the certainty of death, and the awful, the stupendous realities of the invisible world, I am irresistibly led to the conclusion that nothing but the blindest infatuation can regard that as a good education which has reference only to this life, which, abstractly considered, does not contribute one iota in qualifying the immortal soul for the exalted felicity of which it is capable, which affords no aid in preparing us for that inheritance which is incorruptible, undefiled, and that fadeth not away.

Mr. President, I maintain, that that only is a good education which assists in the all-important work of training man for his native skies; for

> Minds, though sprung from heav'nly race,
> Must first be tutor'd for the place.
> The joys above are understood, .
> And relish'd only by the good.

I do not intend to convey the idea that a good education can change the heart from nature to grace—no, sir, far be the impious insinuation! This is the peculiar province of the Holy Spirit. What I mean to say is that a good education is powerfully auxiliary, under God, in working out the salvation of man—in promoting his well-being in time and in eternity.

It is unquestionable, sir, that those children who are early taught to remember their Creator in the days of their youth, who are early taught, both by precept and example, that to fear God and keep his commandments is the whole duty of man, will be far more likely than others, in adult life to be good citizens and exemplary Christians. These, sir, more than impregnable fortifications, powerful fleets, and formidable armies, constitute the true strength and glory of a nation. Their intelligence and virtue render them invincible. A government blessed with such subjects has all the elements of prosperity, happiness, and durability. These are they who, at the sound of the gospel trumpet, flock to the standard of Immanuel and engage heart and hand in all those great moral enterprises of the age, which are the pioneers and harbingers of that day when the nations of the earth shall learn war no more—when they shall beat their swords into ploughshares, and their spears into pruning hooks—when "the kingdoms of this world shall become the kingdoms of our Lord and of his Christ."

In all that I have advanced on a good education, I am not aware of having controverted the maxim that "whatever is useful is good." On the contrary, I have incidentally conceded that the mere cultivation of the intellectual powers has been productive of the most important results to mankind; and I am prepared further to admit that these results may, in a certain sense, be denominated good. But these admissions derogate nothing from the position we have assumed, that, as it respects man's moral relations, his education cannot be regarded as good, nay, it is radically deficient, unless it has specific reference to those relations. And if this assertion needs confirmation, we need instance only the fact that, in too many cases, the most splendid abilities are associated with the most dissolute morals. And, as with individuals, so with nations. An eloquent historian says of the inhabitants of ancient Corinth (a city called by Cicero "the light of all Greece"), "they were very learned, as well as very dissolute."

But though a good education necessarily implies a cultivation of the mind and morals combined, yet as I have hitherto confined myself chiefly to the consideration of the latter, and incidentally noticed some of its advantages, it may not be amiss to attend for a few moments to the advantages resulting from mere intellectual culture.

The cultivation of the intellectual powers alone, has, under Providence, been productive of the grandest and most important results to the human family.

Man, with his wonderfully penetrating and comprehensive powers, has, with singular success, explored the arcana of nature. He has, with untold pleasure to himself, and incalculable advantage to society, made important discoveries in the animal, vegetable, and mineral kingdoms.

He has altered, and is still altering, the very face of nature for his accommodation and happiness. He conceives, for instance, the design of bringing distant cities into neighbourhood union. The difficulties that tower in his path seem insurmountable. He sees, however, that the most beneficial consequences await the successful prosecution of his contemplated enterprise. He resolves that the work shall be done. He summons to the task all the power of his gigantic intellect. His plans are devised with consummate skill, and, at his bidding and direction, executed with facility. Yes, at the sound of his imperative voice, mountains fall and valleys rise—the crooked is made straight, and the rough places smooth—distance is annihilated, and time is gained. Your canals and your railroads are familiar examples.

The utility of these wonderful improvements is obvious in facilitating trade and travel; in promoting social intercourse among those whose interests should be identical; in enabling the citizen to fly over the country as it were on the wings of the wind; in affording mutual protection and support in the hour of calamity and danger.

Those stupendous works of art which are conferring such rich blessings on America, found their way to this continent chiefly by means of two very important agents—the results also of intellectual cultivation—the mariner's compass and the art of printing. The former guided the white-winged messenger across the pathless ocean, and the latter proclaimed the joyful tidings.

The time was when the fearful mariner dared not venture far from land, lest he should be at the mercy of the winds and waves.

All voyages, however long, were performed along the coasts, and in sight of land. But, behold the astonishing change! The enterprising mariner no longer dreads to leave his vernacular shores: by the aid of the compass, he circumnavigates the globe. He visits every clime, supplying the wants, and ministering to the comforts of one country by the superabundant productions of another; nay, bearing with him the lights of science and religion, dispensing the blessings of civilization and the Gospel. See him, in the prosecution of his perilous enterprise, skilfully wending his solitary way through the trackless ocean when neither sun, nor moon, nor stars, can be seen—when the tempest is raging, and the darkness is almost tangible.

And to what are these splendid results mainly attributable? obviously, to the cultivation of the intellectual powers. It was this that brought into existence that invaluable instrument, the mariner's compass.

It was the exercise of his thinking powers that led Columbus to form his theory of an additional continent—that induced the intrepid adventurer to launch forth on a voyage of discovery, braving the dangers of a fearful ocean, encountering difficulties and hardships truly appalling, and, to an undisciplined mind, overwhelming. But see the event: this brilliant enterprise was crowned with the discovery of a new world, to the great joy of happy millions.

We have alluded to the art of printing, as a splendid result of intellectual culture—an art that has been productive of incalculable advantages to mankind. It is this which is the grand medium through which every species of useful knowledge is poured in one incessant flood upon the vast "empire of mind" in this lower world. Without it, we have good reason to believe that a formidable triumvirate of ignorance, superstition, and tyranny would this day be wielding an iron sceptre over some of the fairest and most enlightened portions of our globe. Europe and America would doubtless be enveloped in the deep gloom of the dark ages, ignorant of the high-born destiny of man, and strangers to the fundamental principles of civil and religious liberty.

Yes, sir, the wings of the press are wafting to all lands the glorious tidings, the ennobling, the heaven-born truths, that "God hath made of *one* blood all nations for to dwell on *all* the face of the earth;" that man, *immortal* man, who bears the image of his Maker—who ranks but a little lower than the angels, may not be treated, as a brute, with impunity; "that *all* men are created *equal*, and endowed by their Creator with certain *inalienable* rights; that among these are life, *liberty* and the pursuit of happiness."

These all-conquering truths have not only done much to elevate man to the true dignity of his nature, but they are still, through the medium of the press, undermining the establishment of despotism—liberalizing the views of the imperious; humanizing those insane and bitter prejudices which impiously forbid a large portion of the human race to occupy the stations assigned them by their benevolent Creator. And these truths, I hesitate not to predict, are yet destined, in their resistless march throughout the habitable globe, to shake down kingdoms; to revolutionize empires, and accelerate the ushering in of that glorious jubilee when millions, now prostrate in the dust, writhing under the iron heel of tryanny, will stand erect and walk abroad in all the majesty of freemen, "redeemed, regenerated, and disenthralled."

The art of printing has conferred immense advantages on mankind. The time was when books could be multiplied only by the tardy process of copying. They were of course exceedingly scarce and exorbitantly high. The Bible, sir, that precious boon of heaven, which is a lamp to our feet and a light to our path, could not be purchased but at the enormous price of from 150 to 200 dollars; consequently, as few were able to obtain it, the great mass of the people groped their way through the deepest gloom of ignorance and superstition. But the invention of printing has remedied these evils and introduced a bright day. Books are now teeming from the press with astonishing rapidity and in boundless profusion. They are continually pouring forth a rich flood of mental, moral, and religious light upon our benighted world,—and that too at a trifling expense, and, in some instances, without money and without price.

And I may here ask, to what purpose are books being multiplied, and put into the hands of our children unless they are able to read them: I mean read them, not *mechanically*, as is too much the case, but *understandingly*. Upon this qualification on the part of the rising generation, your Bible societies, tract societies, temperance societies, &c. depend, in a great measure, for their best results.

Other inventions and improvements demonstrating the great utility of a cultivated intellect, might be noticed but for the want of time. We may mention, however, the invention of the telescope—an invention which has brought the heavens as it were down to the earth, and enabled man to make important and wonderful discoveries in the science of astronomy, discoveries which fill the mind with the most sublime conceptions, and, withal, "lessons of heavenly wisdom teach."

We might also consider the invention of, and the important improvements that have been made in, the science of mechanics; a science by which man can exert a most prodigious power—a power incomparably beyond what he can exert by mere natural strength.

In this connexion it may not be amiss to speak of the numerous labour-saving machines that have been invented—a very important one of which, called the "Corn Planter," was recently invented by a coloured Marylander. This machine is thus noticed by the National Intelligencer:

> *The Corn Planter.*—A machine of this name, for which a patent has been obtained by Henry Blair, a free man of color, of an adjoining county of Maryland, is now exhibiting in the Capitol. It is a very simple and ingenious machine, which, as moved by a horse, opens the furrow, drops (at proper intervals, and in an exact and suitable quantity) the corn, covers it, and levels the earth so as, in fact, to plant the corn as rapidly as a horse can draw a plough over the ground. The inventor thinks it will save the labor of eight men. We understand he is about to modify the machine, so as to adapt it to the planting of cotton. If it will accomplish (as we are inclined to believe it will) all which he supposes, it will prove to be an invention of great utility.—*Nat. Intel.*

Thus you perceive, sir, that the coloured man, who has been denied the attributes of humanity, is triumphantly refuting, on the very soil of slavery—a soil which he has doubtless watered with his tears—the oft-refuted calumny that his race is devoid of genius; and this he is doing in a way which the interests of his calumniators will not allow them to overlook. And by what means is he thus signalizing himself, and conferring a distinguished honour upon his people? It is unquestionably owing, to say the least, to the exercise of his thinking powers. And if we would see such men multiplied among us, we must give our children a good education. We must teach them *how* to think—*how* to use and improve the noble powers with which they are happily endowed.

Sir, we live in a very important age of the world, and in a very enlightened portion of the globe. The lessons of wisdom and experience are every where blazing before us. They teach us that intelligence and virtue will, at all times, in all places, and under all circumstances, elevate any people; and that ignorance and vice will as certainly degrade them.

Shall we then, while all classes of society around us are making improvements in everything that is excellent and useful, remain alone stationary? Then indeed would it be true that we are so low in our debasement as scarcely to be reached by the heavenly light. No, sir, we will bestir ourselves—we will shake off our slumbers—we will "lay aside every weight," and resolve in humble reliance on Divine aid, that we will be more intelligent, more useful, more respectable—that our career of improvement shall be onward, and onward, until the declaration of Fabricius in relation to ancient Rome shall be adopted as the motto of every civilized and Christian community: "Rome knows no qualifications for great employments but virtue and ability." And, in carrying out this resolution, we shall remember that all our efforts to ameliorate our condition will be inefficient unless the foundation be laid in a good education. This will not only make us useful and respectable members of society, but will eminently contribute to the increase of our rational enjoyments.

The educated man—the man of a cultivated taste, whose mind is enriched with stores of useful knowledge, has, within himself, an inexhaustible source of refined pleasure. On the contrary, the uneducated man lives in a sort of embryo: he has eyes, sir, but sees not; ears, but hears not; his spiritual senses are sealed; his intellectual powers, for the most part, dormant. But when a flood of mental and moral light is poured upon his benighted vision, his slumbering energies are awakened, and called forth into vigorous exercise: he now enters into a new world and beholds, with ineffable delight, scenes new, beautiful, and grand. Both the works of nature and of art which the unthinking view "with brute unconscious gaze," the educated man beholds with the most pleasurable emotions. He gazes upon the works of genius—the painted canvass or the sculptured marble—and discovers beauties to which others are strangers; beauties that afford him the most exquisite delight. He peruses a well-written book on some interesting subject, or listens to the accomplished orator, or converses with the intelligent, with feelings of pleasure inexpressible, and, to the illiterate, incommunicable. All nature, in every place, in all seasons, under every variety of aspect, in all her diversified operations, furnishes a bounteous feast—a rich entertainment for the man of cultivated taste.

> For him the spring
> Distils her dews, and from the silken gem
> Its lucid leaves unfolds; for him, the hand
> Of autumn tinges every fertile branch
> With blooming gold, and blushes like the morn.
> Each passing hour sheds tribute from her wings
> And still new beauties meet his lonely walk,
> And loves unfelt attract him.
> Not a breeze
> Flies o'er the meadow; not a cloud imbibes

> The setting sun's effulgence; not a strain
> From all the tenants of the warbling shade
> Ascends, but whence his bosom can partake
> Fresh pleasure unreproved.

Such a man, having within himself an opulent fund of intellectual enjoyment, will not be so much inclined as others to seek happiness in the gratification of his appetites and passions.

The attractions of the gambling table and the ale house are not, in his view, to be compared with those to be found in his own domicile—in the rich volumes of a well selected library.

Instead of associating with the vicious and abandoned in those sinks of pollution—those whirlpools of vice, those charnel houses of health, of genius, and of everything lovely in the human character, where too many of the youth of the present generation are revelling in licentiousness and gross sensuality, blasting the prospects and destroying the happiness of their friends and relations, and burying the hopes of their country, and consigning themselves to eternal infamy—I say, instead of thus seeking happiness in the lowest depths of ignominy and disgrace, you will find him in the hall of science, the lecture room, the moral lyceum, or in some useful institution, in all of which, whether he is receiving or imparting instruction, he is increasing his own intellectual enjoyments.

Mr. President, I most firmly believe that a good education is the great *sine qua non* as it regards the elevation of our people. Give them this and they cease to grovel; give them this and they emerge from their degradation, though crushed beneath a mountain weight of prejudice; give them this and they will command respect and consideration from all who respect themselves and whose good opinions are worth having; give them this and they acquire a moral power that will enable them to storm and batter down that great citadel of pride and prejudice, that great Babel of oppression that impiously lifts itself to the clouds, vainly hoping to thwart the designs of Him who is thundering in the heavens. "For the oppression of the poor, for the sighing of the needy, now will I arise: I will set him in safety from him that puffeth at him."

Sir, give the rising generation a good education, and you instruct them in, and qualify them for, all the duties of life—you make them useful citizens and enlightened Christians—you refine the pleasures and increase the happiness of their social circles—you banish from their religion that superstition, and from their devotional exercises that wild, ranting fanaticism, which are the legitimate fruits of ignorance, and which can procure for them no other consideration than the pity of the intelligent, or the ridicule of the unthinking—give them a good education, and then, when liberty, in the full sense of the term, shall be conferred upon them, it will be something more than a "sounding brass or a tinkling cymbal:" they will thoroughly understand its nature, duly appreciate its value, and contribute efficiently to its inviolable preservation.

In conclusion, sir, permit me to say we have much more to animate our hopes than to excite our fears. Ours is a *righteous* cause—that of our enemies, an *un*righteous one. On the one hand we see arrayed against us unblushing impiety, unholy pride, grovelling sinful prejudice, and a short-sighted worldly policy; on the other hand —on the side of unoffending innocence and struggling virtue—we behold arrayed an invincible phalanx of all that is liberal and magnanimous, holy, just, and good—the active sympathies of the civilized world, and the moral energies of the universe. Sir, the unholy alliance must capitulate—they must make a virtue of necessity; for we are divinely assured that "no weapon formed against us shall prosper," so long as "the weapons of our warfare are not carnal, but mighty through God to the pulling down of the strongholds" of wickedness.

Mr. President I shall trespass no longer upon the kind indulgence that has been extended towards me: I move the adoption of the resolution.

Part III

Significant Annual Conferences,
1830–1837

Conferences and conventions of free people of color held during the 1830s marked a new trend in the struggle to abolish slavery. This organized activity signaled a fresh effort to take the initiative in deciding and shaping their own destiny. Education, temperance, moral reform, equal rights, economy, self-help, and above all the quest for unity were the concerns of this period. Not everyone supported these organized gatherings. Some blacks opposed separate conventions because they feared that separation from white abolition societies would undermine the fight against slavery. Whites for their part were not convinced that black people were prepared to assume the helm in such an area of responsibility. Proslavery groups opposed meetings of black people, assuming that such gatherings would serve as vehicles of revolutionary activity which might result in the overthrow of their "peculiar institution." It was within this frame of sentiment that the National Convention Movement—embracing moral reform, church, and temperance conferences held throughout the 1830s—was born, bred and developed.

The establishment on December 21, 1816, of the American Colonization Society, was the spark which forced the free people of color into organized groups. The Society's motives were interpreted by the people of color as a conspiracy to rid America of free blacks whose presence, in the eyes of the slavocracy, presented a threat to slavery.

The first response to the establishment of the American Colonization Society was articulated at a public meeting of free people of color in Richmond, on January 24, 1817.

Almost six months later, on August 10, 1817, James Forten and Russell Parrott called a general meeting in Philadelphia at which they charged that the American Colonization Society had issued

167

false and damaging propaganda against the free black population in order to justify sending them all to Africa.[1] This Philadelphia meeting urged the people of color to counterattack the Society. As a result, protest meetings voicing opposition to the policies of the Society were held throughout the country.

By 1830, free Negroes lived in such a milieu of hostile opinion that many of their leaders felt that organized activity was the only means of bettering their situation. Specifically, black laws enacted in the Northern states severely hampered their ability to gain employment and provide adequate living conditions for their families. The covert aim of these laws was the expulsion of the free population from localities controlled by those interested in the perpetuation of slavery. To some leaders of the black community, emigration loomed as the best way of ameliorating their condition.[2]

Southern Canada was cited as a likely site. The possibility of such a mass emigration project seemed an important enough justification to issue a call for a convention. *The American Society of Free Persons of Colour, for Improving their Condition in the United States; for Purchasing Lands; and for the Establishment of a Settlement in Upper Canada*—the First National Negro Convention—met on September 20, 1830, and elected Richard Allen President.

The impact caused by the publication of David Walker's *Appeal* in 1829 did much to make any mass meetings of black people suspect. The prevailing sentiment of hostility drove the conventioneers of this 1830 meeting underground for five days prior to the public sessions. The delegates, forty in all, were representatives of churches, educational organizations, cultural, and beneficial societies. In their public sessions they deliberated on the feasibility of emigrating to Canada. "The American Society of Free Persons of Colour" grew out of this convention. Its primary purpose was to investigate the possibility of purchasing land in Canada for a settlement. Throughout the sessions, the delegates voiced severe denunciations of the American Colonization Society.

Concrete results of the formation of the American Society of Free Persons of Colour were varied. Eastern cities such as Baltimore, New York, Boston, and Washington held post-convention meetings to reaffirm an anticolonization position. Funds were collected for the proposed Canadian settlement. Efforts to educate and train workers who had been turned out of their jobs as a result of discrimination were initiated. Free-produce societies, whose members vowed to use no

---

[1] See *To the Humane and Benevolent Inhabitants* . . . , p. 265.
[2] See Part IV.

products made with slave labor, were established. These activities by and for the good of the free black population contributed measurably toward fulfillment of the convention's pleas for unity and solidarity against the climate of prejudice and injustice.[3]

In the cities of Baltimore, Wilmington, Salem, New Jersey, and Attleborough, Pennsylvania, Methodist Societies of Free Africans were in process of formation in 1816, the year Richard Allen was elected the First Bishop of the African Methodist Episcopal Church. Bishop Allen felt the need to consolidate them into a strong organization and to extend the work of the A.M.E. Church to the various states. As a result of his correspondence with the various Methodist African Societies a convention was held in Philadelphia on April 9, 1816.

The A.M.E. Church was now an independent organization and a symbol of Negro independence although its leader, Bishop Allen, did not wholly advocate separation or segregation of Negroes in the Church.

Testimony of black ministers of the Church indicates that annual conferences were first held as early as 1817 in Philadelphia and Baltimore, and the first General Conference was held in Philadelphia on July 9, 1820. The minutes and proceedings of these early meetings seem to have been lost. Joseph N. Corr, who served as secretary to the Baltimore and Philadelphia conferences held in 1826 was in 1833 the General Book Steward for the Conferences of the African Methodist Episcopal Church. To him must be given credit for compiling and publishing the minutes of the Third Ohio Annual Conference held in Pittsburgh, Pennsylvania, September 14–23, 1833; the 19th Baltimore Annual Conference held in Washington, D.C., April 19–28, 1834; the 19th Annual Conference of the Philadelphia District held in Philadelphia, May 24, 1834–June 3, 1834; and the 13th Annual Conference of the New York District held in Brooklyn, New York, June 14–23, 1834.

Bishop Morris Brown, ordained in 1828, organized these Conferences and served as the presiding officer from 1832 to 1849. Known as a radical, Morris Brown had helped numerous slaves to purchase their freedom. Because of his sympathy for them he was forced to flee Charleston, South Carolina, where he had a church, in 1822

[3] For an account of the convention movement see: Bella Gross "The First National Convention" *The Journal of Negro History*, Vol. 31, October, 1946, pp. 435–443; Howard H. Bell *A Survey of the Negro Convention Movement, 1830–1861.* (New York, 1969). Also Howard H. Bell, ed.; *Minutes of the Proceedings of the Negro Conventions, 1830–1864* (New York, 1969).

after the Denmark Vesey insurrection and seek refuge in Philadelphia.

While the Conferences and Conventions of the people of color during this period all had similar purposes, and individuals and leaders were in attendance at more than one meeting, at the Church conferences "The Ambassadors of the Cross" urged the importance of "promoting harmony" and the necessity for "study to show themselves in all their pursuits approved of God." At these Conferences recommendations were passed stressing the importance of education and the need to establish both common and Sunday schools, as well as temperance societies. A survey of the number of schools, their location, scholars, and the subjects taught was recommended. The 13th Annual Conference, held in Brooklyn, urged that the buying and selling of lottery tickets be discouraged.

The successful Conference held at Washington in 1834 created much excitement, since it was the first Negro meeting in the capital of the United States. Hundreds of whites and persons of color attended. The city officials offered their protection "should any evil designed persons attempt" to interrupt the proceedings, and the President of the United States wished the Conference success.

The historical, statistical and genealogical data to be gleaned from the *Minutes of the Four Last Annual Conferences* is of utmost importance for tracing the early leaders and their work. Considering the number of copies of this important document that were printed, it is difficult to believe that the only locatable copy is in the New York Historical Society.

The Fifth Annual Convention for the Improvement of the Free People of Colour, held in 1835, established the American Moral Reform Society. After six successive years of annual conventions, prejudice was still rampant in the country and little had been done to improve the condition of the colored population. Their leaders hoped that a National Moral Reform Society might prove to be a means for changing their humiliating situation.

The First Annual Meeting of the American Moral Reform Society was held in Philadelphia on August 14–19, 1837. Its purpose was "to extend the principles of universal peace and good will to all mankind, by promoting sound morality, by the influence of education, temperance, economy and all those virtues that alone can render man acceptable in the eyes of God or the civilized world."

James Forten, Sr., after twenty years of leadership and now 71 years of age, was appointed President of the Society; his son, James Forten, Jr., was appointed Recording Secretary. Perhaps the ablest and certainly the longest address before the meeting was that of James Forten, Jr., whose remarks were limited to the problem of education. He paid tribute to the females, who, he said, "were generally to be found foremost in the cause of Moral Reform." Of those males who opposed extensive education of women he asked, "What just reason can be assigned for her not becoming acquainted with all the branches of polite literature? What signifies external elegance, if the mind within be shrouded in ignorance?"

John Francis Cook of Washington addressed the conference on temperance mainly, but discussed the other objects of moral reform—education, universal love, and economy. William Whipper, in his speech to the Conference, suggested the establishment of a press in order to make known to the world the progress of the people of color in the arts, science, and civilization.

William Whipper's suggestion became a reality and he served as the first editor of *The National Reformer,* which was published by the Board of Managers of the American Moral Reform Society. Only a few issues of the monthly are known to exist. Resolutions passed at the Third Annual Meeting, as reported in *The National Reformer* for September 1839, indicate that the Society was still concerned about slavery, lack of cooperation among the colored people, and the need to raise money to carry out the principles of the Moral Reform Society.

No separately published minutes and proceedings of Annual Meetings of the American Moral Reform Society have been located, except for those of the First Annual Meeting held in 1837.

CONSTITUTION

OF THE

AMERICAN SOCIETY

OF

FREE PERSONS OF COLOUR,

For Improving their Condition in the United States;
for Purchasing Lands; and for the Establishment
of a Settlement in Upper Canada,

ALSO

THE PROCEEDINGS OF THE CONVENTION,

WITH THEIR

ADDRESS

TO

THE FREE PERSONS OF COLOUR

IN THE

UNITED STATES.

PHILADELPHIA:
PRINTED BY I. W. ALLEN, NO 26, STRAWBERRY ST.
1831.

172

MINUTES OF THE CONVENTION

AT a Convention held by adjournments from the 20th day of September, to the 24th of the same inclusive, 1830, in accordance with a public notice issued on behalf of the Coloured Citizens of Philadelphia, and addressed to their brethren throughout the U. States, inviting them to assemble by delegation, in Convention, to be held in the city of Philadelphia, on the 20th day of September, 1830, and signed, on behalf, by the Rev. Bishop *Allen, Cyrus Black, Junius C. Morel, Benjamin Paschall,* jr. and *James Cornish—*

The delegation accordingly met in Bethel church, on the 20th September, at 10 o'clock, A. M. and after a chaste and appropriate prayer by the venerable Bishop *Allen,* the Convention was organized by electing

Rt. Rev. RICHARD ALLEN, President.

Dr. BELFAST BURTON, of Philadelphia, ⎫

AUSTIN STEWARD, of Rochester, N.Y. ⎬ Vice Presidents.

JUNIUS C. MOREL, of Philadelphia, Secretary, and

ROBERT COWLEY, of Maryland, Assistant Secretary.

On motion it was

Resolved, That this Convention do recommend the formation of a Parent Society; and that immediately after its organization, to appoint a general corresponding Agent, to reside at or near the intended purchase in Upper Canada.

On motion it was

Resolved, That this Convention enjoins and requires of each of its members to use their utmost influence in the formation of societies, *auxiliary* to the Parent Society about being established in the city of Philadelphia; and also to instruct the auxiliary societies when formed, to send delegates to the next General Convention.

On motion it was

Resolved, That the next General Convention shall be composed of delegates appointed by the Parent Society and its auxiliaries: provided always, that the number of delegates from each society, shall not exceed *five,* and all other places, where there are no auxiliaries, are hereby invited to send one delegate.

On motion it was

Resolved, That this Convention address the Free People of Colour throughout the United States, and publish in one of the daily papers of this city.

On motion it was

Resolved, That the Convention do adjourn at the invitation of one of the managers of the Lombard-street Free School for coloured children. The Convention were highly gratified at the order, regularity and improvement discoverable in the various departments, among a collection of children, male and female, rising four hundred. Their specimens in writing, needlework, &c. &c. made a deep impression on the Convention, with a desire that the People of Colour may availingly appreciate every extended opportunity for their improvement in the various situations where they may reside.

On motion, the House adjourned *sine die.*

Rt. Rev. RICHARD ALLEN, President.

JUNIUS C. MOREL, Secretary.

The following Delegates composed the Convention, viz.:

Pennsylvania—Rev. Richard Allen, Dr. Belfast Burton, Cyrus Black, Junius C. Morel, Benjamin Paschall, jr. James Cornish, Wm. S. Whipper, Peter Gardiner, John Allen, James Newman, Charles H. Leveck, Frederick A. Hinton.

New-York—Austin Steward, Jos. Adams, George L. Brown.

Connecticut—Scipio C. Augustus.

Rhode-Island—George C. Willis, Alfred Niger.

Maryland—James Deavour, Hezekiah Grice, Aaron Willoon, Robert Cowley.

Delaware—Abraham D. Shad.

Virginia—Arthur M. Waring, Wm. Duncan, James West, jr.

HONORARY MEMBERS.

Robert Brown, William Rogers, John Bowers, Richard Howell, Daniel Peterson, Charles Shorts, of Pennsylvania; Leven Williams, of New York; James P. Walker, of Maryland; John Robinson, of Ohio; Rev. Samuel Todd, of Maryland; John Arnold, of New Jersey; Sampson Peters, of New Jersey; Rev. Anthony Campbell, of Delaware; Don Carolos Hall, of Delaware.

CONSTITUTION

PREAMBLE

In conformity to a resolution of the Delegates of Free Persons of Colour, in General Convention assembled, in the City of Philadelphia, September 20th, 1830, recommending the formation and establishment of a Parent Society in the City of Philadelphia, for the purpose of purchasing land, and locating a settlement in the Province of Upper Canada; and to which all other Societies formed for that purpose, may become auxiliary—We therefore have adopted the following Constitution.

ARTICLE I

This Society shall be called "The American Society of Free Persons of Colour, for improving their condition in the United States; for purchasing lands; and for the establishment of a settlement in the Province of Upper Canada": and shall consist of such Persons of Colour as shall pay not less than *twenty five cents* on entering, and thereafter quarterly, *eighteen and three quarter cents.*

ARTICLE II

The Officers of the Society shall be, a President, and [word missing in original—editor] Vice Presidents, four of whom to be chosen out of the city and county of Philadelphia; a Corresponding, Recording, and two Assistant Secretaries, and a Treasurer: a Board of Managers of fifteen members, a Corresponding Committee of five, a Financial Committee of three, a Soliciting Committee of thirteen, and a Publishing Committee of three; all of whom shall be elected by Ballot, at the annual meeting in October.

The Society shall meet quarterly in the city of Philadelphia, on the first Monday in October, January, April, and July.

The Board of Managers shall meet to transact business on the last Monday of every month; they shall have power to fill all vacancies occurring during the year, in their body, or any of the committees. Nine of their number shall constitute a quorum.

ARTICLE III

The President shall preside at all meetings of the Society, and sign all orders on the Treasurer.

The Vice Presidents shall preside at all meetings of the Society, in the absence of the President.

The President, Vice Presidents, Secretaries, and Treasurer, shall be *ex officio* members of the Board of Managers.

ARTICLE IV

The duty of the Corresponding Secretary shall be to attend the meetings of the Corresponding Committee, keep the minutes of their proceedings; he shall be subject to their order, and shall report and present all letters or communications directed to him, to the chairman of the committee, that they may be convened together. He shall also keep a true copy of all his letters or communications.

The Committee of Correspondence shall open an exchange of views with the different Auxiliary Societies that may be formed; receive intelligence concerning the operations of the different societies throughout the United States, and from other persons aiming to improve the situation and condition of the people of colour; and also receive all essays on the subject, with such other information as may conduce to the accomplishment of the great object of the Society.

All communications shall be directed to the Corresponding Secretary.

ARTICLE V

The Recording Secretary shall attend the meetings of the Society and keep their minutes.

He shall be provided with a book, wherein shall be recorded the proceedings of the Society, of the Board of Managers, and of the Committees, or any persons entrusted with the care or concerns of the Society.

Therefore it shall be the duty of the chairmen of the several committees to aid the Recording Secretary in the discharge of his official duty.

The Assistant Secretaries shall attend the meetings and keep the minutes of the Board of Managers, and assist the Recording Secretary when required.

ARTICLE VI

The Treasurer on entering upon the duties of his office, shall give such security for the faithful performance of his trust as the Board of Managers shall require.

The Treasurer shall not retain in his possession more than $100. All monies above that sum shall be deposited in the United States Bank, that all persons interested in the prosperity of the Institution may be satisfied as to the safety of their funds; and no sum so deposited shall be withdrawn without an order signed by the President, Vice President, and Secretary of the Parent Society, and four of the Board of Managers thereof.

He shall keep fair accounts of his transactions, hold all papers belonging to the Society, and pay, (if in funds,) all such orders drawn by the Board of Managers, signed by the President, and attested by the Recording Secretary.

He shall annually report to the Board of Managers the state of the treasury, or as often as they may direct; and at the expiration of his term, if not re-elected, shall hand over all the books, papers and funds of the Society to his successor, within thirty days.

ARTICLE VII

The Financial Committee shall have under their care the pecuniary concerns of the Society, and everything in relation thereto: they shall also audit the accounts of the Treasurer.

They shall report to the Board of Managers, from time to time, bills or provisions for the increase of the funds, or appropriations of the same, as they may deem in their judgment expedient, that the same may be considered or approved.

ARTICLE VIII

The Soliciting Committee shall be provided with books for the purpose of receiving subscriptions or donations, wherein shall be registered the names, and amount so received.

ARTICLE IX

The several Committees shall record, for the future use of the Society, all important observations that may relate to the subject of their charge.

The Board of Managers shall report to the Society quarterly; and at the annual meeting, their report shall be printed in pamphlet form.

ARTICLE X

All Societies auxiliary to this shall, when formed, duly notify the Board of Managers of the Parent Society, through its Corresponding Secretary, taking care to forward a copy of their organization and proceedings, to be entered upon the records of the Society.

And with the view of more effectually strengthening a general union among the Free People of Colour, it shall be the duty of each auxiliary Society respectively, to elect from among their own members, one individual as Vice President of the Parent Society.

At a meeting of the Parent Society, held on Monday the 30th of November, 1830, the following persons were elected Officers for the ensuing year, viz.:

President—Rev. Richard Allen.

Vice Presidents—Messrs. John Bowers, Rob't Brown, Daniel D. Brownhill, Peter Gardiner.

Corresponding Secretary—William Whipper.

Recording Secretary—Charles H. Leveck.
Assistant Secretaries—John P. Thompson, Samuel D. Potts.
Treasurer—James Johnson.
Board of Managers—Dr. Belfast Burton, Messrs. John P. Burr, Scipio Sewell, John Allen, (Porter,) Richard Howell, Joseph Cassey, Shedrich Basset, James Gibson, Jeremiah Bowser, Richard B. Johnson, James Newman, Henry Beckett, Peter McNeal, James Bird, Abraham Williams.
Corresponding Committee—Dr. Belfast Burton, Messrs. Daniel B. Brownhill, John B. Sammons, Frederick A. Hinton, Rev. Richard Allen.
Financial Committee—Messrs. Charles W. Gardner, John B. Sammons, Thomas Butler.
Soliciting Committee—Rev. Richard Allen, Messrs. Samuel Nickels, William James, Joseph Cassey, Thomas Channock, Thomas Butler, William C. West, Robert Johnson, Joshua Brown, Edward Johnson, Jeremiah Bowser, Prince G. Laws, Samuel Combegy.
Publishing Committee—Dr. Belfast Burton, Messrs. William Whipper, John Dutton.

CONVENTION OF PEOPLE OF COLOUR

AS much anxiety has prevailed on account of the enactment of laws in several States of the Union, especially that of Ohio, abridging the liberties and privileges of the Free People of Colour, and subjecting them to a series of privations and sufferings, by denying them a right of residence, unless they comply with certain requisitions not exacted of the Whites, a course altogether incompatible with the principles of civil and religious liberty.

In consideration of which, a delegation* was appointed from the states of Connecticut, New York, Pennsylvania, Delaware, and Maryland, to meet in Convention in Philadelphia, to consider the propriety of forming a settlement in the province of Upper Canada, in order to afford a place of refuge to those who may be obliged to leave their homes, as well as to others inclined to emigrate with the view of improving their condition.

The said Convention accordingly met in Bethel Church, city of Philadelphia, on the 20th of September, 1830; and having fully considered the peculiar situation of many of their brethren, and the

* In consequence of not having had timely notice, delegates from other sections of the country did not attend; though it is hoped that at the Convention on the first Monday in June next, there will be a more general representation.

advantages to be derived from the proposed settlement, adopted the following

ADDRESS

To the Free People of Colour of these United States

Brethren,

Impressed with a firm and settled conviction, and more especially being taught by that inestimable and invaluable instrument, namely, the Declaration of Independence, that all men are born free and equal, and consequently are endowed with unalienable rights, among which are the enjoyments of life, liberty, and the pursuits of happiness.

Viewing these as incontrovertible facts, we have been led to the following conclusions; that our forlorn and deplorable situation earnestly and loudly demand of us to devise and pursue all legal means for the speedy elevation of ourselves and brethren to the scale and standing of men.

And in pursuit of this great object, various ways and means have been resorted to; among others, the African Colonization Society is the most prominent. Not doubting the sincerity of many friends who are engaged in that cause; yet we beg leave to say, that it does not meet with our approbation. However great the debt which these United States may owe to injured Africa, and however unjustly her sons have been made to bleed, and her daughters to drink of the cup of affliction, still we who have been born and nurtured on this soil, we, whose habits, manners, and customs are the same in common with other Americans, can never consent to take our lives in our hands, and be the bearers of the redress offered by that Society to that much afflicted country.

Tell it not to barbarians, lest they refuse to be civilised, and eject our Christian missionaries from among them, that in the nineteenth century of the Christian era, laws have been enacted in some of the states of this great republic, to compel an unprotected and harmless portion of our brethren, to leave their homes and seek an asylum in foreign climes: and in taking a view of the unhappy situation of many of these, whom the oppressive laws alluded to, continually crowd into the Atlantic cities, dependent for their support upon their daily labour, and who often suffer for want of employment, we have had to lament that no means have yet been devised for their relief.

These considerations have led us to the conclusion that the formation of a settlement in the British province of Upper Canada would be a great advantage to the people of colour. In accordance with these views, we pledge ourselves to aid each other by all honourable

means, to plant and support one in that country, and therefore we
earnestly and most feelingly appeal to our coloured brethren, and to
all philanthropists here and elsewhere, to assist in this benevolent
and important work.

To encourage our brethren earnestly to cooperate with us, we
offer the following, viz. 1st. Under that government no invidious
distinction of colour is recognised, but there we shall be entitled to
all the rights, privileges, and immunities of other citizens. 2d. That
the language, climate, soil, and productions are similar to those in
this country. 3d. That land of the best quality can be purchased at
the moderate price of one dollar and fifty cents per acre, by the
one hundred acres. 4th. The market for different kinds of produce
raised in that colony, is such as to render a suitable reward to the
industrious farmer, equal in our opinion to that of the United States.
And lastly, as the erection of buildings must necessarily claim the
attention of the emigrants, we would invite the mechanics from our
large cities to embark in the enterprise; the advancement of architecture depending much on their exertions, as they must consequently take with them the arts and improvements of our well-
regulated communities.

It will be much to the advantage of those who have large families,
and desire to see them happy and respected, to locate themselves
in a land where the laws and prejudices of society will have no
effect in retarding their advancement to the summit of civil and
religious improvement. There the diligent student will have ample
opportunity to reap the reward due to industry and perseverance;
whilst those of moderate attainments, if properly nurtured, may be
enabled to take their stand as men in the several offices and situations necessary to promote union, peace, order and tranquility. It
is to these we must look for the strength and spirit of our future
prosperity.

Before we close, we would just remark, that it has been a subject
of deep regret to this convention, that we as a people have not
availingly appreciated every opportunity placed within our power
by the benevolent efforts of the friends of humanity in elevating our
condition to the rank of freemen. That our mental and physical
qualities have not been more actively engaged in pursuits more
lasting is attributable in a great measure to a want of unity among
ourselves; whilst our only stimulus to action has been to become
domestics, which at best is but a precarious and degraded situation.

It is to obviate these evils that we have recommended our views
to our fellow citizens in the foregoing instrument, with a desire of
raising the moral and political standing of ourselves; and we cannot

devise any plan more likely to accomplish this end, than by encouraging agriculture and mechanical arts: for by the first, we shall be enabled to act with a degree of independence, which as yet has fallen to the lot of but few among us; and the faithful pursuit of the latter, in connection with the sciences, which expand and ennoble the mind, will eventually give us the standing and condition we desire.

To effect these great objects, we would earnestly request our brethren throughout the United States, to cooperate with us, by forming societies *auxiliary* to the Parent Institution, about being established in the city of Philadelphia, under the patronage of the General Convention. And we further recommend to our friends and brethren, who reside in places where, at present, this may be impracticable, so far to aid us, by contributing to the funds of the Parent Institution; and, if disposed, to appoint one delegate to represent them in the next Convention, to be held in Philadelphia the first Monday in June next, it being fully understood, that organized societies be at liberty to send any number of delegates not exceeding five.

Signed by order of the Convention,

Rev. RICHARD ALLEN, *President*,
Senior Bishop of the African Methodist Episcopal Churches.
JUNIUS C. MOREL, *Secretary*.

MINUTES

OF THE

FOUR LAST ANNUAL CONFERENCES

OF THE

AFRICAN

Methodist Episcopal Church

HELD

At Pittsburg, (Pa.,) Washington, (D.C.,) Philadelphia,
and New York, 1833–4.

PHILADELPHIA:
PUBLISHED BY JOSEPH M. CORR,
General Book Steward for the Conferences of the African Methodist
Episcopal Church in the United States of America.
1834.

THIRD OHIO ANNUAL CONFERENCE
OF THE
AFRICAN METHODIST EPISCOPAL CHURCH,
HELD
AT PITTSBURG, PA., SEPTEMBER 14TH, 1833.

THE third Ohio Annual Conference of the African Methodist
Episcopal Church: met in the city of Pittsburg, on the 14th of
September, and continued by adjournments, until the 23d, inclusive.
Right Reverend Morris Brown, Bishop of the A.M.E.C., called the

Conference to order, and presided during its session: Lewis Woodson, Secretary.

MEMBERS PRESENT.

Rev. *John Boggs,**   Rev. *William P. Quinn,*
Wiley Reynolds,   *Thomas Lawrence,*
Austin Jones,   *James Bird,*
Jeremiah Thomas,   Abraham D. Lewis,
Lewis Woodson,   Samuel Collins,
Samuel Johnson,   George Coleman,
Samuel Enty,   Samuel Clingman,

Pleasant Underwood.

The Bishop delivered an appropriate and impressive address to the members of this Conference, on the importance of promoting harmony and good feeling among themselves, and all Christian people, and that they should study to show themselves in all their pursuits, "approved of God."

The method of proceeding in the Annual Conferences is to inquire,—

Question. 1. What preachers are admitted on trial?

Answer. None.

Q. 2. Who remain on trial?

A. Pleasant Underwood.

Q. 3. Who are admitted into full connexion?

A. James Bird, Samuel Collins, Thomas Lawrence, Jeremiah Thomas, Lewis Woodson, Abraham D. Lewis, George Coleman, Samuel Johnson, Samuel Clingman, Henry Adkerson, Thomas Baldwin, Peter James, Samuel Webster.

Q. 4. Who are the deacons?

A. Samuel Collins, Lewis Woodson, Henry Adkerson, Abraham D. Lewis, Samuel Johnson, George Coleman, Samuel Enty, Jeremiah Thomas,** and Pleasant Underwood.**

Q. 5. Who have been elected and ordained elders this year?

A. None.

Q. 6. Who have located this year?

A. Samuel Enty and James Bird.

Q. 7. Who has been elected by the General Conference to exercise the Episcopal office, and superintend the African Methodist church in America.

---

* Those whose names are Italicised, are travelling ministers.

** The ministers whose names are marked with double asterisks were ordained this year.

A. Morris Brown.
Q. 8. Who have been expelled from the connexion this year.
A. None.
Q. 9. Who have withdrawn this year?
A. None.
Q. 10. Are all the preachers blameless in life, and conversation?
A. They have been examined, one by one, and stood fair.
Q. 11. Who have died this year?
A. *Samuel Madison,* an unordained travelling preacher, who was appointed at the last Conference to Hillsborough circuit, under the charge of James Bird, who finished his course, and his life together, dying in the triumphs of faith.
Q. 12. What numbers are in society?

PITTSBURG CIRCUIT—

Pittsburg,	220
Washington,	50
Uniontown,	36
	306

ZANESVILLE CIRCUIT—

Zanesville,	45
Captien,	50
Mount Pleasant,	40
Smithfield,	20
Steubenville,	24
Wheeling,	26
	205

COLUMBUS CIRCUIT—

Columbus,	60
Urbana,	40
New Lancaster,	40
Circlesville,	12
Springfield,	14
	166

CHILICOTHE CIRCUIT—

Chilicothe,	92
Big Bottom,	16
Jackson,	25
Galloplace,	60
	193

HILLSBOROUGH CIRCUIT—

Hillsborough,	30
Wilmington,	22
Zana,	18
Daton,	24
Harden's Creek,	20
White Oak,	12
	126
Cincinnati,	190

Several other places not returned.

Whole amount returned, 1194.

Q. 13. Where are the preachers stationed this year?

A.

Pittsburg, Pa.,	William P. Quinn.
Zanesville, Ohio,	Austin Jones.
Columbus,	Wiley Reynolds.
Chilicothe,	Jeremiah Thomas.
Hillsborough,	Thomas Lawrence.
Cincinnati,	John Boggs.

Q. 14. Where and when, shall our next Conference be held?

A. Pittsburg, September 20th, 1834.

The following important resolutions were passed at this Conference.

Resolved, As the sense of this Conference, That common Schools, Sunday Schools, and Temperance Societies, are of the highest importance to all people, but more especially to us, as a people.

Resolved, That it shall be the duty of every member of this Conference, to do all in his power to promote and establish these useful institutions among our people.

At the close of this Conference, God was pleased, in a most miraculous manner to display his power at the Love Feast: many souls were added to the Lord.

Adjourned until 1834.

NINETEENTH
BALTIMORE ANNUAL CONFERENCE,
OF THE
AFRICAN METHODIST EPISCOPAL CHURCH,
CONVENED
IN WASHINGTON CITY, D.C., APRIL 19TH, 1834.

The Conference met, according to appointment, Saturday morning, April 19th, 1834; and sat by adjournments until Monday, 28th, inclusive.

The house was called to order, and organized, after singing and prayer by the Right Rev. Morris Brown, Bishop of the A.M.E. Church, who presided during its session, assisted by the Rev. E. Waters; Levin Lee, Secretary.

MEMBERS WHO WERE PRESENT DURING ITS SITTING.

Rev. *E. Waters,*   Walter Proctor,
  William Cornish,   Levin Lee,
  John Cornish,   Jeremiah Durham,
  Noah C. Cannon,   Jeremiah Brown,
  William Moore,   Joseph M. Corr,
  William A. Nicholas,   Jeffrey Goulden,
                    Basil Simms.

Q. 1. What preachers were admitted on trial?
A. Jeffrey Goulden.
Q. 2. Who remain on trial?
A. William Moore, Basil Simms, and Southey Hammonds.
Q. 3. Who are admitted into full connexion?
A. William A. Nichols.
Q. 4. Who are the deacons?
A. Charles Dunn, Levin Lee, Nathaniel Peck, Aaron Wilson, Jeremiah Brown, Stephen Smith, William A. Nichols,* and William Moore.*
Q. 5. Who have been elected and ordained elders this year?
A. None.
Q. 6. Who have located this year?
A. None.
Q. 7. Who have been expelled from the connexion this year?
A. None.
Q. 8. Who have withdrawn this year?
A. None.
Q. 9. Are all the preachers blameless?
A. They were particularly examined, and stood fair.
Q. 10. Who have died this year?
A. 1. Abner Coker, a useful and zealous local deacon, who departed this life, in the full assurance of faith, and full of years, in the city of Baltimore, in the fall of 1833: he has left behind him a widow, and a large number of bereaved children, who "sorrow not as those who have no hope." "The righteous shall be had in everlasting remembrance."
   2. John Gustive, a licensed local preacher, who formerly lived on the Eastern Shore of Maryland. He was a slave until 1830, when he

received permission from his owner to raise means to release himself and a large family from the wretched fetters of slavery: he had only partly accomplished his wishes, in relieving a part with himself; but while in the full pursuit of completing his desires, death arrested his course in the month of November last, and disappointed his calculations. He was a man of sound piety, and died in the earnest expectation of that hope, which St. Paul, declares is the certain portion of all who "love the appearing of our Lord Jesus Christ."

Q. 11. What numbers are in society?

A. Baltimore charge, 1300
   Washington, D.C., 225

CHAMBERSBURG CIRCUIT—

Chambersburg,	114
Mercersburg,	34
Carlisle,	24
Columbia,	106
Lancaster,	41
Marietta,	33
Reading,	32
Lewistown and others not returned	384

FRENCHTOWN CIRCUIT—

Bohemia,	45
Thoroughfareneck,	38
Ironhill,	14
	97

Whole amount returned, 2006

Q. 12. Where are the preachers stationed this year?

A. Baltimore, Rev. Edward Waters,
   Chambersburg, and Columbia circuit, } Francis P. Graham, one to be supplied.
   Washington, D.C., William Cornish.
   Lewistown, Pa., Jeremiah Miller.

Frederick City, and Hagerstown, to be served once in three months, or as often as convenient, by Levin Lee.

Easton, Md., left in the same way with William A. Nichols.

Q. 13. Where, and when, shall our next Conference be held?

A. In the city of Baltimore—1835.

Adjourned until 1835.

The sitting of this Conference was attended with unusual success; it, being the first coloured body that has ever convened in the capital of the United States, caused great excitement. Many hundreds, both of white and coloured, assembled at the preaching hours, especially on the Lord's day, and listened with delight to the ambassadors of the cross; who, on this occasion, were endued with more than usual energy. Several were cut to the heart, and fourteen came forward professing their faith in Christ, and joined the society. The authorities of the city expressed their good feeling, and offered their protection, should any evil designed persons attempt any interruption. His Excellency, the President of the United States, being waited upon, expressed his warmest approbation of the proceedings of the Conference, and wished a hearty success to the cause in which these distinguished followers of Christ were engaged; "peace on earth, and good will to men."

> Let all the sons of Adam raise
> The honours of their God.

NINETEENTH ANNUAL CONFERENCE
OF THE
PHILADELPHIA DISTRICT OF THE AFRICAN METHODIST EPISCOPAL CHURCH,
CONVENED, ACCORDING TO APPOINTMENT, MAY 24TH, 1834,
IN THE CITY OF PHILADELPHIA.

The Conference convened at the usual place on Saturday morning, May 24th, 1834, and was duly organized, and met with adjournments from time to time, until Tuesday, June 3d, 1834, and then adjourned *sine die* until the next year.

MEMBERS PRESENT.
Rev. Bishop Brown, President.
Edward Waters, Assistant.
Joseph M. Corr, Secretary.

Rev. *Samuel Todd,*	*William Moore,*
Jeremiah Miller,	Jeremiah Bulah,
William Cornish,	Samson Peters,
John Cornish,	Clayton Durham,
Peter D. W. Schureman,	Walter Proctor,
Noah C. Cannan,	Jeremiah Durham,
Israel Scott,	Shadrach Bassitt,
Richard, Robison,	Marcus Brown,
Reuben Cuff,	London Turpin,
Moses Robinson,	Stephen Smith,
Joshua P. B. Eddy,	Abraham Marks,

Charles A. Spicer,	Charles Dunn,
Adam Clincher,	Benjamin Potter,
Andrew Massey,	Samuel Edwards,
Wardell Parker,	Henry Brown,
Joseph Oliver,	Aaron Wilson,
Benjamin Wilson,	Robert Evans,
John Hight,	Thomas Hall.

Q. 1. What preachers are admitted on trial?

A. None.

Q. 2. Who remain on trial?

A. Perry Gibson and Benjamin Wilson.

Q. 3. Who are admitted into full connexion?

A. None.

Q. 4. Who are the deacons?

A. Jeremiah Bulah,
Walter Proctor,
Clayton Durham,
Shadrach Bassitt, } Philadelphia.
Adam Clincher,
Marcus Brown,
Joseph M. Corr,
Jeremiah Durham,
William Henry, West-Town, Pa.
Samson Peters, Trenton, N.J.
Andrew Massey, Dagsborough, Del.

Q. 5. Who have been elected, and ordained elders this year?

A. None.

Q. 6. Who have located this year?

A. None.

Q. 7. Who have been expelled from the connexion this year?

A. Lewis Cork and Anthony Campbell, for immoral conduct.

Q. 8. Who have withdrawn this year?

A. None.

Q. 9. Are the preachers blameless?

A. With the exception of the two before named, their characters were individually examined, and stood fair.

Q. 10. Who have died this year?

A. Joseph Harper, who was born in Flushing, Long Island, N.Y. He experienced religion about twelve years of age, and joined the Methodist church; soon after which, he began to exhort. In the year 1823, he joined the travelling connexion of the African Methodist Episcopal Church, and was appointed to the Bucks county, Pa., circuit, under the charge of the Rev. William P. Quinn, was ordained deacon at Philadelphia, 1824, and elder 1825. He successively travelled Bucks, Salem, N.J., Trenton, N.J., Lewiston, Del., Lancaster, and Chambersburg circuits.

Brother Harper, in his various appointments, discharged the duties of a zealous, pious, and persevering travelling minister, and ended his life in the itinerancy, after labouring almost eleven years. He was attacked in the summer of 1833 with a pulmonary complaint, which, at the approach of winter, brought on an afflictive illness. He returned home, after finding his case hopeless, in January, and died without a struggle or groan, on the first day of February, 1834. Brother Harper was a sincere friend, a consistent and uniform Christian, an exemplary preacher, a sincere husband and kind parent. In his last illness he expressed a great confidence in the merits of a Saviour's death, and was often enraptured in the sweet anticipation of an everlasting rest.

"He being dead, yet speaketh."

"Mark the perfect man, and behold the upright, for the end of that man is peace."

II. Joseph Chaine, many years a local deacon. He formerly lived on the eastern shore of Maryland, but removed to Philadelphia, in the year 1832, where he died, after a protracted illness, in January, 1834.

Q. 11. What numbers are in the Society?

PHILADELPHIA CHARGE—

Bethel church,	1500
Union church,	140
Hosanna church,	26
Academy,	22
	1688

BUCKS AND CHESTER COUNTY CIRCUIT—

Frankford,	39
Bensalem,	70
Attleborough,	30
New Hope,	38
Buckingham,	29
Hamilton Village,	24
Tea Chester,	13
Thornbury,	59
West-Town,	69
West Chester,	39
Valley,	65
	475

NEW JERSEY—TRENTON CIRCUIT—

Trenton,	97
Princeton,	54
New Brunswick,	65
Brumagen,	10
Rahway,	40
Elizabeth-Town,	8
	274

BURLINGTON CIRCUIT—

Burlington,	32
Mount Holly,	60
Wescott's Neck,	20
Pemberton,	18
Egypt,	15
Snowhill,	60
Camden,	23
Woodbury,	17
	245

SALEM CIRCUIT—

Salem,	79
Bush-Town,	39
Dutch-Town,	36
Greenwich,	122
Fairfield,	41
Backneck,	24
	341

DELAWARE—LEWISTOWN CIRCUIT—

Lewistown,	29
Georgetown,	25
Slaughterneck,	46
Milton,	18
Indian River,	40
Laurel,	35
Dagsborough,	20
	213

Whole amount, 3236

Q. 12. What has been collected for the contingent expenses, aiding the preachers, &c.?

A. Salem Circuit,	$7.60
Philadelphia,	81.90
	89.50

Q. 13. How has this been expended?

A.

Superintendent's allowance,	25.00
Postage of letters,	6.00
Horses' stabling during session,	18.50
Apportioned for travelling expenses of preachers, &c. &c. &c.,	40.00
	89.50

The "Daughters of Conference Society" presented the travelling ministry with the sum of $50.10, which was divided according to their constitution, in the following manner:

Rev. W. Cornish,	4.81
I. Cornish,	4.81
S. Todd,	4.81
P. D. W. Schureman,	4.81
Israel Scott,	4.81
Richard Robison,	4.81
Jeremiah Miller,	4.81
Jeremiah Bulah,	4.81
Edward Waters,	4.81
William Moore,	4.81
Noah C. Cannon,	2.00
	50.10

Q. 14. Where are the preachers stationed this year?

A. Philadelphia,   } Rev. Mr. Brown, assisted by the Rev. I. Cornish.

Bucks county circuit,	Rev. Israel Scott.
Trenton, N.J., circuit,	Richard Robison.
Burlington circuit,	John Cornish.
Salem circuit,	P. D. W. Schureman.
Lewistown, Del., circuit,	} Peter Lewis and Moses Robison.

Q. 15. Where and when shall our next conference be held?

A. In the city of Philadelphia, 1835.

The following important resolutions were passed at this conference.

Resolved, That the Rev. Richard Robison be received into the travelling connexion.

Resolved, That Charles A. Spicer be received back in the connexion, as a local elder.

Resolved, That Frenchtown circuit be attached to Baltimore district.

Resolved, That it shall be the duty of all the preachers of this Conference strictly and perseveringly to recommend the "Temperance Cause" in their respective circuits or stations, both by example and precept; and should a complaint of default in this particular be made against any preacher, he shall be dealt with by the senior preacher, according to the provisions made for all cases of imprudence and neglect of duty in our form of discipline.

Resolved, That as the subject of education is one that highly interests all people, and especially the coloured people of this country, it shall be the duty of every minister who has the charge of circuits or stations, to use every exertion to establish schools wherever convenient, and to insist upon parents sending their children to school; and to preach occasionally a sermon on the subject of education; and it shall be the duty of all such ministers to make returns yearly of the number of schools, the amount of scholars, the branches taught, and the places in which they are located; and that every minister neglecting so to do, be subject to the censure of the Conference.

Resolved, That all the ministers in charge advise the members of our church, in the circuits and stations within our bounds, to raise the average sum of twelve and a half cents from each member within one year, to aid the publishing fund.

Resolved, That it is the duty of every preacher in charge of this Conference, to take up collections yearly in every principal appointment in his circuit or station, to assist in the promulgation of the gospel, by aiding those who are labouring in the itinerancy; and that, if any minister shall neglect so to do, he shall be liable to the censure of the Conference.

To accomplish this desirable end, they can read and enlarge upon the following hints.

How shall we send labourers into those parts where they are most wanting? Many are willing to hear, but not to bear the expense. Nor can it as yet be expected of them; stay till the word of God has touched their hearts, and then they will gladly provide for those who preach it. Does it not lie upon us, in the mean time, to supply their lack of service? To raise money, out of which, from time to time, that expense may be defrayed. By this means those who willingly offer themselves, may travel through every part, whether there be societies or not, and stay wherever there is a call, without being burdensome to any. Thus may the gospel, in the life and power thereof, be spread from sea to sea.

Which of you will not rejoice to throw in your mite to promote this glorious work? Besides this, in carrying on so large a work through the continent, there are calls for money in various ways, and we must frequently be at considerable expense, or the work must be at a full stop.

The money contributed, will be brought or sent to the ensuing Conference.

THIRTEENTH ANNUAL CONFERENCE,
OF THE
NEW YORK DISTRICT OF THE AFRICAN METHODIST EPISCOPAL CHURCH,
HELD
IN THE CITY OF BROOKLYN, L. I., BY ADJOURNMENTS FROM 14TH, TO 23D JUNE, INCLUSIVE.

The thirteenth New York Annual Conference of the African Methodist Episcopal church, convened in the city of Brooklyn, L. I., according to appointment on Saturday morning June 14th, 1834; after singing and prayer the Conference was organized, by the

Rev. Bishop Brown, President.
Rev. Edward Waters, Assistant.
George Hogarth, Secretary.

MEMBERS WHO WERE PRESENT DURING THE SITTING OF THE CONFERENCE.

Rev. *Richard Williams,*
Samuel Todd,
Richard Robinson,
John Cornish,
Francis P. Graham,
William Moore,
Noah C. Cannon,
Peter D. W. Schureman,
Benjamin Croger,
James Burton,
Edmund Crosby,
Jeremiah Bulah,
John Scott,
Enoch Smith,
Samuel Edwards,
Jacob Smith,
Clayton Durham,
Fortune Matthias,
Abraham Marks,
Henry Brown, of
  Flushing, L. I.
Henry Brown, of P.
London Turpin,
Edward Thompson,
Peter Croger,
James Thompson,
William P. Williams,
Anthony Treadwill,
Eli N. Hall,
Sampson Peters,
Hercules Schureman,
John Morris.

The Bishop, in his usual manner, delivered an impressive lecture, at the opening of the Conference, on the subject of exemplary living, as ministers of the cross of Jesus Christ, and to show to all with whom they have to do, that they are influenced by the Holy Spirit, to go forth, in the promotion of the glorious gospel among the children of men; after which the Conference proceeded to the usual business.

Q. 1. What preachers are admitted on trial?
A. John Scott and Enoch Smith.
Q. 2. Who remain on trial?
A. Francis P. Graham.
Q. 3. Who are admitted into full connexion?
A. Cuffy Spence, Eli N. Hall, and Anthony Treadwill.
Q. 4. Who are the deacons?

A. Fortune Matthias,
London Turpin,
Abraham Marks,
Edmund Crosby,   } New York city.
William P. Williams,
James Burton,

Benjamin Croger,
Peter Croger,   } Brooklyn, L. I.
George Hogarth,

Henry Brown,
Jacob Smith,   } Long Island.

Q. 5. Who have been elected, and ordained elders this year?
A. Francis P. Graham.
Q. 6. Who have located this year?
A. Noah C. Cannon, applied for location and was granted.
Q. 7. Who have been elected by the General Conference, to exercise the Episcopal office, and superintend the African Methodist Church in America?
A. Right Rev. Morris Brown.
Q. 8. Who have been expelled from the connexion this year?
A. None.
Q. 9. Who have withdrawn this year?
A. None.
Q. 10. Are all the preachers blameless in life and conversation?
A. They were examined one by one, and stood fair.
Q. 11. Who have died this year?
A. None.
Q. 12. What numbers are in society?

A. New York city,   380
Brooklyn city,   182
Rock Hall, N.J.,   37
                         ―――
                         599

LONG ISLAND CIRCUIT—

Flushing,	76
Jamaica,	12
Huntington, South,	84
Jericho,	5
Hemstead Harbour,	26
Musquito Cove,	18
	171
Albany city, N.Y.,	45
Whole amount,	815

Q. 13. What has been collected for the contingent expenses, &c.?
A. New York city, $43.25
   Brooklyn city,   20.50
   Long Island circuit,   1.50
   Albany city,   2.05
                            $67.30

Q. 14. How has this been expended?
A. In defraying the expenses of the Conference.
Q. 15. Where are the preachers stationed this year?
A. New York, and Brooklyn,   Rev. Samuel Todd.
   Albany,   Richard Williams.
   Long Island circuit,   William Moore.
Francis P. Graham, transferred to Baltimore Conference.
Q. 16. Where, and when, shall our next Conference be held?
A. In the city of New York, 1835.

The following resolutions were adopted at this Conference.
Resolved, That we will make use of all disciplinary measures, both by precept and example, to promote and extend the temperance cause.
Resolved, That common and Sunday schools, be warmly and perseveringly advocated, and insisted upon, among our members, by the preachers having the charge of circuits or stations in this Conference.
Resolved, That we deprecate the pernicious and baneful effects of lottery dealing, and that the preachers of this Conference use their influence to discourage the buying and selling of lottery tickets.
Resolved, That Abraham Marks be appointed book steward, for New York District, Benjamin Croger having resigned on account of ill state of health.
Resolved, That the Minutes of this Conference be printed.
The "Rock of Wisdom," a book published by the Rev. N. C. Cannon, was taken up by the Conference, and after a thorough investi-

gation of its contents, it was found to contain many erroneous principles, repugnant to the articles of faith, believed and taught by the Methodist church. Brother Cannon came forward and acknowledged that he was convinced thereof, and that he was sorry for it: his acknowledgment was received, and the book condemned by the Conference, as being erroneous and unfit for circulation.

Adjourned until 1835.

A LIST OF PREACHERS WHO WERE IN CONNEXION WITH THE "AFRICAN METHODIST EPISCOPAL CHURCH," BUT WHO HAVE DIED, WITHDRAWN, OR HAVE BEEN EXPELLED.

Right Rev. Richard Allen, first bishop of the "African Methodist Episcopal Church," died 1831.

ELDERS.

Rev. *Enos Adams,*	died,	1832.
William Allen,	expelled,	1831.
Anthony Campbell,	expelled,	1834.
Lewis Cork,	expelled,	1834.
William Cousins,	expelled,	1832.
Joseph Cox,	expelled,	1832.
Stephen Dutton,	withdrawn,	1826.
Moses Freeman,	died,	1825.
Henry Harden,	expelled,	1830.
Joseph Harper,	died,	1834.
Jacob Matthews,	withdrawn,	1828.
William Miller,	withdrawn,	1826.
Charles Pierce,	died,	1833.
Jacob Richardson,	expelled,	1828.
William Richardson,	died,	1832.
Samuel Ridley,	died,	1828.
Thomas Robison,	died,	1824.
David Smith,	withdrawn,	1824.
Nathan Tarman,	expelled,	1833.
James Towson,	expelled,	1833.
Thomas Webster,	died,	1828.
George White,	expelled,	1829.

DEACONS.

Joseph Chainc,	died,	1834.
Abner Coker,	died,	1833.
Charles Corr,	died,	1827.
Henry Drayton,	withdrawn,	1830.

Henry Fox,	died,	1830.
Edward Johnson,	withdrawn,	1824.
William Johnson,	died,	1833.
Reuben Melvin,	expelled,	1828.
James Savin,	withdrawn,	1833.
Jacob Williams,	expelled,	1833.

PREACHERS.

Henry Allen,	expelled,	1831.
Abraham Anderson,	expelled,	1829.
George Anderson,	expelled,	1826.
Philip Brodie,	died,	1829.
David Crosby,	withdrawn,	1826.
Thomas A. Dorsey,	expelled,	1829.
Charles Gray,	expelled,	1827.
John Gustiff,	died,	1834.
George Hicks,	died,	1830.
Michael Parker,	died,	1824.
Stephen Stanford,	died,	1831.
James Scott,	expelled,	1824.
William Shorts,	expelled,	1827.
James Wilson,	died,	1827.
Peter Woods,	died,	1825.

PREACHERS WHO ARE NOW IN CONNEXION, AND WHO WERE IN GOOD
STANDING AS MEMBERS OF THE LAST ANNUAL CONFERENCES.

ELDERS.

Rev. *Edward Waters,*
William Cornish,
Samuel Todd,
Jeremiah Miller,
Richard Williams,
John Cornish,
Israel Scott,
Peter D. W. Schureman,
Francis P. Graham,
William P. Quinn,
Joshua P. B. Eddy,
Charles A. Spicer,

Rev. *John Boggs,*
Austin Jones,
Wiley Reynolds,
Thomas Lawrence,
Richard Robison,
Moses Robison,
Peter Lewis,
Reuben Cuff,
Edward Jackson,
Noah C. Cannon,
James Bird,
George W. Boler,

Isaac Miller.

DEACONS.

Rev. *William Moore,*
Clayton Durham,
Adam Clincher,

Rev. *Jeremiah Thomas,*
Walter Proctor,
Joseph M. Corr,

Marcus Brown,
Shadrach Bassitt,
William Henry,
Benjamin Croger,
George Hogarth,
Jacob Smith,
Abraham Marks,
William P. Williams,
Aaron Wilson,
Charles Dunn,
Jeremiah Brown,
William A. Nichols,
Henry Adkerson,
Abraham D. Lewis,
Samuel Collins,
Samuel Enty,
Jeremiah Durham,
Jeremiah Bulah,
Andrew Massey,
Peter Croger,
Henry Brown,
Edmund Crosby,
James Burton,
Fortune Matthias,
Levin Lee,
Nathaniel Peck,
Stephen Smith,
Lewis Woodson,
Pleasant Underwood,
George Coleman,
Samuel Johnson,
Sampson Peters,

London Turpin.

PREACHERS.

Henry Brown,
Benjamin Potter,
Joseph Oliver,
Benjamin Wilson,
Robert Evans,
Wardel Parker,
Thomas Hall,
John Hight,
John Messer,
Cuffee Spence,
Eli N. Hall,
John Morris,
Edward Thompson,
Thomas Banks,
Jeffrey Goulden,
Fathan Blake,
Jacob Ringold,
Peter James,
Samuel Webster,
Thomas Baldwin,
Samuel Clingman,
Basil Simms,
Enoch Smith,
Samuel Edwards,
James Thompson,
John Scott,
Anthony Treadwill,
Perry Gibson,

Israel Williams.

Preachers, not members of the Conference, [list] not returned.

Minutes and Proceedings

OF THE

FIRST ANNUAL MEETING

OF THE

AMERICAN MORAL REFORM SOCIETY

Held at Philadelphia

In the Presbyterian Church in Seventh Street, below Shippen, from
the 14th to the 19th of August, 1837.

PHILADELPHIA:
PRINTED BY MERRIHEW AND GUNN,
No. 7 Carter's Alley.
1837.

DECLARATION OF SENTIMENT.

That this Convention earnestly deplore the depressed condition of
the coloured population of the United States; and they have in vain
searched the history of nations to find a parallel.

They claim to be the offspring of a parentage, that once, for their
excellence of attainment in the arts, literature and science, stood
before the world unrivalled. We have mournfully observed the fall
of those institutions that shed lustre on our mother country, and
extended to Greece and Rome those refinements that made them
objects of admiration to the cultivators of science.

We have observed, that in no country under Heaven have the
descendants of an *ancestry* once enrolled in the history of fame,
whose glittering monuments stood forth as beacons, disseminating
light and knowledge to the uttermost parts of the earth, been re-

duced to such degrading servitude as that under which we labour from the effect of American slavery and American prejudice.

The separation of our fathers from the land of their birth, earthly ties and early affections, was not only sinful in its nature and tendency, but it led to a system of robbery, bribery and persecution offensive to the laws of nature and of justice.

Therefore, under whatever pretext or authority these laws have been promulgated or executed, whether under parliamentary, colonial, or American legislation, we declare them in the sight of Heaven wholly null and void, and should be immediately abrogated.

That we find ourselves, after the lapse of two centuries on the American continent, the remnants of a nation amounting to three millions of people, whose country has been pillaged, parents stolen, nine generations of which have been wasted by the oppressive cruelty of this nation, standing in the presence of the Supreme Ruler of the Universe, and the civilized world, appealing to the God of nations for deliverance.

Surely there is no people on earth whose patriotic appeals for liberty and justice possess more hallowed claims on the just interposition of Divine Providence, to aid them in removing the most unqualified system of tyranny and oppression under which human beings ever groaned.

We rejoice that it is our lot to be the inhabitants of a country blest by nature with a genial climate and fruitful soil, and where the liberty of speech and the press is protected by law.

We rejoice that we are thrown into a revolution where the contest is not for landed territory, but for freedom; the weapons not carnal, but spiritual; where struggle is not for blood, but for right; and where the bow is the power of God, and the arrow the instrument of divine justice; while the victims are the devices of *reason,* and the prejudice of the human heart. It is in this glorious struggle for civil and religious liberty, for the establishment of peace on earth and good will to men, that we are morally bound by all the relative ties we owe to the author of our being, to enter the arena and boldly contend for victory.

Our reliance and only hope is in God. If success attend the effort, the downfall of Africa from her ancient pride and splendor will have been more than glorious to the establishment of religion; every drop of blood spilt by her descendants under the dominion of prejudice and persecution will have produced peaceful rivers, that shall wash from the soil of the human heart the mountains of vice and corruption under which this nation has long withered.

And if our presence in this country will aid in producing such a desirable reform, although we have been reared under a most debasing system of tyranny and oppression, we shall have been born under the most favourable auspices to promote the redemption of the world; for our very sighs and groans, like the blood of martyrs, will prove to have been the seed of the church; for they will freight the air with their voluminous ejaculations, and will be borne upwards by the power of virtue to the great Ruler of Israel, for deliverance from this yoke of merciless bondage. Let us not lament, that under the present constituted powers of this government, we are disfranchised; better far than to be partakers of its guilt. Let us refuse to be allured by the glittering endowments of official stations, or enchanted with the robe of American citizenship. But let us choose like true patriots, rather to be the victims of oppression than the administrators of injustice.

Let no man remove from his native country, for our principles are drawn from the book of Divine Revelation, and are incorporated in the Declaration of Independence, "that all men are born equal, and endowed by their Creator with certain inalienable rights; that among these are, life, liberty, and the pursuit of happiness." Therefore, our only trust is in the agency of Divine Truth, and the spirit of American liberty; our cause is glorious, and must finally triumph. Though the blighting hand of time should sweep us from the stage of action; though other generations should pass away, our principles will live forever; we will teach our children and our children's children to hand them down to unborn generations, and to the latest posterity; not merely for the release of the bondman from his chains, nor for the elevation of the free coloured man to the privileges of citizenship; nor for the restoration of the world from infidelity and superstition; but from the more fatal doctrine of *expediency*, without which the true principles of religion can never be established, liberty never secure, or the sacred rights of man remain inviolate.

It is our fortune to live in an era, when the moral power of this nation is waking up to the evils of slavery, and the cause of our oppressed brethren throughout this country. We see two rival institutions* invoking the benevolence of nations to aid in changing our condition. The former proposes an indirect action on the sin of slavery, by removing the free to the land of their fathers. The latter, a direct action on the subject of slavery, by denouncing its guilt, while it pleads for the elevation of the free coloured man in the land of his nativity.

The former we reject. First, because it is unnecessary, there being

* The American Colonization Society and American Anti-Slavery Society.

sufficient amount of territory on this continent to contain ten times the number of its present inhabitants. Secondly, because it is anti-republican in its nature and tendency; for if our country were now overflowing with a redundant population, we should deny the right of any one class of men to designate those that should be first re-moved. Thirdly, because if the few be removed, we have no security that slavery would be abolished; besides, if that were achieved, the victims of prejudice would scarcely be removed in a century, while the prejudice itself would still exist. Therefore, we, as ardent lovers of our country's welfare, would be guilty of leaving it to writhe under the dominion of a prejudice inimical to the principles of morality, religion, and virtue, while on the contrary we might have aided in its removal. Therefore we believe and affirm that the duty we owe to the land of our birth, the interest of our suffering breth-ren, the cause of justice, virtue and religion, appeal to us in the most emphatic terms to remain on our soil, and see the salvation of God, and the true principles of freedom.

Therefore we do not desire to see our numbers decreased, but we pray God that we may lawfully multiply in numbers, in moral and intellectual endowments, and that our visages may be as so many Bibles, that shall warn this guilty nation of her injustice and cruelty to the descendants of Africa, until righteousness, justice, and truth shall rise in their might and majesty, and proclaim from the halls of legislation that the chains of the bondsman have fallen; that the soil is sacred to liberty; and that, without distinction of nation or com-plexion, she disseminates alike her blessings of freedom to all mankind.

Then let us rally around her standard, and aid in cementing and perpetuating that bond of union.

As it regards the latter institution, we believe that it is preparing the way for that desirable event. With them we will make one com-mon cause, satisfied to await the same issue. With them we are willing to labour for its achievement, and terminate our lives as martyrs in support of its principles. We will raise our moral flag, bearing for its inscription, "do unto others as you would have them do unto you"; under this banner we will rally our countrymen with-out distinction of caste or complexion.

We therefore declare to the world, that our object is to extend the principles of universal peace and good will to all mankind, by promoting sound morality, by the influence of education, temper-ance, economy, and all those virtues that alone can render man ac-ceptable in the eyes of God or the civilized world.

We therefore consider it due to our friends and our enemies, nay, to the world, that previous to our taking this decided stand, we should make this just exposition of our sentiments. We have drawn our principles of human rights from an authority above human legislation. Therefore we cheerfully enter on this moral warfare in defence of liberty, justice and humanity, conscious that whether we live to witness its completion, or die in anticipation of its glorious results, that it has already been committed to the friends of liberty and Christianity throughout the world, and to them we look for its final consummation. We, therefore, mutually pledge ourselves to these principles, the cause, and the world, to do all that in our power lies, to hasten the period when justice and universal liberty shall sway the sceptre of nations.

TO THE AMERICAN PEOPLE

Fellow Citizens—We form a portion of the people of this continent, on whom an unmeasurable amount of obloquy, and scorn, and contempt have been poured, on account of the depravity of our morals; and who have been educated under the influence of a system that impairs the mental vigour, blights with its blasting influence the only successful hope on which the mind can be reared, that keeps from our grasp the fruits of knowledge, the favour of just and equitable laws, and presents a formidable barrier to the prosecution of the arts and sciences of civilized life. The lucrative avocations, mechanic arts, and civil associations by which men acquire a knowledge of government and the nature of human affairs, have been almost wholly reserved as a dignified reward, suited only to the interest and use of the fairer complexion. Yet, in despite of all these, when all the avenues of privileged life have been closed against us, our hands bound with stationary fetters, our minds left to grope in the prison cell of impenetrable gloom, and our whole action regulated by constitutional law and a perverse public sentiment, we have been tauntingly required to prove the dignity of our human nature, by disrobing ourselves of inferiority, and exhibiting to the world our profound Scholars, distinguished Philosophers, learned Jurists, and distinguished Statesmen. The very expectation on which such a requisition is founded, to say the least, is unreasonable, for it is only when the seed is sown that we can justly hope to reap. If, amidst all the difficulties with which we have been surrounded, and the privations which we have suffered, we presented an equal amount of intelligence with that class of Americans that have been so peculiarly favoured, a very grave and dangerous question would present itself to the world on the natural equality of man, and the best rule of logic would place those who have oppressed us in the scale of inferiority. This we do not desire; we love the appellation that records the natural and universal rights of man (to enjoy all the attributes of human happiness) too well, to deprive a single being on earth of such an heavenly inheritance. We can never consent to degrade the creation of man by even attempting to defend the impartiality of his Author. If there be those who doubt that we are made in the image of God, and are endowed with those attributes which the Deity has given to man, we will exhibit them our "hands and side."

The general assertion that superiority of mind is the natural offspring of a fair complexion arrays itself against the experience of the past and present age and both natural and physiological science. The ignorance that exists on this subject we are not accountable for, nor are we willing to admit a theory alike irreconcilable with philosophy and common sense.

It is in view of these mighty evils that exist in our country, which are truly national, that has caused us to meet in annual convention for six successive years to take into consideration the best method of remedying our present situation by contributing to their removal; during which period we have associated the collected wisdom of our people, in their representative character, from half the states of this Union, extending from Maine to Washington, southernly, and from thence westwardly to Cincinnati, Ohio, and have come to the conclusion to form a National Moral Reform Society, as a means best calculated to reach the wants and improve the condition of our people.

We have selected four valuable subjects for rallying points, viz.: Education, Temperance, Economy, and Universal Liberty. We hope to make our people, in theory and practice, thoroughly acquainted with these subjects, as a method of future action. Having placed our institution on the high and indisputable ground of natural laws and human rights, and being guided and actuated by the law of universal love to our fellow men, we have buried in the bosom of Christian benevolence all those national distinctions, complexional variations, geographical lines, and sectional bounds that have hitherto marked the history, character and operations of men; and now boldly plead for the Christian and moral elevation of the human race. To aid us in its completion, we shall endeavour to enlist the sympathies and benevolence of the Christian, moral, and political world. Without regard to creeds, we shall only ask for the fulfilment of Christian duty, as the surest method of extending righteousness and justice. We shall aim to procure the abolition of those hateful and unnecessary distinctions by which the human family has hitherto been recognised, and only desire that they may be distinguished by their virtues and vices.

We hope to unite the coloured population in those principles of Moral Reform. 1st. As a measure necessary to be practised by all rational and intelligent beings, for the promotion of peace, harmony and concord in society. 2d. As a measure necessary to aid in effecting the total abolition of slavery. And 3d. As having a tendency to effect the destruction of vice universally.

In order to this, we will appoint agents to disseminate these truths among our people, and establish auxiliaries wherever practicable, that the same leaven of righteousness and justice may animate the body politic. We will establish a press, and through it make known to the world our progress in the arts, science, and civilization. For aid in the prosecution of our undertaking we shall appeal to the benevolence of nations, but more particularly to our own. For, as God has so abundantly blessed her with internal resources as a means of gratifying her spiritual and temporal wants, so we believe she should employ them to his honour and glory, in disseminating the blessings of education, peace, happiness and prosperity to her own fellow citizens. And if America is to be instrumental through the providence of Almighty God in blessing other portions of the peopled earth, by extending to the heathen and pagan idolater the knowledge of the true God, a pure science, an unadulterated religion, an exalted and benevolent philanthropy, how necessary is it that she should first purify her own dominions, by extending to all her children those divine and precious gifts; so when she shall have joined other nations in rearing the standard for the redemption of the world, every ray of light that may reach those benighted regions will, when falling on the prism of truth, present one pure, unmixed stream of Christian love, and cease to becloud the horizon of everlasting justice. We will first appeal to the Christian churches to take the lead in establishing the principles of supreme love to God and universal love to man. We will do all in our power to aid her in forming a moral structure against which "the gates of hell cannot prevail."

We plead for the extension of those principles on which our government was formed, that it in turn may become purified from those iniquitous inconsistencies into which she has fallen by her aberration from first principles; that the laws of our country may cease to conflict with the spirit of that sacred instrument, the Declaration of American Independence. We believe in a pure, unmixed republicanism, as a form of government best suited to the condition of man, by its promoting equality, virtue, and happiness to all within its jurisdiction. We love our country, and pray for the perpetuation of its government, that it may yet stand illustrious before the nations of the earth, both for the purity of its precepts, and the mildness and equableness of its laws.

We shall advocate the cause of peace, believing that whatever tends to the destruction of human life is at variance with the precepts of the Gospel, and at enmity with the well being of individuals as well as of society. We shall endeavor to promote education, with sound morality, not that we shall become "learned and mighty," but "great and good." We shall advocate temperance in all things, and total abstinence from all alcoholic liquors. We shall advocate a system of *economy*, not only because luxury is injurious to individuals, but because its practice exercises an influence on society, which in its very nature is sinful. We shall advocate universal liberty, as the inalienable right of every individual born in the world, and a right which cannot be taken away by government itself, without an unjust exercise of power. We shall exhibit our sympathy for our suffering brethren by petitioning Congress to procure the immediate abolition of slavery in the District of Columbia, and her territories. We shall endeavour to strengthen public sentiment against slavery so long as a slave treads the soil of these United States. We shall aim at the extinction of mental thraldom; an evil much more dangerous and exceeding the former, both in extent and power. We shall dissuade our brethren from using the products of slave labor, both as a moral and Christian duty, and as a means by which the slave system may be successfully abrogated. We shall appeal to the coloured churches to take decisive measures to rid themselves of the sin of slavery and immorality. We shall endeavor to pledge all the ministers and elders of our churches to the cause of Moral Reform. We hope to train the undisciplined youth in moral pursuits, and we shall anxiously endeavour to impress on our people everywhere, that in moral elevation true happiness consists. We feel bound to pursue the present course as a duty we owe to ourselves, our God, our common country, and the interests of suffering humanity. The free coloured population of the United States now amount to about 400,000, and are constantly increasing by a double process, and we believe that the philanthropic exertions that are now making in our country for the abolition of slavery will shortly remove the fetters from thousands annually, and these will be continually adding to our number. We are unable to conceive of any better method by which we can aid the cause of human liberty than by improving our general character, and embracing within our grasp the liberated slave for moral and mental culture. By pursuing this course we shall certainly remove many of the objections to immediate emancipation. And we further believe, that all who have either thought or felt deeply on this subject will not only sanction such an organization, but will feel bound to aid in promoting its objects. We shall entreat those that are constantly persecuting and calumniating our general character to cease with their vituperations, and suffer a people already bowed to the dust to breathe out their existence in peace and quietude. We will entreat our brethren to bear with Christian fortitude the scoffs and indignation that may be cast on them on account of their complexion, and pity the source from whence it emanates, knowing it is the offspring of wickedness and ignorance.

In the present state of society, we must expect to endure many difficulties, until the world improves in wisdom, and a polite education and a more liberal and enlightened philosophy supplants the present system of national education. If we but fully rest ourselves on the dignity of human nature, and maintain a bold, enduring front against all opposition, the monster, prejudice, will fall humbly at our feet. Prejudice, like slavery, cannot stand the omnipotence of Truth. It is as impossible for a bold, clear and discriminating mind that can calmly and dispassionately survey the structure upon which prejudice is founded, and the materials of which it is composed, to be chained within its grasp, as it is for the puny arm of rebellious man to control the operations of the universe.

We will endeavour to establish in our people a correct knowledge of their own immortal worth, their high derivation as rational, moral and intelligent beings. We shall appeal to them to abandon their prejudices against all complexion and bury them in oblivion, and endeavor to live in the same country as children of one common father, and as brethren possessing the same holy, religious faith, and with a zeal determined on the promotion of great and glorious objects. We shall endeavor to impress on them, at all times, to maintain in every station of life that affability of manner, meekness, humility and gentleness, that ornaments the Christian character; and finally, we will appeal to Heaven for the purity of our motives, and the rectitude of our intentions, and to men for the means of prosecuting them; to Christians, philanthropists and patriots, without regard to creed, profession, or party. In short, we shall aim to whatever seemeth good, consistent with these principles, for the promotion and welfare of our people.

Having now stated the most prominent objects that will command our attention and support, there are others, that from mere custom and usage, many might suppose it were our duty to vindicate. From these we must respectfully dissent, viz.: We will not stoop to contend with those who style us inferior beings. And as we know of no earthly tribunal of sufficient competency and impartiality to decide on a question involving the natural superiority of individuals and nations, we shall not submit so grave a decision to creatures like ourselves, and especially to our enemies. In the preamble of our constitution, we claim to be American citizens, and we will not waste our time by holding converse with those who deny us this privilege, unless they first prove that a man is not a citizen of that country in which he was born and reared. Those that desire to discuss with us the propriety of remaining in this country, or of the method of our operations, must first admit us, as a cardinal point, their equals by nature, possessing, like themselves, from God, all those inalienable rights that are universally admitted to be the property of his creatures. We will not admit that strength of mind lies concealed in the complexion of the body. Having now performed a duty we owed to the people of these United States, in explaining the whole course of action of an Institution for the improvement of the morals, bearing the broad and illustrious title of American, we view in anticipation the most happy results to our beloved country, and will most heartily rejoice if that in an hour of danger we shall have been fortunate enough to have aided in rescuing her from the evils into which she has fallen; and we do most cordially hope that a moral fabric may be reared that will promote the cause of righteousness and justice throughout the universe.

William Whipper

AMERICAN MORAL REFORM SOCIETY

In view of the most mighty considerations that ever engaged the attention of man, and resting our hopes of a triumphant success on the great Author of all good, we the subscribers, citizens of the United States of America, in Convention assembled, believing that the successful resuscitation of our country from moral degeneracy depends upon a vigilant prosecution of the holy cause of Moral Reform, as in its promotion is involved the interest, happiness and prosperity of the great Republic, and also that the moral elevation of this nation will accelerate the extension of righteousness, justice, truth, and evangelical principles throughout the world: Therefore, in accordance with the recommendation of the fourth annual Convention, held in the city of New York, we do agree to form ourselves into a National Society, based on the principles set forth in the Declaration of Sentiment.

ART. I. This Society shall be called The American Moral Reform Society.

ART. II. Any person may become a member of this institution who shall pledge himself to practise and sustain the general principles of Moral Reform as advocated in our country, especially those of Education, Temperance, Economy, and Universal Liberty, by contributing to its objects.

ART. III. The Annual meeting of this Society shall be on the second Tuesday in August, in each year, in the city of Philadelphia.

ART. IV. The officers of this Society shall consist of one President, four Vice-Presidents, three Secretaries, (Foreign, Home, and Recording,) a Treasurer, and a Board of Managers of seven persons.

ART. V. *Sect. 1st.* It shall be the duty of the Board to supervise and direct the action and operation of the Society, as well as its financial concerns.

Section 2nd. All candidates for membership must apply to the Board of Directors, whose duty it shall be to admit all who subscribe to the principles contained in this Constitution.

ART. VI. Any member violating the principles set forth in this Constitution will be disqualified for membership, and shall be subject as the Board may direct.

ART. VII. The funds of this Society shall be appropriated to the diffusion of light on the subject advocated, and its Constitution may be altered from time to time, so as to keep pace with the great object of Moral Reform.

Signed on behalf of the officers of this Society.

JAMES FORTEN, Sen., *President.*

Vice Presidents.

WM. WATKINS, of Maryland.   WALTER PROCTOR, Pennsylvania.
REUBEN RUBY, Maine.   JACOB C. WHITE.

Treasurer.
JOSEPH CASSEY.

Secretaries.
JOHN F. COOKE, Foreign Corresponding Secretary,
WILLIAM WHIPPER, Home Corresponding Secretary,
JAMES FORTEN, Jr., Recording Secretary.

BOARD OF MANAGERS—*John P. Burr,* Chairman, *Rev. Morris Brown, John B. Roberts, Thomas Butler, Moore Walker, James McCrummill, and James P. Clay.*

The First Annual Report
OF THE
AMERICAN MORAL REFORM SOCIETY.

The Board of Managers, in presenting this their first Annual Report to the public, are duly impressed with the importance of their obligations, and of their dependence on Divine Providence for his aid and assistance in the prosecution of so laudable an enterprise as the one which at present claims our attention. The Board have endeavored during the past year, to do all they could to disseminate and promote the principles of this Institution as far as the means of the Society would admit. The limited state of the funds, however, has prevented us from doing the good we would. There is a large and expansive field open to our view, and for our action; but we cannot effect much without means; we, therefore, hope that this annual meeting, and every friend of the cause, will for the future contribute their aid, or exert their influence, to produce the desirable objects of Moral Reform.

The Minutes of the last special meeting have been very extensively circulated, but the newness and greatness of the enterprise does not as yet appear to be so fully comprehended by our people as we could wish. However, wherever it has been considered it has been measurably received and attended to, as may be seen from the accompanying statement (marked A), from which it appears that several institutions have been formed auxiliary to this, and a great many others have taken up some of the branches of Moral Reform, and are now endeavoring to do something for the cause. A very promising female Society has been formed in this city, and from their past and present laudable exertions, bid fair to effect much. We hope that other females will copy their example, and come out and exert their mighty influence in favour of this heavenly enterprise, as much signal good can be effected by female effort.

The Board have, during the past year, appointed the Rev. Bishop Brown, John B. Roberts and John F. Cook as agents of this Society, to lecture, receive contributions, and promote the objects, and disseminate the principles of this Society, which they have done gratuitously, as far as they have been able in several states, cities, and towns quite to the satisfaction of the Board, for which they have our united thanks. Your Board are of the opinion that if a permanent salaried agent could be located in this city, who would devote his time and attention to the cause, much might be effected, and the march of our Society would be onward and irresistible. We hope, therefore, that this subject will claim your particular attention.

STATEMENT A—*Showing the progress and present state of the coloured population so far as heard from, by the Board of Managers of the Amer. Mor. Ref. Soc., for their first annual report, Aug., 1837.*

Names of States, Towns, &c. which have complied with the circular of the 22d June 1837.		No. of Churches.	Clergymen.	Day Schools.	Teachers.	Sabbath Schools.	S. S. Teachers.	Bible Classes.	Literary Societies.	Debating Societies.	Mutual Relief or Benevolent.	Moral Ref. Societies.	Temperance Societ's.	Dealers.
Massachusetts.	New Bedford.								1				1	
Rhode Island.	Providence.	1		3	2	1		1	1		2	1	1	
New York.	Buffalo.	2	2	1					1	1	2	1		4
"	Troy.	3	3	2	2	2	6		1	1	3	4	2	
"	Utica.													
"	Poughkeepsie.	1	1	1	1	1			1		1		1	
New Jersey.	Trenton.	1	2	2	1						1			8
"	Salem.					1					3			
"	Bridgetown.					1								
"	Newark.	2	2	3		3		2	1		1	1	2	4
Pennsylvania.	Philadelphia.	15	34	21	6	17	125		3	3	64	1	4	Many
"	Pittsburg.	2	10	1		1		1		2	4	2		
"	York.	2		1										1
"	West Chester.	1	2	1		1		1						
"	Columbia.	2	2	2	1	1						1		
"	Wilkesbarre.											1	1	
District of Columbia.		9	10	6	7	6	40	1	1	1	7	2	6	18
Indiana.	Lawrenceburg.													
Tennessee.	Nashville.													

212

	Mechanics.	Real Estate, Taxes, Rents, &c.	Coloured population.	Paupers.	Criminals.	Names of Agents, Reports, &c.
New Bedford.	2		894	40	9	Nathan Johnson.
Providence.			1400	9		Alfred Niger.
Buffalo.	12	$100.000	500	3	6	Abner H. Francis.
Troy.	21	25.000	997	18	2	Daniel A. Payne.
Utica.			200			George L. Brown.
Poughkeepsie.	3	7.000	294		3	Nathan Blount.
Trenton.	9	120.000		2	12	George McMullen.
Salem.		23.397			few	Reuben Cuff.
Bridgetown.	2	14.796				Jesse Gould.
Newark.	13	76.300	800			Amos N. Freeman.
Philadelphia.	78	850.000	25000	few	few	John P. Burr.
Pittsburg.	several.	95.000	2400	3		L. Woodson, W. J. Greenly.
York.	4	12.150	320	11		William Goodrich.
West Chester.	5	15.000	290			Abraham D. Shad.
Columbia.	3	20.000	600	few		William Whipper.
Wilkesbarre.	3		80			William Brewer.
District of Columbia.	40 or more	unknown.	6200	few		J. F. Cook.
Lawrenceburg.			23			Richard Moran.
Nashville.						Reuben Plynhaur.

NOTE.—*Agents, Auxiliaries, or persons who communicate with the Board of Managers will please, in rendering their Quarterly or Annual Reports, comply with the above form.*

The business of the last meeting of this Society has not been so fully carried into effect as was wished, for want of means and men to act, which cannot be expected without means; much, therefore, still remains to be done, and we hope will be, during the ensuing year. The Board have appointed and corresponded with several local agents in various places, and we hope much good will be effected by them, as from their influence and exertions we have already received some cheering communications, giving account of the progress of our people. We can only thank them for their exertions and attention, and hope that they will continue their efforts and effect much for the cause of Moral Reform, as upon the successful promotion of such principles depends our future prospects in the world.

Circulars inviting this annual assemblage have been extensively circulated, and measurably responded to, but not all in time to be embraced fully in this report. The experiment has been, we conceive, fully tried and meets our approbation; for the future we hope to be more competent to discharge our duties, to the satisfaction of ourselves and the people generally.

The statement (marked B) accompanying this report, will exhibit the amount of receipts and expenditures during the past year.

In humble reliance upon the aid of Divine Providence, whose blessings we invoke upon our holy enterprize, we do most cordially submit this brief statement of our doings.

In behalf of the Board of Managers of the American Moral Reform Society.

John P. Burr,
Chairman.

STATEMENT B

Exhibiting the amount of Receipts and Expenditures of the Board of Managers, for the past year, 1836 *and* 1837.

American Moral Reform Society, in account with the Board of Managers.

DR.

To Cash paid Benjamin Lundy for publishing 300 copies of minutes, $12.00

To Cash paid Trustees of Wesley Church for the use thereof during last session,   7.50

To Cash paid for blank minute book.   2.00

To Cash paid Merrihew & Gunn for printing circulars   2.50

To Cash paid do. for printing Watkins' Address on Education.   28.42

To Cash paid for postage and sundry expenses, stationary, &c.   10.00

$62.42

Cr.

By Cash received from auxiliary Society of Baltimore. $ 5.00

By Cash received from W. Watkins for pamphlets.   5.00

By Cash received from selling minutes, pamphlets, and members' contributions.   52.42

$62.42

JOHN P. BURR, *Chairman.*

Philadelphia, August, 1837.

MINUTES

The first annual meeting of the American Moral Society was held at the Presbyterian Church in Seventh Street, below Shippen, on Monday morning, August 14th, 1837, at 10 o'clock, A.M.; President James Forten in the Chair. The house was opened by prayer from the Rev. Charles W. Gardner, Chaplain of the Society. The Secretary then read the Constitution of the Society, together with the Declaration of Sentiment and the Rules and Regulations of the Society. The President then made some very appropriate remarks, inviting our fellow citizens to cooperate in the cause of Moral Reform. The Secretary then commenced the reading of some very interesting communications from Massachusetts, Rhode Island, New Jersey, New York, Pennsylvania, Tennessee, Indiana, and the District of Columbia; after which the credentials were presented, as follows: From the Philadelphia Mechanic Society, Rush Education Society, Annual Conference of the Methodist Episcopal Church, Bethel Church Temperance Society, Humane Mechanics Society, Philadelphia Library Company, St. Thomas' Church Temperance Society, Mental and Moral Association of Philadelphia, 14th Presbyterian Church. On motion of J. Forten, jr., all the communications and credentials of the Board were received. On motion, the House adjourned.

Afternoon Session

Prayer by the Rev. C. W. Gardner. Minutes of former meeting were read. The Secretary then read the Constitution of the Society, and the Address to the American People. After singing a few verses, the Rev. C. W. Gardner delivered the opening address, on the subject of Moral Reform.

F. A. Hinton moved, That the President of the Society be authorized to invite the President of the Anti-Slavery Societies, and such other friends of our cause as he may deem proper.

On motion of William Brewer, seconded by F. A. Hinton, it was

Resolved, That a General Committee of one person from each state present, be appointed by the President of this Society to take into consideration such matters as are proper to be submitted to the early deliberation of this assembly. That they report as soon as practicable and embody in a systematic plan, such business as they may deem requisite for the action of this meeting.

The President appointed the committee agreeably to the resolution, as follows: Messrs. Brewer, F. A. Hinton, Moore, Cook, R. Cuff and D. A. Payne.

On motion of F. Cook, a resolution of thanks was returned to the
Rev. Charles W. Gardner, for his interesting address on the subject
of moral Reform. Prayer by the Rev. D. A. Payne.
On motion the House adjourned.

Tuesday Morning, August 15th

Prayer by the Chaplain. The roll was called, and the minutes of
former meeting together with the rules, regulations and Constitution
read. After which the report of the Board of Directors was read and
received. The committee appointed yesterday to report business for
this meeting reported the following, which was received, and after
considerable discussion was unanimously adopted, as follows:

REPORT

The Committee appointed under Mr. Brewer's resolution to prepare such business as in their judgment they may deem proper for
the action of this meeting, submit the following resolutions for consideration and adoption.

1. *Resolved,* That we recommend to our people the propriety of
forming and sustaining Societies, for the mutual instruction of both
young and old, in the branches of a good English education, and
the mechanic arts, in every State, county, city, town, and village,
wherever it may be practicable.

2. *Resolved,* That the Board of Managers of the Society be requested to appoint an agent, in every State, county, city, town, or
village in the Union, wherever practicable, whose duty it shall be
to form auxiliaries, and carry into effect all the objects of this society; he shall make a quarterly return to the President of said
Board, of their progress, and condition of his district, in mental,
and moral improvement.

3. *Resolved,* That the agents named in the above resolution be
and are hereby authorized to open books, and endeavour to obtain
and receive subscriber's names for the purpose of establishing a
Manual Labor School in some suitable place, hereafter to be decided upon; and they shall make their returns quarterly, with the
other information to the Board, for the information of the Society—
and whenever it shall appear that a sufficient amount has been subscribed—there shall be appointed by the Board, some responsible
agent to collect the same for the Society—who shall then take immediate measures to establish the said Manual Labor School for
the instruction of youth.

4. *Resolved,* That this Society recommend to all societies who
are, or shall, become auxiliary, or shall send representatives to the

annual meetings thereof, to adopt and sustain by precept, and example, all the principles of this society, especially that of total abstinence from all intoxicating liquors.

5. *Resolved,* That the agents and members of this Society be, and are hereby requested, to use every exertion in their power by lectures, and addresses, &c., to impress upon our people the propriety of practising the principles of economy in all things.

6. *Resolved,* That the practice of the principles of peace, as exemplified in the life and character of our Blessed Redeemer while on earth, is the most proper example for our people to follow.

7. *Resolved,* That the moral, upright, and correct deportment of our people will be one of the strongest arguments we can present in favor of universal, civil, and religious liberty.

Your committee in submitting this Report, beg leave to say that they are of opinion that too much legislation is rather injurious, and therefore hope that this Society will not adopt any more resolutions than they are able to carry into full and efficient effect.

All of which is most respectfully submitted.

Frederick A. Hinton, *Chairman.*

On motion the Society adjourned.

Afternoon Session

Prayer by the Rev. Daniel A. Payne. Minutes of the former session were read, and the roll called. The business of the morning session was taken up, and an animated discussion on the 1st resolution of the report continued until 6 o'clock, when on motion the House adjourned.

Wednesday Morning, August 16th

The President being absent, the Vice President was called to the Chair. Prayer by the Rev. Mr. Gardner. The Minutes and Constitution were read, and Roll called. The business was then continued in a debate on the second resolution of the report of the committee. On motion of Jacob White, seconded by Robert Purvis, it was agreed:

That the rules of the third annual convention, be the rules for the government of this Society.

While the subject relative to the resolution, was under discussion, On motion the House adjourned.

Afternoon Session

President in the Chair; prayer by the Chaplain; Constitution, Rules and Minutes read, and Roll called. The first resolution of the committee being still under consideration, the debate was continued by Messrs. Whipper, Bowers, Hinton, Purvis and others, for some time.

On motion of James Forten jr., seconded by John P. Burr, it was resolved, that the paper recently established in the city of New York, and edited by the Rev. Samuel E. Cornish, is a valuable acquisition to our cause; we therefore recommend it to the patronage of the people.

The Society then suspended their proceedings for a time, to hear an address from Mr. Wm. Whipper on peace; which he then arose and delivered in a very able and interesting manner. The following resolution was then presented by J. F. Cook, seconded by James Forten, jr., and unanimously carried.

Resolved, That the principles of peace, are worthy our particular attention, consideration, and adoption. Therefore we do hereby tender to Mr. Wm. Whipper, our united thanks for his views, so ably delivered thereon, this afternoon.

Several notices were given out, among which a notice, that this meeting would meet in St. Thomas' Church, 5th Street, this evening at 8 o'clock, to hear addresses, on Temperance, from Messrs. J. F. Cook, and J. C. Bowers—after which Mr. Joshua Leavitt made some very feeling remarks, followed by a Lady, eminent for her untiring zeal in the cause of human rights, and the Rev. Wm. Reynolds. On motion the Society adjourned to meet at 9 o'clock, tomorrow morning.

Thursday Morning

President in the chair. Prayer by the Rev. Mr. Cornish. Constitution, rules and minutes were read and roll called. The first resolution in the report of the committee was again brought up, when, after a protracted and animated discussion, the President decided that the words "Free people of colour" should be stricken out.

On motion of F. A. Hinton seconded by Moore Walker, it was unanimously

Resolved, That the thanks of this meeting be presented to Mr. John F. Cook, for his excellent address on Temperance delivered at St. Thomas' Church last evening, and that a copy of it be requested for publication.

On motion of James M'Crummill, seconded by F. C. Lippins, it was

Resolved, That no individual shall be capable of being a member of this Society, or a representative from any other body to the meetings of this Society, that sells ardent spirits.

On motion of William Whipper seconded by R. Purvis, it was

Resolved, That the thanks of this House and the nation, are due to the Hon. John Quincy Adams, and others for the able, and independent manner in which they have maintained the right of petition irrespective of colour or condition.

Several other resolutions were presented and on motion severally laid on the table.

On motion adjourned till 3 o'clock P.M.

Afternoon Session

Prayer by Rev. Mr. Gardner. Rules and minutes were read, and roll called. At the request of the President, the proceedings of the people, termed "a voice from Philadelphia" passed in the city of Philadelphia, were read. Mr. Cornish at the request of Mr. Leavitt moved that the following resolution thereof be adopted, which was accordingly cordially carried into operation.

Resolved, That we never will separate ourselves voluntarily from the slave population in this country; they are our brethren by the ties of consanguinity, of suffering and of wrong; and we feel that there is more virtue in suffering privations with them here, than in enjoying fancied advantages for a season.

One or two resolutions on various subjects were called up, but on motion were laid on the table.

On motion of J. C. Bowers, it was agreed that the business of this meeting be now suspended, in order to give opportunity to the audience to hear an address from James Forten, Jr. He then arose, and delivered a very eloquent and interesting address on the subject of Education. After which, on motion of J. F. Cook, seconded by R. Purvis, it was unanimously

Resolved, That the thanks of the meeting be, and are hereby tendered to James Forten, Jr., for his very able, eloquent, and interesting address just delivered on the subject of Education, and that it be requested by the Board of Managers for publication.

On motion of William Whipper, seconded by R. Purvis, it was, after being ably supported by the Rev. C. W. Gardner,

Resolved, That those women who are now pleading the cause of humanity, and devoting their time, talents, and industry, to the cause of Universal Freedom, deserve the blessings of Heaven, and the gratitude of posterity.

On motion of D. A. Payne, seconded by W. Whipper, and ably supported by the mover, it was

Resolved, That the rising generation is the only hope, not only of the Church, but also of the Country; that they cannot be brought

too soon into the field of moral action; and that therefore all ministers with whom we have any influence be requested to deliver
special sermons, statedly, to children and youth.

On motion of J. C. White, seconded by James M'Crummill, it was

Resolved, That the proceedings of the last session of the Society
be now taken up, and referred to a committee of three, to report on
tomorrow morning; whereupon Messrs. White, Whipper and
M'Crummill, were appointed.

On motion of R. Purvis, seconded by Wm. Whipper, it was

Resolved, That the gratitude of the friends of humanity throughout the world are due to that distinguished champion of Love,
George Thompson of England, for his successful advocacy of the
principles of human rights in both hemispheres.

On motion of R. Forten, seconded by S. Smith, it was unanimously

Resolved, That for the early, untiring, and uncompromising advocacy of Benjamin Lundy, and others, of the great cause of human
rights, entitles them to the gratitude of this meeting. Several other
resolutions were presented, but were laid over.

On motion, the meeting adjourned to meet at 9 o'clock on Friday
morning.

Friday morning, August 18th

Vice President Jacob C. White, in the Chair; prayer by the Rev.
D. A. Payne; Roll called; Rules and Minutes read. The Committee
who were appointed to examine and report on such business of last
year as remains unattended to, presented the following resolutions
for the consideration and re-adoption of this meeting, which, after
being fully and fairly considered, were adopted in the following
manner.

The first resolution was adopted with the understanding that the
Board appoint, without compensation, the agents already appointed
by another society, viz.:

Resolved, That it is considered necessary and expedient to employ
a suitable agent in the city to make inquiry concerning the education
of children, whose parents are in indigent circumstances; and that he
use all proper means to solicit their attention to this all-important
subject.

Resolved, That this meeting recommend to the Board of Directors
to employ an agent, or agents, to lecture on the subject of Moral
Reform, and establish auxiliaries, wherever practicable.

Resolved, That the members of this meeting pledge themselves to use their best endeavors to raise, during the present year, one thousand dollars, for the promotion of our principles.

Resolved, That we recommend to the Board of Managers to use the columns of the *National Enquirer* as the organ of this society for the present.

Resolved, That we recommend to the Board of Managers the propriety of continuing to secure addresses to be made monthly, on the great principles of Moral Reform.

Whereas, The time-honoured custom of wearing mourning apparel for the dead is frequently attended with much inconvenience, and always with unnecessary expense; and whereas, the money which the poor of our people are obliged to spend in this way, in conformity with the tyranny of fashion, might be applied to purposes of substantial utility; Therefore be it

Resolved, That from motives of economy alone, if from no other, this practice should be abolished among our people.

Resolved, That all unnecessary eclat and parade on funeral occasions are in bad taste, and should be frowned down by the reflecting portion of our community.

Resolved, That the auxiliary Societies are hereby requested to present a copy of the foregoing preamble and resolutions to the Presidents of the different beneficial societies, and others that are in the habit of burying their dead, respectfully requesting the officers to have them read to the institutions over which they preside.

On motion of Moore Walker, seconded by S. E. Cornish, it was

Resolved, That agricultural pursuits be recommended to our coloured population as highly calculated to promote their best interest.

On motion of William Greenly, seconded by F. C. Lippins, it was

Resolved, That this meeting congratulate the young men of this Union in their labor and exertion in forming Literary and Moral Institutions for their mental and moral improvement.

A series of resolutions were presented by James M'Crummill, and seconded by J. Forten, Jr., relative to memorializing the Senate and House of Representatives of the United States against the annexation of Texas to the Union; all of which, after some debate, were adopted, and a committee of three were appointed to draft a memorial and report the same in the afternoon.

On motion, the House adjourned.

Afternoon Session

President in the chair; prayer by the Chaplain; Roll called; Minutes read; a form of the memorial was presented by J. M'Crummill, of the committee, and approved; various motions and resolutions in relation to "Mechanics," and the term "coloured" were indefinitely postponed.

On motion of R. Purvis, seconded by J. M'Crummill, it was

Resolved, That Messrs. Colly, Cook and Smith, be a committee to nominate all the constitutional officers of the Society.

On motion of D. A. Payne, seconded by J. C. White, it was

Resolved, That Messrs. Whipper, Cook and Forten, Jr., be requested to furnish copies of their addresses to the Board of Managers, to be preserved in the archives of this Society.

On motion of John C. Bowers, seconded by Thomas Holland, it was

Resolved, That we recommend to the youth of our land, the propriety of abstaining from all and every fluid that has a tendency in the least degree to intoxicate; and instead thereof, adopt the principles of Moral Reform, viz: Education, Temperance, Economy and Universal Love, and thus aid in carrying out the measures for which this Society was organized.

On motion of C. W. Gardner, seconded by R. Purvis, it was

Resolved, That this Society approve of the course taken by James Bird, and others, for the encouragement given to the mechanics.

On motion of Stephen Smith, seconded by J. Forten, Jr., it was

Resolved, That we recommend the monthly concert of prayer, on the last Monday in each month, for the promotion of the cause of Human Rights, and that ministers are requested to unite their congregations on the occasion.

On motion of J. M. White, seconded by James M'Crummill, it was

Resolved, That this meeting recommend to the young men of the city and county of Philadelphia to assist in the support of the Philadelphia Library Company.

On motion of R. Purvis, seconded by J. M'Crummill, it was

Resolved, That the thanks of this meeting are hereby tendered to the Chaplain and Officers of this church, for their kindness and attention during the sitting of this Society, also to the officers of this Society for the able and dignified manner in which they have presided over its deliberations.

On motion of Mr. S. Smith, seconded by J. F. Cook, it was

Resolved, That this Society adjourn this afternoon, at 6 o'clock, to meet on the second Tuesday in August, 1838, in the city of Philadelphia.

The committee appointed to nominate officers for the ensuing year, reported the following:

JAMES FORTEN, Sen., *President*

Vice Presidents

WM. WATKINS, of Maryland.   WALTER PROCTOR, Pennsylvania.
REUBEN RUBY, Maine.   JACOB C. WHITE.

Treasurer
JOSEPH CASSEY.

Secretaries

JOHN F. COOK, Foreign Corresponding Secretary,
WILLIAM WHIPPER, Home Corresponding Secretary,
JAMES FORTEN, JR., Recording Secretary.

BOARD OF MANAGERS—*John P. Burr, Chairman, Rev. Morris Brown, John B. Roberts, Thomas Butler, Moore Walker, James M'Crummill, and James P. Clay.*

Messrs. Charles W. Gardner, Daniel A. Payne and Wm. Reynolds made some very interesting concluding remarks to the members and children. The hour of 6 having arrived, in conformity with the resolution, the meeting adjourned till the second Tuesday in August, 1838. Prayer by the Rev. Charles W. Gardner.

Signed in behalf of the Society.

JAMES FORTEN, Sen., *President.*

John F. Cook,
Wm. Whipper,   }*Secretaries.*
James Forten, Jr.,

LIST OF DELEGATES

In attendance at the First annual meeting of the American Moral Reform Society, held in the city of Philadelphia, August, 1837.

New York

Daniel A. Payne, *of Troy.*   Joshua Leavitt, of *New York.*
Samuel E. Cornish, *of New York.*

New Jersey

Reuben Cuff, *of Salem,*   Daniel Aytes, *of Salem.*
Peter Doran, do.   Jesse Gould, *Bridgetown,*
Firman Gould, *of Bridgeton.*

Pennsylvania
William Brewer, *of Wilkesbarre.*
William J. Greenly, *of Pittsburg.*

Of the Mechanics Association of Philadelphia.
Parris Saulter,   Morris Brown, Jr.
Daniel Colly,   Robert B. Ayres,
                   William H. Wilson.

Of the Rush Education Society, Philadelphia.
James Bird,   Littleton Hubert,
Harrison H. Sylva,   Henry Cornish,
                   Jehu Champion.

Temperance Society of Bethel Church, Philadelphia.
         E. Beck,   B. W. Wilkins,
         J. J. G. Bias,   Thomas Holland,
                   J. B. Roberts.

Of the Mental and Moral Association of Philadelphia.
      Benjamin Wilson,   Samuel Van Brackle.
David Ware, *Bethel Church Conference Philadelphia.*

Of the Library Association of Philadelphia.
      John C. Bowers,   James Cornish,
                   James White.

The members of the American Moral Reform Society, besides
delegates, were seventy in number from different places.

AN ADDRESS

*Delivered before the American Moral Reform Society, by
James Forten, Jr., Philadelphia, August 17th, 1837.*

Mr. President—Another year has rolled away since last we met to
take into consideration, and to adopt, such measures as would lead
to our future elevation and honour. Yet through the permission of a
kind Providence, we have again assembled for the same grand
purpose; again do we behold brother united with brother in one
great and glorious object—the overthrow of vice and the restoration
of morality. The privilege and opportunity of addressing this audience is one that affords me the most unfeigned pleasure. But how
much greater is the privilege, how much more heightened is the
pleasure, from the fact that I have it in my power to appear before
you, not only as a member, but as an officer, of one of the most
beneficial institutions our people ever issued forth to the world. I
allude to the American Moral Reform Society, the anniversary of
which we now commemorate. As I have the honour to be Recording
Secretary of this Society, I feel it my duty, and shall endeavour to

the best of my abilities, to fulfil the various duties devolving upon me, with credit to the Institution, with satisfaction to my fellow officers, and, above all, with a clear conscience.

This Association, though yet in its infancy, having but just emerged from the confines of a long-buried ambition, we have every reason to believe will be most salutary in its operations; and as it advances on the wheels of time to maturer age, strengthened and invigorated, will unfold itself, exhibiting a rich and abundant harvest. Sir, it has for its basis the elevation of our people from ignorance and superstition, to light and knowledge; and is eminently calculated from its pure and holy designs to place us far beyond the reach of our ungenerous oppressors—to strip them of every chance by which they might assail us—to palsy the Herculean arm of prejudice—to change the scornful look, the invidious frown, into an approving smile—to force the rude laugh of contempt and ridicule into a silence deep and breathless as the eternal sleep of death.

Of all the many things held out by the Society for our benefit, there is none stands more prominent than *Education;* and it is to this subject that I shall chiefly confine my remarks. Sir, the best feelings of our nature, our highest aspirations should be directed towards the illumination of the mind. It is a prize far above all others, and so great is its influence, so irresistible and captivating is its form, that should it come in the glittering mantle of courtly dignity, or in the tattered garb of beggary, or shine beneath the dark colouring of our skin, its potency must be felt and known; proscription cannot live where it lives; the oppressor must wither under it, and be compelled to lift his murderous foot from off the neck of the oppressed. Education moulds the character; it is the food of morality; nourishing the mental faculties, checking the tide of vice, subduing the violent passions and natural depravity which pervade the human breast, it renders man an ornament to society, a beautiful, intellectual and virtuous being; it gives him to know fully his relation to the Deity, inspires him with a dignity, possesses him with a commanding mien, of which no power on earth can disrobe him. Sir, as an evidence that these are some of the wholesome effects produced from cultivating and enriching the mind, we have only to take a retrospective view of things, to glance our eyes over the innumerable pages of history. There it speaks in tones of thunder of the many conquests it has made over barbarism; how it has sown the seed of religion, has caused the ruthless savage to throw down his weapons of hostility; hath awakened the heathen from his lethargy to a sense of the benevolence and incomprehensible wisdom of the Great Spirit; and in the place of gilded baubles, painted and inanimate idols, the ever living God is worshipped and adored. Mr. President, it is an undeniable fact that, wherever the light of Education has been permitted to burst in upon a people, it gives them peace and competency. Indeed, if we call to mind the situation of many governments years past—when we look at the obstinacy and madness of their rulers, men entirely swayed by passion and not by reason, and I may say, in many instances, wrapped in the barbaric darkness of past centuries, we will not wonder at the anarchy, confusion and bloodshed that then prevailed —we will not wonder that all law was unknown. But when civilization was called from her urn, and when knowledge began to beam upon those very people who had been so long subjected to the cruelties of these reigning despots, they shook off the disgraceful load of servility; their blind and infatuated rulers fell from their lofty height; the scene was changed, and they, assuming a more civilized form, exhibited their actions on a different stage. Tranquillity was established, then, through the influence and power of mental light.

That Education promotes peace is evident, I may briefly observe, from the regularity of conduct, the disposition to make every action harmonize one with the other, which we almost invariably perceive, both in private and public, amongst the higher and favoured classes of this community, who have been blessed with an early and moral education. It is this which implants the principles of peace in the bosoms of families, which enables them to maintain a chastity of spirit, and to give to virtue a full supremacy over every irregular and wayward passion. Hence where Education predominates, there no enemy can intrude to spoil or contaminate domestic happiness. That Education is conducive to economy, no one will for a moment question. For we find that when persons' talents have been expanded and their minds properly instructed, they become a thinking people; this noble faculty of thinking is kept constantly in operation; and the result is that wisdom, caution, prudence, firmness, characterize their every action; they generally look twice before they leap, and are seldom found plunging into foolish extravagancies, or rash speculations; but on the contrary, pursue an undeviating and judicious course through life, keeping in sight that imperishable motto, "economy is the road to wealth." Education, then, will enable us to make accurate calculations and correct contracts in our business transactions, and will preserve us against the encroachments of the swindler, the deceitful, and rapacious. Education, then, I firmly believe, is the mighty lever which, if kept constantly and properly in motion, will be the means of turning over into our present scanty coffers sufficient wealth to supply the conveniences of life.

Knowledge is power; and in proportion to the acquirement of it, when fitly and aptly applied, is the progress of morality—discord and strife are laid prostrate, and peace asserts its empire, vice and immorality are immolated, and virtue and reform live to confine, qualify, and regulate the emotions of the heart. Education cannot help but improve the morals; for it and morality go hand in hand; they are in many respects dependent upon each other; in fact, they are almost Siametrically joined. It is far beyond all calculation how much we owe to their power for the little quiet we now enjoy; and without these great essentials to man's best interest, what kind of a world would we have? Why, Society would present naught but continued scenes of derangement; the fury of the elements of profligacy and lawlessness would be forever at work; and we would look in vain for the calm, soothing, life-giving principles of virtue—in vain would we search for the mild lessons of Christianity to strengthen and guide the actions of men. Truly may it be said, that "Knowledge is the hand-maid of virtue, the light of the mind, and places man far above the brutes."

Sir, I must confess that, as I proceed in this subject, I most deeply feel my incompetency to do it that justice which its high importance demands. The weight is almost insupportable; and I would sink under it were it not for a conviction that it is the solemn duty of everyone who has had the slightest opportunity to improve, to use the same to the well-being of their fellow creatures. And, my brethren, it is because I feel devotedly and unalterably attached to you; because I feel an unextinguishable desire to see you prosperous, to see you walking in the exalted and dignified sphere of usefulness, that I am here, offering to you my weak though sincere services. It is for the general good that I wish to unseal my lips; for your interest is my interest, your happiness is my happiness. The same hand that strikes at your liberties strikes at mine; the same proscription to which you are victims falls alike on me. We must be as one, then, in this cause of reform, remembering that "in Union is strength." Under these considerations, I feel at liberty to entreat, nay to beseech, you to lay hold of the inestimable gifts which learning offers. We, above all others, stand in need of them. It requires tenfold the energies, a thousand times the constant, untiring application on our part, to overcome the countless number of difficulties in our path. We have to confront the cold, calculating, stern visage of public opinion. Our advantages to gain a step up the hill of science, are as angels' visits, "few and far between." We are not situated like those of our citizens whose fairer hue entitles them to all the privileges which this country can bestow. They have but to knock, and the door is thrown open to them—to ask, and they receive food fresh from the stores of knowledge. Yet to their shame be it said, that while participating in this mental feast, they forget those whom they have left sitting at the gate, with minds equally capable of developement, yet bereft of nearly every chance—with talents equally as susceptible, yet languishing for want of sustenance. These latter remarks show the situation we are in; and in view of all these obstacles, I ask what are we to do? Why, I know of no better plan than acting for ourselves, and I trust that all who now hear me can at once perceive the necessity of our doing so. Besides, the time has arrived that we should be aware that our opponents, with but a few casual exceptions, have scarcely, if any, sympathy for us, or any regard for the advancement of education among us. It appears to me that they live but for their own personal aggrandizement, their own firesides, their own complexion, and not for God and the human family. They ascend the ladder, and, when on the top, cast it one side, and turn a deaf ear to the innocent suppliant beneath, who, with a heart burning with ambition, pleads for assistance. Does this not plainly show, then, the great need of acting for ourselves? It only requires on our part a greater will to act; to feel the force of the language of that most gifted author Mrs. Child, which, if my memory serves me, is as follows: "The will is a powerful worker, and if mountains were in its way, it would cut a passage through with tools of its own making." We have only, therefore, to clap our own shoulders to the work, and make one united effort in our own behalf, and I will guarantee that something will be accomplished, that we shall have no cause to be ashamed of.

Who is there within these walls so callous, so dead to all that is noble and elevating, as not to see at one glance the immense utility, the immeasurable advantages accruing from the cultivation of the mind? What is this shapened lump of clay, decorate it as we please, but a mere nothing, without a proper culture of that which makes it an object to be adored, which gives it vitality? Its inhabitant mind—

> Mind, mind alone, bear witness earth and heaven!
> The living fountain in itself contains
> Of beauteous and sublime.

There, hand in hand, sit paramount the graces;
There enthroned, celestial Venus, with divinest airs,
Invites the soul to never-fading joy.

Who is there, then, that would be so presumptuous as to deny
that Education is one of the greatest blessings that man can possess?
I trust no one in this assembly would fall so far short of common
reason; does it not check the irregularities of the heart, and remove
the evil propensities which obscure its brightest advances? Does it
not smother the dangerous feelings of vice; improve the taste which
springs from the soul, kindling into operation, and giving a powerful
impetus to the principles of learning and opinion, thereby presenting
an impenetrable shield to the approach of passion with its host of
direful evils? Does it not do all this? Most assuredly. It behoveth us,
then, to be up and doing. What more powerful argument—what
greater bulwark could we throw around our abolition friends—that
noble band of Christian warriors, who, regardless of the scoffs and
sneers of a pitiless world, have avowed themselves the unflinching
advocates of the perishing, unfolding to the eyes of this guilty nation
their sacred charter, which proclaims all free, and entitled to equal
rights and privileges; what more would they want, than to know,
that every step of ours was to virtue—every effort, was to stay the
ravages of depravity in our ranks, and to disseminate the light of
Education more widely among us than heretofore? What more
powerful to the pulling down of the strongholds of prejudice, than
our coming out to the world, notwithstanding our limited chances,
redeemed, unshackled, freed from the chains of ignorance, and
standing in the full majesty of mind—this too by our own hands—this
too by a fearlessness of purpose, by a determination to strike a
deathblow to that supineness which threatened to keep us a people
forever grovelling in the dark. Truly would we then have a glorious
inheritance which we would not blush to transmit to posterity.

Who, then, in anticipation of such happy results, designed to secure to us peace here and eternal happiness hereafter, would remain
silent, or refuse to encourage the promotion of Literature? Who
could be so inconsistent, so utterly destitute of sense, as to have
within his reach the means of destroying the reptile, prejudice,
which lays between him and his elevation, and yet be too indolent
to seize it. Sir, if we can overcome prejudice by mental force, let us
do so; let us go to work and charge ourselves to the muzzle. For too
long, sir, have we been crushed under its iron heel; still does it
pursue us, whichever way we bend our steps, this blighting, soul-
withering prejudice stares us in the face; it comes on the fiery tongue

of slander, and its evil machinations are forever seeking to blast our hopes; it gathers strength from the sulphurous atmosphere of perdition, and in the form of a Devil goes about to destroy the better feelings of man; its hot breath parches up the pure stream of benevolence which encircled and warmed the heart of youth, steals from his bosom all that is noble, generous and patriotic, and implants in their stead the most implacable hatred against his brother.

We have been proclaimed, time after time, an inferior race, utterly incapable of ever rising to an equal footing with the white population, in the scale of moral and intellectual worth; we are also told that we were destined by Providence to be subservient to the will and caprice of others—to bow and kiss the earth at their bidding. What base presumption; what an open insult to the Creator of all things. No, my brethren, if we are inferior in any respect, it is because they have made us so; it arises from their cruel and partial laws, and customs, and prejudices, and not, I can assure you, from any deficiency in our physical, moral or intellectual constitution. God is no respecter of persons. The same hand which, in the strength and might of its own uncreated power, made one man, made another; all are His family; He made all accountable to a moral government, enjoined upon all the sacred duty of living in bonds of charity with each other. The superiority, then, of one part of our population over the other, grows merely out of situation and advantages in life; and, Mr. President, I will here be vain enough to assert that we may gather, even from the imperfect sentiments advanced and the rough colours in which I have portrayed our proscribed state, some conception of the destructiveness, and bitter malignity of prejudice, and see in the mean time the necessity of our strangling the monster; and we can do so, and that too by the agency of the giant power of Education; for I am satisfied, fully satisfied, sir, that this demon is not invincible, as the enemies to the rights of man would feign have us believe. No, the spirit of death is in it, it cannot live—it must die. Yet, my brethren, we should be careful in all our walks, lest we should give the appearance of truth to the illiberal charges brought against us; we must not remain quiet or inactive, but approach as near to perpetual motion as possible. I fear we have been too tardy of late; it is requisite that we should now rally. What! shall we as citizens of America, permit the hateful yoke of indolence to remain unbroken on our shoulders? Are we to suffer that which man should hold near and dear to him, our moral character, to be held up as an object of ridicule? Are we content to wrap the mantle of ignorance around us, and cry out "a little more sleep, a little more slumber, a little more folding together of the arms?" Shall we, when told that we aspire to no other stations than hewers of wood and drawers of water, respond Amen, even be it so?—or shall we give the lie direct to these foul accusations, by examples of talent, genius, honesty, and sobriety, by rearing in our midst the broad standard of education? Be it ours to act thus. Why, sir, we would be really deserving of the severest censure, the bitterest denunciations that language could invent or the tongue of slander utter, if we, when civilization, light, and knowledge are shining around us, when the great principles of reform are penetrating the darkest corners of the earth, are unwilling to make one single effort to save ourselves. We should strain every nerve, should bring into full, active exercise, all the powers that God hath given us, and push onward, striving, if possible, to excel our white brethren in everything designed to "raise the genius and to mend the heart."

It is undoubtedly true that, among some of our young men, there is a disposition to appear conspicuous in the eyes of the world; but I am fearful it is not of the right stamp, and will excite the ridicule, instead of the approbation of the reflecting and respectable. I am exceedingly sorry to find so many of our talented young men, instead of spending their leisure hours in instructing the uninformed, striving their best to imitate the fashionable follies of the day. I would be more explicit did occasion suffer me. But, oh! let me respectfully entreat you to banish such conduct forever; and let our ambition be of that genuine cast, which scorns all low, mean, degrading things, sets its face against all frivolous and unprofitable amusements, and aims only at the more lofty and substantial materials, which are sure to beautify and adorn the intellect. Let us be archers in the Godlike cause of Universal Reform; our target, Literature,—our arrows, Industry. It is to be hoped that no one will take offence at the slight hints I have thrown out, but, on the contrary, view it as a friendly desire of your humble speaker to do good. We all are aware, I trust, that discretion is all important in any undertaking. Then, while we claim the right, as freemen, to indulge in all the innocent recreations of the age, the right, as freemen, to act as we please, so long as we keep within the pale of law, order, and decorum, we should also, in the meanwhile, question the policy of such a step—should ask ourselves whether it be consistent with our abolition principles, whether it looks much like self-denial, or sympathy for the oppressed, or remembering those who are in bonds as bound with them.

But to return. Strict attention to Education is all desirable with us. Besides, it is our indispensable duty as responsible beings, to be studious and diligent. We were not sent here merely to eat, drink, and be merry—to revel over the sparkling champagne or rich Madeira until the watch of the night warns us of the lateness of the hour; but for a higher and nobler purpose. We are imperatively commanded to cultivate the talents which the great Lawgiver of Heaven gave to us; and whenever we neglect our moral, physical, and mental Education, we render ourselves criminal—we are guilty of a downright insult to that Omnipotent Being.

Man was ordained to hold empire over the fowls of the air, the beast of the forest, and the inhabitants of the deep—stamped the noblest work of creation,—made but a little lower than the angels. He was destined to shed the brightest lustre throughout the land, to guide the reins of state, to establish mild and equitable laws, and, from a consciousness of his superior structure, to rise in grandeur like the oak, nourished by the limpid stream which flows beneath it, spreading branches of knowledge far and wide. Be not surprised, my friends, at the immensity of the work you are called upon to perform. The capacity of the human intellect is boundless. It is to be seen in the wonderful contrivance of machinery, in the great discovery of the propelling power of steam, enabling us to travel to all parts of our Union with an almost incredible swiftness, and a thousand other proofs I might mention of the magnitude of the human intellect, did time permit. Let it suffice here to say, that no obstacle can present itself, but what human effort can surmount.

Let us, sir, for a moment, contrast the difference between the literate and the illiterate man. The one resembles a beautiful edifice, adorned and fitted up for occupation; the other an unfinished building, abandoned by the slothful labourer; the materials are there, but not a finger is raised to touch them; the straw is there, but no bricks are made; and instead of carved frames, and richly moulded cornices, the wood remains in its rough, unturned state, without beauty, comeliness, order, or symmetry. The one is courted, admired and respected wherever he goes, for he carries with him an indisputable power. The other is at a loss to know how to act or express his thoughts, and hangs only as a dead weight upon society; when mingling with the enlightened, he renders everything disagreeable around him; his intercourse through life is but a ceaseless exhibition of passion and headlong impetuosity; he cares not for the opinion of others, and seldom lends an attentive ear to the admonitions of the better informed; but, puffed up with conceit, wonders at the daring presumption of anyone differing from him in sentiment or action. My brethren, disguise ignorance as you may—cover it with all the adornments that fancy or art can suggest—still, through all that gorgeous apparel, may be seen its utter destitution of the one thing needful—the renovating, soul-cheering, vital principle of Education. "The soul without reflection, like a pile without inhabitant, to ruin runs." Ignorance in society is always sure to engender mischief of some kind or other; vice of every description is its necessary appendage. It destroys all government in domestic affairs, and deprives the individual under its pernicious influence of the power to regulate, or fully appreciate, the rules of domestic economy. Now, if it be the means of so deranging the finest machinery of society, if it be the parent of the many evils I have attempted to describe, our first act should be to get rid of so dangerous an enemy. In the nervous language of the eloquent Thompson, we should "cut down the pestiferous tree, eradicate it root and branch, annihilate now, annihilate forever."

But, Mr. President, I am not ignorant of the fact that there are many, who, as an excuse for their idleness and carelessness, would say, "oh, we can't do anything; there is so much prejudice against us that there is no use of attending to the cultivation or accomplishment of our minds." Let me beg such to be careful how they venture upon so fatal a conclusion. Why, we should be educated in order to improve and cheapen the pleasures of our own society, to benefit our own people, and to set an example to the rising generation. We should at least be able to teach them that to be useful, their enjoyments must be of an intellectual character—to rise in the estimation of the wise and good, they must look to those pursuits which are sure to nourish and sustain the immortal mind, rather than the dying body. I will grant, however, that we labour under an intolerable burden; that the arm of oppression is laid bare to crush us; that prejudice, like the never-satiated tiger, selects us as its prey; that we have felt the withering blight of tyranny sweeping from before us, in its destructive course, our homes and our property. Yet we can still do something for ourselves; still is there an avenue open, through which we can reach the fountain of wisdom. And parents, for I would here take the liberty of addressing you, it is to this avenue I would have you lead your children; see that they attend strictly to the various schools now open for their reception, and conducted by able, benevolent and kindhearted men, men who have a sincere regard for the future happiness of your children; and, above all, see that they do not neglect their sabbath schools; for, if ever there was anything calculated to bless your children, and make them honourable members of society—the future hope and promise of our land—it is sabbath schools. Oh what a prolific source of good is to be found there, what sweet impressions can there be made on the early germs of character. It is there, can be learned the solemn duty of loving and respecting each other; there, food may be found for the immortal soul. I hail them as a double blessing; as the rock of ages, they stand laden with the gems of Heaven; they come, like the star of Bethlehem, to shed rays of peace and goodwill to all mankind.

Again, let no one say that he cannot do anything, but rather let him try. These "can't do any thing" persons remind me of an anecdote I heard related once of a youth, who had been ordered one day by his father to put the counting room to rights, while he was gone out on business; he promised obedience; but when the father returned, he found his son standing near the table, and every thing in the same topsy-turvy state as when he left. Why, my son! exclaimed he, why did you not do as I desired? I can't, sir, it is so hard; besides, sir—besides what? I'm tied fast to the table here; Tied to the table! who tied you? why, why, sir, I—I—tied myself. Now, often do we find persons imitating the conduct of this foolish youth. They say they cannot accomplish an object, when at the same time they are too indolent, and will stand still and not move hand or foot. No, my friends, we must try. I, for one, will never admit, degraded, fallen though we may be, that we cannot reform. We are men possessing physical and mental powers in common with other men. It only requires industry, to bring into full and beneficial operation these noble qualities with which all men are naturally endowed, and which will enable them to walk in the full stature and dignity of men.

There is one branch of Education that I would earnestly recommend to you, and that is Domestic Education. And how forcibly does the remark which fell from the lips of our respected and beloved friend, Henry C. Wright, rush upon my memory. He said, that "it was in the domestic circles, that a great reformation could be accomplished; that there, a vast amount of good might be done— there, children might be trained up in the many arts and sciences, and in moral duties, free from the eye of hatred, and the pointed finger of scorn." How true are these sentiments of our brother; and how zealously ought we to strive to profit by them, to hoard them up, to watch over them carefully. Parents! for there must be such in this large assembly, pardon me for again appealing to you; let me but adjure you to fit your children in your domestic circles, for public life. Educate them; the little that you have fortunately obtained extend to them; and, while you, despite the veil of darkness which lowers about you, have caught one glimpse of the star of science, point out that same glorious light to the youthful being at your side. In the domestic circle children can be taught prudence and forbearance, so that they will be prepared to buffet the storms of adversity, when they place their feet on the stage where they are to seek a livelihood by their own exertions; and should they be compelled to occupy those humble situations in life, to which that accursed prejudice has driven many an aspiring mind, the lessons they have learned at home will stimulate them to industry, and cause them to be obedient and faithful to those whom they serve.

Again, Mr. President, to be educated we must be persevering. It is perseverance we want; let us get hold of this. What, I ask, would the cause of learning and our country have lost, if a Franklin, a Rittenhouse, a Rush, could have been made to quail before the frowning brow of persecution? Why, our houses, perhaps, would not have been protected from the fury of the lightning of Heaven; the planetary system, which pay their nightly visits to the world, would not have produced such happy contemplations, and caused man's soul to be lifted from earth to his Maker, in admiration of the sublimity of the starry firmament; and our medical academies, there is no doubt, would not have been thronged, as they now are, by ambitious youths studying the complicated machinery of man, exploring the "arcana of the healing art." What would have been this vast metropolis, with its extensive internal improvements, if our reformers of old had refused to lay their hands to the plough—if the first settlers had thought that the clearing of the land could not be effected. Why, our splendid cities would not have been here, the proud boast of America. Our inimitable waterworks, with their inimitable facilities for supplying us with the pure stream from the Schuylkill, imparting health and vigour to the body, would not have been here to gladden the eye of the stranger, and to induce him to start with wonder and surprise. Our canals, railroads and locomotives—powerful helpers in the facilities of commerce, and the rapid transmission of private and public information—would never have been introduced to the world; but, on the contrary, our whole country would still be in its rude and uncultivated state.

But aspiring ambition was working in the hearts of men. They saw that a reform was wanting. The axe was applied, blow upon blow was struck, and the proud sycamore, the graceful elm, and stately oak trembled and fell; in a little while the once impenetrable forest was changed into verdant and widely extended meadows, richly laden fields, and beautiful flower gardens. The voice of William Penn spoke, and the council fires of the Red Men were extinguished; the wild song of the young hunter of the woods was hushed; and the blood-freezing war-whoop ceased to echo and re-echo over mountain and crag, startling the timid deer as he lay reposing in his lair; superstition was prostrated in the dust, and mind has ever since reigned triumphant. All this great revolution was wrought by dint of perseverance. We have, then, to imitate the example of these departed spirits, and persevere in all that our hands find to do; and soon shall we behold the clouds of ignorance that now, with threatening aspect, hang over our heads, vanishing before the bright sunshine of Literature. Let every one feel it his duty, then, to press forward; there is no cause to be fainthearted; friends are pouring in to our aid every day. Have we not enough to encourage us? Go with me back to the earliest ages, and if I must again advert to history, turn over and over again, the leaves of that ancient chronicler of the times, and tell me if it has there treasured a single instance where a people situated as we are, have ever equally borne up against the torrent of oppression, outrage and insult. Is it not encouraging to think that, despised and scoffed at as we are, we have nevertheless set our calumniators a lesson of resignation to the wrongs they have inflicted on us? Injuries which might have demanded revenge on our part we have buried eternally in the depths of our bosoms; we have clothed ourselves in the panoply of nonresistance, and submitted patiently to mobocracy and lynch law. Let us not despair, then; but, relying on the never-failing anchor of Hope, let our motto be, *Education;* our watchword, *Perseverance.*

Sir, we are even now on the march to the Temple of Fame. As proof of this I would point you to our many Literary institutions. Some of these, I am happy to say, are creditably conducted by the females, who are generally to be found foremost in the cause of Moral Reform. It must have been a gratifying sight, to all who were present on the evening that a member of this church addressed the Ladies' Literary Society, entitled the "Edgeworth Society," to see so large a number of our respectable females collected together, all uniting in one grand purpose—the diffusion of knowledge; to hear them reading and reciting in a manner that would reflect honour upon any community. Much opposition has of late existed in relation to females being educated on a more extensive scale than formerly. I regret to see this, and am fearful it originates from an unmanly and selfish motive. For it appears to me that our sex startle at the idea of woman rising equal to them in the sphere of intellectual strength. But why should she not? What just reason can be assigned for her not becoming acquainted with all the branches of polite Literature? Would it not give her additional beauties? What is it that adds charms to society, and sheds a potent brilliancy around it, but an accomplished woman? What signifies external elegance, if the mind within be shrouded in ignorance? Woman should be well-instructed in all the higher branches, if it were only to check that false pride and unpardonable vanity which we are too apt to assume towards her and which ungenerously prompts us to look with contempt upon her slender abilities. Now if we are truly sincere in our endeavors to do good—in promulgating the blessings of Education—we will not hesitate to act because woman wishes to cooperate with us. It is not for us to place a stumbling block in the path of any one who is desirous to enlist in the same cause which we are endeavoring to promote; it is not for us to belie our principles; to cry aloud against persecution, and in the meanwhile play the part of persecutors; to be the first to draw a line of demarkation, and prevent the "divinest work of creation" from a free use of her reasoning faculties. Such a state of things will never do. Let us at least keep in her good graces, by looking with approval upon every step she takes in polite learning; let us exhibit a mutual interest, a universal desire, to widen and extend every rational enjoyment. Such should be our highest aspirations, and I sincerely trust they will. Ladies, I would say to you, then, go on conquering and to conquer in all that will increase your pleasures, refine your taste, and polish both head and heart.

Our Library Association is gaining strength every day; we have a well supplied stock of books collected from the most useful and varied productions of the age. It has received the countenance and approbation of the most choice, intellectual, and influential of our citizens; and, as a mark of their esteem for us, they have contributed liberally to our reading department. This one circumstance is sufficient to show us the necessity of being enlightened. Here we have the fact that as soon as we engage in any enterprise having for its foundation the mighty principles of mental illumination, we are at once noticed and respected. Thus we see that, whatever tends to disseminate the principles of education, tends to raise us above the tide of popular prejudice; and whatever tends to raise us above the chilling influence of prejudice, must of reason tend to elevate our condition; and whatever has been prominent in any degree in effecting such results, must be productive of good. Such, I conceive, our Literary Institutions to have the power of doing. It seems to me, then, that the main object is to accomplish an intellectual and moral reformation. And I know of but few better ways to effect this than by reading, by examining, by close comparisons and thorough investigations, by exercising the great faculty of thinking; for, if a man can be brought to think, he soon discovers that his highest enjoyment consists in the improvement of the mind; it is this that will give him rich ideas, and teach him, also, that his limbs were never made to wear the chains of servitude; he will see too that equal rights were intended for all. Then who would not wish to become inspired with a taste for reading, if it has the ability to create so happy a state of things as I have just described. Yet we should be particular what kind of works we select. They should be those that would be sure to yield us profitable information, and teach us sound practical lessons—Natural History, Natural Philosophy, Astronomy, Chemistry, Geography and Grammar, for instance. These are delightful studies, and perfectly accessible; but it is to be deeply regretted that they are not more countenanced, and more extensively sought after by us. Rest assured, these would give us a character, would throw a wall of brass around us, too high to be overleaped, too powerful to be overcome. We all know, however, that the best Education can be perverted; for how many of the youth of our land who have been cradled in the lap of ease, raised in the very midst of science, upon whom hundreds have been lavished, in order to make them learned and useful men—bright stars in the constellation in which they were destined to move—have, after all, exhibited the very worst specimens of human depravity, have turned out to be a disgrace to their parents, and a scourge to their country. Education, then, can be often abused for the want of proper discipline, and is dangerous when acquired to the exclusion of moral instruction. The great benefit, therefore, to be derived from Education, depends upon the manner we apply it; for it will in the end avail a man but little happiness, unless he connects with it his great moral obligations. In a word, if we want virtue to predominate over vice, we must possess a moral education.

But while I submit these essential things to your consideration and due attention, far be it from me to discountenance or discourage some other branches of Education, in which our people are exceedingly fond of participating, such as the art of music and singing. I am extravagantly partial to them; indeed, devoid of taste must that mind be which is insensible to the charms of music. It must (as an eminent writer observes) be a "mind which is either absorbed in some one overwhelming idea, which for a season engrosses all its faculties, and harrows its feelings with an endless train of vexatious recollections, or a mind which nature has not cast in the common mould of humanity"—and a mind, too, which nature has forgotten to invest with a capacity for progressive improvement and social intercourse. Music and singing are certainly refined and intellectual arts, and are essentially necessary to buoy us up as recreations of life; but we must all admit that, unless they are accompanied by something more substantial, less adapted to attract only the attention without producing any lasting impression, they would soon grow insipid and lose their sweetness.

Mr. President, when we reflect for a moment upon what Education has achieved, what is to prevent us from arriving to any given height in prosperity, if we only continue in the path of industry and enterprise. But I fear, sir, that I have already intruded too far upon your kindness, have put the patience of this audience to too severe a test, and will therefore conclude with a few desultory remarks on the merits of the general principles of our Moral Reform Society. If ever there was a day dawned, teeming with glory and future grandeur to our people, it was that which ushered in that messenger of peace. The trumpet of reform sounded, and our hills echoed back its melodious tones; the sun of Heaven shone not on a fairer creature; all creation seemed to gather a brighter radiance from her presence. The altars of bigotry fell crumbling before its omnipotent power, and they that were dead in iniquity awoke, and have come forth redeemed, clad in the armour of morality. Its portentous blast has struck terror to the remorseless tyrant; day after day, he feels its mightiness and trembles; while, at the same time, the hapless captive, prostrate at his feet, catches the heavenly notes, expiring hope rallies—mounts high in his bosom—rushes through every channel of his heart—circulates in every vein, and he looks forward with a brighter eye to the day of deliverance. Yes, my brethren, I firmly believe that one of the greatest means to lead to the overthrow of the dreadful system of soul trafficking is moral reform among us. When this becomes general, the whole north will be abolitionists. They will perceive that we are an industrious people, equal to them in all that is moral and elevating, equally capable of self-government. Their finer feelings will be touched, and they will cry out with one voice to the south, "undo the heavy burden, break every yoke, and let the oppressed go free," that they may share with their brethren in the sweets of liberty, peace and plenty. Oppression must fall before the power of such principles as are contained in the declaration of this Society; principles imposing a solemn obligation upon all those who enlist under them; principles, while they urge upon a guilty nation the claims of perishing millions, bringing before our eyes the frightful criminality of the tyrannical oppressor; principles safe and sure to unite every creed and clime and colour in the universe in one unalterable link of justice and humanity.

To possess morality in its purity, we must be careful in our walks; remembering that she should be held sacred as her ancient parent, Religion. Brethren, a great work remains for us to perform. Look you into the south part of our city, and there you will find a great field of labour; there you will behold wretchedness which beggars description—wretchedness that will make the eye of pity weep, to witness the image of God defaced, brutalized, trampled in the dust.

Oh! it is to be devoutly hoped that the committee of vigilance, appointed by this Society to examine into the condition of those people, will spare no pains and relax none of their energies, in striving to reclaim their fallen brethren, and bring them over to the path of honesty and soberness; that they will point out to them their deplorable situation, reason with them mildly and as becometh Christians, and bid them at once to dash the bitter cup of Intemperance for ever from their lips—bid them touch it not, for it contains a deadly liquid fresh from the boiling cauldron of the damned. Do this, and you will receive the prayers of many a broken-hearted mother; do this, and you will secure the bounteous smiles of Heaven. Sir, we have been too dilatory; too long have our ministers suffered this degradation to dwell among us. It is time they were calling them in from our lanes and alleys, and expostulating with them. For our own credit we should rally. What! shall envy, strife and dissentions destroy us? I trust not; oh! let us not be a scourge to the world instead of an example. Up, up, while it is yet time; clear your streets of the corruption now suffered to pollute them; show not a craven spirit and sound a retreat, but charge home upon the monster, Vice. Let us seize the sceptre of Moral Reform, and make these sacred walls the place of resuscitation; here, let us unite hand to hand, and with the sword of love, and animated by light and knowledge, go forth to battle with sin, and to lay waste the strong places of Satan. Yes, let America behold the reformation of our people. Be it ours to make but one era of the triumph of Reform and the revival of Virtue; be it ours to do this, and we will have gained a glorious conquest—a conquest over ourselves.

REMARKS

On the subject of Temperance, by John Francis Cook, delivered before the American Moral Reform Society, in St. Thomas' Church, Philadelphia, August 16th, 1837.

"*Resolved,* That the successful promotion of all the principles of the Moral Reform Society, viz.: Education, Temperance, Economy, and Universal Love, depends greatly upon the practical prosecution of the Temperance reform."

Mr. President: In presenting this resolution, permit me to say that the present state of my physical constitution, and the very short time I have had to prepare, will not permit me to trespass upon the patience of this respectable assembly by a long and elaborate argument to prove the subject of my resolution. But, in compliance with the request of some of the leading members here, I have prepared a few simple remarks, to present for your charitable consideration, on the very common subject of Temperance. Notwithstanding my inability to do justice to the subject, the triteness thereof, and my disposition to be only a quiet listener in this venerable assembly, yet I do not feel at liberty to decline the proffered invitation, lest I might be considered a recreant to the stand I have taken, the cause I love, the principles I avow and cherish, and, by God's grace, shall endeavour humbly to support. I congratulate this Society on its again assembling together. Happy am I, friends, once more to meet you this side of eternity, for the purpose of joining, I trust, our harmonious considerations for the promotion of the glorious causes of Education, Temperance, Economy, and Universal Love. It is natural that we should hail this event with no small feelings of joy and exultation, with feelings of gratitude to Him who has spared us for the glorious purpose of promoting His cause. Is it unnatural for us to indulge the hope that this Society, though an infant in age, will speedily advance with untiring zeal to a greater and more elevated rank; that the great object of mental and moral advancement will cheer us on, and upon the basis of Education, Temperance, Economy, and Universal Love, will be reared an edifice that will endure with our time, and prove the home of religion, virtue and truth? Let, then, our exercises on this occasion adorn our character as a body of men, sweeten our social deliberations by uniting the charms of friendship, and so bring into one harmonious sphere of mutual action all the moral abilities with which we have been gifted by our good and Almighty Father, in pushing forward and disseminating the principles of our worthy institution. In efforts so laudable, every encouragement awaits us. Knowledge, virtue, philanthropy, and charity—all present themselves robed in all that is honourable and useful in life, and spread before you the prospects of their rich reward; while our true friends are looking on, waiting to see us take our stand and press our principles among our people, and by those means aid them in advancing the cause of human rights, of righteousness and truth. With these bright prospects then before us, it will not, I trust, be deemed inappropriate to the present occasion, or an unpleasant theme, notwithstanding its triteness, to present to this respected assembly a few broken thoughts on the subject of Temperance, especially as it regards its connection with the other great and fundamental principles of this society.

Firstly, when we take a view of the powerful effect which intemperance has in retarding the progress of the first great principles of our Society, we can but condemn it, and use every exertion in promoting the glorious principles of temperance. It is an enemy to Education, because it destroys reason, and wholly unfits a man or child for any growth in knowledge. That it makes men ignorant and keeps them so is a truth that is self-evident; it needs no argument to prove or qualify the assertion, as all present are well acquainted with, or eye-witnesses of the fact. And no one will dare deny that intemperance destroys all incentives to the acquisition of knowledge, and therefore subverts the principles of a good Education, by the attainment of which, ignorance and its concomitant evils, prejudice and superstition, will pass away, and we would be enabled to obtain and enjoy the privileges and blessings we are now unjustly deprived of. If the progress of Education was not so much retarded by the influence of the intoxicating cup, the grog shops, taverns and other haunts of intemperance and vice, how many young men of colour who are now the inmates of these places, might be useful in diffusing the principles of a virtuous education, and correct and enlightened sentiments among our people? Education, as a great and pervading influence in exalting, sustaining and supporting us as a people, in this our native country, would be beyond computation, immense. Yes, if we could cause the influence of the intemperate, and the millions of money expended by them, to be exerted in favour of the cause of education, even among our own people, every child of colour in our land would have a liberal education. We would soon shine forth and become lights in our country, happy citizens, honest patriots, and useful men. To secure these valuable objects, and endeavor to turn the scale in favor of education, is one of the noble objects of the American Moral Reform Society. We call on you, then, by every generous emotion of the heart—by the duties we owe ourselves and our friends, and by the claims of our common country, by the gratitude we owe to Him who has permitted us to enjoy the privileges we now enjoy, by all the anticipations of better times and privileges, to endeavor to use all our exertions to promote this great object of our Society, Education, by the destruction of intemperance.

Secondly, The next great object of our Society is the promotion of Temperance in all things, which cannot be more effectually accomplished than by abandoning the intoxicating fluid, which, besides destroying reason, creates intemperate habits and appetites. And nothing can aid it more than by every friend of moral reform coming out, and uniting in the exertion of their individual efforts—advocating in private and public the blessings of Temperance and unfolding the evils of intemperance, and by the habitual practice of sobriety, without which no man can be safe, happy, useful, respectable or intelligent; for intemperance is the germinating source of a long train of pernicious diseases, horrible pains, and causes us to be the miserable and disgusting victims of hatred and scorn. This is not all. Aside from its destroying reason, character, health, moral sensibility, virtue, the faculties of the mind, the affections of the heart— it brings high and low, rich and poor, noble and ignoble, through scorn, contempt, disease, anguish and remorse, to a maniac's death, and then leads them from the frown of man, to the bar of a righteous and sin-avenging God, who does not behold sin with any degree of allowance, and who has, by his sacred word, declared that "no drunkard shall inherit the kingdom of heaven." If such is a mere glimpse of a few of the evils connected with intemperance, does it not go very conclusively to show that intemperance is a great obstruction to the successful promotion of all the principles of Moral Reform; and is it not the duty of every man, of whatever caste or complexion, or in whatever condition, to use every exertion to promote the cause of Temperance, and resolutely declare by precept and example, at every opportunity, that they will "neither touch, taste nor handle the unclean thing."

Now, if we are temperate ourselves, let us go and teach our poor fellow man the absurdity of the doctrine which he has been taught, that the intoxicating fluid is necessary for to strengthen, to entertain, to warm, to cool; that, on the contrary, it is a certain and sure destroyer of the human body and soul. Teach him that the temptations held out, under the shadow of the license law, for filthy lucre's sake, if followed, will lead through a gateway to the damned. Tell him of the tempting influences of ardent spirit in its various forms as administered at the tavern, grog shops, at the festive board, and too often in the social circle. Tell him, that though he may be strongly tempted thereby, this does not destroy or diminish his guilt; and then remind him that the inebriate is driven by the temptations of Bacchus to deeds of violence and death; that by intemperance he robs on the highway, by it the sudden passion of the murderer is sharpened, by it the cherished revenge of the assassin is made stronger, and he is made ready to plunge the instrument of death into the bosom of the object of his hate—perhaps his own mother, father, brother, sister, wife, or child. Tell him that by the influence of the intoxicating cup, we are prepared to violate the whole moral and Christian law of God; to bow down and worship images, the idol of Bacchus, forgetting the true God, taking his name in vain, violating his holy sabbath, dishonouring father and mother and bringing their gray hairs down to the grave with sorrow; that we are made ready to kill, murder, commit adultery, steal, lie, and defraud our neighbour, and covet what is his; that we are rendered wholly incapable of regarding the Christian virtues—love to God, universal love to man, or a proper regard for ourselves. Tell him that by it, immediately after the deluge, was Canaan cursed, which curse has been entailed on his posterity even unto this day. Tell him that doubtless by it David, Solomon, and many others were tempted to do many of their offensive acts in the sight of God. Tell him that through the influence of intemperance we strip ourselves of decency, order, decorum and honour; we extinguish reason, throw off the character of men and put on that of brutes, rush into wickedness and insanity, and become a disgrace to mankind, loathsome even to our beggared families, corrupting youth and teaching them debauchery and crime—cursed upon the earth, and we fear cursed from the presence of Him who hath declared that he will not receive any drunkard into his kingdom. Who is there, then, in this enlightened assembly that will not accord with the language of the resolution, and the position I have taken, and have been endeavoring to sustain, that the successful promotion of all the principles of this Society depends greatly upon the advancement of the Temperance reformation—the second position being, I think, clearly brought to bear, that Temperance in general depends upon the abolition of intoxicating liquors.

Let us, then use every exertion in our power to abolish the liquid poison, and by that means not only the recommendation of the apostle to "be temperate in all things" would be followed, but we should at the same time promote education, and the third great object of our Society—Economy—which is also a great virtue. One of the greatest luxuries of life appears to consist in the bowl, both among rich and poor, noble and ignoble. They spend their earnings, sometimes hard earnings, "to revel in a brutish bliss, to find an age of wo." Yes, with the hundred millions spent annually for intemperance, we could redeem every slave from under the yoke of an iron-handed oppression, educate every child in our land, and promote happiness among all who are now in wretchedness, poverty and misery. Let us then endeavor to promote economy by the suppression of intemperance, and we shall be able to do more for God, ourselves, and our fellow man. It is a virtue of much importance to us as a people, especially in our present situation, as it enables us to keep within our proper limits or means, and by so doing we are enabled to sustain and promote Education, Temperance and Charity. It will not permit us to ape the fashionable appearances of the times; but our pride will be the adorning of the mind and heart, in moral and mental qualifications. It is a virtue generally regarded as having a tendency to make us mean, ungenerous and selfish. This is not the case; it may be of avarice, but not properly of economy. "True economy is a careful treasure in the service of benevolence, and when they are united, respectability, prosperity and peace will follow as so many native streams." Let us endeavor to promote economy by destroying intemperance and bringing our influence to bear in favor thereof. Every one present must agree with me, that intemperance presents a great barrier to the promotion of economy.

The last proposition I shall very briefly attempt to urge is, that intemperance in the use of intoxicating liquors is an enemy to the successful promotion of the fourth grand object of Moral Reform, which I shall take the liberty here to term Universal Love, which I think equal if not much better than the term now used; at least, I think it might be the means of extending the influence of this Society over every portion of our beloved country, whereas now its direct influence is only known and felt in what are commonly called the free states; at any rate it would be more agreeable to the section of country where I have the pleasure of residing, and doubtless to every part of the country. For the term now used can be maliciously or wilfully construed as an unlimited control of all the passions, without regard to law, decency or order; but if we were to substitute the term Universal Love, I think it would answer every purpose of the term now used, for there is no one here, I presume, willing to doubt the language of inspiration which says, that "wherever the spirit of love is, there is liberty."

Universal Love consists not in speculative ideas of benevolence— and in being free from malice, envy, &c.; but in the language of Blair, "it is an active principle, residing in the heart as a fountain, from whence all the heavenly virtues of benignity, candor, forbearance, generosity, compassion and philanthropy flow, as so many homogeneous streams." This principle of love teaches us to extend and exert all our good influence in our respective communities and neighborhoods, by the glorious principles of peace, virtue, and philanthropy. It prompts us to do all we can for the amelioration of the condition of ourselves, and our fellow men. It breathes candor and liberality of sentiment toward all men. It forms good manners, tempers, habits, actions and sympathies. In the language of an inspired penman, it enables us "to rejoice with them that rejoice, and weep with them that weep." In short, it is the sum and substance of all our duty on record in the Bible, for it teaches us to love God with all our minds, and our fellow men as ourselves. It is, then, the soul of all our social, moral and political enjoyments—it is the sum that enlivens, enlightens, and cheers our pathway through the transitory scenes of time, and accompanies us to the Elysian fields of the paradise of God. Or, in the language of the Psalmist, "it is like the dew of Hermon, and the dew that descended on the mountains of Zion, even when the Lord commanded the blessing, even life for ever more." Can any one doubt for a moment, then, that the inebriate can enjoy this holy principle of God, of angels, and (should be) of men? You will all agree with me in the assertion that intemperance greatly impedes the progress of Universal Love, and therefore greatly obstructs all the principles of Moral Reform. Let us, then, notwithstanding the triteness of the subject, as I before said, continue our hostility against it, while intemperance stalks abroad in our land. Let us use every exertion in our power to promote the principles of temperance; as, by so doing, we will greatly aid the cause of Education, Temperance, Economy and Universal Love.

Having very briefly, and I trust satisfactorily, endeavored to bring before you the subject of my resolution, permit me to thank you for your attention, and appeal to you, and to all present, as you value education, knowledge, science and the arts, as you value temperance in all things, as you value economy, industry and benevolence, as you value the principles of love, yea, as you love the Lord himself (for "God is love"), to adopt and sustain the Temperance reformation, and, in so doing, exhibit to our enemies and the world that we are capable of enjoying the great blessings bestowed upon us by the great parent of all, but denied by man, namely, civil and religious liberty.

I again appeal to you, fathers and mothers, as you value the future prospects of your sons and daughters, their probity, chastity, and well being, to use all your efforts to promote this holy cause. I appeal to you, young men and maidens, to promote this cause, as you value your future prospects in the world, as you hope for better times, when persecution shall cease, and when you and I shall, by the promulgation of correct moral sentiments, be enabled to enjoy the rights and privileges of American citizens; which can be done, if you will exert your influence at the polls, at the festive board, in the social circle, and in every place where an opportunity can be found.

I cannot resume my seat, Mr. President, without giving the passing attention to the ladies which their influence demands. As your influence is great in the prosecution of every good cause, permit me to appeal to you, Ladies—you who inspired the great Thompson, the champion of Human Rights, to cross the great briny waters of the Atlantic, to plead the cause of suffering humanity in "this land of liberty"—you, who inspired a Dickson, a Slade, and an Adams, and many others, to rise in our nation's councils, to plead the cause of

3,000,000 of oppressed men in our land—you, who followed the Saviour up and down while upon earth doing good—you, who were last at the cross, and first at the sepulchre, will you not reach out your arm (the arm of your influence) and raise poor degraded human nature from the mire of Ignorance, Intemperance, Vice, Luxury, Voluptuousness and Oppression.

And, finally, I appeal to high Heaven, in the name of our Great Redeemer, and invoke the blessings of our Heavenly Father, upon the holy cause of Education, Temperance, Economy and Universal Love.

Part IV

To Emigrate or Remain at Home?

1773–1833

The years between 1817 and 1840 provide an interesting format for analyzing thought among free blacks regarding colonization, whether to Guiana, Canada, Haiti, Honduras, Demerara, Trinidad, Texas, or elsewhere. Their opinions were expressed in many arguments for and against leaving the land of their birth. They utilized to the maximum the press, conventions and mass meetings, correspondence from emigrees, and the public platform and pulpit. The subject of emigration, especially to Africa as proposed by the American Colonization Society, was characterized by vigorous debate reflecting the overwhelming endorsement of the Society's object by some to extreme hostility towards it by others. Paul Cuffe, free Negro shipowner and navigator, firmly believed that American Negroes should return to Africa as colonists and traders in order to escape the horrors of slavery and discrimination. He explored Sierra Leone in 1811 for purposes of colonization and trade, and actually established thirty-eight Negroes in West Africa at his own expense. Cuffe died in 1817, only months after the American Colonization Society was formed.[1]

On the other hand, Richard Allen, Nathaniel Paul, and James Forten, Sr., who were at first unopposed to emigration, viewed the work of the Colonization Society as a nefarious scheme of the slaveocracy and various prejudiced elements of America to eliminate all free people of color, and thereby place the institution of slavery on a firmer foundation. Possibly the earliest request of slaves to return to Africa and freedom was made by Peter Bestes and others of Boston in their petition dated April 20, 1773. Other free persons of color such as the respectable "Free Men of Colour" in Charleston, South Carolina, equated the emigration of blacks to Liberia to the emigra-

[1] Henry N. Sherwood, "Paul Cuffe" *Journal of Negro History* Vol. 8, No. 2, (April, 1923), pp. 153–232.

tion of Europeans to America, where the end result of the latter was inevitably wealth.

The first meeting of the American Colonization Society was held on December 25, 1816. Its constitution was adopted December 31, 1816 and the election of its first officers occurred January 1, 1817.[2] Three weeks later, on January 24, 1817, the free colored people of Richmond, Virginia expressed their general approval of the colonization idea, but preferred "being colonized in the most remote corner of the land of our nativity, to being exiled to a foreign country." This was the first demonstration of hostility to the Colonization Society and its objectives.

On August 10, 1817, James Forten, a wealthy sailmaker of Philadelphia, declared in a meeting of free people of color in Philadelphia that "we have no wish to separate from our present homes for any purpose whatever."[3] Thus he aroused his listeners, and the campaign to fight the colonization movement was begun.

Debates on the subject to emigrate or not to emigrate were stimulated by critical situations which daily confronted free people of color in their efforts to survive. Laws in both Northern and Southern states were calculated to provide as uncomfortable living conditions as possible for them. In Ohio, laws almost entirely limiting the immigration of free blacks more or less typified Northern attitudes. Campaigns in Southern states existed for the removal of free blacks, or the levying of almost unpayable fines on them, with the penalty of sale into slavery if the fine went unpaid. To many, the intolerable conditions they faced daily were ample justification of emigration or actual financial support of the Colonization Society; John Mosely, a wealthy colored man, upon his death in June, 1825, was found to have willed 1000 dollars to the American Colonization Society.[4]

---

[2] John W. Cromwell, *The Negro in American History* (Washington, D.C.: The American Negro Academy, 1914), p. 19.

[3] James Forten in a letter to the Editor of the *New England Spectator*, dated June 10, 1835 made a brief statement concerning the meetings held by people of color in Philadelphia in 1817, to express their opinion of emigration to Liberia. See *Report of the Discussion on American Slavery, in Dr. Wardlow's Chapel, Between Mr. George Thompson and Rev. R. J. Brookinridge . . .* (Glasgow, 1836), pp. 37–38. See also Robert Purvis *Remarks on the Life and Character of James Forten* (Philadelphia, 1842); Esther Douty *James Forten, The Sail Maker, Pioneer Champion of Negro Rights* (Chicago, 1968); Ray A. Billington, "James Forten: Forgotten Abolitionist," *Negro History Bulletin*, Vol. 13, 1949.

[4] *African Repository and Colonial Journal*, Vol. 1, No. 4 (June, 1825), p. 128.

The exposure of the Colonization "delusion" by the American Anti-Slavery Society extended to England. Many Britishers had been convinced that the object of the American Colonization Society was the abolition of slavery and the civilization of Africa and had donated money to an agent, Elliott Cresson, of the Colonization Society to aid it in its objectives.

The Reverend Nathaniel Paul, at one time minister of the First African Baptist Society in Albany, New York (1820–1830), who had gone to England to raise money for the Wilberforce Settlement in Upper Canada. He delivered a speech at the large Anti-Colonization Meeting held in Exeter Hall, London, on July 13, 1833, in which he launched a scathing two-pronged attack against the Colonization Society, deeming it cruel because it sought expulsion of an innocent and patriotic element "who contributed blood, sweat and tears to the development of the United States" primarily because they were of a "different complexion." Furthermore, he argued that the propaganda perpetuated by the Colonization Society sought to destroy all political, civil, and religious liberties guaranteed by the Constitution to the free people of color. Nathaniel Paul asserted that the Society was hypocritical because it had painted a distorted picture of its intentions to the British public, by professing to be a friend of the people of color while at the same time opposing their education. Paul ended his speech with a remark about the Society's design with regard to Africa. "Africa," he said, "is enveloped in darkness, infinitely deeper than the sable hue of its degraded sons . . . this society represents it as their object to let in the rays of the gospel, and enlighten the people . . . they select as instruments, to spread civilization and Christianity, people not fit to live in America . . . let us send men who are enlightened themselves. If we mean to evangelize Africa, let us at least send Christians there to do the work."[5]

Thomas Paul, a brother of Nathaniel Paul, noted various reasons that made Haiti a suitable country for emigration of the emancipated. He had resided there as a missionary for several months in 1823 and was well respected. Not only was Haiti a beautiful country, but it had all of the "necessaries and luxuries of life"—staple products, forests, pastures covered with herds, and fresh fish. The Haitians were

[5] Immediately after the meeting, a repudiation of the principles of the American Colonization Society was published by a group of distinguished British abolitionists including William Wilberforce, Zachary Macaulay, Thomas F. Burton and others. See *The Abolitionists*, Vol. 1, No. 10 (October, 1833), pp. 157–158. Nathaniel Paul went with his brother, Benjamin, to Wilberforce at the time of the founding of the Settlement.

also mechanics and manufacturers; the country was favorable to trade and commercial enterprise. Its inhabitants were "determined to live free or die gloriously in defense of freedom." Peter Williams, Rector of St. Philips Church in New York City, convinced that colonization—but not to Africa—was good, urged in 1830 the establishment of a Colony in Wilberforce, Canada, as a place of asylum "for his exiled brethren in Cincinnati." Since opposition to emigration as the best alternate to conditions at home was still strong, Negro leaders decided that Canada as a target destination of emigrees would be used only as a refuge and was to be supported accordingly. At the same time, new black laws were passed to control the mobility of the free black population. More money was appropriated for colonization projects. Public clamor for compulsory emigration laws to force free blacks out of the country mounted. Nat Turner's abortive revolt in Virginia contributed to the fears of the white population that conventions were "instruments and vehicles of insurrection and ruin."

"A Colored Female in Philadelphia" expressed her support, on January 2, 1832, of emigration to Mexico, where "all men are born free and equal," where "the climate is healthy and warm" and where "the soil is rich and fertile," and where the country "would afford us a large field of speculation, were we to remove thither." Furthermore, she wrote "who can say, that the day will not soon arrive, when the flag of our colored American merchants' ships from the Mexican ports shall be seen proudly waving in the breeze of the American harbors? And shall not our sons feel proud to enlist under the Mexican banner, and support her government? Surely they will."[6]

Persuasive and logical arguments by articulate persons of color convinced some to emigrate and others to remain at home. These debates occurred across the nation. One of the most interesting was a debate between David Ruggles, the distinguished black abolitionist, and David M. Reese, a strong advocate of colonization, in New York City.[7]

Between the years 1820 and 1830, a total of 1430 Negroes left for Liberia, and in 1832, when conditions of suppression were intensified after the Nat Turner Insurrection, 1037 emigrated to Liberia.

[6] See *Freedom's Journal*, Vol. 1, No. 17 (July 6, 1827), p. 66, for two letters written by "A Coloured Baltimorean" and a "Free Coloured Virginian" for suggestions of better means of providing for free people of color than colonization in Africa.
[7] David Ruggles, *"Extinguisher" Extinguished! or David M. Reese, M.D., "Used Up."* (New York, 1834).

Of these, 247 were manumitted slaves and 790 were free persons of color who chose to leave the country. These figures certainly lend credibility to the contention that the intensification of crisis situations of the colored population, slave and free, strongly influenced the emigration movement.

Petition of Peter Bestes, Sambo Freeman, Felix Holbrook, and Chester Joie.

BOSTON, *April 20th*, 1773.

SIR,

THE efforts made by the legislative of this province in their last sessions to free themselves from slavery, gave us, who are in that deplorable state, a high degree of satisfaction. We expect great things from men who have made such a noble stand against the designs of their fellow-men to enslave them. We cannot but wish and hope Sir, that you will have the same grand object, we mean civil and religious liberty, in view in your next session. The divine spirit of freedom, seems to fire every humane breast on this continent, except such as are bribed to assist in executing the execrable plan.

WE are very sensible that it would be highly detrimental to our present masters, if we were allowed to demand all that of right belongs to us for past services; this we disclaim. Even the Spaniards, who have not those sublime ideas of freedom that English men have, are conscious that they have no right to all the services of their fellowmen, we mean the Africans, whom they have purchased with their money; therefore they allow them one day in a week to work for themselve, to enable them to earn money to purchase the residue of their time, which they have a right to demand in such portions as they are able to pay for (a due appraizment of their services being first made, which always stands at the purchase money.) We do not pretend to dictate to you Sir, or to the honorable Assembly, of which you are a member: We acknowledge our obligations to you for what you have already done, but as the people of this province seem to be actuated by the principles of equity and justice, we cannot but expect your house will again take our deplorable case into serious consideration, and give us that ample relief which, as men, we have a natural right to.

BUT since the wise and righteous governor of the universe has permitted our fellow men to make us slaves, we bow in submission to him, and determine to behave in such a manner, as that we may have reason to expect the divine approbation of, and assistance in, our peaceable and lawful attempts to gain our freedom.

WE are willing to submit to such regulations and laws as may be made relative to us, until we leave the province, which we determine to do as soon as we can from our joynt labours procure money to transport ourselves to some part of the coast of Africa, where we propose a settlement. We are very desirous that you should have instructions relative to us, from your town, therefore we pray you to communicate this letter to them, and ask this favor for us.

In behalf of our fellow slaves in this province,
And by order of their Committee.
PETER BESTES,
SAMBO FREEMAN,
FELIX HOLBROOK,
CHESTER JOIE.

For the Representative of the town of Thompson.

A

BRIEF ACCOUNT

OF THE

SETTLEMENT AND PRESENT SITUATION

OF

THE COLONY

OF

SIERRA LEONE,

IN AFRICA;

AS COMMUNICATED BY PAUL CUFFEE (A MAN OF COLOUR)
TO HIS FRIEND IN NEW YORK: ALSO, AN EX-
PLANATION OF THE OBJECT OF HIS VISIT,
AND SOME ADVICE TO THE PEOPLE OF
COLOUR IN THE UNITED STATES.

TO WHICH IS SUBJOINED,

An address to the people of colour, from the Con-
vention of Delegates from the Aboli-
tion Societies in the United States.

NEW YORK:
PRINTED BY SAMUEL WOOD,
NO 357 PEARL-STREET.
1812.

256

HAVING been informed that there was a settlement of people of colour at Sierra Leone under the immediate guardianship of a civilized power, I have for these many years past felt a lively interest in their behalf, wishing that the inhabitants of the colony might become established in the truth, and thereby be instrumental in its promotion amongst our African brethren. It was these sentiments that first influenced me to visit my friends in this colony, and instead of repenting, I have cause to rejoice in having found many who are inclined to listen and attend to the precepts of our holy religion. Nevertheless, I am convinced that further help will be requisite to establish them in the true and vital spirit of devotion; for although there are many who are very particular in their attendance of public worship, yet I am apprehensive that the true substance is too much overlooked; and by thus mistaking the form for the substance, that their religious exercise is rendered rather a burden than a pleasure. It is not however my object to extend these observations at present. I merely wish to convey a brief account of the situation of the colony as I found it, hoping the information may prove serviceable and interesting to some of my friends in the United States.

Sierra Leone is a country on the west coast of Africa. Its situation is inviting, and its soil generally very productive. A river of the same name passes through the country, and the land for a great extent on each side is peculiarly fertile, and with the climate well calculated for the cultivation of West India and other tropical productions. In the year 1791 an act passed the British parliament incorporating a company called the Sierra Leone Company, whose object was to settle and cultivate these lands, and open a trade with other countries in the products of the soil. The first settlers amounted to about 200 white persons, and a number of free blacks or people of colour from North America; and their experiments in sugar, cotton, &c. soon convinced them that they would be abundantly rewarded for their labour. The promising appearance of the settlement soon attracted the attention of the neighbouring chiefs, who with their subjects generally, became very friendly. The colony is now considerably increased, and continues to be in a flourishing situation. The population at present as taken by order of Governor Columbine in the 4th mo. 1811, is as follows, viz.

Europeans,	22	4	2
Nova Scotians,	188	295	499
Maroons,	165	195	447
Africans,	20	43	37
	395	537	985
Making together,			1917

Besides which there are 601 Crue Men, so called from their being natives of a part called Crue Country, from which they have emigrated since the establishment of this colony.

These people have not yet been enrolled in the list of citizens, but are generally hired by the inhabitants as labourers. The disposition prevails very generally to encourage new settlers who may come amongst them either for the purpose of cultivating the land, or engaging in commercial enterprise. A petition, of which the following is an outline, was lately presented to his excellency governor Columbine, and signed by several of the most respectable inhabitants, viz.

1st. That encouragement may be given to all our brethren, who may come from the British colonies or from America, in order to become farmers, or to assist us in the cultivation of our land.

2d. That encouragement may be given to our foreign brethren who have vessels for the purpose, to establish commerce in Sierra Leone.

3d. That those who may undertake to establish the whale fishery in the colony may be encouraged to persevere in that useful and laudable enterprise.

There are at this time 7 or 8 schools established throughout the colony. One of these is for the instruction of grown persons, and the others contain together about 230 children, who are instructed in all the necessary branches of education.

The inhabitants have likewise six places of public worship, which are generally well attended. Their times for meeting on the sabbath are at 5 and 10 o'clock in the morning, and at 2 and 6 o'clock in the evening. Also, the week through, many of their meetings are attended at 5 in the morning and 6 in the evening. There was also a society formed here some time since for the further promotion of the Christian religion. I have met with one of their epistles, which I shall insert at the close of my communication.

An institution was formed on the 1st of the 12th mo. last for the relief of the poor and disabled. It is now regularly held on the 1st second day in every month, at which time proper persons are appointed to take charge of those under the care of the institution. A general meeting is held once every six months. Everyone can judge of the happy effect of such institutions as these in improving the dispositions and softening the manners of our native brethren.

The colonists have instituted 5 courts, consisting, first, of the

Court of Quarter Sessions, which is held four times in the course of the year. The governor always presides as judge, and is attended by a justice of the peace, sheriff's clerk, messengers of the bailiff and constables. The petit jury consists of 12 men selected from the Europeans, Nova-Scotians, and Maroons.

2d. Mayor's Court. This formerly sat on the 5th day of every week; but the time for holding it has since been prolonged to every three months.

3d. The Court of Requests which is held on the 7th day of every week. The power of this court is confined to the trial of debts not exceeding two pounds. 12 men are selected for this purpose, and four out of the number transact the business of a sitting.

4th. The Police Court, which is likewise held on the 7th day of every week, and is constituted of the same number of persons as the court of requests. Their business is confined to the trial of persons for disorderly conduct.

5th. The Court of Vice Admiralty, which is held as occasion may require.

The inhabitants are governed entirely by the British law, and are generally peaceable and willing to abide by the decisions of their civil magistrates. Governor Columbine lately issued a proclamation in which he offers the protection of these laws to any slave who may arrive in the colony with the consent of his or her owners, and leaves them at liberty to remain or go elsewhere, as they may think proper.

On the 18th of the 3d month, I travelled in amongst the natives of Africa. The first tribe I met with was called the Bullone Tribe. Their king, whose name is George, appeared to be very friendly. He could speak but very little English himself, but had a young man with him by the name of Peter Wilson, who had received his education in England, and appeared to be a man of very good information. This tribe, from what I could gather, have adopted the mode of circumcision, and seem to acknowledge by words the existence of a Deity. So accustomed are they to wars and slavery that I apprehend it would be a difficult task to convince them of the impropriety of these pernicious practices. I gave the king a Testament and several other books, and let him know by the interpreter the useful records contained in those books, and the great fountain they pointed unto.

The Mendingo Tribe professes Mahometanism. I became acquainted with two men of this tribe who were apparently men of considerable learning; indeed this tribe generally, appeared to be a people of some education. Their learning appeared to be the Arabic. They do not allow spirituous liquors to be made use of in this tribe.

They have declined the practice of selling their own tribe; but notwithstanding this, they continue to sell those of other tribes, and thought it hard that the traffic in slaves should be abolished, as they were made poor in consequence thereof. As they themselves were not willing to submit to the bonds of slavery, I endeavoured to hold this out as a light to convince them of their error. But the prejudice of education had taken too firm hold of their minds to admit of much effect from reason on this subject.

ADDRESS.
To my scattered brethren and fellow countrymen at Sierra Leone.

Grace be unto you and peace be multiplied from God our Father, and from the Lord Jesus Christ, who hath begotten a lively hope in remembrance of you; and for which I desire ever to be humbled, world without end. Amen.

Dearly beloved friends and fellow countrymen,

I earnestly recommend to you the propriety of assembling yourselves together for the purpose of worshipping the Lord your God. God is a spirit, and they that worship him acceptably must worship him in spirit and in truth; in so doing you will find a living hope which will be as an anchor to the soul and a support under afflictions. In this hope, may Ethiopia stretch out her hand unto God. Come, my African brethren and fellow countrymen, let us walk together in the light of the Lord—That pure light which bringeth salvation into the world, hath appeared unto all men to profit withal. I would recommend unto all the saints, and elders, and sober people of the colony, that you adopt the mode of meeting together once every month in order to consult with each other for your mutual good. But above all things, let your meetings be owned of the Lord, for he hath told us that "where two or three are gathered together in his name, there he would be in the midst of them." And I would recommend that you keep a record of your proceedings at those meetings in order that they may be left for the benefit of the young and rising generation. In these meetings let it be your care to promote all good and laudable institutions, and by so doing you will increase both your temporal and spiritual welfare. That the Prince of Peace may be your preserver, is the sincere desire of one who wishes well to all mankind.   PAUL CUFFEE.

The following advice, though detached from the foregoing address, appears to be intended to accompany it.

ADVICE.

First. That sobriety and steadfastness, with all faithfulness, be recommended, that so professors may be good examples in all things; doing justly, loving mercy, and walking humbly.

Secondly. That early care be extended towards the youth, whilst their minds are young and tender, that so they may be redeemed from the corruptions of the world—such as nature is prone to—not swearing, following bad company and drinking of spirituous liquors. That they may be kept out of idleness, and encouraged to be industrious, for this is good to cultivate the mind, and may you be good examples therein yourselves.

Thirdly. May servants be encouraged to discharge their duty with faithfulness; may they be brought up to industry; may their minds be cultivated for the reception of the good seed, which is promised to all that will seek after it. I want that we should be faithful in all things, that so we may become a people, giving satisfaction to those, who have borne the heat and burden of the day, in liberating us from a state of slavery. I must leave you in the hands of him who is able to preserve you through time, and to crown you with that blessing that is prepared for all those who are faithful unto death.

Farewell,   PAUL CUFFEE.

Copy of an epistle from the society of Sierra Leone, in Africa, to the saints and faithful brethren in Christ.

Grace be unto you and peace from God our Father and from the Lord Jesus Christ.

We desire to humble ourselves with that thankful acknowledgment to the Father and fountain of all mercies for the liberty and freedom we enjoy, and our prayer to God is, that our brethren who live in distant lands and are held in bondage, and groan under the galling chain of slavery; that they may be liberated, and enjoy the liberty which God has granted unto all his faithful saints. Dearly beloved brethren in the Lord, may the power and peace of God rule in all your hearts, for we feel from an awful experience the distresses that many of our African brethren groan under. Therefore we feel our minds engaged to desire all the saints and professors in Christ to diligently consider our cause, and to put our cause to the Christian query, whether it is agreeable to the testimony of Jesus Christ for one professor to make merchandise of another. We desire that this may be made manifest to all professors of all Christian denominations who have not abolished the holding of slaves.

We salute you, beloved brethren, in the Lord with sincere desire, that the work of regeneration may be more and more experienced. It would be a consolation to us to hear from the saints in distant lands; and we could receive all who are disposed to come to us with open arms.

Our dearly beloved Brethren, we also salute in the love of God, to be obedient unto your masters with prayers lifted up to God, in whom we would recommend you to confide, who is just as able in these days to deliver you from the yoke of oppression, as he hath in time past brought your forefathers out of the Egyptian bondage. Finally, brethren, may the power and peace of God rest in all your hearts. Grace be unto you and peace from God our Father and from the Lord Jesus Christ. Amen.

Signed by John Gordon, preacher, Warrick Francis, James Reed, Joseph Brown, Moses Wilkinson, Larsus Jones, John Ellis, Adam Jones, George Clarke, Peter Frances, George Carrell, Edward Wiliboughly, Thomas Richardson, senr. Eli Achim, John Stevenson, James Wise.

To the free Africans and other free people of colour in the United States.

The convention of deputies from the abolition societies in the United States, assembled at Philadelphia, have undertaken to address you upon subjects highly interesting to your prosperity.

They wish to see you act worthily of the rank you have acquired as freemen, and thereby to do credit to yourselves, and to justify the friends and advocates of your colour in the eyes of the world.

As the result of our united reflections, we have concluded to call your attention to the following articles of advice. We trust, they are dictated by the purest regard for your welfare, for we view you as friends and brethren.

In the first place, we earnestly recommend to you, a regular attention to the important duty of public worship, by which means you will evince gratitude to your Creator, and, at the same time, promote knowledge, union, friendship, and proper conduct amongst yourselves.

Secondly, We advise such of you, as have not been taught reading, writing, and the first principles of arithmetic, to acquire them as early as possible. Carefully attend to the instruction of your children in the same simple and useful branches of education. Cause them, likewise, early and frequently to read the holy Scriptures; they contain, among other great discoveries, the precious record of the original equality of mankind, and of the obligations of universal justice and benevolence, which are derived from the relation of the human race to each other in a common Father.

Thirdly, Teach your children useful trades, or to labour with their hands in cultivating the earth. These employments are favourable to health and virtue. In the choice of masters, who are to instruct them in the above branches of business, prefer those who will work with them: by this means they will acquire habits of industry, and be better preserved from vice, than if they worked alone, or under the eye of persons less interested in their welfare. In forming contracts, for yourselves or children, with masters it may be useful to consult such persons as are capable of giving you the best advice, who are known to be your friends, in order to prevent advantages being taken of your ignorance of the laws and customs of our country.

Fourthly, Be diligent in your respective callings, and faithful in all the relations you bear in society, whether as husbands, wives, fathers, children or hired servants. Be just in all your dealings. Be simple in your dress and furniture, and frugal in your family expenses. Thus you will act like Christians as well as freemen, and by these means, you will provide for the distresses and wants of sickness and old age.

Fifthly, Refrain from the use of spirituous liquors; the experience of many thousands of the citizens of the United States has proved that those liquors are not necessary to lessen the fatigue of labour, nor to obviate the extremes of heat or cold; much less are they necessary to add to the innocent pleasures of society.

Sixthly, Avoid frolicking, and amusements that lead to expense and idleness; they beget habits of dissipation and vice, and thus expose you to deserved reproach amongst your white neighbours.

Seventhly, We wish to impress upon your minds the moral and religious necessity of having your marriages legally performed; also to have exact registers preserved of all the births and deaths which occur in your respective families.

Eighthly, Endeavour to lay up as much as possible of your earnings for the benefit of your children, in case you should die before they are able to maintain themselves—your money will be safest and most beneficial when laid out in lots, houses, and small farms.

Ninthly, We recommend to you, at all times and upon all occasions, to behave yourselves to all persons in a civil and respectful manner, by which you may prevent contention, and remove every just occasion of complaint. We beseech you to reflect it is by your good conduct alone that you can refute the objections which have been made against you as rational and moral creatures, and remove many of the difficulties which have occurred in the general emancipation of such of your brethren as are yet in bondage.

With hearts anxious for your welfare, we commend you to the guidance and protection of that Being who is able to keep you from all evil, and who is the common Father and friend of the whole family of mankind.

By order and on the behalf of the convention,

THEODORE FOSTER, President.

Attest. THOMAS P COPE, Secretary.

Philadelphia, January 6th, 1796.

have reason to expect the divine approbation of, and assistance in, our peaceable and lawful attempts to gain our freedom.

WE are willing to submit to such regulations and laws as may be made relative to us, until we leave the province, which we determine to do as soon as we can from our joynt labours procure money to transport ourselves to some part of the coast of Africa, where we propose a settlement. We are very desirous that you should have instructions relative to us, from your town, therefore we pray you to communicate this letter to them, and ask this favor for us.

In behalf of our fellow slaves in this province,
And by order of their Committee.

PETER BESTES,
SAMBO FREEMAN,
FELIX HOLBROOK,
CHESTER JOIE.

For the Representative of the town of Thompson.

To the humane and benevolent Inhabitants of the city and county of Philadelphia.

The free people of color, assembled together, under circumstances of deep interest to their happiness and welfare, humbly and respectfully lay before you this expression of their feelings and apprehensions.

Relieved from the miseries of slavery, many of us by your aid, possessing the benefits which industry and integrity in this prosperous country assure to all its inhabitants, enjoying the rich blessings of religion, by opportunities of worshipping the only true God, under the light of Christianity, each of us according to his understanding; and having afforded to us and to our children the means of education and improvement; we have no wish to separate from our present homes, for any purpose whatever. Contented with our present situation and condition, we are not desirous of increasing their prosperity but by honest efforts, and by the use of those opportunities for their improvement, which the constitution and laws allow to all. It is therefore with painful solicitude, and sorrowing regret, we have seen a plan for colonizing the free people of color of the United States on the coast of Africa, brought forward under the auspices and sanction of gentlemen whose names give value to all they recommend, and who certainly are among the wisest, the best, and the most benevolent of men, in this great nation.

If the plan of colonizing is intended for our benefit, and those who now promote it will never seek our injury, we humbly and respectfully urge, that it is not asked for by us: nor will it be required by any circumstances, in our present or future condition, as long as we shall be permitted to share the protection of the excellent laws and just government which we now enjoy, in common with every individual of the community.

We, therefore, a portion of those who are the objects of this plan, and among those whose happiness, with that of others of our color, it is intended to promote, with humble and grateful acknowledgments to those who have devised it, renounce and disclaim every connexion with it; and respectfully but firmly declare our determination not to participate in any part of it.

If this plan of colonization now proposed, is intended to provide a refuge and a dwelling for a portion of our brethren who are now held in slavery in the south, we have other and stronger objections to it, and we entreat your consideration of them.

The ultimate and final abolition of slavery in the United States, by the operation of various causes, is, under the guidance and protection of a just God, progressing. Every year witnesses the release of numbers of the victims of oppression, and affords new and safe assurances that the freedom of all will be in the end accomplished. As they are thus by degrees relieved from bondage, our brothers have opportunities for instruction and improvement; and thus they become in some measure fitted for their liberty. Every year, many of us have restored to us by the gradual, but certain march of the cause of abolition—parents, from whom we have been long separated—wives and children whom we had left in servitude—and brothers, in blood as well as in early sufferings, from whom we had been long parted.

But if the emancipation of our kindred shall, when the plan of colonization shall go into effect, be attended with transportation to a distant land, and shall be granted on no other condition; the consolation for our past sufferings and of those of our color who are in slavery, which have hitherto been, and under the present situation of things would continue to be, afforded to us and to them, will cease for ever. The cords, which now connect them with us, will be stretched by the distance to which their ends will be carried, until they break; and all the sources of happiness, which affection and connexion and blood bestow, will be ours and theirs no more.

Nor do we view the colonization of those who may become emancipated by its operation among our southern brethren, as capable of producing their happiness. Unprepared by education and a knowledge of the truths of our blessed religion for their new situation, those who will thus become colonists will themselves be surrounded by every suffering which can afflict the members of the human family.

Without arts, without habits of industry, and unaccustomed to provide by their own exertions and foresight for their wants, the colony will soon become the abode of every vice, and the home of every misery. Soon will the light of Christianity, which now dawns among that portion of our species, be shut out by the clouds of ignorance, and their day of life be closed, without the illuminations of the gospel.

To those of our brothers who shall be left behind, there will be assured perpetual slavery and augmented sufferings. Diminished in numbers, the slave population of the southern states, which by its magnitude alarms its proprietors, will be easily secured. Those among their bondmen who feel that they should be free, by rights which all mankind have from God and from nature, and who thus may become dangerous to the quiet of their masters, will be sent to the colony; and the tame and submissive will be retained, and subjected to increased rigor. Year after year will witness these means to assure safety and submission among their slaves, and the southern masters will colonize only those whom it may be dangerous to keep among them. The bondage of a large portion of our brothers will thus be rendered perpetual.

Should the anticipations of misery and want among the colonists, which with great deference we have submitted to your better judgment, be realized, to emancipate and transport to Africa will be held forth by slaveholders as the worst and heaviest of punishments; and they will be threatened and successfully used to enforce increased submission to their wishes, and subjection to their commands.

Nor ought the sufferings and sorrows which must be produced by an exercise of the right to transport and colonize such only of their slaves as may be selected by the slaveholders, escape the attention and consideration of those whom with all humility we now address. Parents will be torn from their children—husbands from their wives—brothers from brothers—and all the heart-rending agonies which were endured by our forefathers when they were dragged into bondage from Africa will be again renewed, and with increased anguish. The shores of America will, like the sands of Africa, be watered by the tears of those who will be left behind. Those who shall be carried away will roam childless, widowed, and alone, over the burning plains of Guinea.

Disclaiming, as we emphatically do, a wish or desire to interpose our opinions and feelings between all plans of colonization, and the judgment of those whose wisdom as far exceeds ours as their situations are exalted above ours; we humbly, respectfully, and fervently intreat and beseech your disapprobation of the plan of colonization now offered by 'the American Society for colonizing the free people of color of the United States.'—Here, in the city of Philadelphia, where the voice of the suffering sons of Africa was first heard; where was first commenced the work of abolition, on which heaven has smiled, for it could have had success only from the Great Maker; let not a purpose be assisted which will stay the cause of the entire abolition of slavery in the United States, and which may defeat it altogether; which proffers to those who do not ask for them what it calls benefits, but which they consider injuries; and which must insure to the multitudes whose prayers can only reach you through us, misery, sufferings, and perpetual slavery.

JAMES FORTEN, Chairman.

RUSSELL PARROTT, Secretary.

[Source: *Minutes of the Proceedings of a Special Meeting of the Fifteenth American Convention for Promoting the Abolition of Slavery, and Improving the Condition of the African Race, Assembled at Philadelphia, on the Tenth Day of December, 1818* . . . (Philadelphia: Hall and Atkinson, 1818), pp. i–iv; also included in *Resolutions and Remonstrances of the People of Colour Against Colonization to the Coast of Africa* (Philadelphia, 1818), pp. 5–8.]

A

MEMOIR

PRESENTED TO

THE AMERICAN CONVENTION

FOR PROMOTING

THE

ABOLITION OF SLAVERY,

AND

Improving the Condition of the African Race,

DECEMBER 11TH 1818;

CONTAINING

Some Remarks upon the civil Dissentions of the hitherto afflicted People of Hayti, as the Inhabitants of that Island may be connected with Plans for the Emigration of such Free Persons of Colour as may be disposed to remove to it, in case its Reunion, Pacification and Independence should be established.

TOGETHER WITH

Some Account of the Origin and Progress of the Efforts for effecting the Abolition of Slavery in Pennsylvania and its neighbourhood, and throughout the World.

BY PRINCE SAUNDERS.

PHILADELPHIA: PRINTED BY DENNIS HEARTT. 1818

Respected Gentlemen and Friends,

AT a period so momentous as the present, when the friends of abolition and emancipation, as well as those whom observation and experience might teach us to beware to whom we should apply the endearing appellations, are professedly concerned for the establishment of an Asylum for those Free Persons of Colour who may be disposed to remove to it, and for such persons as shall hereafter be emancipated from slavery, a careful examination of this subject is imposed upon us.

So large a number of abolitionists convened from different sections of the country, is at all times and under any circumstances an interesting spectacle to the eye of the philanthropist; how doubly delightful then is it to me, whose interests and feelings so largely partake in the object you have in view, to behold this convention engaged in solemn deliberation upon those subjects employed to promote the improvement of the condition of the African race.

It was in this city and its vicinity that the eccentric, the humane, the pious, and the practically philanthropic lay, was the first who laboured to draw aside that thick, and then impenetrable veil, with which prejudice and avarice had obscured the enormities of the slave-trade; being seemingly conscious that it was only necessary that its iniquitous and barbarous character should be discovered and known in order to effect its condemnation and abolition by every community of practical Christians.

This commonwealth was also the scene of a great portion of the benevolent exertions of that early and zealous advocate for the injured descendants of Africa, the candid and upright Sandiford.

Philadelphia had the honour and the happiness of being for years adorned and illumined by the beneficent light of the precepts and example of that distinguished philanthropist, the late venerable and excellent Benezet. Those rays of the light of truth and justice, which had beamed upon his own mind and heart, and which he communicated to the public through the medium of the press in this country, were sent across the Atlantic; and Anthony Benezet's historical account of Guinea seems to have done much towards interesting the mind of the celebrated Thomas Clarkson upon the great subject of the abolition. This city and its neighbourhood were the region which was enlightened by the residence and labours of that illustrious pattern of practical beneficence, the pious and humane Woolman.

Among other distinguished abolitionists, who were contemporaries with Woolman and Benezet, the late Warner Mifflin, of Kent county in Delaware, stands preeminently conspicuous. So deeply did he become impressed with a sense of the injustice and the inhumanity of holding slaves, that he fixed upon a day for the emancipation of thirty-seven persons of colour, who were received from his father. On that interesting occasion it appears that he called them into his chamber, one after the other, and that the following is the substance of the conversation which took place between him and one of them: "Well, my friend James, how old art thou?" "My master," said he, "I am twenty-nine years and a half old." The master replied, "Thou shouldst have been free at twenty-one years of age, as our white brethren are. Religion and humanity enjoin it upon me this day to give thee thy liberty, and justice commands me to pay thee for eight and a half year's services: which, at 21*l.* 5*s.* per year, including thy food and raiment, makes the sum of 95*l.* 12*s.* 6*d.* which I owe thee." Would that every slave holder would "go and do likewise."

The names of Pemberton, Wistar, and Rush, who have been successively called to preside over the interests of the Abolition Society in this city, will be cherished in affectionate remembrance, in conjunction with those of many other eminently distinguished abolitionists, in different parts of the United States, who have also passed the bourn of that more elevated scene of human destiny, where the wicked cease from troubling and oppressing their fellow beings, and where the weary have entered upon an interminable state of rest, felicity and immortal peace, in those bright mansions, which the King of Glory has gone to prepare for the reception of all those who have, with religious fidelity and care, assiduously cherished and cultivated that celestial principle, which the inspiration of the Almighty hath lighted up in the soul of every individual; and which, when duly nurtured and improved, must inevitably bring forth the fruits of those beneficent, philanthropic, humane, benevolent and pious affections, which constitute that pure and elevated charity and love, which fulfill all the laws of Christian purity and human excellence.

To those who have thus laboured to discipline their minds and hearts, and to bring them into an entire subjection and imitation of the great example of excellence, by religiously considering the wrongs endured by those persecuted and afflicted children of sorrow, whose liberty has been cloven down by the artifice, intrigue, violence or oppressive cruelty, of the stronger portion of mankind; to such as have so believed, and practised, are the thoughts of an immortality beaming with the lustre of a faith so strong, and a hope so clear and transporting, peculiarly interesting.

To those excellent men who have exemplified the dignity of human nature by their labour of practical piety and goodness, while sojourning in this state of discipline and probation, by becoming the protectors of the friendless, among all the various descriptions of their brethren of mankind; to them belongs the happiness of looking forward with delightful anticipation to that animating period, when the great and excellent benefactors of the human race shall shine as the stars, for ever and ever, for the illumination of that eternal city, which hath foundation, whose maker and builder is God Almighty, in the heavens.

Many of the most distinguished and enlightened individuals in different regions, and among various nations, are habitual in their labours to unbind the chains of unjust captivity and servitude; and to set the innocent victims of avarice and cupidity upon the broad basis of the enjoyment of those unalienable rights which the universal Parent has entrusted to the care of every individual among his intelligent and accountable children.

And if those who consider the poor, in the ordinary concerns of charity and pious almsgiving, are authorised to look for the favour of providence; with how much more full an assurance may those who have delivered their fellow beings from the inhuman grasp of the unprincipled kidnapper, or saved them from dragging out a miserable existence amidst the thraldoms of the most abject slavery; with what confident expectation of becoming the recipients of that inconceivably glorious recompence of reward which God has prepared for those who love and obey him (and keep his commandments); may such persons anticipate the period when Christ shall reappear, to make up his jewels.

Among the various projects or plans which have been devised or suggested in relation to emigration, there are none which appear to many persons to wear so much the appearance of feasibility, and ultimate successful and practical operation, as the luxuriant, beautiful and extensive island of Hayti (or St. Domingo). This vast island is situated between lat. 17° 40′ and 20° north, and between long. 68° 30′, and 74° 30′ west. Its length from Cape Engano to Cape Tiburon, is 430 miles. Its greatest breadth, from Cape Beata to point Isabella, is said to be 160 miles. It contains about 28,000 square miles.

The merchandise landed in the various ports of France, from the Island of St. Domingo, in the year 1789, were as follows: 84,617,328 lbs. of coffee, 217,463 casks of sugar, white and brown, 5,836 casks of molasses, 3,257,610 lbs. of indigo, 1,536,017 lbs. of cocoa, 11,317,226 lbs. of cotton wool, 1,514 seroons of Spanish cochineal, 6,814 tons of logwood, Nicaragua wood, fustic, and lignumvitæ,

1,685 tons of mahogany, 4,618 bags of black pepper, 2,426 bags of ginger, 380 casks of guiacum and other gums, 248 boxes of aloes, cassia, and China root, 26,948 hides, tanned, 114,639 hides in the hair; from the Spaniards 4,167 lbs. tortoise shell, 27,812 casks of syrup, 1,364 of sweet meats, 1,478 seroons of Jesuit's bark, 2,617,530 dollars, 57,218 ounces of gold in grains. The total value of these products was estimated at 6,094,230 pounds sterling.

According to Mr. Edwards the average exports before the revolution consisted of 58,642,214 lbs. of clayed sugar, 85,549,829 lbs. of Muscovado, 71,663,187 lbs. of coffee, 6,698,858 pounds of cotton, 951,607 hogsheads of indigo, 23,061 hogsheads of molasses, 2,600 hogsheads of an inferior kind of rum called taffia, 6,500 raw hides, and 7,900 tanned ones. The value of which exports was equal to 4,765,129 pounds sterling.

That city, which was formerly called Cape Francois, but now Cape Henry, before the revolution contained between 800 and 900 houses of stone and brick; 8,000 free inhabitants and 12,000 slaves. The duties on exports from that port in 1789 amounted to 253,590 dollars 37 cents.

Port au Prince, in 1790, contained 600 dwelling houses, 2,754 whites, and 12,000 persons of colour; the duties on exports in 1789 amounted to 189,945 dollars 46 cents.

The whole value of exports from France to St. Domingo in 1789 amounted to 4,125,610*l*. During the revolution in the North, or French part of the island, the few remaining part of the white Spaniards emigrated to Porto Rico, and have never yet returned. So that at present, there are but very few, if any, Europeans, or whites of any description, even in that section of the country which is nominally, and in fact, in allegiance to old Spain. That this territory is but little valued by the government of Spain is to be distinctly inferred from a variety of circumstances. The first is this: soon after the subject of emigrating to Hayti was in agitation in this city, our valuable friend, John James, did me the favour to introduce me to his friend, his excellency Louis Don Onis (who was then on his way to Washington), with whom we had a liberal conversation, upon the probability of meeting with success in case an application should be made to his Catholic Majesty's government to procure that part of the island which is in allegiance to Spain. And from the tenor of his excellency's remarks, it was the united opinion of both friend James and myself, that the acquisition of it would not be difficult. Another reason which induces the belief that it is not highly valued by the mother country is that it is said to be an annual bill of expense to her in its present uncultivated condition; and in a recent conversation I had the honour of holding with an intelligent Spanish gentleman, I found that it was principally valued by his countrymen on account of its being the spot which was first discovered by Columbus.*

The French claims we all know are merely nominal, and may easily be forever silenced in the contemplated pacification, as without doubt, may all the political connexions of Spain. In this great island there seems to be some foundation for the hopes of those who are to emigrate to rest upon; as there are already governments established there, which, although they may be arbitrary, and somewhat allied to military despotism in their present features and character, they are still susceptible of being improved, whenever a tranquilized state of society, and their stability and independence as a nation, shall authorize it.

Assembled as this Convention is for the promotion and extension of its beneficent and humane views and principles, I would respectfully beg leave to lay before it a few remarks upon the character, condition and wants of the afflicted and divided people of Hayti, as they, and that island, may be connected with plans for the emigration of the free people of colour of the United States.

God in the mysterious operation of his providence has seen fit to permit the most astonishing changes to transpire upon that naturally beautiful, and, as to soil and productions, astonishingly luxuriant island.

The abominable principles, both of action and belief, which pervaded France during the long series of vicissitudes which until recently she has experienced, extended to Hayti, or St. Domingo; and have undoubtedly had an extensive influence upon the character, sentiments and feelings of all descriptions of its present inhabitants.

This magnificent and extensive island which has by travellers and historians been often denominated the "paradise of the New World," seems from its situation, extent, climate, and fertility, peculiarly suited to become an object of interest and attention to the many distinguished and enlightened philanthropists whom God has been graciously pleased to inspire with a zeal for the promotion of the best interests of the descendants of Africa. The recent proceedings in several of the slave states towards the free population of colour in those states seem to render it highly probable that that oppressed class of the community will soon be obliged to flee to the free states for protection. If the two rival governments of Hayti were con-

* The third, and by no means the least important, fact in support of this opinion is that Spain ceded the eastern part of the island to France, July 22, 1795.

solidated into one well-balanced pacific power, there are many hundreds of the free people in the New England and middle states who would be glad to repair there immediately to settle. And believing that the period has arrived, when many zealous friends to abolition and emancipation are of opinion, that it is time for them to act in relation to an asylum for such persons as shall be emancipated from slavery, or for such portion of the free coloured population at present existing in the United States, as shall feel disposed to emigrate. And being aware that the authorities of Hayti are themselves desirous of receiving emigrants from this country, are among the considerations which have induced me to lay this subject before the Convention.

The present spirit of rivalry which exists between the two chiefs in the French part of the island, and the consequent belligerent aspect and character of the country, may at first sight appear somewhat discouraging to the beneficent views and labours of the friends of peace; but these I am inclined to think are by no means to be considered as insurmountable barriers against the benevolent exertions of those Christian philanthropists whose sincere and hearty desire it is to reunite and pacify them.

There seems to be no probability of their ever being reconciled to each other without the philanthropic interposition and mediation of those who have the welfare of the African race at heart. And where in the whole circle of practical Christian philanthropy, and active beneficence, is there so ample a field for the exertion of those heaven-born virtues as in that hitherto distracted region? In those unhappy divisions which exist in Hayti is strikingly exemplified the saying which is written in the sacred oracles, "that when men forsake the true worship and service of the only true God, and bow down to images of silver, and gold, and four footed beasts and creeping things, and become contentious with each other," says the inspired writer, "in such a state of things trust ye not a friend, put ye not confidence in a guide; keep the doors of thy mouth from her that lieth in thy bosom; for there the son dishonoureth the father, and the daughter riseth up against her mother, the daughter-in-law against her mother-in-law, and a man's enemies shall be those of his own house."

Had the venerable prophet in the foregoing predictions alluded expressly and entirely to the actual moral, political, and above all, to the religious character and condition of the Haytians, he could scarcely have given a more correct description of it.

For there is scarcely a family whose members are not separated from each other, and arrayed under the banners of the rival chiefs, in virtual hostility against each other. In many instances the husband is with Henry, and the wife and children with Boyer, and there are other instances in which the heads of the family are with Boyer, and the other members with Henry.

Let it be distinctly remembered that these divided and distressed individuals are not permitted to hold any intercourse with each other; so that it is only when some very extraordinary occurrence transpires, that persons in the different sections of the country receive any kind of information from their nearest relatives and friends.

"Blessed are the peace-makers," is the language of that celestial law-giver, who taught as never man taught; and his religion uniformly assures the obedient recipients of his spirit, that they shall be rewarded according to the extent, fidelity and sincerity of their works of piety and beneficence.

And if, according to the magnitude of the object in all its political, benevolent, humane and Christian relations, the quantum of recompense is to be awarded and apprised to the just, to how large a share of the benediction of our blessed Saviour to the promoters of peace, shall those be authorised to expect, who may be made the instruments of the pacification and reunion of the Haytian people? Surely the blessings of thousands who are, as it were, ready to perish, must inevitably come upon them.

When I reflect that it was in this city that the first abolition society that was formed in the world was established, I am strongly encouraged to hope that here also there may originate a plan, which shall be the means of restoring many of our fellow beings to the embraces of their families and friends, and place that whole country upon the basis of unanimity and perpetual peace.

If the American Convention should in their wisdom think it expedient to adopt measures for attempting to affect a pacification of the Haytians, it is most heartily believed that their benevolent views would be hailed and concurred in with alacrity and delight by the English philanthropists.

It is moreover believed that a concern so stupendous in its relations, and bearing upon the cause of universal abolition and emancipation, and to the consequent improvement and elevation of the African race, would tend to awaken an active and an universally deep and active interest in the minds of that numerous host of abolitionists in Great Britain, whom we trust have the best interests of the descendants of Africa deeply at heart. Among those distinguished and illustrious philanthropists are the following gentlemen:

Thomas Clarkson, Esq. W. Wilberforce, Esq. M. P. William Smith,

Esq. M. P. William Allen, Esq. Z. M'Caulay, Esq. Sir Samuel Romilly, Mr. Vansittart, Lord Teignmouth, Sir Joseph Banks, the Marquis of Downshire, the Bishops of Gloucester, Norwich, London, Salisbury, and Bristol; James Stephens, Esq. William Roscoe, Esq. the Messrs. Babington, Harrison, &c.

The author of these remarks is personally acquainted with most of the above mentioned gentlemen, and has been assured by many of them that they have considered it as one of their highest honours, as well as its constituting a great portion of pleasing reflection to them, that they have, under Providence, been permitted to aid in affecting the abolition of slavery, and that they were ever ready to unite in any object which might serve to advance the great cause of African improvement and happiness.

It is undoubtedly well known to the Convention, that their Britannic Majesties, the Prince Regent, and, in fact, all the members of the illustrious house of Brunswick (with one solitary exception), have been zealous in the great cause of African emancipation. Some of whom have particularly distinguished themselves in parliamentary debates upon the subject of universal abolition. The Duke of Gloucester is to be numbered among the foremost and most zealous friends to the African cause in the whole united kingdom. His Royal Highness was called to the presidential chair at the first regular meeting of the African institution; and has been indefatigable in his endeavours to promote the interests of an establishment which is designed to remunerate Africa for the evils they as a nation have inflicted on her, by now diffusing along her desolated and benighted shores the blessings of legitimate commerce, and all the cheering lights of civilization and instruction in morality and religion.

The following extract of a letter to me from that distinguished philanthropist and enlightened statesman, the right honourable Sir Joseph Banks, one of his Britannic Majesty's most honourable privy counsellers, will serve to evince the views and sentiments not only of that illustrious personage, but of the abolitionists generally in Great Britain, upon the subject of Haytian affairs.

"Spring Grove, Aug. 13, 1816.

"DEAR SIR,

"I beg leave to offer you my best wishes for a prosperous voyage, and a safe return to the very interesting country you are about to revisit. Allow me to request of you to return my best thanks to the count De Limonade for his obliging letter and present; and assure him that I hold the newly established government of Hayti in the highest respect. It is without doubt in its theory, I mean the Code

Henri, the most moral association of men in existence; nothing that white men have been able to arrange is equal to it. To give to the labouring poor of the country a vested interest in the crops they raise, instead of leaving their reward to be calculated by the caprice of the interested proprietor, is a law worthy to be written in letters of gold, as it secures comfort and a proper portion of happiness to those whose lot in the hands of white men endures by far the largest portion of misery.

"That the present possessors of the island of Hayti hold it by the best of human titles, that of conquest, cannot be doubted; the right by which the French held it, that of having by slow degrees exterminated the aborigines, is neither so honourable nor so equitable a right. We must admit, that the French have a right to reconquer if they are able; but this, in my view of the subject, is not within the bounds of the most extensive probability. I grieve therefore that the governments of white men have hitherto conceived it imprudent to acknowledge that of their fellow men of Hayti. It is a compliment paid to France which she does not deserve; for she can have no title to dominion over the men who have destroyed or driven away her hostile troops, and rid their country from the pollution of those sanguinary wretches who then enjoyed the name of Frenchmen. Perseverance, however, in the line of conduct laid down in the Code Henri cannot but in due time conquer all difficulties, and bring together the black and white varieties of mankind under the ties of mutual and reciprocal equality and brotherhood, which the bountiful Creator of all things has provided for the advantage of both parties."

That portion of the Code Henri alluded to in the foregoing extract, in all its relative departments and bearings, is to be found in my compilation of Haytian documents.

PRINCE SAUNDERS.

The following well written Letter from Thomas Paul, a most intelligent and respectable Minister of the Baptist Society in Boston, is taken from the Columbian Sentinel of July 3, 1824.

MR. EDITOR,

In compliance with the request of several very respectable gentlemen of this city, and the solicitations of persons of my own colour, I am induced to publish the following statement in relation to the country and government of Hayti. I the more cheerfully comply with these requests, in hopes that those free people of colour especially, who are disposed to seek an asylum for the enjoyment of liberty, and the common rights of man in a foreign clime, may be benefitted by this publication.

Having been a resident for some months in the Island of Hayti, I am fully persuaded that it is the best and most suitable place of residence which Providence has hitherto offered to emancipated people of colour, for the enjoyment of liberty and equality with their attendant blessings. At an interview which I had with President Boyer, some months ago, he was pleased to make a verbal statement of the same offers to me, as an organ of communication to the free people of colour in the United States, which he has recently made to the Colonization Society, in answer to several inquiries made by the Rev. Mr. Dewey.

After having made known to his Excellency the object of my visit, and having received permission from him to preach, and discharge the duties of a missionary of the gospel in the Island, I never received the least molestation from any person; but on the contrary, was always treated with the greatest respect by all the officers of the government, and by all classes of the people.

The Island is delightfully situated, abounding with all the necessaries and even the luxuries of life. It presents to the eye the most romantic and beautiful scenery; and while its verdant mountains recall to our minds what we have read of ancient Gilboa, Tabor, Lebanon, Carmel, and Sion, its fertile valleys present us with the rich luxuriance of the valleys of the Israelitish Canaan.

279

The staple productions are coffee, rice, tobacco, indigo, and Indian corn. The forests abound with the best of mahogany, logwood, and fustic; and the pastures are literally covered with flocks and herds.

A yoke of well made oxen, measuring six feet six inches, may be purchased for 17 or $18; a handsome cow and calf, for $7; and swine and poultry at the same rate. The markets are supplied with a plenty of fresh and salt water fish—oysters, lobsters, and turtles. A turtle weighing 80 or 90 lbs. may be purchased for $2. Through the months of June, July, August, and September, I resided upon the Island, and during this time, which is considered the hottest part of years, and the most unhealthy to strangers, I enjoyed as good health as at any period of my life.

The Haytiens have made great progress in the mechanical arts, which receive liberal encouragement. Goldsmiths, silversmiths, blacksmiths, tailors, bootmakers, painters, cabinetmakers, coopers, tanners, curriers, house-carpenters, ship-carpenters, turners, wheelwrights, tin-workers, sugar-manufacturers, and distillers would find constant and profitable employment.

A country, the local situation of which is favourable to trade and commercial enterprise, possessing a free and well regulated government, which encourages the useful and liberal arts, a country possessing an enterprising population of several hundred thousands of active and brave men, who are determined to live free or die gloriously in the defense of freedom, must possess advantages highly inviting to men who are sighing for the enjoyment of the common rights and liberties of mankind. The time, I trust, is not far distant, when all wise and good men will use their influence to place the Free Coloured People of the United States upon the delightful Island of Hayti.

THOMAS PAUL.

Boston, July 1st, 1824.

RESOLUTIONS

OF THE

PEOPLE OF COLOR,

AT A

MEETING HELD ON THE 25TH OF JANUARY, 1831.

WITH AN

ADDRESS TO THE CITIZENS OF NEW YORK,

IN ANSWER TO THOSE OF THE

New York Colonization Society.

New York: 1831.

RESOLUTIONS

AT a public meeting of the colored citizens of New York, held at Boyer Lodge Room, on Tuesday evening, the 25th ult., Mr. Samuel Ennals was called to the Chair, and Mr. Philip Bell appointed Secretary. The Chairman stated that the object of the meeting was to take into consideration the proceedings of an Association, under the title of the "New York Colonization Society." An address to the "Citizens of New York" relative to that Society, was read from the Commercial Advertiser of the 8th ult.; whereupon the following resolutions were unanimously adopted.

Whereas a number of gentlemen in this city, of mistaken views with respect to the wishes and welfare of the people of this State, on the subject of African Colonization, and in pursuance of such

mistaken views are using every exertion to form "African Colonization Societies;" and whereas a public document, purporting to be an
address to the people of the "city of New York" on this subject, contains opinions and assertions regarding the people of color as unfounded as they are unjust and derogatory to them—Therefore

Resolved, That this meeting do most solemnly protest against the
said address, as containing sentiments with respect to the people of
color, unjust, illiberal, and unfounded; tending to excite the prejudice of the community.

Resolved, That in our opinion the sentiments put forth in the
resolutions at the formation of the "Colonization Society of the city
of New York," are such as to impress this community with the belief that the colored population are a growing evil, immoral, and
destitute of religious principles.

Resolved, That we view the resolution calling on the worshippers
of Christ to assist in the unholy crusade against the colored population of this country, as totally at variance with true Christian
principles.

Resolved, That we claim *this country, the place of our birth, and
not Africa,* as our mother country, and all attempts to send us to
Africa, we consider as gratuitous and uncalled for.

Resolved, That a committee of three persons be appointed to
draft an address to the people of New York, and to be published,
together with these resolutions, and the same be signed by the
Chairman and Secretary.

SAMUEL ENNALS, Chairman.

PHILIP BELL, Secretary.

AN ADDRESS TO THE CITIZENS OF NEW YORK.

In protesting against the sentiments and declarations to our prejudice with which the above noticed "address" and "resolutions"
abound, we are well aware of the power and influence we have
attempted to resist. The gentlemen named as officers of the "Colonization Society" are men of high standing, their dictum is law in
morals with our community; but we who feel the effect of their
proscription indulge the hope of an impartial hearing.

We believe many of those gentlemen are our friends, and we
hope they all mean well; we care not how many Colonization Societies they form to send slaves from the south to a place where they
may enjoy freedom; and if they can "drain the ocean with a bucket,"
may send "with their own consent," the increasing free colored population: but we solemnly protest against that Christian philanthropy
which in acknowledging our wrongs commits a greater by vilifying

us. The conscientious man would not kill the animal, but cried "mad dog," and the rabble dispatched him. These gentlemen acknowledge the anomaly of that political ethicks which makes a distinction between man and man, when its foundation is "that all men are born equal," and possess in common "unalienable rights," and to justify the withholding of these "rights" would proclaim to foreigners that we are "a distinct and inferior race," without religion or morals, and implying that our condition cannot be improved here because there exists an unconquerable prejudice in the whites towards us. We absolutely deny these positions, and we call upon the learned author of the "address" for the indications of distinction between us and other men. There are different *colors* among all species of animated creation. A difference of color is not a difference of species. Our structure and organization are the same, and not distinct from other men; and in what respects are we inferior? Our political condition we admit renders us less respectable, but does it prove us an inferior part of the human family? Inferior indeed we are as to the means which we possess of becoming wealthy and learned men, and it would argue well for the cause of justice, humanity, and true religion, if the reverend gentlemen whose names are found at the bottom of President Duer's address, instead of showing their benevolence by laboring to move us some 4000 miles off, were to engage actively in the furtherance of plans for the improvement of our moral and political condition in the country of our birth. It is too late now to brand with inferiority any one of the races of mankind. We ask for proof. Time was when it was thought impossible to civilize the red man. Yet our own country presents a practical refutation of the vain assertion in the flourishing condition of the Cherokees, among whom intelligence and refinement are seen in somewhat fairer proportions than are exhibited by some of their white neighbors. In the language of a writer of expanded views and truly noble sentiments, "the blacks must be regarded as the real authors of most of the arts and sciences which give the whites at present the advantages over them. While Greece and Rome were yet barbarous, we find the light of learning and improvement emanating from this, by supposition, degraded and accursed continent of Africa, out of the midst of this very wooly-haired, flat-nosed, thick-lipped, coal-black race, which some persons are tempted to station at a pretty low intermediate point between men and monkeys."* It is needless to dwell on this topic, and we say with the same writer, the blacks had

---

* Alexander H. Everitt, Esq. Vide his work entitled *America, or a General Survey, &c. &c.*, pp. 212, 225.

a long and glorious day: and after what they have been and done, it argues not so much a mistaken theory, as sheer ignorance of the most notorious historical facts, to pretend that they are naturally inferior to the whites.

We earnestly desire that this address may not be misunderstood. We have no objection in the abstract to the Colonization Society; but we do protest strongly against the means which that Society uses to effect its purposes. It is evident to any impartial observer, that the natural tendency of all their speeches, reports, sermons, &c. is to widen the breach between us and the whites, and give to prejudice a tenfold vigor. It has produced a mistaken sentiment towards us. Africa is considered the home of those who have never seen its shores. The poor ignorant slave who, in all probability, has never heard the name of Christ by the Colonization process, is suddenly transformed into a "missionary," to instruct in the principles of Christianity and the arts of civilized life. The Friends have been the last to aid the system pursued by the society's advocates. And we say (for we feel it) that in proportion as they become Colonizationists they become less active and less friendly to our welfare as citizens of the United States.

There does exist in the United States a prejudice against us, but is it unconquerable? Is it not in the power of these gentlemen to subdue it? If their object is to benefit us, why not better our condition here? What keeps us down but the want of wealth? Why do we not accumulate wealth? Simply because we are not encouraged. If we wish to give our boys a classical education, they are refused admission into your colleges. If we consume our means in giving them a mercantile education, you will not employ them as clerks; if they are taught navigation, you will not employ them as captains. If we make them mechanics, you will not encourage them, nor will white mechanics work in the same shop with them. And with all these disabilities, like a millstone about us, because we cannot point to our statesmen, bankers and lawyers, we are called an inferior race. Look at the glaring injustice towards us. (A Foreigner, before he knows one of our streets from another, mounts a cart under the licence of another man, or is a public porter, a lamplighter, a watchman, &c.)

These gentlemen know but little of a large portion of the colored population of this city. Their opinions are formed from the unfortunate portion of our people whose characters are scrutinized by them as judges of courts. Their patrician principles prevent an intercourse with men in the middle walks of life, among whom a large portion of our people may be classed. We ask them to visit the dwellings of the respectable part of our people, and we are satisfied that they will discover more civilization and refinement than will be found among the same number of white families of an equal standing.

Finally, we hope that those who have so eloquently pleaded the cause of the Indian, will at least endeavor to preserve consistency in their conduct. They put no faith in Georgia, although she declares that the Indians shall not be removed but "with their own consent." Can they blame us if we attach the same credit to the declaration, that they mean to colonize us "only with our consent?" They cannot indeed use force; that is out of the question. But they harp so much on "inferiority," "prejudice," "distinction," and what not, that there will no alternative be left us but to fall in with their plans. We are content to abide where we are. We do not believe that things will always continue the same. The time must come when the declaration of independence will be felt in the heart as well as uttered from the mouth, and when the rights of all shall be properly acknowledged and appreciated. God hasten that time. This is our home, and this our country. Beneath its sod lie the bones of our fathers: for it some of them fought, bled, and died. Here we were born, and here we will die.

SPEECH OF NATHANIEL PAUL

DELIVERED AT

THE ANTI-COLONIZATION MEETING

London, 1833

In rising to address an audience of this description, I shall not offer an apology, because I consider it to be unnecessary. Nature has furnished me with an apology in the complexion that I wear, and that shall speak in my behalf. (Cheers.)

Allow me to say that Mr. Garrison has, for many years past, devoted himself exclusively to the interests of the slaves and the free people of color in the United States of America. He requires, however, no commendation from me, or from any other gentleman whatever; "the tree is known by its fruits," and "out of the abundance of the heart, the mouth speaketh." But if there be any necessity for calling evidence in favor of that gentleman, there is an abundance, demonstrating that he has acted a most disinterested part on behalf of those whose cause he has espoused. It has been his lot to make large sacrifices, in order that he might be enabled to pursue the object of his heart's desire. He might have swum upon the tide of popular applause, and have had the great and the noble of our country on his side, who would now have been applauding him, instead of persecuting him as the disturber of the peace and tranquility of the nation, if he had not lifted up his voice on behalf of the suffering slaves. (Hear, hear.) To my certain knowledge, when he commenced his career, it was under the most unfavorable circumstances. No one stood forward in his defense, and he was under the necessity of adopting and pursuing a system of the most rigid economy, in order that he might be sustained while he was engaged in the important work he had undertaken.

But it is not merely the sacrifice that Mr. Garrison has made, or the rigid system of economy that he has adopted, that speaks on his behalf; but the sufferings that he has endured likewise recommend him to the attention of every philanthropist. This gentleman has suffered forty-nine days incarceration in a prison in the city of Baltimore, in the State of Maryland, because he had the hardihood to engage in defense of the suffering slaves in that State. The fact of Mr. Garrison's imprisonment has been loudly sounded throughout this country. The agent of the American Colonization Society has seen fit to represent Mr. Garrison as a mere pamphleteer, as the editor of a Negro newspaper in the United States, and as a convicted libeller. This is the manner in which this gentleman has been spoken of in this country, by the agent of the American Colonization Society. And does that agent suppose that by such mere slang he can lower Mr. Garrison in the estimation of the British public? The simpleton reminds me of another of whom I have heard, who, for some cause or other, became exceedingly exasperated at the moon, and stood the whole night angrily shaking his fist at it, but could not reach it. (Cheers.)

I make no complaint against the agent of the American Colonization Society for stating the fact that Mr. Garrison was convicted, and thrown into prison in the United States; it is a fact, and he had a right to the advantage of it whenever he saw fit. I only blame him because, in stating it, he did not tell the cause why—who the persons were at whose instigation it was done—or the character of the court that condemned him. Inasmuch as that gentleman did not perform that part of his duty, if you will allow me I will undertake to discharge it for him.

Perhaps it is not generally known that in the United States of America—that land of freedom and equality—the laws are so exceedingly liberal that they give to man the liberty of purchasing as many negroes as he can find means to pay for (hear, hear), and also the liberty to sell them again. In consequence of this, a regular system of merchandise is established in the souls and bodies of our fellow creatures. It so happened that a very large number of mercantile gentlemen resided in the city of Baltimore and its vicinity, who were engaged in this traffic; and Mr. Garrison had the impudence, the unblushing effrontery to state, in a public newspaper, that this traffic was a direct violation of the laws of God, and contrary to the principles of human nature. (Cheers.) This was the crime of which he was convicted. And now I will tell you the character of the judicial tribunal before which the conviction took place. Allow me to say, and let that suffice, that the judges of the court were slaveholders (hear, hear), and the jury likewise. Had it been the case that such men as William Wilberforce, Thomas Clarkson, Thomas Fowell Buxton, James Cropper, and in addition to these, the honorable gentleman who sits on my right (Mr. O'Connell) (cheers), and had these gentlemen in the place where Mr. Garrison resided pursued the course they have adopted in this country, they would have been indicted, convicted, and thrown into prison. In regard to my friend on my right, (Mr. O'Connell,) I know not what they would have done with him: he could have expected no quarters whatever. (Laughter and cheers.) I believe he has more than once arraigned the American Republic before the British community, before God, and before the world, as the most detestable political hypocrite in the world. And this is not all. I may say, in addition, that that Court and that Jury would have convicted the whole Anti-Slavery Society of this country, and would have transported them all to Liberia as the punishment of their crimes. (Laughter and loud cheers.)

These are the causes and these the reasons why our friend, Mr. Garrison, was imprisoned; and as I said before, tho' I have no complaint to make against the agent of that benevolent institution, as it is called—the American Colonization Society—for stating that Mr. Garrison was cast into prison; yet I submit that, in connexion with it, he ought to have told the reason why it took place. But I shall leave this Garrison to itself. It possesses, I believe, ammunition enough to defend itself from any attack that may be made upon it, either by the agent of that Society, or the gentleman who has appeared here to plead on its behalf this morning. (Loud applause.)

I now come directly to express my views in relation to the American Colonization Society.

As a colored man, and as a citizen of the United States, it necessarily follows that I must feel more deeply interested in its operation, than any other individual present. In relation to the Society, I know not which is the most detestable in my view—its cruelty, or its hypocrisy. Both of these are characteristics of its whole operation.

I brand it as a *cruel* institution, and one of the most cruel that has ever been brought into existence by the ingenuity of man. If I am asked, why it is cruel? I answer, in the first place, because it undertakes to expel from their native country hundreds of thousands of unoffending and inoffensive individuals, who, in time of war, have gone forth into the field of battle, and have contended for the liberties of that country. Why does it seek to expel them? Because the God of heaven has given them a different complexion from themselves. (Cheers.) I say it is a *cruel* institution, because it seeks to rob the colored men in that country of every right, civil, political or religious, to which they are entitled by the American Declaration of Independence. It is through the influence of that Society, to the everlasting disgrace of a land boasting of liberty and equality, that there are laws enacted which absolutely forbid the instruction of the slave, or even the free person of color, in the use of letters. I say it is a *cruel* institution, because in addition to this, it has also been the means of having laws enacted which prevents them from meeting together to pay homage to their Creator, and worship the God who made them. I might go on enumerating instances of cruelty, and show to this meeting that even combinations have been formed in what are called the free States, under the influence of this Society, not to give to the colored man employment, but to rob him of the means of gaining his livelihood, that he may thereby be compelled to leave the land of his nativity, and go to Africa.

In the next place, I condemn the Society on account of its *hypocrisy;* and this, I believe, will be detested wherever it appears, by every honest man. And wherein does that hypocrisy consist or appear? I mean more particularly in regard to the representations which have been made of the Society in this country. It comes to Great Britain, and begins to talk about the evils of slavery, pitying the condition of the unhappy victims of cruelty and oppression in the United States of America; and it tells the British public that its object is to do away with slavery, and to emancipate those who are in bondage. What Briton's heart is there but responds to such a sentiment as this? (Cheers.) Englishmen are seeking for the liberation of the slaves; and, giving credit to the reports which they have heard respecting the American Colonization Society, without examining its principles, many benevolent individuals in this country have come forward and freely contributed to its funds. But instead of the institution being the enemy of slavery; instead of its being formed for the purpose of annihilating the system; its object is to perpetuate it, and render more secure the property of man in man. I will show to the meeting, in a few words, that its object cannot be the abolition of slavery, because through a hundred of its organs it has over and over again denounced the proposition of liberating the slaves, except on condition of their being transported to Africa. And now let the audience understand that, at the present time, there are upwards of 2,000,000 of slaves in the United States, and that their annual increase is more than 60,000. If slavery, therefore, is to be abolished only as those who shall be emancipated are transported from the United States to Africa, we ask, when is slavery to cease in that country? The Colonization Society, with all the efforts that it can bring to bear, cannot transport the annual increase of the slaves (hear, hear), and, therefore, if no other means be adopted for the abolition of slavery in America, its extinction will not take place until the last trumpet shall sound. (Immense applause.)

Again I repeat it, it is *hypocritical,* because it professes to be the friend of the free people of color, and to pity their present condition; and hence it says, "It seeks to promote their welfare." That gentleman (Mr. Abrahams) tells us that he is acquainted with the people of North America, and that this Society is formed, in part, for the benefit of the free people of color. Does that gentleman know that when an effort was made at New Haven, two or three years since, to establish a College for the instruction of the free people of color,—notwithstanding New Haven is within the boundaries of that part of the country which is called the "free States,"— yet the supporters of the Society came forward, held a meeting, and passed the most spirited resolutions against the establishment of that institution in the city? (Hear, hear!) Does that gentleman know that in the same State, a white female, in endeavoring to establish a school for the instruction of colored females, has been most inhumanly assailed by the advocates of the Colonization Society, who, in town meetings, passed resolutions against her benevolent object, as spirited as if the cholera were about to break out in the village, and they by a single effort of this kind could hinder its devastations? They could not have acted with more promptness, and energy, and violence, than they did in persecuting this excellent lady, because her compassion led her to espouse the cause of the suffering blacks. (Cheers.) They were ready to expel her from the country. I could relate many facts with regard to that part of the country for which the Rev. gentleman contends, and show that, instead of the American Colonization Society seeking the welfare of the free people of color, it is their most bitter enemy. Whenever it speaks of this class, both in public and in private, it calumniates and abuses them in the most extravagant manner, as its reports will abundantly show.

Wishing to be brief, and knowing that there are gentlemen present who will address you with more interest than I can (hear, hear), I will make but one remark more, and that respects the designs of this Society with regard to Africa. O, bleeding, suffering Africa! We hear of the sad condition which that country is in; it is enveloped in darkness infinitely deeper than the sable hue of its degraded sons. The vilest superstition there abounds; and hence this Society represents it as their object to let in the rays of the gospel, and enlighten the people. But, according to their own reports, whom do they select as instruments to spread civilization and christianity? People not fit to live in America—people who are a disgrace to that country. (Hear, hear.) I pity Africa as much as any man; I want her to be enlightened; but let us send men who are enlightened themselves. If we mean to evangelize Africa, let us at least send Christians there to do the work. (Cheers.)

Mr. Garrison has well remarked that the free people of color in the United States are opposed to this Society. I will venture to assert that I am as extensively acquainted with them, throughout both the free and slave States, as any man in that country; and I do not know of a solitary colored individual who entertains the least favorable view of the American Colonization Society; but, in every way they possibly could, they have expressed their disapprobation of it. They have said to the Society, *"Let us alone."*

The argument which is brought by the friends of the Society in favor of colonization is, that the white population of America can never amalgamate or live on terms of equality with the blacks. Be it so. Let it be admitted that their prejudices are strong. All that I will say is, that if such be the case, they ought not to send an agent to this country to ask assistance to enable them to gratify a prejudice of which they ought to be ashamed.

[Source: *Speeches Delivered at the Anti-Colonization Meeting in Exeter Hall, London, July 13, 1833, by James Cropper, Esq., William Lloyd Garrison, Rev. Nathaniel Paul, Daniel O'Connell, Esq. M.P., Mr. Buckingham, M.P., Mr. Hunt, Rev. Mr. Abrahams, George Thompson, Esq. etc., etc.* (Boston: Garrison and Knapp, 1833), pp. 12–15.]

Emigration to Mexico

Mr. Editor—I am happy to learn that the sentiments of some of my Trenton brethren are in accordance with my own, in regard to our locating in Mexico and Upper Canada; for, in my humble opinion, one thing is needful for us as a people, even emigration; but not to Africa, nor to place ourselves as a distinct people anywhere, but to attach ourselves to a nation already established. The government of these United States is not the only one in this hemisphere that offers equal rights to men; but there are others under whose protection we may safely reside, where it is no disgrace to wear a sable complexion, and where our rights will not be continually trampled upon, on that account. We profess to be republicans, and such I hope we are; but wherein do we show our republican spirit, by sitting still and sighing for that liberty our white brethren tell us we never shall obtain, or in hoping that in some fifty or a hundred years hence, our children's children will be made free? I think we do not evince republicanism by this conduct, but verily believe that the time has arrived when we, too, ought to manifest that spirit of independence which shines so conspicuously in the character of Europeans, by leaving the land of oppression and emigrating where we may be received and treated as brothers; where our worth will be felt and acknowledged; and where we may acquire education, wealth and respectability, together with a knowledge of the arts and sciences; all of which may be in our power—of the enjoyment of which the government of the separate states in the union is adopting means to deprive us.

The author of this article is aware, that the subject is not popular, and perhaps will not be kindly received; but it is one that I hope will be deeply pondered in the mind of every colored citizen of this country before he passes sentence against it.

Some of your readers may inquire, where is that country to which we may remove, and thus become free and equal? I believe that country to be Mexico. There is an independent nation, where indeed "all men are born free and equal," possessing those inalienable rights which our constitution guarantees. The climate is healthy and warm, and of course adapted to our nature; the soil is rich and fertile, which will contribute to our wealth; and there we may become a people of worth and respectability; whereas in this country we are kept poor, and of course, cannot aspire to anything more than what we always have been. I have been waiting to hear of some way being pointed out that will tend to better the present generation; but, as yet, have heard of nothing that appears to be permanent. I would not wish to be thought pleading the cause of colonization, for no one detests it more than I do. I would not be taken to Africa, were the Society to make me queen of the country; and were I to move to Canada, I would not settle in the colony, but take up my abode in some of the cities where a distinction is not known; for I do not approve of our drawing off into a separate body anywhere. But, I confess, I can see no just reason why we should not cultivate the spirit of enterprise as well as the whites. They are found in every quarter of the globe, in search of situations to better their condition; and why may we not "go and do likewise?"

I am informed that the population of Mexico is eight millions of colored, and one million of whites; and by the rapid growth of amalgamation amongst them, there is every probability that it will ere long become one entire colored nation. I am of opinion that Mexico would afford us a large field for speculation, were we to remove thither; and who can say that the day will not soon arrive when the flag of our colored American merchants' ships from the Mexican ports shall be seen proudly waving in the breeze of the American harbors? And shall not our sons feel proud to enlist under the Mexican banner, and support her government? Surely they will.

There is one objection, however, that may arise in the minds of some; that is, the religion of that nation being Papist; but we can take with us the Holy Bible, which is able to make us wise unto salvation; and perhaps we may be made the honored instruments, in the hands of an all-wise God, in establishing the holy religion of the Protestant Church in that country; and that alone might be a sufficient inducement for the truly pious.

A COLORED FEMALE OF PHILADELPHIA.
Philadelphia, January 2, 1832.

[Source: *Liberator,* Vol. 2, No. 4 (January 28, 1832), p. 14.]

A

DISCOURSE

DELIVERED IN

ST. PHILIP'S CHURCH,

FOR THE BENEFIT OF THE

Coloured Community of Wilberforce,

IN UPPER CANADA,

ON THE FOURTH OF JULY, 1830.

BY REV. PETER WILLIAMS,
RECTOR OF ST. PHILIP'S CHURCH.

NEW-YORK:
PRINTED BY G. F. BUNCE, 224 CHERRY-STREET.
1830.

At a regular meeting of the Vestry of St Philip's Church, the 13th July, 1830, the following preamble and resolve was passed.

Whereas, in the opinion of the Vestry, the discourse delivered by our Rector, the Rev. PETER WILLIAMS, on the 4th, in favour of the colony of coloured people in Upper Canada, contains information that will (if circulated) be of service to said colony:

Therefore, resolved that the Rev. Peter Williams be requested to furnish the Secretary of this Vestry, with the manuscript of said discourse, for publication. A copy from the minutes.

PETER VOGELSANG, *Secretary.*

DISCOURSE

ECCLESIASTES xi. 1, 2.—Cast thy bread upon the waters: for thou shalt find it after many days. Give a portion to seven and also to eight, for thou knowest not what evil shall be upon the earth.

ON this day, the fathers of this nation declared, "We hold these truths to be self-evident, that all men are created equal, that they are endowed by their Creator with certain unalienable rights, among which are life, liberty, and the pursuit of happiness."

These truly noble sentiments have secured to their author a deathless fame. The sages and patriots of the revolution subscribed them with enthusiasm, and "pledged their lives, their fortunes, and their sacred honour" in their support.

The result has been the freedom and happiness of millions, by whom the annual returns of this day are celebrated, with the loudest and most lively expressions of joy.

But although this anniversary affords occasion of rejoicing, to the mass of the people of the United States, there is a class, a numerous class, consisting of nearly three millions, who participate but little in its joys, and are deprived of their unalienable rights, by the very men who so loudly rejoice in the declaration, that "all men are born free and equal."

The festivities of this day serve but to impress upon the minds of reflecting men of colour a deeper sense of the cruelty, the injustice, and oppression of which they have been the victims. While others rejoice in their deliverance from a foreign yoke, they mourn that a yoke a thousandfold more grievous is fastened upon them. Alas, they are slaves in the midst of freemen; they are slaves to those who boast that freedom is the unalienable right of all; and the clanking of their fetters, and the voice of their wrongs make a horrid discord in the songs of freedom which resound through the land.

No people in the world profess so high a respect for liberty and equality as the people of the United States, and yet no people hold so many slaves, or make such great distinctions between man and man.

From various causes (among which we cheerfully admit a sense of justice to have held no inconsiderable rank) the work of emancipation has, within a few years, been rapidly advancing in a number of the states. The state we live in, since the 4th of July 1827, has been able to boast that she has no slaves, and other states where there still are slaves appear disposed to follow her example.

These things furnish us with cause of gratitude to God; and encourage us to hope that the time will speedily arrive when slavery will be universally abolished. Brethren, what a bright prospect would there be before us in this land, had we no prejudices to contend against, after being made free.

But alas! the freedom to which we have attained, is defective. Freedom and equality have been "put asunder." The rights of men are decided by the colour of their skin; and there is as much difference made between the rights of a free white man and a free coloured man, as there is between a free coloured man and a slave.

Though delivered from the fetters of slavery, we are oppressed by an unreasonable, unrighteous, and cruel prejudice, which aims at nothing less than the forcing away of all the free coloured people of the United States, to the distant shores of Africa. Far be it from me to impeach the motives of every member of the African Colonization Society. The civilizing and christianizing of that vast continent, and the extirpation of the abominable traffic in slaves (which, notwithstanding all the laws passed for its suppression, is still carried on in all its horrors) are no doubt the principal motives which induce many to give it their support.

But there are those, and those who are most active and most influential in its cause, who hesitate not to say that they wish to rid the country of the free coloured population, and there is sufficient reason to believe that, with many, this is the principal motive for supporting that Society; and that whether Africa is civilized or not, and whether the slave trade be suppressed or not, they would wish to see the free coloured people removed from this country to Africa.

Africa could certainly be brought into a state of civil and religious improvement without sending all the free people of colour in the United States there.

A few well-qualified missionaries, properly fitted out and supported, would do more for the instruction and improvement of the natives of that country than a host of Colonists, the greater part of whom would need to be instructed themselves, and all of whom for a long period would find enough to do to provide for themselves, instead of instructing the natives.

How inconsistent are those who say that Africa will be benefitted by the removal of the free people of colour of the United States there, while they say they are the most vile and degraded people in the world.—If we are as vile and degraded as they represent us, and they wish the Africans to be rendered a virtuous, enlightened and happy people, they should not think of sending us among them, lest we should make them worse instead of better.

The colonies planted by white men on the shores of America, so far from benefitting the aborigines, corrupted their morals, and caused their ruin; and yet those who say we are the most vile people in the world, would send us to Africa, to improve the character and condition of the natives. Such arguments would not be listened to for a moment, were not the minds of the community strangely warped by prejudice.

Those who wish that that vast continent should be compensated for the injuries done it, by sending thither the light of the gospel, and the arts of civilized life, should aid in sending and supporting well-qualified missionaries, who should be wholly devoted to the work of instruction, instead of sending colonists, who would be apt to turn the ignorance of the natives to their own advantage, and do them more harm than good.

Much has also been said by Colonizationists about improving the character and condition of the people of colour of this country by sending them to Africa. This is more inconsistent still. We are to be improved by being sent far from civilized society. This is a novel mode of improvement. What is there in the burning sun, the arid plains, and barbarous customs of Africa, that is so peculiarly favourable to our improvement? What hinders our improving here, where schools and colleges abound, where the gospel is preached at every corner, and where all the arts and sciences are verging fast to perfection? Nothing, nothing but prejudice. It requires no large expenditures, no hazardous enterprises, to raise the people of colour in the United States to as highly improved a state as any class of the community. All that is necessary is that those who profess to be anxious for it, should lay aside their prejudices, and act towards them as they do by others.

We are natives of this country, we ask only to be treated as well as foreigners. Not a few of our fathers suffered and bled to purchase its independence; we ask only to be treated as well as those who fought against it. We have toiled to cultivate it, and to raise it to its present prosperous condition; we ask only to share equal privileges with those who come from distant lands to enjoy the fruits of our labour. Let these moderate requests be granted, and we need not go to Africa nor anywhere else, to be improved and happy. We cannot but doubt the purity of the motives of those persons who deny us these requests, and would send us to Africa to gain what they might give us at home.

But they say the prejudices of the country against us are invincible; and as they cannot be conquered, it is better that we should be removed beyond their influence. This plea should never proceed from the lips of any man who professes to believe that a just God rules in the heavens.

The African Colonization Society is a numerous and influential body. Would they lay aside their own prejudices, much of the burden would be at once removed; and their example (especially if they were as anxious to have justice done us here, as to send us to Africa) would have such an influence upon the community at large, as would soon cause prejudice to hide its deformed head.

But alas! the course which they have pursued has an opposite tendency. By the scandalous misrepresentations which they are continually giving of our character and conduct, we have sustained much injury, and have reason to apprehend much more.

Without any charge of crime, we have been denied all access to places to which we formerly had the most free intercourse; the coloured citizens of other places, on leaving their homes, have been denied the privilege of returning; and others have been absolutely driven out.

Has the Colonization Society had no effect in producing these barbarous measures?

They profess to have no other object in view than the colonizing of the free people of colour on the coast of Africa, with their *own consent;* but if our homes are made so uncomfortable that we cannot continue in them, or if, like our brethren of Ohio and New Orleans, we are driven from them, and no other door is open to receive us but Africa, our removal there will be any thing but voluntary.

It is very certain that very few free people of colour wish to go to that land. The Colonization Society know this, and yet they do certainly calculate that in time they will have us all removed there.

How can this be effected, but by making our situation worse here, and closing every other door against us?

God, in his good providence, has opened for such of us as may choose to leave these States an asylum in the neighbouring British province of Canada.

There is a large tract of land on the borders of Lake Huron, containing a million of acres, which is offered to our people at $1.50 per acre. It lies between the 42nd and 44th degrees of north latitude. The climate is represented as differing but little from this; the soil as good as any in the world, well timbered and watered. The laws are good, and the same for the coloured man as the white man. A powerful sympathy prevails there in our behalf, instead of the prejudice which here oppresses us; and everything encourages the hope that, by prudence and industry, we may rise to as prosperous and happy a condition as any people under the sun.

To secure this land as a settlement for our people, it is necessary that a payment of $6000 be made on or before the 10th of November next.

This sum it is proposed to lay out in the purchase of 4000 acres, and when paid, will secure the keeping of the remainder in reserve for coloured emigrants, ten years. The land so purchased is to be sold out by agents, or trustees to emigrants, and the monies received in return, to be appropriated to a second purchase, which is to be sold as at first, and the returns again laid out in land, until the whole tract is in their possession; and then the capital so employed is to be expended on objects of general utility.

The persons who have bargained for the land have found it necessary to apply to the citizens of the United States to aid them, by their donations, in raising the amount necessary to make their first purchase; and also to aid a number of emigrants who were driven away in a cruel manner and in a destitute condition from Cincinnati, to seek a home where they might, and who have selected the Huron tract as their future abode.

Each of these particulars present powerful claims to your liberality. "Cast thy bread upon the waters," says the wise man in the text, "and thou shalt find it after many days. Give a portion to seven and also to eight, for thou knowest not what evil shall be upon the earth." Oh! truly we "know not what evil shall be upon the earth."

When we look at the course of events relative to our people in this country, we find reason to conclude that it is proper we should provide a convenient asylum to which we and our children may flee, in case we should be so oppressed as to find it necessary to leave our present homes. The opinion is daily gaining ground, and has been often openly expressed, that it would be a great blessing to the country if all its free coloured population could be removed to Africa. As this opinion advances, recourse will naturally be had to such measures as will make us feel it necessary to go. Its operation has been already much felt in various states.

The coloured population of Cincinnati were an orderly, industrious and thriving people, but the white citizens, having determined to force them out, first entered into a combination that they would give none of them employment; and finally resorted to violent measures to compel them to go. Should the anxiety to get rid of us increase, have we not reason to fear that some such courses may be pursued in other places?

Satan is an inventive genius. He often appears under the garb of an angel of light, and makes religion and patriotism his plea for the execution of his designs. Our Lord foretold his disciples that "the time cometh, when whosoever killeth you, will think that he doeth God service." Brethren, the time is already come when *many* think that whosoever causeth us to remove from our native home does service to his country and to God.

Ah! to many in other places beside Cincinnati and New Orleans, the sight of free men of colour is so unwelcome that we know not what they may think themselves justifiable in doing, to get rid of them. Will it not then be wise for us to provide ourselves with a convenient asylum in time? We have now a fair opportunity of doing so; but if we neglect it, it may be too late; the lands now offered us may be occupied by others, and I know of none likely to be offered which promises so many advantages. Indeed I feel warranted in saying, that if they are not speedily secured, attempts will be made to prevent our securing them hereafter, and that propositions have actually been made, by influential men, to purchase them, in order that the coloured people may not get them in their possession.

It is true that Africa and Hayti, and perhaps some other countries, will still afford us a place of refuge, yet it will not certainly be amiss to have Canada also at our choice. Some may prefer going there to any other place. But suppose we should never stand in need of such an asylum (and some think that our having provided it will make it less necessary; an effect we should all rejoice in, as we have no wish to go, if we can stay in comfort)—suppose we should never stand in need of such an asylum, still the amount required to secure it is so small that we can never regret parting with it for such an object. What is $6000 to be raised by the coloured people throughout the United States? How few are so poor that they cannot give a few shillings without missing it? Let it have the amount which is usually spent by our people in this city on the 4th of July, in celebrating the national independence, and it will make up a very considerable part of it.

I have been informed that, at the suggestion of one of our coloured clergymen, the members of one of the societies, who intended to dine together tomorrow, have agreed to give the money which would have been paid for dinner-tickets to this object. This is truly patriotic. I would say to each of you, brethren "go and do likewise." Give what you would probably expend in celebrating the 4th of July, to the colony of your brethren in Canada; and on the birthday of American freedom, secure the establishment of a colony in which you and your children may rise to respectability and happiness.—

Give it, and you will be no poorer than if you gave it not; and you will secure a place of refuge to yourselves in case of need.—"Give a portion to seven and also to eight, for thou knowest not what evil shall be upon the earth."

You are strongly urged to liberality on this occasion by a regard to your future welfare. No scheme for our colonization that has ever yet been attempted has so few objections, or promises so many advantages; but if you withhold your aid until every imaginable objection is removed, you will never effect any object beneficial to yourselves or to your brethren.

Brethren, it is no time to cavil, but to help. If you mean to help the colony, help now. The amount of the first purchase must be paid by the 10th of November, or not at all. Brethren, this scheme of colonization opens to us a brighter door of hope than was ever opened to us before, and has a peculiar claim upon our patronage, because it has originated among our own people. It is not of the devising of the white men, nor of foreigners, but of our own kindred and household. If it succeeds, ours will be the credit. If it succeeds not, ours will be the fault. I am happy, however, to find that it meets the approbation of most, if not of all, of those wise and good men who have for many years been our most zealous and faithful friends, and it evidently appears to be specially favoured by Providence. But the occasion has not only an appeal to your interest, but to your charity.

Your brethren exiled from Cincinnati, for no crime, but because God was pleased to clothe them with a darker skin than their neighbours, cry to you from the wilderness for help. They ask you for bread, for clothing, and other necessaries to sustain them, their wives and their little ones, until by their industry they can provide themselves the means of support. It is true, there are some among them that are able to help themselves; but for these we do not plead. Those who can help themselves, will; but as the ablest have been sufferers in the sacrifice of their property, and the expenses and dangers of their forced and hurried removal, they are not able to assist their destitute brethren.

Indeed, most of the wealthy men of colour in Cincinnati arranged so as to remain until they could have a chance of disposing of their property to advantage; but the poor were compelled to fly without delay, and consequently need assistance. Brethren, can you deny it to them? I know you too well to harbour such a thought. It is only necessary to state to you their case, to draw forth your liberality. Think then, what these poor people must have suffered, in being driven with their wives and their little ones, from their comfortable homes, late in autumn, to take up their residence in a wide and desolate wilderness. O, last winter, must have been to them a terrible one indeed. We hope that they, by their own efforts, will be better prepared for the next; but they must yet stand in need of help. They have the rude forest to subdue; houses to build; food to provide. They are the pioneers for the establishment of a colony which may be a happy home for thousands and tens of thousands of our oppressed race. O think of the situation of these your brethren, whom the hand of oppression has driven into exile, and whom the providence of God, has perhaps doomed like Joseph to suffering, that at some future day, much people may be saved alive.—Think of them, and give to their relief as your hearts may dictate. "Cast thy bread upon the waters," &c.

Opinions of a Freeman of Colour in Charleston

We have received a communication from a respectable free coloured man of Charleston, which contains some thoughts which merit the serious consideration of all his brethren. May the noble spirit of devotedness which he manifests to the good of mankind, soon animate ten thousand of his coloured brethren, that they may go forth, not merely to improve their own condition, but to relieve and bless the long afflicted and degraded children of Africa. We have omitted some sentences in this article, and made some slight corrections; not affecting materially the sense of the writer. His remarks have reference to the three following heads.

I. *A Brief Inquiry into the propriety of the Free People of Colour migrating to Liberia or elsewhere.*

II. *The objections urged by many of the Coloured People against emigration.*

III. *The good likely to result to those who may determine to emigrate.*

1st. When we reflect upon the laws of Ohio, that expel from her territory our brethren—when we look to Virginia, to Maryland, to Alabama and to Tennessee, we must candidly confess that we have much fearful apprehension in regard to the laws that may be enacted bearing heavily upon us, even in our own dear Carolina, which generously cherishes all her inhabitants and gives them support and employment in all of the various and useful branches of mechanism, without regard to colour or condition. There are many callings in which the coloured people in Carolina have a decided preference; in some cases they have no competitors; how long this favorable state of things will remain, we are not prepared to say—time alone can correctly decide in this matter. This is an era, however, in our affairs, that we cannot shut our eyes to, and it must appear to the philosopher, the Christian, and the sagacious politician, a period of deep and anxious solicitude as regards the future prospects, hopes, and interests of a people little known but as a nuisance—mere laborers in the most menial capacity; at best a people who seldom deserve notice, or the exercise of charitable acts bestowed on them. Their friends and their foes both desire the removal of the free people of colour; although it is a fact not denied but by a very few, that the descendants of Africa, when transplanted in a country favorable to their improvement, and when their advantages are equal to others, seldom fail to answer all of the ends suited to their capacity, and in some instances rise to many of the virtues, to the learning and piety of the most favored nation. Yet, alas! the prevalence of popular prejudice against our colour (which is the more surprising, as it is well known that God alone creates different classes of men, that he may be adored and worshipped by all in the spirit of truth, without regard to complexion) has almost invariably stood as a barrier to our advancement in knowledge. Hence some of us appear to be useless,* and when it is considered that we are a large body of people, growing rapidly every day, without that improvement which the present age seems to require, in moral virtue and intellectual attainments; indeed, when we examine our own conduct and that of our brethren, and compare the advantages we do actually possess, with so many bright examples before us of christianizing and improving the condition of mankind, both far and immediately under our eyes, we cannot but enquire "how can these things be?" My friends, if we will venture to look around us, we will behold the most encouraging proofs of happiness in the emigrants from Europe to this country. You have no call to look farther than our city (Charleston) to witness the most lively encouragements given to emigrants.† Many who arrive here very poor, are soon made rich (and so it will be with us in Liberia): enterprising, industrious individuals, also families incorporating themselves in the community, enjoying all the blessings peace can confer on society, and soon successfully advancing on the high road to wealth and respectability, whilst we sink daily in the estimation of all.

Our apparently inactive habits may, in a great measure, be attributed to this reason—"That we have no opportunity for the cultivation of our minds by education." As a matter of course, generally speaking, we lose all regard for any, but our individual self * * * * * * *—satisfied with every moral privation, with this certain conviction in our hearts: that our children are likely to be much worse situated than we are, as we ourselves are not as well situated in many respects as our parents were. The next enquiry is, what are we to do? I answer honestly and without hesitation, mi-

---

* Except it may be when we are employed as laborers.
† Without any tax whatever, whilst we pay a heavy one.

grate to Liberia, in preference to any other country, under the protecting hand and influence of the Colonization Society. *Here comes my second proposition;* a consideration of the objections many have to emigrating to a country whose inhabitants are shrouded in deep ignorance—whom long and deep-rooted custom forbids us to have social intercourse with in the various relations of civilized life upon fair and equal terms of husband and wife, and whose complexion is darker than many of ours. But in all this, my friends, there is no reasonable ground of objection to your removal to a country more adapted to promote your interests, because a very plain reason presents itself for such removal—and that is, in Liberia you will enjoy moral and political liberty. Besides, the heralds of the cross who first preached salvation to the benighted sons of Africa, were white men, and numbers of ladies also withdrew themselves from the beauties of highly polished circles in Europe to accompany their husbands in spreading the light in dark places. Those who contribute in money to carry on the splendid work of colonization and religion, who sacrifice their health on the shrine of humanity and deprive themselves of all earthly comforts, even stare death in the face, and prefer to die in the attempt, rather than relinquish the spread of virtue and religion amongst this very people you affect to despise— they are white. Who are they at this very period, rearing up an establishment at Liberia, that bids fair under the protecting smiles of Providence, to crush forever the monster (the slave trade) that has led to captivity, and chains, and perpetual disgrace, our brethren, who, although formed in the image of God, are doomed in most countries, Liberia excepted, to degradation and servitude? They are white men. Surely this is at least one strong reason that should induce you, cheerfully to migrate to a country, where you can possess *all* of the importance of free citizens; in fact, all your objections dwindle into insignificance, in view of this one fact stated above. Besides, locating in Liberia does not necessarily compel you to form private alliance in families that you dislike; on the contrary, there is no country where you could indulge your own opinions in this respect with more freedom, than in that land of equality.

If you do go, and I hope in my heart all of us may speedily go— will we not go with our families and friends; cementing more strongly the bond of our connections, our customs, and our habits? Look for example to the Jews and other ancient people, scattered all over the world; look at our own situation, wherever we are placed: we see no innovation, nothing likely to break in and change the existing face of society.

III. Much good is likely to result to those who are meek and humble, who can see the advantages of liberty and equality, with the courage to embark in an enterprise, under such favorable circumstances. *This is the truth,* which is useful for all of us to know, and I have endeavored briefly to lay it before you, for your reflection, and if you once bring your minds to serious reflection, your friends will never blush—no—never under any circumstances, on account of dissensions on your part. Surely, my brethren, there are very strong reasons for us to go—yes go—and invoke Jehovah for his favorable protection to you, and to that country which holds out to us, and to our children, forever, protection, in life, liberty, and property—beside every honor of office, within the gift of a free people. He who holds in the hollow of his hand the destiny of nations, will be with you, and will bless you with health and vigor to contribute your personal services of pious example, to improve the country that invites you to possess its soil. Moreover, you will have the great privilege of sharing in your own government, and finally of becoming a perfectly free and independent people. And where would you go (go you must, sooner or later) to look for this noble privilege—the power of electing your officers or removing them when need requires. Yes, my brethren, perhaps much depends on your present zeal and activity for success—and if God be with us, and I have a lively hope that he influences and directs you in this matter, before long the emigrants to Liberia will become a distinguished nation; and who can prophesy and foretell the future destiny of Liberia? The day, however, may not be far distant, when those who now despise the humble, degraded emigrants to Liberia, will make arrangements with them, to improve navigation, to extend commerce, and perhaps we may soon conduct and carry on our trade with foreign nations in our own bottoms without molestation or fear. Such, my brethren, are some of the high expectations to be derived from a well established colony in Liberia, and to you Carolinians, all eyes are directed, all hearts are uplifted to God in prayer, to know what course your good sense will induce you to pursue, under existing circumstances. Your reputation as a body of first-rate mechanics is well known; distinguished for your industry and good behaviour, you have with you, carpenters, millers, wheel-wrights, ship builders, engineers, cabinet makers, shoe makers, tailors, and a host of others, all calculated at once to make you a great people. In Liberia you can erect a temple to worship God in the beauty of holiness; without fear you can set up and protect your sacred altars, and pour out the orisons of the devout and pious heart before them, in praise and thanksgiving to God. In Liberia, you can establish Academies and

Colleges, to instruct youth in Theology, in Physic, and in Law. You will there know no superiors but virtue, and the laws of your country—no religion but the revealed revelation of God—and recollect all of this is for you yourselves.

A SOUTH CAROLINIAN.

[Source: *The African Repository, And Colonial Journal*, Vol. VIII, October 1832, pp. 239–243.]

The first woman to petition the A.M.E. Church for the authority to preach, **Jarena Lee** was an itinerate preacher who ministered throughout the northeastern United States.

An abolitionist and a Masonic leader,
Absalom Jones was the first African
American priest of the Protestant
Episcopal Church.

A minister of the Boston Baptist
Society, **Thomas A. Paul**
established the African Meeting
House. The meeting house served
as both a church and school and
was the only building in Boston
controlled by Blacks at that time.

Richard Allen was an abolitionist and the founder of the Free African Society and the African Methodist Episcopal Church where he was consecrated as the church's first Bishop.

Among the early antislavery orators, pamphleteers, and publicists, there was none more uncomprimisingly opposed to slavery than **David Ruggles** (center).

An educational, religious, and political leader, **Rev. John Francis Cook** helped to establish two of the most important churches in Washington, D.C., Union Bethel and the First Colored Presbyterian Church of Washington.

A soldier in the Revolutionary War, **Rev. Lemuel Haynes** was a Congregational minister and preached to white congregations for most of his life.

Staunchly opposed to the colonization of free Blacks, **James Forten** was a businessman, abolitionist, leader of reform movements, and champion of Black rights.

The fourth Bishop of the African Methodist Episcopal Church, **Rev. William Paul Quinn** was a minister in the A.M.E. Church for more than sixty years.

A moral reformer and businessman in Pennsylvania, **William Whipper** was the editor of the National Reformer, the journal of the American Moral Reform Society, and one of the society's leading organizers.

Phillis Wheatley's first collection of poems, entitled *Poems On Various Subjects, Religious and Moral*, was published in London in 1773.

Part V

Spokesmen in Behalf of Their
"Colored Fellow Citizens,"
1787–1815

Throughout this volume, many intelligent and persuasive men of color plead the cause of their oppressed brethren, appearing as their advocate before groups or congregations in churches and assembly halls. They gave sound advice, suggested hope under adversity, indicated their points of view on current conditions, on religion, political matters, education, morals, and economics.

These spokesmen summarized the thinking of thousands of their brethren who were unable to formulate their own ideas in writing or to articulate fluently their feelings and reactions to their situation. Only a few writings by Negroes during this period are extant, and then often only as single copies. The majority of the documents written by spokesmen for the free person of color that are included in this section emanate from the New York and Philadelphia area.

The earliest title included was written by Jupiter Hammon and directed to the members of the African Society in New York City in 1786. In it he stated that liberty was a "great thing and worth seeking for," if it could be obtained by "good conduct" which might "prevail upon our masters to set us free." Slaves, particularly those young ones with a little education, were certainly not resigned to a life of servitude. Hammon's fanatical appeal for obedience, honesty, Godliness and faithfulness may have been of consolation to the old slaves who would not be able to take care of themselves if set free. He warned his readers against being lazy, idle, or drunk; he spoke against stealing as "this will hurt those of us who are slaves and prevent their being freed."

Jupiter Hammon was born October 17, 1711. He remained a slave all of his life, belonging to the Lloyd family of Long Island. Unedu-

309

cated, he was satisfied with his status as a slave and did not desire his freedom.[1] In contrast to the life of Jupiter Hammon, Benjamin Banneker, born near Baltimore, November 9, 1731, was free and owned a few acres of land. He acquired some learning and had facility in astronomical calculations. He attracted the attention of the Elliott family who loaned him books relating to astronomy and some instruments which enabled him to use his leisure in research on astronomy. Banneker studied French, German, Greek, and Latin, as well as other subjects. He was considered the most learned man in the small town of Ellicott City, near Baltimore, where he lived. He compiled almanacs similar to others of his day. He sent to Thomas Jefferson, then Secretary of State, a manuscript copy of his first almanac, together with a letter concerning the emancipation of the Negro. A copy of the letter, dated August 19, 1791, was published in Philadelphia in 1792. He stated that he hoped Jefferson would "embrace every opportunity to eradicate that train of absurd and false ideas and opinions which so generally prevails with respect to us; and that your sentiments are concurrent with mine, which are, that one universal Father hath given being to us all; and that he hath not only made us all of one flesh, but that he hath also without partiality, afforded us all the same sensations and endowed us all with the same faculties; and that however variate we may be in society or religion, however diversified in situation or color, we are all of the same family." Banneker urged Jefferson to recognize the true worth of the Negro. Jefferson replied, "Nobody wishes more than I do to see such proofs as you exhibit, that nature has given to our black brethren talents equal to those of other colours of men; and that the appearance of the want of them, is owing merely to the degraded condition of their own existence, both in Africa and America.[2]

For twenty or more years on January 1, beginning in 1808, sermons and addresses were delivered by Negro leaders in commemoration of the abolition of the African slave trade. Passed in 1807, the Congressional Act abolishing the slave trade did not become effective until January, 1808. One of the most memorable of many "thanksgiving sermons" was written and delivered by Absalom Jones, rector

---

[1] See Stanley A. Ransom, *America's First Negro Poet.* (Port Washington, New York, 1970).

[2] Banneker's Almanacs appeared from 1792 to 1797 and were printed in New Jersey, Pennsylvania, Maryland, Delaware, and Virginia. For biographical data see Henry Baker, "Benjamin Banneker, the Negro Mathematician and Astronomer," *Journal of Negro History*, Vol. 3 (April 1918), pp. 99–118.

of St. Thomas' Church in Philadelphia, which he helped to found. Grateful to God for what He had done for the African, he beseeched Him, on the part of his brethren, for the completion of "His begun goodness" and he further implored the Holy Spirit to influence the legislature to pass laws to "ameliorate the condition of our brethren who are still in bondage."[3]

Peter Williams' January 1, 1808, oration, written at the age of twenty-one, was so well written that there was some doubt that he had written it. Williams, minister of St. Philip's Episcopal Church for twenty years and an able representative of his people, contributed many practical ideas to newspapers of the day. Several of his pamphlets have been preserved and are still available in libraries. William C. Nell noted that Williams' style was so clear and concise that few men twice his age with every advantage could excell it.[4] The committee on publication of Williams' speech stated that they hoped it "might be the means of enlightening the minds of some and of promoting the great work of emancipation, as it relates to the African race in general, who are still held in bondage in the United States and other parts of the world."

Because of the lack of education of most people of color, Joseph Sidney, in his oration delivered before the Wilberforce Philanthropic Association on January 2, 1809, stated that immediate emancipation was impractical, but that gradual emancipation, as had occurred in New England, was possible. He stated that free persons had duties as well as rights. The right of suffrage carried the duty to vote wisely. He concluded his speech by reminding the audience that its highest duty was to convince the world that free men are capable of self-government because they are sober, honest and industrious. Joseph Sidney was spoken of as "the wit, the pure patriot, the almost self-taught scholar, cut off, alas! in the very bloom of his most promising youth."[5]

On the first anniversary of the abolition of the slave trade, Henry Sipkins humbly inscribed his oration to "the Friends of Humanity whose assiduity and disinterested Philanthropy, have been conspicuous in the propagation of emancipation."

After describing the plundering of Africa, the hardships of the

---

[3] For a sketch of Absalom Jones, see William Douglass, *Annals of the First African Church* (Philadelphia, 1862), pp. 118–123; George F. Bragg, *Men of Maryland* (Baltimore, 1914).

[4] William C. Nell, *Colored Patriots of the American Revolution* (Boston, 1855), p. 320.

[5] Henry Highland Garnet, *A Memorial Discourse* (Philadelphia, 1865), p. 23.

"middle passage," the misery of life as a slave in America, Henry Sipkins gave thanks to those who aided the abolition cause. He ended his speech with the wish that the time would arrive "when slavery of every species shall be destroyed—when despotism and oppression shall forever cease—when Africans shall be reinstated in their former joys . . . and all find protection under the fostering wing of Liberty." "Rejoice," he wrote, ". . . that exiles of our race are emerging from the depths of forlorn slavery, in which they have been environed."[6]

On behalf of "Fathers, brethren and Friends" George Lawrence, on the fifth anniversary of th? abolition of the slave trade, appealed to the Father of the Universe "to crush that power that still holds thousands of our brethren in bondage . . . let Liberty unfurl her banners, Freedom and justice reign triumphant in the world universally."

Spokesmen for the free persons of color were grateful to their white friends who had served as advisors and protectors. As they heralded the abolition of the slave trade as one of the greatest events of the times, they lauded such friends as Rush, Sharp, Wilberforce, Clarkson, Gregoire, Benezet and others. Likewise in the early *Petition of the People of Colour*, Absalom Jones is thankful to God and to the government for freedom, and James Forten, on behalf of the "Africans" and "descendants of that unhappy race" thanked George T. Hatcher for "the philanthropic zeal with which you defended our cause when it was brought before the general government." Forten spoke on behalf of the 700,000 people of color considered in the petition: "their thanks, their gratitude to you they now express—their prayers for you will mount to heaven."

[6] Henry Sipkins was described as the "Jefferson" of the people of color. An unlocated address on his life and character was delivered by Thomas Jennings, *Mirror of Liberty*, Vol. 1. No. 2 (January, 1839), p. 35.

AN

ADDRESS

TO THE

NEGROES

In the State of New York,

By Jupiter Hammon,

SERVANT OF JOHN LLOYD, JUN, ESQ; OF THE MANOR OF
QUEEN'S VILLAGE, LONG ISLAND.

"Of a truth I perceive that God is no respecter of persons:
"But in every Nation, he that feareth him and worketh
righteousness, is accepted with him."—*Acts* x. 34, 35.

NEW YORK:
Printed by CARROLL and PATTERSON
No. 32, Maiden-Lane.
1787.

TO THE MEMBERS OF THE AFRICAN SOCIETY
IN THE CITY OF NEW YORK

Gentlemen,

I take the liberty to dedicate an address to my poor brethren to
you. If you think it is likely to do good among them, I do not doubt
but you will take it under your care. You have discovered so much
kindness and good will to those you thought were oppressed, and
had no helper, that I am sure you will not despise what I have
wrote, if you judge it will be of any service to them. I have nothing

to add, but only to wish that "the blessing of many ready to perish, may come upon you."

I am Gentlemen,
Your Servant,
JUPITER HAMMON.

Queen's Village, 24th Sept.
1786

TO THE PUBLIC

As this Address is wrote in a better Stile than could be expected from a slave, some may be ready to doubt of the genuineness of the production. The Author, as he informs in the title page, is a servant of Mr. Lloyd, and has been remarkable for his fidelity and abstinence from those vices, which he warns his brethren against. The manuscript wrote in his own hand, is in our possession. We have made no material alterations in it, except in the spelling, which we found needed considerable correction.

The PRINTERS.

New York, 20th. Feb. 1787.

AN ADDRESS TO THE NEGROES
OF THE STATE OF NEW YORK

When I am writing to you with a design to say something to you for your good, and with a view to promote your happiness, I can with truth and sincerity join with the apostle Paul, when speaking of his own nation the Jews, and say that "I have great heaviness and continual sorrow in my heart for my brethren, my kindsmen according to the flesh." Yes my dear brethren, when I think of you, which is very often, and of the poor, despised and miserable state you are in, as to the things of this world, and when I think of your ignorance and stupidity, and the great wickedness of the most of you, I am pained to the heart. It is at times almost too much for human nature to bear, and I am obliged to turn my thoughts from the subject or endeavour to still my mind, by considering that it is permitted thus to be by that God who governs all things, who seteth up one and pulleth down another. While I have been thinking on this subject, I have frequently had great struggles in my own mind, and have been at a loss to know what to do. I have wanted exceedingly to say something to you, to call upon you with the tenderness of a father and friend, and to give you the last, and I may say dying advice, of an old man, who wishes your best good in this world, and in the world to come. But while I have had such desires, a sense of my own ignorance and unfitness to teach others has frequently discouraged me from attempting to say anything to you; yet when I thought of your situation, I could not rest easy.

When I was at Hartford in Connecticut, where I lived during the war, I published several pieces which were well received, not only by those of my own colour, but by a number of the white people, who thought they might do good among their servants. This is one consideration, among others, that emboldens me now to publish what I have written to you. Another is, I think you will be more likely to listen to what is said, when you know it comes from a Negro, one your own nation and colour, and therefore can have no interest in deceiving you, or in saying anything to you, but what he really thinks is your interest and duty to comply with. My age, I think, gives me some right to speak to you, and reason to expect you will hearken to my advice. I am now upwards of seventy years old, and cannot expect, though I am well, and able to do almost any kind of business, to live much longer. I have passed the common bounds set for man, and must soon go the way of all the earth. I have had more experience in the world than the most of you, and I have seen a great deal of the vanity and wickedness of it. I have great reason to be thankful that my lot has been so much better than most slaves have had. I suppose I have had more advantages and privileges than most of you who are slaves have ever known, and I believe more than many white people have enjoyed, for which I desire to bless God, and pray that he may bless those who have given them to me. I do not, my dear friends, say these things about myself to make you think that I am wiser or better than others; but that you might hearken, without prejudice, to what I have to say to you on the following particulars.

1st. Respecting obedience to matters. Now whether it is right, and lawful, in the sight of God, for them to make slaves of us or not, I am certain that while we are slaves, it is our duty to obey our masters, in all their lawful commands, and mind them unless we are bid to do that which we know to be sin, or forbidden in God's word. The apostle Paul says, "Servants be obedient to them that are your masters according to the flesh, with fear and trembling in singleness in your heart as unto Christ: Not with eye service, as men pleasers, but as the servants of Christ doing the will of God from the heart: With good will doing service to the Lord, and not to men: Knowing that whatever thing a man doeth the same shall he receive of the Lord, whether he be bond or free."—Here is a plain command of God for us to obey our masters. It may seem hard for us, if we think our masters wrong in holding us slaves, to obey in all things, but who of us dare dispute with God! He has commanded us to obey, and we ought to do it cheerfully, and freely. This should be done by us, not only because God commands, but because our own peace and comfort depend upon it. As we depend upon our masters, for what we eat and drink and wear, and for all our comfortable things in this world, we cannot be happy, unless we please them. This we cannot do without obeying them freely, without muttering or finding fault. If a servant strives to please his master and studies and takes pains to do it, I believe there are but few masters who would use such a servant cruelly. Good servants frequently make good masters. If your master is really hard, unreasonable and cruel, there is no way so likely for you to convince him of it, as always to obey his commands, and try to serve him, and take care of his interest, and try to promote it all in your power. If you are proud and stubborn and always finding fault, your master will think the fault lies wholly on your side, but if you are humble, and meek, and bear all things patiently, your master may think he is wrong, if he does not, his neighbours will be apt to see it, and will befriend you, and try to alter his conduct. If this does not do, you must cry to him, who has the hearts of all men in his hands, and turneth them as the rivers of waters are turned.

2d. The particular I would mention, is honesty and faithfulness. You must suffer me now to deal plainly with you, my dear brethren, for I do not meant to flatter, or omit speaking the truth, whether it is for you, or against you. How many of you are there who allow yourselves in stealing from your masters. It is very wicked for you not to take care of your masters goods, but how much worse is it to pilfer and steal from them, whenever you think you shall not be found out. This you must know is very wicked and provoking to God. There are none of you so ignorant, but that you must know that this is wrong. Though you may try to excuse yourselves, by saying that your masters are unjust to you, and though you may try to quiet your consciences in this way, yet if you are honest in owning the truth you must think it is as wicked, and on some accounts more wicked to steal from your masters, than from others.

We cannot certainly, have any excuse either for taking anything that belongs to our masters without their leave, or for being unfaithful in their business. It is our duty to be faithful, *not with eye service as men pleasers.* We have no right to stay when we are sent on errands, any longer than to do the business we were sent upon. All the time spent idly, is spent wickedly, and is unfaithfulness to our masters. In these things I must say, that I think many of you are guilty. I know that many of you endeavour to excuse yourselves, and say that you have nothing that you can call your own, and that you are under great temptations to be unfaithful and take from your masters. But this will not do, God will certainly punish you for stealing and for being unfaithful. All that we have to mind is our own duty. If God has put us in bad circumstances, that is not our fault and he will not punish us for it. If any are wicked in keeping us so, we cannot help it, they must answer to God for it. Nothing will serve as an excuse to us for not doing our duty. The same God will judge both them and us. Pray then my dear friends, fear to offend in this way, but be faithful to God, to your masters, and to your own souls.

The next thing I would mention, and warn you against, is profaneness. This you know is forbidden by God. Christ tells us, "swear not at all," and again it is said "thou shalt not take the name of the Lord thy God in vain, for the Lord will not hold him guiltless, that taketh his name in vain." Now though the great God has forbidden it, yet how dreadfully profane are many, and I don't know but I may say the most of you? How common is it to hear you take the terrible and awful name of the great God in vain?—To swear by it, and by Jesus Christ, his Son—How common is it to hear you wish damnation to your companions, and to your own souls—and to sport with in the name of Heaven and Hell, as if there were no such places for you to hope for, or to fear. Oh my friends, be warned to forsake this dreadful sin of profaneness. Pray my dear friends, believe and realize, that there is a God—that he is great and terrible beyond what you can think—that he keeps you in life every moment —and that he can send you to that awful Hell, that you laugh at, in an instant, and confine you there forever, and that he will certainly do it, if you do not repent. You certainly do not believe, that there is a God, or that there is a Heaven or Hell, or you would never trifle with them. It would make you shudder, if you heard others do it, if you believe them as much, as you believe anything you see with your bodily eyes.

I have heard some learned and good men say, that the heathen, and all that worshiped false Gods, never spoke lightly or irreverently of their Gods, they never took their names in vain, or jested with those things which they held sacred. Now why should the true God, who made all things, be treated worse in this respect, than those false Gods, that were made of wood and stone. I believe it is because Satan tempts men to do it. He tried to make them love their false Gods, and to speak well of them, but he wishes to have men think lightly of the true God, to take his holy name in vain, and to scoff at, and make a jest of all things that are really good. You may think that Satan has not power to do so much, and have so great influence on the minds of men: But the scripture says, "he goeth about like a roaring Lion, seeking whom he may devour—That he is the prince of the power of the air—and that he rules in the hearts of the children of disobedience,—and that wicked men are led captive by him, to do his will." All those of you who are profane, are serving the Devil. You are doing what he tempts and desires you to do. If you could see him with your bodily eyes, would you like to make an agreement with him, to serve him, and do as he bid you? I believe most of you would be shocked at this, but you may be certain that all of you who allow yourselves in this sin, are as really serving him, and to just as good purpose, as if you met him, and promised to dishonor God, and serve him with all your might. Do you believe this? It is true whether you believe it or not. Some of you to excuse yourselves, may plead the example of others, and say that you hear a great many white people, who know more than such poor ignorant Negroes as you are, and some who are rich and great gentlemen, swear, and talk profanely, and some of you may say this of your masters, and say no more than is true. But all this is not a sufficient excuse for you. You know that murder is wicked. If you saw your master kill a man, do you suppose this would be any excuse for you, if you should commit the same crime? You must know it would not; nor will your hearing him curse and swear, and take the name of God in vain, or any other man, be he ever so great or rich, excuse you. God is greater than all other beings, and him we are bound to obey. To him we must give an account for every idle word that we speak. He will bring us all, rich and poor, white and black, to his judgment seat. If we are found among those who *feared his name,* and *trembled at his word,* we shall be called good and faithful servants. Our slavery will be at an end, and though ever so mean, low, and despised in this world, we shall sit with God in his kingdom as Kings and Priests, and rejoice for ever, and ever. Do not then, my dear friends, take God's holy name in vain, or speak profanely in any way. Let not the example of others lead you into the sin, but reverence and fear that great and fearful name, the Lord our God.

I might now caution you against other sins to which you are exposed, but as I meant only to mention those you were exposed to, more than others, by your being slaves, I will conclude what I have to say to you, by advising you to become religious, and to make religion the great business of your lives.

Now I acknowledge that liberty is a great thing, and worth seeking for, if we can get it honestly, and by our good conduct, prevail on our masters to set us free. Though for my own part I do not wish to be free, yet I should be glad if others, especially the young negroes, were to be free, for many of us, who are grown up slaves, and have always had masters to take care of us, should hardly know how to take care of ourselves, and it may be more for our own comfort to remain as we are. That liberty is a great thing we may know from our own feelings, and we may likewise judge so from the conduct of the white people, in the late war. How much money has been spent, and how many lives has been lost, to defend their liberty? I must say that I have hoped that God would open their eyes, when they were so much engaged for liberty, to think of the state of the poor blacks, and to pity us. He has done it in some measure, and has raised us up many friends, for which we have reason to be thankful, and to hope in his mercy. What may be done further, he only knows, for *known unto God are all his ways from the beginning.* But this, my dear brethren, is by no means the greatest thing we have to be concerned about. Getting our liberty in this world, is nothing to our having the liberty of the children of God. Now the Bible tells us that we are all by nature, sinners, that we are slaves to sin and Satan, and that unless we are converted, or born again, we must be miserable forever. Christ says, except a man be born again, he cannot see the kingdom of God, and all that do not see the kingdom of God, must be in the kingdom of darkness. There are but two places where all go after death, white and black, rich and poor; those places are Heaven and Hell. Heaven is a place made for those who are born again, and who love God, and it is a place where they will be happy forever. Hell is a place made for those who hate God, and are his enemies, and where they will be miserable to all eternity. Now you may think you are not enemies to God, and do not hate him. But if your heart has not been changed, and you have not become true Christians, you certainly are enemies to God, and have been opposed to him ever since you were born. Many of you, I suppose, never think of this, and are almost as ignorant as the beasts that perish. Those of you who can read I must beg you to read the Bible, and whenever you can get time, study the Bible, and if you can get no other time, spare some of your time from sleep, and learn what the mind and will of God is. But what shall I say to them who cannot read? This lay with great weight on my mind, when I thought of writing to my poor brethren, but I hope that those who can read will take pity on them and read what I have to say to them. In hopes of this I will beg of you to spare no pains in trying to learn to read. If you are once engaged you may learn. Let all the time you can get be spent in trying to learn to read. Get those who can read to learn you, but remember, that what you learn for, is to read the Bible. If there was no Bible, it would be no matter whether you could read or not. Reading other books would do you no good. But the Bible is the word of God, and tells you what you must do to please God; it tells you how you may escape misery, and be happy forever. If you see most people neglect the Bible, and many that can read never look into it, let it not harden you and make you think lightly of it, and that it is a book of no worth. All those who are really good, love the Bible, and meditate on it day and night. In the Bible God has told us everything it is necessary we should know in order to be happy here and hereafter. The Bible is a revelation of the mind and will of God to men. Therein we may learn what God is. That he made all things by the power of his word; and that he made all things for his own glory, and not for our glory. That he is over all, and above all his creatures, and more above them that we can think or conceive—that they can do nothing without him—that he upholds them all, and will over-rule all things for his own glory. In the Bible likewise we are told what man is. That he was at first made holy, in the image of God, that he fell from that state of holiness, and became an enemy to God, and that since the fall, all the imaginations of the thoughts of his heart, are evil and only evil, and that continually. That the carnal mind is not subject to the law of God, neither indeed can be. And that all mankind, were under the wrath and curse of God, and must have been for ever miserable, if they had been left to suffer what their sins deserved. It tells us that God, to save some of mankind, sent his Son into this world to die, in the room and stead of sinners, and that now God can save from eternal misery all that believe in his Son, and take him for their saviour, and that all are called upon to repent, and believe in Jesus Christ. It tells us that those who do repent, and believe, and are friends to Christ, shall have many trials and sufferings in this world, but that they shall be happy forever, after death, and reign with Christ to all eternity. The Bible tells us that this world is a place of trial, and that there is no other time or place for us to alter, but in this life. If we are Christians when we die, we shall awake to the resurrection of life; if not, we shall awake to the resurrection of damnation. It tells us, we must all live in Heaven or Hell, be happy or miserable, and that without end. The Bible does not tell us of but two places, for all to go to. There is no place for innocent folks that are not Christians. There is no place for ignorant folks, that did not know how to be Christians. What I mean is, that there is no place besides Heaven and Hell. These two places will receive all mankind, for Christ says, there are but two sorts, *he is not with me is against me, and he that gathereth not with me, scattereth abroad.* The Bible likewise tells us that this world, and all things in it shall be burnt up —and that "God has appointed a day in which he will judge the world, and that he will bring every secret thing whether it be good or bad into judgment—that which is done in secret shall be declared on the house top." I do not know, nor do I think any can tell, but that the day of judgment may last a thousand years. God could tell the state of all his creatures in a moment, but then everything that everyone has done, through his whole life is to be told, before the whole world of angels and men. There, Oh how solemn is the thought! You and I must stand, and hear everything we have thought or done, however secret, however wicked and vile, told before all the men and women that ever have been, or ever will be, and before all the angels, good and bad.

Now my dear friends seeing the Bible is the word of God, and everything in it is true, and it reveals such awful and glorious things, what can be more important than that you should learn to read it; and when you have learned to read, that you should study it day and night. There are some things very encouraging in God's word for such ignorant creatures as we are; for God hath not chosen the rich of this world. Not many rich, not many noble are called, but God hath chosen the weak things of this world, and things which are not, to confound the things that are: And when the great and the rich refused coming to the gospel feast, the servant was told, to go into the highways, and hedges, and compel those poor creatures that he found there to come in. Now my brethren it seems to me, that there are no people that ought to attend to the hope of happiness in another world so much as we do. Most of us are cut off from comfort and happiness here in this world, and can expect nothing from it. Now seeing this is the case, why should we not take care to be happy after death? Why should we spend our whole lives in sinning against God, and be miserable in this world, and in the world to come? If we do thus, we shall certainly be the greatest fools. We shall be slaves here, and slaves forever. We cannot plead so great temptations to neglect religion as others. Riches and honours which drown the greater part of mankind, who have the gospel, in perdition, can be little or no temptations to us.

We live so little time in this world that it is no matter how wretched and miserable we are, if it prepares us for heaven. What is forty, fifty, or sixty years, when compared to eternity? When thousands and millions of years have rolled away, this eternity will be no nigher coming to an end. Oh how glorious is an eternal life of happiness! And how dreadful, an eternity of misery. Those of us who have had religious masters, and have been taught to read the Bible, and have been brought by their example and teaching to a sense of divine things, how happy shall we be to meet them in heaven, where we shall join them in praising God forever. But if any of us have had such masters, and yet have lived and died wicked, how will it add to our misery to think of our folly. If any of us who have wicked and profane masters should become religious, how will our estates be changed in another world. Oh my friends, let me intreat of you to think on these things, and to live as if you believed them to be true. If you become Christians you will have reason to bless God forever, that you have been brought into a land where you have heard the gospel, though you have been slaves. If we should ever get to Heaven, we shall find nobody to reproach us for being black, or for being slaves. Let me beg of you my dear African brethren, to think very little of your bondage in this life, for your thinking of it will do you no good. If God designs to set us free, he will do it, in his own time, and way; but think of your bondage to sin and Satan, and do not rest, until you are delivered from it.

We cannot be happy, if we are ever so free or ever so rich, while we are servants of sin, and slaves to Satan. We must be miserable here, and to all eternity,

I will conclude what I have to say with a few words to those negroes who have their liberty. The most of what I have said to those who are slaves may be of use to you, but you have more advantages, on some accounts, if you will improve your freedom, as you may do, than they. You have more time to read God's holy word, and to take care of the salvation of your souls. Let me beg of you to spend your time in this way, or it will be better for you, if you had always been slaves. If you think seriously of the matter, you must conclude, that if you do not use your freedom, to promote the salvation of your souls, it will not be of any lasting good to you. Besides all this, if you are idle, and take to bad courses, you will hurt those of your brethren who are slaves, and do all in your power to prevent their being free. One great reason that is given by some for not freeing us, I understand, is that we should not know how to take care of ourselves, and should take to bad courses. That we should be lazy and idle, and get drunk and steal. Now all those of you, who follow any bad courses, and who do not take care to get an honest living by your labour and industry, are doing more to prevent our being free, than anybody else. Let me beg of you then for the sake of your own good and happiness, in time, and for eternity, and for the sake of your poor brethren, who are still in bondage to lead quiet and peaceable lives in all Godliness and honesty, and may God bless you, and bring you to his kingdom, for Christ's sake, Amen.

COPY

OF A

LETTER

FROM

BENJAMIN BANNEKER

TO THE

Secretary of State,

WITH HIS

ANSWER.

PHILADELPHIA:
PRINTED AND SOLD BY DANIEL LAWRENCE, NO. 33.
NORTH FOURTH-STREET, NEAR RACE.
1792.

Maryland, Baltimore County, August 19, 1791.

SIR,

I am fully sensible of the greatness of that freedom which I take with you on the present occasion; a liberty which seemed to me scarcely allowable, when I reflected on that distinguished and dignified station in which you stand, and the almost general prejudice and prepossession, which is so prevalent in the world against those of my complexion.

I suppose it is a truth too well attested to you, to need a proof here, that we are a race of beings who have long labored under the abuse and censure of the world; that we have long been looked upon with an eye of contempt; and that we have long been considered rather as brutish than human, and scarcely capable of mental endowments.

Sir, I hope I may safely admit, in consequence of that report which hath reached me, that you are a man far less inflexible in sentiments of this nature, than many others; that you are measurably friendly and well disposed towards us; and that you are willing and ready to lend your aid and assistance to our relief from those many distresses and numerous calamities to which we are reduced.

Now Sir, if this is founded in truth, I apprehend you will embrace every opportunity to eradicate that train of absurd and false ideas and opinions which so generally prevails with respect to us; and that your sentiments are concurrent with mine, which are, that one universal Father hath given being to us all; and that he hath not only made us all of one flesh, but that he hath also, without partiality, afforded us all the same sensations and endowed us all with the same faculties; and that however variable we may be in society or religion, however diversified in situation or color, we are all of the same family, and stand in the same relation to him.

Sir, if these are sentiments of which you are fully persuaded, I hope you cannot but acknowledge that it is the indispensable duty of those who maintain for themselves the rights of human nature, and who possess the obligations of Christianity, to extend their power and influence to the relief of every part of the human race from whatever burden or oppression they may unjustly labor under; and this, I apprehend, a full conviction of the truth and obligation of these principles should lead all to.

Sir, I have long been convinced that if your love for yourselves, and for those inestimable laws which preserved to you the rights of human nature, was founded on sincerity, you could not but be solicitous that every individual, of whatever rank or distinction, might with you equally enjoy the blessings thereof; neither could you rest satisfied short of the most active effusion of your exertions, in order to their promotion from any state of degradation, to which the unjustifiable cruelty and barbarism of men may have reduced them.

Sir, I freely and cheerfully acknowledge that I am of the African race, and in that color which is natural to them of the deepest dye; and it is under a sense of the most profound gratitude to the Supreme Ruler of the Universe that I now confess to you that I am not under that state of tyrannical thraldom and inhuman captivity to which too many of my brethren are doomed, but that I have abundantly tasted of the fruition of those blessings, which proceed from that free and unequalled liberty with which you are favored; and which, I hope, you will willingly allow you have mercifully received from the immediate hand of that Being from whom proceedeth every good and perfect Gift.

Sir, suffer me to recall to your mind that time in which the arms and tyranny of the British crown were exerted, with every powerful effort, in order to reduce you to a state of servitude: look back, I entreat you, on the variety of dangers to which you were exposed; reflect on that time in which every human aid appeared unavailable, and in which even hope and fortitude wore the aspect of inability to the conflict, and you cannot but be led to a serious and grateful sense of your miraculous and providential preservation; you cannot but acknowledge, that the present freedom and tranquility which you enjoy you have mercifully received, and that it is the peculiar blessing of Heaven.

This, Sir, was a time when you clearly saw into the injustice of a state of slavery, and in which you had just apprehensions of the horrors of its condition. It was now that your abhorrence thereof was so excited, that you publicly held forth this true and invaluable doctrine, which is worthy to be recorded and remembered in all succeeding ages: "We hold these truths to be self-evident, that all men are created equal; that they are endowed by their Creator with certain unalienable rights, and that among these are, life, liberty, and the pursuit of happiness."

Here was a time in which your tender feelings for yourselves had engaged you thus to declare you were then impressed with proper ideas of the great violation of liberty, and the free possession of those blessings to which you were entitled by nature; but, Sir, how pitiable is it to reflect, that although you were so fully convinced of the benevolence of the Father of Mankind, and of his equal and impartial distribution of these rights and privileges which he hath conferred upon them, that you should at the same time counteract his mercies, in detaining by fraud and violence so numerous a part of my brethren under groaning captivity and cruel oppression, that you should at the same time be found guilty of that most criminal act, which you professedly detested in others, with respect to yourselves.

I suppose that your knowledge of the situation of my brethren is too extensive to need a recital here; neither shall I presume to prescribe methods by which they may be relieved, otherwise than by recommending to you and all others, to wean yourselves from those narrow prejudices which you have imbibed with respect to them, and as Job proposed to his friends, "put your soul in their souls' stead;" thus shall your hearts be enlarged with kindness and benevolence towards them; and thus shall you need neither the direction of myself or others, in what manner to proceed herein.

And now, Sir, although my sympathy and affection for my brethren hath caused my enlargement thus far, I ardently hope that your candor and generosity will plead with you in my behalf, when I make known to you, that it was not originally my design; but having taken up my pen in order to direct to you, as a present, a copy of an Almanac which I have calculated for the succeeding year, I was unexpectedly and unavoidably led thereto.

This calculation is the production of my arduous study, in this my advanced stage of life; for having long had unbounded desires to become acquainted with the secrets of nature, I have had to gratify my curiosity herein, through my own assiduous application to Astronomical Study, in which I need not recount to you the many difficulties and disadvantages which I have had to encounter.

And although I had almost declined to make my calculation for the ensuing year, in consequence of that time which I had allotted therefor, being taken up at the Federal Territory, by the request of Mr. Andrew Ellicott; yet finding myself under several engagements to Printers of this state, to whom I had communicated my design, on my return to my place of residence, I industriously applied myself thereto, which I hope I have accomplished with correctness and accuracy; a copy of which I have taken the liberty to direct to you, and which I humbly request you will favorably receive; and although you may have the opportunity of perusing it after its publication, yet I choose to send it to you in manuscript previous thereto, that thereby you might not only have an earlier inspection, but that you might also view it in my own hand writing.

And now, Sir, I shall conclude, and subscribe myself, with the most profound respect,

Your most obedient humble servant,

BENJAMIN BANNEKER.

To Mr. BENJAMIN BANNEKER.

Philadelphia, August 30, 1791.

SIR,

I THANK you, sincerely, for your letter of the 19th instant, and for the Almanac it contained. Nobody wishes more than I do, to see such proofs as you exhibit, that nature has given to our black brethren talents equal to those of the other colors of men; and that the appearance of the want of them is owing merely to the degraded condition of their existence, both in Africa and America. I can add with truth, that nobody wishes more ardently to see a good system commenced for raising the condition, both of their body and mind, to what it ought to be, as far as the imbecility of their present existence, and other circumstances, which cannot be neglected, will admit.

I have taken the liberty of sending your Almanac to Monsieur de Condozett, Secretary of the Academy of Sciences at Paris, and Member of the Philanthropic Society, because I considered it as a document to which your whole color had a right, for their justification against the doubts which have been entertained of them.

I am with great esteem, Sir,
Your most obedient
Humble Servant,

THOMAS JEFFERSON.

The following account, taken from BANNEKER's Almanac, is inserted here, for the Information of the Public.

Baltimore, August 20, 1791.

BENJAMIN BANNEKER, a free Black, about 59 years of age: he was born in Baltimore county; his father an African, and his mother the offspring of African parents. His father and mother having obtained their freedom, were enabled to send him to an obscure school, where he learned, when a boy, reading, writing, and arithmetic, as far as double position; and to leave him, at their deaths, a few acres of land, upon which he has supported himself ever since, by means of economy and constant labor, and preserved a fair reputation. To struggle incessantly against want, is no ways favorable to improvement: what he had learned, however, he did not forget; for as some hours of leisure will occur in the most toilsome life, he availed himself of these, not to read and acquire knowledge from writings of genius and discovery, for of such he had none, but to digest and apply, as occasions presented, the few principles of the few rules of arithmetic he had been taught at school. This kind of mental exercise formed his chief amusement, and soon gave him a facility in calculation that was often serviceable to his neighbours, and at length attracted the attention of the Messrs. Ellicott, a family remarkable for their ingenuity and turn to the useful mechanics. It is about three years since Mr. George Ellicott lent him Mayer's Tables, Ferguson's Astronomy, Leadbeater's Lunar Tables, and some Astronomic Instruments, but without accompanying them with either hint or instruction, that might further his studies, or lead him to apply them to any useful result. These books and instruments, the first of the kind he had ever seen, opened a new world to Benjamin, and from thenceforward he employed his leisure in Astronomical Researches.

He now took up the idea of the calculations for an Almanac, and actually completed an entire set for the last year, upon his original stock of Arithmetic. Encouraged by his first attempt, he entered upon his calculation for 1792 which, as well as the former, he began and finished without the least information or assistance from any person, or other books than those I have mentioned; so that whatever merit is attached to his present performance, is exclusively and peculiarly his own.

I have been the more careful to investigate those particulars, and to ascertain their reality, as they form an interesting fact in the History of Man; and as you may want them to gratify curiosity, I have no objection to your selecting them for your account of Benjamin.

Petition of Absalom Jones and Seventy-Three Others

To the President, Senate, and House of Representatives.

The Petition of the People of Colour, free men, within the City and Suburbs of Philadelphia, humbly showeth,

That, thankful to God, our Creator, and to the Government under which we live, for the blessings and benefits granted to us in the enjoyment of our natural right to liberty, and the protection of our persons and property from the oppression and violence which so great a number of like colour and national descent are subject to, we feel ourselves bound, from a sense of these blessings, to continue in our respective allotments, and to lead honest and peaceable lives, rendering due submission unto the laws, and exciting and encouraging each other thereto, agreeable to the uniform advice of our friends of every denomination; yet while we feel impressed with grateful sensations for the Providential favour we ourselves enjoy, we cannot be insensible of the condition of our afflicted brethren, suffering under various circumstances, in different parts of these states; but deeply sympathizing with them, are incited by a sense of social duty, and humbly conceive ourselves authorized to address and petition you on their behalf, believing them to be objects of your representation in your public councils, in common with ourselves and every other class of citizens within the jurisdiction of the United States, according to the design of the present Constitution, formed by the General Convention, and ratified in the different states, as set forth in the preamble thereto in the following words, viz. "We, the people of the United States, in order to form a more perfect union, establish justice, insure domestic tranquillity, provide for the common defence, and to secure the blessings of liberty to ourselves and posterity, do ordain, &c." We apprehend this solemn compact is violated, by a trade carried on in a clandestine manner, to the coast of Guinea, and another equally wicked, practised openly by citizens of some of the southern states, upon the waters of Maryland and Delaware; men sufficiently callous to qualify them for the brutal purpose, are employed in kidnapping those of our brethren that are free, and purchasing others of such as claim a property in them:

330

thus, those poor helpless victims, like droves of cattle, are seized, fettered, and hurried into places provided for this most horrid traffic, such as dark cellars and garrets, as is notorious at Northwest-fork, Chestertown, Eastown, and divers other places. After a suffi-cient number is obtained, they are forced on board vessels, crowded under hatches, without the least commiseration, left to deplore the sad separation of the dearest ties in nature, husband from wife, and parents from children; thus packed together, they are transported to Georgia and other places, and there inhumanly exposed to sale. Can any commerce, trade, or transaction so detestably shock the feel-ing of man, or degrade the dignity of his nature equal to this? And how increasingly is the evil aggravated, when practised in a land high in profession of the benign doctrines of our Blessed Lord, who taught his followers to do unto others as they would they should do unto them. Your petitioners desire not to enlarge, though volumes might be filled with the sufferings of this grossly abused part of the human species, seven hundred thousand of whom, it is said, are now in unconditional bondage in these states: but conscious of the recti-tude of our motives in a concern so nearly affecting us, and so effec-tually interesting to the welfare of this country, we cannot but address you as guardians of our rights, and patrons of equal and na-tional liberties, hoping you will view the subject in an impartial, un-prejudiced light. We do not ask for an immediate emancipation of all, knowing that the degraded state of many, and their want of education, would greatly disqualify for such a change; yet, humbly desire you may exert every means in your power to undo the heavy burdens, and prepare the way for the oppressed to go free, that every yoke may be broken. The law not long since enacted by Con-gress, called the Fugitive Bill, is in its execution found to be at-tended with circumstances peculiarly hard and distressing; for many of our afflicted brethren, in order to avoid the barbarities wantonly exercised upon them, or through fear of being carried off by those men-stealers, being forced to seek refuge by flight, they are then, by armed men, under colour of this law, cruelly treated, or brought back in chains to those that have no claim upon them. In the Constitution and the Fugitive Bill, no mention is made of black people, or slaves: therefore, if the Bill of Rights, or the Declaration of Congress are of any validity, we beseech, that as we are men, we may be admitted to partake of the liberties and unalienable rights therein held forth; firmly believing that the extending of justice and equity to all classes would be a means of drawing down the blessing of Heaven upon this land, for the peace and prosperity of which, and the real happi-

ness of every member of the community, we fervently pray. Philadelphia, 30th of December, 1799.

Absalom Jones and others. 73 subscribers.

[Source: John Parrish, *Remarks on the Slavery of the Black People
Addressed to the Citizens of the United States, Particularly to Those
Who are in Legislative or Executive Stations in the General or State
Governments; and Also to Such Individuals as Hold Them in Bond-
age* (Philadelphia: Kimber, Conrad and Co., 1806), pp. 49–51.]

A Letter From James Forten

The following letter from James Forten, as it is known to be genuine, and taken from the author's own handwriting, may properly follow, and serve to show he is not only a man of talents, but of feeling and gratitude.

SIR,

WHEN the hand of sorrow presses heavy upon us, and the generality of mankind turn unpitying from our complaints, if one appears, and feels for, and commiserates our situation, endeavours all in his power to alleviate our condition, our bosoms swell with gratitude, and our tongues instinctively pronounce our thanks for the obligation. We, therefore, sir, Africans and descendants of that unhappy race, respectfully beg leave to thank you for the philanthropic zeal with which you defended our cause when it was brought before the General Government, by which only we can expect to be delivered from our deplorable state. We interested ourselves in the business, because we knew not but ere long we might be reduced to slavery: it might have been said that we viewed the subject through a perverted medium, if you, sir, had not adopted and nobly supported those sentiments which gave rise to our Petition. Though our faces are black, yet we are men; and though many among us cannot write, yet we all have the feelings and passions of men, and are as anxious to enjoy the birth-right of the human race as those who from our ignorance draw an argument against our Petition, when that Petition has in view the diffusion of knowledge among the African race, by unfettering their thoughts, and giving full scope to the energy of their minds. While some, sir, consider us as [so] much property, as a house, or a ship, and would seem to insinuate that it is as lawful to hew down the one as to dismantle the other, you, sir, more humane, consider us part of the human race. And were we to go generally into the subject, would say, that by principles of natural law our thraldom is unjust. Judge what must be our feelings, to find ourselves treated as a species of property, and levelled with the brute creation; and think how anxious we must be to raise ourselves

333

from this degraded state. Unprejudiced persons who read the documents in our possession, will acknowledge we are miserable; and humane people will wish our situation alleviated. Just people will attempt the task, and powerful people ought to carry it into execution. Seven hundred thousand of the human race were concerned in our Petition; their thanks, their gratitude to you, they now express. . . . their prayers for you will mount to heaven; for God knows they are wretched, and will hear their complaints. A deep gloom envelopes us; but we derive some comfort from the thought that we are not quite destitute of friends; that there is one who will use all his endeavours to free the slave from captivity, at least render his state more sufferable, and preserve the free black in the full enjoyment of his rights. This address cannot increase the satisfaction you must derive from your laudable exertions in the cause of suffering humanity, but it serves to show the gratitude and respect of those whose cause you espoused.

JAMES FORTEN.

To the Honourable George Thatcher,
    Member of Congress.

[Source: John Parrish, *Remarks on the Slavery of the Black People* . . . (Philadelphia, 1806), pp. 51–52.]

A

THANKSGIVING SERMON,

PREACHED JANUARY 1, 1808,

In St. Thomas's, or the African Episcopal, Church,
Philadelphia:

ON ACCOUNT OF

THE ABOLITION

OF THE

AFRICAN SLAVE TRADE,

ON THAT DAY,

BY THE CONGRESS OF THE UNITED STATES.

BY ABSALOM JONES,
RECTOR OF THE SAID CHURCH.

PHILADELPHIA:
PRINTED FOR THE USE OF THE CONGREGATION.
FRY AND KAMMERER, PRINTERS.
1808.

EXODUS, iii. 7, 8: And the Lord said, I have surely seen the affliction of my people which are in Egypt, and have heard their cry by reason of their task-masters; for I know their sorrows; and I am come down to deliver them out of the hand of the Egyptians.

THESE words, my brethren, contain a short account of some of the circumstances which preceded the deliverance of the children of Israel from their captivity and bondage in Egypt.

They mention, in the first place, their *affliction*. This consisted in their privation of liberty: they were slaves to the kings of Egypt, in common with their other subjects; and they were slaves to their fellow slaves. They were compelled to work in the open air, in one of the hottest climates in the world; and, probably, without a covering from the burning rays of the sun. Their work was of a laborious kind: it consisted of making bricks, and travelling, perhaps to a great distance, for the straw, or stubble, that was a component part of them. Their work was dealt out to them in tasks, and performed under the eye of vigilant and rigorous masters, who constantly upbraided them with idleness. The least deficiency in the product of their labour, was punished by beating. Nor was this all. Their food was of the cheapest kind, and contained but little nourishment: it consisted only of leeks and onions, which grew almost spontaneously in the land of Egypt. Painful and distressing as these sufferings were, they constituted the smallest part of their misery. While the fields resounded with their cries in the day, their huts and hamlets were vocal at night with their lamentations over their sons; who were dragged from the arms of their mothers, and put to death by drowning, in order to prevent such an increase in their population as to endanger the safety of the state by an insurrection. In this condition, thus degraded and oppressed, they passed nearly four hundred years. Ah! who can conceive of the measure of their sufferings, during that time? What tongue, or pen, can compute the number of their sorrows? To them no morning or evening sun ever disclosed a single charm: to them, the beauties of spring, and the plenty of autumn had no attractions: even domestick endearments were scarcely known to them: all was misery; all was grief; all was despair.

Our text mentions, in the second place, that, in this situation, they were not forgotten by the God of their fathers, and the Father of the human race. Though, for wise reasons, he delayed to appear in their behalf for several hundred years, yet he was not indifferent to their sufferings. Our text tells us that he saw their affliction, and heard their cry: his eye and his ear were constantly open to their complaint: every tear they shed was preserved, and every groan they uttered was recorded, in order to testify, at a future day, against the authors of their oppressions. But our text goes further: it describes the Judge of the world to be so much moved, with what he saw and what he heard, that he rises from his throne—not to issue a command to the armies of angels that surrounded him to fly to the relief of his suffering children—but to come down from heaven in his own person, in order to deliver them out of the hands of the Egyptians. Glory to God for this precious record of his power and goodness: let all the nations of the earth praise him. *Clouds and darkness are round about him,* but *righteousness and judgment are the habitation of his throne. O sing unto the Lord a new song, for he hath done marvellous things: his right hand and his holy arm hath gotten him the victory. He hath remembered his mercy and truth toward the house of Israel, and all the ends of the earth shall see the salvation of God.*

The history of the world shows us that the deliverance of the children of Israel from their bondage is not the only instance in which it has pleased God to appear in behalf of oppressed and distressed nations, as the deliverer of the innocent, and of those who call upon his name. He is as unchangeable in his nature and character as he is in his wisdom and power. The great and blessed event, which we have this day met to celebrate, is a striking proof that the God of heaven and earth is *the same, yesterday, and today, and forever.* Yes, my brethren, the nations from which most of us have descended, and the country in which some of us were born, have been visited by the tender mercy of the Common Father of the human race. He has seen the affliction of our countrymen, with an eye of pity. He has seen the wicked arts, by which wars have been fomented among the different tribes of the Africans, in order to procure captives, for the purpose of selling them for slaves. He has seen ships fitted out from different ports in Europe and America, and freighted with trinkets to be exchanged for the bodies and souls of men. He has seen the anguish which has taken place when parents have been torn from their children, and children from their parents, and conveyed, with their hands and feet bound in fetters, on board of ships prepared to receive them. He has seen them thrust in crowds into the holds of those ships, where many of them have perished from the want of air. He has seen such of them as have escaped from that noxious place of confinement, leap into the ocean, with a faint hope of swimming back to their native shore, or a determination to seek an early retreat from their impending misery, in a watery grave. He has seen them exposed for sale, like horses and cattle, upon the wharves; or, like bales of goods, in warehouses of West India and American sea ports. He has seen the pangs of separation between members of the same family. He has seen them driven into the sugar, the rice, and the tobacco fields, and compelled to work—in spite of the habits of ease which they derived from the natural fertility of their own country—in the open air, beneath a burning sun, with scarcely as much clothing upon them as modesty required. He has seen them faint beneath the pressure of their labours. He has seen them return to their smoky huts in the evening, with nothing to satisfy their hunger but a scanty allowance of roots; and these, cultivated for themselves, on that day only, which God ordained as a day of rest for man and beast. He has seen the neglect with which their masters have treated their immortal souls; not only in withholding religious instruction from them, but, in some instances, depriving them of access to the means of obtaining it. He has seen all the different modes of torture, by means of the whip, the screw, the pincers, and the red-hot iron, which have been exercised upon their bodies, by inhuman overseers: overseers, did I say? Yes: but not by these only. Our God has seen masters and mistresses, educated in fashionable life, sometimes take the instruments of torture into their own hands, and, deaf to the cries and shrieks of their agonizing slaves, exceed even their overseers in cruelty. Inhuman wretches! though You have been deaf to their cries and shrieks, they have been heard in Heaven. The ears of Jehovah have been constantly open to them: He has heard the prayers that have ascended from the hearts of his people; and he has, as in the case of his ancient and chosen people the Jews, *come down to deliver* our suffering countrymen from the hands of their oppressors. He *came down* into the United States, when they declared, in the constitution which they framed in 1788, that the trade in our African fellowmen should cease in the year 1808: He *came down* into the British Parliament, when they passed a law to put an end to the same iniquitous trade in May, 1807: He *came down* into the Congress of the United States, the last winter, when they passed a similar law, the operation of which commences on this happy day. Dear land of our ancestors! thou shalt no more be stained with the blood of thy children, shed by British and American hands: the ocean shall no more afford a refuge to their bodies, from impending slavery: nor shall the shores of the British West India islands, and of the United States, any more witness the anguish of families, parted for ever by a publick sale. For this signal interposition of the God of mercies, in behalf of our brethren, it becomes us this day to offer up our united thanks. Let the song of angels, which was first heard in the air at the birth of our Saviour, be heard this day in our assembly: *Glory to God in the highest,* for these first fruits of *peace upon earth, and good-will to man:* O! let us *give thanks unto the Lord:* let us *call upon his name,* and *make known his deeds among the people. Let us sing psalms unto him and talk of all his wondrous works.*

Having enumerated the mercies of God to our nation, it becomes us to ask, What shall we render unto the Lord for them? Sacrifices and burnt offerings are no longer pleasing to him: the pomp of public worship, and the ceremonies of a festive day, will find no acceptance with him, unless they are accompanied with actions that correspond with them. The duties which are inculcated upon us, by the event we are now celebrating, divide themselves into five heads.

In the first place, Let not our expressions of gratitude to God for his late goodness and mercy to our countrymen, be confined to this day, nor to this house: let us carry grateful hearts with us to our places of abode, and to our daily occupations; and let praise and thanksgivings ascend daily to the throne of grace, in our families, and in our closets, for what God has done for our African brethren. Let us not forget to praise him for his mercies to such of our colour as are inhabitants of this country; particularly, for disposing the hearts of the rulers of many of the states to pass laws for the abolition of slavery; for the number and zeal of the friends he has raised up to plead our cause; and for the privileges we enjoy, of worshiping God agreeably to our consciences, in churches of our own. This comely building, erected chiefly by the generosity of our friends, is a monument of God's goodness to us, and calls for our gratitude with all the other blessings that have been mentioned.

Secondly, Let us unite, with our thanksgiving, prayer to Almighty God, for the completion of his begun goodness to our brethren in Africa. Let us beseech him to extend to all the nations in Europe, the same humane and just spirit towards them, which he has imparted to the British and American nations. Let us, further, implore the influence of his divine and holy Spirit, to dispose the hearts of our legislatures to pass laws, to ameliorate the condition of our brethren who are still in bondage; also, to dispose their masters to treat them with kindness and humanity; and, above all things, to favour them with the means of acquiring such parts of human knowledge, as will enable them to read the holy scriptures, and understand the doctrines of the Christian religion, whereby they may become, even while they are the slaves of men, the freemen of the Lord.

Thirdly, Let us conduct ourselves in such a manner as to furnish no cause of regret to the deliverers of our nation, for their kindness to us. Let us constantly *remember the rock whence we were hewn, and the pit whence we were digged. Pride was not made for man,* in any situation; and, still less, for persons who have recently emerged from bondage. The Jews, after they entered the promised land, were commanded, when they offered sacrifices to the Lord, never to forget their humble origin; and hence, part of the worship that accompanied their sacrifices consisted in acknowledging, *that a Syrian, ready to perish, was their father:* in like manner, it becomes us, publickly and privately, to acknowledge, that an African slave, ready to perish, was our father or our grandfather. Let our conduct be regulated by the precepts of the gospel; let us be sober-minded, humble, peaceable, temperate in our meats and drinks, frugal in our apparel and in the furniture of our houses, industrious in our occupations, just in all our dealings, and ever ready to honour all men. Let us teach our children the rudiments of the English language, in order to enable them to acquire a knowledge of useful trades; and, above all things, let us instruct them in the principles of the gospel of Jesus Christ, whereby they may become *wise unto salvation.* It has always been a mystery, why the impartial Father of the human race should have permitted the transportation of so many millions of our fellow creatures to this country, to endure all the miseries of slavery. Perhaps his design was that a knowledge of the gospel might be acquired by some of their descendants, in order that they might become qualified to be the messengers of it, to the land of their fathers. Let this thought animate us, when we are teaching our children to love and adore the name of our Redeemer. Who knows but that a Joseph may rise up among them, who shall be the instrument of feeding the African nations with the bread of life, and of saving them, not from earthly bondage, but from the more galling yoke of sin and Satan.

Fourthly, Let us be grateful to our benefactors, who, by enlightening the minds of the rulers of the earth, by means of their publications and remonstrances against the trade in our countrymen, have produced the great event we are this day celebrating. Abolition societies and individuals have equal claims to our gratitude. It would be difficult to mention the names of any of our benefactors, without offending many whom we do not know. Some of them are gone to heaven, to receive the reward of their labours of love towards us; and the kindness and benevolence of the survivors, we hope, are recorded in the book of life, to be mentioned with honour when our Lord shall come to reward his faithful servants before an assembled world.

Fifthly, and lastly, Let the first of January, the day of the abolition of the slave trade in our country, be set apart in every year, as a day of publick thanksgiving for that mercy. Let the history of the sufferings of our brethren, and of their deliverance, descend by this means to our children to the remotest generations; and when they shall ask, in time to come, saying, What mean the lessons, the psalms, the prayers and the praises in the worship of this day? let us answer them, by saying, the Lord, on the day of which this is the anniversary, abolished the trade which dragged your fathers from their native country, and sold them as bondmen in the United States of America.

Oh thou God of all the nations upon the earth! we thank thee, that thou art *no respecter of persons,* and that thou *hast made of one blood all nations of men.* We thank thee, that thou hast appeared, in the fullness of time, in behalf of the nation from which most of the worshipping people, now before thee, are descended. We thank thee, that the sun of righteousness has at last shed his morning beams upon them. *Rend* thy *heavens,* O Lord, and *come down* upon the earth; and grant that *the mountains,* which now obstruct the perfect day of thy goodness and mercy towards them, may *flow down at thy presence.* Send thy gospel, we beseech thee, among them. May the nations, which now *sit in darkness,* behold and rejoice in its *light.* May *Ethiopia soon stretch out her hands unto thee,* and lay hold of the gracious promise of thy everlasting covenant. Destroy, we beseech thee, all the false religions which now prevail among them; and grant, that they may soon *cast* their *idols, to the moles and the bats* of the wilderness. O, hasten that glorious time, when the knowledge of the gospel of Jesus Christ, shall cover the *earth, as the waters cover the sea;* when *the wolf shall dwell with the lamb, and the leopard shall lie down with the kid, and the calf and the young lion and the fatling together, and a little child shall lead them; and, when, instead of the thorn, shall come up the fir tree, and, instead of the brier, shall come up the myrtle tree: and it shall be to the Lord for a name and for an everlasting sign that shall not be cut off.* We pray, O God, for all our friends and benefactors in Great Britain, as well as in the United States: reward them, we beseech thee, with blessings upon earth, and prepare them to enjoy the fruits of their kindness to us, in thy everlasting kingdom in heaven; and dispose us, who are assembled in thy presence, to be always thankful for thy mercies, and to act as becomes a people who owe so much to thy goodness. We implore thy blessing, O God, upon the President, and all who are in authority in the United States. Direct them by thy wisdom, in all their deliberations, and O save thy people from the calamities of war. Give peace in our day, we beseech thee, O thou *God of peace!* and grant, that this highly favoured country may continue to afford a safe and peaceful retreat from the calamities of war and slavery, for ages yet to come. We implore all these blessings and mercies, only in the name of thy beloved Son, Jesus Christ, our Lord. And now, O Lord, we desire, with angels and arch-angels, and all the company of heaven, ever more to praise thee, saying, *Holy, holy, holy, Lord God Almighty: the whole earth is full of thy glory.* Amen.

AN

ORATION

ON

THE ABOLITION OF THE SLAVE TRADE;

DELIVERED

IN

The African Church,

IN

THE CITY OF NEW YORK,

JANUARY 1, 1808.

Ethiopia shall soon stretch forth her hands unto God.
Psalm lxviii. 31.

The people that walked in darkness have seen a great light.
Isaiah ix. 2.

BY PETER WILLIAMS, JUN.
A DESCENDANT OF AFRICA.

New York:
Printed by Samuel Wood.
No. 362, Pearl-Street.
1808.

343

To the different societies for the abolition of slavery, this oration is humbly inscribed, as a tribute of sincere gratitude for their assiduous, energetic, and benevolent exertions, in the cause of injured humanity.

THE INTRODUCTORY ADDRESS

By Henry Sipkins

Brethren,

THE object of our assembling at this time is attended with many incentives to mutual gratulation and pious gratitude. The prohibition of the slave trade (which on this auspicious day, becomes an effectual law) allows us to indulge the delightful reflection that justice has not yet forsaken her dominion in this sublunary scene; but that she still pleads with a tone of dignity and in the spirit of truth for the violated rights of humanity, we are now enabled to contemplate the heart of man with more philanthropy; and to relinquish our suspicion of its general propensity to wrong and oppression. We are now confident that unmerited injuries may still excite pity, and that the sufferings of innocence can sometimes awaken an active and helpful commiseration. That sinful traffic which has wrested so many of our brethren from their parent country, and doomed them to painful and incessant servitude, has been recently extirpated by the parliament of Great Britain, and from the ensuing act of the legislature of these United States, we hear those glad tidings, which by divine assistance we may hope will ere long become the unanimous voice of the world.

ORDER OF THE CELEBRATION OF THE DAY

FORENOON SERVICE

1. A solemn address to Almighty God, by the Rev. Mr. Abraham Thompson.
2. An appropriate anthem sung under the direction of William Hamilton.
3. The act read with an introductory address, by Henry Sipkins.
4. The oration delivered by Peter Williams, jun.
5. An appropriate hymn, sung under the direction of William Hamilton.
6. A solemn address to Almighty God, by Mr. Thomas Miller, sen.

1. An appropriate hymn, under the direction of William Hamilton.
2. A prayer, by the Rev. Mr. June Scot.
3. An appropriate hymn.
4. A sermon delivered by Mr. James Varick.
5. A hymn.
6. A prayer, by Mr. James Varick.

ORATION

Fathers, Brethren, and Fellow Citizens,

AT this auspicious moment, I felicitate you, on the abolition of the slave trade. This inhuman branch of commerce, which, for some centuries past, has been carried on to a considerable extent, is, by the singular interposition of Divine Providence, this day extinguished. An event so important, so pregnant with happy consequences, must be extremely consonant to every philanthropic heart.

But to us, Africans, and descendants of Africans, this period is deeply interesting. We have felt, sensibly felt, the sad effects of this abominable traffic. It has made, if not ourselves, our forefathers and kinsmen its unhappy victims; and pronounced on them and their posterity the sentence of perpetual slavery. But benevolent men have voluntarily stepped forward to obviate the consequences of this injustice and barbarity. They have striven assiduously, to restore our natural rights; to guaranty them from fresh innovations; to furnish us with necessary information; and to stop the source from whence our evils have flowed.

The fruits of these laudable endeavours have long been visible; each moment they appear more conspicuous; and this day has produced an event which shall ever be memorable and glorious in the annals of history. We are now assembled to celebrate this momentous era; to recognize the beneficial influences of humane exertions; and by suitable demonstrations of joy, thanksgiving, and gratitude, to return to our heavenly Father, and to our earthly benefactors, our sincere acknowledgements.

Review, for a moment, my brethren, the history of the slave trade, engendered in the foul recesses of the sordid mind, the unnatural monster inflicted gross evils on the human race. Its baneful footsteps are marked with blood; its infectious breath spreads war and desolation; and its train is composed of the complicated miseries of cruel and unceasing bondage.

Before the enterprising spirit of European genius explored the western coast of Africa, the state of our forefathers was a state of simplicity, innocence, and contentment. Unskilled in the arts of dissimulation, their bosoms were the seats of confidence, and their lips were the organs of truth. Strangers to the refinements of civilized society, they followed with implicit obedience the (simple) dictates of nature. Peculiarly observant of hospitality, they offered a place of refreshment to the weary, and an asylum to the unfortunate. Ardent in their affections, their minds were susceptible of the warmest emotions of love, friendship, and gratitude.

Although unacquainted with the diversified luxuries and amusements of civilized nations, they enjoyed some singular advantages from the bountiful hand of nature, and from their own innocent and amiable manners, which rendered them a happy people. But, alas! this delightful picture has long since vanished; the angel of bliss has deserted their dwelling; and the demon of indescribable misery has rioted, uncontrolled, on the fair fields of our ancestors.

After Columbus unfolded to civilized man the vast treasures of this western world, the desire of gain, which had chiefly induced the first colonists of America to cross the waters of the Atlantic, surpassing the bounds of reasonable acquisition, violated the sacred injunctions of the gospel, frustrated the designs of the pious and humane, and, enslaving the harmless aborigines, compelled them to drudge in the mines.

The severities of this employment was so insupportable to men who were unaccustomed to fatigue, that, according to Robertson's "History of America," upwards of nine hundred thousand were destroyed in the space of fifteen years, on the island of Hispaniola. A consumption so rapid must, in a short period, have deprived them of the instruments of labour; had not the same genius, which first produced it, found out another method to obtain them. This was no other than the importation of slaves from the coast of Africa.

The Genoese made the first regular importation, in the year 1517, by virtue of a patent granted by Charles of Austria to a Flemish favourite; since which, this commerce has increased to an astonishing and almost incredible degree.

After the manner of ancient piracy, descents were first made on the African coast; the towns bordering on the ocean were surprised, and a number of the inhabitants carried into slavery.

Alarmed at these depredations, the natives fled to the interior, and there united to secure themselves from the common foe. But the subtle invaders were not easily deterred from their purpose. Their experience, corroborated by historical testimony, convinced them that this spirit of unity would baffle every violent attempt; and that the most powerful method to dissolve it, would be to diffuse in them the same avaricious disposition which they themselves possessed; and to afford them the means of gratifying it by ruining each other. Fatal engine: fatal thou hast proved to man in all ages: where the greatest violence has proved ineffectual, thy undermining principles have wrought destruction. By thy deadly power, the strong Grecian arm, which bid the world defiance, fell nerveless; by thy potent attacks, the solid pillars of Roman grandeur shook to their base; and, Oh! Africans! by this parent of the slave trade, this grandsire of misery, the mortal blow was struck which crushed the peace and happiness of our country. Affairs now assumed a different aspect; the appearances of war were changed into the most amicable pretensions; presents apparently inestimable were made; and all the bewitching and alluring wiles of the seducer were practised. The harmless African, taught to believe a friendly countenance the sure token of a corresponding heart, soon disbanded his fears, and evinced a favourable disposition towards his flattering enemies.

Thus the foe, obtaining an intercourse, by a dazzling display of European finery bewildered their simple understandings, and corrupted their morals. Mutual agreements were then made; the Europeans were to supply the Africans with those gaudy trifles which so strongly affected them; and the Africans in return were to grant the Europeans their prisoners of war, and convicts, as slaves. These stipulations naturally tending to delude the mind, answered the two-fold purpose of enlarging their criminal code, and of exciting incessant war, at the same time that it furnished a specious pretext for the prosecution of this inhuman traffic. Bad as this may appear, had it prescribed the bounds of injustice, millions of unhappy victims might have still been spared. But, extending widely beyond measure, and without control, large additions of slaves were made, by kidnapping, and the most unpalliated seizures.

Trace the past scenes of Africa, and you will manifestly perceive these flagrant violations of human rights. The prince who once delighted in the happiness of his people, who felt himself bound by a sacred contract to defend their persons and property, was turned into their tyrant and scourge: he, who once strove to preserve peace and good understanding with the different nations; who never unsheathed his sword, but in the cause of justice; at the signal of a slave ship, assembled his warriors and rushed furiously upon his unsuspecting friends. What a scene does that town now present, which a few moments past was the abode of tranquillity. At the approach of the foe, alarm and confusion pervade every part; horror and dis-

may are depicted on every countenance; the aged chief starting
from his couch, calls forth his men, to repulse the hostile invader:
all ages obey the summons; feeble youth, and decrepit age, join the
standard; while the foe, to effect his purpose, fires the town.

Now, with unimaginable terror the battle commences: hear now
the shrieks of the women; the cries of the children; the shouts of
the warriors; and the groans of the dying. See with what desperation the inhabitants fight in defense of their darling joys. But, alas!
overpowered by a superior foe, their force is broken; their ablest
warriors fall; and the wretched remnant are taken captives.

Where are now those pleasant dwellings where peace and harmony reigned incessant? where those beautiful fields, whose smiling
crops, and enchanting verdure, enlivened the heart of every beholder? Alas! those tenements are now enveloped in destructive
flames: those fair fields are now bedewed with blood, and covered
with mangled carcasses. Where are now those sounds of mirth and
gladness, which loudly rang throughout the village? where those darling youth, those venerable aged, who mutually animated the festive
throng? Alas! those exhilarating peals are now changed into the dismal groans of inconceivable distress: the survivors of those happy
people, are now carried into cruel captivity. Ah! driven from their
native soil, they cast their languishing eyes behind, and with aching
hearts, bid adieu to every prospect of joy and comfort.

A spectacle so truly distressing is sufficient to blow into a blaze
the most latent spark of humanity: but the adamantine heart of
avarice, dead to every sensation of pity, regards not the voice of the
sufferers, but hastily drives them to market for sale.

Oh, Africa, Africa! to what horrid inhumanities have thy shores
been witness; thy shores, which were once the garden of the world,
the seat of almost paradisiacal joys, have been transformed into
regions of wo: thy sons, who were once the happiest of mortals, are
reduced to slavery, and bound in weighty shackles, now fill the
trader's ship. But, though defeated in the contest for liberty, their
magnanimous souls scorn the gross indignity, and choose death in
preference to slavery. Painful; Ah! painful, must be that existence,
which the rational mind can deliberately doom to self-destruction.
Thus, the poor Africans, robbed of every joy, while they see not the
most transient, glimmering, ray of hope to cheer their saddened
hearts, sink into the abyss of consummate misery. Their lives, em-
bittered by reflection, anticipation, and present sorrows, they feel
burthensome; and death (whose dreary mansions appall the stoutest
hearts), they view as their only shelter.

You, my brethren, beloved Africans, who had passed the days of infancy when you left your country; you best can tell the aggravated sufferings of our unfortunate race: your memories can bring to view these scenes of bitter grief. What, my brethren, when dragged from your native land, on board the slave ship; what was the anguish which you saw, which you felt? what the pain, what the dreadful forebodings, which filled your throbbing bosoms?

But you, my brethren, descendants of African forefathers, I call upon you to view a scene of unfathomable distress. Let your imagination carry you back to former days. Behold a vessel bearing our forefathers and brethren from the place of their nativity to a distant and inhospitable clime: behold their dejected countenances; their streaming eyes; their fettered limbs: hear them, with piercing cries, and pitiful moans, deploring their wretched fate. After their arrival in port, see them separated without regard to the ties of blood or friendship: husband from wife; parent from child; brother from sister; friend from friend. See the parting tear, rolling down their fallen cheeks: hear the parting sigh, die on their quivering lips.

But, let us no longer pursue a theme of boundless affliction. An enchanting sound now demands your attention. Hail! hail! glorious day, whose resplendent rising disperseth the clouds which have hovered with destruction over the land of Africa; and illumines it by the most brilliant rays of future prosperity. Rejoice, Oh! Africans! No longer shall tyranny, war, and injustice, with irresistible sway, desolate your native country: no longer shall torrents of human blood deluge its delightful plains: no longer shall it witness your countrymen wielding among each other the instruments of death; nor the insidious kidnapper, darting from his midnight haunt, on the feeble and unprotected: no longer shall its shores resound with the awful howlings of infatuated warriors, the deathlike groans of vanquished innocents, nor the clanking fetters of wo-doomed captives. Rejoice, Oh, ye descendants of Africans! No longer shall the United States of America, nor the extensive colonies of Great Britain, admit the degrading commerce of the human species: no longer shall they swell the tide of African misery by the importation of slaves. Rejoice, my brethren, that the channels are obstructed through which slavery and its direful concomitants have been entailed on the African race. But, let incessant strains of gratitude be mingled with your expressions of joy. Through the infinite mercy of the great Jehovah, this day announces the abolition of the slave trade. Let, therefore, the heart that is warmed by the smallest drop of African blood glow in grateful transports; and cause the lofty arches of the sky to reverberate eternal praise to his boundless goodness.

Oh, God! we thank thee, that thou didst condescend to listen to the cries of Africa's wretched sons; and that thou didst interfere in their behalf. At thy call humanity sprang forth, and espoused the cause of the oppressed: one hand she employed in drawing from their vitals the deadly arrows of injustice; and the other in holding a shield to defend them from fresh assaults: and at that illustrious moment, when the sons of '76 pronounced these United States free and independent; when the spirit of patriotism, erected a temple sacred to liberty; when the inspired voice of Americans first uttered those noble sentiments, "we hold these truths to be self-evident, that all men are created equal; that they are endowed by their Creator with certain unalienable rights; among which are life, liberty, and the pursuit of happiness;" and when the bleeding African, lifting his fetters, exclaimed, "am I not a man and a brother;" then with re-doubled efforts, the angel of humanity strove to restore to the African race the inherent rights of man.

To the instruments of divine goodness, those benevolent men who voluntarily obeyed the dictates of humanity, we owe much. Surrounded with innumerable difficulties, their undaunted spirits dared to oppose a powerful host of interested men. Heedless to the voice of fame, their independent souls dared to oppose the strong gales of popular prejudice. Actuated by principles of genuine philanthropy, they dared to despise the emoluments of ill gotten wealth, and to sacrifice much of their temporal interests at the shrine of benevolence.

As an American, I glory in informing you that Columbia boasts the first men who distinguished themselves eminently in the vindication of our rights, and the improvement of our state.

Conscious that slavery was unfavourable to the benign influences of Christianity, the pious Woolman loudly declaimed against it; and although destitute of fortune, he resolved to spare neither time nor pains to check its progress. With this view he travelled over several parts of North America on foot, and exhorted his brethren, of the denomination of Friends, to abjure the iniquitous custom. These, convinced by the cogency of his arguments, denied the privileges of their society to the slaveholder, and zealously engaged in destroying the aggravated evil. Thus, through the beneficial labours of this pattern of piety and brotherly kindness, commenced a work which has since been promoted by the humane of every denomination. His memory ought therefore to be deeply engraven on the tablets of our hearts, and ought ever to inspire us with the most ardent esteem.

Nor less to be prized are the useful exertions of Anthony Benezet. This inestimable person, sensible of the equality of mankind, rose superior to the illiberal opinions of the age; and, disallowing an inferiority in the African genius, established the first school to cultivate our understandings, and to better our condition.

Thus, by enlightening the mind, and implanting the seeds of virtue, he banished, in a degree, the mists of prejudice, and laid the foundations of our future happiness. Let, therefore, a due sense of his meritorious actions ever create in us a deep reverence of his beloved name. Justice to the occasion, as well as his merits, forbid me to pass in silence over the name of the honourable William Wilberforce. Possessing talents capable of adorning the greatest subjects, his comprehensive mind found none more worthy his constant attention, than the abolition of the slave trade. For this he soared to the zenith of his towering eloquence, and for this he struggled with perpetual ardour. Thus, anxious in defense of our rights, he pledged himself never to desert the cause; and, by his repeated and strenuous exertions, he finally obtained the desirable end. His extensive services have, therefore, entitled him to a large share of our affections, and to a lasting tribute of our unfeigned thanks.

But think not, my brethren, that I pretend to enumerate the persons who have proved our strenuous advocates, or that I have portrayed the merits of those I have mentioned: No, I have given but a few specimens of a countless number,* and no more than the rude outlines of the beneficence of these. Perhaps there never existed a human institution which has displayed more intrinsic merit than the societies for the abolition of slavery.

Reared on the pure basis of philanthropy, they extend to different quarters of the globe; and comprise a considerable number of humane and respectable men. These, greatly impressed with the importance of the work, entered into it with such disinterestedness, engagedness, and prudence, as does honour to their wisdom and virtue. To effect the purposes of these societies no legal means were

---

* Among the many eminent defenders of African rights, the reader cannot fail to recognize the Rev. Mr. Thomas Clarkson, whose extensive capacities and unremitting zeal have classed him with the most conspicuous and useful advocates of the cause. In his essays in defense of injured humanity, he displays a power of argument which silences every objector. Thus, while Mr. Wilberforce arrested the attention of the national councils on this important subject, the excellent Mr. Clarkson strongly seconded his endeavours by addressing the community at large; and penetrating the flimsy garb in which sophistry had veiled the evils of slavery, he exploded all its fallacious arguments, exposed this monster of deformity in all its nakedness, and confirmed the principle, that it is not only our duty, but our temporal and eternal interest to "do good unto all men."

left untried which afforded the smallest prospects of success. Books were disseminated, and discourses delivered, wherein every argument was employed which the penetrating mind could adduce, from religion, justice, or reason, to prove the turpitude of slavery, and numerous instances related, calculated to awaken sentiments of compassion. To further their charitable intentions, applications were constantly made to different bodies of legislature, and every concession improved to our best possible advantage. Taught by preceding occurrences that the waves of oppression are ever ready to overwhelm the defenseless, they became the vigilant guardians of all our reinstated joys. Sensible that the inexperienced mind is greatly exposed to the allurements of vice, they cautioned us, by the most salutary precepts and virtuous examples, against its fatal encroachments; and the better to establish us in the paths of rectitude, they instituted schools to instruct us in the knowledge of letters and the principles of virtue.

By these and similar methods, with divine assistance they assailed the dark dungeon of slavery; shattered its rugged wall, and enlarging thousands of the captives, bestowed on them the blessings of civil society. Yes, my brethren, through their efficiency, numbers of us now enjoy the invaluable gem of liberty; numbers have been secured from a relapse into bondage; and numbers have attained a useful education.

I need not, my brethren, take a farther view of our present circumstances to convince you of the providential benefits which we have derived from our patrons; for if you take a retrospect of the past situation of Africans, and descendants of Africans, in this and other countries, to your observation our advancements must be obvious. From these considerations, added to the happy event which we now celebrate, let us ever entertain the profoundest veneration for our munificent benefactors, and return to them from the altars of our hearts the fragrant incense of incessant gratitude. But let not, my brethren, our demonstrations of gratitude be confined to the mere expressions of our lips.

The active part which the friends of humanity have taken to ameliorate our sufferings, has rendered them in a measure, the pledges of our integrity. You must be well aware, that notwithstanding their endeavours, they have yet remaining, from interest and prejudice, a number of opposers. These, carefully watching for every opportunity to injure the cause, will not fail to augment the smallest defects in our lives and conversation; and reproach our benefactors with them, as the fruits of their actions.

Let us, therefore, by a steady and upright deportment, by a strict obedience and respect to the laws of the land, form an invulnerable bulwark against the shafts of malice. Thus, evincing to the world that our garments are unpolluted by the stains of ingratitude, we shall reap increasing advantages from the favours conferred; the spirits of our departed ancestors shall smile with complacency on the change of our state; and posterity shall exult in the pleasing remembrance.

May the time speedily commence, when Ethiopia shall stretch forth her hands; when the sun of liberty shall beam resplendent on the whole African race; and its genial influences, promote the luxuriant growth of knowledge and virtue.

HAVING understood that some persons doubt my being the author of this Oration, and thinking it probable that a like sentiment may be entertained by others who may honour this publication with a perusal, I have thought proper to authenticate the fact, by subjoining the following certificates.

PETER WILLIAMS, Jun.

New York, January 16, 1808.

THIS is to certify, all whom it may concern, that the Oration on the Abolition of the slave trade, delivered by PETER WILLIAMS, Jun. in the African Church, was submitted to my inspection while it was in manuscript; that I have every reason to believe it was composed by him, the said Peter Williams; and that it now comes from the press, with only a few immaterial verbal alterations.

BENJAMIN MOORE,
Bishop of the P. E. Church,
in the State of New York.

To whom it may concern: These presents are to certify, that the "Oration on the Abolition of the slave trade; delivered in the African Methodist Episcopal Church, in the City of New York, January 1, 1808; by PETER WILLIAMS, Jun. a descendant of Africa," was inspected by me while in manuscript, and I was present when he delivered the same; and I have satisfactory assurance, and sufficient reason to believe, that the said Oration was composed by the said Peter Williams.

EZEKIEL COOPER,
Minister of the Methodist
Episcopal Church.

New York, January 16, 1808.

PETER WILLIAMS, Jun. a young man of the African race, having delivered on the first of this month, "An Oration on the Abolition of the slave trade," These are therefore to certify, that from my knowledge of him, I believe the production to be his own; though in the revisal of it, he received some small aid.

JOHN MURRAY, Jun.

New York, 1st. mo. 18, 1808.

FROM my knowledge of PETER WILLIAMS, Jun. (a descendant of the African race) and of several of his essays at composition, I have no doubt but that he composed the Oration which he delivered on the 1st inst. on the subject of the Abolition of the slave trade.

WILLIAM T. SLOCUM.

New York, 1st. mo. 18, 1808.

AN

ORATION,

COMMEMORATIVE OF THE

ABOLITION

OF

THE SLAVE TRADE

IN THE UNITED STATES;

DELIVERED BEFORE THE

Wilberforce Philanthropic Association,

IN THE
CITY OF NEW YORK,
ON THE SECOND OF JANUARY, 1809.

BY JOSEPH SIDNEY.

NEW YORK:
PRINTED FOR THE AUTHOR.
J. SEYMOUR, PRINTER.
1809.

*To the members of the Wilberforce Philanthropic Association, in
the city of New York, this oration, delivered and published by their*

request, is respectfully inscribed, by their very obedient humble servant,

J. SIDNEY.

New York, 10th January, 1809.

ORATION

Friends, Countrymen, and Fellow Citizens,

DEEPLY affected with the various sensations and emotions which the occasion is so peculiarly calculated to excite, I rise to address you. We, together with our fellow-citizens at large, this day celebrate the commencement of a new year. This day is observed throughout the United States, as one devoted to joy, to festivity, to mutual good wishes, and to the thousand civilities of social life. But in addition to the general joy which this day occasions to the American empire, and in which we, in common with our fellow-citizens, participate; I say, in addition to this cause of general rejoicing, the return of this day opens to us, my countrymen, a newly discovered source of joy, of which ourselves, and the sympathizing friends of suffering humanity, are the exclusive partakers. On this auspicious day, we celebrate the anniversary of that glorious era, which, in these United States, put a period to that inhuman species of traffic, that, with relentless cruelty, had so long plundered unhappy Africa of her sons.

My friends, 'tis not an illusion of fancy, 'tis a truth recorded in the annals, and enrolled among the statutes of the United States, that no African, nor a single individual descended from African ancestors, shall henceforth be imported into this country as a slave. What a stride is this towards the total abolition of slavery in America! what a progress towards the consummation of our fondest hopes! what a presage that the exertions, the good wishes, and the prayers of the humane and benevolent, will finally triumph! And with what transports of joy may we not hail the return of this memorable, this auspicious day—this jubilee of freedom!!

My countrymen, you will probably expect something from me on the subject of the African slave trade. But to undertake to show its inhumanity and injustice, or to demonstrate its inconsistency with the principles of sound policy, would inevitably lead me too far from what I conceive to be the more immediate duty of an orator on an occasion like the present. Besides, the inhumanity, the injustice, and the inexpediency of the slave trade, have been so often and so illustriously exhibited by so many celebrated champions of African freedom, that for me to insist on these truths, would be merely to recapitulate the arguments which have been variously and successfully urged by others, and which no efforts of mine could possibly enforce. These are truths which seem to have been universally conceded. And the very event which we are assembled to celebrate, proves beyond controversy that in these United States, reason, truth, humanity, and freedom have finally obtained a glorious triumph over sophistry, falsehood, cruelty, and tyranny.

Since, then, the slave trade is by law for ever abolished, may we not, my countrymen, without incurring the imputation of rashness or presumption, look forward to the period when slavery, in this land of freedom, will be unheard of and unknown? Yes! this is what we most ardently desire, what we fondly anticipate, and what, I think, we may with certainty expect to realize.

The immediate emancipation of all our brethren in the United States is an event which we cannot reasonably expect; and, perhaps, ought not to desire. For it is a lamentable fact that our brethren in the South are in a state of deplorable ignorance. Uneducated as they are, and unacquainted with every thing except the plantations on which they toil, and from which they are never suffered to depart, it is incredible that they can possess sufficient information to render their immediate emancipation a blessing either to themselves or to society at large. But a want of information, on the part of our southern brethren, cannot be urged as an argument against their gradual emancipation.

For the purpose of showing that no evils would result from the gradual abolition of slavery, I need only refer you to some facts and considerations which relate to the people of the New England states.

The enlightened people of New England, immediately after the American revolution, feeling that slavery was perfectly irreconcilable with the principles for which they had fought and bled, seriously and deliberately formed a plan for its gradual abolition. Their plan was successful. Their legislatures enacted laws which suddenly inflicted on slavery a death-wound: and in consequence of this, no inconveniences, but blessings incalculable, have resulted to that people.

To thee, New England! to thee, belongs the honour of making the first exertions towards ameliorating the hard condition of my unfortunate countrymen! Yes! thou land of patriots, and thou nation of freemen, in abolishing slavery from within thy borders, thou hast exhibited to the world a signal example of humanity and justice! And oh! may I not indulge the hope, that ere long thy southern sisters may be induced to imitate this splendid exhibition of thy magnanimity!

New York, and several other of the middle states, actuated by a spirit similar to that which animated the sages of New England, have obeyed the voice of humanity; and are gradually abolishing slavery. Would to God that I could say the same of the southern states! but truth compels me to observe, that in the southern section of the United States, and particularly in Virginia, slavery still exists in all its horrors, unrelieved by the slightest degree of mitigation!

Alas! what is man, and of what is he formed! How contradictory in his professions! how strangely inconsistent in his actions!

No people in the world make louder pretensions to "liberty, equality, and the rights of man," than the people of the South! And yet, strange as it may appear, there is no spot in the United States where oppression reigns with such unlimited sway! It is here we may see human nature sunk to the lowest state of degradation; and human misery exalted to a height, which, if transcended, would be beyond human endurance. 'Tis here we may behold our wretched brethren smarting under the lash of tyranny, and retiring in sorrow, to eat their hard-earned pittance, moistened with their tears. 'Tis here that the ear is stunned with the cries of these hapless children of wretchedness, whose sighs and groans are wafted on every breeze. And 'tis here, in sad succession, they spend their days, friendless, comfortless, oppressed, and forlorn, until, at last, the grave, less savage and unfeeling than their remorseless persecutors—the grave, that "house appointed for all the living," compassionates their sufferings, and opens its capacious doors to receive them!

Pardon me, my countrymen, for thus intruding on your joy; but whilst engaged in taking a short survey of our present prospects and of our future hopes, I could not avoid, even on this day of festivity, shedding a tear of commiseration over the cheerless condition of our southern brethren.

Heaven grant that some Wilberforce, some champion of African freedom, whose warm, whose expanded, whose benevolent heart, is capable of beating in unison with their sufferings, may arise in Virginia; assert the long neglected and abused rights of Africa's sons; and institute that plan of gradual emancipation, which has been so successfully adopted and pursued in New England and New York! Then shall their sorrow be turned into rejoicing, their sighs into melody, and their groans into acclamations of joy!

But I shall wave these reflections, and proceed, my countrymen, to suggest to you some of those duties which have devolved on us, in consequence of our having recently obtained our freedom, and which appear to me peculiarly proper to be called to mind on the present occasion.

Freedom has broken down that wall of separation which formerly distinguished our rights and duties from those of the white inhabitants. Our rights and duties have, of course, assimilated to theirs. And, permit me to add, that the judicious exercise of these rights, and the punctual performance of these duties, involve considerations which are all-important, both to ourselves and to our country.

Among the most valuable of our newly acquired rights, is that of suffrage. This right is particularly valuable, inasmuch as it enables us to express our choice with respect to our rulers. Good rulers are a blessing, but bad rulers are, and must be considered, a curse to any nation. The right of suffrage, brings with it a duty of the highest obligation. For as this right gives us the power of voting, so it devolves on us the indispensable duty of bestowing our votes on those, and on those only, whose talents, and whose political, moral, and religious principles, will most effectually promote the best interests of America.

My countrymen, you cannot be unacquainted with the fact, that there has existed, for some time past, in our country, two great political parties. At the head of the Federal Republican Party was the immortal Washington, the Father of his country. Hamilton, Jay, Adams, Pinckney, King, and Pickering, together with most of our old revolutionary officers and soldiers, were among the illustrious characters who attached themselves, through principle and patriotism, to this party.

After achieving the independence of their country, this distinguished band of patriots formed the federal constitution; and from that circumstance, were denominated Federalists, or Federal Republicans. The single object of this party was to preserve the liberty, to promote the happiness, to increase the prosperity, and to extend the respectability of the United States. Being satisfied as to the immense advantages which are to be derived from commerce, and knowing, that the interests of the middle and eastern States are intimately connected with it, this party, while in office, gave to commerce every possible encouragement. To this end, a small navy was built to protect our vessels from the armed ships of foreign nations. So long as Federalists remained in office, so long this country enjoyed an uninterrupted state of increasing prosperity—And so long as this happy state of things continued, so long did agriculture and commerce unite hand in hand, to diffuse their riches, and to extend their blessings to every class of citizens.

'Twas then, that lofty forests bowed their heads, at the approach of agriculture—and the "wilderness and the solitary place blossomed as the rose!" 'Twas then, that the cheerful hum of industry, and the jocund song, were heard throughout our happy land! 'Twas then, that American commerce extended her dominion to every sea, and spread her canvas to every breeze! And 'twas then, that America, being a nation of patriots, was therefore terrible to her enemies, "as an army with banners!"

Such was the state of our affairs, when the Anti-federal or Democratic Party, consisting of a set of ambitious, designing, and office-seeking men, first adventured from its native cave of filth and darkness, into open day. A number of abandoned printérs, mostly foreigners, enlisted in the service of this party: and from that moment, commenced a persecution against federal men; and federal measures; which persecution, for cool and malignant cruelty, can never be exceeded. To destroy the reputation of distinguished federalists, calumnies the most vile were daily circulated through the country. Even the virtues and services of Washington did not prove a shield sufficiently broad, to protect him against the envenomed shafts of malice. The Father of his country, was branded as a "traitor"—and the venerable Adams was stigmatized as "a hoary-headed incendiary!"

Thus feeding on detraction, and fattening on the mangled reputation of federalists, the democratic party became a majority—and thus their leader, Mr. Jefferson, became the President of the United States. And from that inauspicious day, though the current could not instantly leave its wonted channel, yet, the tide of American prosperity soon ceased to flow, and all our goodly prospects vanished.

One of the first acts of the present administration, was to displace those revolutionary officers whom Washington had placed in office, as a small reward for all their labours, toils, and dangers. Washington placed in office real patriots and statesmen, who fought to procure our independence; others have bestowed these high dignities on foreigners, probably as a reward for their insurrection and slander.

Our infant navy, the protector of our commerce, fell an early victim to the fury of the Virginian Junto. Nor could that fury be appeased, until our commerce itself had received the stroke of death. Yes, my countrymen! an unlimited embargo, wielded by the mad democracy of the southern states, has, like the besom of destruction, swept our commerce from the ocean!

Time would fail me, to give even a sketch of the calamities produced by this self-destroying measure.

In the eastern states, it has fallen with tremendous force. To destroy their commerce is to pour out the life-blood of their prosperity.

Nor is it in the eastern states only, that this rash measure is felt.

We all, my countrymen, most sensibly feel it. The poor and the labouring class of people, in every state, are peculiarly its victims. Yes, we do feel, and we shall indubitably continue more and more to feel, its hard and partial operation. Nor do we find a probability of relief, in the partiality of our democratic rulers for undeserving emigrants to our shores.

The middle and New England states are all commercial states. But the southern states, on account of their local situation, can, comparatively speaking, derive but little advantage from commerce, and therefore probably wish to destroy it altogether. Its destruction, they imagine, will put an effectual check to the increasing prosperity and influence of their rivals, the middle and eastern states. Now, the southern states, which comprise the great body of the democratic party in our country, being hostile to commerce, and this party having laid the embargo, and being still the ruling party, we cannot rationally expect that commerce will again flourish, until the general government shall be administered by federalists, the real friends of commerce, and the genuine disciples of Washington. It is not within the limits of probability, that a change of measures for the better will be effected, in any other way than by a change of men.

How important then, that we, my countrymen, should unite our efforts with those of our Federal friends, in endeavouring to bring about this desirable change—this change, so all-important to commerce, to our own best interests, and to the prosperity and glory of our country!

But there is another consideration, which appears to me worthy of being suggested. The great hotbed of democracy is Virginia, and the other southern states. All the democratic members of Congress, who have any considerable influence in directing the machine of government, belong to the South. And almost all the free inhabitants of the southern section of the United States, are of the democratic party. And these are the very people who hold our African brethren in bondage. These people, therefore, are the enemies of our rights. And as the democrats in this state are acting with these, our enemies, we should not only be wanting in duty to ourselves, but we should be destitute of the spirit of freemen, were we not to turn our backs upon democracy, and unite with our Federal friends, to place men in office possessed of humanity, justice, firmness, and American patriotism.

Besides, is the great idol of democracy our friend? That he is not, is evident; else he would respect the rights of our African brethren; several hundreds of whom he keeps as slaves on his plantations. What did Washington? This illustrious and humane man, feeling that slavery was incompatible with the principles for which he fought, most generously emancipated every slave that he owned, and gave to each a portion sufficiently large to answer his exigencies, until he could procure employment.

Can you then, my countrymen, for a moment hesitate in choosing between your enemies and your friends? between slavery and freedom? Will you run into the camp of your enemies? Will you flock to the Slavery-hole of democracy?—Or will you patriotically rally round the standard of liberty?—a standard which was erected by the immortal Washington; and which has been consecrated by the blood of the martyred Hamilton.

Before I conclude, permit me, my countrymen, to impress on your minds a duty, which it is our highest interest ever to observe. This duty consists in endeavouring unceasingly, by pure and upright conduct, to convince the world that we are not only capable of self-government, but also of becoming honourable citizens and useful members of society. Let it be our business to demonstrate to the conviction, even of the enemies of our freedom, that sobriety, honesty, and industry, are among the distinguishing traits in our characters; that we know too well the value of liberty, ever to abuse her inestimable privileges; and that although the "Ethiopian cannot change his skin," yet his heart may, nevertheless, become an habitation for all the virtues which ever adorn the human character.

A conduct, on our part, in all respects dignified and proper, will effectually put to silence every cavil which may be offered against African emancipation, and must eventually convert our enemies into friends.

I need scarcely to remind you, my countrymen, on an occasion like this, that all those whose exertions have, in any degree, contributed to bring about the interesting event which we this day celebrate, and, in particular The Manumission Society of the City of New York, whose kind interference has greatly ameliorated our condition, are all eminently entitled to our warmest gratitude.—Long may they all be remembered, and amply rewarded for their "labours of love!"—May they have the satisfaction of realizing that their efforts for our happiness and usefulness in life, have been crowned with success! And may we always be possessed of that evidence of gratitude to these our benefactors, which springs from pure and upright conduct!

And let me add, that such a conduct is the best evidence which we can possibly produce, of that gratitude which we owe to the God of mercies, for his interposition in our behalf. He has ever been our kindest benefactor; and, as such, we owe him a debt of gratitude, which we can never cancel. While we therefore, my countrymen, in unison, lift up our voices in praise and thanksgiving to this God of mercies, let us supplicate, that by a more general extension of freedom and of pure patriotism throughout our country, every return of this anniversary may be accompanied with additional causes for joy and rejoicing.

CELEBRATION

The Wilberforce Philanthropic Association, assembled at Liberty Hall, together with the Musical and Maritime Associations, agreeably to the orders of the committee of arrangement, appointed by the general meeting of the people of colour; and marched in procession, up Leonard Street, down Broadway, to the Lyceum in Warren Street, in the following order, viz.: The Grand Marshal; two Africans, escorted by the deputy Marshals; the Committee of Arrangement, the Chairman and Secretary, the Orator and Reader, the Wilberforce band of Music, with the Association, the Maritime and Musical Associations, decorated with their badges, and accompanied with their appropriate banners. The novelty of the procession attracted the notice of an immense concourse of citizens, and presented a spectacle both grand and interesting. It was the Jubilee of Liberty; the triumph of Philanthropy.

Previous to the day of celebration, the Committee published the following notice.

"National Jubilee of the Abolition of the Slave-Trade

"The undersigned committee of arrangement, appointed by the general meeting of the people of colour, for the celebration of the national jubilee, most respectfully inform the public, that they will assemble at Liberty Hall, on Monday morning, January 2, 1809, at 9 o'clock, and march in procession, if the weather will permit, with the societies, with their badges and banners, accompanied with a band of music, up Leonard Street, down Broadway, to the Lyceum in Warren Street, where an Oration will be delivered, and anthems sung suitable to the occasion. A collection will then be made to defray the expenses, and the surplus, if any, will be given to the Manumission Society. After the service is over, the procession will form again, and march through Broadway, down Pearl Street, through Wall Street, up Broadway to Liberty Hall, and dismiss. Every exertion has been made to fulfil the intentions of their constituents, to show their gratitude in the most public manner, for so great a blessing; and they cannot but lament that a division should exist, and indulge the flattering hope, that all dissentions will cease.

John Robison,	William Wiltshier,
Peter Bane,	Jupiter Burns,
John Belt,	Samuel Glass,
Alexander Sutlif,	Robert Ash,
John T. Tate,	Aaron Connor,
Thomas Smith,	Samuel Reed,

ROBERT Y. SIDNEY, *Sec'ry.*"

N. B. The committee, after service, shortened their route on account of the numerous spectators, and dismissed at the place of rendezvous, with the greatest acclamations of joy.

AN

ORATION

ON THE

ABOLITION OF THE SLAVE TRADE;

DELIVERED

IN

THE AFRICAN CHURCH,

IN

THE CITY OF NEW YORK,

JANUARY 2, 1809.

By Henry Sipkins,
A DESCENDANT OF AFRICA.

NEW YORK:
PRINTED BY JOHN C. TOTTEN,
NO. 155 CHATHAM-STREET.
1809.

This oration is humbly inscribed to the friends of humanity, whose assiduity, and disinterested philanthropy, have been conspicuous in the propagation of emancipation.

INTRODUCTORY ADDRESS BY HENRY JOHNSON.

Fathers and Brethren,

THE attentive seriousness, the respectable appearance of this crowded audience; and the grandeur that I behold in the countenance of so many in this great assembly: and the solemnity of the cause for which we are this day met together, joined to the consideration of the part that I am to take in the important business of this day, increase the sense which I have had of my unworthiness of gracing this sacred stage.

And now let us Africans and descendants of Africans, with uplifted hands and bended knees make daily prayers and expressions of gratitude to God, for the long lives of those benevolent men who have been so arduously engaged in the abolition of the slave trade. And may that Almighty being mercifully dwell in all our councils; and may he direct us to such proceedings as he himself shall approve and be pleased to bless. And may we ever be favoured of him. And may the whole world be a world of liberty, the seat of virtue, and a refuge for the oppressed. And then will the poor African no longer have to exclaim:

> I long to lay this painful head,
>   And aching heart, beneath the soil;
> To slumber in that dreamless bed,
>   From all my toil.
>
> For misery stole me at my birth,
>   And cast me naked on the wild,
> I perish, O my mother earth;
>   Take home thy child.

ORATION.

Brethren and Fellow-Citizens,

WE are again assembled to tender our sincere thanks, to recount the beneficial exertions of humane men, to venerate the beneficence of the Almighty Father of the universe, and to commemorate the return of a day that has, in some degree, restored the long-lost tranquility of the once happy inhabitants of Africa.

The prohibition of the slave trade, which is the momentous occasion of our convention, is perhaps equal to any inscribed in the page of history. No event therein occurs that so conspicuously points out the magnanimity of spirit by which the advocates of its annihilation were stimulated, whose venerable names will be perpetuated to latest posterity, and receive from them a tribute of unfeigned gratitude; while the exposed pusillanimity of their predecessors and opponents meet its merited reproach and indignation from all upright persons. By means of this nefarious traffic, the delectable scenes of our parent-country have been immersed in the blood of our ancestors. This flagitious infringement on human rights was not confined within the sphere of a single province; its rage was not exhausted by reducing one or two tribes to the most unparalleled miseries; but, clothed in the habiliments of destruction, it spread its unlimited cruelties over the wide-expanded realms of Africa.

The most sanguinary massacres committed by the nations of antiquity, at the taking or subversion of Troy, Babylon, or Jerusalem, notwithstanding their enormous horrors, at which the blood of everything animated by rational feelings, is appalled; yet, when we revert our thoughts to the productive inseparable evils, attendant on the slave trade, we are compelled to attribute to it unequalled cruelty, barbarity and injustice.

Let us for a moment take a retrospective view of Africa in its primitive state.

It exhibits the most blissful regions, productive of all the necessaries and even luxuries of life, almost independent of the arm of husbandry. Its innocent inhabitants regardless of, or unacquainted with the concerns of busy life, enjoyed with uninterrupted pleasure the state in which, by the beneficent hand of nature, they were placed.

But, ah! sad reverse. By this abominable trade they have been forced to bid adieu to their serenity and happiness.

When this envenomed monster of misery explored the passage to their fertile shore, when it reared its hideous head on their luxuriant plains; when with all its dismal concomitants it approached their peaceful abodes, all was consternation and woe.

It owes its being to the Portuguese, who, in the year 1508, by basely kidnapping numbers of the inhabitants, made the first import into the island of Hispaniola, for the purpose of cultivating the possessions of the Spaniards. It owes its rise to the fostering hand of other nations, who, as they acquired settlements in America, adopted the execrable practice which the Spaniards had tolerated. And it owes its maturity to the increasing avarice of all Europeans, who conceived it the most conducive to the enlarging of their fortunes out of the inexhaustible treasures which the new world unfolded.

Although conscious of the turpitude of destroying the liberties of the Africans, which they knew to be as inherent in them, as in the

Europeans, length of time lead them to view it as a matter of right; and no sooner was it so conceived, than it was prosecuted to the greatest possible extent.

It was not until the year 1551 that the English commenced trading to Africa for gold, ivory, &c. And in 1556, Sir John Hawkins sent on shore a number of men to take and enslave the inhabitants.

But, being defeated in the attack, dropt down the river, where he recommenced the enforcing of his inhuman plan; and the better to effect it, burnt the towns.

After repeated efforts, he procured his number and proceeded to the West Indies, where he exposed them for sale. After this, his first adventure, he was pleased with the success of this base employ, from the sight of which human nature revolts with terror. But alas, such was his depravity, as with the utmost composure, to see them linger out a miserable existence.

Hearing that the Africans were a valuable commodity in Hispaniola, he readily expressed his sentiments to his most intimate friends, who promised him their utmost endeavours to facilitate his design.

But finding the slaves purchased at too dear a price, being often at the expense of many lives, he thought it advisable to resort to other means of obtaining them; and conceived it the most effectual by instilling into them a spirit of avarice, and love of luxury. The gratification of which soon became the most powerful incentives to a speedy dissolution. Fatal, indeed, to the peace of Africa was this devised plan.

The harmless Africans, who had ever been strangers to the arts of deception, and unsuspicious of treachery in the bosoms of others, gratefully received the proffers of friendship from their cruel invaders, and consequently became an easy prey to European wiles.

Stimulated by the promised rewards of the Europeans, and in some cases intoxicated by the excessive use of spirituous liquors, joined them in their cruel depredations against their unhappy countrymen.

Once disunited, and the same stimulus ever remaining, eminently conduced to the waging of perpetual war.

Hence, no sooner than a slave ship presented itself to the view of the inhabitants bordering on the coast, than they beat to arms, and regardless of age or sex, with unequalled violence attacked their neighbouring friends, to whom but a few minutes before they evinced the most amicable disposition.

In some of their hostilities, when they have been obstinately opposed, have been so heated with revenge, as to become insensible of the dictates of avarice, and indiscriminately murder men, women, and children.

Notwithstanding the depredations of these intestine broils, the horrid desolation and ravages which are their constant attendants, yet far is their misery from being at its summit.

Augmented much are their sorrows on board the slave ship, almost inconceptionable must be their sufferings.

Confined in these caverns of despair, their tender limbs in weighty shackles bound, without the most distant hope of release, is truly miserable.

Torn from their native land, the endearing bonds of society are broken by the remorseless hearts of their assailants, whose insatiate thirst for sordid treasure dooms them victims to the most abject slavery.

But here their miseries do not cease. Still are they advancing toward maturity. Once brought into port a new and unbounded field of oppression presents itself to their view.

Here the most relentless tyranny on them is inflicted.

In this scene of their torture is summoned the aggregate distresses of both the former.

The day of sale at length arrives, they are now driven from this abode of distress. The ties of relation and friendship are now dissolved, which were the more strongly cemented by being fellow sufferers for several months.

Severed from their native shore, and after enduring the pain of a long voyage, they are now the victims of a second parting. The sale now over, perhaps without taking the last tender embraces of an eternal separation, they are precipitantly hurried to the estates of their various purchasers. They now become witnesses of scenes the most direful. They are now the subjects of miseries the most replete.

The plantation bell summonses them to the incessant fatigues of the day.

One moment's delay subjects them to the malevolence of their revengeful overseers.

The scorching sun now rising to its high noon meridian, and pouring its intolerable radiance on them, and they languishing under the labour of the field, if they chance to fall a little behind their fellow sufferers, they are reminded of their indolence by the stripes of their brutal drivers.

Nor are these the duties and punishments of the men only; but even feminine weakness and juvenile years are not exempted.

Behold a mother with her helpless infant on her shoulders, a sufferer in these toilsome scenes, or, in despite of the overbearing impulse of maternal affection, forced to lay it on the ground.

Night now approaches, but instead of retiring to habitations to enjoy a frugal repast, to support almost exhausted nature, or to recline their wearied frames on even their sheaf of straw, they are obliged to appropriate part of this cessation from the labour of the field, to the gathering of grass for the cattle.

But why attempt to pourtray, in their true colours, scenes of oppression, which language the most descriptive is inadequate to delineate: or why any longer expatiate on a subject of such complicated misery.

Suffice it to say, that to this deplorable situation, my brethren, descendants of Africans, have millions of our forefathers and brethren fell victims. In this state of hopeless servitude, do many yet remain, who look forward with pleasing expectation to the termination of their lives as the only possible means of emancipating them from servile despotism.

At the bare thought of such unexampled debasement of part of mankind, humanity shudders. The slave trade, in its every stage, unfolds to the view of every beholder, in whose heart glows the most latent particle of sympathy, scenes of woe and detestation. For the destruction of this almost inexhaustible magazine of cruelty, much thanks, my brethren, from us are due. In producing which, America boasts the unrivalled exertions of Woolman and Benezet, whose boundless services in the cause of emancipation have been viewed with admiration by a surrounding world. Wheresoever they turned their eyes, discouraging obstacles presented their withering frowns; but emboldened by a consciousness of rectitude, they resolved to persevere. Also the venerable names of Dillwyn, Sharp, and many others, will ever resplendently embellish the historic page—will ever receive from us the most grateful homage, and will by posterity be heard of with peculiar satisfaction. We can pleasantly anticipate the gratulation with which their virtues will be received. *Oh, our most worthy advocates! we humbly beg you to accept our grateful thanks for your disinterested, indefatigable exertions to ameliorate our state. When we were under the iron hand of oppression, you did generously step forward to ease our burthen. When we trembled at the haughty mandates of imperious tyrants, your consoling whispers offered some shelter. When sinking under the weighty shackles of slavery to the most consummate despondency, with unremitting zeal

* Addressed to the Friends.

you flew to our relief.—These, my brethren, are but a few of innumerable instances in which they have proved our strenuous beneficial advocates. It was their ineffable delight to see mankind restored to primitive parity. And for it the voice of justice and humanity were heard in the Congress of these United States and the British Parliament. At this despair seemed to erect her appalling brow; but, by their dauntless spirits, she was quickly repelled. Their prayers, though often discarded, did not intimidate them. Still was their ardour invigorated—still they remained the firm champions of our cause.

To these philantrophic exertions, my African brethren, we are indebted for our present happiness and prosperity. To these we owe our preservation from a second bondage; and on these depend the prospect of future felicity. Their ever-memorable acts were such as the paternal hand rearing its tender offspring to mature years, and planning for it the edifice of virtue and happiness. By their unabating energy they accomplished the long-sought conquest; at which the votaries of liberty shouted their congratulations; she waved in ecstasies her tallest standards; and calling to the drooping captives of slavery, bade them behold and admire! They disdained the stimulus of pecuniary gains, and felt themselves amply compensated by the smiles of an approving conscience.

My beloved Africans, let us by an upright and steady deportment merit a continuance of former favours, and evince to the world our high sense of gratitude. Eminent respect should, perhaps, be engraven on our hearts for the distinguished lustre with which our advocates, in these United States, have shone. These to their honour have it in their power to boast the first seminary for the cultivation of our understanding, and advancing us in morals. And they have had the gratification to see some make considerable attainments in literature, and become worthy members of civil society.

The benevolent exertions of the persons who are the subjects of the foregoing thanks, although worthy the highest eulogiums of terrestrial praise, can only be considered a secondary cause in the completion of this incomparable epoch. If these merit the greatest encomiums; how infinitely small must be our means of fixing the properties of respect, which infallibly belong to a primary cause? Stunned with astonishment we stand when contemplating the goodness of the divine majesty of heaven, who of his wonderful providence summoned our votaries by a voice of humanity to espouse the cause of the injured African race. In the moments of deliberate reflection on the causes tending to produce this memorable era, we are engulfed in the amazing labyrinth of his unfathomable condescention. Our hearts are lost in the maze of his incalculable benignity. Let us however endeavour to offer our indispensable obligations of unfeigned gratitude to eternal goodness—let us pay our greatest veneration to his matchless beneficence, and impel it loudly to re-echo through the regions of eternity. By his august decree the grossest debasement of mortals was abjured. He saw with piteous eyes our wretched state, and sent his guardian angels to rescue us from our distressed condition. Oh our heavenly Father! deign we beseech thee to accept the thanks of thy humble supplicants. In commiseration to our state thou didst inspire, by the dictates of humanity, men who became the vigilant exterminators of that commerce which has much depopulated the land of our nativity. And which has reduced its inhabitants with all their progeny under the sentence of perpetual bondage.

But rejoice, my brethren, through the efficiency of the friends of humanity this fell sentence has now subsided. It is absorbed in the refulgence of that memorable day, which announced the abolition of the slave trade, the return of which we now celebrate. That day which caused our hearts to dilate with the ideal hope of future bliss.

This day completes the first anniversary of the suspension of that facinerious [i.e., atrociously wicked—editor] traffic, which has made the most indelible blot in the history of nations. May it ever be held as a monument of contempt by rising generations. Rejoice that its baneful effects shall no longer be seen in these United States, nor the British colonies. No longer shall the shores of Africa be drenched with human gore. No longer shall its inhabitants be torn from their native soil; no longer shall they be brought on cruel shipboard, weighed down in chains; nor shall we any longer hear the dreadful recital of their mutilated, fettered limbs; nor shall the dismal groans of dying captives intercept our ears. No longer shall we witness the woeful prospect of an unnatural separation of a loving husband, an affectionate wife; nor a darling child cling to its fond parents, imploring their protection from the impending fury of their merciless owners. Rejoice, that no longer shall the sons of Africa become the subjects of such inhuman drudgery. Rejoice, my brethren, descendants of Africans, that the exiles of our race are emerging from the depths of forlorn slavery, in which they have been environed. The thick fogs of ignorance that have ever encompassed their gloomy mansions are gradually vanishing; they have been dissipated by the superior radiance of increasing knowledge.

But let not our expressions of joy suppress the inestimable obligations of gratitude due to our patrons. For on the most transient survey of our past condition, you must manifestly discover the unshaken constancy with which they have persevered to have established us in our present improved state. Beset with the most insuperable difficulties, arising from the strong imbibed opinion of our inferiority, they nevertheless, with that fortitude which characterises true worth, stemmed the torrent of popular prejudice. May it no longer shed on the mind its wizard darkness; nor the false tongue of envy envenom it by its beguiling insinuations.

But may the long wished for time soon arrive when slavery of every species shall be destroyed—when despotism and oppression shall forever cease—when the Africans shall be reinstated in their former joys—when the exulting shouts of Princes, embracing their long lost oppressed subjects, shall reverberate on our ears—when the bursting acclamations of approbation shall resound from the tombs of our worthy departed ancestors; and all find protection under the fostering wing of Liberty.

ORATION

ON THE

ABOLITION OF THE SLAVE TRADE,

DELIVERED

ON THE

FIRST DAY OF JANUARY, 1813,

IN THE

African Methodist Episcopal Church.

By George Lawrence.

Published by Request.

NEW YORK:
PRINTED BY HARDCASTLE AND VAN PELT,
NO. 36, NASSAU-STREET.
1813.

AN ADDRESS BY PETER MALACHI EAGANS.

January 1st, 1813.

Citizens,

I rise to address the venerable appearance of this crowded audience; the dignity which I behold in the countenances of so many in this general assembly, the solemnity of the occasion upon which we have met together, joined to a consideration of the part I am to take in the important business of this day, fills me with an awe hitherto unknown, and heightens the sense which I have ever had of my unworthiness to fill this sacred stage.

But allured by the call of some of our respected committee with whose request it is always my greatest pleasure to comply, I almost forgot my want of ability to perform what they required; in this situation I find my only support in assuring myself that a generous people will not severely censure what they know was well intended, though its want of merit should prevent them from applauding it.

And I pray that my sincere attachment to the interest of Africa and the descendants of Africans, and my hearty detestation of every design formed against her liberty and justice, may be admitted as some apology for my appearance in this place.

I have always from my earliest youth rejoiced in the felicity of my fellow men, and have ever considered it as the indispensable duty of every member of society to promote as far as in him lies the prosperity of every individual, but more especially of the community to which he belongs; and also as a faithful subject to the abolition of the slave trade, to use our utmost endeavours to detect, and having detected, strenuously to oppose every traitorous plot which its enemies may devise for its destruction.

AN ORATION

Respected Audience,

WE have again assembled with warm and grateful hearts, to celebrate our annual anniversary. It presents a period rendered venerable by the wise and humane fathers of our liberties, who laid the foundation of the happiness we now enjoy, and plucked from the very jaws of destruction, our devoted mother country. Gratitude then towards that veteran band of patriots, whose patriotism was crowned with justice, and shod with humanity, calls aloud. And shall we be backward in showing it? No, God forbid! the name of a Sharp, a Pitt, and a Fox, as the strong tower of our defense, cemented and made still stronger by the aid of many others, shall ever dwell with delight on our memories, and be treasured up in our hearts as the choicest gifts of heaven; for heaven gave them and heaven again shall receive them.

In our behalf they struggled long against a host of powerful and malignant enemies, who, being supplied with the wisdom of Satan, and bound by the impulse of avarice, made an almost impenetrable defense: but that great and all-wise being who holds the reigns of justice and destiny of nations, using them as arrows of his divine will, they passed the brazen walls of their opponents, and brought to light the august era of this thrice blessed and ever memorable day. Animated by the reverse of our hard fortunes, my brethren, and beholding the many blessings incident to our present situations; anticipating the advantages necessarily arising from the good work already begun, as we verge towards the summit of our happiness, it becomes us to make public our joy, for which purpose we are convened. We now celebrate the fifth anniversary of the abolition of the slave trade, and a partial restoration of one of those rights most congenial to the human heart; it becomes the grand epoch of our boast, a day joyful to every bosom through whose veins our noble blood does flow, we hail it as the birthday of justice and triumph over atrocious vice; we rejoice for a nation rising from the dark and dreary gulf of desponding servitude and shining forth conspicuously as she ascends the lofty mount of arts and sciences, giving presages of future greatness; and should we not rejoice when we consider that we make a part of this nation, although we were never exposed to all the piercing blasts of adversity that they were, yet does the refulgent beams of prosperity, dilate our hearts with joy. We rejoice for the abolition of the slave trade; and our joy overflows when we reflect that this heaven-born plant shall bring forth the full fruits of emancipation, and divulge that bright genius so long smothered in slavery.

The subject of this day calls for our serious attention; at the recurrence of this season we rejoice, not because we have gained a victory over our enemies by the arts of war, or that we have become rich and opulent, no, but it is the epoch that has restored to us our long-lost rights. It is a subject congenial with my heart, and I cannot but regret my inability to do it justice, although confident, that were my talents equal to the most eloquent and profound orator that ever graced the world, I could not fully expound it. The task is arduous —even experience might shrink before its magnitude. The field is very extensive, presenting to view various objects of infinite magnitude: such as past sufferings, present mitigation, and future happiness.

All buoyed up to sigh on the sea of reflection, the first forms a melancholy spectacle; a scene fraught with misery and horror. We behold Asia, Europe and America, claiming an authority, as far distant from moral rectitude, or the laws of nature, as heaven is from hell. They usurp the throne of justice, and she takes her flight from off the face of the earth. They commence their traffic in the innocent sons and daughters of Africa. View them divide their spoils dragged from our mother country, a country once rich in the enjoy-

ments of liberty and all the glory nature could afford. Nature there
caused the wild desert to be more fruitful and fragrant than the
best cultivated gardens, the inventions of men, ever could produce.
Her inhabitants was happy, seated in the very temples of bliss and
with nature for their guide. Their employments were innocent,
neither did they seek evil, contented in the enjoyments of their native sports; they sued not for the blood of their fellow men; they
arose in the morning with cheerfulness before their God, and bowed
down their heads at night, fully sensible of his goodness. But ah,
my friends! the scene changes. Alas! the rose was nipt in the bud,
and too soon did the canker worm enter the trunk of its support.
Africa! thou was once free, and enjoyed all the blessings a land and
people could. Once held up as the ornament of the world, on thy
golden shores strayed Liberty, Peace and Equality; but the usurping
power of accursed demagogues brought desolation within thy borders, thy populous cities are laid waste, thy mourning millions,
loaded with chains, are driven from their native homes, and far and
wide does the ravages of merciless power extend like the besom of
destruction, sweeping off thy inhabitants without regard to age or
sex. Thus did the baneful deed of avaricious power pierce the hearts
of our ancestors, separated and dashed asunder the most sacred ties
of nature; and hurled them, my brethren, not only from their native
country, but to enhance their misery, separated them from their
dearest relatives; the aged parent from the tender child; the loving
husband from the affectionate wife. We cast the eye of retrospec-
tion, and behold the field crimsoned with the blood of those slain;
and the earth drinks deeply of the tears of those that yet live, but
to meet a worse fate,* while the heavens reverberate with their
shrieks, and nature stands amazed! Yet the scene does not end
here; misery is still pouring in like a deluge; we view them hurried
on board some floating dungeons, whose rulers, more like fiends,
were never in the shape of men. Yes, that noble name is much degraded when they are called men. Tis here our ancestors drank the
wormwood and the gall!—Tis here they even died for lack of that
care which is due to the most inferior of the brute creation!—Tis
here some noble spirits fired with indignation, and disdaining to submit to savage rules, sought an asylum in the bosom of the sea!—Tis
here death, that grim monster so dreaded by the nations of the
earth, at whose approach crowned monarchs quake and termble; at
whose sight the countenance once flushed with the crimson vigour of
health, turns pale, the vivid eye that flashed with cheerfulness, sinks

* Slavery.

dimly back in its sockets, not willing to meet this ghastly visage. But view the contrast: Here injured innocence leaps to meet him, and receives him as a bosom friend. Yes, death is their only alternative and rescue from a set of beings who, through vicious customs and the impulse of avarice, had trampled under foot the most sacred rights of their nature. They who commenced and supported a trade begun in savage wars, prosecuted with unheard of barbarity, and ended in perpetual exile and slavery. But to harangue you on the sufferings of our ancestors I know is excruciatingly painful, yet bear with me a little; although it rends the tender heart, or forces the silent tear, it is expedient. In reflecting on their situation, our celebration demonstrates itself to be fully sensible of ours; we need but view theirs. They were pressed down beneath the surface of nature; we soar aloft as the towering eagle to an eminence commanding a view of the world, and three fourths we behold drenched in human gore, and the loud clarion of war is forboding their total destruction; thus while the dark clouds of strife and contention are encompassing them in, we enjoy the perpetual sunshine of peace and happiness. Then let us be united, the glory of a people is union; united in the bonds of social love, they become strong and vigorous, wise and discerning; they press undauntedly forward, and are sure of conquest; the sturdy oak fall before them; the stubborn rock yield to their force, and as the sun bursting forth from behind some dark cloud, they disperse the icy mountains of adversity and soar up to the meridian of prosperity. They are not tossed on the tempestuous sea of contention, but sail gently down the course of life, on the silver current of friendship. Union is the foundation of liberty, and its perfection is social love.

> This only can the bliss bestow,
> Immortal souls should prove;
> From one short word all pleasures flow,
> That blessed word is LOVE.

Love shall never fail: the man of love shall be held in everlasting remembrance, his memory shall be blessed; no spices can so embalm a man, no monument can so preserve his name, as works of love. Love gives worth to all its apparent virtues, insomuch that without it, no quality of the heart, no action of the life, is valuable in itself, or pleasing to God. Without love, what is courage but the boldness of a lion, or the fierceness of a tyger? What is power but merciless oppression? What is union but jealous corruption? What is justice but passion or policy? What is wisdom but craft and subtlety? Without love what is riches but a barren shore or a congealed stream?

And what is man, that noble structure, but the ravenous wolfe, or more subtle viper? What is devotion but mockery of God? What is any practice, how auspicious soever in itself, or beneficial to others, but the effect of pride? For, says one of the ancient worthies, though I had faith that I could remove mountains, and had not love, I am nothing. Though I give all my goods to feed the poor, and have not love, it profiteth me nothing. Love is the crystal fountain from whence flows all human happiness; its golden mines shall never be exhausted, its silver brooks shall never run dry. Let this then be our rallying point, for this shall ward against animosities and contentions —this shall bring down the blessings of heaven upon our heads—this shall slay our enemies, and make alive our friends—this shall cause our society to flourish, and this shall break the chain that still holds thousands of our brethren in bondage.

My brethren, the land in which we live gives us the opportunity rapidly to advance the prosperity of liberty. This government founded on the principles of liberty and equality, and declaring them to be the free gift of God, if not ignorant of their declaration, must enforce it; I am confident she wills it, and strong forbodings of it is discernible. The northern sections of the union is fast conceding, and the southern must comply, although so biased by interest, that they have become callous to the voice of reason and justice; yet as the continual droppings of water has a tendency to wear away the hardest and most flinty substance, so likewise shall we, abounding in good works, and causing our examples to shine forth as the sun at noonday, melt their callous hearts, and render sinewless the arm of sore oppression. My brethren, you who are enrolled and proudly march under the banners of the Mutual Relief, and Wilberforce Societies, consider your important standings as incorporated bodies, and walk worthy of the name you bear, cling closely to the paths of virtue and morality, cherish the plants of peace and temperance; by doing this you shall not only shine as the first stars in the firmament, and do honor to your worthy patrons, but immortalize your names. Be zealous and vigilant, be always on the alert to promote the welfare of your injured brethren; then shall providence shower down her blessings upon your heads, and crown your labors with success. It has been said by your enemies that your minds were not calculated to receive a sufficient store of knowledge to fit you for beneficial or social societies; but your incorporation drowned that assertion in contempt; and now let shame cover their heads, and blushes crimson their countenances. In vain they fostered a hope that our unfavorable circumstances would bear them out in their profane insinuations. But is that hope yet alive? No; or do we know where to find it? If it is to be found, it must be in the dark abysses of ignorance and folly, too little, too trifling for our notice.

There could be many reasons given, to prove that the mind of an African is not inferior to that of an European; yet to do so would be superfluous. It would be like adding hardness to the diamond, or lustre to the sun. There was a time whilst shrouded in ignorance, the African was estimated no higher than beasts of burthen, and while their minds were condensed within the narrow compass of slavery, and all their genius damped by the merciless power of cruel masters, they moved in no higher sphere. Their nature was cramped in infancy, and depraved in riper years, vice was showed them for virtue, and for their labor and industry, the scourge was their only reward. Then did they seem dead to a better state, but it was because they were subject to arbitrary power; and then did their proud oppressors assert, though against their better judgment, that they were destined by nature to no better inheritance. But their most prominent arguments are lighter than vanity, for vacuous must the reasons of that man have been, who dared to assert that genius is confined to complexion, or that nature knows difference in the immortal soul of man: No! the noble mind of a Newton could find room, and to spare, within the tenement of many an injured African.

My brethren, the time is fast approaching when the iron hand of oppression must cease to tyrannize over injured innocence, and very different are the days that we see, from those that our ancestors did; yet I know that there are thousands of our enemies who had rather see us exterminated from off the earth, than partake of the blessings that they enjoy; but their malice shall not be gratified; they will, though it blast their eyes, still see us in prosperity. Our daystar is arisen, and shall perform its diurnal revolutions, until nature herself shall change; and my heart glows with the idea, and kindles with joy, as my eye catches its radiant beams dispersing the dark clouds of ignorance and superstition. The spring is come, and the autumn nigh at hand, when the rich fruits of liberty shall be strewed in the paths of every African, or descendant, and the olive hedge of peace encompass them in from their enemies.

Some of the most profound historians inform us, that if there is any truth fully ascertained by reason or revelation, it is this; that man is but to be happy. Then it is evident that the human being never was formed for slavery; for between no two things in existence does there exist so irreconcilable opposition, as between the human mind and slavery. Water and oil, fire and snow, may, by the powerful arts of chemistry, be taught to forget their natural antipathies, and rush together into friendly embraces; but by no arts can human nature, even in the earliest stage of action, be taught to salute slavery as a friend—no! Take the child of three days old, confine him in some obscure cell; and at once you behold anxiety and misery fixed on his countenance; square his life there agreeable to your own rule, with all the tenderness that state will afford, but teach him not to crave liberty if you can. No, there is a something within him, tells him liberty is his own, and to have it is all his study; his noble mind without the help of arts and sciences, soars aloft and beholds throughout creation, to liberty all lay claim, from the almost undiscernible plant to the stately oak their liberty commands, the brute creation through their train enjoying all the liberty they are capable of and shall man who God created free and pronounced lord of his creation be enslaved by his fellow man, heaven forbid; man was made to be happy, therefore liberty is his undoubted right.

In all ages of the world, whether we take the present or retrospective view, we behold mankind worshiping at the shrine of liberty, and willingly sacrificing their all in pursuit of that fair goddess. We behold the rational man walk undauntedly in the very jaws of death to retain his liberty; he surmounts all difficulties; wades through all dangers; he industriously climbs the rough and craggy mount, and undauntedly leaps forth from its lofty and dangerous precipice if he but beholds the most distant gleams of liberty; so attractive, so congenial is liberty with the human heart; from the crowned monarch down to the lowest miscreant the world affords, all sue for this; yes, that particle of creation cannot be found that either by words or actions does not lay strong claim to this celestial good, and it is evident that all creation, both animal and vegetable, were destined to liberty, for neither can thrive or come to perfection without it, and he who called this world to light from the dark and loathsome abodes of chaos, caused liberty to be the golden pillars on which alone can happiness dwell secure.

Then Fathers, Brethren, and Friends, although depressed under many grievances, yet the strong fibres of that pressure must give way, and the time is not far distant when our tree of liberty shall reach the sun, and its branches spread from pool to pool. Then let us stand firm in union, let us transmit to ages yet to come, deeds that shall bear record with time and not find their rival; let us cultivate the minds of youth; let your examples clothed with wisdom be strewed in their paths; by you let their tender minds be impressed with humane principles; let your virtues shine conspicuously before them, as lamps that shall light them to a glorious victory over their enemies, and conduct them to the haven of immortal bliss; let malice and hatred be far from your doors; let your hearts be linked in the chain that bids defiance to the intrigues of your enemies; let not the cries of the widow and the orphan pass you unnoticed: although this happy land abounds with humane institutions, yet has your individual aid, opportunities to alleviate the miseries of thousands. Many are the miseries of our exiled race in this land, and dark are the clouds that shrouds them in woe. O! then, let us call forth our every power, arrayed in wisdom and ornamented with virtue, such as shall gain the applause of men and be sanctioned by God; these shall alleviate their present miseries and finally burst with the refulgent beams of liberty on their devoted heads.

And, O! thou father of the universe and disposer of events, thou that called from a dark and formless mass this fair system of nature, and created thy sons and daughters to bask in the golden streams and rivulets contained therein; this day we have convened under thy divine auspices, it's not to celebrate a political festivity, or the achievement of arms by which the blood of thousands were spilt, contaminating thy pure fields with human gore! but to commemorate a period brought to light by thy wise counsel, who stayed the hand of merciless power; and with hearts expanded with gratitude for thy providences, inundated in the sea of thy mercies, we farther crave thy fostering care. O! wilt thou crush that power that still holds thousands of our brethren in bondage, and let the sea of thy wisdom wash its very dust from off the face of the earth; let Liberty unfurl her banners, Freedom and Justice reign triumphant in the world, universally.

AN

ORATION

OF THE

ABOLITION OF THE SLAVE TRADE.

BY RUSSELL PARROTT.

Delivered on the First of January, 1814.

AT THE

African Church of St. Thomas.

PHILADELPHIA:
PRINTED FOR THE DIFFERENT SOCIETIES,
BY THOMAS T. STILES
1814.

AGAIN selected, my brethren, to bear a conspicuous part in the celebration of the abolition of the slave trade, I should do injustice to my feelings, did I let the present opportunity escape without expressing my warmest thanks for the undeserved honour this second time conferred upon me; and though poor in talent, and one of that unfortunate portion of mankind that unrelenting prejudice has cast in the background of society, my most strenuous effort shall be to portray, in language of unadorned truth, the wrongs and sufferings of unhappy Africa, by that traffic which has long disgraced the civilized world.

The discovery of America opened a new era in the affairs of Europe: the immense treasures that inundated the mother country, the highly coloured descriptions of its soil, climate and resources,

spread such an universal desire of gain, that it pervaded all ranks of
society, from the peasant to the king. It is from this period that we
may date the commencement of the sufferings of the Africans, and
the discovery of the new world; which, to one portion of the human
family, has afforded such advantages, to the unfortunate African, has
been the source of the greatest misery; it was the precursor of his
sufferings, his misery; and it removed him many ages from that state
of civilization which his natural genius entitled him to enjoy.

The infamous barbarities committed by the Spaniards in their
newly discovered possessions upon the unoffending inhabitants,
caused some few pious men, who migrated for the purpose of
promulgating the Christian religion, to lay their sufferings before
the government, who, to save the aborigines from slavery, cast the
shackles upon the African—an inconsistency no way to be reconciled
with those immutable principles of justice, which give stability and
glory to authority. The magnanimous prince who at that time swayed
the united sceptres of Spain and Germany, although by the advice
of bad counsellors, he suffered this horrid traffic to disgrace for a
short time an otherwise splendid reign, he formally declared, that
within his dominions, slavery should not exist. On the abdication of
the throne by Charles, avarice again triumphed over justice, and the
piratical Portuguese, who were the first violators of the rights of the
African, again could find a market, to vend him and his posterity to
perpetual bondage. England, too, at this time, had acquired large
possessions in America; they were not so populous as those of their
neighbour, and it was proposed to Elizabeth, the then reigning
sovereign, to populate her newly acquired domains, by the introduction of Africans: it is said, she expressly forbade any force to be
used; but, such was the profligacy of the times, that the calls of humanity and justice were totally disregarded, and scenes of cruelty
and rapine commenced, that would have disgraced the most gothic
ages of society: man assumed the nature of the savage; plucked
from his bosom every sentiment of pity; and, to gratify his accursed
avarice, devoted to lasting bondage his equal, man.

The slave trade, the partial abolition of which, we this day meet
to celebrate, has filled this earth with more moral turpitude than
any other event that has ever occurred. Its iniquity was great, but
the heart-rending sufferings of the unfortunates who fell within its
vortex are beyond my feeble description. Fancy yourself on the
fertile plains of Africa—see, reposing beneath the luxuriant foliage of
the palm, the child of her soil—say he is a father, surrounded by a
flock of innocents, whose endearing, artless prattle has bound him to
his paternal home with ties stronger than adamant—providence has

blessed him with a competency, and to make that blessing sure, has made him contented—here is the land of his nativity—here dwells his father, his mother, the partner of his affection, and the friend of his heart; when in the midst of his domestic enjoyment, a fiend steals in and mars all his happiness; the slave merchant, whose steps are marked by desolation and dismay, at one stroke destroys all his sublunary joys; tears from the bosom of his family, the poor African! No tears, no entreaties, will avail; in vain he tells him that a numerous offspring depend upon him for sustenance; that an affectionate wife looks with anxious solicitude for his return; he shrieks with all the violence of desperate anguish—all, all, is lost! he is hurried to the bark, prepared for his reception, where begins the career of his ignomy, and his sufferings. Here, with himself, he finds immured hundreds of his unfortunate countrymen, whose agonizing groans, and the terrific sound of whose chains, adds fresh fuel to his grief. Hope, delusive hope, amidst all his sombre prospects, holds out one faint, one glimmering ray, that an opportunity to escape may occur;— how vain, how illusory. The signal for departure is made; he sees the home of his affections, recede from his sight—mute and immoveable, he stands;—the transition, from joy most perfect, to woe, is so sudden, that reason is banished, and wild despair usurps her seat. What language can tell the feelings of his soul? what pen portray the intenseness of his grief? The bustle of departure over, these worse than freebooters, have time to turn their attention to their prey. The cruelties perpetrated on board of the slave ship, are such, that to the superficial observer of human nature, it would appear as the effusion of romance, that within the small compass of a vessel, enormities are committed that would make "angels weep." There decrepit age, bending beneath the weight of years, and new afflictions; there dejected youth, with all his glowing prospects blasted, while yet in his morning—some emaciated with disease, contracted by inhaling an unhealthy atmosphere, rendered so by the multitude that are confined in these receptacles of misery; some suffering from the effects of torture, a mutilated limb, or a lacerated body; some driven to desperation by famine, make an attempt to sacrifice their tyrants. Armed but by frenzy, they are soon driven from the deck, with slaughter and death. Some, impelled by the hope of revisiting their native land, seek a passage to her shores through the yielding waves.—The passage is one continued scene of suffering and barbarity. A cargo (if I must so term it) of slaves, who on account of the badness of the food, and the number that were crowded together, many were daily emancipated from their chains by the kind hand of death, when these monsters in human shape, to recover the insurance from the underwriters, cast into the sea the sick and the disabled. To what lengths will not the love of lucre drive mankind; what crimes will it not cause them to commit.

Instances of individual sufferings are so numerous that their recital would extort a tear from hearts that never wept before. They, whose fortitude or whose constitution bear them through the middle passage, are on the arrival of the ship, exposed for sale. It is now that the bond of relationship, the ties of friendship and affection, more closely cemented by a reciprocity of sufferings, are for a second time to be rent asunder. With the purchaser, it is not whether he separates parents and children, or husband and wife; a thought of this kind never enters his cold, calculating soul; but if such or such a one, will suit him best. The sale ended, conceive the affliction of separation, for my imperfect language cannot tell it—In spite of all the calls of humanity, they are forced from each other's embrace, and doomed to disgrace and labour. The slave is now placed under a code of laws (if laws they can be called); he is considered as a part of the brute creation; the master is invested with a complete control over him; can either sell or kill him; let his oppressions be what they may, there is no tribunal for the slave to apply to for redress; he is entirely at the mercy of his tyrant, for whom he is compelled to spend the remainder of his wretched existence, in ceaseless toil. If labouring under a meridian sun, he should faint, the lash is his restorative. If, after suffering with heroic fortitude an accumulation of wrong and contumelies that would have laid his persecutors in the dust, he should survive, it is called barbarous insensibility. If he celebrates in uncouth strains, the departure of some dear friend from scenes of persecution and distress, it is called inhumanity. His mental faculties are depressed, and ignorance inculcated witih the most studious assiduity, and then he is represented as being incapable of receiving instruction; ingenuity is tortured to assimilate him to the brute, as a justification for his inhuman treatment. Thus depressed, it excites wonder that the least ray of rationality should expand itself. What inducement has the unfortunate slave to call into action those talents which only impart lustre to the character of the freeman; no prospects of reward or honour open to his view; to him, all is hopeless misery. By what right does man thus compel his fellow creature to suffer? my bosom burns with indignation while I make the inquiry. The religion which we profess does not sanction it— the plea that they are principally prisoners taken in war, and who would, according to the custom of savage nations, be put to death if not sold into captivity, will not justify the slave merchant, when it is known that to their corruptive influence are owing most of the wars that have desolated unhappy Africa for more than a century. What right has the conqueror to dispose of the liberties of the captive, whom the fortune of war has thrown in his power? That he has the power we acknowledge, but power and right are terms quite dissimilar in their signification; and as man receives his liberty with his existence, from God, no earthly power has the right to take it from him. Again, it is asserted that many of them are criminals, who have forfeited their lives to the offended laws of their country. They who violate the social compact, deserve punishment; but that punishment should be commensurate with the crime committed. The unhappy culprit, who is doomed to suffer perpetual servitude, and whose guiltless posterity are included in the unhappy number, is punished beyond the measure of his crimes.

They say they save from an ignominious death, those whom they bear into slavery; he whose crimes deserve this dreadful punishment, let him suffer; because there is no virtue in letting loose upon society a wretch whose enormities and whose crimes are such that human nature is disgraced by his existence. But death brings no ignominy with it when it is inflicted in our country's service.

They say the slave's situation is more happy, he is better fed and clad, than the poor of civilized Europe. Can he claim the proud privilege of being a citizen of the country in which he resides, can he lay his hand on his heart, and with honest confidence say, her law is no respecter of persons, and in her eye I enjoy equal privileges with the rich and powerful? No! ye sophists whom avarice has armed in her cause, dress up the Negro's situation in your gayest colours, say he enjoys a paradise on earth; but when you say he is a slave, the visionary description fades before our sight, and shows his truly wretched situation. The baneful effects of the slave trade were diffused through all the mass of society engaged in it. The generous sailor, whose bosom glows with all the social virtues, engaged in the slave trade, becomes quite a different being, loses those traits of generosity that characterize him when engaged in more honourable employment. The man surrounded by an hundred human creatures, whose lives are at his disposal, subject to his caprice, is in miniature, what Nero was in magnitude, the tyrant and oppressor of his species. —That a traffic so marked by iniquity, so replete with every enormity, should have so long existed, excites our wonder and regret.

The oppression of the Africans called down the interposition of Providence, and among the names whom the Deity selected as the accomplishers of the great work of abolition, stand preeminent those

of Sharp, Clarkson, Gregoire, Wilberforce; with our own countrymen, Sewel, Benezet, Delwin, and tho' last mentioned, yet first in
our affection, Rush, the philosopher and the philanthropist, in whom
the cause of humanity has found one of the most indefatigable
friends. The sphere of his usefulness was confined to no particular
science, nor to any particular virtue—he was familiar with all; he,
with true philanthropy, viewed the whole human family as his
brethren! and that vast stock of information which he possessed, as
the peculiar gift of heaven, for their good. When pestilence hovered
over this fair city, shaking from her wings pale disease; when every
avenue was filled with scenes of horror and distress, when the bonds
of consanguinity were not strong enough to bind together families;
when the child forsook his parent, the parent its partner, it was then,
that with unshaken firmness he stood, when all, whose circumstances
would permit, had fled, struck with fear; even then, in the abodes of
penury and sickness, without prospect of fee or reward, he was
found, acting in the double capacity of physician and priest, and
while his skilful hand baffled the power of disease, he poured the
balm of heavenly consolation upon the wounded heart.—In truth,
we may say that he was commissioned from on high, to be thy
guardian angel, Philadelphia, in the darkest hours of peril and
affliction. Early in life, he stepped forward as a friend of the abolition of slavery; and during a period of thirty years, he was the true
friend of the people of colour. The melioration of their situation was
a subject nigh to his heart. The abolition of the slave trade, he knew
to be an act of justice due to the cause of humanity; and the emancipation of those held in slavery, absolutely necessary to secure from
the imputation of inconsistency the character of his country. To a
man of his enlarged and generous mind, these were sufficient excite-
ments to call into action his talents and his virtues. The claims of
the black to the privileges of freedom, he ably and successfully contended for. That they were a portion of the great human family
was a truth that he assisted in establishing on a firm basis.

The loss of this great and good man is sensibly felt by us; he
was our father, our counsellor, and our protector: long shall his name
and his services be remembered with gratitude by the African and
his descendants.

He was a man of such rare and sterling virtue that his name was
familiar to the literati of every country, who conceived themselves
honoured by associating him in their different learned bodies—princes
sought, and thought themselves exalted by, his friendship. After a
life of three score and seven years, a great majority of which was

dedicated to the service of mankind, Rush, the just, sunk into the arms of death.

> The good man's end was peace—how calm his exit.
> Night dews fall not more gently to the ground—
> Nor weary worn out winds, expire so soft.

With such a constellation of talents and virtue opposed to that mass of corruption, the slave trade, we are not surprised that the monster fell, after rioting for more than a century in the blood and tears of millions of the human species.

How diminutive are the glories of the greatest potentates, when compared with the achievements of that host of worthies who accomplished the abolition. They contended, not to enslave, but to liberate; not to depress, but to exalt; they have, by their exertions in this righteous cause, not only secured an immortal name here, but an eternal reward hereafter; and when the names of your Alexanders, your Cæsars, and your Bonapartes, are remembered but to be execrated, theirs shall be cherished with filial reverence. The genius of philanthropy shall be their historian; and shall inscribe in glowing characters, on the grateful heart (more durably than on tablets of marble or brass) their many virtues.

The abolition of the slave trade is one of the greatest events that mark the present age. It was a sacrifice that virtue compelled avarice to make, at the shrine of justice, as her first oblation. And, when to this is added the emancipation of those already in bondage, the triumph of philanthropy will be complete; when man shall no longer be stigmatised by the name of slave, and heaven's first, best gift, be universally enjoyed. That freedom is the natural inheritance of man, is a truth that neither sophistry nor interest can shake; and the being that exists from under her benign rays, can neither be exhilarated by the influence of learning, nor warmed into a proper knowledge of himself, by religion. If the security of a country should rest within her bosom, then it is necessary that each citizen should be a freeman.

Pennsylvania, first in virtue, first in patriotism, to the wisdom of thy councils, and the firmness of thy magistrates, we are indebted for the privileges we now enjoy. By this act of justice, you have secured to yourself a band of citizens who will not forsake you in the hour of danger, whose bosoms are ready to be bared in your service, and whose blood will cheerfully flow in your defense. May you ever remain the sanctuary of liberty, and may your sacred portals never be polluted by the violators of the rights of man.

That we are faithful to our country, we have abundantly proved: where her Hull, her Decatur, and her Bainbridge, fought and conquered, the black bore his part, stimulated by the pure love of country, which neither contempt nor persecution can eradicate from his generous heart. With a jewel of such inestimable value within her bosom, the cheering smiles of that country should not be withheld by narrow-minded prejudice.

Abolition! already are thy blessings diffusing themselves; already Africa experiences its blessed effects; confidence is again restored between man and man—whole villages are no longer depopulated, to glut that insatiable monster, avarice; mild religion begins to unfold her heavenly truth, through this former land of paganism and error— and over the ruins of the altars that idolatry had reared, the sacred temple points its spire towards heaven. Civilization, with her attending handmaids, agriculture and industry, infuses cheerfulness over the face of nature, and inspires the husbandman with gratitude and joy.

Liberty! thou exhilarating soother of human hearts, may thy presence, like the sun, illuminate every soil, and brighten every countenance; may thy animating smiles enliven the humble dwelling of the Negro of Africa, as well as the courts and cottages of more favoured climes; may neither the tide of time obliterate, nor the combination of avarice, inhumanity, and injustice, be ever able to eradicate from the human breast, this heaven-born truth, that man was formed for the enjoyments of thy influence, and that without thee, creation is a cheerless blank.

AN

ORATION,

ON THE

ABOLITION OF THE SLAVE TRADE,

DELIVERED

IN

The Episcopal

Asbury African Church,

IN ELIZABETH-ST.
NEW YORK, JANUARY 2, 1815.

By William Hamilton,
A DESCENDANT OF AFRICA.

NEW YORK:
PRINTED BY C. W. BUNCE,
FOR THE N.Y. AFRICAN SOCIETY:
1815.

IT may not be amiss, my brethren, to commence this part of the
exercise of this day, with a description of the country of our parents.
Here let me observe, that when I first turned my mind on the
subject for this day, I had intended instead of what would be in me,
a vain attempt at oratory, or rhetorical flourishes, to have given as
far as in my power lay, a plain instructive address; but I am sorry

to say, the resources from whence I intended to draw materials for such an address were entirely without my reach. I am therefore obliged to content myself with what I shall now offer.

We shall first give the geographical situation of Africa, that is, its place on this globe or earth. Its latitude is 37 deg. north and 34 deg.° south of the equator, or the middle distance of the sun's perigrination north and south, so that the sun, its extreme distance never 'stretching beyond 23½ deg. north or south of the equator, it never reaches beyond the boundaries of Africa.

We hereby see that Africa lies immediately under the influence of the sun, for its rays fall obliquely, when at its greatest distance, north on Africa's extreme northerly line, only about 13½ deg. and southerly only 10½. (We shall make some use of this directly.) Its longitude is 17 deg. west, and 51 deg. east of London, that is, when the sun is at its meridian, or it is noon at London, from that place in Africa that the sun is at its meridian at the same time to Africa's extreme westerly line, is 17 deg. and extreme easterly line is 51 deg.

The form of Africa is a three-sided figure; its northerly side is bounded by the Mediterranean Sea, which separates it from Europe; its easterly side, by a neck of land called the Isthmus of Suez, which separates it from Asia, by the Red Sea, and by the Indian or Southern Ocean; its westerly side, is bounded by the great Atlantic Ocean, which separates it from America.

Of this description we shall make the following use: first, that Africa, being situated in the middle of the Globe, surrounded by the other continents, to wit, Asia, Europe, and America, in case of an universal Empire, she would make a grand eligible situation for the seat of Authority, and who knows—as she has descended to the ultimate point of degradation—but she may ascend to the zenith of glory and aggrandizement.

Next, as the nations of the Earth generally agree that mankind had an original, and as our religion teaches the same, would not Africa have made (she lying immediately under the fostering care of the sun) an eligible situation for the growth of man in his first state of existence? Let each study the nature of man, and answer the question for himself.

From these speculative thoughts, we turn to give a short account of the history of Africa; here were we disposed to dwell, we have an ample field before us; for Africa has a long, and in some parts, a proud account to give of herself. She can boast of her antiquity, of

° The speaker omitted the minutes exceeding the degrees of latitude and longitude from motives of ease to himself.

her philosophers, her artists, her statesmen, her generals; of her curi-
osities, her magnificent cities, her stupendous buildings, and of her
once widespread commerce. Our account shall be as plain and as
simple as we can give.

That part of the continent known by the name of Egypt is the
part that history gives its first account of; and is divided into what
is called upper and lower Egypt—the one the Southern, the other the
Northern division—of the origin of this settlement we have no
authentic account: the natives claim an antiquity beyond what we
are willing to believe, but of so ancient a date it is, that some of the
most learned believe, for reasons it would be out of our way to give,
that China, that very ancient settlement, was originally a colony
peopled from Egypt; perhaps we cannot do better than here to introduce an account given by a nation found in the interior of the
country (which account agrees with that given by the most learned),
who say they were originally of that part of Egypt where the magnificent City of Thebes was built, which is described as having its
hundred gates.

They tell us that Egypt was anciently settled by an honest, industrious, peaceable and well-disposed people; that they were divided
into distinct parts, or hordes, with a father or chief to each horde,
and one general, chief, or father to the whole, that each horde followed some useful employment, and that some of each horde made
the sciences their particular study, and that these became the teachers of the youth, that they were all rich alike, for that one common
storehouse clothed and fed them, that they lived in peace and quietness, until a wicked nation entered and laid waste their country, making slaves of some of the inhabitants, and put to death others, and
that as many of the hordes as escaped, chose rather to leave the
country in the possession of this savage people, than shed the blood
of their fellow men; of these each family or horde, went to seek a
place for themselves in the interior of the country. The name given
to their invaders is one that agrees with Josephuses, king's shepherds,
or king's beasts.

They further state that this wanton people were driven out by a
hero of mixed blood by the name of Sos (or perhaps the great
Sesostris, famous in the history of Egypt), under whose wise laws
Egypt again enjoyed prosperity and peace; and after a lapse of time,
Egypt was again overrun by a nation more wicked than the first, and
who committed greater enormities; and again the inhabitants sought
an asylum in the interior. The last, my brethren, may be the people
driven out of Canaan by Joshua; for it is said of a people that invaded Egypt, when they were asked of what country they were, we

are of Canaan driven out by Jesus or Joshua the Robber. From this account, we shall draw the following inferences.

First, that those inhabitants that occupy the country from the tropic of Cancer to the cape of Good Hope were originally from Egypt.

Secondly, that they were an industrious, honest, peaceable people.

Thirdly, as it was an attachment to a peaceable life that made them leave their native soil and seek an asylum in another clime, they must have remained the same peaceable, just, and honest, people for a long series of time.

And as Africa, with the exception of her sandy deserts, is very fertile, producing its fruits with very little labour of the husbandman, and as virtue carries with it no corroding thoughts, they must have been a very happy people.

But O! Africa, thou first fair garden of God's planting, thou once delightful field and original nursery for all those delicious fruits, tasteful herbage, and fragrant plants, that man highly prises, thou track of earth over which the blest luminary, the sun, delights to make his daily splendid pass, thou spot of earth, where fair science first descended and the arts first began to bud and grow; how art thou chang'd and fallen.

Yes, my brethren, from once perhaps the most happy people the earth ever knew, to the most miserable under heaven. But such is the nature of the case, that to them that forc'd on her the cup of misery, to them shall be dealt an equal cup of bitterness.

Look at the present state of the present inhabitants of Egypt. Sunk, and they shall continue to sink, until they are on a level with the worm they crush beneath their feet; no effort can save them.

Look at the Portuguese, the first traders in African blood and sinews, and the Spaniards, the base followers of so base an example: have they not for more than a century been sinking into a state of effeminacy, weakness and degradation, do they hold the proud standing in the rank of nations they did two centuries ago? No, and they shall continue to sink, altho they may, like a dying man, sometimes seem to revive, until they are below the Africans they have so debased, or until the memory of them is obliterated from the nations of the earth. It is fortunate for England that she is making something like an atonement for her more than base treatment of the African people.

We would here proceed to give the origin of that trade whose character is marked with African gore, and carried with it rapine and murder, only that its origin has been treated of by those who have addressed us heretofore on these occasions.

I shall content myself with observing that the trade was began by white men, and by Europeans, by men who boast of the proud trust they put in the book that tells us "with what measure you mete to others, shall be meted to you again." By men who boast of their superior understanding, their superior genius, their superior souls.

Their boasted superiority was set to work at the basest employment. When they first explored the western, and eastern shores of Africa, they found the natives a peaceable, simple, unsuspicious people.

They set to work that low, sly, wicked, cunning, peculiar to the Europeans, to the creating of jealousies and animosity, one horde or nation with another. To those princes who were proof against their vile craftiness they administered draughts of their intoxicating spirituous liquor and then distilled in them their base purposes.

Thus they laboured until Africa became one continued scene of suspicion, mad jealousy, confusion, war, rapine, blood and murder.

No longer was the banjo and the drum the call to the dance and to glee, but the signals to the work of destruction; no sooner does those instruments that used to be the call to pleasure strike the ear, than the mother clasps her infant in her arms and flies to the thicket for shelter to hide from the foe: the father and the sons grasp the weapons of defense, and prepare to meet the attack.

O! Africa, what carnage hast thou witnessed; thy flesh, thy bones, thy very vitals have been torn from thee.

The question will hardly arise, what was all this butchery set on foot for? if it should, I will tell you my brethren; for sordid gain, the white man's God.

They purchased the captives taken in war for gewgaws and for draughts of that intoxicating liquor that is sometimes the bane of the peace of families among themselves, and sold them again at an advanced price.

Other base modes were set on foot besides that of war. One of which was they sent out parties, who hid themselves in the thicket by day, and at night, surrounded the peaceful hamlet, and made prisoners of its inhabitants.

The Europeans were not satisfied with planting settlements and carrying off what they ought to have considered the riches of the country: its gold, its dye-woods, its medicinal plants, &c. Nothing would satisfy them but the blood and sinews of its inhabitants. Like Shylock, nothing but a pound of flesh nearest the heart.

Nor were they satisfied with making slaves of them in their own country, and enjoying the benefit of their labour on their own soil.

They were not contented with this, they must prepare their floating dungeons, or rather floating hells manned with fiends. Yes, my brethren, hells manned with fiends, I will not retract, nor ask pardon for the warmth of expression, for they deserve no better name, and it would be impossible for me to talk coolly, when the slave trade is the subject.

Some nations have painted their devil in the complexion of a white man. View the history of the slave trade, and then answer the question, could they have made choice of a better likeness to have drawn from? All that low, sly, artful, wicked, cunning attributed to him, was practised by them. All the insulting scorn, savage cruelty, and tormenting schemes, practised by him, were executed by them.

Yes, my brethren, I repeat it; they prepared their floating hells manned with fiends, to carry the Africans across a wide ocean, to a new-explored continent, to wit, America. Would to God that Columbus with his exploring schemes had perished in Europe ere he touched the American Isles; or that Americus had perished in the ocean ere he explored the southern parts of the Continent; or rather that the hateful Cortes, with his murderous band, had been swallowed by an earthquake ere he reached the City of Mexico. Then might Africa been spared the terrible calamity she has suffered; pardon me my brethren I seem to wander.

On ship-board in their passage from Africa, they were treated with the most horrible cruelty that the imagination can conceive of.

The murderous scenes in Africa were delightful, compared with these. But we will spare your ears the recital of a tale that would curdle your blood, and the wish you had been there with an arm strong enough to have dashed the perpetrators to death, would stiffen your sinews, and like the citizens gathered around Mark Anthony, make you mad for revenge on the murderers of your brethren.

Permit me to relate one of the lightest scenes of this tragical drama. An infant of ten months old, had taken sulk on board of a slave ship, that is, refused to eat; the savage captain with his knotted cat whipped it until its body and legs had much swollen, he then ordered it in water so hot, that its skin and nails came off; he then bound it in oilcloth; he after a few days whipped it again, swearing he would make it eat or kill it; in a few hours after it expired, he then ordered the mother to throw her murdered infant overboard, she refused, he beat her until she took it up, turned her head aside, and dropped it into the sea. Now tell me my brethren, is there in God's domain other and worse fiends than these?

But we will hasten. Our parents were brought originally to this country to supply the place of the aborigines; the Spaniards had found that these could not bear the burden they had put on them.

The Indians were fast dwindling away: they thought that Africans would make better beasts of burden, yes, my brethren, beasts of burden they were, and such they still are.

The European with his bloated pride, conceives himself an order of being above any other order of men, and because ye have found out their vein and sometimes fawn on and flatter them, and call them master, a name they ought to despise, for the odium it carries with it when used between men. They think you have really given into their whim, and acknowledge them a superman, or demigod. But still I wander, yes my brethren, the Africans were brought over to supply the place of Indians, or native Americans, to do the drudgery of the new-found world, as it is sometimes called by way of eminence, but to them a new-found place of misery. Soon were the extensive shores of America covered with the best sons and daughters of Africa; toiling as slaves for men to whom they had never forfeited their right to freedom, and who had no better claim to them than the thief, or the purchaser of stolen goods, knowing them to be such, have to their booty; (and if it was not stepping out of our way we would prove they have not half the right) but the labouring was not all, the more than cruel barbarous treatment they underwent, such as the mind sickens at first glance at; it was not enough that in Africa they should set on foot wars, rapine, and murder! it was not enough to tear from her, her sons and her daughters? it was not enough that on ship-board they should be confined in stenchful holes, crowded together like common lumber, fettered with irons, tortured with thumb-screws and other instruments of cruelty: it was not enough they should be slaves in a foreign country, far from all that was dear to them, and there made to toil and labour and face a scorching sun each day, with a very scanty miserable meal. All this, and the picture is not half drawn. But still, like Shylock, "nothing but the pound of flesh nearest the heart;" nothing would satiate but that an iron-hearted fellow must be placed over them, with his knotted scourge to quicken them with the smart thereof to labour: it was not enough that the father whose heart writhing with anguish, had inadvertently stopped his work to contemplate his misery, in being torn from his loving wife, and dear prattling infants, he should be awakened from his reverie by the whip from the driver, making long furrows in his back: it was not enough that the lad who had been the hope of his father and pride of his mother, when casting a wishful thought toward home, should forget for the moment to work the hoe; should be startled to a sense of his neglect, by the flesh-cutting stroke of the driver's whip: it was not enough that the tender girl, once the pleasure of her mother, and darling of her father, who had stopped to wipe away a fallen tear, at the supposed auguish of her parents, should receive from an arm that ought to have been palsied at the stroke, the heart-stinging lash of the driver, but still the pound of flesh nearest the heart: the mother! the tender mother, with her more tender infant lashed to her back, and her feet clogged with weights. Because, with a mind torn with anguish, her thoughts had turned on him she had each day hailed with joy, the partner of her better days.

She had dropped her hoe; the cruel driver with his lacerating stroke; but we will turn from the scene, it is too disgusting. We seem to catch the blow to save the victim.

If these are some of the marks of superiority may heaven in mercy always keep us inferior: go, proud white men; go, boast of your superior cunning; the fox, the wolf, the tyger, are more cunning than their prey.

But my brethren, we are this day called on to rejoice: to rejoice that the sadness of a long gloomy night is passed away, and that the fair opening of a better day is before us. To rejoice that the venomed monster, that Hydra with seven heads, is expiring. To rejoice that the slave trade, that cursed viper that fed on Africa's vitals; from the Danish, the British, and the American commerce, is swept away. To rejoice, that the friends of humanity have triumphed over our foes. Yes my brethren; among white men, are found, after all this shocking picture of their wickedness, men who are indeed the friends of humanity. Such was the good Anthony Benezet, such is the great, good, and immortal Mr. Wilberforce; and such is that angelically good man, Mr. Tho. Clarkson, whose name ought never to be pronounced by us but with the highest esteem and gratitude. Our children should be taught in their little songs, to lisp the name of Clarkson: he laboured in the field for the abolition of the slave trade, literally day and night, with very little time to refresh himself with sleep. Twenty years did Mr. Clarkson labour for the abolition of the slave trade. His labours were finally successful: too much cannot be said in his praise. In the British Parliament, long and hard was the struggle for the destruction of this trade: and it was shameful for Britain, who boasts so much of her strong attachment to liberty, and humanity, that the struggle should be so long.

Of the Danish nation we can say nothing; except their having agreed to abolish the trade ten years after they passed a law to that effect.

In Congress of these United States, the motion for the abolition of the slave trade was brought on by a Mr. Bradley, a gentleman from Vermont: among our other friends from this State, was that excellent gentleman, and friend of man, Dr. Mitchel* a member from this city; the motion was opposed by members from the southern section of these United States. Why they opposed, we know not: except their guilty souls, fearful that it would bring on Mr. Jefferson's doomsday, that made him tremble for the fate of his country, when he reflected that God was just; and had no attribute wherewith to favour their cause. But they writhed and twisted as long as they could; but the friends of humanity triumphed: it was the Lord's doing, and it is marvelous in our eyes.

To him be the praise, we add no more.

ROBT. F. WILLIAMS.	ADAM CRUMP.
SANDY LATTION.	SAMUEL READ.
JOHN GOFF.	JOHN J. JOHNSON.
RICHARD DEAN.	JAMES JAROME.
BENJAMIN SMITH.	JOHN J. MORRIS.
THOMAS SIPKINS.	ROBT. Y. SYDNEY.
ANDREW SMITH.	

* The motion was brought on in the Senate; Dr. Mitchel seconded it.

Part VI

Saints and Sinners,

1786–1836

The selections collected in this section include a narrative, sermons, letters and addresses, and autobiographies and autobiographical confessions. They are a random sampling of "lives" which were only alike in their resistance to or revolt against capricious and oppressive social conditions or in their quixotic combativeness toward those evils in American society which stood in the way of the righteous and the black. While autobiographical confession can hardly be considered an important class of early Afro-American literature, two specimens are offered here which may contribute to a better understanding of the social obstacles and frustrations which bore down upon some blacks in Colonial times and after. John Green's *Life and Confession* was printed as a broadside and sold by Isaiah Thomas, a master printer of Boston and Worcester. Though the broadside probably had a wide circulation, today only two copies are extant. Richard Allen, to whom John Joyce made his confession, came close to presenting the life and deeds of the condemned man as a morality play in which the proceedings of the trial, the "Confession," and Allen's exhortatory *Address to the Public and People of Colour* were three well-defined parts.

Universal Salvation: A Very Ancient Doctrine, a sermon by Lemuel Haynes, a mulatto Congregational minister who lived nearly all of his life and pursued a churchman's career among whites, has been generally regarded as a choice example of early New England pulpit eloquence. It is also regarded as "most important in a study of the psychological reasons underlying race prejudice in America."[1]

[1] Vernon Loggins, *The Negro Author: His Development in America* (New York: Columbia University Press, 1931), p. 122. For additional information on Haynes, see Timothy M. Cooley, *Sketches of the Life and Character of the Rev. Lemuel Haynes. . .* (New York, 1839).

*The Address to the Wyandot Nation and Letter to William
Walker* reveals a life in interesting contrast to that of Haynes,
though both pursued the path and goals of Christian ministry. John
Stewart's extraordinary conversion from "sinner" to "believer" was
followed almost immediately by a prolonged period of successful
though arduous missionary work among the Wyandot Indians in
Sandusky, Ohio. John Stewart, a free mulatto, was the first successful missionary to the Wyandot Indians. Raised in Powhattan County,
Virginia he was early converted to Christianity and subsequently
licensed to preach in the Methodist Episcopal Church. Accompanied
at times by two Indian chiefs and an interpreter, his life among the
Wyandots is colorful and convincing. Stewart's work among the
Indians led to the establishment of the Methodist Missionary Society
on April 5, 1819, in New York.[2]

The popularity of John Marrant's *Narrative* may have been due
in part to the widespread interest in tales of Indian captivity; much
of the *Narrative* relates to Marrant's life among the Indians. Numerous editions were published between the years 1785 and 1829,
both in England and in the United States. They appeared under
three different though similar titles. The 1802 edition is included in
this work because it includes evidence of authenticity.

John Marrant was born in New York City in 1755 and at the age
of five was taken by his mother to St. Augustine, about seven hundred miles from New York City. He was sent to school and taught
to read and spell. Eighteen months later, his mother took her family
to Georgia where he remained until age eleven. Marrant next went to
Charles Town where he hoped to learn a trade, but became interested in music and eventually learned to play well the French horn
and the violin. It was during one of George Whitefield's fiery
sermons in Charles Town that Marrant was converted to Christianity.
He had gone to the meeting with a companion who had urged him
to blow his French horn while Whitefield was speaking. Marrant
relates in the *Narrative* that, just before he was to blow his horn, the
great divine looked straight at him, saying, "Prepare to meet thy
God, O Israel." The Lord accompanied his word with such power
that Marrant fell to the ground unconscious. Marrant was soon converted to Christianity and became perhaps the first Negro minister

---

[2] His name appears as Steward and Stewart. See Charles Elliott *Indian
Missionary Reminiscences, Principally of the Wyandott Nation* (New
York, 1837); Joseph Mitchell, *The Missionary Pioneer; or, a Brief Memoir
of the Life, Labours and Death of John Stewart (Man of Colour) Founder,
under God of the Mission Among the Wyandotts at Upper Sandusky,
Ohio* (New York, 1827).

of the Gospel in North America. He learned an Indian language from an Indian hunter. Years before John Mitchell preached to the Wyandot Indians, John Marrant carried the teachings of Jesus Christ not only to the Cherokees, but also to the Creeks, the Catawas, and the Housaws.

Marrant served in the Revolutionary War, during which he was carried to the West Indies. After recuperating from illness and wounds suffered in the war, he went to London, where he lived three years with a friendly merchant. At Bath he was ordained. He returned to the United States with the help of the Countess of Huntingdon. Marrant was made a Mason by Prince Hall (in his African Lodge No. 459), who requested Marrant to preach a sermon on the occasion of the festival of St. John the Baptist, June 24, 1789.[3]

The passionate eloquence of Maria W. Stewart—one of the earliest if not the first black woman lecturer, whose published speeches stressed the necessity for self-improvement or education and moral resistance to the oppressor—is by any measure remarkable for a woman of her day. She tried to set an example of heart-searching prayer, prayerful confession, and moral resoluteness by her well-composed meditations, which were undoubtedly modeled on the Psalms of David. *Religion and the Pure Principles of Morality* is one of six speeches published in 1835 under the title Productions of Mrs. Maria W. Stewart. This speech first appeared in 1831 as a pamphlet. Other addresses were published in *The Liberator*.[4]

Theodore Wright's pious and consolatory *Pastoral Letter Addressed to the Colored Presbyterian Church of New York* seems by contrast to have an Apostolic flavor. Wright studied at Princeton University where he was a student between 1825 and 1828. While there he completed a course in Theology. As pastor of the First Colored Presbyterian Church, Wright strongly opposed the colonization movement. With Samuel E. Cornish he published a pamphlet on the colonization scheme that explained why colonization was rejected by the colored people.

Among the early Antislavery orators, pamphleteers and publicists there was none more uncompromisingly opposed to slavery than David Ruggles. *Abrogation of the Seventh Commandment by*

---

[3] See *A Journal of the Rev. John Marrant, from August the 18th, 1785 To The 16th of March 1790*. . . (London: printed for the author, 1790).
[4] For biographical material See *Meditations from the Pen of Mrs. Maria W. Stewart, (widow of the late James W. Stewart,) now Matron of the Freedmen's Hospital, and Presented in 1832 to the First African Baptist Church and Society of Boston, Mass.* (Washington, D.C., 1879). Her name has been spelled as Steward and Stewart.

American Churches is an example of his power to use biblical arguments (more usually resorted to by the slaver on behalf of slavery) quite tellingly against "the enemy." His appeal to virtuous or would-be virtuous American womanhood has an unmistakable bite of irony since it challenges individual conscience and church policy at the same time as it acknowledges and demands the abolition of a moral double standard applied by slavers to black women.[5]

Jarena Lee's autobiography appeared in two editions. The first edition represented here is a brief sketch of her life and appeared in 1836. The second edition, entitled *Religious Experiences and Journal of Mrs. Jarena Lee, Giving an Account of her Call to Preach the Gospel* (1849), describes in detail her career of evangelism. Converted by Richard Allen, she early demanded to preach from the pulpit in spite of regulations forbidding females to do so.

As the "first female preacher of the African Methodist Episcopal Church" she traveled, under the most trying circumstances, thousands of miles, preaching hundreds of sermons to small and large congregations, black, white, and Indian, regardless of ministerial connection. Confronting prejudice towards her sex by A. M. E. preachers and Elders; risking the wrath of white preachers who resented their members attending her revivals; surmounting the laws in places restricting religious groups to congregate and overcoming personal hardships of illness, fatigue, and weather; Jarena Lee illustrates the great fortitude found among Negro women of her day.

---

[5] For accounts of David Ruggles see Dorothy Porter, "David Ruggles, an Apostle of Human Rights," *Journal of Negro History*, Vol. 28 (January, 1943), pp. 23–50; "David Ruggles 1810–1849, Hydropathic Practitioner," *Journal of the National Medical Association*, Vol. 49 (January, 1957), pp. 67–72, Vol. 49 (March, 1957), pp. 130–134.

The Life and Confession of

JOHNSON GREEN,

WHO IS TO BE EXECUTED THIS DAY, AUGUST 17TH, 1786,

FOR THE

Atrocious Crime of Burglary;

TOGETHER WITH HIS

LAST and DYING WORDS.

I, JOHNSON GREEN, having brought myself to a shameful and ignominious death by my wicked conduct, and, as I am a dying man, I leave to the world the following History of my Birth, Education, and vicious Practices, hoping that all people will take warning by my evil example and shun vice and follow virtue.

I was born at Bridgwater, in the County of Plymouth, in the Commonwealth of Massachusetts, was twenty-nine years of age the seventh day of February last. My father was a negro, and a servant to the Hon. Timothy Edson, Esq, late of said Bridgwater, deceased. My mother was an Irish woman named Sarah Johnson. She was a widow, and her maiden name was Green. I have been called Joseph-Johnson Green. When I was five years of age my mother bound me as an Apprentice to Mr. Seth Howard of said Bridgwater, to be instructed in Agriculture. I was used very tenderly, and instructed in the principles of the Christian Religion. Whilst I was an apprentice my mother gave me much good advice, cautioned me against keeping company with those that used bad language and other vicious practices. She advised me not to go to sea nor into the army, foretold what has come to pass since the commencement of the late war, and said it would not come to pass in her day. She died about sixteen years ago, and if I had followed her good advice I might have escaped an ignominious death.

When I was eighteen years of age (contrary to my mother's advice) I enlisted into the American service, and remained in the same for the duration of the war. I would just observe to the world, that my being addicted to drunkenness, the keeping of bad company, and a correspondence that I have had with lewd women, has been the cause of my being brought to this wretched situation.

In March, 1781, I was married at Easton, to one Sarah Phillips, a mustee, who was brought up by Mr. Olney of Providence. She has had two children since I was married to her, and I have treated her exceeding ill.

When I began to steal I was about 12 years old, at which time I stole four cakes of gingerbread and six biscuit out of a horse cart, and afterwards I stole sundry small articles, and was not detected.

When I was about fourteen, I stole one dozen of lemons and one cake of chocolate, was detected, and received reproof. Soon after I stole some hens, and my conduct was so bad that my master sold me to one of his cousins, who used me well.

I continued the practice of stealing, and just before I went into the army I took my master's key, unlocked his chest, and stole two shillings; he discovered what I had done, gave me correction, but not so severely as I deserved.

Sometime after I was engaged in the American service, at a certain tavern in Sherburne I stole fifteen shillings, one case bottle of rum, one dozen of biscuit, and a pillow case with some sugar.

In April, 1781, I stole at the Highlands, near West Point, a pair of silver shoe buckles, was detected, and received one hundred lashes.

In October, the same year, when I was at West Point, and we were extremely pinched for the want of provisions, three of us broke open a settler's markee, stole three cheeses, one small firkin of butter, and some chocolate. I only was detected, and punished by receiving one hundred stripes.

Sometime in the winter of 1783, at Easton, I broke into a grist mill belonging to Mr. Timothy Randall and stole about a bushel of corn, and at sundry times the same year I broke into a cellar belonging to Mr. Ebenezer Howard, of the same place, and stole some meat and tobacco; and I also broke into a cellar and a corn house belonging to Mr. Abiel Kinsley, of the same place, and stole some meat and corn; and at East Bridgewater, the same year, I broke open a grist mill, and stole near a bushel of meal; and at the same time I stole three or four dozen herrings out of a corn house. I also went to a corn house belonging to Mr. Nathaniel Whitman, of Bridgwater, and stole two cheeses out of it.

August 1st, 1784, I broke open a house in Providence and stole goods to the value of forty dollars. Soon after I broke open a shop near Patuxet Falls, stole one pair of cards, two cod fish, and sundry other articles.

In 1784 I also committed the following crimes, viz. I broke into a cellar about a mile from Patuxet Bridge, stole about thirty weight of salt pork, one case bottle, and several other articles. About the same time I stole out of a washing tub in Patuxet a pair of trowsers, three pair of stockings, and a shirt; and at Seaconk I stole two shirts and some stockings through an open window. I stole, at a barn between Seaconk and Attleborough, a woollen blanket, and through an open window near the same place I stole two sheets, one gown, and one shirt. At Mr. Amos Shepherdson's, in Attleborough, I stole out of a wash-tub one shirt, two shifts, one short gown, and one pair of stockings.

At Norton, I broke into a cellar belonging to Col. George Leonard, and stole a quarter of mutton. The same night I broke into another cellar near that place, and stole between twenty and thirty weight of salt pork.

About the same time, I broke into a tavern near the same place, and stole near two dollars in money, and one case bottle of rum.

Between Providence and Attleborough, I broke open two cellars and stole some meat.

I broke into a house in Johnston, and stole betwixt twenty and thirty wt. of salt pork and beef, and one broom.

Some of the things I stole this year, I sold at the market in Providence.

April 23d, 1785, I was imprisoned at Nantucket for striking a truckman and some other persons, at a time when I was intoxicated with liquor: The next day I was released upon my paying a fine and the cost of prosecution.

I broke open a house in Stoughton, stole several aprons, some handkerchiefs, and some other apparel.

I stole about two yards and an half of tow-cloth from Col. David Lathrop, of Bridgewater; and the same night I stole a shirt from a clothier, in the same town; and I also stole one apron, one pocket-handkerchief, one pair of stockings, and one shift from Thomas Howard of East Bridgewater, upon the same night.

The next week I stole a piece of tow-cloth in Halifax, and at the same time I broke into a house, and stole about twenty pounds of salt beef, and three pounds of wool.

October 15th, 1785, I broke open a shop in Walpole, and stole seven pair of shoes.

Nov. 1785, I broke open a store in Natick and stole a quantity of goods from the owner, viz. Mr. Morris.

At Capt. Bent's tavern, in Stoughtonham, I went down chimney, by a rope, opened a window and fastened it up with my jack-knife; immediately after, a man came to the house for a gallon of rum; he called to the landlord, and his daughter (as I took her to be) arose and waited upon him. She discovered the open window, with the jack-knife, and said it did not belong to the house; it was concluded that it belonged to some boys who were gone to a husking, and had called there that evening. It was my design to have made my escape out at the window, when I opened it, in case I should be discovered by any person in the house: But when the man came up to the house, I, fearing I might be discovered, drawed myself up chimney and stood on the cross-bar until he was gone and all the people were asleep; I then descended again, and stole near three dollars out of the bar; then ascended the chimney and escaped without being discovered.

The same month I hid a quantity of goods which I had stole (part of them being the goods I had stolen at Natick) in a barn belonging to Mr. Nathaniel Foster, in Middleborough, and I engaged to come and work for the said Foster: It happened that I was taken up on suspicion that I had stolen a horse (which I had taken and rode about four miles) and committed to gaol in the county of Plymouth, but as no sufficient evidence appeared, I was set at liberty. In the mean time the said Foster found the goods and advertised them. I sent my wife to him; she owned and received the goods, and I escaped undiscovered, by her telling him that I came to his house in the evening preceding the day I had promised to work for him; that as it was late in the night, and the weather rainy, I did not choose to disturb him and his family, by calling them up; that I was obliged to leave the goods and return home, and being taken up on the suspicion aforesaid, I could not take care of the goods, &c.

April 1st, 1786, I broke into a house in Medford and stole two pair of stockings, one scarf, one gown, and one pair of buckles.

The same month I broke into the house of one Mr. Blake, inn-holder, opposite the barracks in Rutland, and stole a bottle of bitters, and three or four dollars in money.

Soon after I broke into Mr. Chickery's house, in Holden, and stole about thirty dollars worth of clothing. The next day I lodged in the woods, and at evening Mr. Chickery took me up after I had got into the high-way, searched my pack, and found his things. On his attempting to seize me, I ran off, and made my escape. I left my pack, and the money I had stolen from Mr. Blake.

Not long after, I went to Mr. Jotham Howe's in Shrewsbury, and opened a window, and stole a blanket.

I then went to another house, broke in, and stole a fine apron out of a desk. The same night I went to a barn belonging to Mr. Baldwin, in said Shrewsbury, and lodged in it the next day, and at evening I broke into his house, and stole about three shillings and three pence in money, and about nine dollars worth of clothing, for which crime I am now under sentence of death.

The same night I broke open the house of Mr. Farror, in said Shrewsbury, and stole in money and goods, to the value of near six dollars.

I also broke into the house of Mr. Ross Wyman, of the same town, and upon the same night, and stole from him near two dollars.

Moreover, I stole a pair of thread stockings at a house just beyond said Wyman's, and hid myself in the woods, where I lay all the next day, and at evening I set off towards Boston, and was taken up by a guard that was placed by a bridge in the edge of Westborough. I was taken before General Ward, confessed the crimes alledged, was committed to gaol, and in April last, I received sentence of death, for the crime aforementioned.

Upon the evening of the first day of June I cleared myself of all my chains, and made an escape from the gaol. And notwithstanding all the admonitions, counsels and warnings that I had received from the good ministers and other pious persons who had visited me under my confinement, I returned again to my vicious practices, "like the dog to his vomit, and the sow that is washed, to her wallowing in the mire;" for the very same evening I stole a cheese out of a press in Holden. And the next Saturday I broke into the house of Mr. James Caldwell, in Barre, and stole near twenty five dollars worth of clothing.

I tarried in Barre about twelve days, and then set off for Natick, and on the way I broke into a cellar in Shrewsbury, and stole some bread and cheese.—Whilst I tarried in Barre, I lived in the woods all the time—when I had got to Natick, I stole two pair of stockings and two pocket handkerchiefs, that were hanging out near a house.

From Natick I went to Sherburne, and broke open a store belonging to Mr. Samuel Sanger, and stole between four and five dozen of buttons.

From thence I went to Mr. John Sanger's house, in the same town, broke it open, and stole a case bottle of rum, one bottle of cherry rum, six cakes of gingerbread, and as many biscuits: I searched for money, but found none.

At another tavern in the same town, I took out a pane of glass, and opened the window, but I was discovered by the landlord, made my escape, and went back to Natick, and tarried there two days.

From Natick I went to Stoughtonham, and at Capt. Bent's (the place where I went down the chimney), the cellar being open, I went through it, and in the bar room I stole fifteen shillings in money, one case bottle of rum, and one half dozen of biscuits.

Afterwards I went to Easton, and on the way I broke open a house and stole some cheese, and two pair of shoes, and two pair of shoe buckles. At Easton I tarried two days, and then made my escape from two men who attempted to take me up on suspicion that I had broken gaol. From thence I went to Attleborough, and through a window I stole two cheeses, and at a tavern near the same place, I stole six shillings and eight pence, one case bottle of rum, a sailor's jacket, and one pair of silver knee buckles.

I then set off for Providence, and by the way I opened a window, and stole one cotton jacket, one jack-knife; and at another house on the same way, I stole through a window, one fine apron, one pocket handkerchief, and one pillow case.

I came to Providence the 26th day of June, and not long after, I broke open a cellar, and stole one bottle of beer, some salt fish, and ten pounds of butter.

A few nights after, I went to Col. Manton's, in Johnston, and the cellar being open, I went into it, and stole twenty pounds of butter, near as much salt pork, one milk pail, one cheese cloth, and one frock.

A few nights after, I went to Justice Belknap's, in the same place, and broke into his cellar, and stole about thirty pounds of salt pork, one neat's tongue, one pair of nippers, one box of awls, and one bag.—It remarkably happened on the 13th ultimo (the day that had been appointed for my execution) that I was committed to gaol in Providence, on suspicion of having stolen the things last mentioned, and on the 18th ult. I was brought back and confined in this gaol again.—Many more thefts and other vicious practices have I been guilty of, the particulars of which might tire the patience of the reader.

Some of the things I have stolen I have used myself—some of them I have sold—some have been taken from me—some I have hid where I could not find them again—and others I have given to lewd women, who induced me to steal for their maintenance. I have lived a hard life, by being obliged to keep in the woods; have suffered much by hunger, nakedness, cold, and the fears of being detected and brought to justice—have often been accused of stealing when I was not guilty, and others have been accused of crimes when I was the offender. I never murdered any person, nor robbed anybody on the highway. I have had great dealings with women, which to their and my shame be it spoken, I often too easily obtained my will of them. I hope they will repent, as I do, of such wicked and infamous conduct. I have had a correspondence with many women, exclusive of my wife, among whom were several abandoned Whites, and a large number of Blacks; four of the whites were married women, three of the Blacks have laid children to me besides my wife, who has been much distressed by my behaviour.

Thus have I given a history of my birth, education and atrocious conduct, and as the time is very nigh in which I must suffer an ignominious death, I earnestly intreat that all people would take warning by my wicked example; that they would shun the paths of destruction by guarding against every temptation; that they would shun vice, follow virtue, and become (through the assistance of the ALMIGHTY) victorious over the enemies of immortal felicity, who are exerting themselves to delude and lead nations to destruction.

As I am sensible of the heinousness of my crimes, and am sorry for my wicked conduct, in violating the laws of the great Governour of the Universe, whose Divine Majesty I have offended; I earnestly pray that he would forgive my sins, blot out my multipled transgressions, and receive my immortal spirit into the Paradise of never ending bliss.

I ask forgiveness of my wife, and of all persons whom I have injured. I return my sincere thanks to the Ministers of the Gospel, and others, who have visited me under my confinement, for their counsels and admonitions, and for the good care they have taken of me: God reward them for their kindness, and conduct us all through this troublesome world to the regions of immortal felicity in the kingdom of Heaven. AMEN.

his

JOHNSON † GREEN.

mark.

Worcester Gaol, August 16, 1786.

The following POEM was written at the request of JOHNSON GREEN, by a prisoner in Worcester Gaol, and is at said GREEN's

*special request, added to his Life and Confession, as a PART of his
DYING WORDS.*

LET all the people on the globe
    Be on their guard, and see
That they do shun the vicious road
    That's trodden been by me.
If I had shun'd the paths of vice;
    Had minded to behave
According to the good advice
    That my kind mother gave,
    Unto my friends I might have been
    A blessing in my days,
And shun'd the evils that I've seen
    In my pernicious ways.
My wicked conduct has been such,
    It's brought me to distress;
As often times I've suffer'd much
    By my own wickedness.
    My lewdness, drunkenness, and theft
    Has often times—(behold)
Caus'd me to wander, and be left
    To suffer with the cold.
Hid in the woods, in deep distress,
    My pinching wants were such,
With hunger, and with nakedness
    I oft did suffer much.
I've liv'd a thief; it's a hard life;
    To drink was much inclin'd;
My conduct has distress'd my wife,
    A wife both good and kind.
Though many friends which came to see
    Me, in these latter times,
Did oft with candour, caution me
    To leave my vicious crimes;
Yet when I had got out of gaol,
    Their labour prov'd in vain;
For then, alas! I did not fail
    To take to them again.
If I had not conducted so;
    Had minded to refrain;
Then I shou'd not have had to go

Back to the gaol again.
Thus in the Devil's service, I
   Have spent my youthful days,
And now, alas! I soon must die,
   For these my wicked ways.
Repent, ye thieves, whilst ye have breath,
   Amongst you let be wrought
A reformation, lest to death,
   You, like myself, be brought.
Let other vicious persons see
   That they from vice abstain;
Lest they undo themselves, like me,
   Who in it did remain.
I hope my sad and dismal fate
   Will solemn warning be
To people all, both small and great,
   Of high and low degree.
By breaking of the righteous laws,
   I to the world relate,
That I thereby have been the cause
   Of my unhappy fate.
As I repent, I humbly pray
   That God would now remit
My sins, which in my vicious way
   I really did commit.
May the old TEMPTER soon be bound
   And shut up in his den,
And peace and honesty abound
   Among the sons of men.
May the great GOD grant this request,
   And bring us to that shore
Where peace and everlasting rest
   Abides for ever more.

his
JOHNSON † GREEN.
mark.

Printed and Sold at the Printing-Office in Worcester.

CONFESSION

OF

JOHN JOYCE, alias DAVIS,

WHO WAS EXECUTED

ON MONDAY, THE 14TH OF MARCH, 1808.

FOR THE

MURDER

OF

MRS. SARAH CROSS;

WITH AN

ADDRESS TO THE PUBLIC,

AND

PEOPLE OF COLOUR,

TOGETHER WITH THE SUBSTANCE OF THE TRIAL,
AND THE ADDRESS
OF CHIEF JUSTICE TILGHMAN, ON HIS CONDEMNATION.

PHILADELPHIA:
PRINTED AT NO. 12 WALNUT-STREET,
FOR THE BENEFIT OF BETHEL CHURCH.
1808.

414

District of Pennsylvania, to wit:

BE IT REMEMBERED, That on the tenth day of March, in the thirty-second year of the Independence of the United States of America, A.D. 1808, RICHARD ALLEN of the said district, hath deposited in this office, the title of a book, the right whereof he claims as proprietor, in the words following, to wit:—"Confession of John Joyce, *alias* Davis, who was executed on Monday, the 14th of March, 1808, for the Murder of Mrs. Sarah Cross, with an address to the public and people of colour, together with the substance of the trial and the address of Chief Justice Tilghman, on his condemnation." In conformity to the Act of the Congress of the United States, entitled "An Act for the encouragement of learning, by securing the copies of maps, charts, and books, to the authors and proprietors of such copies during the times therein mentioned," and extending the benefits thereof to the arts of designing, engraving, and etching historical and other prints.

D. Caldwell, *Clerk of the District of Pennsylvania*

Address to the Public, and People of Colour.

MURDER is one of the most atrocious crimes of which depraved human nature is capable. Happily for the race of Man, excepting when because of its more extensive mischiefs, it receives the name of war, it has in every nation and age been contemplated with horror.

The divine Majesty testified his aversion to the dreadful offence, and his resolution to punish the perpetrator, in the earliest ages of society: nor, at this can we wonder, when we recollect, that the very first Son of our common Parents was a murderer; a mark was set upon Cain. Under the Levitical Economy, an involuntary man-slayer could find safety only by flying to a city of refuge; but as to the murderer, no sacrifice must be offered to God—no Money received by Man for his pardon—the horns of Jehovah's Altar he grasped in vain. The language of the law was "thou shalt take him from mine altar, that he may die."

When a body was found murdered in the open field and the offender unknown, the Rulers of the adjacent city were commanded to bring a "Heifer into a rough valley, that was neither cared or sown," and to "strike off the heifer's neck there in the valley." The valley was perhaps chosen with a view of limiting the horizon, and thereby confining the meditations of the people to the transaction. Its roughness and barrenness taught the desolation this sin produces;

while the striking off the victim's head testified the murderer's desert.

Over the slaughtered heifer the Rulers must wash their hands, solemnly protesting their innocence, and the Priests or Levites supplicate the Lord that against the land there might not be placed the charge of blood.

In the heathen world the belief was popular that the Divine vengeance, that could certainly distinguish, would also fearfully punish the man who shed the blood of his fellow man. When the Viper of Melita fastened itself on the hand of Paul, the Barbarians said among themselves, "no doubt this man is a murderer, whom though he hath escaped the sea, yet vengeance suffereth not to live." The histories of vicious men, and especially the records of Courts of Judicature, discover that to the shedder of blood, Darkness or Solitude, Art or Confederacy, Flight or concealment, afford not protection.

Reader, hast thou conceived murder in thy heart? tremble! tremble! The eye of God is upon thee! his providence will supply a clew for thy detection. "Be sure your sin will find you out."

The path of sin is descending, and for this reason, the feet of the wicked become swifter to do evil, as they approach nearer the bottom of the steep, where the gulf of ruin lies. Would'st thou, O man, avoid the gallows? avoid the ways that lead to it. Thy maker commands "that thou shalt not steal." Labour with thy hands and thou wilt provide things which are honest, and with a good conscience enjoy them. Fly for thy life from the chambers of the harlot. Know, O young man, that her steps take hold of hell. Secret crimes shall be all dragged to light and seen by the eye of the world in their horrid forms. The solemn record is standing: "Whoremongers and adulterers, God will judge." Go not to the tavern; the song of the drunkard will soon be changed to weeping and wailing and gnashing of teeth. Drunkenness hurls reason from the throne, and when she has fallen, vice always stands ready to ascend it. Break off, O young man, your impious companions. If you still grasp their hands they will drag you down to everlasting fire.

Cry out like the ancient Patriarch, "O my soul, come not thou into their secret, to their assembly mine honour be not thou united." Perhaps the person at this moment reading is a female of ill-fame —if thy reputation be not yet quite blasted, pause, thou art on the way to ruin. The midnight revel, the polluted couch, thy diseased body, and thy affrighted conscience, testify against thee. Perhaps thy Mother's heart is already broken!

Poor miserable Creature! it is not yet too late. Hast thou made some guilty assignation this very night? Break it off, for thy soul's sake break it off; tomorrow thou may'st be in Hell. Ask the protection of the Magdalene Society, lately established in this City; above all, let the eyes that have been full of fornication become fountains of tears; smite on thy breast and cry, "God be merciful to me a sinner!"

People of Colour: To you, the murder of Mrs. Cross speaks as with a voice of thunder. Many of you fear the living God, and walk in his commandments; but, oh, how many are slaves of Sin. See the tendency of dishonesty and lust, of drunkenness and stealing, in the murder, an account of which is subjoined. See the tendency of midnight dances and frolics. While the lustful dance is delighting thee, forget not, that "for all these things God will bring thee into judgment." Be these, O man, O woman of colour, thy resolutions:

"In God's name and strength, I will never more attend a frolic. Drunkards and swearers, Whoremongers and Sabbath-breakers, I have done with you for ever. These hands supply my wants. I will seek the recovery of the character I have lost. Next Lord's day I will go to divine worship. If my cloths are not so good as my industry shall, with God's blessings, soon make them, I will nevertheless go. My Creator, and all good men, would rather see me in rags, in the house of God than in the gayest attire in a riotous tavern, or in the chambers of pollution. Who can tell, but that my injured, my offended Maker, may have mercy on my soul, for Christ's sake, who came to save the lost. O my injured parents, my unhappy wife, my miserable children, I pray I may be enabled to do all that can be done, for repairing the evils I have made you suffer. God of heaven, have mercy upon me!"

Go, pray for strength to put these resolutions into execution. At the feast of the gospel there yet is room. But if thou wilt fill up the measure of thy iniquity, and despise knowledge, be assured, this little book, in the day of judgment, shall be a swift Witness against thee.

The Following Is the Substance of the Trial, as it appeared in one of the public Papers.

At a court of Oyer and Terminer, for the City and County of Philadelphia, held on the 15th February, by Chief Justice *Tilghman*, and Mr. justice *Smith*, came on the trial of *John Joyce* and *Peter Mathias*, two black men, charged with the murder of *Sarah Cross*.

The indictment charged *Joyce* with being the actual perpetrator of the crime, and *Peter* with being present, aiding, abetting, and assisting it.

Mrs. *Cross,* the deceased, was a widow of about the age of fifty. She lived in a small two story brick house, in Black-Horse Alley near Second Street, Philadelphia; kept a little shop; by industry and care, lived comfortably, and saved a little money. *Anne Messinger,* a girl of between 13 and 14 years of age, was the principal witness on the part of the commonwealth. Although so young, she gave her testimony with striking distinctness and precision. She stated, that about 7 o'clock of the evening of the alleged murder, which happened on the 18th of December last, she was sent by her guardian to the house of the deceased, to buy some liquorice. That when she got there, she perceived, contrary to custom, that the window shutters were closed. That this led her to look through the key-hole of the door before she went into the house. That on doing so, she saw one of the prisoners, Joyce, Shaking Mrs. Cross by the neck; that she pushed the door open and went in; that a candle was burning in the room; that the instant she entered, Joyce let Mrs. Cross fall, came to the door, and locked it, and put the key in his pocket; that when he came to the door he held in his hand a rope, part of which appeared to be tied round the neck of Mrs. Cross; that Mrs. Cross, at this time, was lying on the floor dead; that Peter was in the room with Joyce; that Joyce opened the drawer of the counter, and took out all the money; that he then lighted another candle and went up stairs; that the witness being terrified, tried to make her escape through the window, but could not; that Joyce came down stairs, but soon went up again, Peter going with him; that they compelled the witness to go up too, and made her hold the candle, while they were engaged in plundering; that having gathered up all the articles worth taking, they came down stairs, treading in their way over the body of the deceased; that they were preparing to go out, but hearing the sound of footsteps passing the door, they paused, and bade the witness put out the candles; that after waiting a little while, they unlocked the door and went out; Joyce holding the witness tight by the hand, that when she got outside of the door she gave wild screams, and cried Murder; that the prisoners immediately ran off, dropping in the street the cumbrous articles they had stolen. The witness was, in all about half an hour in the house, and spoke with confidence as to the prisoners being the same men who were there. Joyce she had often seen before, and knew his face well. He had been a servant in a family in Laetitia court near Black-horse Alley; and within a few doors of the house where the witness lived. On the day following that on which the murder took place, she identified them both before the examining magistrate.

Several witnesses were examined who had seen the body of the deceased, after the prisoners had left the house. It appeared she had been strangled with a rope coiled three or four times round her neck very tight, and had been wounded and bruised on the head with a stick, or perhaps with some sharp instrument.

The prisoners went to the house of Peter in Southwark, after they left the house of the deceased, and counted and displayed the booty they had brought off. Joyce was arrested the same evening. Peter was taken up the next day, a mile or two out of town in the garret of a house where he had secreted himself. Several of the stolen articles were found upon him, and he confessed that he had been at the house of the deceased the night before. A piece of rope which appeared on comparison to be the counterpart of that used in effecting the murder was found, the same evening, with the prisoners.

The evidence for the commonwealth seem thus complete, and the prisoners had no testimony to impeach it.

Their counsel said they rose, in compliance with a professional duty which the court had been pleased to devolve upon them: that they did so with embarrassment and regret, as the weight, and clearness of the testimony against them constrained them to acknowledge the criminality of the prisoners. The defence, therefore, could only aim at mitigating the severity of their fate. The counsel then entered into an examination of the evidence, and endeavoured to shew, that although it proved the homicide, it did not fix upon the prisoners such a previously formed design to take away life, as, under the statute of Pennsylvania was required to warrant the punishment of death. They endeavoured so to expound this statute as to shew that the offence of the prisoners had not in it those ingredients of malice and premeditation which constitute murder in the first degree, but was reducible to that form of it which the law punishes with solitary confinement for 18 years.

Mr. *Rush* spoke one hour and a half; Mr. *Biddle* three quarters of an hour. If a profound knowledge of the human heart, a brilliant display of Forensic elequence, and great legal knowledge would have meliorated the verdict of the jury, it would have been done; but, in this dreadful transaction, there was no loop upon which to hang a doubt. Law, humanity, and self defence had guarded every avenue to compassion; the Angel of mercy hid her face in the bosom of pity, and resigned to justice its victims.

The Attorney General, in his summing up, declared there was the fullest proof in this case, of that wilful, deliberate, and premeditated intention to kill, that constituted a murder, under its most attrocious form, to shew which, he went through a discussion of the testimony. That the prisoners had justly forfeited their lives by the laws of their country, and could not escape its awful doom. He replied to, and obviated the objections to his interpretation of the law of Pennsylvania, urged by the counsel for the prisoners.

The Chief Justice, in his charge, stated the evidence, told the jury the extension of mercy did not fall within their province. That if they thought the facts proved a murder in the first degree, they should say so. That it was his duty though a painful one, to say, the facts had made that impression on the mind of the court, tho' it was the right of the jury exclusively to decide. He said the act of assembly did not make it necessary, in order to constitute a murder in the first degree, that a scheme should have been concerted, long antecedent, to destroy life. That if there be a perfect, complete intent to kill, formed only a minute before, it is sufficient, and such had frequently been declared by judicial authority, to the meaning of the act.

The Jury retired from the box, and returned with a verdict of murder in the first degree against both the prisoners.

ADDRESS

Of Chief Justice Tilghman,

on their

CONDEMNATION.

John Joyce and Peter Matthias!

YOU have been convicted, after an impartial trial, of an offence of the blackest dye—the only offence which by the law is punished with death. You have taken that life, which can never be restored, from a harmless, industrious old woman, a widow, helpless, and incapable of resistance; whom it was your duty rather to have protected than to have injured. Your crime is attended with the most aggravating circumstances. Others have committed murder in the heat of passion, to revenge insults or injuries real or supposed; but you have no such excuse. Actuated by no motive but the base desire of possessing yourselves of the little property this poor woman possessed, you calmly and deliberately contrived the means of her death—you carried with you the rope which was the instrument of your abominable deed—and in her own house you knocked down and strangled her, without pity or remorse!—But this was not all—you rifled her house of her money, clothing and bed; and proving yourselves utterly destitute of human feelings, you went fresh from this scene, at the bare recital of which the heart recoils, to partake of the amusement of a dance. You have injured society in general, and the people of your own colour in particular, by rendering them objects of public disgust and suspicion. I am happy however to be informed, that they view your conduct with horror, and I hope they will profit by your example. I mention not these things with a view of wounding your feelings at this unhappy moment, for I consider you as objects of the greatest compassion: But it is of importance that you should be roused to a quick sense of your guilt, and of the necessity of immediate repentance.

Let no man hope to commit murder with impunity. In vain did you flatter yourselves that you were covered by the darkness of night. Before that God, with whom there is no night, the bloody deed appeared in full day! And in the course of his Providence, the eyes of an innocent little child was directed towards you, while you thought yourselves in perfect security. Her simple, artless story carried conviction to the minds, not only of the respectable jury who condemned you, but of the court, and the numerous audience who attended your trial. You are guilty beyond a doubt; and I exhort you to employ the short period for which you are to remain in this world in such a manner as will prove your sincere repentance. Make a full confession of your crime, and pray for forgiveness. It would be presumptuous for any man to say on what terms, or to what extent, that forgiveness is to be obtained. But we are taught by our religion to hope that to those who truly repent, the mercy of God is without bounds.

It remains that I pronounce the awful judgment the law has ordained for your crime. It is this: That you, and each of you be taken from hence to the prison of the city and county of Philadelphia from whence you came, and from thence to the place of execution; and that you be there hanged by the neck till you be dead.—And may God have mercy on you!

CONFESSION

I, JOHN JOYCE, *alias* DAVIS, (about 24 years of age,) was born at West River, state of Maryland; a slave in the service of Sarah Saunders, I left her about 9 years and an half since, to go into the service of the United States.* Went to Boston, and from thence

* My parents were piously inclined. My uncle had religious meetings held

went on board the ship Boston, M'Neal commander, on a cruise to
the Straits. I continued in the service about 7 years, during which
period I sailed with Commodore Preble, Captain Chauncy, Captain
Cox, and Commodore Barron. I returned to the city of Washington
and lived there about twelve months in the family of Dr. John Bullus,
married a hired woman in the family, and had by her 2 children (and
2 others by other women). I went out to sea again on a cruise to the
Straits, and returned with Captain Decatur in the Congress to Washington. While absent on this voyage, my wife was unfaithful to me,
and cohabited with another man in consequence of which I left her.
The first crime against the laws of my country was the stealing of
a horse at Washington, from Lawrence Hays, about eighteen months
ago, on which I came up to Philadelphia, and sold him to a white
man by the name of ————, for eighteen dollars. I boarded with
Margaret Tucker, a black woman, in Fourth below South-streets,
about a week, and then hired with Adam Guyer to keep horses and
take care of his stable, corner of Filbert and Eleventh-streets, where
I stayed near two months. I then hired as a servant at Dr. B————'s,
in Sansom-streets, where I continued about two months. I then went
to live with Mr. W————, in Second between Vine and Race-streets,
as a coachman, where I stayed about two months, during which
period I drove Mr. W———— twice to Lancaster, to visit his son-in-
law Mr. R————. While at Lancaster the last time, I entered the
house adjoining Mr. R————'s and stole a watch, which being
missed by the owners who suspected me as the thief, they sent one
of the Lancaster stage drivers to Mr. W———— to demand the watch,
which I gave up. In consequence of this transaction, Mr. W————
turned me away: from thence I went to live with David Kennedy,
in Laetitia Court, as a waiter in the tavern, with whom I lived
about two months; the cause of my leaving his service was my going
out to a dance late at night, and leaving the door open. While I
lived at Mr. Kennedy's I became acquainted with Mrs. Cross, who
kept a shop in Blackhorse-alley, being frequently sent there on errands. After leaving Mr. Kennedy's I engaged with Mrs. Scott, to
drive her carriage, the day on which, in the evening, I perpetrated
the horrid crime for which I am condemned to die. On Friday the
18th December last, early in the evening, I went down to the house
of Peter Matthias or Matthews, in Fifth below Small-street: while

---

at his house—my father is living in Maryland—I was depraved in my
morals, and never belonged to any religious society.—On parting with my
mother, after giving me much good advice, she observed she "was afraid
that I would be hanged one day or other."

there, I conceived the plan of the murder, but did not relate it to Peter, at that, or any other time; and he (Peter) is innocent. I asked Peter to go with me up to Kennedy's, to receive money due me for wages. Peter declined, saying he "was engaged that evening to play for a dance." I prevailed upon him to accompany me, by promising him as much, or more money than he could get by playing the fiddle: I then saw a rope, or clothes line, which I told Hester Cook (the woman of the house with whom Peter lived,) that I wanted, and of which I cut off a part and took with me. Leaving the house with Peter, we went together to a shop in Shippen-street, and I bought an half pint of gin, the most of which I drank myself; and from thence proceeded towards Laetitia Court. While walking up Front-street, saw some wood which had been sawed, and took a small stick of it in my hand and carried it with me. We went to another shop in Market near Water-street, and I got a gill of gin; and thence I and Peter went to Laetitia Court to Mr. Kennedy's. I looked in at the window and saw Cyrus Porter, a black man, who was a waiter at nights, and assisted me while I had lived there. I then asked Peter to go with me to Mrs. Cross', in Blackhorse-alley: I bought half a dozen of apples, gave Peter a part, and he ate his at the counter. While conversing with Mrs. Cross, she observed to me, that, "I had left my place" (Mr. Kennedy's). She asked Peter to "come by the stove and warm himself." I felt tempted to commit the act. Peter was desirous to go, and proposed it. I asked "what is your hurry?" Peter then went out of the house. I called after him to tarry a little, and I would go along with him in a few minutes. The door was shut to by Peter. I then, holding the stick in my hand, felt strongly tempted to perpetrate the horrid act: I struck her on the head with the stick, she cried out "Lord, John, what did you do that for," and she fell to the floor. I then took the rope out of my pocket, made a noose in it, put it round her neck, and drew it tight. I then took the candle and went up stairs to look for the money. Under the pillow, between the bed and sacking bottom, I found a handkerchief containing a purse of dollars and a crown or two, and another containing gold and some silver, which I took, and came down stairs, and found in the drawer of the counter a small purse with silver and small change, and took that also. Peter then came to the door, to see if I was ready to go, and I let him in.—On Peter's coming in, and seeing the situation of Mrs. Cross, lying on the floor, he said, "Lord! John, what have you been about? have you killed the woman?" To which I replied, "no, she is not dead." Then a little girl came in, and asked for a penny's worth of liquorice. No reply was made to her. The door was then shut and locked by me.

I asked Peter and the girl to go up stairs to help me tie up the bed. The girl held the candle. I took the bed down stairs, put it out of doors, and left it in the alley. Coming down stairs, I demanded of the little girl whether she knew me? She said "no." I asked her if she would go with me? She replied "yes." I came out of the house with a bundle of cloths, and a looking glass, at the same time held the girl by the hand, and came into Second-street; she then cryed out "murder." I let go of her hand, and I and Peter ran up Second to Market-street, and up Market to Fifth streets, and down Fifth to Peter's house: found there Hester Cook, with whom Peter lived. I sat down, and put the looking glass on the table. Peter put the bundle down. I then took the money out of my pocket, and told Peter to count it. Peter did so, and it was put in the purse again. I then requested Hester Cook to take the money and the clothes, and put them away for me, which she did, by putting them in a trunk. After a short pause, I asked Peter what he would drink. Each gave a quarter of a dollar, and sent Hester Cook for a quart of brandy, which she brought. Two women of colour who lived up stairs came down (they are of loose character.) I asked them to drink, but I did not drink myself. I then went with Peter to Margaret Tucker's; Peter went from there to Jenny Miller's in Pine Alley, where he had been engaged to play the fiddle that evening.

While I was at Margaret Tucker's, Hester Cook came there after me, and shortly after (about 10 o'clock) the Watchmen came in, apprehended me, and brought me to prison.

In a conversation with Mr. Allen, prior to his making this Confession, he (John) enquired, "whether any thing could be done for that innocent man, Peter." He said, "three things laid heavy on his mind: he had murdered that Old Lady, and was the cause of the death of that innocent man." Mr. Allen demanded, "how he, (Peter) could be innocent? Was he not consulted in the plot? Was he not present when you struck Mrs. Cross with the stick, and put the rope round her neck?" to which he replied, "No my dear Mr. Allen, he is clear of it as G...d is himself. The poor Old Woman was snatched off in her sins, with scarce time to say, Lord have mercy on me; but we, miserable sinners, have time to repent. It is better with Peter than with me, for he is innocent, and I am the guilty wretch." On being again questioned by Mr. Allen, whether "Peter was present when he struck the woman, or when he put the rope round her neck," he replied, "No, he was not."

his
JOHN † JOYCE,
mark.

THE person who wrote the above confession on the 2nd inst, as dictated by the prisoner, visited him on Saturday last and after adverting to the near approach the solemn hour of Execution, informed him, that they now saw each other perhaps for the last time, before they should meet at the judgment seat of Christ. That since the confession had been copied, and read to him, to which he had put his signature, or mark, he had ample time for reflection on its contents: that he had called on him, for the express purpose of affording him an opportunity to take from, to add to, to alter, or amend, any part of the confession, which might not yet be strictly consistent with truth (if any such there should be); at the same time warning him of the awful consequences of publishing what might be false to the world: to which the prisoner replied that "he had well considered the contents of his confession, and that it contained nothing but what was strictly true." On being requested to consider that part of it, which related to his fellow-sufferer; he declared, "that it was also true, and that he intended at the place of Execution to address the people, if he was able, and there tell all the circumstances of the awful transaction, as far as he could recollect them.* He professed to have attained from a merciful God, through the atoning merits of the

---

* It is to be remarked, that after the Prisoner had given his confession, he was visited by the Mayor, who closely interrogated him as to the guilt of his fellow prisoner, Peter Matthias, or Methews; and when the question was propounded whether Peter was present when he committed the murder, when he struck Mrs. Cross on the head, and put the rope round her neck: John answered "that he was, and also a second time, repeated it, on the same question being proposed." But, as soon as the Mayor had withdrawn from the cell, an awful horror seemed to seize his mind, he exclaimed, "Lord forgive me, for I have told the Mayor a falsehood." Being asked by one present, what he had told, he answered, "I have told him, Peter was present, when I killed Mrs. Cross, but he was not. Lord! Forgive me for it, as he is an innocent man."

When the pious are informed of the departure of any from this world, the first enquiry arising in their minds, is, *How did they seem prepared?* In answer to such we can say, concerning this unfortunate man, that having been visited by clergymen of several denominations, who faithfully warned him of the danger of covering his crimes with falsehood, and also admonished him to repent of his sins, and to implore mercy from the hands of that Omniscient Being from whose notice nothing can be hid, and before whose bar he must shortly stand. By means of these admonitions (to all human appearances) he was brought to a discovery of his lost and deplorable condition, not merely under sentence of that law, which can only inflict its penalties on the body, but that more awful one which roars in thunder, *"The soul that sinneth, it shall die."* From every appearance he felt much disquietude of mind, until some days before the day appointed for his execution, when he professed to find great relief.

Saviour of sinners, a lively hope of acceptance; that the fears of death and consequences were removed from his mind, and that he was ready and willing to die, even before the time appointed, which sentiment he had many times repeated to those who visited him, for three or four days before. If those hopes and views were well founded in the prisoner, notwithstanding, every one must view the horrid crime, for which he has justly forfeited his life to the injured laws of his country, in all its enormous malignancy; yet who can withhold that tribute of praise, which is due to the Sovereign Lord of all, who has revealed himself to his creature, man, as "The Lord, the Lord God gracious and merciful, slow to anger, abundant in loving kindness, forgiving iniquity, transgression and sin!"

It is certain there was a visible change in his behaviour, his language was often expressive of joy. His countenance did not wear that gloomy appearance it had done. But a solemn cheerfulness seemed to express, a tranquility of mind. The tears that copiously flowed from his eyes, ready to fall with looking upward, seemed now to be wiped away, while hope sprung up in his soul.

About 10 o'clock he was brought out of prison, and walked to the place of execution singing hymns, attended by the following Clergymen: viz. Rev. Dr. Staughton, Rev. Seely Bunn, Rev. Thos. Dunn, Rev. Richard Allen, and Jeffery Buelah. He seemed cheerful all the way to the place of execution, frequently expressing his hopes and expectations of being shortly received in the world of bliss. At the gallows he still seemed doubtless of his acceptance through the atoning blood of Christ. He there requested that the audience should be informed that the confession he had made (which was in the hands of Mr. Allen) was a true confession, and he wanted no alteration to be made.

Also, that he had hopes of happiness beyond the grave; and had no enmity in his heart against the witnesses, or any other person, but freely forgave all. He expressed his gratitude to the Sheriff, Coroner, Keepers, and others, for the kindness and attention that had been shown him during his imprisonment. He had confirmed his confession in the presence of the Sheriff and Coroner, between nine and 10 o'clock the night before his execution, as he did under the gallows.

A

NARRATIVE

OF THE

LORD'S WONDERFUL DEALINGS

WITH

JOHN MARRANT,

A BLACK,

(Now gone to preach the Gospel in Nova Scotia)

BORN IN NEW YORK, IN NORTH AMERICA.

TAKEN DOWN FROM HIS OWN RELATION,

ARRANGED, CORRECTED, AND PUBLISHED,
BY THE LATE

Rev. Mr. Aldridge.

THE SEVENTH EDITION,
WITH ADDITIONS AND NOTES EXPLANATORY.

Thy People shall be willing in the Day of thy Power, Psalm cx. 3

Declare his Wonders among all People, Psalm xcvi. 3

London:
Printed by T. Plummer, Seething-Lane;
For T. WILLIAMS, Stationer's Court, Ludgate-Hill; and
sold by all Booksellers in the United Kingdom.
Price One Shilling.
1802.

PREFACE

Reader,

THE following Narrative is as plain and artless as it is surprising and extraordinary. Plausible reasonings may amuse and delight, but facts, and facts like these, strike, are felt, and go home to the heart. Were the power, grace and providence of God ever more eminently displayed, than in the conversion, success, and deliverances of John Marrant? He and his companion enter the meeting at Charlestown together; but the one is taken, and the other is left. He is struck to the ground, shaken over the mouth of hell, snatched as a brand from the burning; he is pardoned and justified; he is washed in the atoning blood, and made happy in his God. You soon have another view of him, drinking into his master's cup; he is tried and perplext, opposed and despised; the neighbours hoot at him as he goes along; his mother, sisters, and brother hate and persecute him; he is friendless, and forsaken of all. These uneasy circumstances call forth the corruptions of his nature, and create a momentary debate, whether the pursuit of ease and pleasure was not to be preferred to the practice of religion, which he now found so sharp and severe? The stripling is supported and strengthened. He is persuaded to forsake his family and kindred altogether. He crosses the fence which marked the boundary between the wilderness and the cultivated country; and prefers the habitations of brutal residence to the less hospitable dwellings of enmity to God and godliness. He wanders, but Christ is his guide and protector. Who can view him among the Indian tribes without wonder? He arrives among the Cherokees, where gross ignorance wore its rudest forms, and savage despotism exercised its most terrifying empire. Here the child, just turned fourteen, without sting or stone, engages, and with the arrow of prayer pointed with faith, wounded Goliah, and conquers the king.

The untutor'd monarch feels the truth, and worships the God of the Christians; the seeds of the Gospel are disseminated among the Indians by a youthful band, and Jesus is received and obeyed.

The subsequent incidents related in this Narrative are great and affecting; but I must not anticipate the reader's pleasure and profit.

The novelty or magnitude of the facts contained in the following pages may dispose some readers to question the truth of them. My answer to such is—1. I believe it is clear to great numbers, and to some competent judges, that God is with the subject of them; but if he knowingly permitted an untruth to go abroad in the name of God, whilst it is confessed the Lord is with him, would it not follow,

that the Almighty gave his sanction to a falsehood?—2. I have observed him to pay a conscientious regard to his word.—He appeared
to me to feel most sensibly, when he related those parts of his Narrative, which describe his happiest moments with God, or the most
remarkable interpositions of Divine Providence for him; and I have
no reason to believe it was counterfeited.

I have always preserved Mr. Marrant's ideas, tho' I could not his
language; no more alterations, however, have been made, than were
thought necessary.

I now commit the whole to God. That he may make it generally
useful is the prayer of thy ready servant, for Christ's sake,

W. ALDRIDGE.

London,
July 19th, 1785.

A NARRATIVE, &c.

I, JOHN MARRANT, born June 15th, 1755, in New York, in
North America wish these gracious dealings of the Lord with me to
be published, in hopes they may be useful to others, to encourage
the fearful, to confirm the wavering, and to refresh the hearts of true
believers. My father died when I was little more than four years of
age, and before I was five my mother removed from New York to
St. Augustine, about seven hundred miles from that city. Here I was
sent to school, and taught to read and spell; after we had resided
here about eighteen months, it was found necessary to remove to
Georgia, where we remained; and I was kept to school until I had
attained my eleventh year. The Lord spoke to me in my early days,
by these removes, if I could have understood him, and said, "Here
we have no continuing city." We left Georgia, and went to Charlestown, where it was intended I should be put apprentice to some
trade. Some time after I had been in Charlestown, as I was walking
one day, I passed by a school, and heard music and dancing, which
took my fancy very much, and I felt a strong inclination to learn
the music. I went home, and informed my sister, that I had rather
learn to play upon music than go to a trade. She told me she could
do nothing in it, until she had acquainted my mother with my desire. Accordingly she wrote a letter concerning it to my mother,
which, when she read, the contents were disapproved of by her, and
she came to Charlestown to prevent it. She persuaded me much
against it, but her persuasions were fruitless. Disobedience either to

God or man, being one of the fruits of sin, grew out from me in
early buds. Finding I was set upon it, and resolved to learn nothing
else, she agreed to it, and went with me to speak to the man, and to
settle upon the best terms with him she could. He insisted upon
twenty pounds down, which was paid, and I was engaged to stay
with him eighteen months, and my mother to find me everything
during that term. The first day I went to him he put the violin into
my hand, which pleased me much, and, applying close, I learned
very fast, not only to play, but to dance also; so that in six months
I was able to play for the whole school. In the evenings after the
scholars were dismissed, I used to resort to the bottom of our garden,
where it was customary for some musicians to assemble to blow the
French horn. Here my improvement was so rapid, that in a twelvemonth's time I became master both of the violin and of the French
horn, and was much respected by the gentlemen and ladies whose
children attended the school, as also by my master. This opened to
me a large door of vanity and vice, for I was invited to all the balls
and assemblies that were held in the town, and met with the general
applause of the inhabitants. I was a stranger to want, being supplied
with as much money as I had any occasion for; which my sister
observing, said, "You have now no need of a trade." I was now in
my thirteenth year, devoted to pleasure, and drinking in iniquity like
water; a slave to every vice suited to my nature and to my years.
The time I had engaged to serve my master being expired, he persuaded me to stay with him, and offered me anything, or any money,
not to leave him. His entreaties proving ineffectual, I quitted his
service, and visited my mother in the country; with her I staid two
months, living without God or hope in the world, fishing and hunting on the Sabbath-day. Unstable as water I returned to town, and
wished to go to some trade. My sister's husband, being informed of
my inclination, provided me with a master, on condition that I
should serve him one year and a half on trial, and afterwards be
bound, if he approved of me. Accordingly I went, but every evening
I was sent for to play on music, somewhere or another; and I often
continued out very late, sometimes all night, so as to render me incapable of attending my master's business the next day; yet in this
manner I served him a year and four months, and was much approved of by him. He wrote a letter to my mother to come and have
me bound, and whilst my mother was weighing the matter in her
own mind, the gracious purposes of God, respecting a perishing sinner, were now to be disclosed. One evening I was sent for in a very
particular manner to go and play for some gentlemen, which I
agreed to do, and was on my way to fulfill my promise; and passing

by a large meetinghouse I saw many lights in it, and crowds of people going in. I enquired what it meant, and was answered by my companion, that a crazy man was hallooing there; this raised my curiosity to go in, that I might hear what he was hallooing about. He persuaded me not to go in, but in vain. He then said, "If you will do one thing I will go in with you." I asked him what that was? He replied, "Blow the French horn among them." I liked the proposal well enough, but expressed my fears of being beaten for disturbing them; but upon his promising to stand by and defend me, I agreed. So we went, and with much difficulty got within the doors. I was pushing the people to make room, to get the horn off my shoulder to blow it, just as Mr. Whitefield was naming his text, and looking round, and, as I thought, directly upon me, and pointing with his finger, he uttered these words, "Prepare to meet thy God, O Israel." The Lord accompanied the word with such power that I was struck to the ground, and lay both speechless and senseless near half an hour. When I was come a little too, I found two men attending me, and a woman throwing water in my face, and holding a smelling-bottle to my nose; and when something more recovered, every word I heard from the minister was like a parcel of swords thrust into me, and what added to my distress, I thought I saw the devil on every side of me. I was constrained in the bitterness of my spirit to halloo out in the midst of the congregation, which disturbing them, they took me away; but finding I could neither walk or stand, they carried me as far as the vestry, and there I remained till the service was over. When the people were dismissed Mr. Whitefield came into the vestry, and being told of my condition he came immediately, and the first word he said to me was, "Jesus Christ has got thee at last." He asked where I lived, intending to come and see me the next day; but recollecting he was to leave the town the next morning, he said he could not come himself, but would send another minister; he desired them to get me home, and then taking his leave of me, I saw him no more. When I reached my sister's house, being carried by two men, she was very uneasy to see me in so distressed a condition. She got me to bed, and sent for a doctor, who came immediately, and after looking at me, he went home, and sent me a bottle of mixture, and desired her to give me a spoonful every two hours; but I could not take anything the doctor sent, nor indeed keep in bed; this distressed my sister very much, and she cried out, "The lad will surely die." She sent for two other doctors, but no medicine they prescribed could I take. No, no; it may be asked, a wounded spirit who can cure? as well as who can bear? In this distress of soul I continued for three days without any food, only a little water now and then. On the fourth day, the minister* Mr. Whitefield had desired to visit me came to see me, and being directed upstairs, when he entered the room, I thought he made my distress much worse. He wanted to take hold of my hand, but I durst not give it to him. He insisted upon taking hold of it, and I then got away from him on the side of the bed; but being very weak I fell down, and before I could recover he came to me and took me by the hand, and lifted me up, and after a few words desired to go to prayer. So he fell upon his knees, and pulled me down also; after he had spent some time in prayer he rose up, and asked me now how I did; I answered much worse; he then said, "Come, we will have the old thing over again," and so we kneeled down a second time, and after he had prayed earnestly we got up, and he said again, "How do you do now?" I replied worse and worse, and asked him if he intended to kill me? "No, no," said he, "you are worth a thousand dead men, let us try the old thing over again," and so falling upon our knees, he continued in prayer a considerable time, and near the close of his prayer, the Lord was pleased to set my soul at perfect liberty, and being filled with joy I began to praise the Lord immediately; my sorrows were turned into peace, and joy, and love. The minister said, "How is it now?" I answered, all is well, all happy. He then took his leave of me; but called every day for several days afterwards, and the last time he said, "Hold fast that thou hast already obtained, till Jesus Christ come." I now read the Scriptures very much. My master sent often to know how I did, and at last came himself, and finding me well, asked me if I would not come to work again? I answered no. He asked me the reason, but receiving no answer he went away. I continued with my sister about three weeks, during which time she often asked me to play upon the violin for her, which I refused; then she said I was crazy and mad, and so reported it among the neighbours, which opened the mouths of all around against me. I then resolved to go to my mother, which was eighty-four miles from Charlestown. I was two days on my journey home, and enjoyed much communion with God on the road, and had occasion to mark the gracious interpositions of his kind providence as I passed along. The third day I arrived at my mother's house, and was well received. At supper they sat down to eat without asking the Lord's blessing, which caused me to burst out into tears. My mother asked me what was the matter? I answered, I wept because they sat down to supper without asking the Lord's blessing. She bid me, with much surprise, to ask a blessing. I remained with her fourteen days without inter-

* Mr. HALL, a Baptist minister, at Charlestown.

ruption; the Lord pitied me, being a young soldier. Soon, however, Satan began to stir up my two sisters and brother, who were then at home with my mother; they called me every name but that which was good. The more they persecuted me, the stronger I grew in grace. At length my mother turned against me also, and the neighbours joined her, and there was not a friend to assist me, or that I could speak to; this made me earnest with God. In these circumstances, being the youngest but one of our family, and young in Christian experience, I was tempted so far as to threaten my life; but reading my Bible one day, and finding that if I did destroy myself I could not come where God was, I betook myself to the fields, and some days staid out from morning to night to avoid the persecutors. I staid one time two days without any food, but seemed to have clearer views into the spiritual things of God. Not long after this I was sharply tried, and reasoned the matter within myself, whether I should turn to my old courses of sin and vice, or serve and cleave to the Lord; after prayer to God, I was fully persuaded in my mind that if I turned to my old ways I should perish eternally. Upon this I went home, and finding them all as hardened, or worse than before, and everybody saying I was crazy; but a little sister I had, about nine years of age, used to cry when she saw them persecute me, and continuing so about five weeks and three days, I thought it was better for me to die than to live among such people. I rose one morning very early, to get a little quietness and retirement. I went into the woods, and staid till eight o'clock in the morning; upon my return I found them all at breakfast; I passed by them, and went upstairs without any interruption; I went upon my knees to the Lord, and returned him thanks; then I took up a small pocket Bible and one of Dr. Watts's hymnbooks, and passing by them went out without one word spoken by any of us. After spending some time in the fields I was persuaded to go from home altogether. Accordingly I went over the fence, about half a mile from our house, which divided the inhabited and cultivated parts of the country from the wilderness. I continued travelling in the desert all day without the least inclination of returning back. About evening I began to be surrounded with wolves; I took refuge from them on a tree, and remained there all night. About eight o'clock next morning I descended from the tree, and returned God thanks for the mercies of the night. I went on all this day without anything to eat or drink. The third day, taking my Bible out of my pocket, I read and walked for some time, and then being wearied and almost spent I sat down, and after resting awhile I rose to go forward; but had not gone above a hundred yards when something tripped me up, and I fell down; I prayed to the Lord upon the ground that he would command the wild beasts to devour me, that I might be with him in glory. I made this request to God the third and part of the fourth day. The fourth day in the morning, descending from my usual lodging, a tree, and having nothing all this time to eat, and but a little water to drink, I was so feeble that I tumbled half way down the tree, not being able to support myself, and lay upon my back on the ground an hour and a half, praying and crying; after which getting a little strength, and trying to stand upright to walk, I found myself not able; then I went upon my hands and knees, and so crawled till I reached a tree that was tumbled down, in order to get across it, and there I prayed with my body leaning upon it above an hour, that the Lord would take me to himself. Such nearness to God I then enjoyed, that I willingly resigned myself into his hands. After some time I thought I was strengthened, so I got across the tree without my feet or hands touching the ground; but struggling I fell over on the other side, and then thought the Lord will now answer my prayer, and take me home. But the time was not come. After laying there a little, I rose, and looking about, saw at some distance bunches of grass, called deer-grass; I felt a strong desire to get at it; though I rose, yet it was only on my hands and knees, being so feeble, and in this man-ner I reached the grass. I was three quarters of an hour going in this form twenty yards. When I reached it I was unable to pull it up, so I bit it off like a horse, and prayed the Lord to bless it to me, and I thought it the best meal I ever had in my life, and I think so still, it was so sweet. I returned my God hearty thanks for it, and then lay down about an hour. Feeling myself very thirsty, I prayed the Lord to provide me with some water. Finding I was something strengthened I got up, and stood on my feet, and staggered from one tree to another, if they were near each other, otherwise the journey was too long for me. I continued moving so for some time, and at length passing between two trees, I happened to fall upon some bushes, among which were a few large hollow leaves, which had caught and contained the dews of the night, and lying low among the bushes, were not exhaled by the solar rays; this water in the leaves fell upon me as I tumbled down and was lost. I was now tempted to think the Lord had given me water from Heaven, and I had wasted it. I then prayed the Lord to forgive me. What poor unbelieving creatures we are! though we are assured the Lord will supply all our needs. I was presently directed to a puddle of water very muddy, which some wild pigs had just left; I kneeled down, and asked the Lord to bless it to me, so I drank both mud and water mixed together, and being satisfied I returned the Lord thanks, and went on my way rejoicing. This day was much chequered with wants and supplies, with dangers and deliverances. I continued travelling on for nine days, feeding upon grass, and not knowing whither I was going; but the Lord Jesus Christ was very present, and that comforted me through all. The next morning, having quitted my customary lodging, and returned thanks to the Lord for my preservation through the night, reading and travelling on, I passed between two bears, about twenty yards distance from each other. Both sat and looked at me, but I felt no fear; and after I had passed them, they both went the same way from me without growling, or the least apparent uneasiness. I went and returned God thanks for my escape, who had tamed the wild beasts of the forest, and made them friendly to me: I rose from my knees and walked on, singing hymns of praise to God, about five o'clock in the afternoon, and about 55 miles from home, right through the wilderness. As I was going on, and musing upon the goodness of the Lord, an Indian hunter, who stood at some distance, saw me; he hid himself behind a tree; but as I passed along he bolted out, and put his hands on my breast, which surprised me a few moments. He then asked me where I was going? I answered I did not know, but where the Lord was pleased to guide me. Having heard me praising God before I came up to him, he enquired who I was talking to? I told him I was talking to my Lord Jesus; he seemed surprised, and asked me where he was? for he did not see him there. I told him he could not be seen with bodily eyes. After a little more talk, he insisted upon taking me home; but I refused, and added, that I would die rather than return home. He then asked me if I knew how far I was from home? I answered, I did not know. You are 55 miles and a half, says he, from home. He farther asked me how I did to live? I said I was supported by the Lord. He asked me how I slept? I answered, the Lord provided me with a bed every night; he further enquired what preserved me from being devoured by the wild beasts? I replied, the Lord Jesus Christ kept me from them. He stood astonished, and said, you say the Lord Jesus Christ do this, and do that, and do every thing for you, he must be a very fine man, where is he? I replied, he is here present. To this he made me no answer, only said, I know you, and your mother and sister, and upon a little further conversation I found he did know them, having been used in winter to sell skins in our town. This alarmed me, and I wept for fear he would take me home by force; but when he saw me so affected, he said he would not take me home if I would go with him. I objected against that, for fear he would rob me of my comfort and communion with God: But at last, being much pressed, I consented to go. Our employment for ten weeks and three days, was killing deer, and taking off their skins by day, which we afterwards hung on the trees to dry till they were sent for; the means of defense and security against our nocturnal enemies always took up the evenings: We collected a number of large bushes, and placed them nearly in a circular form, which uniting at the extremity, afforded us both a verdant covering, and a sufficient shelter from the night dews. What moss we could gather was strewed upon the ground, and this composed our bed. A fire was kindled in the front of our temporary lodging-room, and fed with fresh fuel all night, as we slept and watched by turns; and this was our defense from the dreadful animals, whose shining eyes and tremendous roar we often saw and heard during the night.

By constant conversation with the hunter, I acquired a fuller knowledge of the Indian tongue: This, together with the sweet communion I enjoyed with God, I have considered as a preparation for the great trial I was soon after to pass through.

The hunting season being now at an end, we left the woods, and directed our course towards a large Indian town, belonging to the Cherokee nation; and having reached it, I said to the hunter, they will not suffer me to enter in. He replied, as I was with him, nobody would interrupt me.

There was an Indian fortification all round the town, and a guard placed at each entrance. The hunter passed one of these without molestation, but I was stopped by the guard and examined. They asked me where I came from, and what was my business there? My companion of the woods attempted to speak for me, but was not permitted; he was taken away, and I saw him no more. I was now surrounded by about 50 men, and carried to one of their chiefs to be examined by him. When I came before him, he asked me what was my business there? I told him I came there with a hunter, whom I met with in the woods. He replied, "Did I not know that whoever came there without giving a better account of themselves than I did, was to be put to death?" I said I did not know it. Observing that I answered him so readily in his own language, he asked me where I learnt it? To this I returned no answer, but burst out into a flood of tears, and calling upon my Lord Jesus. At this he stood astonished, and expressed a concern for me, and said I was young. He asked me who my Lord Jesus was? To this I gave him no answer, but continued praying and weeping. Addressing himself to the officer who stood by him, he said he was sorry; but it was the law, and it must not be broken. I was then ordered to be taken away, and put into a place of confinement. They led me from their court into a low dark place, and thrust me into it, very dreary and dismal; they made fast the door, and set a watch. The judge sent for the executioner, and gave him his warrant for my execution in the afternoon of the next day. The executioner came, and gave me notice of it, which made me very happy, as the near prospect of death made me hope for a speedy deliverance from the body. And truly this dungeon became my chapel, for the Lord Jesus did not leave me in this great trouble, but was very present, so that I continued blessing him, and singing his praises all night without ceasing. The watch hearing the noise, informed the executioner that somebody had been in the dungeon with me all night; upon which he came in to see and examine, with a great torch lighted in his hand, who it was I had with me; but finding nobody, he turned round, and asked me who it was? I told him it was the Lord Jesus Christ; but he made no answer, turned away, went out, and locked the door. At the hour appointed for my execution I was taken out, and led to the destined spot, amidst a vast number of people. I praised the Lord all the way we went, and when we arrived at the place I understood the kind of death I was to suffer, yet, blessed be God, none of those things moved me. The executioner shewed me a basket of turpentine-wood, stuck full of small pieces, like skewers; he told me I was to be stripped naked, and laid down in the basket, and these sharp pegs were to be stuck into me, and then set on fire, and when they had burnt to my body,* I was to be turned on the other side, and served in the same manner, and then to be taken by four men and thrown into the flame, which was to finish the execution. I burst into tears, and asked what I had done to deserve so cruel a death! To this he gave me no answer. I cried out, Lord, if it be thy will that it should be so, thy will be done: I then asked the executioner to let me go to prayer; he asked me to whom? I answered, to the Lord my God; he seemed surprised, and asked me where he was? I told him he was present; upon which he gave me leave. I desired them all to do as I did, so I fell down upon my knees, and mentioned to the Lord his delivering of the three children in the fiery furnace, and of Daniel in the lion's den, and had close communion with God. I prayed in English a considerable time, and about the middle of my prayer, the Lord impressed a strong desire upon my mind to turn into their language, and pray in their tongue. I did so, and with remarkable liberty, which wonderfully affected the people. One circumstance was very singular, and strikingly displays the power and grace of God. I believe the executioner was savingly converted to God. He rose from his knees, and embraced me round the middle, and was unable to speak for

---

* These pegs were to be kindled at the opposite end from the body.

about five minutes; the first words he expressed, when he had utterance, were, "No man shall hurt thee till thou hast been to the king."

I was taken away immediately, and as we passed along, and I was reflecting upon the deliverance which the Lord had wrought out for me, and hearing the praises which the executioner was singing to the Lord, I must own I was utterly at a loss to find words to praise him. I broke out in these words, what can't the Lord Jesus do! and what power is like unto his! I will thank thee for what is passed, and trust thee for what is to come. I will sing thy praise with my feeble tongue whilst life and breath shall last, and when I fail to sound thy praises here, I hope to sing them round thy throne above: And thus, with unspeakable joy, I sung two verses of Dr. Watts's hymns:

> My God, the spring of all my joys,
>   The life of my delights;
> The glory of my brightest days,
>   And comfort of my nights.
> In darkest shades, if thou appear,
>   My dawning is begun;
> Thou art my soul's bright morning star,
>   And thou my rising sun.

Passing by the judge's door, he stopped us, and asked the executioner why he brought me back? The man fell upon his knees, and begged he would permit me to be carried before the king, which being granted, I went on, guarded by two hundred soldiers with bows and arrows. After many windings I entered the king's outward chamber, and after waiting some time he came to the door, and his first question was, how came I there? I answered, I came with a hunter whom I met with in the woods, and who persuaded me to come there. He then asked me how old I was? I told him not fifteen. He asked me how I was supported before I met with this man? I answered, by the Lord Jesus Christ, which seemed to confound him. He turned round, and asked me if he lived where I came from? I answered, yes, and here also. He looked about the room, and said he did not see him; but I told him I felt him. The executioner fell upon his knees, and entreated the king, and told him what he had felt of the same Lord. At this instant the king's eldest daughter came into the chamber, a person about 19 years of age, and stood at my right hand. I had a Bible in my hand, which she took out of it, and having opened it, she kissed it, and seemed much delighted with it. When she had put it into my hand again, the king asked me what it was? and I told him, the name of my God was recorded there;

and, after several questions, he bid me read it, which I did, particularly the 53d chapter of Isaiah, in the most solemn manner I was able; and also the 26th chapter of Matthew's Gospel; and when I pronounced the name of Jesus, the particular effect it had upon me was observed by the king. When I had finished reading, he asked me why I read those names* with so much reverence? I told him, because the Being to whom those names belonged made heaven and earth, and I and he; this he denied. I then pointed to the sun, and asked him who made the sun, and moon, and stars, and preserved them in their regular order? He said there was a man in their town that did it. I laboured as much as I could to convince him to the contrary. His daughter took the book out of my hand a second time; she opened it, and kissed it again; her father bid her give it to me, which she did; but said, with much sorrow, the book would not speak to her. The executioner then fell upon his knees, and begged the king to let me go to prayer, which being granted, we all went upon our knees, and now the Lord displayed his glorious power. In the midst of the prayer some of them cried out, particularly the king's daughter, and the man who ordered me to be executed, and several others seemed under deep conviction of sin: This made the king very angry; he called me a witch, and commanded me to be thrust into the prison, and to be executed the next morning. This was enough to make me think, as old Jacob once did, "All these things are against me;" for I was dragged away, and thrust into the dungeon with much indignation; but God, who never forsakes his people, was with me. Though I was weak in body, yet was I strong in the spirit: The Lord works, and who shall let it? The executioner went to the king, and assured him, that if he put me to death, his daughter would never be well. They used the skill of all their doctors that afternoon and night; but physical prescriptions were useless. In the morning the executioner came to me, and, without opening the prison door, called to me, and hearing me answer, said, "Fear not, thy God who delivered thee yesterday, will deliver thee to-day." This comforted me very much, especially to find he could trust the Lord. Soon after I was fetched out; I thought it was to be executed; but they led me away to the king's chamber with much bodily weakness, having been without food two days. When I came into the king's presence, he said to me, with much anger, if I did not make his daughter and that man well, I should be laid down and chopped into pieces before him. I was not afraid, but the Lord tried my faith

---

* Or what those parts were which seemed to affect me so much, not knowing what I read, as he did not understand the English language.

sharply. The king's daughter and the other person were brought out into the outer chamber, and we went to prayer; but the heavens were locked up to my petitions. I besought the Lord again, but received no answer: I cried again, and he was entreated. He said, "Be it to thee as thou wilt;" the Lord appeared most lovely and glorious; the king himself was awakened, and the others set at liberty. A great change took place among the people; the king's house became God's house; the soldiers were ordered away, and the poor condemned prisoner had perfect liberty, and was treated like a prince. Now the Lord made all my enemies to become my great friends. I remained nine weeks in the king's palace, praising God day and night: I was never out but three days all the time. I had assumed the habit of the country, and was dressed much like the king, and nothing was too good for me. The king would take off his golden ornaments, his chain and bracelets, like a child, if I objected to them, and lay them aside. Here I learnt to speak their tongue in the highest style.

I began now to feel an inclination growing upon me to go farther on, but none to return home. The king being acquainted with this, expressed his fears of my being used ill by the next Indian nation, and, to prevent it, sent 50 men, and a recommendation to the king, with me. The next nation was called the Creek Indians, at 60 miles distance. Here I was received with kindness, owing to the king's influence, from whom I had parted; here I staid five weeks. I next visited the Catawar Indians, at about 55 miles distance from the others: Lastly, I went among the Housaw Indians, 80 miles distant from the last mentioned; here I staid seven weeks. These nations were then at peace with each other, and I passed among them without danger, being recommended from one to the other. When they recollect that the white people drove them from the American shores, the three first nations have often united, and murdered all the white people in the back settlements which they could lay hold of, man, woman, and child. I had not much reason to believe any of these three nations were savingly wrought upon, and therefore I returned to the Cherokee nation, which took me up eight weeks. I continued with my old friends seven weeks and two days.

I now and then found, that my affections to my family and country were not dead; they were sometimes very sensibly felt, and at last strengthened into an invincible desire of returning home. The king was much against it; but feeling the same strong bias towards my country, after we had asked Divine direction, the king consented, and accompanied me 60 miles with 140 men. I went to prayer three times before we could part, and then he sent 40 men with me a hundred miles farther; I went to prayer, and then took my leave of them, and passed on my way. I had 70 miles now to go to the back settlements of the white people. I was surrounded very soon with wolves again, which made my old lodging both necessary and welcome. However it was not long, for in two days I reached the settlements, and on the third I found a house: It was about dinner-time, and as I came up to the door the family saw me, were frightened, and ran away. I sat down to dinner alone, and ate very heartily, and, after returning God thanks, I went to see what was become of the family. I found means to lay hold of a girl that stood peeping at me from behind a barn. She fainted away, and it was upwards of an hour before she recovered; it was nine o'clock before I could get them all to venture in, they were so terrified.

My dress was purely in the Indian style; the skins of wild beasts composed my garments; my head was set out in the savage manner, with a long pendant down my back, a sash round my middle, without breeches, and a tomahawk by my side. In about two days they became sociable. Having visited three or four other families, at the distance of 16 or 20 miles, I got them altogether to prayer on the Sabbath days, to the number of 17 persons. I staid with them six weeks, and they expressed much sorrow when I left them. I was now one hundred and twelve miles from home. On the road I sometimes met with a house, then I was hospitably entertained; and when I met with none, a tree lent me the use of its friendly shelter and protection from the prowling beasts of the woods during the night. The God of mercy and grace supported me thus for eight days, and on the ninth I reached my uncle's house.

The following particulars, relating to the manner in which I was made known to my family, are less interesting; and yet, perhaps, some readers would not forgive their omission: I shall, however, be as brief as I can. I asked my uncle for a lodging, which he refused. I enquired how far the town was off; three quarters of a mile, said he. Do you know Mrs. Marrant and family, and how the children do? was my next question. He said he did, they were all well, but one was lately lost; at this I turned my head and wept. He did not know me, and upon refusing again to lodge me, I departed. When I reached the town it was dark, and passing by a house where one of my old schoolfellows lived, I knocked at the door; he came out, and asked me what I wanted? I desired a lodging, which was granted: I went in, but was not known. I asked him if he knew Mrs. Marrant, and how the family were? He said, he had just left them, they were all well; but a young lad, with whom he went to school, who, after he had quitted school, went to Charlestown to learn some trade; but came home crazy, and rambled in the woods, and was torn to pieces by the wild beasts. How do you know, said I, that he was killed by wild beasts? I, and his brother, and uncle, and others, said he, went three days into the woods in search of him, and found his carcase torn, and brought it home, and buried it, and they are now in mourning for him. This affected me very much, and I wept; observing it, he said, what is the matter? I made no answer. At supper they sat down without craving a blessing, for which I reproved them; this so affected the man, that I believe it ended in a sound conversion. Here is a wild man, says he, come out of the woods to be a witness for God, and to reprove our ingratitude and stupefaction! After supper I went to prayer, and then to bed. Rising a little before daylight, and praising the Lord, as my custom was, the family were surprised, and got up: I staid with them till nine o'clock, and then went to my mother's house in the next street. The singularity of my dress drew everybody's eyes upon me, yet none knew me. I knocked at my mother's door, my sister opened it, and was startled at my appearance. Having expressed a desire to see Mrs. Marrant, I was answered, she was not very well, and that my business with her could be done by the person at the door, who also attempted to shut me out, which I prevented. My mother being called, I went in, and sat down, a mob of people being round the door. My mother asked, "what is your business?" Only to see you, said I. She was much obliged to me, but did not know me. I asked, how are your children? how are your two sons? She replied, her daughters were in good health, of her two sons, one was well, and with her, but the other,— unable to contain, she burst into a flood of tears, and retired. I was overcome, and wept much; but nobody knew me. This was an affecting scene! Presently my brother came in: He enquired who I was, and what I was? My sister did not know; but being uneasy at my presence, they contrived to get me out of the house, which, being overheard by me, I resolved not to stir. My youngest sister, eleven years of age, came in from school, and knew me the moment she saw me: She goes into the kitchen, and tells the woman her brother was come; but her news finding no credit there she returns, passes through the room where I sat, made a running curtsey, and says to my eldest sister in the next room, it is my brother! She was then called a foolish girl, and threatened; the child cried, and insisted upon it. She went crying upstairs to my mother, and told her; but neither would my mother believe her. At last they said to her, if it be your brother, go and kiss him, and ask him how he does? She ran and clasped me round the neck, and, looking me in the face, said, "Are not you my brother John?" I answered yes, and wept. I was then made known to all the family, to my friends, and acquaintances, who received me, and were glad, and rejoiced:* Thus the dead was brought to life again; thus the lost was found. I shall now close the Narrative, with only remarking a few incidents in my life, until my connection with my Right Honourable Patroness, the Countess of Huntingdon.

I remained with my relations till the commencement of the American troubles. I used to go and hear the Word of God, if any Gospel ministers came into the country, though at a considerable distance, and thereby got acquainted with a few poor people, who feared God in Will's-Town, and Borough Town, Dorchester Town, and other places thereabouts; and in those places we used to meet and associate together for Christian conversation, and, at their request, I frequently went to prayer with them, and at times enjoyed much of the Lord's presence among them; and yet, reader, my soul was got into a declining state. Don't forget our Lord's exhortation, "What I say unto you, I say unto all, WATCH."

About this time I was an eyewitness of the remarkable conversion of a child seven and a half years old, named Mary Scott, which I shall here mention, in hopes the Lord may make it useful and profitable to my young readers. Her parents lived in the house adjoining to my sister's. One day, as I was returning from my work, and passing by the school where she was instructed, I saw the children coming out, and stop'd and looked among them for her, to take her home in my hand; but not seeing her among those that were coming out, I supposed she was gone before, and went on towards home; when passing by the churchyard, which was in my way, I saw her very busy walking from one tomb to another, and went to her, and asked her what she was doing there? She told me, that in the lesson she had set her at school that morning, in the Twentieth of the Revelations, she read, "I saw the dead, small and great, stand before God," &c. and she had been measuring the graves with a tape she then held in her hand, to see if there were any so small as herself among them, and that she had found six that were shorter. I then said, and what of that? She answered, "I shall die, Sir." I told her I knew she would, but hoped she would live till she was grown a woman; but she continued to express her desire to depart, and be with Christ, rather than to live till she was grown up. I then took her by the hand and brought her home with me. After this, she was observed to be always very solid and thoughtful, and that passage ap-

* I had been absent from them about 23 months.

peared always to be fresh upon her mind. I used frequently to be with her when in town, and at her request we often read and prayed together, and she appeared much affected. She never afterwards was seen out at play with other children; but spent her leisure time in reading God's word and prayer. In about four months after this she was taken ill, and kept her room about three weeks; when first taken, she told me she should never come downstairs alive. I frequently visited her during her illness, and made light of what she said about her dying so soon; but in the last week of her illness she said to me, in a very solemn manner, "Sir, I shall die before Saturday-night." The physicians attended her, but she took very few (if any) medicines, and appeared quite calm and resigned to God's will. On Friday morning, which was the day she died, I visited her, and told her that I hoped she would not die so soon as she said; but she told me that she should certainly die before six o'clock that evening. About five o'clock I visited her again. She was then sitting in a chair, and reading in her Bible, to all appearance pretty well recovered. After setting with her about a quarter of an hour, she got up, and desired me to go down, and send her mother up with a clean shift for her, which I did; and after a little time, when I went up again, I found her lying on the bed, with her eyes fixed up to Heaven; when turning herself and seeing me, she said, "Mr. Marrant, don't you see that pretty town, and those fine people, how they shine like gold?—O how I long to be with my Lord and his redeemed Children in Glory!" and then turning to her parents and two sisters (who were all present, having by her desire been called to her) she shook hands with them, and bade them farewell; desiring them not to lament for her when she was dead, for she was going to that fine place where God would wipe away all tears from her eyes, and she should sing Hallelujahs to God and the Lamb for ever and ever, and where she hoped afterwards to meet them; and then turning again to me, she said, "Farewell, and God bless you," and then fell asleep in the arms of Jesus. This afterwards proved the conversion of her mother.

In those troublesome times, I was pressed on board the *Scorpion*, sloop of war, as their musician, as they were told I could play on music. I continued in his Majesty's service six years and eleven months; and with shame confess, that a lamentable stupor crept over all my spiritual vivacity, life and vigour; I got cold and dead. My gracious God, my dear Father in his dear Son, roused me every now and then by dangers and deliverances. I was at the siege of Charlestown, and passed through many dangers. When the town was taken, my old royal benefactor and convert, the king of the Cherokee

Indians, riding into the town with general Clinton, saw me, and knew me: He alighted off his horse,* and came to me; said he was glad to see me; that his daughter was very happy, and sometimes longed to get out of the body.

Some time after this I was cruising about in the American seas, and cannot help mentioning a singular deliverance I had from the most imminent danger, and the use the Lord made of it to me. We were overtaken by a violent storm; I was washed overboard, and thrown on again; dashed into the sea a second time, and tossed upon deck again. I now fastened a rope round my middle, as a security against being thrown into the sea again; but, alas! forgot to fasten it to any part of the ship; being carried away the third time by the fury of the waves, when in the sea, I found the rope both useless and an encumbrance. I was in the sea the third time about eight minutes, and the sharks came round me in great numbers; one of an enormous size, that could easily have taken me into his mouth at once, passed and rubbed against my side. I then cried more earnestly to the Lord than I had done for some time; and he who heard Jonah's prayer, did not shut out mine, for I was thrown aboard again; these were the means the Lord used to revive me, and I began now to set out afresh.

I was in the engagement with the Dutch off the Dogger Bank, on board the *Princess Amelia,* of 84 guns.† We had a great number killed and wounded; the deck was running with blood; six men were killed, and three wounded, stationed at the same gun with me; my head and face were covered with the blood and brains of the slain: I was wounded, but did not fall till a quarter of an hour before the engagement ended, and was happy during the whole of it. After being in the hospital three months and 16 days, I was sent to the West Indies, on board a ship of war, and, after cruising in those seas, we returned home as a convoy. Being taken ill of my old wounds, I was put into the hospital at Plymouth, and had not been there long, when the physician gave it as his opinion, that I should not be capable of serving the king again; I was therefore discharged, and came to London, where I lived with a respectable and pious mer-

* Though it is unusual for Indians to have a horse, yet the king accompanied the general on the present successful occasion riding on horseback.—If the king wished to serve me, there was no opportunity; the town being taken on Friday afternoon, Saturday an express arrived from the commander in chief at New-York, for a large detachment, or the town would fall into the hands of the Americans, which hurried us away on Sunday morning.

† This action was on the 5th of August, 1781.

chant three years,* who was unwilling to part with me. During this time I saw my call to the ministry fuller and clearer; had a feeling concern for the salvation of my countrymen: I carried them constantly in the arms of prayer and faith to the throne of grace, and had continual sorrow in my heart for my brethren, for my kinsmen, according to the flesh. I wrote a letter to my brother, who returned me an answer, in which he prayed some ministers would come and preach to them, and desired me to show it to the minister whom I attended. I used to exercise my gifts on a Monday evening in prayer and exhortation, and was approved of, and ordained at Bath. Her Ladyship having seen the letter from my brother in Nova Scotia, thought Providence called me there: To which place I am now bound, and expect to sail in a few days.

I have now only to intreat the earnest prayers of all my kind Christian friends, that I may be carried safe there; kept humble, made faithful, and successful; that strangers may hear of and run to Christ; that Indian tribes may stretch out their hands to God; that the black nations may be made white in the blood of the Lamb; that vast multitudes, of hard tongues, and of a strange speech, may learn the language of Canaan, and sing the song of Moses, and of the Lamb; and, anticipating the glorious prospect, may we all with fervent hearts, and willing tongues, sing hallelujah; the kingdoms of the world are become the kingdoms of our God, and of his Christ. Amen and Amen.

London,
Prescot-Street, No. 60,
July 18, 1785.

Since Mr. Marrant's arrival at Nova Scotia, several letters have been received from him by different persons, and some by Mr. Aldridge, the Editor of this Narrative; from which it appears, that Mr. Marrant has travelled through that province, preaching the Gospel, and not without success; that he has undergone much fatigue, and passed through many dangers; that he has visited the Indians in their Wigwams, who, he relates, were disposed to hear and receive the Gospel. This is the substance of the letters transmitted by him to the Editor above-mentioned:

London, August 16, 1785.

Mr. John Marrant liv'd with us about 3 years, which he did with honesty and sobriety—he feared God, and had a desire to save his

* About three years; it might be a few weeks over or under.

soul before he ever came to live with us;—he showed himself to be such while he lived with us, by attending the means of Grace diligently, and by being tender hearted to the poor, by giving them money and victuals if he had left himself none. He left us with no misunderstanding whatever, about April last.

This is nothing but the truth.

(Signed)

Cotton-Merchant,
No. 38, Dowgate-Hill.

John Marsden,
H. Marsden.

UNIVERSAL SALVATION,

A VERY ANCIENT DOCTRINE:

WITH SOME ACCOUNT OF THE LIFE AND CHARACTER

OF ITS AUTHOR.

A

SERMON,

DELIVERED AT RUTLAND, WEST PARISH,

VERMONT,

IN THE YEAR 1805.

BY LEMUEL HAYNES, A. M.

SEVENTH EDITION.

NEW-YORK:
PRINTED FOR CORNELIUS DAVIS.
1810.

PREFACE.

THERE is no greater folly than for men to express anger and resentment because their religious sentiments are attacked. If their characters are impeached by their own creed, they only are to blame. All that the antagonists can say, cannot make falsehood truth, nor truth falsehood.

The following discourse was delivered at Rutland, in June, 1805, immediately after hearing Mr. Ballou, a Universal Preacher, zealously exhibit his sentiments. The author had been repeatedly solicited to hear and dispute with the above Preacher; and had been charged with dishonesty and cowardice for refusing. He felt that some kind of testimony, in opposition to what he calls error, ought to be made; and has been urged to let the same appear in print. But whether on the whole it is for the interest of truth is left to the judgment of the candid.

Rutland, Dec. 30, 1805.

From the Panoplist.

THE following are some of the excellencies of this sermon.

1. The text is very aptly chosen.

2. It is a very impressive and convincing sermon. What could more strongly prove the falsehood of universalism, than to show from scripture, that the devil was its author, and first preacher.

3. The satire, which runs through the sermon, is founded on truth and justice, and managed with Christian sobriety.

4. The sermon displays much originality.

5. It is a very popular sermon. Of this, there is sufficient proof in the six editions of it which have been printed within two years.

6. It is a very useful sermon, especially to those, who want leisure, ability, or patience to follow with advantage a long chain of reasoning.

A SERMON, &c.

Genesis III. 4:
And the Serpent said unto the Woman, Ye shall not surely die.

THE holy Scriptures are a peculiar fund of instruction. They inform us of the origin of creation; of the primitive state of man; of his fall, or apostasy from God. It appears that he was placed in the garden of Eden with full liberty to regale himself with all the delicious fruits that were to be found, except what grew on one tree—if he eat of that he should surely die, was the declaration of the Most High.

Happy were the human pair amidst this delightful paradise; until a certain preacher, in his journey, came that way, and disturbed their peace and tranquillity, by endeavouring to reverse the prohibition of the Almighty, as in our text—"Ye shall not surely die."

She pluck'd, she ate;
Earth felt the wound: nature from her seat,
Sighing through all her works, gave signs of wo,
That all was lost.

Milton.

We may attend to the *character* of the preacher—to the *doctrine* inculcated—to the *hearer* addressed—to the *medium* or *instrument* of the preaching.

I. As to the preacher, I would observe, he has many names given him in the sacred writings, the most common is the *Devil*. That it was he that disturbed the felicity of our first parents, is evident from 2 Cor. xi. 3. and many other passages of Scripture. He was once an angel of light, and knew better than to preach such doctrine; he did violence to his own reason.

But to be a little more particular, let it be observed,

1. He is an *old* preacher. He lived above one thousand seven hundred years before Abraham—above two thousand four hundred and thirty years before Moses—four thousand and four years before Christ. It is now five thousand eight hundred and nine years since he commenced preaching. By this time he must have acquired great skill in the art.

2. He is a very *cunning*, artful preacher. When Elymas, the sorcerer, came to turn away people from the faith, he is said to be *full of all subtlety, and a child of the devil*—not only because he was an enemy of all righteousness, but on account of his carnal cunning and craftiness.

3. He is a very *laborious* unwearied preacher. He has been in the ministry almost six thousand years; and yet his zeal is not in the least abated. The apostle Peter compares him to a roaring lion, *walking* about, seeking whom he may devour. When God inquired of this persevering preacher, Job ii. 2. "From whence camest thou?" he "answered the Lord, and said, From *going to and fro* in the earth, and from *walking up and down in it*." He is far from being circumscribed within the narrow limits of parish, state, or continental lines; but his haunt and travel is very large and extensive.

4. He is a *heterogeneous* preacher, if I may so express myself. He makes use of a Bible when he holds forth, as in his sermon to our Saviour, Matt. iv. 6. He mixes truth with error, in order to make it go well, or to carry his point.

5. He is a very *presumptuous* preacher. Notwithstanding God had declared in the most plain and positive terms, "Thou shalt surely

die"—or "In dying thou shalt die"—yet, this audacious wretch had the impudence to confront Omnipotence, and say, "Ye shall not surely die!"

6. He is a very *successful* preacher. He draws a great number after him. No preacher can command hearers like him. He was successful with our first parents—with the old world. Noah once preached to those spirits that are now in the prison of hell; and told them from God, that they should surely die: but this preacher came along and declared the contrary—"Ye shall not surely die." The greater part, it seems, believed him, and went to destruction. So it was with Sodom and Gomorrah—Lot preached to them; the substance of which was, "Up, get ye out of this place; for the Lord will *destroy* this City." Gen. xix. 14. But this old declaimer told them, No danger! no danger! "Ye shall not surely die." To which they generally gave heed; and Lot seemed to them as one who *mocked*—They believed the Universal preacher, and were consumed—agreeably to the declaration of the apostle Jude, "Sodom and Gomorrah, and the cities about them, suffering the vengeance of eternal fire."

II. Let us attend to the doctrine inculcated by this preacher, "Ye shall not surely die." Bold assertion! without a single argument to support it. The death contained in the threatening, was doubtless *eternal* death,—as nothing but this would express God's feelings towards sin, or render an infinite atonement necessary. To suppose it to be spiritual death, is to blend crime and punishment together. To suppose temporal death to be the curse of the law, then believers are not delivered from it, according to Gal. iii. 13. What Satan meant to preach was, that there is no hell; and that the wages of sin is not death, but eternal life.

III. We shall now take notice of the hearer addressed by the preacher. This we have in the text—"And the serpent said unto the *Woman,* ye shall not surely die." That Eve had not so much experience as Adam, is evident; and so not equally able to withstand temptation. This doubtless was a reason why the tempter chose her, with whom he might hope to be successful. Doubtless he took a time when she was separated from her husband.

That this preacher has had the greatest success in the dark and ignorant parts of the earth, is evident: his kingdom is a kingdom of darkness. He is a great enemy to light. St. Paul gives us some account of him in his day, 2. Tim. iii. 6, "For of this sort are they which creep into houses, and lead captive *silly* women, laden with sins, led away with divers lusts." The same apostle observes, Rom. xvi. 17, 18, "Now I beseech you brethren, mark them which cause divisions and offences contrary to the doctrine which ye have learned, and avoid them. For they that are such serve not our Lord Jesus Christ, but their own belly; and by good words and fair speeches deceive the hearts of the *simple*."

IV. The instrument or medium made use of by the preacher will now be considered. This we have in the text—"And the *Serpent* said unto the Woman, ye shall not surely die." But how came the devil to preach through the serpent?

1. To save his own character, and the better to carry his point. Had the devil come to our first parents personally and unmasked, they would have more easily seen the deception. The reality of a future punishment is at times so clearly impressed on the human mind that even Satan is constrained to own that there is a hell; although at other times he denies it. He does not wish to have it known that he is a liar; therefore he conceals himself, that he can the better accomplish his designs and save his own character.

2. The devil is an enemy to all good, to all happiness and excellence. He is opposed to the felicity of the brutes. He took delight in tormenting the swine. The serpent, before he set up preaching Universal Salvation, was a cunning, beautiful and happy creature; but now his glory is departed. "And the Lord said unto the serpent, because thou hast done this, thou art cursed above all cattle, and above every beast of the field: upon thy belly shalt thou go, and dust shalt thou eat all the days of thy life." There is therefore, a kind of duplicate cunning in the matter—Satan gets the preacher and hearers also.

> And is not this triumphant treachery,
> And more than simple conquest in the foe!
>
> Young.

3. Another reason why Satan employs instruments in his service is because his empire is large, and he cannot be everywhere himself.

4. He has a large number at his command, that love and approve of his work, delight in building up his kingdom, and stand ready to go at his call.

INFERENCES.

1. The devil is not dead, but still lives; and is able to preach as well as ever, "Ye shall not surely die."

2. Universal salvation is no new fangled scheme, but can boast of great antiquity.

3. See a reason why it ought to be rejected, because it is an ancient devilish doctrine.

4. See one reason why it is that Satan is such a mortal enemy to the Bible, and to all who preach the Gospel, because of that injunction, Mark xvi. 15, 16. "And he said unto them, Go ye into all the world, and preach the Gospel to every creature. He that believeth and is baptized, shall be saved; but he that believeth not shall be *damned.*"

5. See whence it was that Satan exerted himself so much to convince our first parents that there was no hell—because the denunciation of the Almighty was true, and he was afraid that Adam and Eve would continue in the belief of it. Was there no truth in future punishment, or was it only a temporary evil, Satan would not be so busy in trying to convince men that there is none. It is his nature and element to lie. "When he speaketh a lie, he speaketh of his own; for he is a liar, and the father of it." John viii. 44.

6. We infer that ministers should not be proud of their preaching. If they preach the true Gospel, they only in substance, repeat Christ's sermons. If they preach, "Ye shall not surely die," they only make use of the Devil's old notes that he delivered almost six thousand years ago.

7. It is probable that the doctrine of Universal Salvation will still prevail, since this preacher is yet alive, and not in the least superannuated; and every effort against him only enrages him more and more, and excites him to new inventions and exertions to build up his cause.

To close the subject: As the author of the foregoing discourse has confined himself wholly to the character of Satan, he trusts no one will feel himself personally injured by this short sermon; but should any imbibe a degree of friendship for this aged divine, and think that I have not treated this Universal Preacher with that respect and veneration that he justly deserves, let them be so kind as to point it out, and I will most cheerfully retract; for it has ever been a maxim with me *"Render unto all their dues."*

The following lines, taken from the *Theological Magazine,* were repeated after the delivery of the preceding discourse.

A later writer in favour of Universal Salvation, having closed his piece with these last lines of Pope's *Messiah,*

> The seas shall waste, the skies in smoke decay,
> Rocks fall to dust, and mountains melt away;
> But fixt his word, his saving power remains,
> Thy realm forever lasts, thy own Messiah reigns;

his antagonist made the following addition to them:

UNIVERSALISM INDEED.

"When seas shall waste, and skies in smoke decay,
"Rocks fall to dust, and mountains melt away;
"In adamantine chains shall death be bound,
"And hell's grim tyrant feel the eternal wound."
But all his children reach fair Eden's shore,
Not e'er to see their father Satan more.
The tottering drunkards shall to glory reel,
And common strumpets endless pleasure feel.
Blest are the haughty, who despise the poor,
For they're entitled to the heavenly store.
Blest all who laugh and scoff at truth divine,
For bold revilers endless comfort find.
Blest are the clam'rous and contentious crew,
To them eternal rest and peace are due.
Blest all who hunger, and who thirst to find
A chance to plunder and to cheat mankind:
Such die in peace—for God to them has given
To be unjust on earth, and go to heaven.
Blest is the wretch whose bowels never move
With generous pity, or with tender love;
He shall find mercy from the God above.
Blest all who seek to wrangle and to fight;
Such mount from seas of blood to worlds of light.
Go riot, drink, and ev'ry ill pursue,
For joys eternal are reserved for you.
Fear not to sin, till death shall close your eyes;
Live as you please, yours is th' immortal prize,
Old Serpent, hail! thou mad'st a just reply
To mother Eve, "Ye shall not surely die!"
But, Reader, stop!—and in God's holy fear,
With sacred truth these tenets first compare;
Our Saviour's Sermon on the mount peruse—
Read with attention, and the bane refuse!

An Address to the Wyandott Nation

and Accompanying Letter to William Walker

DATED MAY 25, 1817

BY JOHN STEWART

"Marietta, (O.) May 25th, 1817.

WILLIAM WALKER, ESQ.

Sir, I have taken the liberty of enclosing to your care the within written address, directed to the Wyandott nation, for their information and edification, hoping that it will (through the blessing of God) impress on their minds, religious and moral sentiments. I have taken the liberty to address it to you, hoping that you will have the goodness to read it, or cause it to be read in their hearing, and in their own language, that they may understand its true meaning; and moreover, that you will try to impress on their minds the necessity of adhering strictly to the laws of God—that their hearts should be constantly set upon the Supreme Being who created them; and that it is their duty to raise their voices in praising, adoring, and loving that *Jesus,* who has suffered and died for them, as well as for those who are more enlightened. Inform them that although their brother is far from them in body, yet his anxiety for their safety and future happiness is very great; in doing this you will confer a favour upon me which I shall ever remember with gratitude. My engagements, you no doubt recollect, were, that I should return about the last week in June, but owing to misfortunes and disappointments to which we are all liable, together with a wound I accidentally received on my leg, will prevent my having the pleasure of seeing or being with you until the middle of July; at which time I hope, by the grace of God, to have the pleasure of seeing you and the Wyandott people generally. At that time I shall not fail to offer verbally my gratitude to you and your dear family for the services you and they have rendered me.

May I ask you to have the goodness to write to me? and please inform me of the general state of those persons that have reformed since I first went among them, and how many have evidenced a change since I came away, and whether they continue to conduct themselves with that sincerity of heart, that would be acceptable in the eyes of God; finally, whether they appear as anxious for my return as they appeared to be for my stay when I was coming away. In attending to these requests of mine, you will confer an obligation which will be ever remembered with every mark of gratitude and respect.

I remain your humble servant, and in every instance sincerely hope, not only to meet with your approbation, but that also of my God.

JOHN STEWART.

THE ADDRESS

My dear and beloved Friends:

I, your brother traveller to eternity, by the grace and mercy of God, am blessed with this opportunity of writing to you; although I be far distant from you in body, yet my mind is oft times upon you. I pray you to be watchful that the enemy of souls do not ensnare you; pray to the Lord both day and night with a sincere heart, and he will uphold you in all your trials and troubles. The words that I shall take as a standard to try to encourage you from, may be found in the 5th chapter of Matthew, 6th verse, "Blessed are they who hunger and thirst after righteousness, for they shall be filled." These words were spoken by our Saviour Jesus Christ, and they are firm and sure; for his words are more firm than the heavens or the earth. Likewise the promise appears to be permanent; it does not say it may be, or perhaps, so as to leave it doubtful; but, "they *shall* be filled." This man, Jesus Christ, spake like one who possessed power to fill and satisfy the hungering soul, and we have no reason to dispute his ability to do so; knowing that he made all things that are made, and made man for his service, then we are bound to believe that he is a Being of all power, able to fulfil all his promises to all mankind. Though he made us for his service, we have all gone astray into the forbidden paths of sin and folly; therefore the promise appears to be held out to a particular class of people, who, happy are they, if they find themselves in this hungering and thirsting after the righteousness of the Lord Jesus Christ. In the first place, my friends, I shall endeavour to show you who it is that this gracious promise is made to, or how it is that we have a right to this promise; according to the light the Lord has given me, it is not him that is living in open rebellion against God, and going contrary to his commands —that closes his eyes against the light—that is barring the door of his heart against the strivings of the blessed Spirit, that is continually admonishing him to forsake the ways of sin, and turn and seek the salvation of his soul; it is that man or woman who has called upon that God that hears sinners pray, and who will have mercy upon such as will call upon him with sincerity of heart, really desiring to receive and believing that he is able to give you. The Lord by his goodness will begin to take off the veil that the enemy has veiled you with, then you begin to see how thou hast strayed from the right way, this causes the sinner to be more and more engaged: this good and great Saviour, who sees and knows the secrets of every heart, seeing the poor soul willing to forsake the service of the devil, moves nearer and nearer to the sinner, his glorious light shines into his heart, he gives him to see the pool of crime that he has committed against the Blessed Saviour who hung on the tree for the sins of the world; this makes him mourn and grieve over his sins, and calling on the mighty Saviour, as his last, his best refuge, for help; finding that there is no help in and of himself, seeing that all he has done is nothing, this causes the soul to try to make his last prayer, crying "Lord save, or I perish;" thou wouldst be just in sending me to destruction, but Lord save, for Christ's sake; Lord, I have done all I can do, take me, do thy will with me, for thou knowest better what to do with me than I can desire. This blessed Saviour shows his face with ten thousand smiles—lays his hand to the work—breaks the snares of sin—unlooses him from the fetters and chains of unbelief— sets the soul at liberty—puts a new song in his mouth—makes the soul rejoice with joy unspeakable and full of glory; it is then he desires to go to his friend who has done so much for him, and leave this troublesome world; but the soul has to stay until it has done its duty on earth, which will not be long. After a few more rolling suns of this life, the tempter beings to tempt him; the world, the flesh, and the devil all unite; the poor soul begins to mourn and grieve, because he cannot do as he would wish; when he would do good, evil is present; then it is the soul begins to hunger and thirst after righteousness. My friends, be glad and rejoice in the Lord, for this promise is to you and to all mankind; yes, they shall be filled with water issuing from the throne of God. O, my friends, pray to God to give you a hungering and thirsting after righteousness! seek for it and you shall find it, for you shall reap in due season if you faint not. If you persevere in the way of well doing, you will find in your path clusters of sweet fruits, that will satisfy your hungering souls, and being faithful to your Lord's commands, when you have made your way through much tribulation, and lie down on your dying bed, you will be filled with the glorious prospect of the reward that awaits you; guardian angels wait around your bed, to bear your soul away to those bright worlds of everlasting day, where the friend of poor sinners reigns. This fills the soul with the sweets of love divine; this methinks, will make the dying bed of the man or woman, "soft as downy pillows are." Therefore, my friends, if you hold out faithful, you will have part in the first resurrection; then it will be that you will see your Lord and master face to face; then it will be that you will hear that blessed sentence "Come ye blessed of my Father, inherit the kingdom prepared for you from the foundation of the world." Then shall you sit down with the people of God in that kingdom, where your Saviour with his soft hand will wipe all tears from your eyes. There you shall see and be with him, and praise him to all eternity. Having, after a broken and imperfect manner, my friends, shown you the characters of those who hunger and thirst after righteousness, I shall endeavour to say a few words to that class of people, who I, in the foregoing part of my discourse said, had no part in the promise. A few words of consolation to the sinner; that is, the Lord is willing to save all who will call upon him with a sincere heart, at the same time having determined to forsake all sin, and to seek the salvation of their souls. Now, my friends, you who have been at war against this great friend of sinners, now turn, for behold now is the accepted time, now is the day of salvation. Take into consideration, realize how long the Lord has spared your lives, and all this time you have been resisting his holy and blessed Spirit—this Spirit the Lord has sent to warn you, and entreat you to turn to the Lord; But oh! my friends, how often have you thrust that good spirit away, and forced it to depart from you! Let me inform you, if you continue to resist this good spirit, it will after a while leave you, never more to return; for God hath said, "my spirit shall not always strive with man." Therefore, my friends, though you have caused the spirit to go away grieved, now begin to encourage and attend to its admonitions; he that receives it and obeys its directions, receives Christ, and at the same time receives God the Father. My friends, if you will not adhere to the Lord's Spirit, neither to the entreaties of your friend, the time draws on when you will wish you had spent this glorious opportunity the Lord has given you, in preparing to meet Him who is to judge the world. Then it will be you will have to hear and abide by that dreadful sentence "Depart ye cursed—ye workers of iniquity, for I never knew you." Oh! my friends, consider you must go into fire prepared for the devil and his angels, where the worm dieth not and the fire is not quenched. Some of you may put off this and think it is a long time yet before it comes to pass; but consider, if the Lord does not call you by judgment, death is always near, and he taking off our friends both on our right and on our left hands. Ah! we must all, sooner or later, be called to lie on a sickbed, when no physician can effect a cure, when death—cold and dreary death—will lay hold on us; then will we have a view of awful eternity, and if unprepared, horrow will seize upon the soul, while our friends wait around our bed, to see us bid the world adieu. Oh! what anguish will tear the soul of the sinner! What bitter lamentations will then be made for mis-spent opportunities, slighted mercies! Oh! that I had spent my time more to the Lord! Then you will say, farewell my friends, I have got to go, for devils are waiting round my bed, to drag my soul away to hell. Then will you remember how often you grieved the good Spirit of the Lord, how often you drove it from you, but too late, you must go to endure the horrors of everlasting burnings. Then, my friends, accept of my feeble advice; bear constantly in mind the necessity of obtaining this blessed promise, and ever let your hearts and conduct be guided by the directions of that blessed Saviour who died for you, that you might live. You who have set out in the way of well doing, be faithful unto death, and you will be conveyed by angels to Abraham's bosom, and there meet the sweet salutation of "well done good and faithful servant, enter thou into the joy of thy Lord." And may God bless you and keep you in the path of righteousness, until he shall see fit to close your eyes in death. Now may the blessing, &c.,

JOHN STEWART

[Source: Joseph Mitchell, *The Missionary Pioneer; or, a Brief Memoir of the Life, Labours, and Death of John Stewart (Man of Colour), Founder Under God of The Mission Among the Wyandotts at Upper Sandusky, Ohio* (New York: printed by J. C. Totten, 1827), pp. 53–63.]

RELIGION

AND THE

PURE PRINCIPLES OF MORALITY

THE SURE FOUNDATION

ON WHICH WE MUST BUILD

PRODUCTIONS FROM THE PEN OF

MRS. MARIA W. STEWARD,

WIDOW OF THE LATE JAMES W. STEWARD, OF BOSTON.

INTRODUCTION.

FEELING a deep solemnity of soul, in view of our wretched and degraded situation, and sensible of the gross ignorance that prevails amongst us, I have thought proper thus publicly to express my sentiments before you. I hope my friends will not scrutinize these pages with too severe an eye, as I have not calculated to display either elegance or taste in their composition, but have merely written the meditations of my heart as far as my imagination led; and have presented them before you, in order to arouse you to exertion, and to enforce upon your minds the great necessity of turning your attention to knowledge and improvement.

I was born in Hartford, Connecticut, in 1803; was left an orphan at five years of age; was bound out in a clergyman's family; had the seeds of piety and virtue early sown in my mind; but was deprived of the advantages of education, though my soul thirsted for knowledge. Left them at 15 years of age; attended Sabbath Schools until I was 20; in 1826, was married to James W. Steward; was left a widow in 1829; was, as I humbly hope and trust, brought to the knowledge of the truth, as it is in Jesus, in 1830; in 1831, made a public profession of my faith in Christ.

From the moment I experienced the change, I felt a strong desire, with the help and assistance of God, to devote the remainder of my days to piety and virtue, and now possess that spirit of independence, that, were I called upon, I would willingly sacrifice my life for the cause of God and my brethren.

All the nations of the earth are crying out for Liberty and Equality. Away, away with tyranny and oppression! And shall Afric's sons be silent any longer? Far be it from me to recommend to you either to kill, burn, or destroy. But I would strongly recommend to you to improve your talents: let not one lie buried in the earth. Show forth your powers of mind. Prove to the world that

> Though black your skins as shades of night,
> Your hearts are pure, your souls are white.

This is the land of freedom. The press is at liberty. Every man has a right to express his opinion. Many think, because your skins are tinged with a sable hue, that you are an inferior race of beings; but God does not consider you as such. He hath formed and fashioned you in his own glorious image, and hath bestowed upon you reason and strong powers of intellect. He hath made you to have dominion over the beasts of the field, the fowls of the air, and the fish of the sea. He hath crowned you with glory and honor; hath made you but a little lower than the angels; and, according to the Constitution of these United States, he hath made all men free and equal. Then why should one worm say to another, "Keep you down there, while I sit up yonder; for I am better than thou?" 'Tis not the color of the skin that makes the man, but it is the principles formed within the soul.

Many will suffer for pleading the cause of oppressed Africa, and I shall glory in being one of her martyrs; for I am firmly persuaded, that the God in whom I trust is able to protect me from the rage and malice of mine enemies, and from them that will rise up against me; and if there is no other way for me to escape, he is able to take me to himself, as he did the most noble, fearless, and undaunted David Walker.

Never Will Virtue, Knowledge, and True Politeness Begin to Flow, Till the Pure Principles of Religion and Morality Are Put into Force.

My Respected Friends,

I feel almost unable to address you; almost incompetent to perform the task; and, at times, I have felt ready to exclaim, O that my head were waters, and mine eyes a fountain of tears, that I might weep day and night for the transgressions of the daughters of my people. Truly, my heart's desire and prayer is that Ethiopia might stretch forth her hands unto God. But we have a great work to do. Never, no, never will the chains of slavery and ignorance burst, till we become united as one, and cultivate amongst ourselves the pure principles of piety, morality and virtue. I am sensible of my ignorance; but such knowledge as God has given to me, I impart to you. I am sensible of former prejudices; but it is high time for prejudices and animosities to cease from amongst us. I am sensible of exposing myself to calumny and reproach; but shall I, for fear of feeble man who shall die, hold my peace? Shall I, for fear of scoffs and frowns, refrain my tongue? Ah, no! I speak as one that must give an account at the awful bar of God; I speak as a dying mortal, to dying mortals. O, ye daughters of Africa, awake! awake! arise! no longer sleep nor slumber, but distinguish yourselves. Show forth to the world that ye are endowed with noble and exalted faculties. O, ye daughters of Africa! what have ye done to immortalize your names beyond the grave? what examples have ye set before the rising generation? what foundation have ye laid for generations yet unborn? where are our union and love? and where is our sympathy, that weeps at another's wo, and hides the faults we see? And our daughters, where are they? blushing in innocence and virtue? And our sons, do they bid fair to become crowns of glory to our hoary heads? Where is the parent who is conscious of having faithfully discharged his duty, and at the last awful day of account, shall be able to say, Here, Lord, is thy poor, unworthy servant, and the children thou hast given me? And where are the children that will arise, and call them blessed? Alas, O God! forgive me if I speak amiss: the minds of our tender babes are tainted as soon as they are born; they go astray, as it were, from the womb. Where is the maiden who will blush at vulgarity? And where is the youth who has written upon his manly brow a thirst for knowledge; whose ambitious mind soars above trifles, and longs for the time to come, when he shall redress the wrongs of his father, and plead the cause of his brethren? Did the daughters of our land possess a delicacy of manners, combined with gentleness and dignity; did their pure minds hold vice in abhorrence and contempt; did they frown when their ears were polluted with its vile accents. Would not their influence become powerful? Would not our brethen fall in love with their virtues? Their souls would become fired with a holy zeal for freedom's cause. They would become ambitious to distinguish themselves. They would become proud to display their talents. Able advocates would arise in our defense. Knowledge would begin to flow, and the chains of slavery and ignorance would melt like wax before the flames. I am but a feeble instrument. I am but as one particle of the small dust of the earth. You may frown or smile. After I am dead, perhaps before, God will surely raise up those who will more powerfully and eloquently plead the cause of virtue and the pure principles of morality than I am able to do. O Virtue! how sacred is thy name! How pure are thy principles! Who can find a virtuous woman? For her price is far above rubies. Blessed is the man who shall call her his wife; yea, happy is the child who shall call her mother. O woman, woman, would thou only strive to excel in merit and virtue; would thou only store thy mind with useful knowledge, great would be thine influence. Do you say you are too far advanced in life now to begin? You are not too far advanced to instill these principles into the minds of your tender infants. Let them by no means be neglected. Discharge your duty faithfully in every point of view: leave the event with God. So shall your skirts become clear of their blood.

When I consider how little improvement has been made the last eight years; the apparent cold and indifferent state of the children of God; how few have been hopefully brought to the knowledge of the truth as it is in Jesus; that our young men and maidens are fainting and drooping, as it were, by the wayside for the want of knowledge; —when I see how few care to distinguish themselves either in religious or moral improvement, and when I see the greater part of our community following the vain bubbles of life with so much eagerness, which will only prove to them like the serpent's sting upon the bed of death, I really think we are in as wretched and miserable a state as was the house of Israel in the days of Jeremiah.

I suppose many of my friends will say, "Religion is all your theme." I hope my conduct will ever prove me to be what I profess, a true follower of Christ: and it is the religion of Jesus alone, that will constitute your happiness here, and support you in a dying hour. O then do not trifle with God and your own souls any longer. Do not presume to offer him the very dregs of your lives; but now, whilst you are blooming in health and vigor, consecrate the remnant of your days to him. Do you wish to become useful in your day and generation? Do you wish to promote the welfare and happiness of your friends, as far as your circle extends? Have you one desire to become truly great? O, then, become truly pious, and God will endow you with wisdom and knowledge from on high.

> Come, turn to God, who did thee make,
> And at his presence fear and quake:
> Remember him now in thy youth,
> And let thy soul take hold of truth.
> The devil and his ways defy;
> Believe him not, he doth but lie;
> His ways seem sweet; but youth, beware!
> He for thy soul hath laid a snare.

Religion is pure; it is ever new; it is beautiful; it is all that is worth living for; it is worth dying for. O, could I but see the church built up in the most holy faith; could I but see men spiritually minded, walking in the fear of God, not given to filthy lucre, not holding religion in one hand and the world in the other, but diligent in business, fervent in spirit, serving the Lord, standing upon the walls of Zion, crying to passers by, ho, every one that thirsteth, come ye to the waters, and he that hath no money; yea, come and buy wine and milk without money and without price—Turn ye, turn ye, for why will ye die?—could I but see mothers in Israel, chaste, keepers at home, not busybodies, meddlers in other men's matters, whose adorning is of the inward man, possessing a meek and quiet spirit, whose sons were like olive-plants, and whose daughters were as polished corner-stones; could I but see young men and maidens turning their feet from impious ways, rather choosing to suffer affliction with the people of God than to enjoy the pleasures of sin for a season; could I but see the rising youth blushing in artless innocence; then could I say, Now, Lord, let thine unworthy handmaiden depart in peace, for I have seen the desire of mine eyes, and am satisfied.

PRAYER.

O Lord God, the watchmen of Zion have cried peace, peace, when there was no peace; they have been, as it were, blind leaders of the blind. Wherefore hast thou so long withheld from us the divine influences of thy Holy Spirit? Wherefore hast thou hardened our hearts and blinded our eyes? It is because we have honored thee with our lips, when our hearts were far from thee. We have polluted thy sabbaths, and even our most holy things have been solemn mockery to thee. We have regarded iniquity in our hearts, therefore thou wilt not hear. Return again unto us, O Lord God, we beseech thee, and pardon this the iniquity of thy servants. Cause thy face to shine upon us, and we shall be saved. O visit us with thy salvation. Raise up sons and daughters unto Abraham, and grant that there might come a mighty shaking of dry bones amongst us, and a great ingathering of souls. Quicken thy professing children. Grant that the young may be constrained to believe that there is a reality in religion, and a beauty in the fear of the Lord. Have mercy on the benighted sons and daughters of Africa. Grant that we may soon become so distinguished for our moral and religious improvements, that the nations of the earth may take knowledge of us; and grant that our cries may come up before thy throne like holy incense. Grant that every daughter of Africa may consecrate her sons to thee from the birth. And do thou, Lord, bestow upon them wise and understanding hearts. Clothe us with humility of soul, and give us a becoming dignity of manners: may we imitate the character of the meek and lowly Jesus; and do thou grant that Ethiopia may soon stretch forth her hands unto thee. And now, Lord, be pleased to grant that Satan's kingdom may be destroyed; that the kingdom of our Lord Jesus Christ may be built up; that all nations and kindreds and tongues and people might be brought to the knowledge of the truth as it is in Jesus, and we at last meet around thy throne, and join in celebrating thy praises.

I have been taking a survey of the American people in my own mind, and I see them thriving in arts, and sciences, and in polite literature. Their highest aim is to excel in political, moral and religious improvement. They early consecrate their children to God, and their youth indeed are blushing in artless innocence: they wipe the tears from the orphan's eyes, and they cause the widow's heart to sing for joy! and their poorest ones, who have the least wish to excel, they promote! And those that have but one talent, they encourage. But how very few are there amongst them that bestow one thought upon the benighted sons and daughters of Africa, who have enriched the soils of America with their tears and blood! few to promote their cause, none to encourage their talents. Under these circumstances, do not let our hearts be any longer discouraged; it is no use to murmur nor to repine; but let us promote ourselves and improve our own talents. And I am rejoiced to reflect that there are many able and talented ones amongst us, whose names might be recorded on the bright annals of fame. But, "I can't" is a great barrier in the way. I hope it will soon be removed, and "I will" resume its place.

Righteousness exalteth a nation, but sin is a reproach to any people. Why is it, my friends, that our minds have been blinded by

ignorance, to the present moment? 'Tis on account of sin. Why is it
that our church is involved in so much difficulty? 'Tis on account of
sin. Why is it that God has cut down, upon our right hand and upon
our left, the most learned and intelligent of our men? O, shall I say,
it is on account of sin! Why is it that thick darkness is mantled upon
every brow, and we, as it were, look sadly upon one another? It is
on account of sin. O, then, let us bow before the Lord our God, with
all our hearts, and humble our very souls in the dust before him;
sprinkling, as it were, ashes upon our heads, and awake to righteousness and sin not. The arm of the Lord is not shortened, that it cannot save; neither is his ear heavy, that it cannot hear; but it is your
iniquities that have separated you from me, saith the Lord. Return,
O ye backsliding children, and I will return unto you, and ye shall be
my people, and I will be your God.

O, ye mothers, what a responsibility rests on you! You have souls
committed to your charge, and God will require a strict account of
you. It is you that must create in the minds of your little girls and
boys a thirst for knowledge, the love of virtue, the abhorrence of
vice, and the cultivation of a pure heart. The seeds thus sown will
grow with their growing years; and the love of virtue thus early
formed in the soul will protect their inexperienced feet from many
dangers. O, do not say you cannot make any thing of your children;
but say, with the help and assistance of God, we will try. Do not
indulge them in their little stubborn ways; for a child left to himself
bringeth his mother to shame. Spare not, for their crying; thou shalt
beat them with a rod, and they shall not die; and thou shalt save
their souls from hell. When you correct them, do it in the fear of
God, and for their own good. They will not thank you for your false
and foolish indulgence; they will rise up, as it were, and curse you
in this world, and, in the world to come, condemn you. It is no use
to say, you can't do this, or, you can't do that: you will not tell your
Maker so, when you meet him at the great day of account. And you
must be careful that you set an example worthy of following, for you
they will imitate. There are many instances, even amongst us now,
where parents have discharged their duty faithfully, and their children now reflect honor upon their gray hairs.

Perhaps you will say, that many parents have set pure examples
at home, and they have not followed them. True, our expectations
are often blasted; but let not this dishearten you. If they have faithfully discharged their duty, even after they are dead, their works
may live: their prodigal children may then return to God, and become heirs of salvation: if not, their children cannot rise and condemn them at the awful bar of God.

Perhaps you will say that you cannot send them to high schools and academies. You can have them taught in the first rudiments of useful knowledge, and then you can have private teachers, who will instruct them in the higher branches; and their intelligence will become greater than ours, and their children will attain to higher advantages, and *their* children still higher; and then, though we are dead, our works shall live. Though we are mouldering, our names shall not be forgotten.

Finally, my heart's desire and prayer to God is that there might come a thorough reformation amongst us. Our minds have too long grovelled in ignorance and sin. Come, let us incline our ears to wisdom, and apply our hearts to understanding: promote her, and she shall exalt thee; she shall bring thee to honor when thou dost embrace her. An ornament of grace shall she be to thy head, and a crown of glory shall she deliver to thee. Take fast hold of instruction; let her not go; keep her, for she is thy life. Come, let us turn unto the Lord our God, with all our heart and soul, and put away every unclean and unholy thing from amongst us, and walk before the Lord our God, with a perfect heart, all the days of our lives: then we shall be a people with whom God shall delight to dwell; yea, we shall be that happy people whose God is the Lord.

I am of a strong opinion that the day on which we unite, heart and soul, and turn our attention to knowledge and improvement, that day the hissing and reproach amongst the nations of the earth against us will cease. And even those who now point at us with the finger of scorn, will aid and befriend us. It is of no use for us to sit with our hands folded, hanging our heads like bulrushes, lamenting our wretched condition; but let us make a mighty effort, and arise; and if no one will promote or respect us, let us promote and respect ourselves.

The American ladies have the honor conferred on them, that by prudence and economy in their domestic concerns, and their unwearied attention in forming the minds and manners of their children, they laid the foundation of their becoming what they now are. The good women of Wethersfield, Connecticut, toiled in the blazing sun, year after year, weeding onions, then sold the seed and procured money enough to erect them a house of worship; and shall we not imitate their examples, as far as they are worthy of imitation? Why cannot we do something to distinguish ourselves, and contribute some of our hard earnings that would reflect honor upon our memories, and cause our children to arise and call us blessed? Shall it any longer be said of the daughters of Africa, they have no ambition, they have no force? By no means. Let every female heart become united, and let us raise a fund ourselves; and at the end of one year and a half, we might be able to lay the corner-stone for the building of a high school, that the higher branches of knowledge might be enjoyed by us; and God would raise us up, and enough to aid us in our laudable designs. Let each one strive to excel in good house-wifery, knowing that prudence and economy are the road to wealth. Let us not say, we know this, or, we know that, and practise nothing; but let us practise what we do know.

How long shall the fair daughters of Africa be compelled to bury their minds and talents beneath a load of iron pots and kettles? Until union, knowledge and love begin to flow amongst us. How long shall a mean set of men flatter us with their smiles, and enrich themselves with our hard earnings,—their wives' fingers sparkling with rings, and they themselves laughing at our folly? Until we begin to pro-mote and patronize each other. Shall we be a byword amongst the nations any longer? Shall they laugh us to scorn forever? Do you ask, What can we do? Unite, and build a store of your own, if you cannot procure a license. Fill one side with dry goods, and the other with groceries. Do you ask, where is the money? We have spent more than enough for nonsense, to do what building we should want. We have never had an opportunity of displaying our talents; there-fore the world thinks we know nothing. And we have been possessed of by far too mean and cowardly a disposition, though I highly dis-approve of an insolent or impertinent one. Do you ask the disposi-tion I would have you possess? Possess the spirit of independence. The Americans do, and why should not you? Possess 'the spirit of men, bold and enterprising, fearless and undaunted. Sue for your rights and privileges. Know the reason that you cannot attain them. Weary them with your importunities. You can but die, if you make the attempt; and we shall certainly die if you do not. The Americans have practised nothing but head-work these 200 years, and we have done their drudgery. And is it not high time for us to imitate their examples, and practise head-work too, and keep what we have got, and get what we can? We need never to think that any body is going to feel interested for us, if we do not feel interested for ourselves. That day we, as a people, hearken unto the voice of the Lord our God, and walk in his ways and ordinances, and become distinguished for our ease, elegance and grace, combined with other virtues,—that day the Lord will raise us up, and enough to aid and befriend us, and we shall begin to flourish.

Did every gentleman in America realize, as one, that they had got to become bondmen, and their wives, their sons, and their daughters, servants forever to Great Britain, their very joints would become loosened, and tremblingly would smite one against another; their countenance would be filled with horror; every nerve and muscle would be forced into action; their souls would recoil at the very thought; their hearts would die within them, and death would be far more preferable. Then why have not Afric's sons a right to feel the same? Are not their wives, their sons, and their daughters, as dear to them as those of the white man's? Certainly, God has not deprived them of the divine influences of his Holy Spirit, which is the greatest of all blessings, if they ask him. Then why should man any longer deprive his fellow-man of equal rights and privileges? Oh, America, America, foul and indelible is thy stain! Dark and dismal is the cloud that hangs over thee, for thy cruel wrongs and injuries to the fallen sons of Africa. The blood of her murdered ones cries to heaven for vengeance against thee. Thou art almost become drunken with the blood of her slain; thou hast enriched thyself through her toils and labours; and now thou refuseth to make even a small return. And thou hast caused the daughters of Africa to commit whoredoms and fornications; but upon thee be their curse.

O, ye great and mighty men of America, ye rich and powerful ones, many of you will call for the rocks and mountains to fall upon you, and to hide you from the wrath of the Lamb, and from him that sitteth upon the throne; whilst many of the sable-skinned Africans you now despise, will shine in the kingdom of heaven as the stars forever and ever. Charity begins at home, and those that provide not for their own, are worse than infidels. We know that you are raising contributions to aid the gallant Poles; we know that you have befriended Greece and Ireland; and you have rejoiced with France, for her heroic deeds of valor. You have acknowledged all the nations of the earth, except Hayti; and you may publish, as far as the east is from the west, that you have two millions of negroes, who aspire no higher than to bow at your feet, and to court your smiles. You may kill, tyrannize, and oppress as much as you choose, until our cry shall come up before the throne of God; for I am firmly persuaded, that he will not suffer you to quell the proud, fearless and undaunted spirits of the Africans forever; for in his own time, he is able to plead our cause against you, and to pour out upon you the ten plagues of Egypt. We will not come out against you with swords and staves, as against a thief; but we will tell you that our souls are fired with the same love of liberty and independence with which your souls are fired. We will tell you that too much of your blood flows in our veins, and too much of your color in our skins, for us not to possess your spirits. We will tell you, that it is our gold that clothes you in fine linen and purple, and causes you to fare sumptuously every day; and it is the blood of our fathers and the tears of our brethren that have enriched your soils. AND WE CLAIM OUR RIGHTS. We will tell you that we are not afraid of them that kill the body, and after that can do no more; but we will tell you whom we do fear. We fear him who is able, after he hath killed, to destroy both soul and body in hell forever. Then, my brethren, sheathe your swords, and calm your angry passions. Stand still, and know that the Lord he is God. Vengeance is his, and he will repay. 'Tis a long lane that has no turn. America has risen to her meridian. When you begin to thrive, she will begin to fall. God hath raised you up a Walker and a Garrison. Though Walker sleeps, yet he lives, and his name shall be had in everlasting remembrance. I, even I, who am but a child, inexperienced to many of you, am a living witness to testify unto you this day that I have seen the wicked in great power, spreading himself like a green bay tree, and lo, he passed away; yea, I diligently sought him, but he could not be found; and it is God alone that has inspired my heart to feel for Afric's woes. Then fret not yourselves because of evildoers. Fret not yourselves because of the men who bring wicked devices to pass; for they shall be cut down as the grass, and wither as the green herb. Trust in the Lord, and do good; so shalt thou dwell in the land, and verily thou shalt be fed. Encourage the noble-hearted Garrison. Prove to the world that you are neither orang-outangs, nor a species of animals, but that you possess the same powers of intellect as those of the proud-boasting American.

I am sensible, my brethren and friends, that many of you have been deprived of advantages, kept in utter ignorance, and that your minds are now darkened; and if any of you have attempted to aspire after high and noble enterprises, you have met with so much opposition that your souls have become discouraged. For this very cause, a few of us have ventured to expose our lives in your behalf, to plead your cause against the great; and it will be of no use, unless you feel for yourselves and your little ones, and exhibit the spirits of men. Oh, then, turn your attention to knowledge and improvement; for knowledge is power. And God is able to fill you with wisdom and understanding, and to dispel your fears. Arm yourselves with the weapons of prayer. Put your trust in the living God. Persevere strictly in the paths of virtue. Let nothing be lacking on your part; and, in God's own time, and his time is certainly the best, he will surely deliver you with a mighty hand and with an out-stretched arm.

I have never taken one step, my friend, with a design to raise myself in your esteem, or to gain applause. But what I have done, has been done with an eye single to the glory of God, and to promote the good of souls. I have neither kindred nor friends. I stand alone in your midst, exposed to the fiery darts of the devil, and to the assaults of wicked men. But though all the powers of earth and hell were to combine against me, though all nature should sink into decay, still would I trust in the Lord, and joy in the God of my salvation. For I am fully persuaded, that he will bring me off conqueror, yea, more than conqueror, through him who hath loved me and given himself for me.

Boston, October, 1831.

A

PASTORAL LETTER,

ADDRESSED TO THE

COLORED PRESBYTERIAN CHURCH,

In the city of New York,

JUNE 20TH, 1832.

By Rev. Theodore S. Wright,

PASTOR OF SAID CHURCH.

NEW YORK.
PRINTED BY SEARS AND MARTIN, 2 FRANKFORT STREET.
1832.

The following consoling letter was addressed to the session and members of the "Colored Presbyterian Church," of the city of New York, by their faithful and beloved pastor, the Rev. Theodore S. Wright, who to recover his health, has been compelled, reluctantly, to leave for a time the people of his charge.

The session, at the request of several members of the church, have, with the pastor's consent, put it in such a form, that they may preserve it for their future benefit.

Praying, dear brethren, that it may tend, under God, as designed by the writer, for our consolation and support, under present trials, it is now placed in your hands.

BENJAMIN WILLIAMS, ⎫
WILLIAM THOMPSON, ⎬ ELDERS.
CHARLES MORTIMER, ⎭

New-York, October 1st, 1832.

472

SCHENECTADY, JUNE 20th, 1832.

To the Session and Members of the Colored Presbyterian Church, of the city of New-York:

DEARLY BELOVED BRETHREN,

I have no doubt but you are anxious to hear from me, for whose well-being, in body and spirit, you pray. You have some reason to believe that I care for your best interest. With me, you are afflicted. With me, you feel solicitous for the safety of the ark which God has set up in the midst of you, and for the flock he has gathered, and for the wants of poor sinners, whose souls are perishing, needing the awakening and sanctifying influences of the spirit of God.

Beloved kindred, mysterious are the ways of God toward us. Clouds and darkness envelope his ways. But blessed be his name, righteousness and judgment are the habitations of his throne. Let us therefore confide in him under all circumstances. Yes, though storms of adversity beat upon us, though death threaten, and every thing looks dark, still may we unreservedly commit ourselves to him.

With the hand of affliction that rests upon me, your spiritual guide, God touches you, with me; you smart under his chastising rod; with me, therefore, go to those sources of consolation which God has provided for those to whom he hath said, "Let not your heart be troubled." "I will not leave you comfortless." Remember, the adversary of God and of souls is on the alert. O! my brethren and sisters! O! my soul! be watchful, be wise! The tempter is ready to incite us, as he did ancient Israel, to murmur against God and to find fault with his dealings towards us, and thus to lure us from the cross of Christ. Come with me, repair to the sacred scriptures and to God's dealings with us—the only true sources of consolation. Here we may learn that God's ways are not as ours; and that however adverse they may seem to us, he doeth all things well. Everything, yes, our present afflictions, are working real good to us. Therefore "despise not the chastening of the Lord." O! let us, with the holy man of old, say, in view of our trials, "It is the Lord, it is the Lord, let him do with us as seemeth him good." When I discover a murmuring thought arising in my mind in consequence of my being deprived of the privilege of laboring in the field of the Lord, I at once say to it, "Peace, be still; shall I receive good at the hand of the Lord, and shall I not receive evil?"

Another idea, which I find calculated to prevent murmuring in the time of affliction, is this: not to let the mind rest too exclusively upon the dark side, and upon present trials. Fix it upon past and present blessings. And here I am free to confess, that it is sometimes trying to me to be deprived of the privilege of ministering to you statedly [regularly] in the house which God has so graciously given to us. And you no doubt regret that you do not now hear the voice of him who often has broken to you the bread of life, and attempted to comfort you in your Christian pilgrimage. But here let us think of the thousands of our brethren, without a bible—without a temple —without a spiritual guide, groaning in fetters and crushed to the earth, in this day of light, in this land of boasted liberty. O! this is calculated at once to suppress our murmuring against God—yes, to excite us to thanksgiving and praise.

Think what we were, as a church and congregation, three years since. Recollect our little room in Duane Street. Recollect how happy we were, when we saw our congregation swelled to fifty or sixty in number; "a little flock" indeed, without friends, without influence, and with very little sympathy from the Christian community. And as you reflect upon those days of trial and anxiety, those days of small things, turn your attention to our church and congregation now; and then tell me, if the past and present mercies are not sufficient to calm every ungrateful thought that may arise in view of present afflictions.

The same Father that now afflicts us is the Father of all our mercies. O! had it not been for him, we would not now have an existence as a church and congregation. Ye fathers and mothers of our Israel, ye well remember when ye trembled for the safety of the ark of God, and hardly dared to hope that you would be able to exist as a church. But the power of Omnipotence has been gloriously displayed for us. Then the Christian community, which had been almost insensible to our wants, awoke. The sympathies of thousands were called forth. They wept and prayed; and decreed that this people, too long neglected, should have a house in which to worship God. More than this; they have evinced the sincerity of their prayers and good desires for us, by their liberal contributions, which, by God's blessing, has secured to our use the house in which we are so prosperously gathered. Remember, all this has been accomplished within one year. Dare you, dear brethren; O! dare I, notwithstanding present trials, murmur against God? Truly it is of the Lord's doing, and it is marvellous in our eyes.

But again, can we not discover something in the spiritual aspect of our flock, which, in these days of trial, will serve as a corrective to those restless emotions in which we may be tempted to indulge? Here, brethren, we find a change infinitely more important, and a cause for corresponding gratitude. Not far from three years since, the standard of faith and piety was so low among us, that to talk of a revival of religion, however desirable, was to speak of that which you could by no means at all expect. You have witnessed the happy change. The cloud of mercy discovered in May, 1830, hanging over us no larger than a man's hand, as it has expanded, has dropped down fatness. O! have not your hearts been refreshed from the mercy drops that have fallen upon you like rain upon the mown grass? How have you been led to pray, to weep and to rejoice, over the heart-smitten and returning prodigal? Recollect, that for more than three years we have been blessed with a continual shower of divine grace, as the fruits of which, the first year, God in great kindness gave us twenty souls, the second thirty, and during the last year one hundred and twenty, over whom we have rejoiced and still do rejoice.

What a change, wrought by Almighty grace, do we now witness in individuals and families, and in our male and female prayer-meetings! The same is witnessed at the sacramental table. Where once sat forty, now two hundred and twenty unite in singing the "Loving Kindness of God." This mighty transformation, blessed be God, is witnessed in our own happy experience. O! how have our hearts burned within us, as we walked by the way, and sat together in heavenly places in Christ Jesus.

My dear young brethren and sisters, who have been the subjects of this soul-renewing work; who have been gathered, as you hope, as trophies of divine grace; you have felt, and I trust still do sensibly feel, the heavenly influence of this change. "Whereas once you were blind, now you see." Once to you there was no beauty in the character of Christ; O! how precious does he now appear! How cordially you now unite in singing the following expressive lines:

> Hail, my ever-blessed Jesus—
>   Only thee I wish to sing;
> To my soul thy name is precious,
>   Thou my prophet, priest and king.
> O! what mercy flows from heaven,
>   O, what joy and happiness;
> Love I much, I've much forgiven,
>   I'm a miracle of grace.

You felt the force of these lines, when your Redeemer first spoke peace to your troubled spirits, and poured heavenly consolation into your souls. And ye fathers and mothers of our Israel, who clung to the standard that God erected among you, when that standard was well nigh fallen—yes, when ye emphatically were a "little flock;" and when despairing of the permanent establishment of a church, save that hope you gathered from the "bow of promise" which encircles the throne of God. O! I am sensible that you realize the good, the blessed change, divine grace has wrought among you; and that with grateful hearts, you will trust God for the future.

Contemplate for a moment the goodness of God, as manifested in our present affliction. Instead of this affliction sent upon your pastor, your pulpit, brethren, to-day might have been hung with the weeds of mourning, and my voice have been hushed in the silence of the grave; and the interesting relation existing between us would have forever ceased. At no time since I have been connected with you, could my affliction have been sent with so little detriment to the church. No doubt you now feel and regret my absence from you, as much as I do. But suppose God had laid his hand upon me one year ago, when the burden of our undertaking was upon me; when duty called me to visit the churches of our denomination in this city, to present the claims of our enterprise. It might have proved fatal to the whole work. My affliction then would have been tenfold more painful. But blessed be God, he then withheld his hand. And although it has pleased the Great Husbandman, for the past few months, to arrest me in my delightful work, not permitting me to comfort you, nor to warn and exhort sinners to flee from the wrath to come, but for whom I, nevertheless, "have great heaviness, and continual sorrow in my heart;" still, in great kindness he has supplied you with the preaching of the word. Almost every Sabbath, you have been fed from the Master's table. Let these facts have their due influence upon your minds, and never be forgotten.

Dearly beloved, in view of these things, ought not you, ought not your feeble brother, to banish every murmuring, every ungrateful thought against God, under his afflictive dispensations? O! let your heart melt and flow out in gratitude to God, our great benefactor. Let every voice respond with the psalmist: "The Lord has done valiantly, the Lord has done valiantly. Praise the Lord, praise the Lord; call upon his name, make known his deeds among the people. Bless thou the Lord, O my soul."

My health is still quite delicate. I cannot tell what is to be the result of my indisposition. God alone knows. He will do that which is best, both for you and me. Do continue your prayers for me, that if it be possible, this affliction may pass away from me, and that ere long I may be restored to my labours among you. But whatever becomes of me, whether I live or die, do not become weary in well-doing. Hold on at the throne of grace. "Live in peace; live in peace." Love the brethren. Remember, I beseech you, that you are not your own, that in view of three worlds, you made a voluntary surrender of yourselves to Christ, to be his, entirely and forever. Remember, that the high honor is yours, "to be workers together with him." As you know, He lived, groaned and expired, and now lives, to save sinners. O! then, brethren, importunately pray, and exert all your powers to rescue from the agonies of the second death, the souls for whom He died. Do all you can to promote the interest of the particular branch of the church to which you belong. Your companions, your children, your neighbors, your parents, while unreconciled to God, however orderly or amiable their natural or acquired qualities may be, if even equal to those of that youth whom Christ loved, yet they are in danger of eternal death, for they yet lack the one thing needful—a new heart, the thing essentially necessary to qualify them to enter heaven; that which must be obtained, or the soul is irrecoverably lost. Think of this, dear brethren, and contemplate the motives everywhere presented, urging you on in the way of well-doing. Think of the constraining love of Christ; the expansive powers, and the inconceivable worth of the soul; the boundless duration of eternity; the ineffable glories of heaven, and of the unutterable and ceaseless horrors of hell; all urge you to fidelity in the service of your Lord and Master.

What you accomplish to honor God or for the salvation of sinners, must be done quickly: must be done now. Time is short—life is uncertain. There is but one step between you and death. The chances of human life are every day lessening. You no doubt before this time have heard that the cholera, that awful pestilence, which within a few years has swept its millions into the grave, in Europe and Asia, has crossed the Atlantic, and is now wasting the inhabitants on the borders of our state in Canada. This is the judgment of the Lord; the destroying angel sent forth with his slaughtering weapon—the scourge of nations. Now whatever may be our anticipations as to its ravages in our country, we cannot even hope that our great commercial city will be exempt from it. I expect to see in the place of your habitation, even among the people of my prayers and affections, such a time of sadness and gloom as never before has been witnessed. How important to be ready. O! let these things lead you to gird up the reins of your mind and urge you to thorough self-examination. Rest not—rest not without a lively sense of that love which is perfect, and lasteth out fear.

In conclusion, dearly beloved, I beseech you by the mercy of God, that ye walk worthy of the high vocation wherewith ye are called.

O! be stedfast, immovable, always abounding in the work of the Lord.

Now may the grace of the Lord Jesus Christ, the love of God and the communion and fellowship of the Holy Ghost, be with you all, Amen.

THE

ABROGATION

OF THE

SEVENTH COMMANDMENT,

BY THE

AMERICAN CHURCHES.

*"When thou sawest a thief, then thou consentedst with him,
and hast been partaker with adulterers."—Psalm l. 18.*

NEW YORK:

DAVID RUGGLES, 47 HOWARD STREET.

1835.

FELLOW CHRISTIANS—
Nothing is more easily demonstrable than the fact that slavery
owes its continuance in the United States chiefly to the women. Had
American females come forward in all the mightiness of their legitimate and resistless influence, and imperatively demanded the extirpation of that complicated iniquity, long ere now the term "American
Slavery" would have been used only to express a dead monster,
loathed amid universal execration. I shall not attempt to demonstrate that slavery is impious, and unjust, and cruel, and ruinous
both to the oppressor and his victim; but it is my design, with all
plainness, but decorum, concisely to illustrate the operation of slavery in reference to females, in domestic and social life, and in professedly Christian relations.
This subject, from false delicacy, or an improper squeamishness,
has never been presented in that palpable form, through which it is

indispensable that we should discern the scowling glances of a slave driver's sensuality, and the hideous features of that evil which destroys the morals, the comfort, and the prosperity of those who are participants in the horrors of slavery. It may not be accurately comprehended by you, that in addition to all the other most odious and criminal attributes of American slaveholding, a licentiousness of intercourse between the sexes, constant, incestuous, and universal, exists; the aggravated corruptions of which, no pen can describe, and no unpolluted imagination conceive; and that this direful calamity is an essential portion—or rather the very heart's blood—of that debasing bondage in which the colored women are held, and by which they are defiled and destroyed. As was justly remarked of the merciless treatment which all slaves experience, "cruelty is the rule, and kindness the exception;" so it must be declared, purity is the exception, and dissoluteness the rule.

It must be remembered, if you would grasp at once all the hideous and awful deformity and wickedness of slaveholding in this Republic, that there are now nearly two millions and a half of slaves in the United States, or five hundred thousand adult colored females, not only "kept in ignorance, and compelled to live without God, and die without hope, by a people professing to reverence the obligations of Christianity"—but that all those females are ever subject to violation in the most flagrant forms of turpitude, without the possibility of complaint or redress.

The pillage and profligacy connected with the storming of a town by a military force, are always perused with shuddering at the outrages which it includes; but the whole history of mankind does not afford a parallel in iniquity to the awful fact which exists in our country, that five hundred thousands of women, by our wicked laws, are surrendered to the unbridled lusts of their worse than Egyptian taskmasters.

A mere enumeration of four of the principal facts connected with the condition of female slaves, affords an inexhaustible source for pungent reflections and appalling fears.

1. The increasing multitudes of the mixed people, who, by their diversity of color, American features, and physical conformation, betray their parental origin, incontestably demonstrate the wide spread and incessant licentiousness of the white population.

2. Colored females cannot offer any resistance to the attempts of their masters, when they choose to coerce them to submission, or to wheedle them into a compliance with their lascivious inclinations; for there is no law to preserve them, and no protecting authority to which they can appeal.

3. The temptation from pecuniary advantage with all rapidity to multiply slaves, is equivalent to a bribe for impurity. Vast numbers of persons in Maryland and Virginia now riot in splendour and luxury, solely through the increase and traffic of slaves. Many plantations are equally devoted to the rearing of slaves, as a Northern farm is set apart for the products of a dairy or of grain.

4. The matrimonial connection among the slaves is altogether nullified. There are fathers, mothers, and children, but there are no families! There are men, women, and youth, but the relation, even the name of lover, husband, and wife, according to the ordinance of Jehovah in Paradise, is scarcely more of a reality, from Pennsylvania to the Gulf of Mexico, than the phantom of Aladdin's wonder working lamp. The pestilential effects of these principles, and of this system in practice, are too evident to every person who has investigated the state of society in the Southern States. The natural instinctive delicacy with which God has imbued mankind, for the purest and most endearing purpose, withers away before the blight of slavery, as it is witnessed by youth while advancing to maturity. It would be criminal longer to conceal from Northern inspection the every day and sun light exhibitions which are performed at the South. Travellers know that the large taverns in the slave States combine all corrupt doings in their most mischievous and degrading effects; and not only in taverns, but in boarding houses, and the dwellings of individuals, boys and girls verging on maturity altogether unclothed, wait upon ladies and gentlemen, without exciting even the suffusion of a blush on the face of young females, who thus gradually become habituated to scenes of which delicate and refined Northern women cannot adequately conceive.

But all the complicated evils which are comprised within the above four general topics in their most extensive wickedness, are hidden from contemplation by the operation of another principle in the system of slavery. Those abominable practices probably would not be directly defended by any persons; and are palliated only by the excuses that the slaves are no better than brutes, and that as the multiplication of them is profitable, therefore everything which tends to that advantage may justifiably be adopted. We therefore advert chiefly to that universal dissoluteness among the white and colored population which is sanctioned and perpetuated by the nominal disciples of the Lord Jesus.

It cannot be too deeply impressed upon your minds, that all attempts to abolish slavery, or to diminish the iniquities which are inseparable from it, must be utterly inefficient, unless you combat that monster with *evangelical weapons.* Arguments drawn from political evils, or prospective dangers however certain, are of no importance among worldly sensual men, when put in competition with present emolument and lascivious indulgences. All reasonings concerning the future are nugatory upon men who live only for the present, and who "neither fear God nor regard man!"

To the Christian churches appertain the stigma and the crime of having fostered and prolonged the curse of slavery in the United States; and if it is ever eradicated, it must be achieved by gospel principles, and be commenced by regenerating the temple of Jeho-vah, so that the house of prayer shall no longer be a den of thieves and adulterers. In no point of view does the inordinate wickedness of slavery appear more glaring and offensive than in its practical justifi-cation by the professors of religion. This most unchristian departure from all that is righteous and holy is exemplified not only in the con-federacies of slaveholders, who are called churches of different de-nominations, and of which every member is a slavedriver or a slave; but also in the sanction given to their most ungodly practices by the Northern Christians, who admit slaveholding preachers into their pul-pits, and slavite professors to their communion, as acknowledged fel-low disciples of that Prince of liberators and emancipators, "Jesus, who went about doing good."

It is incontestable that slaveholding ladies, who occupy the first rank both in religious and civil society, are notoriously inexorable in their exaction of unremitting and the severest labor, and that they will inflict most torturing and unmerited punishments with an inde-scribable savageness of ferocity. If it were publicly known in New England, that a woman used the ordinary language only which many Southern ladies apply to their "colored wenches," they would not be admitted as members of any Christian church; and if they were to whip a cat or a dog as the Southern ladies scourge and lacerate their slaves, instead of being estimated as women they would be discarded as monsters.

This hypocritical system imposes upon Christian ladies in New England. There is as much moral difference between a slaveholding lady, when on the Northern summer tour, and when she is at home on the plantation, as there is in the planter's own children, who are reared in the domicile and in the "slave quarter." For that deceitful-ness, for that hard heartedness, and for that violation of every prin-ciple of feminine sensibility, and Christian morals and philanthropy, there is no effectual cure, but by the indignant denunciations of the gospel, in all their most pungent and strictly individualized application, which certify that all pretensions to Christianity by a slaveholder are only startling proofs of shameless dissimulation and obdurate depravity.

It is deceptive and useless for the wives and daughters of Southern slaveholders to profess ignorance of the atrocious overflowings of impurity which are everywhere visible; equally in the houses of Christian professors, as on the plantations of the profligate slave dealer. There may be one black man and woman, or more of either sex around the house; but it is most marvellous, if there are not some naked children also playing about, whom, by the touch, a blind man even would decide that they were not the offspring of those colored persons. Would Northern Christian ladies for one day tolerate the adoption of a system which would recognize as their domestic servants, the spurious offspring of their own husbands, brothers and sons, borne under their own eyes by their constant female attendants? Can young women grow up with all that unceasing contamination ever obtruding itself upon their hearing and inspection, and retain their virgin ignorance and purity? It is impossible; and although they may not disclose all that they knew, yet some elderly matrons have divulged enough to render it certain that the operation of the system poisons domestic comfort and confidence even at its fountain. The Southern ladies are inexcusably criminal for the prolongation of this system. Virtue, talents, continency, and piety, weigh little or nothing in the estimate of a genuine Southern planter, or his daughter, who has been trained up in indolence and voluptuousness, when contrasted with "a gang of slaves." It is not asked how he obtained them, or what is their color; the more fair and numerous they are, the stronger the recommendation; and that they may live in ease and show, the ladies sacrifice all their dignity and honour, and often dwindle into characters very little superior to the superintendents of a Harem for promiscuous concubinage, and the multiplication of human beings for the slave market. What they experience cannot easily be conceived; but what they suffer cannot be described; and how they are punished, their irrepressible emotions frequently disclose. If after marriage, by the grace of God, they become Christians, then it is that they realize all the tortures of an agonized conscience, combined with an abiding sense of their utter helplessness to prove the sincerity of their change of heart, by bringing forth fruits meet for repentance.

It is not a sufficient excuse for the Southern ladies to plead, that they cannot destroy the system of slavery. *They can do it;* and if they were not callous to their own natural feminine instincts, *they would do it.* They know all the odious and accursed miseries to which the colored women are subject; and they connive at those violations of female honor and affection, by raising no voice of outcry, and making no effort for their deliverance.

It is evident therefore, that no expectations can be indulged respecting the cooperation of Southern women for the immediate extirpation of slavery. They cry "tomorrow." They live in hope that the evil day of emancipation and retribution will not arrive in their time, and transfer to their daughters and granddaughters the agonies which they are assured await their posterity, unless slavery shall be swept from our Republic. Consequently the appeal is made to female Christians; and by the lofty honour of your sex, by your sympathies as women, by your character as wives, mothers, and sisters, and by the imperative claims of "pure religion and undefiled," we conjure you to arise, and with all the authority of Christian principles, and with all the steadfastness of Christian perseverance, we urge you to demand the immediate and total abolition of that nefarious domestic servitude, which fills every Southern state with all diversified ungodliness and anguish. We ask you not to engage in this contest with crime, using carnal weapons. We call upon you to look at the system, not so much as it is illustrated among infidels, or the avowedly irreligious, but as it is exemplified among professing Christians. We do not invite you to enter into any collision with men and women, who, in the scriptural sense, are emphatically part of that world "which lieth in wickedness;" but we earnestly solicit you constantly to remember, and incessantly to practice the apostolic admonition, 1 Cor. v. 9–13: "Not to company with fornicators." In its Christian influence and connections only do we wish you to regard the subject, and we solemnly appeal to your feelings and your consciences. Would you listen to a preacher, would you unite in avowed Christian fellowship with a church or churches which enforced the members either to nullify the marriage covenant, or deliberately to approve every species of crime by which the seventh commandment is violated? You instinctively and with aversion answer, No, not for one moment. Then how can you patiently sit and listen to preachers from the Southern States, who abrogate all connubial ties between colored persons in their own houses; and ever admit persons guilty of uncleanness, in various aggravations, to the Lord's table? Upon the principle of expediency, they justify the constant separation of persons who would live faithfully, according to the divine matrimonial institution; and by the forced separations of those persons, and even Christian members, absolutely compel them to a life of unchastity, and still recognize, as exemplary Christians, all the parties, the slave dealer who sells the woman or the man, and thus separates lovers and friends, and the persons disjoined, who cohabit with others, contrary to propriety, duty, and religion.

This awful criminality is universal in all the slaveholding States. Mr. Jay, in his "Inquiry" lately published, thus describes the fact, page 126. "A necessary consequence of slavery, is the absence of the marriage relation. No slave can commit bigamy, because the law knows no more of the marriage of slaves, than it does of the marriage of brutes. A slave, indeed, may be formally married, but, so far as legal rights and obligations are concerned, it is an idle ceremony. His wife at any moment may be legally taken from him and sold in the market. The slave laws utterly nullify the injunction of the Supreme Lawgiver—"What God hath joined together, let not man put asunder." Of course, those laws recognize not the parental relation as belonging to slaves. A slave has no more legal authority over his child, than a cow over her calf." Mr. Jay probably was not acquainted with another fact, that no minister of the gospel, or other functionary, dare to solemnize matrimony between two slaves, or a free person and a slave, without the consent of the slaveholder. It is true, the form, as Mr. Jay states, would be "an idle ceremony;" but in some extreme cases that might be supposed, the evidence of a white minister to an actual marriage could obtrude an impediment; but it would be unavailing, for who would enter a caveat against the sale of either or both the parties? Who could hinder the transfer of the human flesh to another receiver of stolen men? In present circumstances, with few exemptions, that man or that woman who would lift up the voice against the beastly corruptions which are inseparable from slavery, would receive the same recompense which all reformers have ever enjoyed; and probably in addition, the manstealing assassin's dagger or rifle ball.

Are you aware that men living in direct contradiction to the law of God in concubinage, without any other restraint than their own consciences and inclinations, and with every possible inducement always to infringe upon both, are members of Christian churches? Are you apprized that women equally unrestrained by the matrimonial law and obligations, and only controlled by their attachments or modesty, and often obliged to submit to the wanton desires of their licentious masters and overseers, are also numbered among the disciples of Him who decided that a lascivious glance only comprised a flagrant violation of his holy commandment? Have you ever duly realized the peculiar qualities of that devotion which Christian women must feel when they recollect that they are seated in the house of prayer where a congregation assemble, one portion of which is composed of the notoriously impure, and the other portion, of those who connive at their turpitude, and denominate sins against chastity, pure religion? Did you ever attempt to comprehend the nature of that spirituality of mind which must attend the Christian communicant when she realizes, in all its fearful certainty, that she is seated at the Lord's table among menstealers, who solemnly adjudge that habitual fornication, adultery, and bigamy are not sufficient causes for exclusion from the Redeemer's ordinance. If this does not comprise that consent with thieves and that participation with adulterers which are condemned in Psalm l. 18, then there is no meaning in language.

One actual occurrence will abundantly elucidate this subject. A colored member of a church in Augusta, I believe, lived with a woman, but whether she was also a member, I do not recollect; from the circumstances, that fact may be presumed. His master sent him away to a distance for a length of time, and there he formed a connection with another female: the man still retaining his membership in the church. After a season, he was restored to his first residence, and the second companion was permitted to go with him; and thus he was an associate for both women. When his mode of life was understood, the church called him to an account, and informed him that his cohabitation with both women could not be allowed; he must choose one of them or his relation to the church would be dissolved. The man preferred his second choice, and the first was dismissed to obtain a new lover. Upon this condition, the man's Christian profession was pronounced good, and he retained his membership.

This is the very point to which I direct your serious attention; for you must deeply feel that all attempts to reform or extirpate slavery will be utterly unavailing as long as such a course of life as that which I have described is admitted to be consistent with a profession of Christianity. Whatever exceptions there may be, they are of no consequence at all in this argument. It is the system to which we advert: and the slavery which is now predominant in the Southern States directly and completely eradicates all the provisions of the Seventh Commandment; not only among the colored people, by the absolute prohibition of marriage, but also among the whites, by rendering it impossible to adduce evidence of their guilt. No colored person, free or a slave, is admitted as evidence against a white citizen; and the rule is not less rigidly adhered to in the administration of church discipline than in courts of law. Besides, the moral code, in its application to white and colored persons, is of a totally different character in the decision of slaveholders, not less in its abstract theory, than in its practical application. A very heinous crime, if perpetrated upon a white female, friend or acquaintance, loses all its repugnance and guiltiness if the girl be colored; because in the former case it might be discovered and punished, while the latter act could not be known, or cannot be proved, and at all events can be accomplished with sure impunity.

All white men can habitually violate their nuptial vows and the laws of chastity, if they please, without forfeiting their moral or Christian character; because the enactments of slavery preclude the proof, and consequently that disgrace which conviction of the fact might produce. But in the case of the slave, the transgression of the seventh commandment is not only tolerated, it is *enforced,* and *cannot be avoided until slavery is abolished.* That promiscuous licentiousness of intercourse is not a morbid excrescence which has unnaturally been engrafted upon the tree of slavery, it is the very sap which gives life, vigour, and perpetuity to the whole system. Not only do slaveholders fulfil the delineation of the prophet Joel, chap. iii. 3: "they have cast lots for my people; and have given a boy for a harlot, and sold a girl for wine, that they might drink,"—but they also practice the transgressions for which the Lord threatens: "I will not turn away the punishment thereof: because they sold the righteous for silver, and the poor for a pair of shoes; that pant after the dust of the earth on the head of the poor, and turn aside the way of the meek; and a man and his father will go in unto the same maid, to profane my holy name." Amos ii. 6, 7.

You will remember also, that all those hideous and crying sins are the unavoidable result of the dissolution of the marriage compact: which overthrow of the will and government of God, as it was announced at the creation of mankind, is sanctioned by the professed disciples of Christ; and by all those ecclesiastical associations who recognize slaveholders and slaves as good and acceptable members.

Here then we take our stand; and we maintain that it is the most tremendous and heaven-defying dishonor to "the high and lofty One that inhabiteth eternity, whose name is Holy," to denominate any part of such a polluted system compatible with "the commandment of the Lord," which is pure; and any persons who participate in it, directly or indirectly, Christians who possess that "fear of the Lord" which is clean.

To the female members of our Northern Christian churches, it primarily belongs to make their voices heard upon this appalling and most momentous subject. By no other method can the public mind, and especially the consciences of the Redeemer's disciples, be effectually and adequately roused to the proper tone of feeling, until the devout women in our churches openly exemplify their indignant detestation of that system which levels the female sex particularly with the beasts that perish. But you are probably ready to inquire, what can we effect? How can we slay this hydra-headed monster of corruption and wo? We reply; the iniquity which we condemn must receive the indelible brand of condign ignominy from the Christian churches, by denouncing slaveholding; and by the believing women especially, that portion of it which more immediately affects the marriage relation and the seventh commandment; in the language of Job, chap. xxxi. 11, 12, as a "heinous crime, and an iniquity to be punished by the judges; for it is a fire that consumeth to destruction." But you will probably retort, how can we express our opinions, for "women are not permitted to speak in the church?"

In answer to this interesting query, we recommend to you the immediate adoption of a declaratory act and testimony, and if subsequently necessary, the execution of a measure which would "make the ears of every one who heareth it to tingle."

1. All the female members should formally sign a deliberate protest against the admission of any slaveholder to preach in the respective churches to which they belong; and against the reception of any slavedrivers to the communion of saints. *The declaration should be comprehensive, full, and without any exception!* Nothing can be more preposterous in a Christian survey, than the idea of investigating the proportions of guilt contracted by perpetual and impenitent transgressors of the seventh and eighth commandments. It is lamentable to know that *all slaveholders are guilty;* and it is not within human jurisdiction, nor is it of any importance to discriminate their comparative turpitude. The fact alone decisively terminates all discussion. All those persons, therefore, of whatever office, dignity, and denomination, should be discarded from Christian fellowship peremptorily; and Christian females should sign a formal demand upon the officers of the church with which they are united, that those persons should not be acknowledged as Christians. To that testimony should be subjoined a plain and unalterable avowal, that neither the principles, nor character, nor the religious profession of Christian females permit them to tolerate, much less formally to approve of so gross a perversion of piety and decorum, as to honor, as brethren and sisters in Christ Jesus, persons whose life is one continuous and flagrant violation of the seventh and eighth commandments; and therefore, if the pastor or officers of the church will permit so palpable an infringement of evangelical propriety and obligations, whenever they hear that a slave driving preacher is to lead the devotional exercises, that they will absent themselves from the house of worship, and whenever they see a slaveholder in the pulpit or among the communicants, that they will one and all instantly retire from the assembly. That determination should be expressed in such a categori-

cal manner, that the officers of the church might be assured that the
resolve of the Christian sisters would be the counterpart of the ancient "law of the Medes and Persians, which altereth not." A requisition so peaceful and according to the gospel, it is believed, all the
ministers and officers of the Christian churches north of the Pennsylvania line and the river Ohio would instantly ratify.

2. But if an attempt was made to evade that most righteous and
consistent proceeding, then the Christian females should fulfil their
averment; and if a slave driver was discovered either officiating in
the church, or at a meeting for social prayer, they should instantly
and simultaneously withdraw; and then *the knell of slavery would
commence to be resounded.*

Christian sisters! Would you stay in your parlor with a minister of
the gospel, or a church officer, who endeavoured to persuade you
that the marriage relation might justly be set aside to gratify a sup-
positious expediency, or for the sake of gain and sensual indulgence?
Not at all. You would denounce them as atrocious impostors and
scandalous hypocrites. But is the atmosphere of the house of prayer
less hallowed than that of your domestic residence? How then can
you associate with men and honor them in the temple consecrated to
the worship of Jehovah, from whom in a private habitation you
would instinctively recoil, and whose contaminating presence you
would most cautiously shun?

It is therefore self-evident, that the female communicants with
Christian churches have it in their power to accomplish the wondrous
revolution which you so anxiously desire. This hope is cherished and
strengthened by the exhilarating fact, that the members of the Anti-
Slavery societies, both male and female, are mostly Christians; and
consequently that in all cases the ladies will have a powerful cooperation from those brethren. It is nugatory to ask, what can a small
number of women do? *What cannot they do?* When our Redeemer
had not where to lay his head, devout women "ministered to him of
their substance." When all men deserted Paul, the Roman sisters supplied him. When the Apostles forsook the Saviour and fled, women
were last at the cross, and first at the sepulchre. The faith, zeal, fortitude, and perseverance of Christian women have triumphed, where
the lukewarmness, pusillanimity, and irresolution of men had failed.
Men are afraid, or perplexed with their social interests, or making
calculations without or contrary to the book of God's word; and
therefore they are vacillating and uncertain. With all those contradictory motives, female Christians have no connection. They can
come up to the help of the Lord against the mighty, and like Deb-
orah encourage and fortify Barak, until another Jael shall arise and

nail the Sisera of domestic slavery fast to the ground, to die amid execrations for his crimes, mingled with the song of the inspired prophetess—"So let all thine enemies perish, O Lord! but let them that love him be as the sun when he goeth forth in his might!" Judges v. 31.; and *the land shall have rest.*

A passage in the recently published work entitled *Picture of Slavery in the United States of America* is so intimately connected with the object of this address, that I have transcribed it for your perusal. It was written by a minister of the Southern States, who furnishes the result of his own extended scrutiny, and the information obtained from other Christians. The extracts commence on page 87 of that volume.

"The third natural effect of slavery upon slaveholders is this— *They become sensual; and lose that instinctive pudicity which God, for the wisest and holiest purposes, has implanted in the hearts of mankind.*

"No topic connected with slavery requires a more complete and barefaced exposure than the duties and transgressions which are included in the seventh commandment. The time has arrived when the true state of domestic society, and the inexpressible wretchedness of woman's degradation, as they exist among the slaveholders, must be fully developed. For that most *frightful* licentiousness the females among the slaveholding families are chiefly responsible. They would rather connive at the grossest sensuality in their husbands, sons, fathers, and brothers, than abandon the system which enables them to live in luxury and indolence.

"Among all the natural effects of slavery upon the slaveholders, the sensuality and its concomitant vices with which it fills them are the most pernicious in their present influence, and the most appalling and dangerous in their future consequences. Every Southern woman, the member of a slave driver's family, if she had any correct feminine and Christian feeling, would live in a continuous shudder. In the word of God, the great Creator teaches us that female purity is the subject of his constant care, and that the violation of it, without repentance, insures his tremendous retribution. The Scriptures are replete with examples. Upon this principle, what may not the females of the South expect in the day of award? The fact stands before us in all its resistless truth. Generation after generation of the Southern females have witnessed their fellow creatures, even the children of their own fathers and husbands, living as the mere tools of unbridled lust, and often violated with a savage barbarity, of which the legal annals of crime afford no parallel. Against that inconceivable, widespread, and enormous load of guilt, the white women have never yet spoken so as to be heard. Now therefore, let them boldly advance and say to this desolating flood—'Thou shalt go no further.'

"How can they expect to escape, if the Lord should ever permit our Southern States to be convulsed with a resolute struggle on the part of the slaves to be free? What plea could they offer to a colored man against his atrocious assault, which would not recoil upon them with overwhelming force?

"What then shall be done? To whom shall we recur? We must look to the Northern ladies. At present there is no prospect of cooperation from Southern preachers and Southern women. Our Christian sisters at the North must form an impenetrable phalanx, not to be driven from truth and their dignified self-possession by infidel debauchees and profligate slavites; and must take up the arms which they can successfully wield, with matronly purity, dignity, and authority, until they have exterminated that devastating pestilence which is filling the Southwestern country with a flood of iniquity that in its meanders pollutes the farthest boundaries of the United States."

Northern Christian ladies alone can eradicate the moral pestilence which destroys female purity and domestic comfort and endearments in the slaveholding States, and only through the evangelically appointed means. If their husbands and fathers will introduce slaveholders into their habitations, they can scarcely avoid meeting them, however repugnant it may be to their sensibilities and convictions, but no terrestrial power can coerce them to commune with slave drivers at the Lord's table. If I were a woman, I would rather abandon all membership in a Christian church, than have it understood that I recognized as a gospel preacher, or a follower of Jesus of Nazareth, men and women who destroy the marriage contract; extirpate the sanctity of connubial life by annulling all its obligations, vows, and duties; formally justify the most inordinate concubinage; and sanction with an evangelical title, open adultery, with all its compound and most aggravated offences.

Christian sisters! To you the arduous but indispensable duty of purifying the churches from this noisome pestilence appropriately belongs. It only requires a commencement. There are many existing Female Anti-Slavery Societies. Combine your energies without delay! Adopt your measures with promptitude, energy and perseverance! Let the ladies of New York who belong to the several churches at once aloud proclaim, that unless a rule be instantly enacted by which all slaveholders of every grade and name shall be peremptorily excluded from the pulpit and the Lord's table, in the churches to which they respectively belong, they will constitute new Christian societies, with which habitual transgressors of the seventh and eighth commandments shall have no fellowship; and within one year, not an evangelical church north of the Ohio and the Pennsylvania line would own as a disciple of Jesus any Slave Driver. As the immediate consequence, every Southern man and woman who is the subject of redeeming grace, would join the noble army of champions for the truth; and within two years the church of God would be reformed; the sanctuary would be cleansed; the sons of Levi would be purified and purged as gold and silver, Mal. iii. 3; and all American Christians would "offer unto the Lord an offering in righteousness." Then the men of the world would be alone. Slavery would speedily be renounced as the monster of tyranny, robbery, pollution and murder. Divested of its Christian name and Christian garb, it would stand exposed in all its hideous deformity and loathsome corruption, the mark against which the arrows of truth would be shot, until it effused its expiring groan amid the shouts of disenthralled man, and of the enraptured multitudes of emancipated Christians.

Experience has proved that all appeals to justice, honor, patriotism, and safety are in vain. Against present gratifications, prospective calamities are of no weight with obdurate and reckless sinners. It is also most melancholy that, in reference to those slaveholders who profess the Christian religion, every attempt to impress their consciences by enforcing the law of God, and the spirit of Christianity, and the example of that most adorable Philanthropist, its divine founder, and the inconceivable anguish of future retribution, have been totally ineffectual. Thus is exemplified one of the most remarkable contradictions in the history of human depravity; that the difficulty of convincing a criminal of his guilt is exactly proportioned to the magnitude of his sins. It would be deemed a waste of time to prove that a man who enters a baker's shop and secretly carries away a six cent loaf is a thief; but learning, genius, and piety all have poured forth their treasures in vain, to convince a Slaveholder that he who robs a man of his labor, rights, children, lover and even of himself is a Mansteler. No argument would be requisite to demonstrate that carnal intercourse between unmarried persons or under any other sanction than that of the matrimonial institution is a flagrant transgression of the seventh commandment; and yet all the existing splendor of gospel day has not poured sufficient light upon the Southern churches to enable them to comprehend that promiscuous concubinage, incestuous cohabitation, and all that is meant by conjugal infidelity, when practised by colored persons, or by white men with colored females, are fornication or adultery—for if they so judged, they would not certainly hallow that deep pollution with a Christian name, and prolong an accursed system which equally subverts the laws of our country, and the revealed mandates of the Almighty.

Is there no remedy for this evil? Is there no cure for this deadly and desolating plague? Well may an American philanthropist adopt the lamentation of Jeremiah: "For the hurt of the daughter of my people am I hurt; I am black; astonishment hath taken hold upon me. Is there no balm in Gilead? is there no physician there? why then is not the health of the daughter of my people recovered?"— Why? *for the physician there has been no desire; and the balm has never been applied.*

The gospel alone is the only efficient antidote to all the moral maladies of mankind, and that sovereign balm has never been administered. In truth, respecting the system of slavery connected with the Christian church, the language of the Lord Jesus Christ is emphatically appropriate. "The light shineth in darkness, and the darkness comprehendeth it not. Light is come into the world, and men love darkness rather than light, because their deeds are evil. Every one that doeth evil hateth the light, neither cometh he to the light, lest his deeds should be reproved. The light of the body is the eye; but if thine eye be evil, thy whole body shall be full of darkness. If therefore the light that is in thee be darkness, how great is that darkness?" There is the infallible solution of the whole complicated wickedness of Slavery. Preachers, with officers and members of the churches in the Southern States, wilfully close their eyes and dare not come to the light; because they know that their deeds are not "wrought in God." John iii. 19–21.

What then can be done? *Nothing more,* than to pour upon the citizens of our republic the blaze of evangelical irradiation—*nothing less,* than indelibly to brand the system of female violation, adultery, incest, bigamy, concubinage, and polygamy, which predominates throughout the regions where Slavery reigns, with its own infamous names; and to inscribe the revolting stigma so deeply and plainly that every man may be induced to forsake that iniquity, and deliver his soul—and *nothing else,* than for all Northern Christians and churches without delay "not to keep company if any man that is called a brother be a fornicator, &c. and to put away from among yourselves that wicked person." 1 Cor. v. 9–13.

Wherefore, Christian Sisters, come forth in "the unity of the Spirit, in the strength of the Lord, and in the power of his might, wrestling against the rulers of darkness of this world, and against spiritual wickedness in high places." Remember, there are 500,000 women in this republic exposed to the most fearful tortures which your sex can suffer—that myriads of them constantly realize that pollution and anguish over which modesty blushes, humanity shudders, and religion wails—and that you alone as instruments in Divine providence can promptly and effectually banish from our country a mass of woe, mental and bodily, of which probably no exact counterpart or parallel, either in horrors or atrocity or continuance, is recorded in the annals of excruciated victims, or triumphant depravity. Now is your time for labor and for success. Join together all of you with one heart—and in humble reliance upon Him who has promised to bless the efforts and fidelity of his servants, solemnly vow unto the Captain of Salvation who came "to heal the broken hearted, and to preach deliverance to the captives," that you will never more dishonor the holy religion which you profess, and disgrace your own incorruptible principles and irreproachable characters, by practically declaring that you are the Christian associates of men who systematically justify the most outrageous and scarlet colored infractions of the law of God, which prohibits adultery and theft; and that in future you will "have no fellowship with the unfruitful works of darkness." May God bless your "work of faith, and labor of love, and patience of hope," so that you may be more than conquerors through Christ Jesus our Lord!

A PURITAN.

New York, 4th May, 1835.

THE

LIFE

AND

RELIGIOUS EXPERIENCE

OF

JARENA LEE,

A Coloured Lady,

GIVING AN ACCOUNT OF HER CALL TO PREACH THE GOSPEL.

REVISED AND CORRECTED FROM THE ORIGINAL MANUSCRIPT,
WRITTEN BY HERSELF.

PHILADELPHIA:
PRINTED AND PUBLISHED FOR THE AUTHOR.
1836.

And it shall come to pass . . . that I will pour out my Spirit
upon all flesh; and your sons, and your *daughters* shall prophecy.
Joel ii. 28.

I was born February 11th, 1783, at Cape May, state of New Jersey. At the age of seven years I was parted from my parents, and
went to live as a servant maid, with a Mr. Sharp, at the distance of
about sixty miles from the place of my birth.

My parents being wholly ignorant of the knowledge of God, had
not therefore instructed me in any degree in this great matter. Not
long after the commencement of my attendance on this lady, she had

bid me do something respecting my work, which in a little while after, she asked me if I had done, when I replied, yes—but this was not true.

At this awful point, in my early history, the spirit of God moved in power through my conscience, and told me I was a wretched sinner. On this account so great was the impression, and so strong were the feelings of guilt, that I promised in my heart that I would not tell another lie.

But notwithstanding this promise my heart grew harder after a while; yet the spirit of the Lord never entirely forsook me, but continued mercifully striving with me, until his gracious power converted my soul.

The manner of this great accomplishment, was as follows: In the year 1804, it so happened that I went with others to hear a missionary of the Presbyterian order preach. It was an afternoon meeting, but few were there, the place was a school room; but the preacher was solemn, and in his countenance the earnestness of his master's business appeared equally strong, as though he were about to speak to a multitude.

At the reading of the Psalms, a ray of renewed conviction darted into my soul. These were the words, composing the first verse of the Psalms for the service:

> Lord, I am vile, conceived in sin,
> Born unholy and unclean.
> Sprung from man, whose guilty fall
> Corrupts the race, and taints us all.

This description of my condition struck me to the heart, and made me to feel in some measure, the weight of my sins, and sinful nature. But not knowing how to run immediately to the Lord for help, I was driven of Satan, in the course of a few days, and tempted to destroy myself.

There was a brook about a quarter of a mile from the house, in which there was a deep hole, where the water whirled about among the rocks; to this place it was suggested, I must go and drown myself.

At the time I had a book in my hand; it was on a Sabbath morning, about ten o'clock; to this place I resorted, where on coming to the water I sat down on the bank, and on my looking into it; it was suggested, that drowning would be an easy death. It seemed as if some one was speaking to me, saying put your head under, it will not distress you. But by some means, of which I can give no account, my thoughts were taken entirely from this purpose, when I went from the place to the house again. It was the unseen arm of God which saved me from self murder.

But notwithstanding this escape from death, my mind was not at rest—but so great was the labour of my spirit and the fearful oppressions of a judgment to come, that I was reduced as one extremely ill. On which account a physician was called to attend me, from which illness I recovered in about three months.

But as yet I had not found him of whom Moses and the prophets did write, being extremely ignorant: there being no one to instruct me in the way of life and salvation as yet. After my recovery, I left the lady, who during my sickness, was exceedingly kind, and went to Philadelphia. From this place I soon went a few miles into the country, where I resided in the family of a Roman Catholic. But my anxiety still continued respecting my poor soul, on which account I used to watch my opportunity to read in the Bible; and this lady observing this, took the Bible from me and hid it, giving me a novel in its stead—which when I perceived, I refused to read.

Soon after this I again went to the city of Philadelphia; and commenced going to the English Church, the pastor of which was an Englishman, by the name of Pilmore, one of the number, who at first preached Methodism in America, in the city of New York.

But while sitting under the ministration of this man, which was about three months, and at the last time, it appeared that there was a wall between me and a communion with that people, which was higher than I could possibly see over, and seemed to make this impression upon my mind, *this is not the people for you.*

But on returning home at noon I inquired of the head cook of the house respecting the rules of the Methodists,—as I knew she belonged to that society—who told me what they were; on which account I replied that I should not be able to abide by such strict rules not even one year. However, I told her that I would go with her and hear what they had to say.

The man who was to speak in the afternoon of that day, was the Rev. Richard Allen, since Bishop of the African Episcopal Methodists in America. During the labors of this man that afternoon, I had come to the conclusion, that this is the people to which my heart unites, and it so happened, that as soon as the service closed he invited such as felt a desire to flee the wrath to come, to unite on trial with them —I embraced the opportunity. Three weeks from that day, my soul was gloriously converted to God, under preaching, at the very outset of the sermon. The text was barely pronounced, which was: "I perceive thy heart is not right in the sight of God," when there appeared to *my* view, in the centre of the heart *one* sin; and this was *malice*, against one particular individual, who had strove deeply to injure me, which I resented. At this discovery I said, *Lord* I forgive *every* creature. That instant it appeared to me as if a garment, which had entirely enveloped my whole person, even to my fingers' ends, split at the crown of my head, and was stripped away from me, passing like a shadow from my sight; when the glory of God seemed to cover me in its stead.

That moment, though hundreds were present, I did leap to my feet, and declare that God, for Christ's sake, had pardoned the sins of my soul. Great was the ecstasy of my mind, for I felt that not only the sin of *malice* was pardoned, but all other sins were swept away together. That day was the first when my heart had believed, and my tongue had made confession unto salvation. The first words uttered, a part of that song, which shall fill eternity with its sound, was *glory to God*. For a few moments I had power to exhort sinners, and to tell of the wonders and of the goodness of him who had clothed me with *his* salvation. During this, the minister was silent, until my soul felt its duty had been performed, when he declared another witness of the power of Christ to forgive sins on earth was manifest in my conversion.

From the day on which I first went to the Methodist church, until the hour of my deliverance, I was strangely buffetted by that enemy of all righteousness—the devil.

I was naturally of a lively turn of disposition; and during the space of time from my first awakening until I knew my peace was made with God, I rejoiced in the vanities of this life, and then again sunk back into sorrow.

For four years I had continued in this way, frequently labouring under the awful apprehension that I could never be happy in this life. This persuasion was greatly strengthened, during the three weeks which was the last of Satan's power over me, in this peculiar manner: on which acount, I had come to the conclusion that I had better be dead than alive. Here I was again tempted to destroy my life by drowning; but suddenly this mode was changed, and while in the dusk of the evening, as I was walking to and fro in the yard of the house, I was beset to hang myself with a cord suspended from the wall enclosing the secluded spot.

But no sooner was the intention resolved on in my mind than an awful dread came over me, when I ran into the house; still the tempter pursued me. There was standing a vessel of water; into this I was strongly impressed to plunge my head, so as to extinguish the life which God had given me. Had I have done this, I have been always of the opinion that I should have been unable to have released myself; although the vessel was scarcely large enough to hold a gallon of water. Of me may it not be said, as written by Isaiah, (chap. 65, verses 1, 2.) "I am sought of them that asked not for me; I am found of them that sought me not." Glory be to God for his redeeming power, which saved me from the violence of my own hands, from the malice of Satan, and from eternal death; for had I have killed myself, a great ransom could not have delivered me; for it is written, "No murderer hath eternal life abiding in him." How appropriately can I sing

> Jesus sought me, when a stranger,
>   Wandering from the fold of God;
> He to rescue me from danger,
>   Interposed his precious blood.

But notwithstanding the terror which seized upon me, when about to end my life, I had no view of the precipice on the edge of which I was tottering, until it was over, and my eyes were opened. Then the awful gulf of hell seemed to be open beneath me, covered only, as it were, by a spider's web, on which I stood. I seemed to hear the howling of the damned, to see the smoke of the bottomless pit, and to hear the rattling of those chains which hold the impenitent under clouds of darkness to the judgment of the great day.

I trembled like Belshazzar, and cried out in the horror of my spirit, "God be merciful to me a sinner." That night I formed a resolution to pray; which, when resolved upon, there appeared, sitting in one corner of the room, Satan, in the form of a monstrous dog, and in a rage, as if in pursuit, his tongue protruding from his mouth to a great length, and his eyes looked like two balls of fire; it soon, however, vanished out of my sight. From this state of terror and dismay I was happily delivered under the preaching of the Gospel as before related.

This view which I was permitted to have of Satan in the form of a dog is evidence, which corroborates in my estimation, the Bible account of a hell of fire, which burneth with brimstone, called in Scripture the bottomless pit, the place where all liars, who repent not, shall have their portion; as also the Sabbath breaker, the adulterer, the fornicator, with the fearful, the abominable, and the unbelieving, this shall be the portion of their cup.

This language is too strong and expressive to be applied to any state of suffering in *time*. Were it to be thus applied, the reality could nowhere be found in human life; the consequence would be,

that *this* scripture would be found a false testimony. But when made
to apply to an endless state of perdition, in eternity, beyond the
bounds of human life, then this language is found not to exceed our
views of a state of eternal damnation.

During the latter part of my state of conviction, I can now apply
to my case, as it then was, the beautiful words of the poet:

> The more I strove against its power,
> I felt its weight and guilt the more;
> Till late I hear'd my Saviour say,
> Come hither soul, I am the way.

This I found to be true, to the joy of my disconsolate and despairing
heart, in the hour of my conversion to God.

During this state of mind, while sitting near the fire one evening,
after I had heard Rev. Richard Allen, as before related, a view of
my distressed condition so affected my heart, that I could not refrain
from weeping and crying aloud; which caused the lady with whom
I then lived to inquire with surprise, what ailed me; to which I answered that I knew not what ailed me. She replied that I ought to
pray. I arose from where I was sitting, being in an agony, and weeping convulsively, requested her to pray for me; but at the very
moment when she would have done so, some person rapped heavily
at the door for admittance; it was but a person of the house, but this
occurrence was sufficient to interrupt us in our intentions; and I believe to this day, I should then have found salvation to my soul. This
interruption was doubtless also the work of Satan.

Although at this time, when my conviction was so great, yet I
knew not that Jesus Christ was the Son of God, the second person
in the adorable trinity. I knew him not in the pardon of my sins,
yet I felt a consciousness that if I died without pardon, that my lot
must inevitably be damnation. If I would pray—I knew not how.
I could form no connexion of ideas into words; but I knew the
Lord's prayer; this I uttered with a loud voice, and with all my
might and strength. I was the most ignorant creature in the world; I
did not even know that Christ had died for the sins of the world, and
to save sinners. Every circumstance, however, was so directed as
still to continue and increase the sorrows of my heart, which I now
know to have been a godly sorrow which wrought repentance, which
is not to be repented of. Even the falling of the dead leaves from
the forests, and the dried spires of the mown grass, showed me that
I too must die in like manner. But my case was awfully different
from that of the grass of the field, or the widespread decay of a
thousand forests, as I felt within me a living principle, an immortal

spirit, which cannot die, and must forever either enjoy the smiles of its Creator, or feel the pangs of ceaseless damnation.

But the Lord led me on. Being gracious, he took pity on my ignorance; he heard my wailings, which had entered into the ear of the Lord of Sabaoth. Circumstances so transpired that I soon came to a knowledge of the being and character of the Son of God, of whom I knew nothing.

My strength had left me. I had become feverish and sickly through the violence of my feelings, on which account I left my place of service to spend a week with a coloured physician, who was a member of the Methodist society, and also to spend this week in going to places where prayer and supplication was stately [regularly] made for such as me.

Through this means I had learned much, so as to be able in some degree to comprehend the spiritual meaning of the text which the minister took on the Sabbath morning, as before related, which was, "I perceive thy heart is not right in the sight of God." Acts, chap. 8, verse 21.

This text, as already related, became the power of God unto salvation to me, because I believed. I was baptized according to the direction of our Lord, who said, as he was about to ascend from the mount, to his disciples, "Go ye into all the world and preach my gospel to every creature, he that believeth and is baptized shall be saved."

I have now passed through the account of my conviction, and also of my conversion to God; and shall next speak of the blessing of sanctification.

A time after I had received forgiveness flowed sweetly on; day and night my joy was full, no temptation was permitted to molest me. I could say continually with the psalmist, that "God had separated my sins from me, as far as the east is from the west." I was ready continually to cry

> Come all the world, come sinner thou,
> All things in Christ are ready now.

I continued in this happy state of mind for almost three months, when a certain coloured man, by name William Scott, came to pay me a religious visit. He had been for many years a faithful follower of the Lamb; and he had also taken much time in visiting the sick and distressed of our colour, and understood well the great things belonging to a man of full stature in Christ Jesus.

In the course of our conversation, he inquired if the Lord had justified my soul. I answered, yes. He then asked me if he had sanctified me. I answered, no; and that I did not know what that was. He then undertook to instruct me further in the knowledge of the Lord respecting this blessing.

He told me the progress of the soul from a state of darkness, or of nature, was threefold; or consisted in three degrees, as follows: First, conviction for sin. Second, justification from sin. Third, the entire sanctification of the soul to God. I thought this description was beautiful, and immediately believed in it. He then inquired if I would promise to pray for this in my secret devotions. I told him, yes. Very soon I began to call upon the Lord to show me all that was in my heart, which was not according to his will. Now there appeared to be a new struggle commencing in my soul, not accompanied with fear, guilt, and bitter distress, as while under my first conviction for sin; but a labouring of the mind to know more of the right way of the Lord. I began now to feel that my heart was not clean in his sight; that there yet remained the roots of bitterness, which if not destroyed, would ere long sprout up from these roots, and overwhelm me in a new growth of the brambles and brushwood of sin.

By the increasing light of the Spirit, I had found there yet remained the root of pride, anger, self-will, with many evils, the result of fallen nature. I now became alarmed at this discovery, and began to fear that I had been deceived in my experience. I was now greatly alarmed, lest I should fall away from what I knew I had enjoyed; and to guard against this I prayed almost incessantly, without acting faith on the power and promises of God to keep me from falling. I had not yet learned how to war against temptation of this kind. Satan well knew that if he could succeed in making me disbelieve my conversion, that he would catch me either on the ground of complete despair, or on the ground of infidelity. For if all I had passed through was to go for nothing, and was but a fiction, the mere ravings of a disordered mind, then I would naturally be led to believe that there is nothing in religion at all.

From this snare I was mercifully preserved, and led to believe that there was yet a greater work than that of pardon to be wrought in me. I retired to a secret place (after having sought this blessing, as well as I could, for nearly three months, from the time brother Scott had instructed me respecting it) for prayer, about four o'clock in the afternoon. I had struggled long and hard, but found not the desire of my heart. When I rose from my knees, there seemed a voice speaking to me, as I yet stood in a leaning posture—"Ask for sanctification." When to my surprise, I recollected that I had not even thought of it in my whole prayer. It would seem Satan had hidden

the very object from my mind, for which I had purposely kneeled
to pray. But when this voice whispered in my heart, saying, "Pray
for sanctification," I again bowed in the same place, at the same
time, and said, "Lord *sanctify* my soul for Christ's sake?" That very
instant, as if lightning had darted through me, I sprang to my feet,
and cried, "The Lord has sanctified my soul!" There was none to
hear this but the angels who stood around to witness my joy—and
Satan, whose malice raged the more. That Satan was there, I knew;
for no sooner had I cried out "The Lord has sanctified my soul,"
than there seemed another voice behind me, saying, "No, it is too
great a work to be done." But another spirit said, "Bow down for
the witness—I received it—*thou art sanctified!*" The first I knew of
myself after that, I was standing in the yard with my hands spread
out, and looking with my face toward heaven.

I now ran into the house and told them what had happened to
me, when, as it were, a new rush of the same ecstasy came upon me,
and caused me to feel as if I were in an ocean of light and bliss.

During this, I stood perfectly still, the tears rolling in a flood from
my eyes. So great was the joy that it is past description. There is no
language that can describe it, except that which was heard by St.
Paul, when he was caught up to the third heaven, and heard words
which it was not lawful to utter.

MY CALL TO PREACH THE GOSPEL

Between four and five years after my sanctification, on a certain
time, an impressive silence fell upon me, and I stood as if some one
was about to speak to me, yet I had no such thought in my heart.
But to my utter surprise there seemed to sound a voice which I
thought I distinctly heard, and most certainly understood, which said
to me, "Go preach the Gospel!" I immediately replied aloud, "No
one will believe me." Again I listened, and again the same voice
seemed to say, "Preach the Gospel; I will put words in your mouth,
and will turn your enemies to become your friends."

At first I supposed that Satan had spoken to me, for I had read
that he could transform himself into an angel of light, for the purpose
of deception. Immediately I went into a secret place, and called
upon the Lord to know if he had called me to preach, and whether
I was deceived or not; when there appeared to my view the form
and figure of a pulpit, with a Bible lying thereon, the back of which
was presented to me as plainly as if it had been a literal fact.

In consequence of this, my mind became so exercised that during
the night following, I took a text and preached in my sleep. I

thought there stood before me a great multitude, while I expounded to them the things of religion. So violent were my exertions, and so loud were my exclamations, that I awoke from the sound of my own voice, which also awoke the family of the house where I resided. Two days after, I went to see the preacher in charge of the African Society, who was the Rev. Richard Allen (the same before named in these pages) to tell him that I felt it my duty to preach the gospel. But as I drew near the street in which his house was, which was in the city of Philadelphia, my courage began to fail me; so terrible did the cross appear, it seemed that I should not be able to bear it. Previous to my setting out to go to see him, so agitated was my mind that my appetite for my daily food failed me entirely. Several times on my way there, I turned back again; but as often I felt my strength again renewed, and I soon found that the nearer I approached to the house of the minister, the less was my fear. Accordingly, as soon as I came to the door, my fears subsided, the cross was removed, all things appeared pleasant—I was tranquil.

I now told him that the Lord had revealed it to me that I must preach the gospel. He replied by asking, in what sphere I wished to move in? I said, among the Methodists. He then replied, that a Mrs. Cook, a Methodist lady, had also some time before requested the same privilege; who it was believed, had done much good in the way of exhortation, and holding prayer meetings; and who had been permitted to do so by the verbal license of the preacher in charge at the time. But as to women preaching, he said that our Discipline knew nothing at all about it—that it did not call for women preachers. This I was glad to hear, because it removed the fear of the cross—but not no sooner did this feeling cross my mind, than I found that a love of souls had in a measure departed from me; that holy energy which burned within me as a fire, began to be smothered. This I soon perceived.

O how careful ought we to be, lest through our bylaws of church government and discipline, we bring into disrepute even the word of life. For as unseemly as it may appear nowadays for a woman to preach, it should be remembered that nothing is impossible with God. And why should it be thought impossible, heterodox, or improper for a woman to preach, seeing the Saviour died for the woman as well as the man?

If the man may preach, because the Saviour died for him, why not the woman, seeing he died for her also? Is he not a whole Saviour, instead of a half one, as those who hold it wrong for a woman to preach, would seem to make it appear?

Did not Mary *first* preach the risen Saviour, and is not the doctrine of the resurrection the very climax of Christianity—hangs not all our hope on this, as argued by St. Paul? Then did not Mary, a woman, preach the gospel? For she preached the resurrection of the crucified Son of God.

But some will say that Mary did not expound the Scripture, therefore she did not preach, in the proper sense of the term. To this I reply, it may be that the term *preach*, in those primitive times, did not mean exactly what it is now *made* to mean; perhaps it was a great deal more simple then, than it is now: if it were not, the unlearned fishermen could not have preached the gospel at all, as they had no learning.

To this it may be replied by those who are determined not to believe that it is right for a woman to preach, that the disciples, though they were fishermen, and ignorant of letters too, were inspired so to do. To which I would reply, that though they were inspired, yet that inspiration did not save them from showing their ignorance of letters, and of man's wisdom; this the multitude soon found out, by listening to the remarks of the envious Jewish priests. If then, to preach the gospel, by the gift of heaven, comes by inspiration solely, is God straitened; must he take the man exclusively? May he not, did he not, and can he not inspire a female to preach the simple story of the birth, life, death, and resurrection of our Lord, and accompany it too, with power to the sinner's heart. As for me, I am fully persuaded that the Lord called me to labour according to what I have received, in his vineyard. If he has not, how could he consistently bear testimony in favour of my poor labours, in awakening and converting sinners?

In my wanderings up and down among men, preaching according to my ability, I have frequently found families who told me that they had not for several years been to a meeting, and yet, while listening to hear what God would say by his poor coloured female instrument, have believed with trembling, tears rolling down their cheeks—the signs of contrition and repentance towards God. I firmly believe that I have sown seed in the name of the Lord, which shall appear with its increase at the great day of accounts, when Christ shall come to make up his jewels.

At a certain time I was beset with the idea that soon or late I should fall from grace, and lose my soul at last. I was frequently called to the throne of grace about this matter, but found no relief; the temptation pursued me still. Being more and more afflicted with it, till at a certain time when the spirit strongly impressed it on my mind to enter into my closet, and carry my case once more to the Lord; the Lord enabled me to draw nigh to him, and to his mercy seat, at this time, in an extraordinary manner; for while I wrestled with him for the victory over this disposition to doubt whether I should persevere, there appeared a form of fire, about the size of a man's hand, as I was on my knees; at the same moment, there appeared to the eye of faith a man robed in a white garment, from the shoulders down to the feet; from him a voice proceeded, saying: "Thou shalt never return from the cross." Since that time I have never doubted, but believe that God will keep me until the day of redemption. Now I could adopt the very language of St. Paul, and say that nothing could have separated my soul from the love of God, which is in Christ Jesus. From that time, 1807, until the present, 1833, I have not yet doubted the power and goodness of God to keep me from falling, through sanctification of the spirit and belief of the truth.

MY MARRIAGE

In the year 1811, I changed my situation in life, having married Mr. Joseph Lee, Pastor of a Coloured Society at Snow Hill, about six miles from the city of Philadelphia. It became necessary therefore for me to remove. This was a great trial at first, as I knew no person at Snow Hill, except my husband; and to leave my associates in the society, and especially those who composed the band of which I was one. Not but those who have been in sweet fellowship with such as really love God, and have together drank bliss and happiness from the same fountain, can tell how dear such company is, and how hard it is to part from them.

At Snow Hill, as was feared, I never found that agreement and closeness in communion and fellowship, that I had in Philadelphia among my young companions, nor ought I to have expected it. The manners and customs at this place were somewhat different, on which account I became discontented in the course of a year, and began to importune my husband to remove to the city. But this plan did not suit him, as he was the Pastor of the Society; he could not bring his mind to leave them. This afflicted me a little. But the Lord soon showed me in a dream what his will was concerning this matter.

I dreamed that as I was walking on the summit of a beautiful hill, that I saw near me a flock of sheep, fair and white, as if but newly washed; when there came walking toward me a man of a grave and dignified countenance, dressed entirely in white, as it were in a robe, and looking at me, said emphatically, "Joseph Lee must take care of these sheep, or the wolf will come and devour them." When I awoke, I was convinced of my error, and immediately, with a glad heart, yielded to the right way of the Lord. This also greatly strengthened my husband in his care over them, for fear the wolf should by some means take any of them away. The following verse was beautifully suited to our condition, as well as to all the little flocks of God scattered up and down this land:

> Us into Thy protection take,
> And gather with Thine arm;
> Unless the fold we first forsake,
> The wolf can never harm.

After this, I fell into a state of general debility and in an ill state of health; so much so, that I could not sit up; but a desire to warn sinners to flee the wrath to come burned vehemently in my heart, when the Lord would send sinners into the house to see me. Such opportunities I embraced to press home on their consciences the things of eternity, and so effectual was the word of exhortation made through the Spirit, that I have seen them fall to the floor crying aloud for mercy.

From this sickness I did not expect to recover; and there was but one thing which bound me to earth, and this was, that I had not as yet preached the gospel to the fallen sons and daughters of Adam's race, to the satisfaction of my mind. I wished to go from one end of the earth to the other, crying, Behold, behold the Lamb! To this end I earnestly prayed the Lord to raise me up, if consistent with his will. He condescended to hear my prayer, and to give me a token in a dream, that in due time I should recover my health. The dream was as follows: I thought I saw the sun rise in the morning, and ascend to an altitude of about half an hour high, and then become obscured by a dense black cloud, which continued to hide its rays for about one-third part of the day, and then it burst forth again with renewed splendour.

This dream I interpreted to signify my early life, my conversion to God, and this sickness, which was a great affliction, as it hindered me, and I feared would forever hinder me from preaching the gospel, was signified by the cloud; and the bursting forth of the sun, again, was the recovery of my health, and being permitted to preach.

I went to the throne of grace on this subject, where the Lord made this impressive reply in my heart, while on my knees: "Ye shall be restored to thy health again, and worship God in full purpose of heart."

This manifestation was so impressive that I could but hide my face, as if someone was gazing upon me, to think of the great goodness of the Almighty God to my poor soul and body. From that very time I began to gain strength of body and mind, glory to God in the highest, until my health was fully recovered.

For six years from this time I continued to receive from above such baptisms of the Spirit as mortality could scarcely bear. About that time I was called to suffer in my family by death—five, in the course of about six years, fell by his hand; my husband being one of the number, which was the greatest affliction of all.

I was now left alone in the world, with two infant children, one of the age of about two years, the other six months, with no other dependence than the promise of Him who hath said, "I will be the widow's God, and a father to the fatherless." Accordingly, he raised me up friends, whose liberality comforted and solaced me in my state of widowhood and sorrows. I could sing with the greatest propriety the words of the poet.

> He helps the stranger in distress,
> The widow and the fatherless,
> And grants the prisoner sweet release.

I can say even now, with the Psalmist, "Once I was young, but now I am old, yet I have never seen the righteous forsaken, nor his seed begging bread." I have ever been fed by his bounty, clothed by his mercy, comforted and healed when sick, succoured when tempted, and every where upheld by his hand.

THE SUBJECT OF MY CALL TO PREACH RENEWED

It was now eight years since I had made application to be permitted to preach the gospel, during which time I had only been allowed to exhort, and even this privilege but seldom. This subject now was renewed afresh in my mind; it was as a fire shut up in my bones. About thirteen months passed on, while under this renewed impression. During this time, I had solicited of the Rev. Bishop Richard Allen, who at this time had become Bishop of the African Episcopal Methodists in America, to be permitted the liberty of holding prayer meetings in my own hired house, and of exhorting as I found liberty, which was granted me. By this means, my mind was relieved, as the house was soon filled when the hour appointed for prayer had arrived.

I cannot but relate in this place, before I proceed further with the above subject, the singular conversion of a very wicked young man. He was a coloured man, who had generally attended our meetings, but not for any good purpose; but rather to disturb and to ridicule our denomination. He openly and uniformly declared that he neither believed in religion, nor wanted anything to do with it. He was of a Gallio disposition, and took the lead among the young people of colour. But after a while he fell sick, and lay about three months in a state of ill health; his disease was a consumption. Toward the close of his days, his sister who was a member of the society, came and desired me to go and see her brother, as she had no hopes of his recovery; perhaps the Lord might break into his mind. I went alone, and found him very low. I soon commenced to inquire respecting his state of feeling, and how he found his mind. His answer was, "O tolerable well," with an air of great indifference. I asked him if I should pray for him. He answered in a sluggish and careless manner, "O yes, if you have time." I then sung a hymn, kneeled down and prayed for him, and then went my way.

Three days after this, I went again to visit the young man. At this time there went with me two of the sisters in Christ. We found the Rev. Mr. Cornish, of our denomination, labouring with him. But he said he received but little satisfaction from him. Pretty soon, however, brother Cornish took his leave; when myself, with the other two sisters, one of which was an elderly woman named Jane Hutt, the other was younger, both coloured, commenced conversing with him, respecting his eternal interest, and of his hopes of a happy eternity, if any he had. He said but little; we then kneeled down together and besought the Lord in his behalf, praying that if mercy were not clear gone forever, to shed a ray of softening grace upon the hardness of his heart. He appeared now to be somewhat more tender, and we thought we could perceive some tokens of conviction, as he wished us to visit him again, in a tone of voice not quite as indifferent as he had hitherto manifested.

But two days had elapsed after this visit, when his sister came for me in haste, saying, that she believed her brother was then dying, and that he had sent for me. I immediately called on Jane Hutt, who was still among us as a mother in Israel, to go with me. When we arrived there, we found him sitting up in his bed, very restless and uneasy, but he soon laid down again. He now wished me to come to him, by the side of his bed. I asked him how he was. He said, "Very ill;" and added, "Pray for me, quick?" We now perceived his time in this world to be short. I took up the hymnbook and opened to a hymn suitable to his case, and commenced to sing. But there seemed to be a horror in the room—a darkness of a mental kind, which was felt by us all; there being five persons, except the sick young man and his nurse. We had sung but one verse, when they all gave over singing, on account of this unearthly sensation, but myself. I continued to sing on alone, but in a dull and heavy manner, though looking up to God all the while for help. Suddenly, I felt a spring of energy awake in my heart, when darkness gave way in some degree. It was but a glimmer from above. When the hymn was finished, we all kneeled down to pray for him. While calling on the name of the Lord, to have mercy on his soul, and to grant him repentance unto life, it came suddenly into my mind never to rise from my knees until God should hear prayer in his behalf, until he should convert and save his soul.

Now, while I thus continued importuning heaven, as I felt I was led, a ray of light, more abundant, broke forth among us. There appeared to my view (though my eyes were closed) the Saviour in full stature, nailed to the cross, just over the head of the young man, against the ceiling of the room. I cried out, brother look up, the Saviour is come, he will pardon you, your sins he will forgive. My sorrow for the soul of the young man was gone; I could no longer pray—joy and rapture made it impossible. We rose up from our knees, when lo, his eyes were gazing with ecstasy upward; over his face there was an expression of joy; his lips were clothed in a sweet and holy smile; but no sound came from his tongue; it was heard in its stillness of bliss, full of hope and immortality. Thus, as I held him by the hand his happy and purified soul soared away, without a sigh or a groan, to its eternal rest.

I now closed his eyes, straightened out his limbs, and left him to be dressed for the grave. But as for me, I was filled with the power of the Holy Ghost—the very room seemed filled with glory. His sister and all that were in the room rejoiced, nothing doubting but he had entered into Paradise; and I believe I shall see him at the last and great day, safe on the shores of salvation.

But to return to the subject of my call to preach. Soon after this, as above related, the Rev. Richard Williams was to preach at Bethel Church, where I with others were assembled. He entered the pulpit, gave out the hymn, which was sung, and then addressed the throne of grace; took his text, passed through the exordium, and commenced to expound it. The text he took is in Jonah, 2d chap. 9th verse,—"Salvation is of the Lord." But as he proceeded to explain, he seemed to have lost the spirit; when in the same instant, I sprang, as by an altogether supernatural impulse, to my feet, when I was aided from above to give an exhortation on the very text which my brother Williams had taken.

I told them that I was like Jonah; for it had been then nearly eight years since the Lord had called me to preach his gospel to the fallen sons and daughters of Adam's race, but that I had lingered like him, and delayed to go at the bidding of the Lord, and warn those who are as deeply guilty as were the people of Ninevah.

During the exhortation, God made manifest his power in a manner sufficient to show the world that I was called to labour according to my ability, and the grace given unto me, in the vineyard of the good husbandman.

I now sat down, scarcely knowing what I had done, being frightened. I imagined, that for this indecorum, as I feared it might be called, I should be expelled from the church. But instead of this, the Bishop rose up in the assembly, and related that I had called upon him eight years before, asking to be permitted to preach, and that he had put me off; but that he now as much believed that I was called to that work, as any of the preachers present. These remarks greatly strengthened me, so that my fears of having given an offence and made myself liable as an offender subsided, giving place to a sweet serenity, a holy joy of a peculiar kind, untasted in my bosom until then.

The next Sabbath day, while sitting under the word of the gospel, I felt moved to attempt to speak to the people in a public manner, but I could not bring my mind to attempt it in the church. I said, Lord, anywhere but here. Accordingly, there was a house not far off which was pointed out to me; to this I went. It was the house of a sister belonging to the same society with myself. Her name was Anderson. I told her I had come to hold a meeting in her house, if she would call in her neighbours. With this request she immediately complied. My congregation consisted of but five persons. I commenced by reading and singing a hymn, when I dropped to my knees by the side of a table to pray. When I arose I found my hand resting on the Bible, which I had not noticed till that moment. It now occurred to me to take a text. I opened the Scripture, as it happened, at the 141st Psalm, fixing my eye on the 3d verse, which reads: "Set a watch, O Lord, before my mouth, keep the door of my lips." My sermon, such as it was, I applied wholly to myself, and added an exhortation. Two of my congregation wept much, as the fruit of my labour this time. In closing I said to the few, that if any one would open a door, I would hold a meeting the next sixth-day evening; when one answered that her house was at my service. Accordingly I went, and God made manifest his power among the people. Some wept, while others shouted for joy. One whole seat of females, by the power of God, as the rushing of a wind, were all bowed to the floor at once, and screamed out. Also a sick man and woman in one house, the Lord convicted them both; one lived, and the other died. God wrought a judgment—some were well at night, and died in the morning. At this place I continued to hold meetings about six months. During that time I kept house with my little son, who was very sickly. About this time I had a call to preach at a place about thirty miles distant, among the Methodists, with whom I remained one week, and during the whole time not a thought of my little son came into my mind; it was hid from me, lest I should have been diverted from the work I had to do, to look after my son. Here by the instrumentality of a poor coloured woman, the Lord poured forth his spirit among the people. Though, as I was told, there were lawyers, doctors, and magistrates present to hear me speak, yet there was mourning and crying among sinners, for the Lord scattered fire among them of his own kindling. The Lord gave his handmaiden power to speak for his great name, for he arrested the hearts of the people, and caused a shaking amongst the multitude, for God was in the midst.

I now returned home, found all well; no harm had come to my child, although I left it very sick. Friends had taken care of it which was of the Lord. I now began to think seriously of breaking up housekeeping, and forsaking all to preach the everlasting Gospel. I felt a strong desire to return to the place of my nativity, at Cape May, after an absence of about fourteen years. To this place, where the heaviest cross was to be met with, the Lord sent me, as Saul of Tarsus was sent to Jerusalem, to preach the same gospel which he had neglected and despised before his conversion. I went by water, and on my passage was much distressed by sea sickness, so much so that I expected to have died, but such was not the will of the Lord respecting me. After I had disembarked, I proceeded on as opportunities offered, toward where my mother lived. When within ten miles of that place, I appointed an evening meeting. There were a goodly number came out to hear. The Lord was pleased to give me light and liberty among the people. After meeting, there came an elderly lady to me and said she believed the Lord had sent me among them; she then appointed me another meeting there two weeks from that night. The next day I hastened forward to the place of my mother, who was happy to see me, and the happiness was mutual between us. With her I left my poor sickly boy, while I departed to do my Master's will. In this neighborhood I had an uncle who was a Methodist, and who gladly threw open his door for meetings to be held there. At the first meeting which I held at my uncle's house, there was, with others who had come from curiosity to hear the coloured woman preacher, an old man, who was a deist, and who said he did not believe the coloured people had any souls—he was sure they had none. He took a seat very near where I was standing, and boldly tried to look me out of countenance. But as I laboured on in the best manner I was able, looking to God all the while, though it seemed to me I had but little liberty, yet there went an arrow from the bent bow of the gospel, and fastened in his till then obdurate heart. After I had done speaking, he went out, and called the people around him, said that my preaching might seem a small thing, yet he believed I had the worth of souls at heart. This language was different from what it was a little time before, as he now seemed to admit that coloured people had souls, as it was to these I was chiefly speaking; and unless they had souls, whose good I had in view, his remark must have been without meaning. He now came into the house, and in the most friendly manner shook hands with me, saying he hoped God had spared him to some good purpose. This man was a great slave holder, and had been very cruel; thinking nothing of knocking down a slave with a fence stake, or whatever might come to hand. From this time it was said of him that he became greatly altered in his ways for the better. At that time he was about seventy years old, his head as white as snow; but whether he became a converted man or not, I never heard.

The week following, I had an invitation to hold a meeting at the Court House of the County, when I spoke from the 53d chap of Isaiah, 3d verse. It was a solemn time, and the Lord attended the word; I had life and liberty, though there were people there of various denominations. Here again I saw the aged slaveholder, who notwithstanding his age, walked about three miles to hear me. This day I spoke twice, and walked six miles to the place appointed. There was a magistrate present, who showed his friendship by saying in a friendly manner that he had heard of me: he handed me a hymn-book, pointing to a hymn which he had selected. When the meeting was over, he invited me to preach in a schoolhouse in his neighbourhood, about three miles distant from where I then was. During this meeting one backslider was reclaimed. This day I walked six miles, and preached twice to large congregations, both in the morning and evening. The Lord was with me, glory be to his holy name. I next went six miles and held a meeting in a coloured friend's house, at eleven o'clock in the morning, and preached to a well behaved congregation of both coloured and white. After service I again walked back, which was in all twelve miles in the same day. This was on Sabbath, or as I sometimes call it, seventh-day; for after my conversion I preferred the plain language of the Quakers: On fourth day, after this, in compliance with an invitation received by note, from the same magistrate who had heard me at the above place, I preached to a large congregation, where we had a precious time: much weeping was heard among the people. The same gentleman, now at the close of the meeting, gave out another appointment at the same place, that day week. Here again I had liberty, there was a move among the people. Ten years from that time, in the neighbourhood of Cape May, I held a prayer meeting in a school house, which was then the regular place of preaching for the Episcopal Methodists; after service, there came a white lady of the first distinction, a member of the Methodist Society, and told me that at the same schoolhouse, ten years before, under my preaching, the Lord first awakened her. She rejoiced much to see me, and invited me home with her, where I staid till the next day. This was bread cast on the waters, seen after many days.

From this place I next went to Dennis Creek meeting house, where at the invitation of an elder, I spoke to a large congregation of various and conflicting sentiments, when a wonderful shock of God's power was felt, shown everywhere by groans, by sighs, and loud and happy amens. I felt as if aided from above. My tongue was cut loose, the stammerer spoke freely; the love of God, and of his service, burned with a vehement flame within me; his name was glorified among the people.

But here I feel myself constrained to give over, as from the smallness of this pamphlet I cannot go through with the whole of my journal, as it would probably make a volume of two hundred pages; which, if the Lord be willing, may at some future day be published. But for the satisfaction of such as may follow after me, when I am no more, I have recorded how the Lord called me to his work, and how he has kept me from falling from grace, as I feared I should. In all things he has proved himself a God of truth to me; and in his service I am now as much determined to spend and be spent, as at the very first. My ardour for the progress of his cause abates not a whit, so far as I am able to judge, though I am now something more than fifty years of age.

As to the nature of uncommon impressions, which the reader cannot but have noticed, and possibly sneered at in the course of these pages, they may be accounted for in this way: It is known that the blind have the sense of hearing in a manner much more acute than those who can see: also their sense of feeling is exceedingly fine, and is found to detect any roughness on the smoothest surface, where those who can see can find none. So it may be with such as I am, who has never had more than three months schooling; and wishing to know much of the way and law of God, have therefore watched the more closely the operations of the Spirit, and have in consequence been led thereby. But let it be remarked that I have never found that Spirit to lead me contrary to the Scriptures of truth, as I understand them. "For as many as are led by the *Spirit* of God are the sons of God."—Rom. viii. 14.

I have now only to say, May the blessing of the Father, and of the Son, and of the Holy Ghost, accompany the reading of this poor effort to speak well of his name, wherever it may be read. AMEN.

Part VII

Creative Literature—Narratives, Poems, and Essays, 1760–1835

In the mid-eighteenth century, a new type of literature made its appearance in the United States. Small pamphlets and broadsides published by authors were identified on the title pages of their books as written by "a Black," "a Man of Colour," "an Ethiopian Poetess," "a Descendant of Africa," and "the African." Briton Hammon, the earliest of these authors, published his narrative—a small pamphlet of 14 pages—in 1760. It is an amazing story of the "many hardships" he underwent after leaving his master's house, in Marshfield, Massachusetts, on December 25, 1747, until he returned to Boston several years later. Hammon was probably a member of the household of General John Winslow (1703–1774), Colonial soldier and captain at one time of a company in the West India Expedition. No doubt Hammon, intrigued by the stories of military affairs he heard from visitors to the house, with his master's permission set out for a sea voyage to Jamaica on Christmas day, 1747. In spite of shipwrecks, encounters with unfriendly Indians who captured him and threatened to roast him alive, and his serving four years and seven months in a "close dungeon," he lived to return to Boston and relate his almost unbelievable story, which was printed and sold by Green and Russell in Boston. Two copies of the original of this narrative are known to exist today. One is in the Library of Congress and the other is in the New York Historical Society.

It is a strange coincidence that Jupiter Hammon, whose surname was the same as Briton Hammon's, also published his first poem in 1760. It was a broadside entitled *An Evening Thought, Salvation by Christ, With Penetential Cries,* and was first distributed on December 25, 1760. We may assume that Briton Hammon's Narrative appeared earlier in 1760 than December. He might therefore be considered the earliest black American writer whose work appeared in print.

The slave narrative, a peculiar genre of American literature, had as a rule two primary functions: first, that of portraying the author's hardships while he lived in slavery—for no picture of slavery could be more vivid than that experienced by the slave himself—and second, propaganda against human slavery. In many instances, proceeds from the sale of these narratives were used to help support the writer and to enable him to pay for the freedom of members of his family. Naturally, the character and quality of genuine narratives varied with the temperament and ability of their authors, as well as of the persons to whom some of them dictated their stories. Authenticity of many slave narratives can only be checked on the basis of internal evidence. Fortunately, the publishers of the narrative of Venture Smith and Solomon Bayley provide evidence of authenticity. Bayley's narrative would probably never have been published if Robert Hurnard—an Englishman visiting in Wilmington, Delaware, where Bayley had been born a slave—had not heard about his escape in 1820 from slavery and the trials and tribulations connected with it from respectable inhabitants of Wilmington. Hurnard sought Bayley out, interviewed him, and asked him to write his story. Since Hurnard could not remain in Wilmington until Bayley finished his narrative, Bayley sent it to Hurnard in sections. Hunard finally published it, stating that "it appeared too interesting and valuable to be restricted to the circle of my own acquaintances." A singular feature of Bayley's narrative is that it was undoubtedly composed and sold with the view of financially aiding its author. Hurnard stated in his introduction that he intended to transmit all of the income from the publication to America for the benefit of Bayley and his wife, who were then aged. He hoped that "the friends of Humanity generally would assist in promoting the extensive circulation of the tract; by so doing they will also contribute to place slavery in a new and appaling light."[1]

The publisher of the *Narrative of the Life and Adventures of Venture* vouched for its authenticity, and the doubting reader was re-

---

[1] Bayley subsequently went to Haiti and from there he migrated to Monrovia, Liberia. In the meantime all of his children died. While in Monrovia his wife died. Bayley then returned to America where he remarried. It is said that, though aged, he became a preacher to a society and was considered a father and a counselor. See A. Mott, *Biographical Sketches and Interesting Anecdotes of Persons of Color* (New York, n.d.), pp. 46–65; Abstracts of this narrative appeared in the *Liberator*, Vol. 4, February 8, 1834, p. 23, and February 22, 1834, p. 31, with a plea that it be reprinted.

ferred to living persons who were acquainted with most of the facts mentioned in the story of Venture. The African writer was born at Dukandarra, Guinea, about 1729. His father's name was Saungm Furro, and Venture was originally named Brotter. Venture was the name given him by Robertson Mumford, steward of the vessel on which he was placed after being kidnapped from his home and sold for a piece of calico and four gallons of rum. Venture selected for his surname Smith; this was the name of his master, Colonel Oliver Smith, who may have been the brother of Joseph Smith, father of Sophia Smith, founder of Smith College. Venture writing at age 59 reveals a clear memory of his home in Africa and his capture into slavery. At age 69, he was living with his wife and children, all of whom he had purchased, in the town of East Haddam, Connecticut, on land and in a home he had purchased. Venture's story, the publisher states, "exhibits a pattern of honesty, prudence and industry, to people of his own colour; and perhaps some white people would not find themselves degraded by imitating such example." Venture Smith died on September 19, 1805. A brown inscribed slab marks his grave in East Haddam. It contains this inscription:

> Sacred to the memory of Venture Smith,
> African though son of a king he was
> kidnapped and sold as a slave, but by
> his industry he acquired enough money
> to purchase his freedom—who died
> September 19, 1805, in ye 77th year
> of his age.

In 1834, *The Origin, Horrors and Results of Slavery,* by William Paul Quinn, was published in Pittsburgh. Its author, a colleague of Richard Allen, was the fourth Bishop of the African Methodist Episcopal Church, having been consecrated May 19, 1844. The place of his birth is not exactly known, although Payne states it was in Honduras, S. A.[2] Licensed to preach in 1812, Quinn was sent to Western Pennsylvania—where he rode on horseback from place to place. He became the first A.M.E. itinerant preacher or "circuit rider," having enlisted as such on December 25, 1817.

By 1832, Quinn, now a Deacon, traveled across the Alleghany mountains preaching in Indiana, Illinois, Michigan, Kentucky, Missouri, and Iowa. He later established the Western missions between

[2] Daniel A. Payne *Recollections of Seventy Years.* (Nashville, Tenn., A. M. E. Sunday School Union, 1888.) p. 101. A. B. Hyde in his *The Story of Methodism throughout the World.* (Springfield, Mass., 1896) states he was born in Calcutta, Hindustan about 1795, p. 758.

1840 and 1842, which included eight circuits and stations with a membership of 7900. Quinn's report to the Methodist General Conference of 1844 stated that he had traveled from Pittsburgh to the West 300 miles beyond the Missouri line. Quinn faced many dangers while searching for souls in the wilderness, and he no doubt observed the results of slavery and its accompanying horrors, as well as acquiring knowledge on conditions relating to free Negroes.

The Origin, Horrors and Results of Slavery is divided into sections: an introduction, on the irrationality of slavery; an address to the legislators of South Carolina; a hint to the Congress of the United States; treatment of slaves in the Dutch settlements; and a conclusion.

No doubt the distressing laws enacted in South Carolina in 1834 inspired Quinn to prepare this booklet for publication, believing, perhaps, that his thoughts would circulate more widely if published, since he moved from place to place.[3]

Quinn was an intelligent preacher in the African Methodist Episcopal Church for over sixty years and a senior Bishop for twenty-four years.[4] The only copy of his original essay which seems to have been preserved is at Howard University Library.

An examination of the writings of David Ruggles will show that he was one of the most articulate of the early Negro abolitionists. Of his publications, which appeared as pamphlets or in the columns of newspapers such as the *Liberator* and *Emancipator*, none was more significant than his *Appeal to the Colored Citizens of New York and Elsewhere in Behalf of the Press* which appeared in six parts in the *Emancipator* beginning January 13, 1835, and ending February 17, 1835. Ruggles urged his people to strongly support the press whether they could read or not—and wrote, "every paper that is circulated by your means goes forth as an Ambassador to settle the all important question of *Liberty* and *Slavery*."[5]

The very existence of eighteenth century Afro-American poets

---

[3] In 1834, South Carolina enacted laws preventing the education of Negroes, as well as for the destruction of their schools. They were also not permitted to work as clerks or salesmen in shops or stores used for trading. Carter G. Woodson, *The Education of the Negro Prior to 1861* (Washington, D.C.: The Association for the Study of Negro Life and History, 1919), p. 167.

[4] References to Paul Quinn's activities as a presiding Bishop over the various conferences of the A. M. E. Church in the Mid-West, South and East will be found in James A. Handy, *Scraps of Methodist Episcopal History* (Philadelphia: A. M. E. Book Concern); and Daniel A. Payne, *Recollections of Seventy Years* (Nashville, Tenn.: A. M. E. Sunday School Union, 1888).

[5] See earlier references to David Ruggles.

makes the words of Countee Cullen seem pointedly significant: "Yet do I marvel at this curious thing: To make a poet black and bid him sing!" For each of the poets whose works are included herein was not only black but a slave. We have already mentioned Jupiter Hammon's poem, *An Evening Thought, Salvation by Christ, With Penetential Cries*. The one known copy of the original broadside is preserved in the New York Historical Society. The poem had been described as "something of a shout-hymn filled with religious sentiment amounting almost to piety in its somewhat turgent style of poetic declamation." Disregarding the somewhat unsophisticated and occasional crudity of the poem, it embodies some of the qualities found in Richard Allen's *Spiritual Song*. No doubt both were chanted during the delivery of a sermon.

Eighteen years later Jupiter Hammon composed another poem on August 4, 1778 in Hartford, Connecticut. This was also first published as a broadside. In it he pays tribute along with a number of his friends to Phillis Wheatley. The Connecticut Historical Society has preserved a copy of Hammon's *An Address to Miss Phillis Wheatly* (*sic*).[6]

Phillis Wheatley—far more versatile and productive than Jupiter Hammon—is today well known, and her poetry is read by students and literary critics. She was spoken of as the "first Negro poet" until Oscar Wegelin discovered Hammon's *An Evening Thought* in the New York Historical Society in 1915. Phillis Wheatley's first published poem appeared ten years after that of Hammon. *An Elegiac Poem on the Death of that Celebrated Divine and Eminent Servant of Jesus Christ, the Reverend and Learned George Whitefield*, a funeral elegy, was published as a broadside and as a pamphlet of eight pages in 1770.

Phillis Wheatley's poems appeared as collections of poems as well as broadsides. Her first collected edition of poetry appeared in London in 1773 under the title of *Poems on Various Subjects, Religious and Moral*.[7]

Thirteen years later, in 1786, Joseph Crukshanks reprinted the London edition in Philadelphia—the first American edition. The popularity of funeral elegies in Wheatley's day accounts for the fact that she composed at least six that were published. Phillis Wheatley was far more imaginative and better equipped than Jupiter Hammon

---

[6] See Stanley A. Ransom, editor, *America's First Negro Poet, the Complete Works of Jupiter Hammon of Long Island* (Port Washington, N.Y.: Kennikat Press, 1970).

[7] Julian D. Mason, editor, *The Poems of Phillis Wheatley* (Chapel Hill: University of North Carolina, 1966).

as well as able to make use of a variety of experiences unknown to him. The creative aspect of Negro writing begins with the work of these pioneer poets.

George Moses Horton's collected poems *The Hope of Liberty* was published in 1829 when he was age 32 and a slave of Mr. James Horton of Chatham County, North Carolina. Only five poems from that book have been selected for reproduction here. They show his hatred of slavery and his desire for liberty, his keen observation of the beauties of nature and his sentimental attitude towards love.

George Moses Horton was born of slave parents in Northampton County, North Carolina, about 1797. About 1803 his owner moved to Chatham County, near Chapel Hill, the location of the University of North Carolina. Horton was able to learn the alphabet by hearing children repeat it. He taught himself to read and spell. As he could write only a very little, he committed his poems to memory until he was able to dictate them to an amanuensis. Horton's verses appeared in *Freedom's Journal* in August, 1828.

For many years Horton was a familiar figure on the campus of the University of North Carolina, where he was employed as a servant and where he earned extra money by composing poems requested by students. It had been hoped that sufficient funds would have been realized from the sales of copies of *The Hope of Liberty* to secure Horton's freedom and enable him to emigrate to Liberia as a colonist. This did not happen, however. In the 1837 edition of *The Hope of Liberty*—published in Philadelphia, under the title *Poems by a Slave*—a statement in the preface suggested that the publisher of *The Hope of Liberty*, Weston R. Gales, had kept the money realized from its sale. We learn that Horton many years later did escape from slavery and settled in Philadelphia. He second book *Naked Genius* was published in Raleigh in 1865. It includes a short biographical sketch of Horton.[8]

The short poems composed by young students and originally published in the *Catalogue of Exercises from the New York African Free School* are included not because they are fine creative efforts, but to indicate what a little education could do for aspiring black youths who were encouraged to write about and against slavery or on freedom—if only as school exercises, or as exhibition pieces for such gatherings as the American Convention held in Baltimore in November, 1828. The anthems and hymns included are examples of compositions prepared for programs celebrating the abolition of the slave trade.

[8] For biographical data see Stephen B. Weeks, "George Moses Horton: Slave Poet," *Southern Workman*, Vol. 43 (1914), pp. 571–577.

Richard Allen, founder and first Bishop of the African Methodist Episcopal Church, sold his undated *Spiritual Song*, printed as a broadside in Philadelphia, certainly before 1801. In this religious chant he warned his congregation against loud "groaning and shouting"; such religion, he states, is "only a dream." The original of this broadside is in the William L. Clements Library.

The creative writings assembled in this section and throughout this volume, show black men and women making use of their pens as weapons to combat slavery, colonization, and ignorance.

A

NARRATIVE

OF THE

Uncommon Sufferings,

AND

Surprising Deliverance

OF

BRITON HAMMON,

A NEGRO MAN,—SERVANT TO

General Winslow,

OF MARSHFIELD, IN NEW ENGLAND;

WHO RETURNED TO BOSTON, AFTER HAVING

BEEN ABSENT ALMOST THIRTEEN YEARS.

CONTAINING

An account of the many hardships he underwent from the time he left his master's house, in the year 1747, to the time of his return to Boston.—How he was cast away in the capes of Florida,—the horrid Cruelty and inhuman Barbarity of the Indians in murdering the whole ship's crew,—the manner of his being carry'd by them into captivity. Also, an account of his being confined four years and seven months in a close dungeon,—And the remarkable manner in which he met with his good old master in London; who returned to New England, a passenger, in the same ship.

BOSTON, Printed and sold by GREEN & RUSSELL,
in Queen-Street, 1760.

To the Reader,

AS my capacities and condition of life are very low, it cannot be expected that I should make those remarks on the sufferings I have met with, or the kind Providence of a good God for my preservation, as one in a higher station; but shall leave that to the reader as he goes along, and so I shall only relate matters of fact as they occur to my mind.

ON Monday, 25th day of *December,* 1747, with the leave of my master, I went from Marshfield, with an Intention to go a voyage to sea, and the next day, the 26th, got to Plymouth, where I immediately ship'd myself on board of a Sloop, Capt. John Howland, Master, bound to Jamaica and the Bay. We sailed from Plymouth in a short time, and after a pleasant passage of about 30 days, arrived at Jamaica; we was detain'd at Jamaica only 5 days, from whence we sailed for the Bay, where we arrived safe in 10 days. We loaded our vessel with logwood, and sailed from the Bay the 25th day of May following, and the 15th day of June, we were cast away on Cape Florida, about 5 leagues from the shore; being now destitute of every help, we knew not what to do or what course to take in this our sad condition. The captain was advised, entreated, and beg'd on, by every person on board, to heave over but only 20 ton of the Wood, and we should get clear, which if he had done, might have sav'd his vessel and cargo, and not only so, but his own life, as well as the Lives of the mate and nine hands, as I shall presently relate.

After being upon this reef two days, the captain order'd the boat to be hoisted out, and then ask'd who were willing to tarry on board? The whole crew was for going on shore at this time, but as the boat would not carry 12 persons at once, and to prevent any uneasiness, the captain, a passenger, and one hand tarry'd on board, while the mate, with seven hands besides myself, were order'd to go on shore in the boat, which as soon as we had reached, one half were to be landed, and the other four to return to the sloop, to fetch the captain and the others on shore. The captain order'd us to take with us our arms, ammunition, provisions and necessaries for cooking, as also a sail to make a tent of, to shelter us from the weather; after having left the sloop we stood towards the shore, and being within two leagues of the same, we espy'd a number of canoes, which we at first took to be rocks, but soon found our mistake, for we perceiv'd they moved towards us; we presently saw an English colour hoisted in one of the canoes, at the sight of which we were not a little rejoiced, but on our advancing yet nearer, we found them, to our very great surprise, to be Indians of which there were sixty; being now so near them we could not possibly make our escape; they soon came up with and boarded us, took away all our arms, ammunition, and provision. The whole number of canoes (being about twenty) then made for the sloop, except two which they left to guard us, who order'd us to follow on with them; the eighteen which made for the sloop, went so much faster than we that they got on board above three hours before we came along side, and had kill'd Captain Howland, the passenger and the other hand; we came to the larboard side of the sloop, and they order'd us round to the starboard, and as we were passing round the bow, we saw the whole number of Indians advancing forward and loading their Guns, upon which the mate said, "my Lads we are all dead Men," and before we had got round they discharged their small arms upon us, and kill'd three of our hands, viz. Reuben Young of Cape Cod, mate; Joseph Little and Lemuel Doty of Plymouth, upon which I immediately jump'd overboard, chusing rather to be drowned, than to be kill'd by those barbarous and inhuman savages. In three or four minutes after, I heard another volley which dispatched the other five, viz. John Nowland and Nathaniel Rich, both belonging to Plymouth, and Elkanab Collymore and James Webb, strangers, and Moses Newmock, Mulatto. As soon as they had kill'd the whole of the people, one of the canoes paddled after me, and soon came up with me, hawled me into the canoe, and beat me most terribly with a cutlass; after that they ty'd me down, then this canoe stood for the sloop again and as soon as she came alongside, the Indians on board the sloop betook themselves to their canoes, then set the vessel on fire, making a prodigious shouting and hallowing like so many devils. As soon as the vessel was burnt down to the water's edge, the Indians stood for the shore, together with our boat, on board of which they put 5 hands. After we came to the shore, they led me to their huts, where I expected nothing but immediate death, and as they spoke broken English, were often telling me, while coming from the sloop to the shore, that they intended to roast me alive. But the Providence of God order'd it otherways, for He appeared for my help, in this Mount of Difficulty, and they were

better to me than my fears, and soon unbound me, but set a guard
over me every night. They kept me with them about five weeks, during which time they us'd me pretty well, and gave me boil'd corn,
which was what they often ate themselves. The way I made my
escape from these villains was this; A Spanish schooner arriving
there from St. Augustine, the master of which, whose Name was
Romond, asked the Indians to let me go on board his vessel, which
they granted, and the captain knowing me very well,* weigh'd anchor and carry'd me off to the Havana, and after being there four
Days the Indians came after me, and insisted on having me again, as
I was their prisoner. They made application to the governor, and demanded me again from him; in answer to which the governor told
them, that as they had put the whole crew to death, they should not
have me again, and so paid them ten dollars for me, adding, that he
would not have them kill any person hereafter, but take as many of
them as they could of those that should be cast away, and bring
them to him, for which he would pay them ten dollars a head. At
the Havana I lived with the governor in the castle about a twelvemonth, where I was walking thro' the street, I met with a press-gang
who immediately prest me, and put me into gaol, and with a Number of others I was confin'd till next Morning, when we were all
brought out, and ask'd who would go on board the King's ships, four
of which having been lately built, were bound to Old Spain, and on
my refusing to serve on board, they put me in a close dungeon,
where I was confin'd four years and seven months; during which
time I often made application to the governor, by persons who came
to see the prisoners, but they never acquainted him with it, nor did
he know all this time what became of me, which was the means of
my being confin'd there so long. But kind Providence so order'd it,
that after I had been in this place so long as the time mention'd
above, the captain of a merchantman, belonging to Boston, having
sprung a leak was obliged to put into the Havana to refit, and while
he was at dinner at Mrs. Betty Howard's, she told the captain of my
deplorable condition, and said she would be glad, if he could by
some means or other relieve me; the captain told Mrs. Howard he
would use his best endeavours for my relief and enlargement.

Accordingly, after dinner, came to the prison, and ask'd the keeper
if he might see me; upon his request I was brought out of the dungeon, and after the captain had interrogated me, told me, he would

---

* The way I came to know this gentleman was, by his being taken last war
by an English privateer, and brought into Jamaica while I was there.

intercede with the governor for my relief out of that miserable place, which he did, and the next day the governor sent an order to release me; I lived with the governor about a year after I was delivered from the dungeon, in which time I endeavour'd three times to make my escape, the last of which proved effectual; the first time I got on board of Captain Marsh, an English twenty-gun ship, with a number of others, and lay on board conceal'd that night; and the next day the ship being under sail, I thought myself safe, and so made my appearance upon deck, but as soon as we were discovered the captain ordered the boat out, and sent us all on shore. I entreated the captain to let me, in particular, tarry on board, begging, and crying to him, to commiserate my unhappy condition, and added, that I had been confin'd almost five years in a close dungeon, but the captain would not hearken to any entreaties, for fear of having the governor's displeasure, and so was obliged to go on shore.

After being on shore another twelvemonth, I endeavour'd to make my escape the second time, by trying to get on board of a sloop bound to Jamaica, and as I was going from the city to the sloop, was unhappily taken by the guard, and ordered back to the castle, and there confined. However, in a short time I was set at liberty, and order'd with a number of others to carry the Bishop* from the castle, thro' the country, to confirm the old people, baptize children, &c, for which he receives large sums of money. I was employ'd in this service about seven months; during which time I lived very well, and then returned to the castle again, where I had my liberty to walk about the city, and do work for myself;—The Beaver, an English Man of War, then lay in the harbour, and having been informed by some of the ship's crew that she was to sail in a few days, I had nothing now to do but to seek an opportunity how I should make my escape.

Accordingly one Sunday night the lieutenant of the ship with a number of the barge crew were in a tavern, and Mrs. Howard, who had before been a friend to me, interceded with the lieutenant to carry me on board. The lieutenant said he would with all his heart, and immediately I went on board in the barge. The next day the Spaniards came along side the Beaver and demanded me again, with a number of others who had made their escape from them, and got on board the ship, but just before I did; but the captain, who was a true Englishman, refus'd them, and said he could not answer it, to

---

* He is carried (by Way of Respect) in a large two-arm chair; the chair is lin'd with crimson velvet, and supported by eight persons.

deliver up any Englishmen under English Colours. In a few days we set sail for Jamaica, where we arrived safe, after a short and pleasant passage.

After being at Jamaica a short time we sail'd for London, as convoy to a fleet of merchantmen, who all arrived safe in the Downs. I was turned over to another ship, the Arcenceil, and there remained about a month. From this ship I went on board the Sandwich of 90 guns; on board the Sandwich, I tarry'd 6 Weeks, and then was order'd on board the Hercules, Capt. John Porter, a 74-gun ship, we sail'd on a cruise, and met with a French 84-gun ship, and had a very smart engagement,* in which about 70 of our hands were kill'd and wounded, the captain lost his leg in the engagement, and I was wounded in the head by a small shot. We should have taken this ship, if they had not cut away the most of our rigging; however, in about three Hours after, a 64-gun ship came up with and took her.

I was discharged from the Hercules the 12th day of May 1759 (having been on board of that ship 3 months) on account of my being disabled in the arm and render'd incapable of service, after being honourably paid the wages due to me. I was put into the Greenwich Hospital where I stay'd and soon recovered. I then ship'd myself a cook on board Captain Martyn, an arm'd ship in the King's Service. I was on board this ship almost two months, and after being paid my wages, was discharg'd in the month of October. After my discharge from Captain Martyn, I was taken sick in London of a fever, and was confin'd about 6 Weeks, where I expended all my money, and left in very poor circumstances; and unhappy for me I knew nothing of my good Master's being in London at this my very difficult time. After I got well of my sickness, I ship'd myself on board of a large ship bound to Guinea, and being in a publick house one evening, I overheard a number of persons talking about rigging a vessel bound to New England; I ask'd them to what part of New England this vessel was bound? they told me, to Boston; and having ask'd them who was commander? they told me, Capt. Watt. In a few minutes after this the mate of the ship came in, and I ask'd him if Captain Watt did not want a cook, who told me he did, and that the captain would be in, in a few minutes; and in about half an hour the captain came in, and then I ship'd myself at once, after begging off from the ship bound to Guinea; I work'd on board Captain Watt's ship almost three months before she sail'd, and one day being at work in the

* A particular account of this engagement has been publish'd in the Boston newspapers.

hold, I overheard some persons on board mention the name of Winslow, at the name of which I was very inquisitive, and having ask'd what Winslow they were talking about? they told me it was General Winslow; and that he was one of the passengers. I ask'd them what General Winslow? For I never knew my good Master, by that title before; but after enquiring more particularly I found it must be Master, and in a few days' time the truth was joyfully verify'd by a happy sight of his person, which so overcome me that I could not speak to him for some time—*My* good master was exceeding glad to see me, telling me that I was like one arose from the dead, for he thought I had been dead a great many years, having heard nothing of me for almost thirteen years.

I think I have not deviated from truth in any particular of this my narrative, and tho' I have omitted a great many things, yet what is wrote may suffice to convince the reader, that I have been most grievously afflicted, and yet thro' the Divine Goodness, as miraculously preserved, and delivered out of many dangers; of which I desire to retain a grateful remembrance, as long as I live in the World.

And now, That in the Providence of that God, who delivered his servant David out of the paw of the lion and out of the paw of the bear, I am freed from a long and dreadful captivity, among worse savages than they; And am return'd to my own native land, to show how great things the Lord hath done for me; I would call upon all men, and say, O magnifiy the Lord with me, and let us exalt his Name together! O that men would praise the Lord for His Goodness, and for his Wonderful Works to the children of men!

AN

EVENING THOUGHT

Salvation by Christ,

WITH

PENETENTIAL CRIES:

Composed by Jupiter Hammon, a Negro belonging to Mr. Lloyd, of
Queen's Village, on Long Island, the 25th of December, 1760.

> Salvation comes by Jesus Christ alone,
>   The only Son of God;
> Redemption now to every one,
>   That love his holy Word.
> Dear Jesus we would fly to Thee,
>   And leave off every Sin,
> Thy tender Mercy well agree;
>   Salvation from our King.
> Salvation comes now from the Lord,
>   Our victorious King;
> His holy Name be well ador'd,
>   Salvation surely bring.
> Dear Jesus give thy Spirit now,
>   Thy Grace to every Nation,
> That han't the Lord to whom we bow,
>   The Author of Salvation.
> Dear Jesus unto Thee we cry,
>   Give us thy Preparation;
> Turn not away thy tender Eye;
>   We seek thy true Salvation.
> Salvation comes from God we know,
>   The true and only One;

It's well agreed and certain true,
   He gave his only Son.
Lord hear our penetential Cry:
   Salvation from above;
It is the Lord that doth supply,
   With his Redeeming Love.
Dear Jesus by thy precious Blood,
   The World Redemption have:
Salvation comes now from the Lord,
   He being thy captive Slave.
Dear Jesus let the Nations cry,
   And all the People say,
Salvation comes from Christ on high,
   Haste on Tribunal Day.
We cry as Sinners to the Lord,
   Salvation to obtain;
It is firmly fixt his holy Word,
   Ye shall not cry in vain.
Dear Jesus unto Thee we cry,
   And make our Lamentation:
O let our Prayers ascend on high;
   We felt thy Salvation.
Lord turn our dark benighted Souls;
   Give us a true Motion,
And let the Hearts of all the World,
   Make Christ their Salvation.
Ten Thousand Angels cry to Thee,
   Yea louder than the Ocean.
Thou are the Lord, we plainly see;
   Thou art the true Salvation.
Now is the Day, excepted Time;
   The Day of Salvation;
Increase your Faith, do not repine:
   Awake ye every Nation.
Lord unto whom now shall we go,
   Or seek a safe Abode;
Thou hast the Word Salvation too
   The only Son of God.
Ho! every one that hunger hath,
   Or pineth after me,
Salvation be thy leading Staff,
   To set the Sinner free.
Dear Jesus unto Thee we fly;

Depart, depart from Sin,
Salvation doth at length supply,
    The Glory of our King.
Come ye Blessed of the Lord,
    Salvation gently given;
O turn your Hearts, accept the Word,
    Your Souls are fit for Heaven.
Dear Jesus we now turn to Thee,
    Salvation to obtain;
Our Hearts and Souls do meet again,
    To magnify thy Name.
Come holy Spirit, Heavenly Dove,
    The Object of our Care;
Salvation doth increase our Love;
    Our Hearts hath felt thy fear.
Now Glory be to God on High,
    Salvation high and low;
And thus the Soul on Christ rely,
    To Heaven surely go.
Come Blessed Jesus, Heavenly Dove,
    Accept Repentance here;
Salvation give, with tender Love;
    Let us with Angels share.

An Elegiac

POEM,

On the death of that celebrated Divine,

and eminent Servant of Jesus Christ,

the late Reverend and pious

GEORGE WHITEFIELD,

CHAPLAIN TO

THE RIGHT HONOURABLE THE COUNTESS OF

HUNTINGDON, &C &C.

Who made his exit from this transitory state, to dwell in the celestial Realms of Bliss, on Lord's-Day, 30th of September, 1770, when he was seiz'd with a fit of the asthma, at Newbury-Port, near Boston, in New-England. In which is a Condolatory Address to his truly noble benefactress the worthy and pious Lady Huntingdon, and the Orphan-children in Georgia; who, with many thousands, are left, by the death of this great man, to lament the loss of a Father, Friend, and Benefactor.

By Phillis, a Servant Girl of 17 Years of Age, belonging to Mr. J. Wheatley, of Boston, and has been but 9 years in this country from Africa.

Hail happy Saint on thy immortal throne!
To thee complaints of grievance are unknown;

532

We hear no more the music of thy tongue,
Thy wonted auditories cease to throng.
Thy lessons in unequal'd accents flow'd!
While emulation in each bosom glow'd;
Thou didst, in strains of eloquence refin'd,
Inflame the soul, and captivate the mind.
Unhappy we, the setting Sun deplore!
Which once was splendid, but it shines no more;
He leaves this earth for Heaven's unmeasur'd height:
And worlds unknown, receive him from our sight;
There WHITEFIELD wings, with rapid course his way,
And sails to Zion, through vast seas of day.

When his AMERICANS were burden'd sore,
When streets were crimson'd with their guiltless gore!
Unrival'd friendship in his breast now strove:
The fruit thereof was charity and love
Towards *America*—couldst thou do more
Than leave thy native home, the *British* shore,
To cross the great Atlantic's wat'ry road,
To see *America*'s distress'd abode?
Thy prayers, great Saint, and thy incessant cries,
Have pierc'd the bosom of thy native skies!
Thou moon hast seen, and ye bright stars of light
Have witness been of his requests by night!
He pray'd that grace in every heart might dwell:
He long'd to see *America* excell;
He charg'd its youth to let the grace divine
Arise, and in their future actions shine;
He offer'd THAT he did himself receive,
A greater gift not GOD himself can give:
He urg'd the need of HIM to every one;
It was no less than GOD's co-equal SON!
Take HIM ye wretched for your only good;
Take HIM ye starving souls to be your food.
Ye thirsty, come to this life-giving stream:
Ye Preachers, take him for your joyful theme;
Take HIM, "my dear AMERICANS," he said,
Be your complaints in his kind bosom laid;
Take HIM ye *Africans*, he longs for you;
Impartial SAVIOUR, is his title due;
If you will chuse to walk in grace's road,
You shall be sons, and kings, and priests to GOD.

Great COUNTESS! we *Americans* revere
Thy name, and thus condole thy grief sincere:
We mourn with thee, that TOMB obscurely plac'd,
In which thy Chaplain undisturb'd doth rest.
New-England sure, doth feel the ORPHAN's smart;
Reveals the true sensations of his heart:
Since this fair Sun, withdraws his golden rays,
No more to brighten these distressful days!
His lonely *Tabernacle*, sees no more
A WHITEFIELD landing on the *British* shore:
Then let us view him in yon azure skies:
Let every mind with this lov'd object rise.
No more can he exert his lab'ring breath,
Seiz'd by the cruel messenger of death.
What can his dear AMERICA return?
But drop a tear upon his happy urn,
Thou tomb, shalt safe retain thy sacred trust,
Till life divine re-animate his dust.

HARTFORD, AUGUST 4, 1778

An ADDRESS to Miss Phillis Wheatly, Ethiopian Poetess, in Boston, who came from Africa at eight years of age, and soon became acquainted with the gospel of Jesus Christ.

Miss Wheatly; pray give leave to express as follows:

1.
O Come you pious youth to adore
   The wisdom of thy God,
In bringing thee from distant shore,
   To learn his holy word.

Eccles. xii.

2.
Thou mightst been left behind,
   Amidst a dark abode;
God's tender mercy still combin'd,
   Thou hast the holy word.

Psal. cxxxv.
2, 3.

3.
Fair wisdom's ways are paths of peace,
   And they that walk therein,
Shall reap the joys that never cease,
   And Christ shall be their king.

Psal. i. 1, 2,
Prov. iii. 7.

4.
God's tender mercy brought thee here,
   Tost o'er the raging main;
In Christian faith thou hast a share,
   Worth all the gold of Spain.

Psal. ciii. 1,
3, 4.

5.
While thousands tossed by the sea,
   And others settled down,
God's tender mercy set thee free
   From dangers still unknown.

Death.

6.
That thou a pattern still might be,
   To youth of Boston town,
The blessed Jesus set thee free,
   From every sinful wound.

2 Cor. v. 10.

535

7.

The blessed Jesus, who came down,
   Unvail'd his sacred face,   Rom. v. 21.
To cleanse the soul of every wound,
   And give repenting grace.

8.

That we poor sinners may obtain
   The pardon of our sin;   Psal. xxxiv. 6,
Dear blessed Jesus now constrain,   7, 8.
   And bring us flocking in.

9.

Come you, Phillis, now aspire,
   And seek the living God,   Mat. vii. 7, 8.
So step by step thou mayst go higher,
   Till perfect in the word.

10.

While thousands mov'd to distant shore,
   And others left behind,   Psal. lxxxix. 1.
The blessed Jesus still adore,
   Implant this in thy mind.

11.

Thou hast left the heathen shore,
   Thro' mercy of the Lord,   Psal. xxxiv. 1,
Among the heathen live no more,   2, 3.
   Come magnify thy God.

12.

I pray the living God may be,
   The shepherd of thy soul;   Psal. lxxi.
His tender mercies still are free,   2, 3.
   His mysteries to unfold.

13.

Thou, Phillis, when thou hunger hast,
   Or pantest for thy God;   Psal. xlii.
Jesus Christ is thy relief,   3.
   Thou hast the holy word.

14.

The bounteous mercies of the Lord,
   Are hid beyond the sky,   Psal. xvi.
And holy souls that love his word,   11.
   Shall taste them when they die.

15.

These bounteous mercies are from God,
   The merits of his Son;   Psal. xxxiv.

The humble soul that loves his word,
    He chooses for his own.
                16.
Come, dear Phillis, be advis'd,
    To drink Samaria's flood: John iv. 13.
There nothing is that shall suffice,
    But Christ's redeeming blood.
                17.
While thousands muse with earthly toys,
    And range about the street,   Mat. vi.
Dear Phillis, seek for heaven's joys,
    Where we do hope to meet.
                18.
When God shall send his summons down,
    And number saints together,   Psal. cxvi.
Blest angels chant, (triumphant found)
    Come live with me for ever.
                19.
The humble soul shall fly to God,
    And leave the things of time,   Mat. v. 3.
Start forth as 'twere at the first word,
    To taste things more divine.
                20.
Behold! the soul shall waft away,
    Whene'er we come to die,   Cor. xv.
And leave its cottage made of clay,   52, 53.
    In twinkling of an eye.
                21.
Now glory be to the Most High,
    United praises given,   Psal. cl. 6.
By all on earth, incessantly,
    And all the host of heav'n.

Composed by Jupiter Hammon, a Negro Man belonging to Mr.
Joseph Lloyd, of Queen's Village on Long Island, now in Hartford.
    The above lines are published by the Author, and a number of his
friends, who desire to join with him in their regards to Miss Wheatly.

A

NARRATIVE

OF THE

LIFE AND ADVENTURES

OF

VENTURE,

A NATIVE OF AFRICA:

But resident above sixty years in the United States of America.

RELATED BY HIMSELF.

NEW LONDON:
PRINTED BY C. HOLT, AT THE BEE-OFFICE,
1798.

PREFACE

THE following account of the life of Venture is a relation of simple facts, in which nothing is added in substance to what he related himself. Many other interesting and curious passages of his life might have been inserted; but on account of the bulk to which they must necessarily have swelled this narrative, they were omitted. If any should suspect the truth of what is here related, they are referred to people now living who are acquainted with most of the facts mentioned in the narrative.

The reader is here presented with an account, not of a renowned politician or warrior, but of an untutored African slave, brought into this Christian country at eight years of age, wholly destitute of all education but what he received in common with other domesticated animals, enjoying no advantages that could lead him to suppose himself superior to the beasts, his fellow servants. And if he shall derive no other advantage from perusing this narrative, he may experience those sensations of shame and indignation that will prove him to be not wholly destitute of every noble and generous feeling.

The subject of the following pages, had he received only a common education, might have been a man of high respectability and usefulness; and had his education been suited to his genius, he might have been an ornament and an honor to human nature. It may, perhaps, not be unpleasing to see the efforts of a great mind wholly uncultivated, enfeebled and depressed by slavery, and struggling under every disadvantage. The reader may here see a Franklin and a Washington in a state of nature, or rather in a state of slavery. Destitute as he is of all education, and broken by hardships and infirmities of age, he still exhibits striking traces of native ingenuity and good sense.

This narrative exhibits a pattern of honesty, prudence, and industry to people of his own colour; and perhaps some white people would not find themselves degraded by imitating such an example.

The following account is published in compliance with the earnest desire of the subject of it, and likewise a number of respectable persons who are acquainted with him.

CHAPTER I

Containing an account of his life, from his birth to the time of his leaving his native country.

I WAS born at Dukandarra, in Guinea, about the year 1729. My father's name was Saungm Furro, Prince of the Tribe of Dukandarra. My father had three wives. Polygamy was not uncommon in that country, especially among the rich, as every man was allowed to keep as many wives as he could maintain. By his first wife he had three children. The eldest of them was myself, named by my father, Broteer. The other two were named Cundazo and Soozaduka. My father had two children by his second wife, and one by his third. I descended from a very large, tall, and stout race of beings, much larger than the generality of people in other parts of the globe, being commonly considerable above six feet in height, and every way well proportioned.

The first thing worthy of notice which I remember, was a contention between my father and mother, on account of my father's marrying his third wife without the consent of his first and eldest, which was contrary to the custom generally observed among my countrymen. In consequence of this rupture, my mother left her husband and country, and travelled away with her three children to the eastward. I was then five years old. She took not the least sustenance along with her, to support either herself or children. I was able to travel along by her side; the other two of her offspring she carried; one on her back, and the other being a sucking child, in her arms. When we became hungry, my mother used to set us down on the ground, and gather some of the fruits which grew spontaneously in that climate. These served us for food on the way. At night we all lay down together in the most secure place we could find, and reposed ourselves until morning. Though there were many noxious animals there, yet so kind was our Almighty protector, that none of them were ever permitted to hurt or molest us. Thus we went on our journey until the second day after our departure from Dukandarra, when we came to the entrance of a great desert. During our travel in that we were often affrighted with the doleful howlings and yellings of wolves, lions, and other animals. After five days travel we came to the end of this desert, and immediately entered into a beautiful and extensive interval country. Here my mother was pleased to stop and seek a refuge for me. She left me at the house of a very rich farmer. I was then, as I should judge, not less than one hundred and forty miles from my native place, separated from all my relations and acquaintance. At this place my mother took her farewell of me, and set out for her own country. My new guardian, as I shall call the man with whom I was left, put me into the business of tending sheep, immediately after I was left with him. The flock, which I kept with the assistance of a boy, consisted of about forty. We drove them every morning between two and three miles to pasture, into the wide and delightful plains. When night drew on, we drove them home and secured them in the cote. In this round I continued during my stay there. One incident which befel me when I was driving my flock from pasture, was so dreadful to me in that age, and is to this time so fresh in my memory, that I cannot help noticing it in this place. Two large dogs sallied out of a certain house and set upon me. One of them took me by the arm, and the other by the thigh, and, before their master could come and relieve me, they lacerated my flesh to such a degree that the scars are very visible to the present day. My master was immediately sent for. He came and carried me home, as I was unable to go myself on account of my wounds. Nothing remarkable happened afterwards until my father sent for me to return home.

Before I dismiss this country, I must just inform my reader what I remember concerning this place. A large river runs through this country in a westerly course. The land for a great way on each side is flat and level, hedged in by a considerable rise of the country at a great distance from it. It scarce ever rains there, yet the land is fertile; great dews fall in the night which refresh the soil. About the latter end of June or first of July, the river begins to rise, and gradually increases until it has inundated the country for a great distance, to the height of seven or eight feet. This brings on a slime which enriches the land surprisingly. When the river has subsided, the natives begin to sow and plant, and the vegetation is exceeding rapid. Near this rich river my guardian's land lay. He possessed, I cannot exactly tell how much, yet this I am certain of respecting it, that he owned an immense tract. He possessed likewise a great many cattle and goats. During my stay with him I was kindly used, and with as much tenderness—for what I saw—as his only son, although I was an entire stranger to him, remote from friends and relations. The principal occupations of the inhabitants there, were the cultivation of the soil and the care of their flocks. They were a people pretty similar in every respect to that of mine, except in their persons, which were not so tall and stout. They appeared to be very kind and friendly. I will now return to my departure from that place.

My father sent a man and horse after me. After settling with my guardian for keeping me, he took me away and went for home. It was then about one year since my mother brought me here. Nothing remarkable occurred to us on our journey until we arrived safe home.

I found then that the difference between my parents had been made up previous to their sending for me. On my return, I was received both by my father and mother with great joy and affection, and was once more restored to my paternal dwelling in peace and happiness. I was then about six years old.

Not more than six weeks had passed after my return, before a message was brought by an inhabitant of the place where I lived the preceding year to my father, that that place had been invaded by a numerous army from a nation not far distant, furnished with musical instruments, and all kinds of arms then in use; that they were instigated by some white nation who equipped and sent them to subdue and possess the country; that his nation had made no preparation for war, having been for a long time in profound peace that they could not defend themselves against such a formidable train of invaders, and must therefore necessarily evacuate their lands to the fierce enemy, and fly to the protection of some chief; and that if he would permit them they should come under his rule and protection when they had to retreat from their own possessions. He was a kind and merciful prince, and therefore consented to these proposals.

He had scarcely returned to his nation with the message, before the whole of his people were obliged to retreat from their country and come to my father's dominions.

He gave them every privilege and all the protection his government could afford. But they had not been there longer than four days before news came to them that the invaders had laid waste their country, and were coming speedily to destroy them in my father's territories. This affrighted them, and therefore they immediately pushed off to the southward, into the unknown countries there, and were never more heard of.

Two days after their retreat, the report turned out to be but too true. A detachment from the enemy came to my father and informed him that the whole army was encamped not far out of his dominions, and would invade the territory and deprive his people of their liberties and rights, if he did not comply with the following terms. These were to pay them a large sum of money, three hundred fat cattle, and a great number of goats, sheep, asses, &c.

My father told the messenger he would comply rather than that his subjects should be deprived of their rights and privileges, which he was not then in circumstances to defend from so sudden an invasion. Upon turning out those articles, the enemy pledged their faith and honor that they would not attack him. On these he relied and therefore thought it unnecessary to be on his guard against the enemy. But their pledges of faith and honor proved no better than those of other unprincipled hostile nations; for a few days after, a certain relation of the king came and informed him that the enemy who sent terms of accommodation to him and received tribute to their satisfaction, yet meditated an attack upon his subjects by surprise, and that probably they would commence their attack in less than one day, and concluded with advising him, as he was not prepared for war, to order a speedy retreat of his family and subjects. He complied with this advice.

The same night which was fixed upon to retreat, my father and his family set off about break of day. The king and his two younger wives went in one company, and my mother and her children in another. We left our dwellings in succession, and my father's company went on first. We directed our course for a large shrub plain some distance off, where we intended to conceal ourselves from the approaching enemy until we could refresh and rest ourselves a little. But we presently found that our retreat was not secure. For having struck up a little fire for the purpose of cooking victuals, the enemy, who happened to be encamped a little distance off, had sent out a scouting party who discovered us by the smoke of the fire, just as we were extinguishing it and about to eat. As soon as we had finished eating, my father discovered the party, and immediately began to discharge arrows at them. This was what I first saw, and it alarmed both me and the women, who, being unable to make any resistance, immediately betook ourselves to the tall thick reeds not far off, and left the old king to fight alone. For some time I beheld him from the reeds defending himself with great courage and firmness, till at last he was obliged to surrender himself into their hands.

They then came to us in the reeds, and the very first salute I had from them was a violent blow on the head with the fore part of a gun, and at the same time a grasp round the neck. I then had a rope put about my neck, as had all the women in the thicket with me, and were immediately led to my father, who was likewise pinioned and haltered for leading. In this condition we were all led to the camp. The women and myself, being pretty submissive, had tolerable treatment from the enemy, while my father was closely interrogated respecting his money which they knew he must have. But as he gave them no account of it, he was instantly cut and pounded on his body with great inhumanity, that he might be induced by the torture he suffered to make the discovery. All this availed not in the least to make him give up his money, but he despised all the tortures which they inflicted, until the continued exercise and increase of torment obliged him to sink and expire. He thus died without informing his enemies of the place where his money lay. I saw him while he was thus tortured to death. The shocking scene is to this day fresh in my mind, and I have often been overcome while thinking on it. He was a man of remarkable stature. I should judge as much as six feet and six or seven inches high, two feet across his shoulders, and every way well proportioned. He was a man of remarkable strength and resolution, affable, kind and gentle, ruling with equity and moderation.

The army of the enemy was large, I should suppose consisting of about six thousand men. Their leader was called Baukurre. After destroying the old prince, they decamped and immediately marched towards the sea lying to the west, taking with them myself and the women prisoners.

In the march a scouting party was detached from the main army.

To the leader of this party I was made waiter, having to carry his gun, &c. As we were a scouting we came across a herd of fat cattle, consisting of about thirty in number. These we set upon, and immediately wrested from their keepers, and afterwards converted them into food for the army. The enemy had remarkable success in destroying the country wherever they went. For as far as they had penetrated they laid the habitations waste and captured the people. The distance they had now brought me was about four hundred miles. All the march I had very hard tasks imposed on me, which I must perform on pain of punishment. I was obliged to carry on my head a large flat stone used for grinding our corn, weighing, as I should suppose, as much as 25 pounds, besides victuals, mat and cooking utensils. Though I was pretty large and stout of my age, yet these burthens were very grievous to me, being only about six years and an half old.

We were then come to a place called Malagasco. When we entered the place we could not see the least appearance of either houses or inhabitants, but upon stricter search found that instead of houses above ground they had dens in the sides of hillocks, contiguous to ponds and streams of water. In these we perceived they had all hid themselves, as I suppose they usually did upon such occasions. In order to compel them to surrender, the enemy contrived to smoke them out with faggots. These they put to the entrance of the caves and set them on fire. While they were engaged in this business, to their great surprise some of them were desperately wounded with arrows which fell from above on them. This mystery they soon found out. They perceived that the enemy discharged these arrows through holes on the top of the dens directly into the air. Their weight brought them back, point downwards on their enemies' heads, whilst they were smoking the inhabitants out. The points of their arrows were poisoned, but their enemy had an antidote for it, which they instantly applied to the wounded part. The smoke at last obliged the people to give themselves up. They came out of their caves, first spatting the palms of their hands together, and immediately after extended their arms, crossed at their wrists, ready to be bound and pinioned. I should judge that the dens above mentioned were extended about eight feet horizontally into the earth, six feet in height and as many wide. They were arched overhead and lined with earth, which was of the clay kind, and made the surface of their walls firm and smooth.

The invaders then pinioned the prisoners of all ages and sexes indiscriminately, took their flocks and all their effects, and moved on their way towards the sea. On the march the prisoners were treated with clemency, on account of their being submissive and humble. Having come to the next tribe, the enemy laid seige and immediately took men, women, children, flocks, and all their valuable effects. They then went on to the next district which was contiguous to the sea, called in Africa, Anamaboo. The enemies provisions were then almost spent, as well as their strength. The inhabitants knowing what conduct they had pursued, and what were their present intentions, improved the favorable opportunity, attacked them, and took enemy, prisoners, flocks and all their effects. I was then taken a second time. All of us were then put into the castle, and kept for market. On a certain time I and other prisoners were put on board a canoe, under our master, and rowed away to a vessel belonging to Rhode Island, commanded by Capt. Collingwood, and the mate Thomas Mumford. While we were going to the vessel, our master told us all to appear to the best possible advantage for sale. I was bought on board by one Robertson Mumford, steward of said vessel, for four gallons of rum and a piece of calico, and called Venture, on account of his having purchased me with his own private venture. Thus I came by my name. All the slaves that were bought for that vessel's cargo, were two hundred and sixty.

CHAPTER II

Containing an account of his life, from the time of his leaving Africa, to that of his becoming free.

AFTER all the business was ended on the coast of Africa, the ship sailed from thence to Barbadoes. After an ordinary passage, except great mortality by the smallpox which broke out on board, we arrived at the island of Barbadoes: but when we reached it, there were found, out of the two hundred and sixty that sailed from Africa, not more than two hundred alive. These were all sold, except myself and three more, to the planters there.

The vessel then sailed for Rhode Island, and arrived there after a comfortable passage. Here my master sent me to live with one of his sisters until he could carry me to Fisher's Island, the place of his residence. I had then completed my eighth year. After staying with his sister some time, I was taken to my master's place to live.

When we arrived at Narraganset, my master went ashore in order to return a part of the way by land, and gave me the charge of the keys of his trunks on board the vessel, and charged me not to deliver them up to anybody, not even to his father, without his orders. To his directions I promised faithfully to conform. When I arrived

with my master's articles at his house, my master's father asked me
for his son's keys, as he wanted to see what his trunks contained.
I told him that my master entrusted me with the care of them until
he should return, and that I had given him my word to be faithful
to the trust, and could not therefore give him or any other person
the keys without my master's directions. He insisted that I should
deliver to him the keys, threatening to punish me if I did not. But
I let him know that he should not have them, let him say what he
would. He then laid aside trying to get them. But notwithstanding
he appeared to give up trying to obtain them from me, yet I mis-
trusted that he would take some time when I was off my guard,
either in the daytime or at night to get them, therefore I slung them
round my neck, and in the daytime concealed them in my bosom,
and at night I always lay with them under me, that no person might
take them from me without being apprised of it. Thus I kept the
keys from everybody until my master came home. When he returned
he asked where Venture was. As I was then within hearing, I came,
and said, here sir, at your service. He asked me for his keys, and
I immediately took them off my neck and reached them out to him.
He took them, stroked my hair, and commended me, saying in
presence of his father that his young Venture was so faithful that he
never would have been able to have taken the keys from him but by
violence; that he should not fear to trust him with his whole fortune, for that he had been in his native place so habituated to keeping his word that he would sacrifice even his life to maintain it.

The first of the time of living at my master's own place, I was
pretty much employed in the house at carding wool and other household business. In this situation I continued for some years, after
which my master put me to work out of doors. After many proofs
of my faithfulness and honesty, my master began to put great confidence in me. My behavior to him had as yet been submissive and
obedient. I then began to have hard tasks imposed on me. Some of
these were to pound four bushels of ears of corn every night in a
barrel for the poultry, or be rigorously punished. At other seasons of
the year I had to card wool until a very late hour. These tasks I had
to perform when I was about nine years old. Some time after I had another difficulty and oppression which was greater than any I had
ever experienced since I came into this country. This was to serve
two masters. James Mumford, my master's son, when his father had
gone from home in the morning, and given me a stint to perform
that day, would order me to do *this* and *that* business different from
what my master directed me. One day in particular, the authority

which my master's son had set up, had like to have produced melancholy effects. For my master having set me off my business to perform that day and then left me to perform it, his son came up to me in the course of the day, big with authority, and commanded me very arrogantly to quit my present business and go directly about what he should order me. I replied to him that my master had given me so much to perform that day, and that I must therefore faithfully complete it in that time. He then broke out into a great rage, snatched a pitchfork and went to lay me over the head therewith; but I as soon got another and defended myself with it, or otherwise he might have murdered me in his outrage. He immediately called some people who were within hearing at work for him, and ordered them to take his hair rope and come and bind me with it. They all tried to bind me but in vain, tho' there were three assistants in number. My upstart master then desisted, put his pocket handkerchief before his eyes and went home with a design to tell his mother of the struggle with young Venture. He told her that their young Venture had become so stubborn that he could not control him, and asked her what he should do with him. In the meantime I recovered my temper, voluntarily caused myself to be bound by the same men who tried in vain before, and carried before my young master, that he might do what he pleased with me. He took me to a gallows made for the purpose of hanging cattle on, and suspended me on it. Afterwards he ordered one of his hands to go to the peach orchard and cut him three dozen of whips to punish me with. These were brought to him, and that was all that was done with them, as I was released and went to work after hanging on the gallows about an hour.

After I had lived with my master thirteen years, being then about twenty-two years old, I married Meg, a slave of his who was about my age. My master owned a certain Irishman, named Heddy, who about that time formed a plan of secretly leaving his master. After he had long had this plan in meditation he suggested it to me. At first I cast a deaf ear to it, and rebuked Heddy for harboring in his mind such a rash undertaking. But after he had persuaded and much enchanted me with the prospect of gaining my freedom by such a method, I at length agreed to accompany him. Heddy next inveigled two of his fellow servants to accompany us. The place to which we designed to go was the Mississippi. Our next business was to lay in a sufficient store of provisions for our voyage. We privately collected out of our master's store, six great old cheeses, two firkins of butter, and one whole batch of new bread. When we had gathered all our own clothes and some more, we took them all about midnight, and went to the water side. We stole our master's boat, embarked, and then directed our course for the Mississippi river.

We mutually confederated not to betray or desert one another on pain of death. We first steered our course for Montauk Point, the east end of Long Island. After our arrival there we landed, and Heddy and I made an incursion into the island after fresh water, while our two comrades were left at a little distance from the boat, employed at cooking. When Heddy and I had sought some time for water, he returned to our companions, and I continued on looking for my object. When Heddy had performed his business with our companions who were engaged in cooking, he went directly to the boat, stole all the clothes in it, and then travelled away for East-hampton, as I was informed. I returned to my fellows not long after. They informed me that our clothes were stolen, but could not determine who was the thief, yet they suspected Heddy as he was missing. After reproving my two comrades for not taking care of our things which were in the boat, I advertised Heddy and sent two men in search of him. They pursued and overtook him at South-ampton and returned him to the boat. I then thought it might afford some chance for my freedom, or at least a palliation for my running away, to return Heddy immediately to his master, and inform him that I was induced to go away by Heddy's address. Accordingly I set off with him and the rest of my companions for our master's, and arrived there without any difficulty. I informed my master that Heddy was the ringleader of our revolt, and that he had used us ill. He immediately put Heddy into custody, and myself and companions were well received and went to work as usual.

Not a long time passed after that, before Heddy was sent by my master to New London gaol. At the close of that year I was sold to a Thomas Stanton, and had to be separated from my wife and one daughter, who was about one month old. He resided at Stonington-point. To this place I brought with me from my late master's, two johannes, three old Spanish dollars, and two thousand of coppers, besides five pounds of my wife's money. This money I got by cleaning gentlemen's shoes and drawing boots, by catching muskrats and minks, raising potatoes and carrots, &c., and by fishing in the night, and at odd spells.

All this money, amounting to near twenty-one pounds York currency, my master's brother, Robert Stanton, hired of me, for which he gave me his note. About one year and a half after that time, my master purchased my wife and her child, for seven hundred pounds old tenor. One time my master sent me two miles after a barrel of molasses, and ordered me to carry it on my shoulders. I made out to carry it all the way to my master's house. When I lived with Captain George Mumford, only to try my strength, I took up on my knees a tierce of salt containing seven bushels, and carried it two or three rods. Of this fact there are several eye witnesses now living.

Towards the close of the time that I resided with this master I had a falling out with my mistress. This happened one time when my master was gone to Long Island a-gunning. At first the quarrel began between my wife and her mistress. I was then at work in the barn, and hearing a racket in the house induced me to run there and see what had broken out. When I entered the house, I found my mistress in a violent passion with my wife, for what she informed me was a mere trifle; such a small affair that I forbear to put my mistress to the shame of having it known. I earnestly requested my wife to beg pardon of her mistress for the sake of peace, even if she had given no just occasion for offence. But whilst I was thus saying my mistress turned the blows which she was repeating on my wife to me. She took down her horsewhip, and while she was glutting her fury with it, I reached out my great black hand, raised it up and received the blows of the whip on it which were designed for my head. Then I immediately committed the whip to the devouring fire.

When my master returned from the island, his wife told him of the affair, but for the present he seemed to take no notice of it, and mentioned not a word about it to me. Some days after his return, in the morning as I was putting on a log in the fireplace, not suspecting harm from any one, I received a most violent stroke on the crown of my head with a club two feet long and as large round as a chairpost. This blow very badly wounded my head, and the scar of it remains to this day. The first blow made me have my wits about me you may suppose, for as soon as he went to renew it, I snatched the club out of his hands and dragged him out of the door. He then sent for his brother to come and assist him, but I presently left my master, took the club he wounded me with, carried it to a neighboring Justice of the Peace, and complained of my master. He finally advised me to return to my master, and live contented with him till he abused me again, and then complain. I consented to do accordingly. But before I set out for my master's, up he come, and his brother Robert, after me. The Justice improved this convenient opportunity to caution my master. He asked him for what he treated his slave thus hastily and unjustly, and told him what would be the consequence if he continued the same treatment towards me. After the Justice had ended his discourse with my master, he and his brother set out with me for home, one before ·and the other behind me. When they had come to a bye place, they both dismounted their respective horses and fell to beating me with great violence. I became enraged at this and immediately turned them both under me, laid one of them across the other, and stamped both with my feet what I would.

This occasioned my master's brother to advise him to put me off. A short time after this I was taken by a constable and two men. They carried me to a blacksmith's shop and had me handcuffed. When I returned home my mistress enquired much of her waiters whether Venture was handcuffed. When she was informed that I was, she appeared to be very contented and was much transported with the news. In the midst of this content and joy, I presented myself before my mistress, showed her my handcuffs, and gave her thanks for my gold rings. For this my master commanded a negro of his to fetch him a large ox chain. This my master locked on my legs with two padlocks. I continued to wear the chain peaceably for two or three days, when my master asked me with contemptuous hard names whether I had not better be freed from my chains and go to work. I answered him, No. Well then, said he, I will send you to the West Indies or banish you, for I am resolved not to keep you. I answered him I crossed the waters to come here, and I am willing to cross them to return.

For a day or two after this not any one said much to me, until one Hempsted Miner, of Stonington, asked me if I would live with him. I answered him that I would. He then requested me to make myself discontented and to appear as unreconciled to my master as I could before that he bargained with him for me; and that in return he would give me a good chance to gain my freedom when I came to live with him. I did as he requested me. Not long after Hempsted Miner purchased me of my master for fifty-six pounds lawful. He took the chain and padlocks from off me immediately after.

It may here be remembered, that I related a few pages back, that I hired out a sum of money to Mr. Robert Stanton, and took his note for it. In the fray between my master Stanton and myself, he broke open my chest containing his brother's note to me, and destroyed it. Immediately after my present master bought me, he determined to sell me at Hartford. As soon as I became apprised of it, I bethought myself that I would secure a certain sum of money which lay by me; safer than to hire it out to a Stanton. Accordingly, I buried it in the earth a little distance from Thomas Stanton's, in the road over which he passed daily. A short time after, my master carried me to Hartford, and first proposed to sell me to one William Hooker of that place. Hooker asked whether I would go to the German Flats with him. I answered, No. He said I should, if not by fair means I should by foul. If you will go by no other measures, I will tie you down in my sleigh. I replied to him that if he carried me in that manner no person would purchase me, for it would be thought that he had a murderer for sale. After this he tried no more, and said he would not have me as a gift.

My master next offered me to Daniel Edwards, Esq., of Hartford, for sale. But not purchasing me, my master pawned me to him for ten pounds, and returned to Stonington. After some trial of my honesty, Mr. Edwards placed considerable trust and confidence in me. He put me to serve as his cupbearer and waiter. When there was company at his house, he would send me into his cellar and other parts of his house to fetch wine and other articles occasionally for them. When I had been with him some time, he asked me why my master wished to part with such an honest negro, and why he did not keep me himself. I replied that I could not give him the reason, unless it was to convert me into cash, and speculate with me as with other commodities. I hope that he can never justly say it was on account of my ill conduct that he did not keep me himself. Mr. Edwards told me that he should be very willing to keep me himself, and that he would never let me go from him to live, if it was' not unreasonable and inconvenient for me to be parted from my wife and children; therefore he would furnish me with a horse to return to Stonington, if I had a mind for it. As Miner did not appear to redeem me I went, and called at my old master Stanton's first to see my wife, who was then owned by him. As my old master appeared much ruffled at my being there, I left my wife before I had spent any considerable time with her, and went to Colonel O. Smith's. Miner had not as yet wholly settled with Stanton for me, and had before my return from Hartford given Col. Smith a bill of sale of me. These men once met to determine which of them should hold me, and upon my expressing a desire to be owned by Col. Smith, and upon my master's settling the remainder of the money which was due to Stanton for me, it was agreed that I should live with Col. Smith. This was the third time of my being sold, and I was then thirty-one years old. As I never had an opportunity of redeeming myself whilst I was owned by Miner, though he promised to give me a chance, I was then very ambitious of obtaining it. I asked my master one time if he would consent to have me purchase my freedom. He replied that he would. I was then very happy, knowing that I was at that time able to pay part of the purchase money, by means of the money which I some time since buried. This I took out of the earth and tendered to my master, having previously engaged a free negro man to take his security for it, as I was the property of my master, and therefore could not safely take his obligation myself. What was wanting in redeeming myself, my master agreed to wait on me for, until I could procure it for him. I still continued to work for Col. Smith. There was continually some interest accruing on my master's note to my friend the free negro man above named, which I received, and with some besides which I got by fishing, I laid out in land adjoining my old master Stanton's. By cultivating this land with the greatest diligence and economy, at times when my master did not require my labor, in two years I laid up ten pounds. This my friend tendered my master for myself, and received his note for it.

Being encouraged by the success which I had met in redeeming myself, I again solicited my master for a further chance of completing it. The chance for which I solicited him was that of going out to work the ensuing winter. He agreed to this on condition that I would give him one quarter of my earnings. On these terms I worked the following winter, and earned four pounds sixteen shillings, one quarter of which went to my master for the privilege, and the rest was paid him on my own account. This added to the other payments made up forty-four pounds, eight shillings, which I had paid on my own account. I was then about thirty-five years old.

The next summer I again desired he would give me a chance of going out to work. But he refused and answered that he must have my labor this summer, as he did not have it the past winter. I replied that I considered it as hard that I could not have a chance to work out when the season became advantageous, and that I must only be permitted to hire myself out in the poorest season of the year. He asked me after this what I would give him for the privilege per month. I replied that I would leave it wholly with his own generosity to determine what I should return him a month. Well then, said he, if so two pounds a month. I answered him that if that was the least he would take I would be contented.

Accordingly I hired myself out at Fisher's Island and earned twenty pounds; thirteen pounds six shillings of which my master drew for the privilege, and the remainder I paid him for my freedom. This made fifty-one pounds two shillings which I paid him. In October following I went and wrought six months at Long Island. In that six months' time I cut and corded four hundred cords of wood, besides threshing out seventy-five bushels of grain, and received of my wages down only twenty pounds, which left remaining a larger sum. Whilst I was out that time, I took up on my wages only one pair of shoes. At night I lay on the hearth, with one coverlet over and another under me. I returned to my master and gave him what I received of my six months' labor. This left only thirteen pounds eighteen shillings to make up the full sum for my redemption. My master liberated me, saying that I might pay what was behind if I could ever make it convenient, otherwise it would be well. The amount of the money which I had paid my master towards redeeming my time, was seventy-one pounds two shillings. The reason of my master for asking such an unreasonable price, was he said, to secure himself in case I should ever come to want. Being thirty-six years old, I left Col. Smith once for all. I had already been sold three different times, made considerable money with seemingly nothing to derive it from, been cheated out of a large sum of money, lost much by misfortunes, and paid an enormous sum for my freedom.

CHAPTER III

Containing an account of his life, from the time of his purchasing his freedom to the present day.

MY wife and children were yet in bondage to Mr. Thomas Stanton. About this time I lost a chest containing, besides clothing, about thirty-eight pounds in paper money. It was burnt by accident. A short time after I sold all my possessions at Stonington, consisting of a pretty piece of land and one dwelling house thereon, and went to reside at Long Island. For the first four years of my residence there, I spent my time in working for various people on that and at the neighboring islands. In the space of six months I cut and corded upwards of four hundred cords of wood. Many other singular and wonderful labors I performed in cutting wood there, which would not be inferior to those just recited, but for brevity's sake I must omit them. In the aforementioned four years what wood I cut at Long Island amounted to several thousand cords, and the money which I earned thereby amounted to two hundred and seven pounds ten shillings. This money I laid up carefully by me. Perhaps some may enquire what maintained me all the time I was laying up money. I would inform them that I bought nothing which I did not absolutely want. All fine clothes I despised in comparison with my interest, and never kept but just what clothes were comfortable for common days, and perhaps I would have a garment or two which I did not have on at all times, but as for superfluous finery I never thought it to be compared with a decent homespun dress, a good supply of money and prudence. Expensive gatherings of my mates I commonly shunned, and all kinds of luxuries I was perfectly a stranger to; and during the time I was employed in cutting the aforementioned quantity of wood, I never was at the expense of sixpence worth of spirits. Being after this labour forty years of age, I worked at various places, and in particular on Ram Island, where I purchased Solomon and Cuff, two sons of mine, for two hundred dollars each.

It will here be remembered how much money I earned by cutting wood in four years. Besides this I had considerable money, amounting in all to near three hundred pounds. When I had purchased my two sons, I had then left more than one hundred pounds. After this I purchased a negro man, for no other reason than to oblige him, and gave for him sixty pounds. But in a short time after, he run away from me, and I thereby lost all that I gave for him, except twenty pounds which he paid me previous to his absconding. The rest of my money I laid out in land, in addition to a farm which I owned before, and a dwelling house thereon. Forty-four years had then completed their revolution since my entrance into this existence of servitude and misfortune. Solomon my eldest son, being then in his seventeenth year, and all my hope and dependence for help, I hired him out to one Charles Church, of Rhode Island, for one year, on consideration of his giving him twelve pounds and an opportunity of acquiring some learning. In the course of the year, Church fitted out a vessel for a whaling voyage, and being in want of hands to man her, he induced my son to go, with the promise of giving him, on his return, a pair of silver buckles, besides his wages. As soon as I heard of his going to sea, I immediately set out to go and prevent it if possible.—But on my arrival at Church's, to my great grief, I could only see the vessel my son was in almost out of sight going to sea. My son died of the scurvy in this voyage, and Church has never yet paid me the least of his wages. In my son, besides the loss of his life, I lost equal to seventy-five pounds.

My other son being but a youth, still lived with me. About this time I chartered a sloop of about thirty tons burthen, and hired men to assist me in navigating her. I employed her mostly in the wood trade to Rhode Island, and made clear of all expenses above one hundred dollars with her in better than one year. I had then become something forehanded, and being in my forty-fourth year, I purchased my wife Meg, and thereby prevented having another child to buy, as she was then pregnant. I gave forty pounds for her.

During my residence at Long Island, I raised one year with another, ten cart loads of watermelons, and lost a great many every year besides by the thievishness of the sailors. What I made by the watermelons I sold there amounted to nearly five hundred dollars. Various other methods I pursued in order to enable me to redeem my family. In the night time I fished with setnets and pots for eels and lobsters, and shortly after went a whaling voyage in the service of Col. Smith. After being out seven months, the vessel returned, laden with four hundred barrels of oil. About this time, I become possessed of another dwelling-house, and my temporal affairs were in a pretty prosperous condition. This and my industry was what alone saved me from being expelled [from] that part of the island in which I resided, as an act was passed by the selectmen of the place, that all negroes residing there should be expelled.

Next after my wife, I purchased a negro man for four hundred dollars. But he having an inclination to return to his old master, I therefore let him go. Shortly after I purchased another negro man for twenty-five pounds, whom I parted with shortly after.

Being about forty-six years old, I bought my oldest child Hannah of Ray Mumford, for forty-four pounds, and she still resided with him. I had already redeemed from slavery myself, my wife and three children, besides three negro men.

About the forty-seventh year of my life, I disposed of all my property at Long Island, and came from thence into East Haddam. I hired myself out at first to Timothy Chapman, for five weeks, the earnings of which time I put up carefully by me. After this I wrought for Abel Bingham about six weeks. I then put my money together and purchased of said Bingham ten acres of land, lying at Haddam neck, where I now reside. On this land I labored with great diligence for two years, and shortly after purchased six acres more of land contiguous to my other. One year from that time I purchased seventy acres more of the same man, and paid for it mostly with the produce of my other land. Soon after I bought this last lot of land, I set up a comfortable dwelling-house on my farm, and built it from the produce thereof. Shortly after I had much trouble and expense with my daughter Hannah, whose name has before been mentioned in this account. She was married soon after I redeemed her, to one Isaac, a free negro, and shortly after her marriage fell sick of a mortal disease; her husband, a dissolute and abandoned wretch, paid but little attention to her in her illness. I therefore thought it best to bring her to my house and nurse her there. I procured her all the aid mortals could afford, but notwithstanding this she fell a prey to her disease, after a lingering and painful endurance of it.

The physician's bills for attending her during her illness amounted to forty pounds. Having reached my fifty-fourth year, I hired two negro men, one named William Jacklin, and the other Mingo.

Mingo lived with me one year, and having received his wages, ran in debt to me eight dollars, for which he gave me his note. Presently after he tried to run away from me without troubling himself to pay up his note. I procured a warrant, took him, and requested him to go to Justice Throop's of his own accord, but he refusing, I took him on my shoulders, and carried him there, distant about two miles. The justice asking me if I had my prisoner's note with me, and replying that I had not, he told me that I must return with him and get it. Accordingly I carried Mingo back on my shoulders, but before we arrived at my dwelling, he complained of being hurt, and asked me if this was not a hard way of treating our fellow creatures. I answered him that it would be hard thus to treat our honest fellow creatures. He then told me that if I would let him off my shoulders, he had a pair of silver shoe-buckles, one shirt and a pocket hand-kerchief, which he would turn out to me. I agreed, and let him return home with me on foot; but the very following night, he slipped from me, stole my horse and has never paid me even his note. The other negro man, Jacklin, being a comb-maker by trade, he requested me to set him up, and promised to reward me well with his labor. Accordingly I bought him a set of tools for making combs, and procured him stock. He worked at my house about one year, and then run away from me with all his combs, and owed me for all his board.

Since my residence at Haddam neck, I have owned of boats, canoes, and sail vessels not less than twenty. These I mostly employed in the fishing and trafficking business, and in these occupations I have been cheated out of considerable money by people whom I traded with taking advantage of my ignorance of numbers.

About twelve years ago, I hired a whaleboat and four black men, and proceeded to Long Island after a load of round clams. Having arrived there, I first purchased of James Webb, son of Orange Webb, six hundred and sixty clams, and afterwards, with the help of my men, finished loading my boat. The same evening, however, this Webb stole my boat, and went in her to Connecticut river, and sold her cargo for his own benefit. I thereupon pursued him, and at length, after an additional expense of nine crowns, recovered the boat; but for the proceeds of her cargo I never could obtain any compensation.

Four years after, I met with another loss, far superior to this in value, and I think by no less wicked means. Being going to New London with a grandchild, I took passage in an Indian's boat, and went there with him. On our return, the Indian took on board two hogsheads of molasses, one of which belonged to Capt. Elisha Hart, of Saybrook, to be delivered on his wharf. When we arrived there, and while I was gone, at the request of the Indian, to inform Captain Hart of his arrival, and receive the freight for him, one hogshead of the molasses had been lost overboard by the people in attempting to land it on the wharf. Although I was absent at the time, and had no concern whatever in the business, as was known to a number of respectable witnesses, I was nevertheless prosecuted by this conscientious gentleman (the Indian not being able to pay for it) and obliged to pay upwards of ten pounds lawful money, with all the costs of court. I applied to several gentlemen for counsel in this affair, and they advised me, as my adversary was rich, and threatened to carry the matter from court to court till it would cost me more than the first damages would be, to pay the sum and submit to the injury; which I accordingly did, and he has often since insultingly taunted me with my unmerited misfortune. Such a proceeding as this, committed on a defenseless stranger, almost worn out in the hard service of the world, without any foundation in reason or justice, whatever it may be called in a Christian land, would in my native country have been branded as a crime equal to highway robbery. But Captain Hart was a *white gentleman,* and I a *poor African,* therefore it was *all right, and good enough for the black dog.*

I am now sixty-nine years old. Though once strait and tall, measuring without shoes six feet one inch and an half, and every way well proportioned, I am now bowed down with age and hardship. My strength which was once equal if not superior to any man whom I have ever seen, is now enfeebled so that life is a burden, and it is with fatigue that I can walk a couple of miles, stooping over my staff. Other griefs are still behind, on account of which some aged people, at least, will pity me. My eyesight has gradually failed, till I am almost blind, and whenever I go abroad one of my grandchildren must direct my way; besides for many years I have been much pained and troubled with an ulcer on one of my legs. But amidst all my griefs and pains I have many consolations; Meg, the wife of my youth, whom I married for love, and bought with my money, is still alive. My freedom is a privilege which nothing else can equal. Notwithstanding all the losses I have suffered by fire, by the injustice of knaves, by the cruelty and oppression of false-hearted friends, and the perfidy of my own countrymen whom I have assisted and redeemed from bondage, I am now possessed of more than one hundred acres of land, and three habitable dwelling houses. It gives me joy to think that I *have* and that I *deserve* so good a character, especially for *truth* and *integrity*. While I am now looking to the grave as my home, my joy for this world would be full—IF my children, Cuff for whom I paid two hundred dollars when a boy, and Solomon who was born soon after I purchased his mother—If Cuff and Solomon—O! that they had walked in the way of their father. But a father's lips are closed in silence and in grief! —Vanity of vanities, all is vanity!

CERTIFICATE

Stonington, November 3, 1798.

THESE certify, that Venture, a free negro man, aged about 69 years, and was, as we have ever understood, a native of Africa, and formerly a slave to Mr. James Mumford, of Fisher's Island, in the state of New York; who sold him to Mr. Thomas Stanton, 2d, of Stonington, in the state of Connecticut, and said Stanton sold said Venture to Col. Oliver Smith, of the aforesaid place. That said Venture hath sustained the character of a faithful servant, and that of a temperate, honest and industrious man, and being ever intent on obtaining his freedom, he was indulged by his masters after the ordinary labour on the days of his servitude, to improve the nights in fishing and other employments to his own emolument, in which time he procured so much money as to purchase his freedom from his late master Col. Smith; after which he took upon himself the name of Venture Smith, and has since his freedom purchased a negro woman, called Meg, to whom he was previously married, and also his children who were slaves, and said Venture has since removed himself and family to the town of East Haddam, in this state, where he hath purchased lands on which he hath built a house, and there taken up his abode.

NATHANIEL MINOR, Esq.
ELIJAH PALMER, Esq.
Capt. AMOS PALMER,
ACORS SHEFFIELD,
EDWARD SMITH.

SPIRITUAL·SONG.

Good morning brother Pilgrim, what marching to Zion,
What doubts and what dangers have you met to-day,
Have you found a blessing, are your joys increasing?
Press forward my brother and make no delay;
Is your heart a-glowing, are your comforts a-flowing,
And feel you an evidence, now bright and clear;
Feel you a desire that burns like a fire,
And longs for the hour that Christ shall appear.

I came out this morning, and now am returning,
Perhaps little better than when I first came,
Such groaning and shouting, it sets me to doubting,
I fear such religion is only a dream;
The preachers were stamping, the people were jumping,
And screaming so loud that I neither could hear,
Either praying or preaching, such horrible screaching,
'Twas truly offensive to all that were there?

Perhaps my dear brother, while they pray'd together,
You sat and consider'd and prayed not at all,
Would you find a blessing, then pray without ceasing,
Obey the command that was given by Paul,
For if you should reason at any such season,
No wonder if Satan should tell in your ears,
The preachers and people they are but a rabble,
And this is no place for reflection and pray'rs.

No place for reflection, I'm fill'd with distraction,
I wonder that people could bear for to stay,
The men they were bawling, the women were squaling,
I know not for my part how any could pray;
Such horrid confusion, if this be religion,
Sure 'tis something new that never was seen,
For the sacred pages that speak of all ages,
Does no where declare that such ever has been.

Don't be so soon shaken, if I'm not mistaken,
Such things have been acted by christians of old,

559

When the ark was a-coming, King David came running,
And dancing before it by scripture we're told,
When the Jewish nation had laid the foundation,
And rebuilt the temple at Ezra's command,
Some wept and some prais'd, and such a noise there was rais'd,
It was heard afar off, perhaps all through the land.

And as for the preacher, Ezekiel the teacher,
Was taught for to stamp and to smite with his hand,
To shew the transgression of that wicked nation,
That they might repent and obey the command.
For scripture quotation in the dispensation,
The blessed Redeemer had handed them out,
If these cease from praying, we hear him declaring,
The stones to reprove him would quickly cry out.

The scripture is wrested, for Paul hath protested,
That order should be kept in the houses of God,
Amidst such a clatter who knows what they're after,
Or who can attend to what is declared;
To see them behaving like drunkards a-raving,
And lying and rolling prostrate on the ground,
I really felt awful and sometimes was fearful,
That I'd be the next that would come tumbling down.

You say you felt awful, you ought to be careful,
Least you grieve the Spirit and make it depart,
For from your expressions you felt some impressions,
The sweet melting showers has tender'd your heart;
You fear persecution, and that's the delusion,
Brought in by the devil to turn you away;
Be careful my brother, for bless'd is no other,
Than creatures who are not offended in me.

When Peter was preaching, and boldly was teaching,
The way of salvation in Jesus' name,
The spirit descended and some were offended,
And said of the men they were fill'd with new wine.
I never yet doubted but some of them shouted,
While others lay prostrate by power struck down,
Some weeping, some praying, while others were saying,
They are as drunk as fools, or in falsehood abound.

Our time is a-flying, our moments a-dying,
We are led to improve them and quickly appear,

For the bless'd hour when Jesus in power,
In glory shall come is now drawing near,
Methinks there will be shouting, and I'm not doubting,
But crying and screaming for mercy in vain:
Therefore my dear Brother, let's now pray together,
That your precious soul may be fill'd with the flame.

Sure praying is needful, I really feel awful,
I fear that my day of repentance is past;
But I will look to the Saviour, his mercies for ever,
These storms of temptation will not always last,
I look for the blessing and pray without ceasing,
His mercy is sure unto all that believe,
My heart is a glowing, I feel his love flowing,
Peace, comfort, and pardon, I now have received.

Printed for and Sold by the Rev. RICHARD ALLEN, No. 150 Spruce
Street, Philadelphia.

ANTHEMS AND HYMNS, 1808–1814

BY

Michael Fortune

Robert Y. Sidney

Peter Williams

William Hamilton

NEW YEAR'S ANTHEM,

SUNG IN THE AFRICAN EPISCOPAL CHURCH OF ST. THOMAS,
JAN. 1, 1808.

WRITTEN BY MICHAEL FORTUNE.

I.

To Thee, Almighty, gracious power,
   Who sit'st enthron'd, in radiant heaven;
On this bless'd morn, this hallow'd hour,
   The homage of the heart be given!

II.

Lift up your souls to God on high,
   The fountain of eternal grace,
Who, with a tender father's eye,
   Looked down on Afric's helpless race!

III.

The nations heard His stern commands!
   Britannia kindly set us free;
Colombia tears the galling bands,
   And gives the sweets of Liberty.

IV.

Then strike the lyre! your voices raise!
   Let gratitude inspire your song!
Pursue religion's holy ways,
   Shun sinful Pleasure's giddy throng!

V.

From Mercy's seat may grace descend,
   To wake contrition's heartfelt sighs!
O! may our pious strains ascend,
   Where ne'er the sainted spirit dies!

VI.

Then, we our freedom shall retain,
  In peace and love, and cheerful toil:
Plenty shall flow from the wide main,
  And golden harvests from the soil.

VII.

Ye nations that to us restore
  The rights which God bestow'd on all;
For you His blessing we implore:
  O! listen further to His call!

VIII.

From one parental stem ye spring,
  A kindred blood your bosoms own;
Your kindred tongues God's praises sing,
  And beg forgiveness at his throne:

IX.

O, then, your mutual wrongs forgive,
  Unlock your hearts to social love!
So shall ye safe and happy live,
  By grace and blessings from above.

ANTHEMS,

COMPOSED BY R. Y. SIDNEY,

For the National Jubilee of the Abolition of the

Slave Trade, January 1st, 1809.

ANTHEM I.

1 DRY your tears, ye sons of Afric,
   God has shown his gracious power;
   He has stopt the horrid traffic,
   That your country's bosom tore.
   See through clouds he smiles benignant,
   See your nation's glory rise;
   Though your foes may frown indignant,
   All their wrath you may despise.

CHORUS.

Dry your tears ye hapless nation,
Banish all your cares away;
God has given great salvation,
On this ever glorious day.

SOLO.

O raise to heaven a grateful voice,
Through every age rejoice, rejoice.

RECITATIVE.

What objects meet the piteous eye,
   What passions fill the soul of man,
To see a hapless nation rise,
   And all its various actions scan,
In deep disgrace, depriv'd of peace,
   And every blessing dear,

565

Now blest with peace, rais'd up in fame,
And free from every fear.

2 Thus the clouds the light obscuring,
Vainly try to veil the day:
Thus shall you all toils enduring,
See your troubles pass away.
Though the clouds of night have hover'd,
On your nation's hapless head:
See the blushing morn discover'd,
See the dawn of glory shed.

CHORUS.—Dry your tears, &c. &c.

3 See each science round you blooming,
Like the flowers at dawn of day,
With their sweets the air perfuming,
With their beauties cheer the way.
See with eagle wings expanded,
See each hidden talent rise;
See each slavish fear disbanded,
See your genius mount the skies.

CHORUS.—dry your tears, &c. &c.

ANTHEM II.

YE sons of Afric, loud rejoice,
In songs of triumph raise your voice;
The night of slavery now is past,
The dawn of freedom shines at last.

CHORUS.

Rejoice that you were born to see,
This glorious day, your jubilee.

O praise the Lord enthron'd on high,
The Lord that heard your piercing cry;
That made his wond'rous light to spread,
And shed his blessings on your heads.

CHORUS.—Rejoice, &c. &c.

FINALE.

The worthy friends our thanks receive,
'Tis all that Afric's sons can give;
And for the kindness you have shown,
May GOD receive you as his own.

CHORUS.—Rejoice, &c. &c.

HYMN

BY ROBERT Y. SIDNEY.

I.
WHEN ruddy morn dispels the clouds
    That veil the rising day,
To thee, Almighty Power, I'll sing,
    To thee I'll raise the lay.

II.
Awake, my bangor, twin'd with flow'rs,
    Thou pride of Afric's race!
The night is past, o'er are the show'rs
    That dew'd creation's face.

III.
Ye sable nations all rejoice!
    O! wipe your tears away;
Afric, your glory shines once more,
    This is your Jubilee!

IV.
Let all creation join the song,
    Great joy to thee is given;
Whilst circling years shall roll along,
    O! praise the Lord in heaven!

V.
O! let thy servant, Lord, return,
    Since thy Salvation's given,
Back unto his primeval clay,
    And wing his flight to heaven!

HYMN I.

BY PETER WILLIAMS JR.

I.

TO the Eternal LORD,
By saints on earth ador'd
  And saints above.
Let us glad honors rear,
In strains of praise and pray'r
His glorious name declare,
  The God of Love.

II.

When the oppressor's hands
Bound us in iron bands
  Thou didst appear.
Thou saw our weeping eyes,
And list'ning to our cries,
In mercy didst arise,
  Our hearts to cheer.

III.

Thou did'st the trade o'erthrow,
The source of boundless woe,
  The world's disgrace,
Which ravag'd Afric's coast,
Enslaved its greatest boast,
A happy num'rous host,
  A harmless race.

IV.

In diff'rent parts of earth
Thou called the HUMANE forth,
  Our rights to plead,
Our griefs to mitigate,
And to improve our state,
An object truly great,
  Noble indeed.

V.

Thou didst their labours bless,
And gave them great success,
  in FREEDOM's cause.

They prov'd to every sight
By truth's unerring light,
All men are free by right
Of Nature's laws.

VI.

They to insure our bliss,
Taught us that happiness
Is from above.
That it is only found
On this terrestrial ground,
Where virtuous acts abound,
And Mutu'l Love.

HYMN II.

BY PETER WILLIAMS JR.

I.

THE Sov'reign ruler of the skies,
To bless the human kind,
Implanted in the breast of man,
A sympathetic mind.
Hence we, participating woe,
Each other's griefs alloy,
And by reciprocating bliss,
We swell the tide of joy.

II.

Instructed thus by Nature's God,
The good and great first cause;
We find that Fellowship and Love
Stand high in Nature's Laws.
As brethren are to brethren near,
So let us be combin'd:
Knit by the bonds of Mutu'l Love,
In social compact joined.

III.

With unremitting tender care,
Let us the sick attend;
Defend from want the fatherless,
And prove the Widow's friend.
So shall we cheer affliction's night,
And soothe the fiercest grief;

So shall we ease the aching heart,
By MUTUAL RELIEF.

HYMN

BY WILLIAM HAMILTON.

I.

HAIL this auspicious day,
Ye sons of Africa,
  With joyful sounds;
The Slave Trade now doth cease,
That injured the peace,
And which destroy'd the bliss
  Of Afric's sons!

II.

A philanthropic band
Came forth at God's command,
  And stopt its course;
Powerful arguments
They us'd in our defence,
Join'd with the eloquence
  Of WILBERFORCE.

III.

No more do prosperous gales
Distend the slave ship's sails
  On Afric's coast;
To widely spread dismay
Through injur'd Africa,
And waft her sons away,
  Their country's boast.

IV.

Thou Supreme God and King,
From whom our blessings spring
  And goodness flows;
When we were fraught with grief,
Thou send'st to our relief
Friends, who destroy'd the chief
  Of all our woes.

V.

High in thy Courts above,
Where Saints and Angels move,

And Cherubs sing,
Melodious notes we'll raise,
In chanting hymns of praise,
Till death shall end our days,
To thee our King.

[Sources: The anthem by Michael Fortune appears in Absalom Jones, *A Thanksgiving Sermon, Preached January 1, 1808, in St. Thomas's, or the African Episcopal, Church, Philadelphia: On Account of the Abolition of the African Slave Trade, On That Day, By the Congress of the United States* (Philadelphia: Fry and Kammerer, 1808), pp. 22–23. Robert Sidney's anthems appear in Joseph Sidney, *An Oration, Commemorative of the Abolition of the Slave Trade in the United States: Delivered before the Wilberforce Philanthropic Association, in the City of New York, on the Second of January, 1809* (New York: J. Seymour, 1809), pp. 19–20. Peter Williams's hymns appear in William Hamilton, *An Address to the New York African Society, for Mutual Relief, Delivered in the Universalist Church, January 2, 1809* (New York, 1809), p. 4. William Hamilton's hymn appears in Joseph Sidney, *An Oration, Commemorative of the Abolition of The Slave Trade in the United States; Delivered in the African Asbury Church, in the City of New York, on the First of January, 1814* (New York: Printed for the Author, J. S., Pudney, Printer, 1814), pp. 14–15.]

ESSAY, TO THE AMERICAN CONVENTION

FOR

PROMOTING THE ABOLITION OF SLAVERY,

AND

IMPROVING THE CONDITION OF

THE AFRICAN RACE

BY GEORGE R. ALLEN, 1828

POEM,
ON SLAVERY
BY GEORGE R. ALLEN, 1828

POEM,
ON FREEDOM
BY THOMAS S. SIDNEY, 1828

GEORGE R. ALLEN'S ESSAY

To the American Convention for promoting the Abolition of Slavery, and improving the condition of the African Race.

GENTLEMEN:

When I consider that I have the honour of addressing so large an assembly of distinguished gentlemen of this enlightened country, and that I am only a poor little descendant of Africa, I am struck with fear, humility and awe.

In the first place, I return thanks to that Supreme Being, who has put it into your hearts to advocate the cause of our injured race, and to promote their emancipation from slavery.

What sound can be more delightful to the ear of a slave than the expression, "The Laws have made you free?" This is the happy case with us in the state of New York. Liberty is an invaluable blessing to us; and we often feel compassion for the thousands of our brethren in the South who are groaning under the chains of bondage, while we are enjoying the benefits of freedom, and one of the most important of these, I conceive to be education.

I have the happiness to belong to a school which was instituted by the Manumission Society of this city about 40 years ago. There are about 700 scholars, male and female, belonging to this Institution; and although I am but twelve years old, I have made some progress in reading, writing, arithmetic, geography, English grammar, navigation, and astronomy.

The school has frequently been visited by gentlemen from the South and other parts of the country; and I and several of my schoolmates have been called up and examined by them upon the several branches that we were acquainted with, and they have always expressed themselves highly gratified with our performances. I trust the time is not far distant when the blessings that we enjoy shall be the happy portion of all our colored brethren, and then the language in the following lines will have their full weight: "We hold these truths to be self evident, that all men are created equal, and endowed by their Creator with certain unalienable rights; among these, are life, liberty, and the pursuit of happiness; that to secure these rights, governments were instituted, deriving their just powers from the consent of the governed."

That you may prosper in your arduous but glorious undertaking; and that all your labours may be crowned with success, you have, gentlemen, the wishes of myself and fellow schoolmates in the New York African Free School.

GEORGE R. ALLEN.

New York, October 21st, 1828.

Having at the suggestion of some of the Trustees of the School under my charge, informed my pupils that the American Convention was soon to meet in Baltimore, and intimated its objects and its labours, I proposed to the senior boys the propriety of their attempting something in the form of an Address from them to that body; promising to forward such essay as I should judge to be the most appropriate. I certify that the foregoing communication is the original production of the boy who has signed it, with no other correction or alteration than the *erasure of a few superfluous words.*

CHARLES C. ANDREWS.

The undersigned, members of the New York Manumission Society, appointed to draft an Address to the American Convention, have full faith in the above attestation of C. C. Andrews, and from what we have known of the performances of this, and other boys in his school, we are fully convinced that the said Address is the genuine, unaided production of George R. Allen, a very black boy of pure African descent, who is now between 12 and 13 years old, and was born in this city.

MAHLON DAY,
GOOLD BROWN,
THOMAS LEGGETT, Jun.
WILLIAM L. STONE,
ISRAEL CORSE.

New York, 10th mo. 21st, 1828.

George R. Allen and Thomas Sidney's Verses on Slavery and Freedom, produced in a given time.

ON SLAVERY.

Slavery, oh, thou cruel stain,
Thou dost fill my heart with pain:
See my brother, there he stands
Chained by slavery's cruel bands.

Could we not feel a brother's woes,
Relieve the wants he undergoes,
Snatch him from slavery's cruel smart,
And to him freedom's joy impart?

George R. Allen, aged 12 years, *Oct. 21st, 1828.*
New York African Free School.

ON FREEDOM.

Freedom will break the tyrant's chains,
And shatter all his whole domain;
From slavery she will always free
And all her aim is liberty.

Thomas S. Sidney, aged 12 years, *Oct. 21st, 1828.*
New York African Free School.

I

The above verses were composed and. written by the boys who have signed them; George R. Allen was required to produce something on Slavery, either in prose or verse in half an hour, and he, within the time, handed me the above lines. Thomas S. Sidney occupied one hour on freedom.

New York African Free School.

CHARLES C. ANDREWS.

[Source: The preceding essay and poems appear in the *Minutes of the Adjourned Session of the Twentieth Biennial American Convention for Promoting the Abolition of Slavery and Improving the Condition of the African Race, Held at Baltimore, Nov., 1828* (Philadelphia: Samuel Parker, 1828).]

ESSAY, 1828

BY

Isaiah G. DeGrass

GENTLEMEN,

I feel myself highly honoured by addressing you in behalf of myself and the African race. I am but a poor descendant of that injured people. When I reflect upon the enormities which continue to be practised in many parts of our otherwise favoured country, on the ill-fated Africans, and their descendants, who are torn by the hands of violence from their native country, and sold like brutes to tyrannical slave-holders in different countries, where they are held in slavery and bondage, I ought to return thanks unto Almighty God, for having put it into the hearts of such distinguished men as you, to undertake the cause of the Abolishing of Slavery; and I ought to feel myself greatly blessed for enjoying the many privileges I do; while there are so many in the southern States chained in slavery, who perhaps, have left mothers, fathers, sisters and brothers, to mourn their loss. I feel myself greatly blessed in belonging to a school which has been established for many years by the Manumission Society. The different branches that are taught in this school, are reading, writing, arithmetic, geography, navigation, astronomy, and map drawing. Our schools which now contain 700 male and female scholars, continue to be conducted on the Lancasterian system, and the improvement of the scholars is such, as to be satisfactory to the trustees, and all visitors who come to the school. Next to the Supreme Being, gentlemen, you deserve the gratitude and thankfulness of our whole race. When I reflect on the great things that you have done for us, I can but with gratitude fall at your feet and thank you. It makes my heart burn within me, when I think of the poor Africans who are torn from their homes and relatives; deprived of the protection and advice of their friends, and forced to a distance from the means of proving and defending their rights; these wretched victims of avarice and cruelty languish a long time in bondage before they can procure assistance.

You gentlemen, who are advocates for the abolition of such, deserve the gratitude and thanks of our whole race. May Divine Providence assist you in all your proceedings, is the wish of a descendant of Africa.

ISAIAH G. DeGRASS, aged 15 years.

New York African Free School, Oct. 21st, 1828.

[Source: *Minutes of the Adjourned Session of the Twentieth Biennial American Convention* . . . , pp. 67–68.]

Four Selections from

THE HOPE OF LIBERTY

THE HOPE

OF

LIBERTY

CONTAINING

A NUMBER OF POETICAL PIECES

BY

George M. Horton.

RALEIGH: PRINTED BY J. GALES & SON. 1829.

EXPLANATION

GEORGE, who is the author of the following poetical effusions, is a slave, the property of Mr. James Horton, of Chatham County, North Carolina. He has been in the habit, some years past, of producing poetical pieces, sometimes on suggested subjects, to such persons as would write them while he dictated. Several compositions of his have already appeared in the Raleigh Register. Some have made their way into the Boston newspapers, and have evoked expressions of approbation and surprise. Many persons have now become much interested in the promotion of his prospects, some of whom are elevated in office and literary attainments. They are solicitous that efforts at length be made to obtain by subscription, a sum sufficient for his emancipation, upon the condition of his going in the vessel which shall first afterwards sail for Liberia. It is his earnest and only wish to become a member of that Colony, to enjoy its privileges, and apply his industry and mental abilities to the promotion of its prospects and his own. It is upon these terms alone, that the efforts of those who befriend his views are intended to have a final effect.

To put to trial the plan here urged in his behalf, the paper now exhibited is published. Several of his productions are contained in the succeeding pages. Many more might have been added, which would have swelled into a larger size. They would doubtless be interesting to many, but it is hoped that the specimens here inserted will be sufficient to accomplish the object of the publication. Expense will thus be avoided, and the money better employed in enlarging the sum applicable for his emancipation.

It is proposed, that in every town or vicinity where contributions are made, they may be put into the hands of some person, who will humanely consent to receive them, and give notice to Mr. Weston R. Gales, in Raleigh, of the amount collected. As soon as it is ascertained that the collections will accomplish the object; it is expected that they will be transmitted without delay to Mr. Weston R. Gales. But should they ultimately prove insufficient, they will be returned to subscribers.

None will imagine it possible that pieces produced as these have been, should be free from blemish in composition or taste. The author is now 32 years of age, and has always laboured in the field on his master's farm, promiscuously with the few others which Mr. Horton owns, in circumstances of the greatest possible simplicity. His master says he knew nothing of his poetry, but as he heard of it from others. George knows how to read, and is now learning to write. All his pieces are written down by others; and his reading, which is done at night, and at the usual intervals allowed to slaves, has been much employed on poetry, such as he could procure, this being the species of composition most interesting to him. It is thought best to print his productions without correction, that the mind of the reader may be in no uncertainty as to the originality and genuineness of every part. We shall conclude this account of George, with an assurance that he has been ever a faithful, honest and industrious slave. That his heart has felt deeply and sensitively in this lowest possible condition of human nature, will easily be believed, and is impressively confirmed by one of his stanzas,

> Come, melting Pity, from afar,
> And break this vast enormous bar
> Between a wretch and thee;
> Purchase a few short days of time,
> And bid a vassal soar sublime,
> On wings of Liberty.

Raleigh, July 2, 1829.

Praise of Creation

Creation fires my tongue!
    Nature thy anthems raise;
And spread the universal song
    Of thy Creator's praise!

Heaven's chief delight was Man
    Before Creation's birth—
Ordained with joy to lead the van,
    And reign the lord of earth.

When Sin was quite unknown,
    And all the woes it brought,
He hailed the morn without a groan
    Or one corroding thought.

When each revolving wheel
    Assumed its sphere sublime,
Submissive Earth then heard the peal,
    And struck the march of time.

The march in Heaven begun,
    And splendor filled the skies,
When Wisdom bade the morning Sun
    With joy from chaos rise.

The angels heard the tune
    Throughout creation ring:
They seized their golden harps as soon
    And touched on every string.

When time and space were young,
    And music rolled along—
The morning stars together sung,
    And Heaven was drown'd in song.

Ye towering eagles soar,
    And fan Creation's blaze,
And ye terrific lion's roar,
    To your Creator's praise.

Responsive thunders roll,
    Loud acclamations sound,

And show your Maker's vast control
  O'er all the worlds around.

Stupendous mountains smoke,
  And lift your summits high,
To him who all your terrors woke,
  Dark'ning the sapphire sky.

Now let my muse descend,
  To view the march below—
Ye subterraneous worlds attend
  And bid your chorus flow.

Ye vast volcanoes yell,
  Whence fiery cliffs are hurled;
And all ye liquid oceans swell
  Beneath the solid world.

Ye cataracts combine,
  Nor let the paean cease—
The universal concert join,
  Thou dismal precipice.

But halt my feeble tongue,
  My weary muse delays:
But, oh my soul, still float along
  Upon the flood of praise!

On the silence of a young lady, on account of the imaginary flight of her suitor

Oh, heartless dove! mount in the skies,
  Spread thy soft wing upon the gale,
Or on thy sacred pinions rise,
  Nor brood with silence in the vale.

Breathe on the air thy plaintive note,
  Which oft has filled the lonesome grove,
And let thy melting ditty float—
  The dirge of long lamented love.

Coo softly to the silent ear,
  And make the floods of grief to roll;
And cause by love the sleeping tear,
  To wake with sorrow from the soul.

Is it the loss of pleasures past
    Which makes thee droop thy sounding wing?
Does winter's rough, inclement blast
    Forbid thy tragic voice to sing?

Is it because the fragrant breeze
    Along the sky forbears to flow—
Nor whispers low amidst the trees,
    Whilst all the vallies frown below?

Why should a frown thy soul alarm,
    And tear thy pleasures from thy breast?
Or veil the smiles of every charm,
    And rob thee of thy peaceful rest.

Perhaps thy sleeping love may wake,
    And hear thy penitential tone;
And suffer not thy heart to break,
    Nor let a princess grieve alone.

Perhaps his pity may return,
    With equal feeling from the heart,
And breast with breast together burn,
    Never—no, never more to part.

Never, till death's resistless blow,
    Whose call the dearest must obey—
In twain together then may go,
    And thus together dwell for aye.

Say to the suitor, Come away,
    Nor break the knot which love has tied—
Nor to the world thy trust betray,
    And fly forever from thy bride.

On Liberty and Slavery

Alas! and am I born for this,
    To wear this slavish chain?
Deprived of all created bliss,
    Through hardship, toil and pain!

How long have I in bondage lain,
    And languished to be free!
Alas! and must I still complain—
    Deprived of liberty.

Oh, Heaven! and is there no relief
This side the silent grave—
To soothe the pain—to quell the grief
And anguish of a slave?

Come Liberty, thou cheerful sound,
Roll through my ravished ears!
Come, let my grief in joys be drowned,
And drive away my fears.

Say unto foul oppression, Cease:
Ye tyrants rage no more,
And let the joyful trump of peace,
Now bid the vassal soar.

Soar on the pinions of that dove
Which long has cooed for thee,
And breathed her notes from Afric's grove,
The sound of Liberty.

Oh, Liberty! thou golden prize,
So often sought by blood—
We crave thy sacred sun to rise,
The gift of nature's God!

Bid Slavery hide her haggard face,
And barbarism fly:
I scorn to see the sad disgrace
In which enslaved I lie.

Dear Liberty! upon thy breast,
I languish to respire;
And like the Swan unto her nest,
I'd to thy smiles retire.

Oh, blest asylum—heavenly balm!
Unto thy boughs I flee—
And in thy shades the storm shall calm,
With songs of Liberty!

*On hearing of the intention of a gentleman to purchase
the Poet's freedom*

When on life's ocean first I spread my sail,
I then implored a mild auspicious gale;

And from the slippery strand I took my flight,
And sought the peaceful haven of delight.

Tyrannic storms arose upon my soul,
And dreadful did their mad'ning thunders roll;
The pensive muse was shaken from her sphere,
And hope, it vanish'd in the clouds of fear.

At length a golden sun broke thro' the gloom,
And from his smiles arose a sweet perfume—
A calm ensued, and birds began to sing,
And lo! the sacred muse resumed her wing.

With frantic joy she chaunted as she flew,
And kiss'd the clement hand that bore her thro'
Her envious foes did from her sight retreat,
Or prostrate fall beneath her burning feet.

'Twas like a proselyte, allied to Heaven—
Or rising spirits' boast of sins forgiven,
Whose shout dissolves the adamant away
Whose melting voice the stubborn rocks obey.

'Twas like the salutation of the dove,
Borne on the zephyr thro' some lonesome grove,
When Spring returns, and Winter's chill is past,
And vegetation smiles above the blast.

'Twas like the evening of a nuptial pair,
When love pervades the hour of sad despair—
'Twas like fair Helen's sweet return to Troy,
When every Grecian bosom swell'd with joy.

The silent harp which on the osiers hung,
Was then attuned, and manumission sung:
Away by hope the clouds of fear were driven,
And music breathed my gratitude to heaven.

Hard was the race to reach the distant goal,
The needle oft was shaken from the pole;
In such distress, who could forbear to weep?
Toss'd by the headlong billows of the deep!

The tantalizing beams which shone so plain,
Which turn'd my former pleasures into pain—

Which falsely promised all the joys of fame,
Gave way, and to a more substantial flame.

Some philanthropic souls as from afar,
With pity strove to break the slavish bar;
To whom my floods of gratitude shall roll,
And yield with pleasure to their soft control.

And sure of Providence this work begun—
He shod my feet this rugged race to run;
And in despite of all the swelling tide,
Along the dismal path will prove my guide.

Thus on the dusky verge of deep despair,
Eternal Providence was with me there;
When pleasure seemed to fade on life's gay dawn,
And the last beam of hope was almost gone.

A

NARRATIVE

OF SOME REMARKABLE INCIDENTS

IN THE LIFE OF

SOLOMON BAYLEY,

FORMERLY

A SLAVE,

IN THE STATE OF DELAWARE, NORTH AMERICA;
WRITTEN BY HIMSELF,
AND PUBLISHED FOR HIS BENEFIT;
TO WHICH ARE PREFIXED, A FEW REMARKS BY

ROBERT HURNARD.

*"Persecuted, but not forsaken; cast down,
but not destroyed."—II. Cor. v. 9.*

SECOND EDITION.
LONDON:
PRINTED FOR
HARVEY AND DARTON, GRACECHURCH STREET;
W. BAYNES & SON, PATERNOSTER-ROW;
AND P. YOUNGMAN, WITHAM AND MALDON.
1825.

587

PREFACE

IN presenting the following fragments to the attention of the public, it appears necessary to state the manner in which they came into my possession, and to give the reader a brief account of the Author, Solomon Bayley.

During the early part of my residence in America in the year 1820, I met with the piece containing the account of his escape from slavery, with the mental and bodily trials he underwent, resulting from that step: being much interested in the perusal of this simple and unadorned narrative, I was induced to make some inquiry into the character and circumstances of a man, the recital of whose sufferings and wrongs had deeply excited my sympathy. The information which, in consequence, I obtained from many respectable inhabitants of Wilmington, where I then resided, was in all respects gratifying, so far as related to his character; and was, besides, such as to induce a hope that his situation in life was about to become comparatively easy and independent.

I learned that at one period of his life he had been instructed in the business of a cooper, and for some time had wrought at that trade; but feeling some scruples in his mind with regard to following an occupation which he believed had a tendency, though a remote one, to promote the sale and consumption of ardent spirits, he conscientiously forsook that employment, under the persuasion that the frequent and indiscriminate use of distilled spirituous liquors had proved as injurious to the moral and religious growth of society as it was admitted to be subversive of health and the bane of domestic happiness. He then engaged himself as a labourer in husbandry; and while deriving his support from this employment, he one day happened to meet with the Governor of the State of Delaware; and believing it to be his duty to speak to him on the great responsibility of the station in which he was placed, and on the importance of a faithful occupation of the talents committed to his charge, the worthy Governor was so well pleased with his communication, that he shortly after promoted Solomon to the oversight of one of his farms, admitting him as a joint sharer with himself in the profits. This mode of farming, which requires great confidence on one side, and skill and industry on the other, is not uncommon in America; the landlord usually finding all the necessary implements and stocking the farm, and the tenant, the requisite labour to manage the concern. But I subsequently learned that he did not long enjoy the above-mentioned situation, as the Governor was soon

after removed by death. He then engaged himself in the employment of a person at Camden, where with his wife he now resides.
Solomon was moreover described to be estimable as a religious character, remarkably humble, patient of wrong, poor as to worldly
possessions, but rich in faith and in many other Christian virtues:
such was the account which was given me of this extraordinary man.

Feeling a strong inclination to see and converse with one, whom,
from the description of his character, I already esteemed; I requested a friend who had know him many years, and whom he
sometimes visited, to introduce me to his acquaintance, when he
should next come to Wilmington; this he did, and on a more intimate knowledge obtained in subsequent interviews, the favourable
sentiments I at first conceived of his integrity and worth, were fully
and satisfactorily confirmed, heightened as they were, by his solid
instructive conversation, and I may add, the just sense he appeared
to entertain of divine things.

It was in some of these interviews that, among other circumstances of his life, he related the affecting account of the sale and
purchase of his only son, whom he afterwards lost by death; he also
mentioned several particulars of his two daughters, whom he had
placed out in the service of respectable families, but who, on account of ill health, had returned home, and died within a short
period of each other. While narrating in my family the particulars
of these severe domestic bereavements, which he did with great
feeling and sensibility, it was evident that he was no stranger to the
source from whence true consolation is derived.

In common with my brethren of the same religious profession, and
with many philanthropists of other persuasions, I had long felt a
warm interest towards the descendants of Africa generally: but the
peculiar regard which was awakened in my mind towards this deserving individual, made me anxious to obtain more of his history,
especially when I had a prospect of returning to my native country.
I therefore determined to obtain from him as much of it as he should
be free to communicate, and wrote to him two or three times on the
subject. We lived fifty miles apart, and my avocations, as well as his,
precluded our meeting again. I wished to possess it in his own
simple, unvarnished style; but Solomon being a self-taught penman,
and ignorant of orthography, though willing to oblige me if he could,
made many objections on the ground of his incapacity and the advanced period of his life: he was, however, at length induced to
comply with my request, and in a while forwarded me such parts as
I had particularly requested.

I cannot but regret that the manuscript is so disjointed and incomplete, being written and forwarded to me at different times; but imperfect as it is, it appeared too interesting and valuable to be restricted to the circle of my own acquaintance; and I offer it to a candid public, presuming that every indulgence on this score will be granted to a man whose life has been chiefly spent in slavery and servitude.

Solomon is in connexion with that body of Christians called Methodists; and my last communication from him sufficiently evinces on what grounds he has believed himself called to the ministry. From the general tenor of his writings, and from this letter in particular, I leave the serious reader to form his own judgment, whether he be not rightly called and qualified to be engaged in that important service.

I wish it to be understood that it is intended to transmit the whole of the profits of the publication to America, for the benefit of the aged couple; and I hope the friends of humanity generally, will, for this purpose, assist in promoting an extensive circulation of the tract; by so doing, they will also contribute to place Slavery in a new and appalling light.

This narrative discloses the melancholy and incontrovertible fact that the rights of Slaves are shamefully invaded in a country where a man is suffered to go unpunished who has dared to sell and transport those who are legally entitled to their freedom, by his own voluntary act: and if such be the case in America, notwithstanding all the vigilance of her abolition societies, it may be asked, what presumption have the friends of this injured people to hope that any real benefit can result from the tardy and temporizing measures, which have been introduced into the British West India Colonies, where no public bodies are organised to take cognizance of their wrongs.

A period of nearly twenty years has elapsed, during which the friends of gradual manumission have been lulled by hope, and cheated by disappointed expectation; and when it is considered that at this moment England retains nearly eight hundred thousand human beings, and America more than fifteen hundred thousand, in this cruel state of bondage, it remains even now a doubt whether the present generation will witness the end of this aggravated evil, unless prompt and more vigorous measures be taken for its immediate extinction.

R. HURNARD.

KELVEDON, ESSEX,
1ST MONTH, 1825.

FIRST PART

SOLOMON BAYLEY, unto all people, and nations, and languages, grace be unto you, and peace from God our Father, and from the Lord Jesus Christ.

Having lived some months in continual expectation of death, I have felt uneasy in mind about leaving the world without leaving behind me some account of the kindness and mercy of God towards me. But when I go to tell of his favours, I am struck with wonder at the exceeding riches of his grace. O! that all people would come to admire him for his goodness and declare his wonders which he doth for the children of men. The Lord tried to teach me his fear when I was a little boy; but I delighted in vanity and foolishness, and went astray. But the Lord found out a way to overcome me, and to cause me to desire his favour, and his great help; and although I thought no one could be more unworthy of his favour, yet he did look on me, and pitied me in my great distress.

I was born a slave in the state of Delaware, and was one of those slaves that were carried out of Delaware into the state of Virginia; and the laws of Delaware did say that slaves carried out of that state should be free; whereupon I moved to recover my freedom. I employed lawyers, and went to court two days, to have a suit brought to obtain my freedom. After court I went home to stay until the next court, which was about six weeks off. But two days before the court was to sit, I was taken up and put on board of a vessel out of Hunting Creek, bound to Richmond, on the western shore of Virginia, and there put into Richmond jail, and irons were put on me; and I was brought very low. In my distress I was often visited with some symptoms of distraction. At length I was taken out of jail, and put into one of the back country waggons, to go toward the going down of the sun. Now consider how great my distress must have been, being carried from my wife and children, and from my natural place, and from my chance for freedom.

On the third day my distress was bitter, and I cried out in my heart, "I am past all hope." And the moment I said I was past all hope, it pleased the father of all mercy to look on me, and he sent a strengthening thought into my heart, which was this: that he that made the heavens and the earth, was able to deliver me. I looked up to the sky, and then to the trees and ground, and I believed in a moment, that if he could make all these, he was able to deliver me. Then did that scripture come into my mind, which I had heard before, and that was, "they that trust in the Lord, shall never be confounded." I believed that was a true word, and I wanted to try that word, and got out of the waggon; but I thought I was not fit to lay hold of the promise: yet another thought came into my mind, and that was, that I did not know to what bounds his mercy would extend. I then made haste and got out of the waggon, and went into the bushes; I squatted down to see what would follow. Now there were three waggons in company, and four white people; they soon missed me, and took out one of the horses and rode back, and were gone about three-quarters of an hour, and then returned, and put the horse in the waggon again, and went on their way; and that was the last I ever saw or heard of them. I sat still where I was till night, and then walked out into the road and looked up to the sky, and I felt very desolate. Oh! the bitterness of distress which I then felt, for having sinned against God; whom if I had been careful to obey in all things, he would have spared me all my troubles. Oh! it is a dangerous thing to cast off fear, and to restrain prayer before God. If we do that which we believe will please him, with a desire to obtain his favour, it is a real prayer; but if we do, or say, that which we believe will displease him, that is to cast off fear, and to restrain prayer before him.

When night came and I walked out of the bushes, I felt very awful. I set off to walk homewards, but soon was chased by dogs, at the same house where the man told the waggoner he had taken up a runaway three days before. But it pleased the highest to send out a dreadful wind, with thunder and lightning and rain; which was the means by which I escaped, as I then thought, as I travelled along that night. Next day I was taken with the dysentery, which came on so bad, I thought I must die; but I obtained great favour, and kept on my feet, and so I got down to Richmond; but had liked to have been twice taken, for twice I was pursued by dogs.

But after I got to Richmond, a coloured man pretended to be my friend, and then sent white people to take me up; but a little while before they came, it came expressly into my mind, that he would prove treacherous and betray me. I obeyed the impression immediately, and left the place I was in, and presently there came with clubs to take me, as it did appear, two white men and a coloured man. When I saw them I was in an hollow place on the ground, not far from where the coloured man left me: at sight of them I was struck with horror and fear, and the fear that came into my soul, took such an impression on my animal frame that I felt very weak: I cried to the Maker of heaven and earth to save me, and he did so. I lay there and prayed to the Lord, and broke persimmon tree bushes, and covered myself: when night came on, I felt as if the great God had heard my cry. Oh! how marvellous is his loving-kindness toward men of every description and complexion. Though he is high, yet hath he respect unto the lowly, and will hear the cry of the distressed when they call upon him, and will make known his goodness and his power.

I lay there till night, and then with great fear I went into the town of Richmond, and enquired the way over the river to go to Petersburgh, where I staid near three weeks, in which time, severe and painful were my exercises: I appeared to be shut up in such a straight case, I could not see which way to take. I tried to pray to the Lord for several days together, that he would be pleased to open some way for me to get along. And I do remember, that when I was brought to the very lowest, suddenly a way appeared, and I believe it was in the ordering of a good providence.

It was so; there came a poor distressed coloured man to the same house where I had taken refuge: we both agreed to take a craft, and go down James' River, which was attended with great difficulty, for we met with strict examination twice, and narrowly escaped; we had like to have been drowned twice, once in the river, and once in the bay. But how unable were we to offer unto God that tribute of praise due to his name, for the miracle of grace shewn to us in our deliverance! Surely wisdom and might are his, and all them that walk in pride he is able to abase. Oh!

> Let all the world fall down and know
> That none but God such power can shew.

We got safe over to the eastern shore of the Chesapeake Bay, where his wife and mine were. And now, reader, I do not tell thee how glad I was, but will leave thee to judge, by supposing it had been thy own case. We landed near Nandew, and then started for Hunting Creek, and we found both our wives; but we found little or no satisfaction, for we were hunted like partridges on the mountains.

My companion got to work on board of a vessel to get clams, perhaps to get some money to bring suit for his freedom (as he had been sold like me, out of the state of Delaware) if his master should come after him from the back countries, who, he said, lived about three hundred and thirty miles from the eastern shore; but, poor fellow, they went on board of the vessel where he had been at work, and talked of taking him up and putting him in jail, and of writing to his master in the back countries. He was said to tell them that he had rather die than to be taken and carried away from his wife again: and it was said, they went down into the cabin and drank, and then came up on deck and seized him, and in the scuffle he slipped out of their hands, and jumped overboard, and tried to swim to an island that was not far off; but they got out the tow boat and went after him, and when they overtook him, he would dive to escape, and still he tried to reach the island: but they watched their opportunity as he rose, when they struck him with the loom of the oar, and knocked his brains out, and he died. And now, reader, consider if you had been carried away from your wife and children, and had got back again, how hard it would seem to be, to be thus chased out of the world; but the great God, whose eyes behold the things that are equal, he continues to make such repent, either in this world, or in the world to come. And now, readers, you have heard of the end of my fellow-sufferer, but I remain as yet, a monument of mercy, thrown up and down on life's tempestuous sea; sometimes feeling an earnest desire to go away and be at rest; but I travel on, in hopes of overcoming at my last combat.

But I will go on to tell of my difficulties. After I came over the bay, I went to see my wife, but was still in trouble; and it was thought best to leave the state of Virginia and go to Dover, and then if my master came after me, to bring suit at Dover, and have a trial for my freedom. The distance from where I then was to Dover was about one hundred and twenty miles: so I started and travelled at nights, and lay by in the daytime. I went on northwards, with great fear and anxiety of mind. It abode on my mind that I should meet with some difficulty before I got to Dover: however, I tried to study on the promises of the Almighty, and so travelled on until I came to a place called Anderson's Cross-Roads; and there I met with the greatest trial I ever met with in all my distress. But the greater the trial, the greater the benefit, if the mind be but staid on that everlasting arm of power, whom the winds and the waves obey. It was so, that I called at them cross-roads to enquire the way to Camden, and I thought I would go to the kitchen where the black people were; but when the door was opened, it was a white man I saw, of a portly appearance, with a sulky down look. Now the day was just a-breaking: he raised up out of his bed, and came towards the door and began to examine me, and I did not know what to say to him; so he soon entangled me in my own talk, and said, I doubt you are a lying: I said I scorn to lie; but I felt very weak and scared, and soon bid him farewell and started. I went some distance along the road, and then went into the woods, and leaned my back against a tree to study, and soon fell to sleep; and when I waked, the sun was up, and I said to myself, if I stand sleeping about here, and that man that examined me in the morning comes to look for me and finds me, he may tie me before I get awake; for the poor fellow that came across the bay with me told me that he travelled all night, and in the morning he met a coloured man, and passed on, and went into the woods and lay down, and went to sleep; and he said there came white men and tied him, and waked him up to go before the justice; but so it was, he got away from them and found me at Petersburgh. So considering on what he had told me, and that man's examining me in the morning, made me I did not know what to do. I concluded to look for a thick place and lay down, and then another thought came into my mind, and that was, to look for a thin place, and there lie down. So I concluded to do so; withal I thought to take a sally downwards, as I enquired of the man to go upwards, I thought by going a little downwards, would be a dodge, and so I should miss him: I thought this plan would do. I then looked for a thin place, and lay down and slept till about nine o'clock, and then waked; and when I awoke, I felt very strange: I said to myself I never felt so in all my distress: I said something was going to happen to me today. So I studied about my feelings until I fell to sleep, and when I awoke, there had come two birds near to me; and seeing the little strange looking birds, it roused up all my senses; and a thought came quick into my mind that these birds were sent to caution me to be away out of this naked place; that there was danger at hand. And as I was about to start, it came into my mind with great energy and force, "if you move out of this circle this day, you will be taken;" for I saw the birds went all round me: I asked myself what this meant, and the impression grew stronger, that I must stay in the circle which the birds made. At the same time a sight of my faults came before me, and a scanty sight of the highness and holiness of the great Creator of all things. And now, reader, I will assure thee I was brought very low, and I earnestly asked what I should do: and while I waited to be instructed, my mind was guided back to the back countries, where I left the waggons about sixty or seventy miles from Richmond, towards the sun-setting; and a question arose in my mind, how I got along all that way, and to see if I could believe that the great God had helped me notwithstanding my vileness. I said in my heart, it must be the Lord, or I could not have got along, and the moment I believed in his help it was confirmed in my mind; if he had begun to help me, and if he did send those birds, he would not let anything come into the circle the birds had made. I therefore tried to confirm myself in the promises of God, and concluded to stay in the circle; and so being weary, travelling all night, I soon fell to sleep; and when I awaked, it was by the noise of the same man that examined me in the morning, and another man, an old conjuror, for so I called him. And the way they waked me was by their walking in the leaves, and coming right towards me. I was then sitting on something about nine inches high from the ground, and when I opened my eyes and saw them right before me, and I in that naked place, and the sun a shining down on me about eleven o'clock, I was struck with dread, but was afraid to move hand or foot: I sat there, and looked right at them; and thought I, here they come right towards me; and the first thought that struck my mind was, am I a going to sit here until they come and lay hands on me? I knew not what to do; but so it was, there stood a large tree about eleven or twelve yards from me, and another big tree had fallen with the top limbs round it: and so it was, through divine goodness, they went the other side of the tree, and the tree that had fallen was between them and me. Then I fell down flat upon my face on the ground; as I raised up my head to look, I saw the actions of this old craftsman. He had a stick like a surveyor's rod; he went along following his stick very diligently. The young man that examined me in the morning had a large club, with the big end downwards and the small end in his hand; he looked first one side, and then on the other. The old man kept on away past me about sixty yards, and then stopped; and I heard him say, "he h'ant gone this way." Then he took his stick and threw it over his shoulder, and pointed this way and that way, until he got it right towards me; and then I heard him say, "come let us go this way." Then he turned his course and came right towards me: then I trembled, and cried in my heart to the Lord, and said, what shall I do? what shall I do? and it was impressed on my mind immediately, "Stand still and see the salvation of the Lord;" the word that was spoken to the children of Israel when at the Red Sea. And I said in my heart, bless the Lord, O my soul; I will try the Lord this time. Here they come; and still that word sounded in my heart; "Stand still and see the salvation of the Lord." They came not quite so near me as the circle the birds had made, when the old man sheered off, and went by me; but the young man stopped and looked right down on me, as I thought, and I looked right up into his eyes; and then he stood and looked right into my eyes, and when he turned away, he ran after the old man, and I thought he saw me; but when he overtook the old man, he kept on, and then I knew he had not seen me. Then I said, bless the Lord; he that gave sight to man's eyes hath kept him from seeing me this day. I looked up among the trees, and said, how dreadful is this place. I said, two great powers have met here this day; the power of darkness, and the power of God; and the power of God has overthrown the power of darkness for me a sinner. I thought I must jump and shout, but another thought struck my mind, that it was not a right time to shout; I therefore refrained. But my heart was overwhelmed at the sight of the goodness and power of God, and his gracious readiness to help the stranger in distress: though he is high, yet hath he respect unto the lowly. It is a solemn truth, he is nigh to all them that call on him, with a view to his greatness and their own nothingness: I felt greatly at loss to know how to adore him according to his excellent greatness. I said, has the maker of heaven and earth took my part? I said again, what could all the world do in comparison with him? I now believed if everybody in the world was engaged against me, that he was able to deliver me out of their hands.

After a while I moved out of that place, and went away to a small stream of water, and staid there a little while, and then went out of that neighbourhood. But whether I did right or not, I know not; for in moving out of that circle so quickly, I became so bewildered as to be quite lost, and did not know what course to take, or what to do; and I thought it was because my faith failed me so quickly. Oh! what pains God doth take to help his otherwise helpless creatures. O that his kindness and care were more considered and laid to heart, and then there would not be that cause to complain that "the ox knoweth his owner, and the ass his master's crib, but Israel doth not know, my people doth not consider." Oh! how marvellous is his loving-kindness toward people of every description, both high and low, rich and poor. O that all people would study to please him, for his goodness and his power; for his wisdom is great, and he knoweth how to deliver all those that look unto him, and will pass by none, no not the least of all his human creatures; and he will make them see that they are of more value than many sparrows; and that they are not their own, but that they are bought with a price.

Now unto the king immortal, invisible, the only wise God, be glory and honour, dominion and power, now and for ever. Amen.

After this, my understanding was opened to see for what purpose this last trial had happened unto me; and it was impressed on my mind that I had come through difficulties and troubles, in order that my faith and confidence might be tried; and that I might be made strong in the faith to believe that so high and holy an one, who had thus marvellously preserved me, would hereafter help so poor an object as me, out of his great mercy and condescension, and that I might be afraid again to sin against his majesty, who had suffered me to be thus sorely tried, that I might see the greatness of my past transgressions, and his boundless loving-kindness and mercy.

SECOND PART

[What follows, was written and communicated to me at my request, but without any idea on the part of the writer, of the purpose to which I designed it; the originals of which, if desired, may be seen by application to me, in order to satisfy any who might feel a doubt with regard to the faithfulness of the transcript. I can, however, assure the reader, that the alterations I have ventured to make, have been almost altogether confined to the spelling.—R. H.]

7th Mo. 24, 1799, I got to Camden. I will yet go on to show the reader my uneasiness of mind after I got to Camden. I then thought I wanted a preparation to adore the goodness of God that had begun with me in the back countries, and had brought me through so many difficulties; but with shame I must confess, I sang his praise, but soon forgot his works: yet the great God pitied me, and exercised a careful constant mind towards me, for my good: Oh! how deceitful is the heart of man.

But not long after I got to Camden, my master came from the state of Virginia, to Camden, Kent County, state of Delaware, where he found me; whereas he had not seen me since he put me aboard of the back country waggon, which, as I suppose, is near three or four hundred miles from Camden. Upon first sight he asked me what I was a going to do? I says, how, master? he asked me, how did I think I was a going to get free, by running and dodging about in that manner? I said, why, master, I have suffered a great deal, and seen a great deal of trouble; I think you might let me go for little or nothing. He said, I won't do that, but I will give you the same chance I gave you before I sent you away; give me forty pounds bond and security, and you may be free: but I replied, I work hard at nights to get a little money to fee my lawyers, and if it had been right for me to be free, I ought to have been free without so much trouble; he asked me who I blamed for my trouble? I answered, I did not consider that I was to blame: Ah! said he, you can see other people's faults, but cannot see your own. I said, master, you can't blame me for a thing I never did; Ah! said he, my wrongs don't make your's right, and that word put me to silence; but I thought, where the laws of the land made liberty the right of any man, he could not be wrong in trying to recover it: but finally he sold me my time for eighty dollars and I dropped the lawsuit. I went to work, and worked it out in a shorter time than he gave me, and then I was free from man.

And when I came to think that the yoke was off my neck, and

how it was taken off, I was made to wonder, and to admire, and to adore the order of kind providence, which assisted me in all the way. But I found in me a disposition to wander from the path of life, and forget the favour bestowed upon me, and went astray too shameful to be mentioned.

But in this lost condition there came a reasoning to me, to consider where I was a going, and where I should end; and to consider on the shortness of time, and the length of eternity: and a thought came into my mind, assuring me that my life was in the hand of God, and that he was looking for better behaviour from me; and that he was angry with me every day; and that he had whetted his sword, and made ready his arrows to shoot at me. Then my understanding began to be enlightened, to see my dreadful state by nature; and the more I considered on the nature and heinousness of my sin, both in thought, word, and deed, the more I was distressed in mind; but I found the sentence of death was passed against me, and it pressed on my mind, if I kept on going against light, I should soon feel the heat of the burning lake, or the misery of those that are driven to darkness at death. And when I considered the power of God, and for that power to be poured out upon me to all eternity, I began then to examine into my state and condition, and I found I had a falling spirit, prone to evil as the sparks fly upward; then I set myself to think how I could escape the misery that was coming on me. I considered my punishment would be as bad as those that went to darkness in old time: then I began to consider what God had done to save mankind from that fearful condition; and while I thought on the many ways he had taken to show his earnest mind to save sinners, this consideration moderated my distress; but when I remembered my own ways that were not good, I felt ashamed even to lift my eyes to heaven to ask pardon for my sins; but the shortness of time, and the length of awful eternity, so arrested my mind that I was made to realize eternal misery, and to cry like Jonah, as out of the belly of hell, for mercy and for pardon for all my sins. Oh! the thought of being amongst that black crew, when the Lord rains down snares, fire, and brimstone, and horribleness, terrified me much.

And now, reader, I will here record that God is rich in mercy towards sinners of the deepest die; for when every other method failed, to show his steadfast mind to save me, he sent a little boy to me with his finger at a text in a sermon book, "The wicked is driven away in his wickedness, but the righteous hath hope in his death;" the same text I had heard a Methodist preacher take on a funeral occasion; then that little boy coming to me with his finger pointing at the same in the sermon book, it was about noon, the people nearly all gone to meeting, and I reading very earnest in the Testament. I took the book and began to read, and it pleased infinite goodness to look on me from the throne of his highness, and being unwilling that I should perish eternally, he sent down his awakening power, and I was made to quake and tremble; and an impression abode on my mind, that God was a true, and a just, and a holy God, and that no unclean thing could rest in his holy habitation. I saw I was a sinner condemned to die, but a call reached my soul, "take heed that you entertain no hopes of heaven, but what are built on a solid foundation;" a question arose in my mind, what foundation I had to hope for heaven? I examined and found I had none but what was built on the sand, and at death I must fall into hell; which caused a cry to be started from my heart to my maker, what I should do? A thought passed through my mind to make a resolution to amend my way, and turn and be good, but a second thought came powerfully into my mind, if I made another resolution and broke it as I had done, the door of mercy would be for ever shut against me. Then the good spirit brought to my mind the dangers and deaths from which I had been delivered, through the mercy of an indulgent God, and how I had called on him in trouble and he delivered me, and had answered me in the secret place of thunder; and it was pressed on my mind, that it was too dangerous to make another fool's start: then I seemed to be in the wilderness, not knowing what to do. A thought arose in my mind, you have got into a pretty fix now, afraid even to make a resolution of amendment; then an enquiry again arose in my heart, from that depth of thought, what I should do? at the same time the handwriting of God appeared against me, and that power that once shook the earth shook my soul and body: it pressed on my mind that it was the great power of God: and that word came into my mind, "they that resist shall receive to themselves damnation;" at the same time, the spirit of truth brought all things to my remembrance, my sins old and new, little and big, and I saw how hateful they all were in the sight of a holy God. Now let the Lord be praised both now and for ever, for the exceeding riches of his grace to all who will look at their sins, and his goodness, and consider and think, before it be too late, and be sorry, and turn from the evil of their ways that they may understand the truth.

And now, reader, attend to the word sent to me in my distress, which was this: "believe on the name of the Lord Jesus Christ, and thou shalt be saved." Oh! then, and not till then, did I ever desire saving faith; but I could not attain to it by all the exertion I could make: but Oh! reader, I found here in my distress, that faith is the gift of God, and that grace is not sown in the heart, till the heart is broken and contrite: that is, in earnest to study and enter into the saving plan of life and salvation, which is: "Let the wicked forsake his way, and the unrighteous man his thoughts, and let them turn unto the Lord, and he will have mercy upon him, and abundantly pardon all that is passed." But when I was put to the test to try my faith, I found I had none: then in the bitterness of my spirit, I desired the Lord to give me to feel the power of saving faith; and I struggled to lay hold on that word, "Ask and ye shall receive, seek and ye shall find;" but a question made me quake—which question was this: is your heart right? then I trembled, but could not tell whether my heart was right or not; and while I desired to know myself, this form passed through my mind; "Are you willing now to renounce the devil and all his works, and all the pomp and vanity of this wicked world, and all the sinful lusts of the flesh;" and I was enabled in my sinking, distressed state, to forsake every forbidden way for the sake of peace and pardon.—Then did God send down the power of saving faith, then, Oh! how terrible I saw the length, and breadth, and depth, and height of God's eternal law: I also saw that heaven and earth would pass away, before one jot or title of his law should fail, or fall to the ground. Man must be converted, or never enter into the kingdom of heaven. A thought came into my heart, to go out to some secret place to pray; and as I walked I trembled, and when I got to the place, I could only pray, "Lord have mercy upon me." I cried as if falling into black despair, and having consented to forsake every wrong way, God, for Christ's sake, had mercy on me, and pardoned my sins: Glory be to God, for ever and ever, Amen. Oh! praise the Lord, whose mercy is over all his works, from generation to generation, who hath put down the mighty from their seats, and hath exalted them of low degree, and ever holds his servant Israel in remembrance of his mercy. Oh! how faithful and true he is, to all who will yield to the striving of his spirit in their own hearts, before it takes its everlasting flight. Oh! how careful ought we to be, for fear we be left to ourselves; then blindness of mind, and hardness of heart will take place, and the soul be left to stumble on the dark mountains of unbelief, on which many have stumbled since the world began for not following the light that visits their mind; which appeareth in youth, and continueth with some shorter, and some longer, according to the entertainment this heavenly messenger gets in the hearts of all people. Oh! reader, think how many are now in the road to ruin, who are still slighting the call of grace; and if they keep on, must overtake them that are there already; and now I pray that none that sees this, may ever go another step towards the pit, from whence there is no return.

> Oh! that all may taste and see
> The riches of his grace:
> The arms of love that compass me,
> Would all mankind embrace!

Having given the reader a short account of the abundant mercy bestowed on me by a bountiful God, who is engaged to raise poor sinners from a depth of sin and shame to the height of happiness and glory; and if they yield to him he will do it, for faithful is he that has called you, who also will do it, if ye be willing and obedient. I now return to give the reader an account of the difficulties I met with in buying my wife.

She was born a slave, and continued a slave till she was about thirty-two years of age, and I about twenty-eight years old; and having paid for myself, and got a little money beforehand, I was provoked to purpose buying of her. Before this, she and her master had fallen out, and he purposed to send her, and our first daughter, about three months old, away to the back countries; and how to do I did not know: to go with her I knew not where, or buy her at his price, brought me to a stand: and while I was perplexed, there came a messenger to me, who said her master had carried the negro buyer with him from court, in order to sell her to him; but when they were about to count out the money, his daughter broke out and cried in such a distressing manner for my little daughter, that it caused him to recant at that time; but he made two more attempts, but was misput [disconcerted] most providentially. At the same time, her master and I were both on one class-paper, which made it very trying to me to keep up true love and unity between him and me in the sight of God: this was a cause of wrestling in my mind; but that scripture abode with me, "He that loveth father or mother, wife or children, more than me, is not worthy of me;" then I saw it became me to hate the sin with all my heart, but still the sinner love: but I should have fainted, if I had not looked to Jesus, the author of my faith: but I would remark that at the very moment I was about to give up, the Lord appeared for my help, to my great surprise. It pleased almighty goodness, to give my wife's mistress that power which cut Rahab and wounded the Dragon; and she spoke with such concern of mind and said, "Oh do let Solomon have her; I have been afraid to speak, but I want him to have her, he appears to want to have her;" and these words, with a few more I omit, were attended with such force to her master's mind, that he gave up with a whining tone, and said "He may have her;" so I hired her, and took her away the same day. After the year was out I went to pay him his money for her hire, and it being on a meeting day, some friends there who saw me pay the money, said to me, "you had better buy your wife at once;" her master answered, "I want him to buy her:" then they insisted on knowing his price; he said, "a hundred dollars, and give in all the hire;" which was fifty dollars less than ever he had mentioned before: I then said I would undertake it: then they insisted we should have it in writing, and we had it so. Thus I entered purchase of my wife, one hundred and three dollars and a third, which is thirty-one pounds Virginia money. When the articles were drawn, I desired the writer to put down what was paid, and what was due; and then went on working and paying, until I had paid all but forty dollars and fourpence.

But here I will mention a remarkable circumstance: I grew uneasy about my wife and me living together without being married; and while I was studying how to bring it about, a tradition arose in the Methodist Church, to turn out all free members that lived together as man and wife without being married: at the same time, preaching being held at her master's house, the day came round for meeting; after public meeting, the class was called, when to my great surprise, the preacher asked me if I was free? I answered "yes:" he asked "if I had a wife?" I said "yes:" he asked, "are you married?" I answered "no:" he asked "if my wife was free?" I said "no, not properly so:" he asked "who had any claim on her?" The class leader said "Brother Melson:" the preacher asked me "if I was willing to be married?" I answered "yes," and added, "I had been concerned about it, but did not know how to bring it to pass:" the preacher said, "it is easy driving when we are willing;" and then, before the society, added his reason as above, and said, "I suppose Brother Melson will have no objection." Melson, her master, answered, "they may be married, and welcome, for what I care:" then said the preacher, "you can just give him an instrument to the clerk of the court, and he can get a licence and be married, and finish your business afterwards:" he then wrote to the same effect, and I went and got a licence, and we were married according to law.

Now the reader may take notice, that when we bargained, her master agreed to free her upon my paying him his money, or give me a bill of sale to empower me to free her; but after I had paid him about sixty-three dollars, he then took pet, and said he would take her away, without I paid him all, which was forty dollars and fourpence due: now he had given me receipts for all the money I had paid him, but no bill of sale or freedom. By this time my wife had one child after we bargained: he said he "would have the negroes or money;" but we being married, according to law, it made her mine; and the Judge of the court told me that "her master could not get her, nor any more money:" but I felt easiest to do according to bargain, if he would fulfill according to agreement: but it was with great difficulty I got him to fix the business; when done, then I paid him, and then she was manumitted free, and I desired rest.

But I had one child in bondage, my only son, my first-born son; and having worked through the purchase of myself and wife, I thought I would give up my son to the ordering of divine providence. So we worked on and got to farming, and were favoured, so that we did not fall through in twelve or thirteen years, renting land, and paying up, and keeping clear of the world.

Now the reader may take notice, that as I was going on thus, my son's master died; and his property had to be sold, and my son had to be sold, as the other property, at public sale: the backwoodsmen being come over, and giving such large prices for slaves, it occasioned a great concern to come over my mind; and I began to tell my concern to some friends, white and coloured, rich and poor; and they all with one accord persuaded me to buy him, that is, my son: I answered I could have no heart, because he was appraised at the death of his master at four hundred dollars. It being the latter end of the war in America, 1813, and the times dark and dull, I was much afraid to attempt to buy him, but I told my friends what was like to befall me; that when my son was nine months old, then I was sent away from him, as I told the reader in the beginning of my journal, and then I went through a fit of distress, and now he is like to be sent away from me, and then I shall have to go through another fit, and it will seem like double trouble. But my friends and neighbours continued pressing it on me, to meet the day of sale, and buy him; and finally I concluded to do it, and met the day of sale.

Then the crier made a noise in the courtyard, before the courthouse door, and said, "a likely young negro fellow for sale," and then asked for a bid; the second time he asked for a bid, I bid two hundred dollars, which was half what he was appraised to, at the death of his master. As soon as ever I had bid two hundred dollars, the man I feared would buy and sell him to the back-country men, bid three hundred and thirty-three dollars and a third, which was thirty-three dollars and a third more than I had intended to bid, which beat down all my courage. But a thought struck me, don't give out so, so don't; so I bid a shilling: then the same man bid twenty dollars, which was three hundred and fifty-four dollars: at that I sighed, and thought I must give him up, and let him go; but

a thought came into my mind, to bid one time more, and not bid
any more, if he went to the West Indies: so I bid a cent; but the
crier said, no Solomon, not a cent, a shilling: well says I, let it go.
As soon as my bid was confirmed, the same man went on, and I
gave up then. My son had chosen a master, a justice of peace in
town, said to be a good master, who had promised me before the
sale began, that if he saw me give up, he would try and buy him;
so he began and moved him up to three hundred and fifty-seven
dollars, then he gave up. Then three great men, who had agreed to
be my securities, were standing by; one of them was a Methodist
preacher, very rich; he looked at me as if he pitied me, and when
he saw my son was likely to go off the wrong way, he says, "three
shillings;" and when he spoke I cried, and turned off, and went and
leaned against the courthouse, under a weight of concern; and as I
was considering, that word came into my mind, "this is their hour
and the power of darkness," so I gave him up then. Now it did appear, the very moment I gave him up, and hope left me, then help
came; for it pleased the Most High, who pitieth every sorrowful
soul, in the riches of his mercy, to look on two young men that were
acquainted with me, and to touch their hearts, with such a sense of
sympathy and pity towards my case, that they could not endure;
and the dear young neighbour man, a great man's son, says to my
young master, who were both standing in the ring looking on, he
says, "I had rather give twenty dollars out of my own pocket, than
Solomon should not get him; but if Solomon will bid once more, I
will give him four dollars:" my young master answered, "if you will
give him five dollars, I will give him five dollars," and says, "let us
go and tell him;" so they both came to me, as I was leaning against
the courthouse wall, and said in a moving tone, "Solomon, if you
will bid one more bid, we will give you five dollars apiece;" I turned
round and says, "a shilling," which was a shilling upon three hundred and sixty dollars. Then a great man said, "there, let the old
man have him, he is his son, he wants him, he can get security:" so
they kept at that till the switch went down; so he was knocked off
to me at three hundred and sixty dollars and a shilling. Then the
tenderhearted young man that first proposed to my young master,
went into the store, and brought five round silver dollars, and gave
to me in the office, where I went to sign the bond; then three of
my securities agreed upon the spot to make me up twenty dollars
at the day of payment.

By this time I got raised up from my sadness and went out after
I had signed the bond, so much revived and clothed with such a
spirit of faith and courage, believing a way would be opened for

me to get through, though I could not tell how; but as I came out
of the office, I met the executor and administrator who said to me,
"well, Solomon, you have got Spence after all;" I said, "yes, master
George, but I gave up, and if it had not been for those men who
pitied me, and who did as they did, I never should have got him,
and now what will you give me?" He put his hand into his pocket,
and pulled out a round silver dollar and gave me, which caused me
to rejoice more for that one dollar, than for the twenty dollars promised me just before in the office: and now I will give the reader my
reason why I rejoiced more for the one than for the twenty dollars;
because two days before the sale, he, the executor and administrator,
offered a challenge to me and to them I trusted in, touching the sale
of my son; now, as he was the first that put me in heart to try to buy
my son, I thought it right, two days before the sale, to go to him
and hear what he had to say to me; and when I got there, he says,
"well Solomon, where are you going?" I said, "I am come down to
meet the day of sale;" he said, "well, what are you going to do?" I
answered, I want to buy my son if I can; he says, "you do?" and
added, "you will have a hard time of it;" I answered, "I have been
thinking so;" he says, "Solomon, there are four men who say they
will give four hundred dollars for your son;" then says I "they will
get him;" he says, "Solomon what are you willing to give?" I answered, "not more than two hundred and fifty dollars;" he says, "you
will not get him for that, but I suppose you are so much in favour
with the people, nobody will bid against you; but if nobody will bid
against you, I will; you need not think you are going to get him for
nothing," and he seemed angry; then I was very sad at that saying,
and says, "master George, you was the very first man that put me in
heart, and now you seem to put me out of heart;" then he, in an
angry gust of manner, said, "well Solomon, try your faith, and
added, you remember the birds, and how you exercised faith, and
was delivered; now try your faith;" as though he felt as if he could
defy the armies of the living God: but when he gave me the dollar,
then I thought of the challenge "now try your faith." I then believed
that God could work and none could hinder him: although it appeared this man had done what he could to bring me into that
difficulty, yet, when through the goodness of the Highest I was encouraged, as above described, and being brought down as it were to
nothing before the Lord, I was enabled to ask him in such a way
that his hand and heart appeared to be opened, so that he gave me
that dollar, for which I rejoiced more than for the twenty dollars
promised me just before, as above stated: then was I enabled to
sing aloud the praises of our king in spirit and in truth, who ever

sits above, till all his foes submit and bow to his command and fall beneath his feet: I confess the eyes of my mind appeared to be dazzled, as I was let into a sight of the great goodness of the Highest in undertaking for me: but Oh! reader, I felt a fear, lest my behaviour should not be suitable to the kindness and favour showed towards me.

Now there was an impression on my mind, that the Father of Mercy would do greater things for me, for his own honour and praise, and my everlasting advantage, if my behaviour was right before him: it was impressed on my mind that he was unchangeable in his purposes and designs, which are to set the captive souls at liberty, if they will follow him in the path of obedience; and no degrees of grace will destroy man's capability of choosing, whether he will do right or wrong; doing right gives a secret satisfaction to the mind; but doing wrong is followed by a secret uneasiness, because God will be a swift witness against the wrong, and will justify what is right in man's words and deeds, when done with right views. Oh! that all men would study the end of their creation, and act accordingly; then they would walk in the light of his countenance indeed, and "in his name they would rejoice all the day, and in his righteousness for ever be exalted;"

> Then should their sun in smiles decline,
> And bring a peaceful night;

which, may all who read these lines, desire, seek, and obtain, through Jesus Christ our Lord. Amen, and Amen.

Extract of a letter to R. H. dated, Camden, 1st of 2nd month, 1824.

ESTEEMED FRIEND,

"I received thy* book and pens, with a letter unsealed, yesterday, dated 1st month, 17th, 1824, requesting some account of my deceased mother and daughters. Dear Robert, thy letter discovered a sign of generosity, or concern, for the good of all people; and this concern enables thee to be condescending to men of low estate; wherefore I pray, that the condescending grace of God that has begun with thee may continue with thee all the days of thy life; and that through the all-sufficient merits of Christ, both thee and

---

* The reader will observe that Solomon frequently makes use of the pronoun "thee," when addressing an individual; this occurs simply from the circumstance that it is a mode of speech not unusual in some parts of America with people of different denominations, and does not arise from any connexion that he has ever had with the society of friends.—R. H.

thy family, all may be brought to Sion's hill; and that you may be enabled to join the blessed company, to sing redeeming love, for ever and ever, Amen.

"If thou go home to England, then I shall see thee no more; but I trust to see you in the land of rest, where partings are no more, ° ° ° ° ° the grace of our Lord Jesus Christ, be with your spirits. Amen.

SOLOMON BAYLEY.

I now proceed to give some brief account of the nativity, life, and death of my mother. She was born of a Guinea Woman, who was brought from Guinea about the year 1690, as near as I can guess; and said to be about eleven years old when brought to America. But oh! how different is the situation of things towards the coloured people since that day; the Lord certainly is at work in the rising generations, to have more pity and compassion than in ages past. My Grandmother was bought into one of the most barbarous families of that day; and although treated hard, was said to have fifteen sons and daughters: she lived to a great age, until she appeared weary of life.

My mother had thirteen sons and daughters; she served the same cruel family, until they died. Then great distress and dispersion took place: our young mistress married, and brought our family out of the state of Virginia into the state of Delaware. After some years her husband removed back into Virginia: after that law took place against moving slaves, which entitled all of us to freedom; we made a move to recover it by that law, but we soon were all sold and scattered very wide apart, some to the east, and some west, north, and south. My father and mother they pretended to set free, to stop a trial in court, and after they had been free about eleven months, they came upon them unawares; my father Abner, sister Margaret, and brother Abner, were taken in the night, and carried to Long Island, one of the West India Islands, and sold to Abner Stephen; he has sent two letters here, or we never should have known what had become of them.

On the same night as above cited, my mother being in the house, they meant to take her; but she made an excuse to go out at the door, and ran and left her sucking child, and her two other children, and her husband my father: now it being winter time, the child cried; they therefore left it and carried away my father and the other two children. Then some friend took the child and carried it to mother; then mother took her son, about eleven months old, and travelled near a hundred miles from the State of Virginia to

Dover in Kent County, State of Delaware; and from thence to New Jersey.

In this time she testified she experienced great affliction both of body and mind; but at length, like Hagar, she was enabled to see Him who had seen her in all her affliction, and not only to see him in the works of creation, but also in the works of his providence; and her mind was enlightened to see into the nature and largeness of her sins. She also testified that the view of eternity and of eternal consequences so distressed her mind that it swallowed up her present distress, and so she was induced to give up the lesser, and attend to the greater; namely, to find peace and rest in the life to come: she was enabled to go on in search after truth until she experienced peace of mind, and evidence of pardon for all her sins, which was her greatest concern till death.

Now the number of years that we were parted, mother and I, was about eighteen; except that once in a great hurry, I travelled more than a hundred miles to see her; at the same time I left keeping of a saw mill, my wife, and young child about a month old, and taking with me seventeen or eighteen dollars, which all became a sacrifice with my time, to the relief of my mother; but I was favoured to find that satisfaction which I esteemed more than time or money.

Now it came to pass after eighteen years, my mind was visited with a concern to go to Africa, after that Paul Cuffee had been there, and brought good tidings from that place;* therefore I thought it good to put out my children in good families, where they could get some schooling, and learn how to work, and then get my wife in with some good sort of people; and being advised to wait till it should seem proper to recommend me to that service, I thought it right to engage in some profitable business, and was hired to attend a mill, in which time the case of my mother came before me, and I sent for her to the State of Delaware from New Jersey; and when brought together, it was indeed like heaven on earth begun; we could sit and tell of the dangers and difficulties we had been brought through; so my mother was favoured to end her days with me: she, like my grandmother, lived to a great age, and appeared weary of affliction, and of this troublesome world; her mind became disordered; she desired a short illness, which was granted; she died the third day after she was taken sick, with very little complaint or struggle; but was thought to have fallen asleep.

* This concern was doubtless of a religious character: the death of the pious and enterprising Paul Cuffee, was the probable cause of the visit being relinquished.—R. H.

A brief account of my eldest daughter, Margaret Bayley, who died in the twenty-fourth year of her age.

She was a pleasant child in her manners and behaviour, yet fond of gay dress and new fashions; yet her mind was much inclined to her book, and to read good lessons.

And it pleased the Father of mercy to open her understanding, to see excellent things out of his law, and to convince her that it was his will she should be holy here and happy hereafter; but custom, habit, and shame seemed to chain her down, so that she appeared like one that was halting between two opinions.

But about a month before she was taken for death, she went to Meeting under a concern about her future state; and the Meeting appeared to be favoured with the outpouring of the spirit of love and of power: Margaret came home under great concern of mind, and manifested a wonderful change in her manners and behaviour; I believe the whole family were affected at the sight of the alteration, which indeed appeared like that of the prodigal son coming home to his father; for my own part I felt fear and great joy; such was her delight to read the Bible, and ask the meaning of certain texts of Scripture, which evidenced a concern to make sure work for eternity.

In this frame of mind she was taken for death; she appeared very desirous to live for the first four weeks, but was very patient, and of a sweet temper and disposition all the time: I recollect but one instance when she was known to give way to peevish fretfulness; then I, feeling the evil spirit striving to get the advantage of her, very tenderly and earnestly admonished her not to regard trifles, but to look to that power which was able to save her; and from that time she became passive and resigned.

The following two weeks her pain was great, and baffled all the force of medicine: a few days before her departure, she was urged with much brokenness of heart to make confession; when she was let into a view of the vanity of the world, with all its glittering snares; and said she could not rest till her hair was cut off; for she said, "I was persuaded to plait my hair against my father's advice, and I used to tie up my head when father would come to see me, and hide ruffles and gay dress from him, and now I cannot rest till my hair is cut off." I said, "no, my daughter, let it be till thee gets well:" she answered, "Oh! no, cut it now:" so I to pacify her took and cropped it.

After this she appeared filled with raptures of joy, and talked of going, as if death had lost its sting; this was about three days before her departure; she seemed to have her senses as long as she could speak: a little before her speech left her, she called us all, one by one, held out her hand, bade us farewell, and looked as if she felt that assurance and peace that destroyed the fear of death; and while she held out her hands, she earnestly charged us to meet her in heaven.

Thus ends the account of Margaret Bayley, daughter of Solomon and Thamar Bayley, who departed this life the 26th of the 3rd month, 1821, aged twenty-three years, eleven months, and twenty-eight days.

To the pious reader: I desire to give the pious a brief account of the life and death of my youngest daughter, Leah Bayley, who departed this life the 27th of the 7th month, 1821, aged twenty-one years, six months, and one day.

She, from a child, was more weak and sickly than her sister Margaret, and the thought of leaving her here in this ill-natured world caused me many serious moments; but the great Parent of all good, in the greatness of his care, took her away, and relieved me of the care of her forever.

Weakness of body and mind appeared in her as she grew up; and an inclination to vanity and idleness; but being bound out under an industrious mistress, to learn to work and to have schooling, her mind soon became much inclined to her book and then to business. Her school mistress gave her a little book, concerning some pious young people that lived happily and died happily, and were gone to heaven: namely,

> Young Samuel, that little child,
> Who served the Lord, liv'd undefiled.
> Like young Abijah I must be,
> That good things may be found in me.
> Young Timothy, that blessed youth,
> Who sought the Lord and loved the truth.
> I must not sin as others do
> Lest I lie down in sorrow too.

These blessed examples won her heart, so as to bury every other enjoyment: she seemed to possess as great a deadness to the world as any young woman I ever observed: she seemed not ashamed to read in any company, white or coloured; and she read to the sick with intense desire, which appeared from her weeping, and solid manner of behaviour. She seemed to desire to walk in the fear of the

Lord all the day long: everybody that observed her remarked her serious steady behaviour; she seemed as if she was trying to imitate those good children whom she read about; and so continued until she was taken sick; and although her sickness was long and sharp, yet she bore it like a lamb.

A few days before her decease, I was noticing how hard she drew her breath: she looked very wistful at me, and said, "O! father, how much I do suffer:" I answered, "yes, my dear, I believe thee does:" then, after a long pause, she said, "but I think I never shall say I suffer too much:" this I apprehend was extorted from a view of the sufferings of Christ, and her own imperfections: this was about three days before her decease. The day she died, she called us all, one by one, and like her sister Margaret, held out her hand, and with much composure of mind bade us farewell, as if she was only going a short walk, and to return.

Extract of a letter to R. H., dated 3rd month, 26th, 1824.

I thank thee, dear Robert, for spending a thought on so poor and unworthy a thing as I am; but I especially thank your God and my God, for putting it into thy heart to enquire anything about the work of grace on my mind. I trust it is with gratitude I now write unto thee of my call to the ministry: and first I may say,

> God works in a mysterious way,
> His wonders to perform.

Secondly, he knows how to get himself honour and praise by the most feeble; for to undertake to make such a creature as I am, work in his vineyard, was amazing to me; but there was a great work to do, to make me fit for anything at all; surely he called me oftener than he did Samuel, when he was a child: but after I was savingly converted to God, he was pleased to pour into my heart a measure of his universal love; and when my heart was filled with love towards God, and good will towards all mankind, then a longing desire that all people might taste and see the riches of his grace continued with me day and night; then a strong impression to go in the fear of the Lord and speak to men of all descriptions seemed to be required of me.

But Oh! dear friend, after my mind was thus prepared, I had a great warfare and strife; first, with man-fear, and a man-pleasing spirit, then with shame, desire of praise, and a good name.

Now, dear friend, in this exercise of mind there were some scriptures came into my mind, to encourage and strengthen me; such as the II. Corinthians, xii. 9—II. Kings, v. 4—I. Corinthians, i. 21, 27, 28, and chapter xi. 3. also chapter ix. 16, 22—II. Corinthians, xi, 29—Daniel xii. 3—Isaiah vi. 5—Jeremiah i. 6—John i. 15, and chapter iii. 2—Hebrews xi. 34; all these scriptures mightily helped to encourage me to go forward in speaking to a dying people the words of eternal life. Oh! what an affecting view of the worth of souls came into my mind; and I thought, if I could be made instrumental in the hand of the Lord in saving one soul, it would be matter of rejoicing to all eternity. So I went out trusting in the Lord; but I should soon have fainted in mind, if it had not been for the encouragement I met with, both from God and man. Now to Him that sits upon the throne be honour and praise, world without end. Amen.

With good wishes to thee and thine, I conclude, thy friend,

SOLOMON BAYLEY.

*The Sword of Truth going "forth,
conquering and to conquer."*

THE

ORIGIN, HORRORS, AND RESULTS

OF

SLAVERY,

FAITHFULLY AND MINUTELY DESCRIBED,
IN A SERIES OF FACTS,
AND ITS ADVOCATES PATHETICALLY ADDRESSED.

BY THE REV. W. PAUL QUINN,
OF AFRICAN DESCENT.

"Gird thy sword upon thy thigh, O most mighty, with thy glory
and thy majesty. And in thy majesty ride prosperously, because of
truth, and meekness, and righteousness; and thy right hand shall
teach thee terrible things. Thine arrows are sharp in the heart of
the king's enemies; whereby the people fall under thee."—Ps. xlv.

PITTSBURGH. 1834.

INTRODUCTION

My dearly beloved fellow countrymen, and courteous reader, from
whatever nation you may be the honorable descendant, suffer me to
lay before you a subject which is calculated to awaken your tenderest commiseration, and Christian exertions for a portion of no less
than two and a half millions of Africans, who are in a state of servitude, suffering, and degradation truly lamentable! The theme of

liberty is always inspiring. The song of liberty is always enrapturing. The enjoyment of liberty is always elevating. The attainment of liberty is always exhilarating. The cause of liberty is always becoming, to all nations, more and more endearing, and the unbounded diffusion of civil and religious liberty is always becoming more and more interesting, and worthy of the achievement of the combined operation of the whole world. Millions of philanthropists and patriots in many nations are diffusing to the South, North, East, and West the grand and glorious principles of civil and religious liberty; and whole nations, in various parts of the world, are awakening to a perception of the grandeur, the inestimable value, and the heaven-derived origin and excellence of liberty; therefore it is equally our duty as our dignity, our privilege as our happiness, and our safety as our interest, to stir ourselves from our lethargy, embark in the cause of freedom—to rank ourselves on the Lord's side, and fight the good fight of faith.

My dearly beloved fellow countrymen, what the Apostle Paul said respecting his patriotic and Christian feelings, in behalf of his fellow countrymen, the Jews, I now can safely say in behalf of all the two millions and a half of my brothers and sisters, who are in the most ignominious bondage and cruelly oppressive slavery, "Brethren, my heart's desire and prayer to God for Afric's sons and daughters is, that they may be saved." "I say the truth in Christ, I lie not, my conscience also bearing me witness in the holy spirit, that I have great heaviness and continual sorrow in my heart. For I could wish myself accursed from Christ for my brethren, my kinsmen according to the flesh." My dear fellow countrymen, admire the grand patriotic spirit that so eminently distinguished and immortalized Queen Esther, when the King said unto her, at the banquet of wine, "What is thy petition, Queen Esther, and it shall be granted thee; and what is thy request, and it shall be performed, even to half of the kingdom? Then Esther the Queen answered and said, if I have found favor in thy sight, O King, and if it please the King, let my life be given at my petition, and my people at my request: for we are sold, I and my people, to be destroyed, to be slain, and to perish; but if we had been sold for bond men and bond women I had held my tongue, although the enemy could not countervail the King's damage." I say the grand and patriotic spirit that so gloriously distinguished and immortalized the soul of Queen Esther, should fill, distinguish, and characterize every male and female in America. We should cherish and manifest a spirit of sympathy for every brother and sister in slavery. And in attempting to communicate my views, feelings, and desires in this tract, I hope the spirit of God and of glory will most copiously and mightily rest upon me and you. I have faithfully given you a few of my thoughts on Slavery, and have endeavored in a few pages to give you, from the pen of a most faithful witness, a description of Slavery as it has existed in various parts and ages of the world. Therefore I invite you to a careful perusal of these pages, and beseech you to acquire a greater measure of the spirit of unfeigned patriotism, or love to those who are our kinsmen according to the flesh. Powerfully and daily beseech our One Common and Almighty Father to pour on all the planters, and their two millions and a half of human and immortal beings in the most heart-rending slavery, "the spirit of grace and supplication, that they may look on him whom they have pierced, and mourn for him as a man mourneth for an only son, and be in bitterness for him, as one that is in bitterness for his first born." Cherish, teach, and widely diffuse a spirit of enquiry and sympathy respecting the bereavements, sufferings, degradation, and rights of our fellow brethren in bondage. Beloved reader, may God Almighty soon address the captive sons and daughters of Africa as he addressed the captive daughter of Zion: "Shake thyself from the dust; arise, and sit down, O Jerusalem: loose thyself from the bonds of thy neck, O captive daughter of Africa. For thus saith the Lord, ye have been sold for nought to your profit, but ye shall be redeemed without money. For thus saith the Lord God, my people went down aforetime into Egypt to sojourn there; and the Assyrian oppressed them without cause. Now, therefore, what have I here, saith the Lord, that my people is taken away for nought? They that rule over them make them howl, saith the Lord; and my name continually every day is blasphemed; therefore my people shall know my name: therefore they shall know in that day that I am he that doth speak; behold it is I."

Not only one quarter, but every quarter of the world, is the object of God's love; not only one nation, but every nation, was foretold by God to Abraham, "that in him and in his seed, viz. Christ, all nations of the earth should be blessed;" therefore, if God's almighty and infinitely munificent love is fixed on the whole world, the sable sons and daughters of Africa are a portion of that world; and they, as a nation, are within the range of the most glorious and precious of all promises. Now, my esteemed reader, if there are such wonderful, glorious, and enriching blessings in store for the African nation, and the mighty wheel of Providence is about to make a revolution which will deluge the whole world with the moral glory of God; then what are we not to expect from our heavenly Father in these latter days? "O'er the gloomy hills of darkness, look, my soul, be still and gaze, all the promises do travel with a glorious day of grace; blessed jubilee, let thy glorious morning dawn."

My object in thus addressing you by the press, is to excite you to watch and pray daily at God's throne, until the spirit of light, love and liberty shall be poured down on every soul of the eight hundred millions that people our globe. O, reader, may you have the spirit of God, for where it is there is liberty. I now leave you and my little book to God and his blessing.

W. P. QUINN

ON THE IRRATIONALITY OF SLAVERY

SLAVERY originates, diversifies, augments, and perpetuates the greatest physical and mental sufferings, with the provision of the fewest and feeblest consolations to sustain the mind under them.

Where human suffering of the most aggravated and appalling nature exists, on a scale of no less magnitude than between two and three millions of our dark-complexioned fellow-brethren of mankind, without being counteracted or counterbalanced by an opposite scale of felicities, or joyful considerations of an equal or superior magnitude, then it is a system possessing a dreadfully preponderating power in annihilating all good, and of creating evil and misery of every form, and of every degree, and as such is most justly worthy of the supreme and universal abhorrence of the population of the whole world, and should be regarded as a system most equitably doomed to everlasting extinction.

If slavery in its present form, under its present reign, and in its extensive empire over such a large mass of the human species, had bodily and moral good commensurable to its necessary and peculiar evils, it might be tolerated; but since its direful consequences, and tremendous moral destruction, are its ruling and degrading properties, its verdict should be pronounced, its execution should be carried into effect, and its funeral dirge should be sung by the whole of the above two millions of Afric's sons and daughters; and then the real Church of Christ, which is a true, complete, and invincible anti-slavery society, might adopt the apocalyptic strains of the angel respecting Babylon, and apply them to her cause, "Who came down from heaven, having great power, and the earth was lightened with his glory." And he cried mightily, with a loud voice, Slavery the Great is fallen! is fallen!

Slavery, with the utmost acts of severity and cruelty, compels her more than two millions of unhappy victims to toil and labour in sultry climes, and under tropical suns, without being qualified to gain human love, the strongest principle, and the main spring of all moral action on its side, or to set it in motion.

Had America two millions and a half of steamboats trading between the northern and southern extremities of this great and grand continent, all loaded with the blessings, wealth, and multitudes of human lives of its citizens, if the engineers of all these boats had agreed, when at sea, that they would extinguish their fires, and thereby destroy their steam, what then could be expected? Could the proprietors of these two millions and a half of steamboats expect that their vessels could move in the same direction, with the same safety, and with the same velocity, without as with steam? How can two millions of steamboats, with the most valuable cargoes, be managed, when the motions they make are as the currents, winds, and tempests of the heaven and sea are pleased to drive them?

If the two millions and a half of male and female slaves who are compelled to work under a tropical sun, without human love, the tenderest, strongest, and sweetest principle of their nature, being set in motion, then how unutterably melancholy is their condition! They are contemned, anathematized, and tormented with horrid injuries, for being lazy, for not doing their work fast enough, and more abundantly; but how can they work? They have no moral steam, no moral fire; their cruel drivers, that mangle their flesh, shed their blood, and disfigure their persons, and so frequently violate their chastity, compel them to labour. But need I tell you, tender-hearted reader, that such very cruel usage extinguishes the fire of love in male and female slaves to their drivers, and to their proprietors, who approve and sanction such barbarities?

Slavery is only another word for brutal cruelty. How can the love of two millions and a half of male and female human and immortal beings be moved, be excited, be concentrated, be strengthened, and be unceasingly operative, by cruelty? It is impossible, for it is unphilosophical, irrational, and diametrically repugnant to the moral constitution of man.

Can slavery expect her two millions and a half of oppressed victims to give their love to her, and to perform all their toils, and endure all their dreadful wrongs, from this principle? This is utterly and practicably impossible; for disrespect, contempt, and cruelty alienate the heart: it cannot love hatred; it cannot love brutality; it cannot love the deepest of all wrongs; it cannot love the ugliest and most abominable of all vices; therefore, if a system of physical exertion is so constituted that it drives and compels all its victims to unceasing toil, without attracting and commanding the love of two millions and a half of human hearts, which love lightens our burdens—sweetens our bitter afflictions—oils the wheels of industry, which, by its irresistible power, constrains us to activity—then I say such a system is unfit for a spot on God's earth to rest on, because it is unfit for one human being to be employed in its service; for what is unfit to gain the love of man, is unfit for the labour of man, and such is the nature of slavery!

How exceedingly lamentable, then, is the state of two millions and a half of our brothers and sisters of the human family, who are compelled to labour, from their birth to their death, with the principle of their love bleeding, without being capable of loving their labour, or the character of those who cruelly hold them in bondage. And if slavery, from its enormous cruelty, cannot gain or command the love of its stolen and degraded victims, consequently, and unavoidably, it must have their hatred and indignation; and if these should go into action, how alarming would it be! How horrid to heaven and earth, to God and man, is that system that has not one attraction to exhibit to its two millions and a half of slaves! How ignominious and irrational is that system which drives two millions and a half of God's human children to bodily labour, but cannot move their love! which is universally confessed to be the tenderest, sweetest, and strongest principle of the human soul! Shall this system of fell and mutual hatred of slaves and their oppressors be suffered still to operate? No. We will sap its foundation, and never rest until it terminates in its total and eternal extinction, and love becomes the reigning principle of every man's heart.

Slavery demands with stern inflexibility, and inhumanly exacts bodily servitude, from the birth to the death, of two millions and a half of the human family, but furnishes no compensation for the whole amount of their labour, although it is incessantly accompanied with all manner of privations and sufferings!

Then is this system of all work and no pay, of a lifetime of labour, accompanied with. the most heart-rending sorrows of such a vast portion of rational and immortal beings, without any recompense calculated to cheer, or inspire to activity, or to render slavery amiable in the eyes of impartial justice or enlightened reason? Certainly not. Is it not the dictate of reason, as well as the precept of revelation, that "the labourer is worthy of his hire?" If each slave of the two millions and a half that are in the cruelest bondage is worthy of his hire, is deservedly entitled to a fair and honourable remuneration, then what a system is that which has stolen two millions and a half of human beings, infinitely dear to Jesus and the Deity, and is exacting labour from them from their birth to their death; but there is no reward, and they are alike plundered of the value of their services as their freedom?

Shall we suffer these wrongs to remain? Shall we negligently allow this injustice to be so extensively practised? Shall we not, as patriots, as philanthropists, as freemen, and as Christians, stir ourselves, and be resolved to seek the entire extirpation of a system that is equally alike destitute of all justice as of mercy; that demands human labour, human blood, human tears, and the lives of more than two millions, without pay? What nation in the whole world would suffer itself to be thus served, insulted, wronged, and trodden under foot by any set of men-stealers? How can slaves be expected to labour, when it has not one attraction to their hearts, nor one moral incentive to their industry?

Slavery inflicts the heaviest wrongs, the most accumulated sufferings, and the most heart-rending bereavements on its innocent victims, but furnishes no comforter, and shows no sympathy. How tremendously heavy is the wrong, and how peculiarly galling the suffering, to be deprived of civil and religious liberty! Not to be allowed to live in our native country, but to be kidnapped from it! To be driven from our homes—dragged from our friends—torn from our children—severed from our parents—divided from our wives—transported, in horrid forms, across the seas*—sold, and treated like the

---

* The following instance of the cruelty that is sometimes practised towards the slaves on board slave-ships was, in the most unexpected and providential manner, discovered during a trial at Guildhall, in the year 1783. The master, I ought to have said inhuman monster, of a slave-ship had overshot his port in Jamaica, and, under pretext of wanting water before he could beat up again, ordered his mate to throw over forty-six slaves handcuffed; and his diabolical order was immediately executed. Two days after he commanded thirty-six more to be thrown overboard; and at the end of other two days, forty more: all which infernal orders were instantly obeyed. Afterwards ten others, who had been permitted, unfettered, to take an airing on deck, indignantly plunged into the ocean after their countrymen. After all, this murderous crew brought into port with them four hundred and eighty gallons of water. This monster of a captain had the effrontery to commence a suit against the underwriters, in order to recover the neat value of the slaves he had, with such unexampled barbarity, murdered; and his mate, who gave evidence against him in court, had the impudence, even at the bar of one of the most august tribunals on earth, to boast, and to boast with impunity, of his prompt obedience to the master's commands. Human nature, how art thou fallen! how degraded and brutalized! Africans, hard is your lot! We have heard of slave-traders, after purchasing their slaves from the African chiefs, treating them with more than brutal cruelty, in their own country, during a fatiguing journey of hundreds of miles, through woods and forests, to the Guinea-ships. We have heard of their flogging some

brute creation—and doomed to the most brutal treatment of wrong and wo as long as life shall last!

And all this suffering to be unmercifully inflicted, and continued among two millions and a half of human beings, without a comforter to soothe their sorrows—assuage their miseries—brighten their prospects—lighten their galling yoke, or to inform them that their bondage shall be turned to liberty, their toil to spontaneous exertion —their wormwood and gall into the sweets and pleasures of freemen and Christians.

It is almost incredible what a load of accumulated wo men and women are capable of enduring for many years; but there is some inspiring principle, there is some buoyant property of the soul of man, that still plants the bow of a promise, or the object of hope on the bosom of the most threatening cloud, which has a mighty animating influence on the life and mind of man; which influences his faith, hope, and magnanimity—but the two millions and a half of Afric's sons and daughters have no inspiring principle; they have no hope of universal emancipation that is based on a sure foundation —their prospects are overcast—the darkest and most dismal gloom settles down around them, and despair preys on the vitals of their hope!

Slavery is no comforter. It cannot comfort. What was said of the Jews antiently, by the weeping prophet, may with great propriety be said of the African slaves: "Is it nothing unto you, all ye that pass by; behold, and see if there be any sorrow like to ours?"

The Holy Scriptures represent the Most High God as a free, kind, almighty, condescending, and unchanging comforter: they represent his dearly beloved Son Jesus Christ as coming from him with an unrivalled measure of the spirit of God, "To comfort all that mourn in Zion; to give them that mourn beauty for ashes, the oil of joy for mourning, and the garment of praise for the spirit of heaviness." They represent the spirit of God, and of Jesus, as being pre-eminently a soothing, sympathising, loving, forgiving, and comforting spirit; hence it is called "the comforter." But slavery, by legislative enactments, will not allow the ministers of the gospel to go among her two millions and a half of mourning captives and pro-

---

to death; and others, because they refused food, they cut in pieces, and forced their companions to eat them. We have, in short, heard of individual slaves being thrown overboard alive; but the above instance seems to exceed every thing we have either seen, read, or heard. The monster, the master of the ship, might have two objects in view; to gratify his own more than infernal malevolence, and to defraud the underwriters.

claim liberty, joy, and salvation! Slavery will neither suffer her afflicted population to be comforted by others, nor will she comfort it herself! How many millions, hundreds, and thousands of millions has the Holy Bible comforted; and how mighty, strong, abundant, and all-sufficient, have their consolations been, to enable them to "reckon that their light afflictions were but for a moment, and that they were working out for them a far more exceeding and eternal weight of glory?" But the slaves in the various States of this Union cannot so view their sufferings, for they have no teachers, and no comforter. Slavery is deaf and dumb to that golden sentiment, "Blessed are they that mourn, for they shall be comforted."

Slavery punishes its innocent and unjustly recriminated victims with the most horrid cruelties, without the least partiality or lenity to the tenderness, delicacy, weakness, constitution, or circumstances of the female; whether she is old or young, the delicate virgin, the pregnant wife, or the tender mother. Had slavery chose its unhappy victims simply from the male sex, then they, being, physically, "the stronger vessels," would be constitutionally capacitated to bear the wrongs, woes, and horrors of slavery with greater ability than the other sex, and the odium of slavery would have been less horribly disgusting; but for females to be subjected to the cruelest bondage, whose tender frames are unfit to perform its duties, and to be flogged, with horrid indecency, and bloody cruelty, for little or no reason, and these sufferings to be inflicted altogether irrespective of the health or circumstances of these sadly oppressed females, constitute such a feature of slavery as excites our horror and indignation. Pregnancy or motherhood, virginity or old age, are no exceptions from the unsuitable toils and insufferable wrongs and hardships of slavery! If we are worthy our name as men, or Americans, let us be inspired with one spirit, which will never tire, nor terminate its efforts, until the jubilee trumpet of liberty shall sound in the ears and hearts of the two millions and a half of the slave population.

Great Britain has blown her jubilee trumpet, and proclaimed the universal emancipation of all her slaves; the chains of their bondage are snapt asunder; and she has freely consented to purchase their freedom for twenty millions sterling. Let the Southern States, yes, let Congress, and every American, "go and do likewise."

AN ADDRESS TO THE LEGISLATORS
OF SOUTH CAROLINA

Your conduct, in the recent legislative enactments, I can assure you, have excited astonishment and consternation from one end of the Federal Union to the other. Daring step! The period is not distant, at which, I am confident, your own consciences will reprobate your conduct with greater severity than I am either able or willing to do it. However, on this painful occasion I cannot be altogether silent. Vice, in all the multifarious forms of which it is susceptible, ever has had, and ever will have, its reprovers. Were reprovers totally to cease, methinks that, on such an occasion, the stones of the wall, or the beams of the house, could not forbear to cry out. Were you in the full exercise of your judgment and recollection when you passed the execrable act? Bodies of men, as well as individuals, have their moments of infatuation, and insanity; I do not say ebriety [intemperance]. Do your own consciences, in your moments of serious reflection, if any such moments you have, approve your conduct? Or do they, in unison with the general voice of your nation and of mankind, reprobate it? Do you know the origin and natural effects of slavery? Have you ever investigated the nature and tendency of the commerce and slavery of the human species, to sanction and promote which you have exerted your highest legislative authority? Or is your detested act a sin of ignorance?

Have you never been informed of the contented and happy situation of your wretched slaves, while they were in their own country? Did they leave it of choice? You know, or ought to know, that they were forced, and dragged from it, as if they had been horses or hogs. Do you know who brought them into existence, and put them in possession of the country, from which, by your instigation, they have been torn? Who authorized you, or any set of men on earth, forcibly to deprive them of the country, of which Heaven gave them ample possession? Show your authority, if any authority you can pretend. Are not all your slave-traders, whom you encourage by what you call law, robbers? Robbers such men certainly are; and robbers of the most infamous kind. Men did I call them? Have they not forfeited the honorable appellation? Shall I call them *miscreants?* Do you know the means, the inhuman and base means, by which your traders procure these wretches for you? I advise you, before you pass any more laws in support of slavery, to employ proper means for obtaining better information on the subject, than you seem now to possess.

Is there a *grain*, one small *grain*, of either justice or benevolence in your conduct to the unhappy slaves? Do you employ, or encourage traders to procure them, or do you purchase them, with an intention to render their condition in the world better than it was? Do you intend to make them any compensation for the injustice and oppression to which you have compelled them to submit? I do not want an answer. I will not either put you to the blush, or tempt you to become guilty of the most abominable hypocrisy.

But where, by whom, has a law been recently passed, to authorize and encourage the commerce and slavery of the African race? Is there a government on earth; can there be one in Christendom, in the now enlightened and improved state of the world, that could have passed such a law? Is it possible that any government could sanction such a law? The fact does not admit of a doubt. That such a law has lately been passed, and is now in full force and operation, we all know—the world knows. The fact cannot be concealed or denied. It has been passed in one of the free and independent states of America. Passed in America! Enacted in a free and independent state! Call it no more a state of freedom. Slavery in a free state! Are not freedom and slavery diametrically opposite! Americans! talk no more of Asiatic or European despotism and tyranny; talk no more of the freedom of America. A country free, while a considerable part of its inhabitants are in a state of the most humiliating and abject slavery! What a burlesque! What an insult to common sense! Your noble struggle for liberty, a few years ago, did you honor among your foes as well as your friends. For liberty, Americans fought, and bled, and died. Rather than become slaves to an European power, you were willing to shed the last drop of your blood. And why, in the name of wonder, should Africans be made slaves to you? Have not Africans as valid a natural title to liberty, as either Europeans or Americans? Are not the former children of the same Almighty Father, who, great in goodness, and good in greatness, is no respecter of persons? Are they not radically legitimate members of his august family equally with the latter? Is not Africa, in fertility and natural advantages, a country not inferior either to Asia, Europe, or America? Have not the Africans, in former times, been, both in a philosophical and theological point of view, equal to the inhabitants of the other quarters of our terraqueous globe, in mental capacities and powers?

That the beasts of the earth, the fowls of the air, and the fishes of the sea were made to be at the disposal, and subservient to the use, of man, revelation expressly informs us. But that one part of mankind was made to be at the disposal and subservient to the use of another, revelation and reason, by their joint suffrage, deny; and I defy all creation to prove it.

Gentlemen, for your own sakes, for the sake of suffering humanity, for the sake of your country, for the sake of all Europe, the benevolent inhabitants of which view your recent official act with painful sensations, and the tyrannical inhabitants of which exhibit your cruel measures as an excuse for their own barbarity, bethink yourselves; review your late legislative conduct; investigate the criminal nature, the fatal tendency, and ruinous effects of the commerce and subsequent slavery of your human brethren. May the Father of light open the eyes of your minds, to see the atrocity and turpitude of such dreadfully degrading commerce! Do I seem to treat you with uncommon asperity of language? Scurrility of language I abhor; but, on such a topic, asperity of language is unavoidable. Nay, on such a subject we labor under a penury of language. Language fails; and is almost unmeaning. The enormity of your conduct, I confess, I know no words sufficient to express. Conception, in this case, is too big for expression. The time is coming, when you will see the deformity and detestable nature of your conduct in more striking colours than the flowers of rhetoric, than mortal eloquence, than the greatest master of description can now paint it.

You talk loud of the tyrants of Europe, and hold out your country as an asylum for the refugees from European oppression. But ask emigrants from Europe, after they have seen the many hundreds and thousands among you whom you have forced into the most grievous servitude, and confined to the hardest labor, their comparative opinion of European and American freedom. Their sentiments and emotions I know. With indignation against you, and commiseration to their poor fellow mortals whom you oppress, their breasts swell, their hearts overflow. You disgrace your country and miserably disappoint them. Nay, your legislative conduct is both unjust and ungenerous; unjust, as it respects the poor Africans, who have to toil for their indolent, dissipated tyrants; and ungenerous as it respects the poor white people, who have to labor for their own support.

What do you think of the conduct of your fellow citizens in the eastern states? What a contrast between their conduct and yours! By the emancipation of their slaves, they have done a lasting honor to themselves, to their country, and to human nature. They have made glad the hearts of all the friends of humanity and religion. But you have brought a stigma on your character, which, to the mortification of your posterity, history will transmit to the latest times. You have made sad the hearts of all your cotemporaries, who have any regard either for humanity or religion. Of the recent arrival of three vessels from Africa, with eight hundred and seventy-two wretched victims to your avarice and cruelty, who were landed in Charleston, we heard some time ago. Unhappy beings! May the Father of mercies, to whose control all despots, tyrants, and oppressors are necessarily subjected, commiserate your condition!

Do you ever, gentlemen, peep through the curtain of futurity? Possible future occurrences, the human mind can anticipate. Do you ever advert to the probable and dreadful effect of the continued oppression, and the increase of slaves in your country?* To occasion or encourage insurrection or sedition, is infinitely remote from my intention. Everything of the kind, all good men detest, and, to the utmost of their power, suppress. But the nature of the Africans, no less than that of other nations, is human. What human nature is, we all know; and what effect oppression necessarily has upon it, we know. That the Africans are as capable of gratitude and revenge as any other people in the world, does not admit of a dispute; and that they have more political information than any of their colour in the West Indies, might easily be demonstrated. Facts are ir- refragable proofs. The fate of St. Domingo is fresh in all their minds, as well as in all our memories, and if you are not judicially infatu- ated, will prove a solemn warning to you. That the tragical, the bloody scene which has recently been acted in that unhappy island, should ever be re-acted among us, God forbid! I do not prophecy; I caution and warn; nay, I studiously avoid both the oriental style of antiquity, and the prophetical language of divinity. May the in- habitants of your, and of the neighboring states, take *timous* [timely] warning.

Gentlemen, for God's sake! review your late legislative conduct; be ashamed; and speedily recall what you have done. Know that the commerce of human beings is utterly subversive of the specific and essential prerogatives of human nature, and politically pregnant with the most fatal and inevitable consequences. When you make a human being a slave, you disgrace your own natures, and virtually militate against your own interest. Remember, that cruelty of every kind is the object of the strongest aversion of that Being whose high attribute, whose brightest glory, is mercy. Of the oppressed he ever has been, and ever will be, the patron and the friend. While you oppress his creatures, you affront him, and may expect him to be your enemy; and a most dangerous enemy he is. Recollect the fear- ful doom and punishment of the oppressors of former times, and other countries. Read the history of the world, and tremble! Your guilt is flagrant; your crime is attended with high aggravations. Let your repentance, therefore, be speedy; and your reformation exem- plary. For which you shall not cease to have my warmest wishes, and

---

* To demonstrate this topic, many incontestible arguments might be ad- duced, but prudence forbids the investigation; people should prudently think for themselves, what would be considered impolitic for me to write.

most ardent prayers. May universal liberty, civil and religious, prevail in South Carolina, in all her sister states, and throughout the whole world!

A HINT TO THE CONGRESS OF THE UNITED STATES

I must, once more, beg the indulgence of my readers, while I suggest a hint, and only a hint, to the Congress of the United States. That Congress may, without delay, take this subject into their most serious consideration, and adopt such judicious measures, as to them shall appear the most proper and eligible, for meliorating the condition of the poor slaves, and putting a period, with all convenient speed, to slavery in their territories, is my earnest wish, devout prayer, and pleasing expectation. With great satisfaction do I reflect that the year 1835 is not now very distant. The approach of it opens a pleasing prospect to me, and to the other friends of humanity, and diffuses a degree of joy through the whole soul. That our prospects should be disappointed, or our anticipated happiness frustrated, God forbid! Yet alas, before that auspicious period arrives, what thousands of Africans will be imported into South Carolina; what thousands of mortal enemies scattered through other states. Is not Congress under every obligation, which duty or interest can confer, to embark in the cause? The safety, the very existence of the nation, seem to require it. Have we not among us, and intermixed with us, five hundred thousand persons, who were, at least in their progenitors, dragged from their own beloved country; forced into a grievous servitude in this land; and, contrary to their most earnest desires, detained in it? Is not liberty a most desirable thing, and the yoke of bondage galling, to every human being? Do not our slaves consider themselves as oppressed most cruelly, as well as unjustly oppressed? Do they not meditate revenge? For wishing, for attempting, by just measures, to regain their liberty, who can blame them? To their liberty they have as indisputable a title, as to the vital air they breathe. Who can blame an individual man, or an army of men, for attempting, by every lawful means, to recover what is their own? If a man be robbed, is it not lawful for him to recover the property of which he was unjustly and forcibly deprived? The English have been deeply and shamefully concerned in the slave trade; but their situation, humanly speaking, was far less dangerous than ours. They allowed slaves abroad; but they tolerated none at home. To provide for the general safety of the nation is, doubtless, the duty of Congress. Let them take warning from the fate of others. Examples of national judgments occur in every page of the history of the world. Hispaniola in general, and St. Domingo in particular, will long continue to be remembered. Impolitic in the highest degree, as well as intrinsically criminal, is the oppression of the African slaves. Here an ample range of arguments opens. In a variety of views, and from a variety of topics, might the impolicy of it be evinced. But I must, at present, forbear, and postpone the discussion.

That a period is approaching, in which liberty, peace and religion will universally flourish, is truly a consolatory consideration. But the Most High fulfils his designs, and accomplishes his promises, by the intervention and agency of instruments and means. Happy would it be for themselves, and for the world, if Christian powers would advert to what is competent for them, and incumbent upon them, for the happiness of mankind, and the honor of that great Being who is the common friend and father of all men, black as well as white. Does the one color naturally entitle to a life of idleness and dissipation; and the other subject to a life of cruel servitude and oppression? God is not, and why should man be, a respecter of persons? Shall I not entertain the fond, the pleasing hope, that Congress will, at their ensuing session, enter on the consideration of this truly important subject, and begin to make arrangements for the effectual relief of the oppressed, exiled sons and daughters of Africa?

ADDITION.—The preachers and people of the United States form societies against freemasonry and intemperance, and write against sabbath breaking, sabbath mails, infidelity, &c. &c. But the fountain head,* compared with which all those other evils are comparatively nothing, and from the bloody and murderous head of which they receive no trifling support, as hardly noticed by the Americans. This is a fair illustration of the state of society in this country—it shows what a bearing avarice has upon a people, when they are nearly given up by the Lord to a hard heart and a reprobate mind, in consequence of afflicting their fellow creatures. God suffers some to go on until they are ruined forever! Will it be the case with our brethren the whites of the United States of America? We hope not—we would not wish to see them destroyed, notwithstanding they have and do now treat us more cruel than any people (with the exception of the French and Dutch) have treated another on this earth since it came from the hands of its Creator. The will of God must however, in spite of us, be done.

The English are the best friends the coloured people have upon earth. Though they have oppressed us a little, and have colonies now in the West Indies which oppressed us sorely—yet, notwith-

* Slavery and oppression.

standing, they (the English) have done one hundred times more for the melioration of our condition than all the other nations of the earth put together. The blacks cannot but respect the English as a nation, notwithstanding they have treated us a little cruel.

There is no intelligent black man, who knows anything, but esteems a real Englishman, let him see him in what part of the world he will—for the English are the greatest benefactors we have upon earth. We have here and there, in other nations, good friends—but, as a nation, the English are our friends.

How can the preachers and people of America believe the Bible? Does it teach them any distinction on account of a man's colour? Hearken, Americans! to the injunctions of our Lord and Master to his humble followers:

† "And Jesus came and spake unto them, saying, all power is given unto me in heaven and in earth.

"Go ye, therefore, and teach all nations, baptizing them in the name of the Father, and of the Son, and of the Holy Ghost.

"Teaching them to observe all things whatsoever I have commanded you: and lo, I am with you always, even unto the end of the world. Amen."

I declare, that the very face of these injunctions appears to be of God, and not of man. They do not show the slightest degree of distinction. "Go ye therefore," says my divine master, "and teach all nations" (or, in other words, all people), "baptizing them in the name of the Father, and of the Son, and of the Holy Ghost." Do you understand the above, Americans? We are a people, notwithstanding many of you' doubt it. You have the Bible in your hands, with this very injunction. Have you been to Africa, teaching the inhabitants thereof the words of the Lord Jesus? "Baptizing them in the name of the Father, and of the Son, and of the Holy Ghost." Have you not, on the contrary, entered among us, and learned us the art of throat-cutting, by setting us to fight one against another, to take each other as prisoners of war, and sell them to you for small bits of calico, old swords, knives, &c. to make slaves for you and your children? This being done, have you not brought us among you, in chains and handcuffs, like brutes, and treated us with all the cruelties and rigour your ingenuity could invent, consistent with the laws of your country, which (for the blacks) are tyrannical enough? Can the American preachers appeal unto God, the maker and searcher of hearts, and tell him, with the Bible in their hands, that they make no distinction on account of men's colour? Can they say, O God!

† See St. Matthew's Gospel, 28:18, 19, 20; after Jesus was risen from the dead.

thou knowest all things—thou knowest that we make no distinction between thy creatures, to whom we have to preach thy word? Let them answer the Lord; and if they cannot do it in the affirmative, have they not departed from the Lord Jesus Christ, their master? But some may say that they never had, or were in possession of a religion which made no distinction, and of course they could not have departed from it. I ask you then, in the name of the Lord, of what kind can your religion be? Can it be that which was preached by our Lord Jesus Christ from heaven? I believe you cannot be so wicked as to tell him that his gospel was that of *distinction*. What can the American preachers and people take God to be? Do they believe his words? If they do, do they believe that he will be mocked? Or do they believe, because they are whites and we blacks, that God will have respect to them? Did not God make us all as it seemed best to himself? What right, then, has one of us to despise another, and to treat him cruel, on account of his colour, which none but the God who made it can alter? Can there be a greater absurdity in nature, and particularly in a free republican country? But the Americans, having introduced slavery among them, their hearts have become almost seared, as with an hot iron, and God has nearly given them up to believe a lie in preference to the truth! and I am awfully afraid that pride, prejudice, avarice, and blood, will, before long, prove the final ruin of this happy republic, or land of liberty! Can any thing be a greater mockery of religion than the way in which it is conducted by the Americans? It appears as though they are bent only on daring God Almighty to do his best—they chain and hand-cuff us and our children, and drive us around the country like brutes, and go into the house of the God of justice to return Him thanks for having aided them in the infernal cruelties inflicted upon us. Will the Lord suffer this people to go on much longer, taking his holy name in vain? Will he not stop them, preachers and all? O Americans! Americans! I call God—I call angels—I call men—to witness that your destruction is at hand, and will be speedily consummated, unless you *repent*.

TREATMENT OF SLAVES IN THE DUTCH SETTLEMENTS

The Dutch mode of treating the slaves in their colonies coincides, in many particulars, with that of others. It is not more mild; but, alas, still more sanguinary and cruel. Their principal settlements in the West Indies I have visited, and therefore can speak with certainty. In the Dutch settlements, as well as other European colonies, offences, on the one hand, and, on the other, punishments, are distributed into two classes; ordinary and extraordinary. Offences called ordinary are such as these—neglect of orders, absence from work, stealing food, eating the sugar-cane, breaking a plate, looking with displeasure or contempt at the tyrant, their master. For such offences the ordinary punishments are—flogging with a cartwhip; beating with a stick; the breaking of bones; a heavy chain; tying two or three together; a large iron ring round the ankle; an iron collar, with prongs, round the neck; confinement in a dungeon; slitting the ears; breaking the limbs, so as to render amputation necessary; beating out the eyes; castration, &c. In Surinam they have a method of flogging the slaves which seems to be of infernal origin, and certainly is a master-piece of diabolical cruelties. They tie the wrists of the culprit tight, and press his knees together; his bound arms he is obliged to put round his knees; then a long stick is put through behind his knees, and one end of it fastened in the ground. In this situation he can neither move hand nor foot. In this manner have I often seen the wretched slaves flogged till their wounds were an inch deep, and they were unable to move for a whole month. Another most barbarous practice in these colonies is this—one hand of the slave is tied to a tree, and the other to another, so high that his toes can barely touch the ground. While he is suspended in this manner, two unfeeling wretches, as executioners, stand, the one on his right hand, and the other on his left, each having a whip in his hand, with which they alternately lash him, till he is, in a manner hardly to be conceived, cut from head to foot. Such are the barbarities and cruelties which those devils in human form, the proprietors and managers of slaves in the Dutch settlements, commit. Execrable monsters! Hated are they of God, of angels, and of all good men. Heaven rejects, and has already began to repay them; the earth, no longer able to bear, spues them out.

CONCLUSION

My much esteemed reader, I must now draw this communication to a close, and in so doing, kindly suffer me to speak to you, as one that loves your invaluable soul, and the eternal interests of our dark coloured people, who are in the most unhappy bondage. You need to be addressed in the language of *Instruction, Caution, Encouragement, Command, Affection, and Comfort;* and in such strains I will take my leave of you at present. In the language of *instruction,* I would beseech you to consider, that all the innumerable hosts of angels and archangels, cherubim and seraphim, that people the immense regions of the third heaven, that celebrate the praises of the

Sovereign Father of the universe, in perfect and perpetual harmony, are *all free,* and all their services and adorations are performed in the fullest enjoyment of the most glorious *liberty.* Do you and I pray every day that God's "will may be done on earth as it is done in heaven?" Now God's will is done in heaven by none but free angels, or free and happy spirits; for there is no slavery or bond angel or spirit in heaven: If heaven is the theatre of freedom, and all its countless millions are enjoying the most blessed, dignified, and glorious, and immortal freedom, then, pray that every male and female African may be free in soul from sin, and free in person in civil liberty; and that each person in every nation, and the whole world may be free in mind and body, and do God our heavenly Father's "will on earth as it is done in heaven." Oh! how wonderfully honorable will that people be, and how wonderfully happy will that period be, when all people and nations will worship God on earth as the angels worship God in heaven!

This petition "thy will be done on earth as it is done in heaven," is the prayer of freedom. It is the spirit of freedom. It is the heaven-born principle of freedom.

All the innumerable millions that are glorified around the throne, who came out of great tribulation, and have washed their robes, and made them white in the blood of the Lamb, are all in the possession of the most wonderful freedom. They are free from toils, temptations, tears, suffering, and all manner of misery; and they serve God night and day, in the exercise of freedom, "which eye has not seen, nor ear heard, nor hath it entered into the heart of man to conceive."

If millions unnumbered of our brethren of mankind are now enjoying the glorious liberty of the children of God, in that land where bondage and misery, weeping and wo, are not known, and they worship God in the enjoyment of such freedom, then let us try, by every possible exertion, to free our fellow creatures from slavery in body and soul, and to establish them in that liberty whereby Christ has made his people free.

Is Christ free? Did he come to preach liberty to the captives? Is his gospel the jubilee trumpet that proclaims the liberty of the world? Did Jesus pray, preach, travel, weep, agonize and die, and rise again, that liberty, in body and soul, should be enjoyed by every child of Adam, of every clime, country and colour; then to be like Jesus in heart and life, in principle and practice, in desire and object, we must be free, and others must be free, and all must be free. O how delightful to strive to make human and immortal souls like Jesus Christ!

Is the Most High God infinitely free? Does he exercise all his stupendous attributes freely? Is he infinitely free in every action? Is he the Father, the Fountain, the Patron, the Promoter, and the Preserver of Freedom in heaven, in earth, and in the universe? Then cease not using every holy and good exertion until all Africa's sons and daughters shall be made free. O how high is the dignity, and rich the blessedness, to be like the holy angels in freedom; like to the glorified spirits in freedom; to be like to Jesus Christ in freedom; and to be like God in freedom!

My dear reader, suffer me to address you in the language of *caution*. In order to achieve the grand and universal emancipation of our beloved and captive fellow brothers and sisters of the African nation, remember that much will depend on the spirit that you breathe, and the conduct that you manifest. Let your spirit be that of the gospel, and your conduct an imitation of the conduct of Jesus Christ. His gospel and his conduct breathe the same divine and heavenly principle. The motto of the blood-stained banner of the cross is, "glory to God in the highest, and on earth peace and good will towards man;" then, let your will towards all who oppress you, or your fellow brothers and sisters in slavery, be a good will, wish every blessing upon them in body and mind; for if God should condescend to save and bless the planters and all proprietors of slaves, then we may joyfully anticipate a glorious day of liberty. Be mild, yet magnanimous. Be gentle as lambs, but courageous as lions. "Be wise as serpents, and harmless as doves." "Be steadfast and immoveable, always abounding in the work of the Lord, for as much as ye know your labor is not in vain in the Lord."

Be imitators not of fools and madmen, who are governed by feeling, interest, and passion; "but be followers of those who through faith and patience are now inheriting the promises;" yea, "Be ye followers of God, as dear children, and walk in love; even Christ has loved you, and given himself for you an offering to God, a sacrifice of a sweet smelling saviour."

Suffer a word of *encouragement*. You ardently, zealously, and conscientiously pray and hope that ere long the two millions and a half of your dear fellow countrymen may be released from their iron bondage, and spring into the glorious liberty of civil and religious freedom; but be not depressed, yield not in the least to despair, that God who inclined the people, government, and king of Great Britain, to sacrifice twenty millions sterling to purchase the freedom of all the slaves in the British colonies, is able, willing, and ready to incline the people, the planters, and the Congress of the United States of America, to let the captive go free. Hope and trust in God; pray to him, and daily wait upon him. Prove him by a holy spirit and a holy life "if he will not open you the windows of heaven and pour out a blessing, until there shall not be room enough to receive it." The time and the seasons are in his power. He that shall come will come, and will not tarry. When Israel's redemption drew nigh, Moses received his divine commission and credentials, and on the very predicted day all Israel was redeemed, and their enemies were overthrown. God is not man, that he should lie, nor the Son of man, that he should repent; hath he said it and will he not do it; hath he spoken and shall it not come to pass?

Suffer the word of *command*. "Be of one mind." "Live in peace." "Follow peace with all men and holiness, without which no man shall see the Lord." "Watch and pray lest ye enter into temptation." "Put on the whole armour of God." "Stand fast in the faith, quit ye and be strong like men." "Pray without ceasing." "Follow the Lamb through good and through bad report." "Be faithful unto death," says your conquering captain, "and I will give thee a crown of life."

Suffer the word of *affection*. All I say unto you is from a heart sincerely attached to you. I entreat you, in the name of Jesus, to do nothing but what I most willingly wish to do myself. I call upon you to make no exertion but which I wish to put forth myself. Now, my dearly beloved fellow countrymen, seeing that the white people, and nations of white people, are exerting themselves in behalf of our African people, in various parts of the world, as well as in different states of this Union; then, how should we do? Does it become us to do nothing to convince the government, congress, and people of this country, that we are worthy of our freedom and that society, so far from being injured by our liberty, is greatly benefitted thereby? Be good citizens, be industrious, be sober, be good husbands, and be good wives, and be good brothers and sisters, be good parents and children, and be good and honest-hearted Christians. May "the good will of him that dwelt in the bush, be with you."

Finally, suffer the word of *comfort*. There are grand and glorious promises made by God to Jesus Christ, which are upwards of two, three, four, five, and six thousand years old; but, old as they are, they are nothing injured by their antiquity; they rest on the almighty, omnipresent, and all-sufficient attributes of God for their fulfilment. And if the nation and church of the Jews said from experience, not one word that God hath spoken hath failed; then, may we not rest assured, that God's word of promise, that "men shall be blessed in Christ, and all nations shall call him blessed," will be duly and most faithfully fulfilled? Most assuredly.

Jesus has glorified his Father on the earth, and finished the work he gave him to do; but the Father has not fulfilled all his most mag-

nificent promises to Jesus; but ere long the set time will come, when
all the promises made to Jesus shall be accomplished. Jesus will "see
the travail of his soul, and will be satisfied," and this will take place,
when "the heathen shall be given to him for an inheritance, and the
uttermost parts of the earth for his possession." "Every valley shall
be exalted, and every mountain and hill be made low; the crooked
shall be made straight, and the rough places plain, and the glory
of the Lord shall be revealed, and all flesh shall see it together, for
the mouth of the Lord hath spoken it."

With such cheering promises as these, let us comfort and encourage one another, and keep singing and shouting, great is the
Holy One of Israel in the midst of us. Come thou Great Deliverer,
once more awake thine almighty arm, and set thy African captives
free, and let them experimentally feel and fully and eternally enjoy
the glorious liberty of the children of God.

Blessed be the Lord our God, the God of Israel, who only doeth
wondrous things; and blessed be his glorious name forever. Let the
whole earth be filled with his glory, Amen, and Amen.

HYMN

1 YE soldiers of Jesus, pray stand to your arms,
Prepare for the battle, the gospel alarms,
The trumpets are sounding, come, soldiers, and see
The standard and colours of sweet liberty.

2 Tho' Satan's black trumpet is sounding so near,
Take courage, brave soldiers, his armies we dare:
In the strength of King Jesus we dare him to fight,
We'll put his black armies of aliens to flight.

3 In the mount of salvation, in Christ's armory,
There's swords, shields, and breast-plates, and helmets for thee;
O be not faint-hearted, though he roars like a flood,
He'll not stand before the bright armies of God.

4 To battle, to battle, the trumpets doth sound;
The watchmen are crying fair Zion around:
The signal for vict'ry! hark! hark! from the sky;
Shout, shout, ye brave armies, the watchmen all cry.

5 As the great Goliah, Apollyon shall fall;
With the sword of the Spirit we'll conquer them all:
We'll leave no opposers alive in the field:
By the strength of Jehovah we'll force them to yield.

6 Thro' Jesus, our wisdom, we'll baffle his rage:—
  My heart beats for conquest; come, soldiers, engage;
  The trumpets are sounding—the armies appear;
  We'll not leave one standing, from front to the rear.

7 King Jesus is riding the white horse before;
  The watchmen close after; the trumpet doth roar:
  Some shouting, some singing, salvation they cry:
  In the strength of King Jesus all hell we defy.

8 Fair Zion's a shouting to her conq'ring King:
  Salvation to Jesus, the armies doth sing:
  Apollyon we've conquer'd, and sunk in the flood:
  Who can withstand the bright armies of God?

9 Behold all the armies are now marching home,
  God's trumpet is sounding, and bids them to come:
  All Zion's fair armies together doth meet,
  And lay down their armour at Jesus's feet.

10 The angelic army with Zion combines;
   In robes of bright glory eternally shines;
   All shouting and singing on Canaan's bright shore,
   Where wars and commotions can reach them no more.

11 Cheer up, ye dear pilgrims, the time's drawing nigh
   When we shall meet Jesus' bright hosts in the sky:
   Our friends and relations in Jesus so dear,
   Both preachers and people shall then meet us there.

12 We'll join the bright harpers in anthems divine,
   Whose crowns with bright diamonds the sun doth outshine:
   To the praise of King Jesus we'll tune our harps then,
   Salvation and glory to Jesus, AMEN.

Appeals to the colored citizens of New York and elsewhere in behalf of the press. By David Ruggles, a man of color.

No. 1: "It Was"

The old year, with all its important and interesting, its solemn and joyful events, has departed, and we are of the number of those who are spared, and who can say of it, "It Was," and wish each other "a happy new year."

Then let us reflect that although the rapid progress of our cause has far outstripped the anticipations of the most sanguine, the old year has left us as the new year has found us, in the midst of a moral revolution. Though ours is the "Land of Liberty" *we are slaves* whose condition is but a short remove from that of two millions of our race who are pining in their bloody chains, and that our contest is for *freedom* and that the PRESS is the weapon which we wield in behalf of our rights, is the engine that will speed us *on* to the full enjoyment of *freedom's* blessings.

Then let us ask ourselves the question—Have we done our duty in supporting the *press* in rolling on the car of freedom? Or have we impeded its progress by becoming a clog to its wheels? If we have, if we are upon the path of duty, let us continue there to walk, without turning to the right hand or to the left, for to desert it is deserting our own cause—the cause of bleeding humanity. If we have not, let us enter upon it at once and

> Let us to the Press devoted be,
> Its *light* will *shine* and *speak us free.*

Who that has one drop of African blood in his veins can be reconciled to the thought, that the press—that any periodical that advocates our cause, should languish, must die for the want of his support; while two millions of our countrymen—Ah! while our fathers and mothers, brothers and sisters, husbands, wives and children, are crying for us to "help!" "Break every yoke," undo the heavy burden, and let us "go *free.*"

If any such there be, who can be thus reconciled to the idea, that it may be said of any periodical that advocates our cause, "It Was,"

Mark him well, he is not what he ought to be—"He that is not for me is against me."

I am acquainted with the fact that there are those amongst us who are ever ready to offer excuses as reasons why they do not unite in sustaining the press. But to such permit me to say, that in comparison to the importance of our cause, and in consideration of the power of the press, all the excuses that can be offered by us as reasons, why we do not stand shoulder to shoulder in sustaining the press, fall so far short of adequate reasons in favor of our cause, that they are in reality arguments in favor of *slavery itself.* For of all the inventions that have continued to multiply in the world from the first dawn of its existence to the present moment, the art of printing holds the most conspicuous place. Irrespective of the grandness of the discovery, the ingenuity, the patience, and skill in consummating the arts, it stands the first in its inconceivable consequences and tremendous results.

Who that takes a survey of our country is not wonderstruck to behold books, periodicals, papers and pamphlets of a thousand different kinds, spreading over land as a mantle of intelligence to shield a portion of our countrymen from ignorance, superstition, and the curse of slavery. Profuse as the Sybils' leaves, they move on every breath and are wafted by every breeze.

The liberty of OPINION—the liberty of SPEECH—the liberty of the PRESS is guaranteed to us. Then while such facilities for information arise, while so powerful a weapon as the press can be wielded to defend us from slavery and her accursed fruits, the fault is our own if we tamely consent to partake of them.

The press like an engine pouring forth an unceasing tide of information, spreading the knowledge of the present and past ages with the speed of electricity throughout the world; before it ignorance retires and slavery will wield up her ghost.

Then while the tide is high let us "take it at the flood" and ride

> On—till from every vale
> And where the mountain rise,
> The beaconed light of liberty
> Shall kindle to the skies.

I rejoice in the mighty power of the American press, although it has been to us a hard master, capricious, tyrannical, and often as cruel as the slave driver's lash—still I rejoice in its mighty moral power, because I know that "truth is mighty and will prevail."

The press stands confessed not only one great means for disseminating knowledge, but is the great medium itself of knowledge—to it the nations of the world owe their freedom.

OURS is the cause of *freedom*—OUR CAUSE is sacred; its success depends upon the power of the PRESS under God.

> Let him who would be a SLAVE refuse to sustain it,
> Let him who would be FREE; to it devoted be.

Here permit me to adduce the proof, that in consideration to the importance of our cause, in consideration to the power of the PRESS, all the excuses that can be offered by us as reasons why we do not *unite,* and stand *shoulder* to *shoulder* in sustaining the *PRESS,* fall so far short of rational reason in favor of the cause, that they are in reality arguments in favor of *slavery itself.*

Now A, B, or C calls upon D, and requests of him or her to subscribe for the paper. [The answer is,] "I can't take the paper; you know how it is, we have been so long kept down by slavery," etc. I will admit all that D can say against slavery, for the more he says the weaker are his reasons or excuses for not exerting all his every effort to *annihilate slavery.*

The fact that our race have been, for centuries subjected to the tyrannical and bloody reign of *slavery is undeniable.* I will undertake to say that slavery unnerves, crushes, degrades, imbrutes the mind of man whenever and wherever he be found its subject . . . That lofty aspiration peculiar to man is crushed in its infant struggles—under it ambition soars no higher than to wait the beck, and speed the mandates of a haughty, lordling, and every generous emotion of the soul is circumscribed, confined, crushed, and almost *annihilated* by its blighting influence.

Then it is clear that D's excuse for not sustaining the *press*—that engine which will speedily eradicate it root and branch—annihilate it for ever! is conclusive evidence that he will continue to be *kept down by slavery.* The sad tales of our misfortunes—our miserable servitude and oppression, though awful to relate—do not answer the demands of our present situation. The question is not what we *have been* it is what *we are now* and what we *will be* . . . We are human, living

> In our own, our native land,

under a government that proclaims *all men are free and equal.*

Liberty is the magic word, the talismanic word with which from earliest life the American (if forsooth his skin be "not colored like our own") claims the menaces of aggression, and quits with one touch the usurpation of *tyranny.*

'Tis proclaimed throughout the world, the *"Land of Liberty!"* wherever the star spangled banner waves, or the *national pennon* floats on high; there proudly soars the *eagle of liberty,* announcing to every land, that America is the birth place of *freedom.* Why then shall we be *slaves* and lie down in supineness, with our arms folded, singing the song of degradation? I answer, because we are not *united* in sustaining the *press.* The can't word which is always proscribed by slaveholders and colonizationists, as a plaster to heal our wounds and to cure our disease, (though a fatal remedy,) is always applied by ourselves, when it should be remembered that *can't kills, when can cures.*

This word "can't," which seems to attend every effort one makes towards effecting an elevation "according to our equal rights," ought to be colonized; he who yields to its flattering reign, will *live and die an ignorant slave.*

[Source: *Emancipator and Journal of Public Morals,* Vol. III, No. 2 (January 13, 1835), no page given.]

No. 2

Take the following excuses as samples and judge of the amount of reason they contain, in view of the fact that only four cents per week is all that is required to pay for the paper.

A, B, or C calls upon E, and puts the question, "Will you assist in sustaining the cause of suffering humanity by subscribing to this paper?"

Ans. I can't. How much is it?

A. About four cents per week.

Well, that is cheap enough; I spend more than that for tobacco and other things which I can't do without well, and which I *will* have. I believe I am too poor to take the paper!

Here E acknowledges his ability to pay for the paper, but he says he *will have* tobacco, he *will* put his money into the slaveholder's purse, that he may be encouraged to drive his brother, and perhaps his father or mother, who are writhing under the bloody lash, tilling the earth to raise this poisonous weed which he "can't do without," and which he *will have:* and then plead that he is too poor to make an effort to be free himself, or to help remove the yoke and chains from the neck of his brother, but *will* spend his money to keep him a slave.

He calls upon F.

Question. Will you subscribe to this paper which pleads your cause?

Ans. "No, I can't sustain the press, because I can't read."

This is saying, "I can't do anything toward removing slavery; its blighting influence has deprived me of an education. Therefore, I will *let it alone*, that it may crush the rising and future generations!

He calls upon G.

Question. Will you sustain the press by subscribing to this paper?

Answer. "I can't take it; I have no time to read it, and if I had H takes it, and I could read his or her paper."

This is saying, "I can't unite in the mighty struggle against slavery, because time forbids me the pleasure of counting her retiring steps, and if it *did not*, "J" is engaged in the warfare and I can ascertain from him or from her how fast slavery retraces her steps; but "I can't assist in hastening her downfall."

He calls upon K.

Question. Here is a paper that is devoted to our cause; it pleads for our elevation and for the emancipation of our poor enslaved brethren. Will you take it?

Answer. "I can't take the paper; many of my customers are slave-holders and colonizationists, and they don't like it. I take the Courier and Enquirer, and the Commercial Advertiser, and as the public sentiment is against abolition, I can't have anything to do with it. I think I will stand neutral."

Now of all the yielding, retiring, and pusillanimous spirits that anything human can possess, the individual who makes such excuses is in possession of the idea of a man's talking of neutrality in a cause which so earnestly concerns both his temporal and spiritual salvation, is so contemptible that it ought to be buried in the sepulchre that conceived it. What do the Slave say? Why, "I can't do anything toward obtaining my Freedom, because slaveholders and colonizationists don't like it, and the public opinion is against my exercising the rights and attaining the dignity of a man. Therefore I will yield to their insidious smiles, and do nothing toward removing the public opinion, that I may stand erect, but will remain *neutral* under its accursed crushing weight."

Now present your excuses in whatever shape you please; prescribe as many "can'ts" as you will; in consideration to the importance of our cause and the importance of the influence of the press, they cannot reach it, they are lost in the fog that conceives them. The man who refuses to do his duty in His Own Cause is like the man cast away upon the ocean in a leaky boat surrounded by sharks; he has the necessary means by which he can extricate himself; he knows that *"white"* sharks eat *"black men"* like anything; still, he yields to "can't" and sinks to their mercy. Now what is Our Cause? It is the cause of Liberty! Give me Liberty! with all the imaginary evils of poverty, with all the real inconveniences with which man can be subjected to by Poverty, rather than *slavery;* no matter how gaudy be her attire; no matter what be her allurements, she is *slavery still.*

It may be urged that the press cannot alter the laws of our country which make us *slaves;* this I admit. It cannot directly, but it can indirectly, by changing the public opinion which creates the laws. What is the public opinion? It is the opinion of the majority of the intelligent people who inhabit our country, who are of the opinion that *we* ought to be banished to that Sepulchre, LIBERIA, for the crime of wearing a sable skin. It is the opinion of those who repudiate us as being by nature inferior to themselves. The fact of our not being in every respect all that men ought to be in a "Land of LIBERTY!" in consequence of the bleeding wounds inflicted upon us by themselves, and who religiously believe that *we are not men.* It is the opinion of those who say that they "religiously believe" that we are not men, and who stigmatize us as a race upon whose countenance the Maker of man has set his band of infamy and degradation; an opinion which has been created by philosophers and physiologists, who class us midway betwixt *brute* and *man,* somewhere in the neighborhood of monkeys.

The public opinion views us as a race upon whom pains taken to instruct is only labor lost; it is slanderously said that we lack capacity for improvement, and are destitute of capacity to learn.

Now these degrading sentiments never will be entirely obliterated until the fiendish, censorious spirits from the tomb of ignorance (which seems sometimes to infest the community) be *laid,* by the power of an education whose virtue will adorn, elevate and dignify the character of man.

Until we ourselves are *united* in our efforts to rise from our present state of degradation, and demonstrate to the WORLD that no being upon whom God has set the impress of His divinity, can be thus slandered with impunity; that the blighting hand of slavery has thrown us in this degraded condition; that it has deprived us of education and thrown us upon society almost destitute of the means of helping ourselves. That we are daily thrown upon the background by our more intelligent white neighbors, and kept there for the want of a will and superior energy and strength to rise to an equality, I admit. Who does not know, that to ascend an eminence requires more effort than to pace its summit, after you get there?

But all this will not be received as an apology or as an excuse from us. We are *now nominally free*. Freedom and all its blessings are within our reach, and the question is whether we *will obtain it or not*.

The press is the engine which we are to sustain, and it will speed us on to the full enjoyment of its every blessing. The fact is naked before you, that the press has done more in three years in dethroning SLAVERY and her DAUGHTER the Colonization Society, than the mind of man could possibly have conceived, when the swift tide of public opinion was sweeping us down into the gulf "Liberia." All our resolutions and efforts to save ourselves were like the resolutions and efforts of drowning men who catch at straws. When the cry from a thousand voices freighted the air, "Help, O help, or we perish!" Garrison came forth and lent us a helping hand; his voice, like that of a trumpet, was heard through the LIBERATOR from Maine to Georgia. Though attacked by his enemies on every side, though a price was set upon his head, though hunted from place to place like the partridge on the mountains, he was not dismayed. The Liberator, with a boldness only equalled by the truth of the cause which it advocates, has penetrated the very recess of cruelty, and made the soul-murderer tremble in his shambles. Though reproached and calumniated for our sakes, he continues to advocate our cause with the zeal of a martyr and the love of an angel. His motto is, "No reproaches—no dangers shall deter me. At the north or the south, at the east or the west, wherever Providence shall call me, my voice shall be heard in behalf of the perishing slave and against the claims of his oppressor." A host of Christian philanthropists no less zealous; no less firm, have united in the blessed work. They have resolved to stand between us and our oppressors; to vindicate our rights until their voices are closed in death.

Thanks be to Him who said, *"Let there be light;"* light has come; the Liberator and the Emancipator have completely unfrocked the daughter of slavery (the Colonization Society). She is so shamefully exposed that she can find no veil to hide her coquettish face. Slavery's iron fetters begin to yield, and she is *retiring*. Then shall we whose eyes are lighted with the beams of Liberty, stand *"neutral,"* while 2,000,000 of our race are still subjected to Slavery's bloody reign? No. Let us support the press, that light may shine brighter and brighter, until Our Whole Country, the World, shall be illuminated with one hallowed blaze of LIBERTY!

[Source: *Emancipator and Journal of Public Morals*, Vol. III, No. 3 (January 20, 1835), no page given.]

No. 3: Neutrality

In my allusion to the principle of neutrality it may be said that I denounce the principle, and censure those who stand aloof from supporting the *press* and from the great and interesting question of our immediate emancipation from slavery and its accursed fruits, without showing what neutrality is. In order to show what it is, and to remove all doubts of the inconsistency of our standing neutral on a question upon which depends our own and the destinies of generations unborn, I undertake now to show, in a more abstract way, that upon any subject in which man is morally concerned, no matter what be the color of his skin, the idea of neutrality is out of the question:

Now this is a self-evident proposition: Am I concerned in the happiness of my fellow creatures? If I am not, I am worse than a Samaritan or pagan. Who is my neighbor? To admit the plea of neutrality then, is not only renouncing all concern for my fellow beings, but it is actually rejecting all the dictates of humanity and all the injunctions of our most holy religion, and detaching myself from the human species. The Savior of the world himself said, *"he that is not with me is against me,"* and this sentiment is as deeply fraught with philosophy as it is with religion. *"No man can serve two masters,"* &c. Now to get rid of the implications in these texts it will be necessary in the first place to deny any pretension to religion, and in the second place to deny the obligations and the truth of religion. Under this principle, then, are included all questions whether of human agency or moral accountability.

The next thing to be considered is, whether admitting that we are moral agents and accountable beings, we have a duty to perform in relation to ourselves and to the two millions of oppressed brethren who are now "in bounds." Here my subject begins to ramify; and it is in the ramification of this subject, alas, that so many of the great and good are bewildered and lost in the deceitful mazes and byways of colonization and proslavery.

I shall endeavor, however, to keep close to the subject, i.e. the subject of *neutrality*. Now if it be admitted as self-evident that we are concerned in our own happiness and in the happiness of two millions of American bondmen, if our own present and future well-being, and the future well-being of those of our brethren who are now writhing under the slave-driver's lash, is concerned in the discharge of our duty, the inquiry presents itself, how shall we best operate to promote our own and their best interest?

Here I dismiss the preliminary and take it for granted that no two Americans at most, who are despised and oppressed on account of the color of their skin, and whom this appeal shall reach, are in favor of the *American Colonization Society.* It is justly presumed that every enlightened man or woman of the United States, upon whom that poison spider operates, for the crime of wearing a sable hue, rejects the idea of colonization to Africa as a remedy for slavery, or as a relief from its bitter fruits.

Nay, further, we regard it as opposed to the principles and objects of emancipation, consequently disagreeing with every successful effort to benefit our unhappy and trodden-down race.

Now it is morally certain that two societies opposed to each other's principles and doctrines and tendencies, cannot coincide at all, nor both be supported by any individual or class of men.

That the Anti-Slavery and Colonization Societies are thus opposed it is not my object now to prove, nor is it necessary, since it has been proved a thousand times, in a variety of ways, and only waits a due reception in candid minds to be openly acknowledged. And if it was necessary for me to enter into this proof to sustain my position, I should only have to ask the question, Which one of these shoes pinches your foot, the right or the left?

We take it for granted—no, *not* for granted, but won by fair, honest and unanswered argument—that to oppose colonization is to advance abolition, the only principle that will remove slavery and her daughter from our necks, that we may *ourselves* arise up to the full stature of man. My appeal to you is, Which society will you advocate?

Here the question is honestly and fairly stated. Now my brethren, I do not appeal to you to oppose the Colonization Society, as a colonization society in the strict philosophical meaning of the term, but I conjure you to oppose the Colonization Society of America as a society whose accursed face, notwithstanding the number, piety and respectability of its members, is all distorted and awry with the convulsive workings of *prejudice, cupidity, avarice,* and aristocratical *pride* and *despotism.*

But I am wandering from the point. I said it was a fair and true proposition, that no man (no matter what be his complexion) can advocate the Colonization Society, or tolerate it, and be a friend to our elevation and to the emancipation of our enslaved brethren in these United States.

This being granted, I am ready to pronounce censure upon every man professing to advocate one of these societies who does not oppose the other.

Neutrality—If there be such a thing as neutrality, and I shall not stop here to grope in the midst of metaphysics—neutrality is of two kinds.

1st. That which proposes to belong to no party; and 2d. that which proposes to belong to either or all parties. Both are equally absurd, as I shall attempt to show. I hope you will not censure me for attempting to prove my position, or what I have before stated to the self-evident. I am now only going to illustrate the principle already admitted.

1st. Neutrality that proposes to belong to neither party has already been disposed of. I have shown that a man must lose his neutrality and be divorced from a claim to the title of an accountable creature, before he can be neutral upon any moral question.

But 2dly. Neutrality which belongs equally to all parties, though in fact *no neutrality at all* and infinitely absurd, has some show of pretence, some plausibility, a great deal of time-serving complacency, and an infinite degree of good-humored conciliation about it. It is decidedly popular at this age of moral revolution, in this time that tries men's souls, "these days of evil." This kind of neutrality is mightily convenient too, for by its aid a man can advocate whatsoever of any system he chooses, neither implicating himself, nor offending others. It has a mighty plastic and moulding influence, conforming more to his fellow man. It wears off the horns and snags of prejudice and bigotry, cools inflammable zeal, and melts down angry disputation in the crucible of brotherly love. It has a noble expansive power, overlooks the narrow limits of sectional interests, forgets party names in its lofty aspirations, smiles alike at the friend or foe, and speeds its joyous careering way, unconscious and independent. Finally, it has a remarkable assimilating power. No matter how adverse, contradictory or discordant the materials, neutrality, like the alchymist's solvent, converts the mass to unity and union. It is all things to all men.

But seriously, what effect does this neutrality have upon the conduct of men? Or in other words, to give meaning to the question, What is the consequence when a man attempts to be on all sides, and to please all, when his own interest of more than two million of his race are at stake?

The consequence to himself will be, that he will constantly be in hot water. The man who takes this stand, no matter who he be, nor what be the color of his skin, he is in the predicament of one who stands between the fire of two armies. He receives the shafts of both. Sometimes on one side, sometimes on the other; now assailed by a colonizationist, and anon by an abolitionist. But the effect which this course must have upon a man's own mind must be truly pitiable. He is continually shifting, evading, sophisticating and tormenting his brains for a get-out or get-off, from difficulty, until, from habit, he becomes a poor contemptible sophist. This has been exemplified in the history of some of the greatest men of the land on the subject of slavery. I know there are many good men whose skins are "not colored like our own," who would openly espouse our cause were it not for the ridicule and reproach to which they would be exposed. But shall we refuse to do our duty for fear of reproach? Will any good man refuse to do his duty for fear of reproach? Oh no; they would answer, but considering my situation, my relations, etc., etc. I am persuaded that if I were to *come out* on the right side, my usefulness would be greatly diminished, and therefore it is prudent to be mental, and say a good word for both societies. This is serving both God and Mammon with a vengeance. It is defeat, an ignominious defeat at the start, in prosecuting a great moral enterprise. The individual confesses that it is, considering all things, best to let the enterprise alone. God as it is, in itself, he virtually acknowledges that he has not moral courage to put his shoulder to the wheel, although he may wish that Hercules or somebody else would roll on the car.

Now what reason has he to expect that the enterprize will be accomplished if all the friends of abolition were as prudent as he? Will public opinion alter? Yes. What will make it alter? The influence of the press by disseminating the truth. But will truth be disseminated if all are so *prudent* that they think best to be *neutral* and not to promulge it? Come, Mr. Prudence, answer this question, and let me tell you, that while you omit your work the enemy will do his, and public sentiment will accuse your dastardly slumber when liberty shall be bound beneath the ruins of your country. Why not awake to the cause of humanity and vindicate the right of your oppressed countrymen immediately? There is no "lion in the way" which the sound of truth will not avert, no danger which Providence will not avert, and no appalling consequences to which the Omnipotent Ruler of the universe will not interpose a barrier. Come on, then. Gird on the weapons of your warfare. You *"shan't be kil't,"* and depend upon it, if you are ever wounded the mark will not be on your back.

It appears plain enough to me that the man who makes the opinion of the world a barrier to the discharge of a known duty, or who denies the duty of a course which, but, for the opinion of the world, he would account to be a duty, is in a most contemptible state. God only knows what would become of us, or the world, if *all* men were of the same mind—if there were not *some ultraists and* "*fanatics.*"

Now it must be clear to anyone who will look at the subject carefully, that a *consideration of our usefulness or peculiar situations, our relations in society,* and such like, are only modified expressions of "*public sentiment*," and resolvable into that terror-begetting phase.

How then, in the name of common sense, reason and justice, can we be so prudent as to be neutrals, and join in the expressions of a public sentiment that is sweeping us from the face of the earth "like the whirl-wind."

Who that takes the Bible for his guide and the man of his counsel will hesitate to do his duty because public opinion says he must not? I undertake to say that every man who feels and knows the influence of slavery—every man who knows slavery to be wrong, and does thus hesitate, is thus awed by public opinion, and does actually thus *refuse,* rejects the Bible and takes the public opinion as the man of his counsel. Now this is no fiction, nor *poetry* but a true *fact,* because God is the author of it—"*No man can serve God and Mammon.*"

[Source: *Emancipator and Journal of Public Morals,* Vol. III, No. 4 (January 27, 1835), no page given.]

No. 4

Neutrality upon any subject of moral investigation has a direct tendency not only to keep our whole race forever under the blighting influence of slavery, to prevent and corrupt the reasoning faculties, but to weaken the energies of the mind. History and biography are replete with data from which to deduce the fact that the investigation of truth, in all its departments, tends directly "to form the man," and consummate the philosopher.

> *Slaves, though we be enroll'd*
> *Minds are never to be sold.*

Now let this investigation cease; let an individual study to please *all:* he is a *slave* and quickly degenerates into a poor, mean, fallacious sneak—a tool, a sycophant and a fool.

The neutrality not only makes slaves and sneaks, sycophants and fools of us, it is not acquainted with the complexion of its subjects, only with their hearts.

The direct tendency of this neutrality upon men, upon all moral subjects, (no matter what be the complexion of man) is to corrupt the heart. What! be on both sides of a question of morals and religion? Oh no; that wouldn't do, but on both sides of the slavery question is no matter. No matter whether slaves be free or not! Can it be possible that a Christian can argue this? Why yes. Look at the South where Christians and preachers of the Gospel not only argue but *do* this, yes *do* this. But oh, these holy men would be glad to liberate their slaves if they could—yes, *if they could!*—What preposterous language! Tell me of a slave-holding minister of the Gospel who ever once said to his people, slave-holding is an *abomination*, an *iniquitous crime* in the sight of God. Say who can that this is the case!

But I must hasten to conclude my remarks on the principles of neutrality on this head, by noting the dangers incurred by this kind of neutrality. I mean here the danger of God's displeasure visited upon him, both in this world and in the world to come. Were it in my power I would show step by step the progress of iniquity by persons attempting to serve both "God and Mammon." I would adduce Stephen to illustrate my position. I would contrast him with Cain who wanted to please the world by making a show of religion. I would mention Lot who wanted a goodly portion in Sodom, noticing Haman, and concluding with Judas, Ananias, all of whom met a dire catastrophe, except Lot, who was punished and brought to renounce his neutrality. But without meddling with anything out of my province, I flatter myself that I have presented this neutrality so naked before you, that you will bear me out in saying that *two-faced* measures, which must result from a desire to please *all* and be on *all* sides, merit a single defeat, and like all such combustibility will be swept away by the searching ordeal of truth, which "leaves not a wreck behind."

Secondly. The consequences to society will be of a nature similar to those which comes upon himself, and in a degree proportioned to his influence. For want of room, and not to protract my remarks upon neutrality out of proportion to the main subject, I must necessarily be more brief than I could wish to be. Here I only glance at some of the prominent points comprehended under this head.

The general influence of an individual may not be effected by a desire to please all sides and all parties, but the quantity of his influence will be of a specific character totally different from that which is the result of an independent course untrammeled by the opinions of men. "Like will beget like," this will be admitted. Now let us suppose a case. Take, for example, a clergyman, who is beloved of his congregation, and is supposed to have an almost unbounded influence on them. But suppose his apparent influence is of the consequence of having studied their sentiments and conforming his doctrines to their taste, carefully cutting between duty to his divine Master's respect, and conformity to the will of the *other* masters. Tell us, is that man reforming errors, and guiding his flock, or is his flock guiding him? It is plain to everyone that he is nothing more nor less than a mere timeserver.

Suppose now he is convinced that slavery is totally wrong, and that it is the duty of every minister to awaken the minds of his people to an investigation of the subject; but on the other hand, his people, to a man, are colonizationists, or advocates of slavery; you must conclude he is now in a sad predicament. Never accustomed to run counter to public opinion, what will he do in this sad emergency? Why, he will at once fall in with the opinion that the "question must not be agitated." Though slavery is wrong; though emancipation immediate is right; still the question must not be agitated "just *now*." Prudence forbids it, expediency puts it out of the question. The consequence is, his silence on the subject, or rather his abuse of those people who have courage to do their duty, will confirm his people in their errors and crimes. The good Lord deliver our country from such ministers of the Gospel. On the other hand, I have in my mind's eye one, not a supposed one, but one in reality, whose course had been marked by a straightforward discharge of duty; bold, fearless, and independent; swearing never from duty; by the frowns of friends or foes never influenced. He was ardently beloved by his congregation, immensely popular throughout the land, and universally respected for his learning and talents. One condition, or the question of slavery and its remedies was presented to his mind. His benevolent heart bled when he surveyed our wretched condition and the more wretched condition of our poor enslaved brethren.

His eagle vision detected at once the delusion of colonization, and his honest mind acceded heartily to the only remedy for slavery—Immediate Emancipation. But did he consult the opinion of the world in making out his line of duty? Assuredly not. He went to his Bible and read in plain unequivocal characters his duty there.

He sought directions from above, and God told him to "cry aloud and spare not"—to "show his people their transgressions." He breasted the angry storm of popular fury, and though pierced by many a dart came off unscathed and unsullied. Has he lost his popularity? Perhaps he has. He has, I suppose, lost the favor of those whose good opinion no *good* man ought ever to have. But in lieu of these, he has gained friends who are the friends of righteousness.

What now are the probable consequences of such a course? So far as they have been developed, we may safely answer, the happiest results. The fact of this individual's avowing the honest purpose of his soul, and fearlessly promulging his sentiments, though under apparently the most unfavorable circumstances, has done more for the cause of bleeding humanity and the dissemination of truth, than all the efforts of slaveholding, timeserving, and popularity-seeking ministers of the Gospel since the world began.

The plan of crying soft and sparing never answered the purpose of reform, and never will. To go with the current of wrong is to go to destruction. Some must take the lead to change the current of public opinion in any reformation. Duty must be considered irrespective of consequences and in defiance of ridicule, opposition or persecution. The precept, "be wise as a serpent and gentle as doves," is given to guide us *in* our duty, not a prohibition to frighten us *from* it, and it is so understood in all ordinary pursuits; but many that can perceive its application with a Lynx's eye, when their own individual interest is concerned, are yet blind as a bat to its primary and most important meaning. Hence *prudence and expediency* in the colonization and pro-slavery sense of the terms, are merely excuses from duty—the offspring of disobedience and cowardice. Ill fated words! The very death knell of our own and the poor slaves' hope! Thanks be to Him who is the avenger of the oppressed. There are those in this "Land of Liberty" and slavery, who take but one side of two opposing interests, which are vitally interesting to us, and nobly sustain one cause. Our thanks, our hearty thanks be to them, May the blessings of heaven rest upon their heads.

I have now adduced the proof that neutrality upon any moral subject is out of the question. That to be on both sides and please all is a moral impossibility, and that the attempt to do so is fraught with infinite danger; because eternal justice will surely overtake the oppressor and him who vindicates the oppressor.

[Source: *Emancipator and Journal of Public Morals*, Vol. III, No. 5 (February 3, 1835), no page given.]

No. 5

In making an application of these remarks, I appeal to you, my oppressed and downtrodden countrymen, to reflect upon the great necessity of vigorous effort in bringing about that "consummation so devoutly to be wished"—the universal emancipation of our enslaved brethren from the iron bonds of physical servitude, and our own emancipation from the shackles of ignorance and the scorn of prejudice.

That we have been warned by colonizationists to *cease* our efforts lest we be *"cut down like the grass,"* I admit; but what boot it to us whether they "get rid" of us by "cutting us down like grass," or freight our carcasses to manure the barren sands of Africa? If boot there be, it is in falling honorable "one by one" in *Freedom's* ranks. Then be not dismayed by the cowardly menaces of aggression; gird on the armor of faith, shoulder the *press*, enter the ranks, and manfully contend for *victory*.

Our hope for victory, under God, is in the power of the *press*. Then, let us individually and collectively support it, take the paper, and wield it into the ranks of the enemy. Before its power they will fall "like the grass" before the scythe. Liberty will come, and victory! victory! triumphant will be ours.

Ladies, suffer me to make an appeal to you: my hopes for sustenance of the *Press*, for the triumphant success of our cause, is centered in you. The grounds of these hopes rests upon past experience. *Flattery* is not the weapon, but I confess the fact with gratitude, that when all our resources have failed, we have ever found in you a generous support. There is not a female in the community who may not exert an influence that will be felt throughout the world.

Yes, every action is followed by consequences, increasing in importance as they roll on in their development thru *eternal ages*. What an awful thought! Who that reflects can be neutral, an idle spectator in their *own cause*, and the cause of bleeding humanity? Who will refuse to come up boldly to hasten on the chariot wheels of "universal emancipation," and urge on the car of freedom. I trust there are none. But if any there be, I am persuaded that they do not realize or calculate the amount of influence which each female can herself exert. Did Harriet Newell ever dream that she was preparing the embryo seeds of Christian philanthropy? Mark the illustrious names of Moor, and De Steel, and Janeway, and Elizabeth M. Chandler, and a thousand others, and calculate, if you can, the amount of influence which they exerted, and are still exerting. They being dead "yet speak." Your sex have in all ages of the world been the incentives to noble action. To you, I appeal in behalf of our cause, in behalf of our press, which actually languishes for the want of support—Will you bestow your benevolence that *it* may *live*, or will you let *it die?*

[Source: *Emancipator and Journal of Public Morals*, Vol. III, No. 6 (February 10, 1835), no page given.]

No. 6

Who can be reconciled to the thought that anti-slavery periodical "must die" for the want of our support, while the cry from two millions of our countrymen and women freight every southern breeze—Help!—oh help! to deliver us from the "iron that enters into the soul!"

Can your benevolent hearts withstand their cries? Can you refuse them aid when it is your privilege, when it is your power to aid them? Is not freedom to you desirable? Methinks I hear a voice from two millions of my countrymen (mingled with the clanking of their chains) answer yes; Liberty! Liberty! Liberty! thrice-told Liberty! thou art dearer to me than life itself. Then while liberty, which is so interwoven with every fibre of the human heart, be desirable to us and to our poor enslaved brethren, let us form no acquaintance with apathy and supineness. Let no effort be wanting on our part to obtain the full enjoyment of its every blessing. No matter whether we can read or not—no matter whether time forbids us the pleasure of reading or not. Support the *press*, and reflect that every paper that is circulated by your means goes forth as an ambassador to settle the all important question of *liberty* and *slavery*—it is admitted into the "great prison house of slavery," and like a missionary, it addresses itself to the consciences of its haughty tyrannical inmates, in a language not to be misunderstood, though, seared with blood and hardened with iniquity, they yield to its power, and it makes "report of victory!" Then let it be supported, that it may address every family, and instruct every mind in the land, that we ask *not* for amalgamation, but for Freedom!—not for them, their sons and daughters to wed, but to take their iron feet from off our necks, that we may arise *up* and *walk*, like men. The press is the weapon that will instruct with effect; then let us wield it with dexterity—let us not by infidelity and unbelief suffer the richest blessings of nature to "fly"—brightening as it soars from our reach. Let us not seal our own unworthiness, and prove ourselves guilty of ingratitude to those who have ventured their *lives*, their *all* in our cause, by standing *"neutral."* The question admits of no neutrals—with us it is a question of *liberty* or *slavery*—with our friends, the *abolitionists*, it is a question of *right* or *wrong*. Then let us press forward and ascend the lofty summit of *liberty!* and if age, in the morning of our arrival should deliver us up to death, the summit can be paced by those who come after us.

Press forward in our most glorious cause, Angels participate in it—

the best men in Christendom are engaged in it. Female virtue is already enlisted in it. Though you have done much, you can do much more; 'tis your privilege and duty to enter the ranks, and move

On, 'till we reach that eminence
Where Freedom reigns alone,
On, 'till the yoke, the iron band
Shall fall before her Throne.

Though the signs of the times be sometimes turbulent and squally, they augur for good. In a cause like ours difficulties must be welcomed, trials met and endured. We must expect to pass by Stones and Webbs, Frelinghuysen Oaks, and Russian Brambles—we must expect to pass through fogs and smoke, clouds will rise and bust over our heads, but we must not be dismayed—Stones and Webbs, brickbats, "tar and feathers," and declamation cannot obscure the *light. Light* has *come*—a torch have reached the center of slavery's hand, and carried them a dazzling, scorching efficacy. The cry, "*Let us alone*," has been vociferated back to the north. The press, like a sun of light emits its beams to earth's remotest bounds. Come forward then, and contribute your aid and influence, and pledge your unceasing effort to sustain the *press* in the cause of suffering humanity, and administer the cup of consolation to the afflicted, and "wipe the tear from sorrow's eye." Come what will, if *even riot* must come to purge a corrupt public sentiment, like the purifying effects of the hurricane upon a foul atmosphere, "awful though it be," let it come, and rage, and die," anything is better than the "silent, peaceful," soul-damning influence of *slavery-colonization*. Go forward, then, trusting in the mighty arm of Jehovah, and rest assured we shall be helped just in proportion as we help ourselves—we shall be respected just in proportion as we respect ourselves—we shall gain influence just as fast as we acquire merit. Go forward then, in our most sacred cause, and woe to the man who will be a neutral and refuse to "*toe the mark*" and complete the ranks. Though difficulties arise, obstacles withstand, and dangers ensue, the *victory* when won will be more signal, the triumph more illustrious. Go forward then, soon the result of your labors will plant a wreath of honor upon your brow, and the blessings of your memory descend to the latest posterity.

Let *Union* be our watch word, persevering, unremitting, untiring effort be our *Motto*, and success, honor and happiness will be *Our Reward*.

Most truely and affectionately yours,

David Ruggles

Concluded

Who can be reconciled to the thought that any anti-slavery periodical "must die" for the want of our support while the cry for two millions of our countrymen and women flight every southern breeze—Help!—Oh Help! ! to deliver us from the "iron that enters the soul!"
Can your benevolent hearts withstand their cries?

[Source: *Emancipator and Journal of Public Morals*, Vol. III, No. 7 (February 17, 1835), no page given.]

INDEX OF AUTHORS

Allen, George R.: 572, 574
Allen, Richard: 414, 559

Banneker, Benjamin: 324
Bayley, Solomon: 587
Bell, Philip: 281
Bestes, Peter: 254

Cook, John F.: 240
Corr, Joseph M.: 146
Cuffe, Paul: 256

De Grass, Isaiah G.: 576

Eagans, Peter Malachi: 374
Ennals, Samuel: 281

Forten, James, Jr.: 225
Forten, James, Sr.: 265, 333
Fortune, Michael: 563
Freeman, Sambo: 254

Green, Johnson: 405

Hall, Prince: 63, 70
Hamilton, William: 33, 96, 391, 570
Hammon, Briton: 522
Hammon, Jupiter: 313, 529, 535
Haynes, Lemuel: 448
Holbrook, Felix: 254
Horton, George Moses: 578

Johnson, Henry: 366
Joie, Chester: 254
Jones, Absalom: 330, 335
Joyce, John (alias Davis): 414

Lawrence, George: 374
Lee, Jarena: 494

Marrant, John: 427

Parrott, Russell: 265, 383
Paul, Nathaniel: 286
Paul, Thomas: 279

Quinn, William Paul: 614

Ruggles, David: 478, 637

Saunders, Prince: 87, 269
Sidney, Joseph: 355
Sidney, Robert Y.: 565
Sidney, Thomas S.: 574
Sipkins, Henry: 344, 365
Smith, Venture: 538
Stewart, John: 455
Stewart, Maria W.: 129, 136, 460

Watkins, William: 155
Wheatley, Phillis: 532
Whipper, William: 105, 204
Williams, Peter: 294, 343, 569
Wright, Theodore: 472